THE
KING ARTHUR FLOUR
200TH ANNIVERSARY
COOKBOOK

THE
KING ARTHUR FLOUR
200ᵀᴴ ANNIVERSARY
COOKBOOK

by Brinna B. Sands

Dedicated to the Pure Joy of Baking

Countryman Press
Woodstock, Vermont

King Arthur Flour® is a registered trademark
of Sands, Taylor & Wood Co. of Norwich, Vermont.

KING ARTHUR FLOUR 200TH ANNIVERSARY COOKBOOK © 1990
Rev. ed. © 1991
by Brinna Sands
Design & Layout by Liza Bernard
Illustrations by Elizabeth Page

First trade edition published in 1992
by The Countryman Press, PO Box 748, Woodstock, Vermont 05091
Distributed by W. W. Norton & Company, Inc.
500 Fifth Avenue, New York City, New York 10110
Printed in the United States of America
20 19 18 17 16 15 14

Library of Congress Catloging-in-Publication Data

Sands, Brinna.
   King Arthur Flour 200th anniversary cookbook; dedicated to the pure joy of baking/by
Brinna Sands
   p. cm.
 Includes index.
 ISBN 0-88150-247-2
 1. Baking I. Title   II. Title: King Arthur Flour two-hundredth anniversary cookbook.
TX765.S265 1992
641.7'1—dc20   92-17057
                                                                        CIP

Publisher's Note

Sands, Taylor & Wood Company (distributor of King Arthur Flour) celebrated its 200th birthday in 1990 with the publication of their cookbook in a magnificent ring-bound edition for its customers and friends.

We immediately felt that the book should be available to a wide audience of home bakers in a book trade edition, and that our reprint should reproduce the original in its entirety, including the charming company history that opens the text.

This historic company (now *202* years old), operated by generation after generation of the founding family, remains true always to its original values of quality and social consciousness. King Arthur Flour is, after all, a sort of national treasure.

A deluxe ring-bound hard cover edition of The King Arthur Flour 200th Anniversary Cookbook, *of which this edition is a reprint, is available (as are its famous flours and other baking treasures) from* The King Arthur Flour Baker's Catalogue, *R.R. 2, Box 56, Norwich, VT 05055 (1-800-827-6836).*

TABLE OF CONTENTS

Introduction & History
The Once & Future...

1790 • Our company is founded in Boston and begins importing premium flour from England via sailing ships.

1820 • John L. Sands, the first member of the Sands family to join the firm, begins work as a salesman.

1870 • The name Sands appears in the title for the first time as Sands & Fernald.

1890 • The current name, Sands, Taylor & Wood, is adopted.

1896 • A lone rider dressed like King Arthur rides through Boston's streets atop a black stallion waving a symbolic flag as King Arthur Flour is introduced at the Boston Food Fair.

1897 • All of Camelot is reborn on bag and barrel: Round Table Pastry Flour; Queen Guinevere Cake Flour; Merlin Magic Doughnut Mix; and five high-protein bread flours, Sir Lancelot, Squire, Page, Sir Kay, and Excalibur.

1927 • King Arthur rides again, visiting towns and villages in Massachusetts.

1928 • Walter Sands drives a truck with a large calliope and wooden carving of a mounted King Arthur through the streets of New York City.

1930's • Sands, Taylor & Wood turns to radio with "King Arthur Coffee Club" and the "King Arthur Round Table of Song." King Arthur Coffee, Tea and Wheat Germ are introduced.

1932 • The company becomes entirely Sands owned and operated.

1947 • Marjorie Mills, one of New England's foremost food experts, endorses King Arthur Flour.

1963 • Frank E. Sands II enters the firm as a salesman and in 1968 becomes the second youngest president in the company's history.

1966 • King Arthur begins milling stone ground whole wheat flour at the Wayside Inn Grist Mill in Sudbury, Massachusetts.

1970's • Sands, Taylor & Wood acquires the Joseph Middelby Company and then the H.A. Johnson Company to form the subsidiary, Johnson-Middleby, Inc., becoming New England's largest bakery manufacturer and supplier. The number of employees grows to 150 with three labor unions. Interest rates soar to 22%. Frank and Brinna Sands, looking for a new source of vitality and focus, move their family to Norwich, Vermont, and over the next three years sell off all the subsidiaries to refocus solely on retail sales of King Arthur Flour.

1980's • The newly defined company relocates to Norwich, Vermont, and introduces King Arthur Stone Ground Whole Wheat Flour in 5-pound bags. After five years, our Whole Wheat Flour holds a 75% share of the New England market. King Arthur Unbleached All-Purpose Flour becomes the only family flour in America whose sales continue to grow in a declining market.

1990 • Sands, Taylor & Wood celebrates its 200th anniversary creating this cookbook to acknowledge that milestone and our commitment to "Share the Pure Joy of Baking."

1991 • Sands, Taylor & Wood inaugurates a biennial baking tournament, called WinterBake, and creates The King Arthur Flour Baker's Catalogue to launch the company into its third century.

INTRODUCTION & HISTORY
THE ONCE & FUTURE...
I

The two-hundredth anniversary of the founding of Sands, Taylor & Wood Company, distributor of King Arthur Flours, has given us the opportunity to pause and reflect: to take a long look at where we, as individuals and as a company, have come from, where we are today, and where we want to go. We are fortunate to have survived so long and so well. The first reason we have put together this cookbook is to acknowledge and celebrate this history.

In thinking about our company's history, particularly in the last century, some disquieting thoughts have come to mind about our society's collective twentieth-century experience. The following quote by John Fowles sums it up rather well:

> It is almost as if in the last hundred years we left our old planet and found a new one; and we are all, however brashly contemporary, however much we take modern technology for granted, still victims of a profound cultural shock. We are beginning to realize that we have made a very clumsy landing on our new planet and that we left a number of things behind on the old one that we might have done well to bring with us.

Those things that were left behind are very much what our company is about. We are selling an ancient product in a twentieth-century world, trusting that there are enough people out there who feel, as we do, that those things which were "left behind" are worth getting reacquainted with and important enough to take with us into the next century.

• THE COOKBOOK •

THE PURPOSE

We live today in a part of the world and an era in history that is unbe-lievably blessed. For the first time since humans have been cooking, we have almost unlimited resources for ingredients, boundless books of recipes telling us what to do with them, and vast numbers of gadgets to ease their preparation, all of which indicates a tremendous fascination with food. But, as the decades have gone by, we have slowly given up more and more control over this part of our lives. It's almost as if our senses are so overloaded with possibilities that we haven't the time or energy to sort through them and make decisions. In despera-tion, we deal with this overload by buying partially prepared or finished goods from our grocery shelves, food we could easily prepare ourselves.

Before the tremendous communications and technology explosion in this century, we learned how to cook from our parents and grandparents. We carried recipes around in our heads and used whatever was available to dress them up or change them for fun. With fewer options available, cooking used to be a simpler art. But an art it was, and one that was deeply satisfying on many levels.

When Sands, Taylor & Wood Co. first started selling King Arthur Flour, eighty percent of the flour in the country was baked and consumed at home. Today, that has decreased to only five percent. As baking at home has declined, a myth has been created and perpetuated that kitchen pursuits are menial and time consuming, that they tie us down and prevent us from discovering our "true selves." So, as we rush along in this technologically focused century, we have given up many of those things which were our heritage from our parents and grandparents. And in becoming dependent on so many technological wonders, we've lost the satisfaction of doing things by hand and the reassurance of being able to trust our own senses.

Fortunately, there seems to be a growing reaction to the mechanization and mass production of this "modern age" along with a growing desire to relearn some of those old and fundamental arts which link us to the people in our past. Many of us are rediscovering something which our grandparents knew all along: there is nothing as satisfying as the act of creating with one's own hands and sharing what we've created with people we love in a place that we love. So, in addition to celebrating our two hundred years of selling the same fine "old" product, we write this book to rediscover it and celebrate some of those "things that we left behind."

We offer our book as a celebration of our many years as "purveyors of the finest flour in the world" and as a toast to all of you who have experienced and shared the joys of the kitchen, and to all of you who will.

THE DESIGN

The cover of the book contains the original King Arthur logo with which we have taken a bit of license. When our official logo was conceived a century ago, the artist inadvertently placed King Arthur in the Middle East as if he were a crusader. King Arthur may have been a crusader but not in the sense the term is generally accepted. His crusade was in the land of hill fort "castles" and ancient oaks which we have substituted for the palm trees and mosques (which you'll still find on the King Arthur Flour apron).

The framework for the logo on the chapter openings is an example of Celtic interlacing in which geometric whorls and spirals are intricately interwoven with, in this case, King Arthur's sword, Excalibur, but in others, highly stylized people, plants, birds, and animals. These intricate drawings were originally executed and "illuminated" by monks to illustrate religious manuscripts, the most famous of which is the *Book of Kells*.

THE CONTENT

An important aspect of many of the chapters is the "Primer." These were written to give you a basic understanding of each category of baking so you will have an intuitive feeling for it as your grandmothers did. Along with the information in those sections, you'll see King Arthur's wizard, Merlin (or his starry symbol), appear from time to time to cheer you on and let you in on a hint, a secret or some magic.

In the rest of the book we have gathered recipes from the King Arthur Flour archives, our spokesmen and women, our relatives and friends and you, our loyal bakers. Many include profiles of the people from whom they came. But even where none appears, there's a real person in a real kitchen behind the recipe. They are all snapshots of someone's mind after experiencing an "aha!" or an "ummm." And, as all recipes tend to evolve, we hope you will continue the evolution of those in this book.

DESIGN & LAYOUT

Liza Bernard, who has been with the Company since 1987, officially became responsible for the cookbook's Design & Layout almost two years ago. We couldn't have found anyone better to execute this venture, but this doesn't come close to expressing the enormity of the role she has played. Liza put the words of our *200th Anniversary Cookbook* to visual music. She has been conductor and composer at the same time, a combination without which this book would never have existed except in Brinna Sands' mind. Her counsel, suggestions and patience along the way and her commitment to consistency and excellence through all the ups and downs of its incubation and birth made the process and final publication possible.

Liza wears many hats, both at Sands, Taylor and Wood Co. and beyond. As a designer, she has produced and marketed one-of-a-kind fabrics and clothing. She has also managed a number of art galleries. During the past three years, she has developed and organized an exciting educational exhibition of visual arts at Shelburne Farms in Shelburne, Vermont.

ILLUSTRATIONS

Elizabeth Page is responsible for the scratchboard drawings that illustrate this cookbook. Betsy graduated from Colorado College with a B.A. in English and has since gone on to develop her warm and wonderful artistic inclinations. She has done illustrations for *Cricket*, an exceptional literary magazine for children, as well as for other children's publications. One of her most charming creations is *Starry Night*, a tiny alphabet book without words.

Betsy is currently working on new projects and continues to paint, sketch and create collages. She loves to garden and is particularly interested in herbs. After spending so much time on the cookbook, she says she's "getting into serious baking" as well.

Betsy lives across the river in Lyme, New Hampshire, with sheep and many lambs (as of this writing), bees, ducks, a dog and a cat, most of whom you'll find in our book.

Acknowledgements

We wish to extend our thanks:

• to everyone who has given encouragement and counsel and remained patient while this book was being compiled.

• to Frank, Brinna's husband for giving her up for a year and for discovering the "joys of the kitchen" as she explored the joys of the writing.

• to all of Brinna's family and her compatriots at the office as well, for sharing recipes and ideas (and eating their way through many pounds of King Arthur Flour baked into every conceivable form).

• to Whitney Sands for the massive amount of research she did for her senior thesis at Burlington College which put the history of Sands, Taylor & Wood Co. in one book, the source of much of the information in this introduction.

• to Anne Baird, Brinna Sands' sister, a prodigious reader, one of those people who (with no training) can read a billion words a minute and remember everything they read. Her willingness and ability to look with eagle eye at all the words we've written and to make sure they've said what we wanted them to say, has made this a better book by far.

• to Marilyn Magnus, an old friend of Brinna's and an intuitive cook who has always baked all of her family's bread and other goodies from scratch. Her willingness to work her way through all these pages of recipes is appreciated more than we can say.

• to Ruth Sylvester who caught our goofs while she patiently inserted the fractions into the text.

• to Janet Matz, a Vice President at Whitman Press (Lebanon, New Hampshire) who coached and supported us through the labor pains of self-publishing.

Most important, we wish to thank all of you loyal King Arthur Flour bakers for your questions, recipes, tips, suggestions and, most of all, your "love letters" which let us know that there is a lot of joyful baking going on out there. We hope that you will continue this longstanding dialogue with us.

Brinna Sands & the Sands, Taylor & Wood Co.

• THE KING ARTHUR FLOURS •

King Arthur Flour, with the "knight on the horse," has long been a familiar household friend. As a few of you may remember, it used to come in one-hundred and two-hundred-pound barrels with the King Arthur logo on the lid. Then it came in large, one-hundred-pound muslin bags with the King Arthur logo on the side. (These cloth bags were the source of our first King Arthur aprons and the inspiration for the aprons that we make available today.) Now, for sanitation reasons, King Arthur Unbleached All-Purpose Flour comes to you in two-, five-, ten- and twenty-five-pound paper bags with its familiar logo on the front.

King Arthur Stone Ground Whole Wheat Flour was introduced in the early 1970's at the Wayside Inn Grist Mill, in Sudbury, Massachusetts. The Wayside Inn, originally known as the Red Horse Tavern, was made famous by Henry Wadsworth Longfellow in his narrative poems called, collectively, *Tales of a Wayside Inn*. This enterprise was originally a non-profit extension of Sands, Taylor & Wood Co. designed to bring attention both to the history of milling and to the benefits of stone grinding whole wheat flour. From this mill came our first stone ground whole wheat, packaged in small, two-pound bags. It became so popular the Company eventually moved its business to a mill that could handle the demand and began packaging its new whole wheat flour in five-pound bags.

King Arthur Unbleached All-Purpose Flour

King Arthur Unbleached All-Purpose Flour is a hybrid of the various definitions of all-purpose flour you'll find in baking books. First, it is an unbleached white flour. It is ground from the endosperm of the wheat berry (it does not contain the germ or the bran) and it is not treated with chemical bleaching agents. Second, its classification is "all-purpose," which means that it can be used successfully in all baking. The difference between King Arthur Flour and other all-purpose flours starts with the types of wheat from which it is blended.

As a fine wine is blended from prized varieties of grapes, so is a high-quality flour blended from the finest types of wheat. King Arthur Flour is a blend of two of the finest, hard red winter and hard red spring, producing a flour with up to twenty percent more protein than other all-purpose flours. Each time our flour is milled, the blend is carefully balanced so that the protein level and baking characteristics of each batch are always the same. Because the level of ash is so low (another test for purity) King Arthur Flour, with no bleaching necessary, is simply the warm golden color the sun makes the wheat.

If the results of any of the exacting tests that we put a flour through aren't up to our standards, we start over. When all passes muster, the final result is a flour on which we can put the King Arthur label.

King Arthur Stone Ground Whole Wheat Flour

Our whole wheat flour is a blend of high-protein, hard red spring wheats. Its grind is very fine, which makes it easy to substitute for our unbleached all-purpose flour. Whole wheat flour is ground from the entire wheat berry. It contains the wheat bran which is an important source of insoluble dietary fiber (see Appendix). It also contains the wheat germ, or embryo, which would have produced a new wheat seedling had the berry been planted. Wheat germ contains polyunsaturated oils, iron, and vitamins B and E. We stone grind our whole wheat flour, a slow, cool process, to protect these vitamins and minerals.

A Blend of Both

Although there is an enormous culinary history that has developed around white flour, this is, fortunately, beginning to change. For both flavor and nutrition, King Arthur Unbleached All-Purpose and King Arthur Stone Ground Whole Wheat Flours together are an exceptional blend. As the texture and flavor grow on you, you'll discover that this blend can be much more interesting than white flour alone. You can adjust the combination to suit whatever you bake. If you have never used whole wheat flour before, try starting with a ratio of three parts of unbleached all-purpose flour to one of whole wheat. With this, you will have the best of both King Arthur Flours.

The Historical Desirability of "White" Flour

There's a lot of misinformation and myth regarding the merits of "white flour" as well as "white" versus "whole wheat flour." White flour is ground from the endosperm of the wheat berry. The bran has been removed as has the germ. There were two major reasons why it was valued so highly in the past.

• The first reason is no longer relevant. Prior to the development of the high-speed steel roller milling process in the middle of the last century, the "white" part (endosperm) of the wheat berry (seed) was difficult to separate from the seed coat (bran) and the plant embryo (germ). The small amount that was separated was reserved for the wealthy and noble since it made baked goods that were lighter and more appealing. The remainder was used by the lower classes. If you had access to white flour it meant you were part of a select and favored few. Although white flour is now available to everyone, the old associations are still there.

• The second consideration was that by removing the oil-rich germ of the wheat, the keeping quality of the resultant flour was increased significantly. Like any vegetable oil, the oil in wheat germ has a tendency to become rancid in time, making whole wheat flour more sensitive to storage conditions. When flour has had its germ removed it will keep almost indefinitely if it is stored where it is cool and dry.

Additives to "White" Flour

Because white flour was more desirable, the more of a wheat berry that a miller could grind into "white flour," the more profit he could make. A century ago, both here and abroad, millers and bakers "doctored" flour with all kinds of things to make more of it white. Ground lime, chalk and even bone were all used at one time or another. Attempts to regulate these practices were never very successful. Today, the Food and Drug Administration has made these additives illegal. It has sanctioned the following:

Bleaches: The two most common chemical bleaches are chlorine gas (deadly to humans) and benzoyl peroxide (an ingredient in acne medicine). Some of the chemical bleaching agents that were legal earlier in the century have now been banned because of health hazards. In some European countries, all forms of bleaching are illegal.

Chemical bleaches are also added to flour to age (oxidize) it artificially. Like wine, a flour needs to mellow and mature, which will happen naturally over several weeks. The addition of certain of the bleaches can "age" flour immediately, but some vitamins are destroyed in the process and the nature of the protein becomes permanently altered. It is sort of chemically "cooked," which makes it tougher.

Potassium Bromate: Another chemical additive that currently is permitted in flour is potassium bromate, although there are some possible health hazards associated with it. This chemical is added to flour to accelerate the growth of yeast and to chemically fortify the gluten in a dough to make bread rise higher in the heat of an oven. If a flour contains this chemical it must be stated on the bag.

Iron, Niacin, Thiamin and Riboflavin: In the early 1940's the Food and Drug Administration mandated the addition of certain ingredients to white flour. Because consumption of flour was so widespread, it was felt that its "enrichment" was the most direct and effective way to alleviate diseases caused by vitamin deficiencies (pellagra, beri-beri, rickets, etc.). Tiny amounts of iron, niacin, thiamin and riboflavin were, and still are, added to all-purpose flour, much as Vitamins A and D are added to milk.

Malted Barley Flour: Tiny amounts of this natural ingredient are added to flour as a food for yeast. It is made from barley that is first sprouted and then dried at a low heat to prevent destruction of the vitamins and minerals present. The dried barley sprouts are then ground into a flour that is an excellent source of vitamins, minerals and natural sugars, a "health food" long appreciated in Europe.

OUR COMMITMENT TO YOU

The only things you will ever find in King Arthur Unbleached All-Purpose Flour, besides the milled wheat itself, are federally mandated nutritional supplements and malted barley flour. Our flour stands solidly on its own with no chemical additives to change its natural color or its excellent and consistent baking characteristics. Its formula was developed a hundred years ago for the long run. Our commitment, today, is to maintain these same high standards for the next hundred years. Like its namesake, whose leadership created a standard we still honor, King Arthur Flour is indeed the "King Arthur of Flours."

• THE COMPANY •

THE ONCE...

THE 18TH AND 19TH CENTURIES

When the year 1790 opened, our newly formed republic was still recovering from its violent separation from its mother country, and George Washington was about to be inaugurated the first President of the United States. The excitement of independence was high and the energy released by it created fertile ground for the growth of new business.

In that same year of 1790, a man by the name of Henry Wood began importing flour from England. The colonists, despite their distaste for English policy, still had a taste for staples from home. Slowly his business reached out to all regions of the fledgling United States. He did so well that he took on a partner and formed Henry Wood & Company.

Thirty years later, in 1820, John Low Sands was hired as a salesman, the first Sands to join the business. John also did well and eventually acquired a part ownership in the company. He lived a full and long life and attributed his success in business to being scrupulously honest and in giving people a "square deal." These attributes have been part of the company's philosophy ever since.

As the decades went by the company grew and thrived. In 1853, it purchased a building at 13 Long Wharf which extended into Boston Harbor, at that time one of the busiest ports in the world. In the mid-nineteenth century, there were sixty-three wharfs in Boston proper and fourteen in neighboring Charlestown. (In the first decade of the 1700's, Boston's Long Wharf had already been lengthened to almost a half mile.) As the city itself grew, it expanded its geographic limits by filling in the harbor around the base of the wharves. Sometime around 1862 the Company became landlocked and, without moving an inch, changed its address from 13 Long Wharf to 172 State Street.

Two years after Henry Wood & Co. moved into its new quarters on the wharf, John Sands' son, Benjamin Franklin Sands, entered the business at the tender age of fifteen. Ben was a strong-minded character, bold and honest, and not at all shy about expressing his beliefs. When he was still a young man, but after his reputation as a businessman was well established, he was involved in an incident at the North Avenue Congregational Church in Cambridge which clearly illuminated his forthright character. The pastor of the church was delivering a sermon on the evils of "profiteering businessmen." Ben Sands, greatly affronted, and cognizant of the honest way in which he conducted his own business, marched right up to the pulpit and rebuked his pastor in front of the whole congregation.

In 1870, when he was just thirty, Ben Sands acquired some ownership in the Company and took over the reins. Shortly thereafter his name, Sands, became part of the title for the first time. He was an active, vital and successful President who died an unfortunate and untimely death in 1881, at the age of forty-one, only six months after the death of his own father.

Ben's son, Frank Edgar Sands, was only fourteen at the time of his father's death, but unlike his father, was not quite ready for the business world. In 1882, at the age of fifteen, he became one of the youngest students ever to matriculate at the Massachusetts Institute of Technology. After finishing three years later, he opened and ran a haberdashery shop for a number of years.

Upon Ben's death, his younger brother Orin stepped in. Mark Taylor had joined the Company three years before in 1878. George Wood (no relation to Henry) became a partner nine years later in 1890. In 1895, Orin Sands, Mark Taylor and George Wood became partners, which gave the Company its final and lasting name, Sands, Taylor & Wood Co. Even though Taylor and Wood have been gone for many years, the Company has retained this name for almost a century.

The year after the Company was incorporated as Sands, Taylor & Wood, Orin wooed his nephew Frank away from the haberdashery business. On September 10th of this same year at the Boston Food Fair, a rider in chain mail on a black horse introduced King Arthur Flour. Both events played a significant role in determining the course the Company was to take in the next century.

Introduction of King Arthur Flour

During the last decade of the nineteenth century, the flour business was in a state of chaos and change. A new milling technique, developed in Hungary, had made it possible to grind large amounts of wheat into white flour very quickly, which encouraged a great number of people to get involved in the milling business. The result was that the consistency and quality of flour became quite unpredictable. In response to this, the new partnership of Sands, Taylor & Wood Co. made a decision to become distributors of an exceptionally high quality flour. It was to be milled from a unique blend of one hundred percent hard wheats so it would be naturally strong, pure and in need of no additives to enhance its baking qualities or its appearance.

The 1890's were a time when the Arthurian romances were having a renaissance. While Sands, Taylor and Wood were trying to decide on a name for their new and exceptional flour, George Wood attended a musical in Boston called *King Arthur and the Knights of the Round Table.* He came away feeling that the values inherent in the Arthurian legends, purity, loyalty, honesty, superior strength and a dedication to a higher purpose, were the values that most closely expressed their feelings about their new flour. So it was decided that King Arthur would be its symbol.

The immediate success of this new flour was gratifying. Eight years later, in 1904, as the Company grew and thrived, it left 172 State Street and moved up the street to the Custom House where it remained for almost twenty years.

Orin Sands had the reputation in the trade of being a man who could be trusted to produce what he promised. He made good this reputation in the Company's new flour. He remained with the Company until his death in 1917. The city of Cambridge later honored him as a leader and businessman by naming Orin Street after him.

The First Half of the 20th Century

After Orin's death, the presidency passed to his brother Ben's son, Frank Edgar Sands, who, by 1917, had been with Sands, Taylor & Wood Co. for over twenty years. Ed, as his friends called him, was known as an exceptionally intelligent and decent man who "never drank nor swore" and who served for thirty years as deacon of the same Congregational Church in which his father had exhorted the pastor years before.

Ed's elder son, Donald (born the year before King Arthur Flour was introduced) left college early, like many young men during World War I, to join the Army. Among other wartime adventures, he went with General Pershing to the Mexican border in pursuit of Pancho Villa. On his return, he joined the Company as General Manager.

Donald was a man of tremendous energy and vitality and within a very few years had earned great respect from the entire trade. By 1922, the Sands, Taylor & Wood Company had built a reputation within the flour milling community as distributors of what a certain Mr. Gallagher, General Manager of Northwestern Consolidated Milling Company, called "the finest flour in the world."

But in spite of that, Donald recognized that the retail market for flour was in trouble. As home baking declined, so did the flour market. He felt that the solution might be to move into the bakery trade. As a result of this decision, Sands, Taylor & Wood Co. increased its sales and pulled itself out of the World War I slump. In 1923, to accommodate its growth, the Company left the Custom House, moved to Somerville and built a warehouse on a railway line.

During the latter years of his father's presidency, Donald was the Company's driving force. His energy extended well beyond the workplace. In 1932, he refereed the Olympic hockey games at Lake Placid, New York, and later became Commissioner of the Eastern Intercollegiate Hockey League.

Just as his grandfather had died prematurely, Donald died suddenly in 1937 when he was just forty-two, six years before his own father's death. Afterwards, William J. Bingham, Director of Athletics at Harvard, wrote of him saying,

> To be known as a good sport is a tribute. This community has just lost a citizen who lived up to such standards. Donald P. Sands was respected by all who knew him because he always played the game. In business, his energy, discipline and honesty were an inspiration to his fellow workmen. You have given us a great heritage, because you always played the game according to the rules. We shall ever remember you as an energetic and wise executive, a faithful and loving father, an impartial and fair athletic commissioner, a true and loyal friend.

Ed Sands remained President of Sands, Taylor & Wood Co. until 1943. Upon his death, Fred F. Burns, President of the Consolidated Milling Co., wrote,

> Sands, Taylor & Wood Co. has lived and prospered through the War of 1812, the Mexican War, the Civil War, and has withstood all the other trials and vicissitudes including money panics, wheat "corners," depressions, and bank holidays. There has always been a Sands with the firm and usually at the helm. Also, there has always been an unswerving policy of fair dealing. The firm name is known to most milling concerns in the U.S.A. and its brand, "King Arthur," is known to almost every man, woman and child in the six New England states.

We are proud to have been permitted to serve this fine old institution for twenty-two years. We are prouder still to have numbered among our personal friends Mr. Frank E. Sands, who had been connected with the Company since 1896. He passed away last Saturday. He was one of the kindest hearted men the writer was ever privileged to know. He loved his business and was active in the management almost to the day of his death.

Always, as in the past, there is another Sands ready to take over, Walter E., Frank's second son. And the thousands of his father's well-wishers can confidently expect the firm to go on doing business at the old stand in the old way.

Walter Sands (father of Frank E. Sands II, the current President) was an extremely colorful character. He was born five years after Donald and, against all family tradition, went north to New Hampshire to be educated at Dartmouth College. Even more alarming to his family was his burgeoning interest in the theater. Fortunately for the Company (and maybe for the family), Walter's career was short. In 1928, after a year and a half starring with the Duncan sisters in the musical comedy *Topsy and Eva*, he went to work for his father.

Walter put his dramatic energy into the Company just as it was beginning a campaign to capture the New York market. He took to the streets of New York City in a truck outfitted with a calliope and an enormous wooden carving of a mounted King Arthur. (The warehouse he worked out of was where the current United Nations building now stands.) Soon after this debut, he was stopped by the police for driving an illegal vehicle. But Walter, in his inimitable way, made friends with Mayor Jimmy Walker himself, who granted him an "Itinerant Musician's License." So King Arthur rolled on.

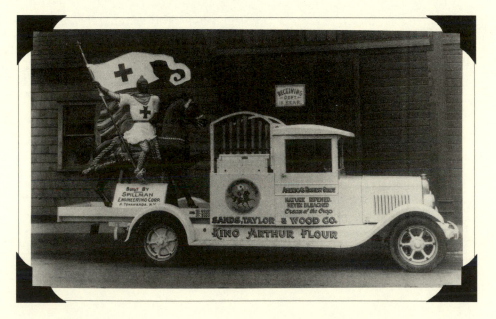

In 1930 Walter left New York to go back to Boston where he was given a mandate to establish the King Arthur Coffee business. When his older brother died seven years later, he took over the flour business in Somerville as well as continuing the coffee business in Boston. (He did so well that in 1938 General Foods tried, without luck, to tempt him away.)

When Ed Sands, Walter's father, died in 1943, Walter took over the entire operation and was elected President of Sands, Taylor & Wood Co. a year later, a position he held until 1968. Alone, he negotiated the Company through the remainder of the difficult war years and then through the postwar years when the pressures on the flour business were many.

In 1955 the Company left Somerville and moved to much more spacious quarters with a railroad siding in Cambridge. It was atop this building, which was clearly visible from one of the major arteries into Boston, that the wooden statue of King Arthur and his horse was to be permanently placed after many years and many miles on the road. Unaware that the pair had been unbolted in preparation for reinstallation, someone attempted to move the truck, leading to an unfortunate and "fatal" accident. Even though the great wooden symbol "fell" on hard times, his spirit lives on in our continuing commitment to all he represented.

Walter's two sons, Frank Edgar Sands II and Robert Graham Sands, both followed in their father's tracks and went north to Dartmouth. Frank spent his military years in the Navy at the Pentagon and then went to Harvard Business School. Bob continued his studies and graduated from Tuck, Dartmouth's business school. After his schooling he became a "green beret" and a paratrooper. During his service in Germany, he guarded Rudoph Hess at Spandau Prison and was photographed by *Time* magazine as a young soldier in front of the construction of the Berlin Wall. (We are exuberant and thankful that 1990 will be remembered as the year the Wall came down.)

Both Frank and Bob went to work for the Company in 1963. They started working in the warehouse lifting and moving hundred-pound bags of flour even before they were allowed to go out on sales calls.

In 1963, Sands, Taylor & Wood Co. had only six percent of the market share of family flour. As retail sales of flour continued to decrease, it seemed to be an astute business move to get into the bakery supply business (the same decision that their Uncle Donald had made in 1922). With Frank and Bob's combined energy, the Company's business grew fivefold by 1968.

That same year, the Company's Board of Directors elected Frank President and Bob Vice President. Eventually Bob chose to pursue a career in government service leaving Frank to operate the business on his own.

Walter Sands (center) and his sons, Robert (left) and Frank (right), in front of the old Wayside Inn Grist Mill, in Sudbury, Massachusetts.

THE COMPANY IN THE 1960's & '70's

At thirty-two, Frank was almost the youngest President in the Company's long history. Because the future of home baking continued to be insecure, Frank made a decision to acquire companies that manufactured bakery supplies rather than function solely as a distributor. Allied Bakery Supply was purchased in the late 1960's. In 1973, the Joseph Middleby Company, which manufactured fillings and other bakery products, was purchased. In 1976, a similar company, H. A. Johnson, was acquired.

In 1976 the Company moved from Cambridge to 155 North Beacon Street in Brighton, where the manufacturing facility of H. A. Johnson was located. Here, Sands, Taylor & Wood Co. and its newly formed subsidiary, Johnson-Middleby, Inc., the largest bakery manufacturer and supplier in New England, took up new headquarters. With these acquisitions, Sands, Taylor & Wood Co. sold every item a bakery could use. Under Frank's tutelage in the '70's, the fortunes of the Company had expanded tenfold.

Although this all seemed like a good idea at the time, several unforeseen problems served to stifle its success. It became increasingly difficult to streamline and manage a complex business whose employees were from three separate entities, some represented by three different labor unions. But the ultimately insurmountable problem was the rise in interest rates to an unaffordable twenty-two percent making it all but impossible to pay off the debt of expansion.

Because it had become almost impossible to focus on what the company was really about, Frank and his wife Brinna decided that there was truth in the axiom "small is beautiful." They decided to sell off their problems and refocus on the thing they knew and loved best, King Arthur Flour. Knowing they could sell their flour from any location, they moved their family and Sands, Taylor & Wood Co. to Norwich, Vermont.

...& Future

Sands, Taylor & Wood remains a small, regional company. Although the market for family flour has been declining for the last century, our share of it continues to grow, thanks to you, our loyal bakers.

The People Behind the Company

In this year of our two-hundredth anniversary, King Arthur Flour (as most people know us) is run by a small group of very able people.

The Norwich Office

• Frank E. Sands II is President, the fifth generation of his family in this business. Although Frank followed his father's tracks north to Dartmouth, he went back to Cambridge where he received his M.B.A. at Harvard in 1963. Frank learned the business literally from the ground up, lugging one-hundred-pound flour bags as a teenager in the summer. Upon joining the company on a full-time basis, he spent his initial years making the early morning calls on retail and wholesale bakers selling bakery supplies. Frank is a natural salesman whose enthusiasm for his product is renowned. When he is in conversation, no matter what the subject, it will somehow always wind up dealing with the superlative qualities of King Arthur Flour. Frank's vitality, knowledge of the flour industry and vision have negotiated us through difficult times and good times. He has kept us focused and urged us on with myriad possibilities for the future.

• Brinna Sands, Frank's wife, has been actively involved with the Company since their move to Norwich in 1978. She has had a long interest in baking, its history and "matters Arthurian." Her early love of the kitchen was given to her by her mother, Mary Baird, and her grandmother, Annie Davis. Her love of writing was stimulated by Wilbur Cheever (her Lexington, Massachusetts, high school English teacher) whose relentless dedication to excellence has permanently imprinted her life. Brinna graduated with a degree in American Literature from Middlebury College. She has actively written about her baking adventures for the last eight years culminating with this *200th Anniversary Cookbook*. Brinna brings you "King Arthur's Kitchen" on "Radio New England Magazine," a weekly show aired on over eighty radio stations throughout the Northeast. She shares recipes, baking instructions, hints for success, as well as stories and anecdotes about life in general. In January of 1987 she was featured as a *Yankee Magazine* "Great New England Cook." She is a member of the American Institute of Culinary Professionals, the American Institute of Wine and Food and the Culinary Historians of Boston.

• Scott Berry is our Vice President and General Manager. Scott grew up across and down the river in Lebanon, New Hampshire, made it to Massachusetts when he went to Williams College and then really broke loose to head for North and South Dakota where he worked for Conagra's Feed Division. After a short stint with Conagra's Export Division in Louisiana and Illinois, he and his wife, Ann, decided that there was no place like home. Shortly thereafter, in August of 1984, he joined Sands, Taylor & Wood Co. and has been here ever since. In the meantime his family has grown to include Emily (now three) and Leah (one).

• Sally Thompson joined us two years later in 1986. Hers is the cheerful voice you hear on the telephone when you call King Arthur's headquarters. Without Sally, the office might not function at all. Worse than that, baking would grind to a halt all over New England because King Arthur Flour would never make it to your grocer's shelf. Along with successfully managing our increasingly busy office, Sally also finds time to be Jason's wife, Jesse and Jenna's mother and a formidable presence in the town of Vershire, Vermont, where they live.

• Liza Bernard, our Consumer Affairs Director, arrived in 1987. Many of you have already met her through correspondence about this cookbook or in response to questions and queries about recipes in particular and baking in general. Liza wears many hats, both at Sands, Taylor & Wood Co. and in her own business as an art consultant. She started working for the Company as a data entry person (a little moonlighting to cushion her "real" vocation as a designer and project co-ordinator). She lives in a home she designed and built six years ago in Pomfret, Vermont, to house herself and her weaving studio. (She also loves to bake and holds the record for variations on the "Cake-Pan" Cake.)

• In 1988, as our two-hundredth anniversary loomed, we hired Ellen Davies, a returnee from Florida, as our Public Relations Director. Her energy and vitality have spread word of the joys of baking with King Arthur Flour all over New England and beyond. Ellen, as a child, was a tomboy so her mother told her that when she was fourteen she would have to stay in the house and learn to cook. Her mother's fears were unfounded. Ellen is a natural cook, loves to bake and knows, from much experience, of which she speaks and writes. She is relatively new to King Arthur Flour but, after much experimentation, is a convert of strong conviction. Her taste for things made with King Arthur has even been passed on to a cockatiel and a lovebird who love to share Sunday biscuits with Ellen and her husband, Bill. One Sunday, Ellen experimented with another brand of flour. She said, "I am not kidding. Those birds turned up their beaks and wouldn't touch them. They must be like those canaries in the mines!" Ellen has three teenage sons and lives across the river in Lebanon, New Hampshire.

• P.J. Hamel (Peggy, but she won't answer to it) joined us in September of 1990. Her arrival came through a bit of serendipity. She had written to us (being a King Arthur sort of person) in hopes that we might have an opening about the time we had begun looking for someone just like her. PJ came to us from the *Camden Herald* in Maine where, as General Manager and Sports Editor (as well as contributing a regular column about her adventures in the kitchen), she did just about everything there that there was to do. So PJ has spent this year making our kitchen sing (she's a baker extraordinaire), editing our new newsletter, *The Baking Sheet*, formatting and writing copy for our new *King Arthur Flour Baker's Catalogue* and just being good company. How did we do without her?

• Martha Douple is one of our part-timers. She is a longtime friend whose presence in our office has been invaluable. She has the ability to see what needs to be done and, with the touch of Merlin, make it happen in the blink of an eye. She's our environmental conscience as well as a proofreader *par excellence*. (Her technique is to read a text backward.) Martha is working her way through Dartmouth College, but Dartmouth is just across the river so we're fortunate to have frequent access to her ready smile and deadly organizational abilities.

Our Advertising Agency

• DiBona, Bornstein & Random, Inc., is a small agency with a combined talent of enormous capacity. Joyce DiBona is its President and Marketing Director whose warmth and energy encompass both her "hominess" and professionalism. Stanley Bornstein is its extremely witty and verbally facile Copy Editor. David Random is its perennially upbeat and smiling Graphic Artist. It's hard to call the time we spend with this trio "work."

Our Food Brokers

• Without the arms and legs and hands and feet of our principal food broker, Morris Alper & Sons, Inc., it would be hard for King Arthur Flour to be in all of the places it is. This organization, run by Fred Alper, the inimitable grandson of the founder, is the finest we've ever worked with. They surprise us every year with how many places those feet have gone and how many times they've been there. Their efforts are truly of heroic proportions as only King Arthur would know. Their belief in us and ours in them creates a music that even Merlin can hear.

• J. P. Luciano & Sons, Inc., is a fast-growing food brokerage agency that handles King Arthur Flour sales in upstate New York. We started working with them in 1986 and our sales have grown steadily since. This agency has focused on handling only top-quality products. We appreciate their vision and commitment to quality because it is so much in keeping with our own. Joe Luciano has often said he models his group on our principal broker, Morris Alper & Sons.

Our Board of Directors

Our Board is small but with many talents. We have three "inside" Directors: Frank Sands, Brinna Sands and Scott Berry. And we have three "outside" Directors: Robert Weiss, E. Clinton Swift and Gary Brooks.

• Bob Weiss has had the longest and most varied association with the company, beginning as our advertising account executive in the mid-1960's. He later headed two advertising agencies which creatively advertised King Arthur Flour for more than a decade. Bob then ran the public relations firm that recognized and promoted the unique talents of our baking spokespeople. Now, heading his own publishing company, he continues to support our company with his creative and sage advice.

• Clint Swift was a corporate lawyer from Philadelphia who found the hills of Vermont and New Hampshire to be the greener side of the fence. His early love of the stock market (he bought his first shares when he was twelve) propelled him out of law and into financial planning where he has successfully developed his early inclinations. His feel for the ebbs and flows of the economy are as valuable for creating perspective as is his sense of humor.

• Gary Brooks is our corporate lawyer whose counsel and enthusiasm for King Arthur Flour are greatly valued. He, too, has found the hills of Vermont to be the green pastures where he and his family want to live. Gary is a meticulous lawyer with an equal devotion to his family. He and his wife, Barbara Duncan (a designer/draftswoman and teacher of ballet), do a whole week's baking together one night a week. You'll find their recommendation for "perfect" cookies in Chapter VI.

Our Advocates in the Past

• Gretchen McMullen was our first spokeswoman. She was a prominent "foodie" in the late 1920's and '30's with her own radio program called "The Boston Food Kitchen."

• Marjorie Mills, billed as "New England's foremost food expert," endorsed King Arthur Flour on the Boston radio station WBZ in 1947. In nine months she received 30,000 requests for "Primers of Bread Baking," a record response at the time.

• Ruth Lenson unwittingly began our demonstration program in the 1960's when she asked for our support for a baking class to teach a group at her Hadassah to make challah. Bert Porter, who was a King Arthur Flour salesman at the time, went along to help. Ruth went on to become a food columnist for the *Jewish Advocate*.

• Bert Porter, with no demonstrator immediately available, approached Walter Sands, current President of the Company, and told him he felt he could also be an effective demonstrator. So, after going to "baking school" under the tutelage of his wife Ruth, Bert, with his Yankee wit, started demonstrating in Burlington, Vermont. Not too long after this, on a show in Providence, Rhode Island, where he was scheduled to visit for less than half an hour, the response of the listeners was so enormous that he ended up staying for the entire afternoon.

When Bert "demonstrated" on the radio, he would arrive with all the ingredients needed to bake bread (even a portable oven). His listeners heard the whole process with Bert explaining as he went. When the timer went off as the bread finished baking and he opened the oven to take it out, listeners swore the aroma came through the radio. Bert finally retired in the late 1970's but it was his success, both over the radio and before a live audience, that committed us to this kind of demonstrating.

Our Advocates Today

Currently we have three wonderful advocates sharing and spreading the "joys of baking."

• Back in 1982, Michael Jubinsky, an avid avocational baker from Preston, Connecticut, wrote to the Sands. Although he was vocationally an engineer for the Navy, he loved to bake and he loved King Arthur Flour. At that point he was writing articles on baking and teaching baking classes as well. His letter began what has become a long and fruitful relationship and friendship between him, his wife, Sandy, the Sands and the Company. Michael and Sandy are a baking team in the true sense of the word.

Today, Michael works full time as the Director of Submarine Safety for the U.S. Navy at the Electric Boat Shipyard in Groton, Connecticut. Additionally (beyond being an advocate for King Arthur Flour), he is on the staff of the Connecticut Culinary Institute in Farmington and is a member of the Connecticut Bakers' Association and the International Association of Cooking Professionals. He writes a bi-weekly food column for *The Day*, a newspaper in New London, Connecticut.

• Barbara Lauterbach joined forces with the Company in 1988. She is an equally enthusiastic and knowledgeable baker and runs an exceptional Bed & Breakfast, Watch Hill, in Centre Harbor, New Hampshire.

Barbara's fascination with food has taken her to cooking schools all over Europe. On this side of the Atlantic she has studied with Julia Child, Chef Jean Louis, Chef Anton Mosiman and Madeleine Kamman, to name only a few.

She received the "Best Cooks in Town Award" from the *Cincinnati Post* and, for directing the "Creative Kitchen Cooking Schools" for Lazarus Department Stores, the "Best of Cincinnati Award" from *Cincinnati Magazine*. Barbara has also done numerous radio and television programs.

Now that she's in the East, beyond teaching many baking classes and doing demonstrations for King Arthur Flour, she's a consultant for "Duck Soup," a gourmet specialty shop in Sudbury, Massachusetts.

• Ken Haedrich has joined us most recently. He is a self-taught baker who has worked in professional bakeries and kitchens along the way. Now that he is married and the father of four children, he is a mellowed, but still earthy, "ex-hippie," as he describes himself, very much dedicated to whole grain baking. These days he will admit that by adding a little, not much, unbleached flour to his baked goods their texture is really lightened and improved. (Where King Arthur Flour's suggested ratio of stone ground whole wheat to unbleached all-purpose flours is about 1 to 3, Ken's is the reciprocal, 3 to 1, which makes hearty, rib-sticking loaves.)

Ken specializes in home baking but he also loves to write. In addition to writing for *Food and Wine Magazine*, *Vermont Magazine*, *Horticulture* and *Country Journal*, he has written *Ken Haedrich's Country Baking* which will be available in the fall of 1990. He has also written *The Great American Cheddar Cheese Cookbook*, *The Maple Syrup Cookbook*, and *A Passion for Bread*. In March of 1988 he was featured by *Yankee Magazine* as a "Great New England Cook."

Here are some of us in revelrous attire at our 200th Anniversary Kick-Off Banquet at the Higgins Armory Museum in Worcester, Massachusetts, in September 1989.

The 1990's and on into the 21st Century

Continued commitment to our King Arthur Flours and two new ventures will provide us with challenges and excitement in the future. We are looking forward to acquainting (and reacquainting) you, in these new ways, with the ordinary but infinitely satisfying joys of baking and of the kitchen.

WinterBake ℠

To help us celebrate and share the joys of baking in the next decade and beyond, we have instituted a baking contest to be held every other year. This year, chefs from the New England Culinary Institute are baking off the recipes that were submitted earlier. The results will be analyzed by an exciting panel of judges. The 1991 WinterBake Award Ceremony will be held at the Inn at Essex, Essex, Vermont, where winners, judges and guests will sample the winning recipes, attend baking workshops and join us in a little revelling.

The King Arthur Flour Baker's Catalogue™

A second venture, which evolved during the writing of this book, was our entrance into the world of direct marketing through the acquisition of *The Breadbasket, The Catalogue for Home Breadbakers*. Along with the *Breadbasket*, we are acquiring the friendship and expertise of its previous owner, Betsy Oppenneer, whose enthusiasm for baking bread appears to be boundless. She and her husband, Keith, are moving to New England from their home ground of Issequah, Washington, and will continue to consult on all catalogue issues. Betsy flies all over the United States giving bread-baking classes and will even slow down enough to do some for us here in the Northeast.

Our catalogue, renamed *The King Arthur Flour Baker's Catalogue*, will continue to offer a wide variety of freshly ground whole grain flours, extracts and spices, books on baking, and baking equipment which your grandchildren will love to inherit from you.

The Baking Sheet™

Betsy also sent out a quarterly newsletter called *The Baking Sheet*, which will retain its name but will continue as a collaboration of her and our expertise in baking matters. We intend it to be a forum for all of you who love to bake and who would love to share your ideas, breakthroughs, knowledge and even problems with us. It will also contain recipes, lore and arcane information about baking that you won't find in most cookbooks.

We are very excited at having these opportunities to share our enthusiam for baking directly with you.

• A SHORT HISTORY OF ARTHUR •

BRITAIN BEFORE ARTHUR

The period in British history in which King Arthur lived is a mysterious one known as Britain's "Dark Ages." It is "dark" because there are very few written documents that tell us what went on. There is significantly more knowledge of the events that led up to that period.

In the fifty years after the birth of Christ, Rome began an occupation of Britain that lasted almost four hundred years, about the same length of time that North America has been "occupied" by non-native peoples. During this period, Britain enjoyed a high level of culture, learning and material wealth which, after the Romans left, was not seen for another thousand years.

As Rome began to disintegrate from within, and in response to increasing aggression from without, she began to call back her legions to protect her. So Britain ultimately was left without access to Roman military protection and had to rely on her own resources. This came at a time when the whole western world, not just Rome and Britain, was being pressed by "barbarian" cultures from outside: Saxon, Angle, Vandal, Jute and Goth.

TRACES OF ARTHUR

The period that is associated with Arthur came right after Rome disassociated herself from Britain during the time that Saxons began to come across from the continent to pillage and plunder. Although there is almost no written history from this period, there is a very strong oral tradition about someone called Arthur who stepped into this military void to organize the remaining Britons and who subsequently held off the Saxon threat long enough to create a period of stability and peace. These oral tales, which are much older than any written record, originated and persist today in the western, Celtic regions of Britain, Ireland and France (Brittany).

Arthur first appeared in literature around 800 A.D., when a monk named Nennius wrote about Britons plagued by Saxon invaders sometime in the late fifth or early sixth century. In his record, a hero named Arthur united the divergent kingdoms and moved successfully against the invaders.

In 1136, a monk known as Geoffrey of Monmouth wrote an ambitious work called *The History of the Kings of England*. With this, Arthur became a "King" and a part of English "history." This history, however, contained only a few threads of truth woven into a much larger fabrication. The result was an Arthurian tapestry blended of ancient Celtic tradition with the Christian traditions of the Middle Ages. Through his "history" Geoffrey introduced this new King Arthur to a much larger audience which took him as their own.

THE LEGENDARY ARTHUR

The evolution of the legend of King Arthur is like the growth of a pearl. Inside there is something real, but the original reality is no longer visible. Whatever really happened a millennium and a half ago has been layered with tale after tale, each one tempered by the age in which it was told, until it has become a luminous epic whose heroes and adventures are permanently woven into the culture of the British people. Each tale has become beloved in its own right and each is a fascinating lens into one part of the vast and complex history of Celtic and, subsequently, Christian Britain.

In the thousand years since Geoffrey's *History*, King Arthur has been celebrated in prose, poetry, art and opera. New writers tell his story from every conceivable point of view. Whatever the original reason for the tale, Arthur's story has come to mean the struggle for light in the face of darkness. The following is a generic and simplified outline.

A STORY OF ARTHUR

Foreseeing Britain's need for a hero/king, Merlin creates by magic the circumstances of Arthur's conception. Uther Pendragon, having fallen in love with Ygerne (wife of Gorlois, Duke of Cornwall), is transformed by Merlin to appear as Gorlois himself. He gains admittance to the castle on the rocky coast of Cornwall at Tintagel, and Arthur is conceived.

After Arthur's birth, Merlin, via a cave accessible by water below the castle, spirits him away to the western lowlands of Scotland to bring him up and prepare him for his future role as king. When Arthur is a young man, he challenges other contenders for the kingdom by pulling the magic sword, Excalibur, out of a stone. As he is the only one who is able, he is accepted as King of the Britons.

Arthur creates alliances among the many small kingdoms of his island and unites them to drive out the Saxon invaders. He weds Guinevere, holds court at Camelot and gathers his knights around the Round Table. A period of peace is achieved during which his knights accomplish many heroic deeds, one of them the search for the Holy Grail.

After many years, Arthur fights his final battle. He is gravely wounded and as he lies waiting for his end, he exhorts his knight, Bedivere, to throw his magic sword, Excalibur, into the waters of Dozmary Pool. The arm of the Lady of the Lake emerges from the surface, receives the sword and then disappears with it forever beneath the water. Arthur is then taken away to Avalon so his wounds might be healed.

In ancient, oral Celtic tradition, Arthur never dies. There are many sites in the west country of England, Scotland and Wales where it is said he lies with his men, waiting. It is the belief that he will return that has given him the epithet, "The Once & Future King."

Although the tale has many versions and diversions, this is part of its essence. It appeals to a universal desire for a leader who can fight a war, real or symbolic, against overwhelming odds, and win because of the justice of the cause. Arthur has thus become a symbol for honesty, goodness and strength. He is revered as Merlin foretold and Merlin, a symbol of our own longing for wisdom and power, is ever present to guide his way.

THE ONCE & FUTURE KING

Because of the universal appeal of his story, the legend of Arthur has developed a life of its own apart from its basis in reality. But the possibility that a person really did exist to set this story in motion electrifies the legends and continues to tantalize and excite the scholar.

To search for Arthur is to look for what is real in a house of mirrors, but mirrors with many facets that never reflect exactly the same thing twice. There are the images that you see, the tales that are told, but of all those images, it is a daunting task to separate what is real from what is just a slightly altered reflection of another reflection.

There are scholars today who pore over newly discovered medieval documents looking for the clues that will finally substantiate this "King" named Arthur who lived so long ago. Even in the last decade there are people whose research seems to be finding real traces of the "original image." But again, clues are few and theories are many. The fact that the search continues means that Arthur does, in fact, still "live" and really may be "The Once & Future King."

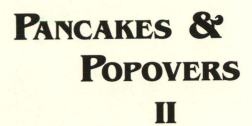

PANCAKES & POPOVERS

II

PANCAKES & POPOVERS
WAFFLES & CRÊPES

• To ensure that your pancakes are light, make sure your cups of flour weigh 4 ounces. See the top of the King Arthur Unbleached All-Purpose Flour bag or page 597 for directions. The second thing you can do to ensure light pancakes is to mix the wet and dry ingredients together for only 20 seconds, just enough to blend the two.

• Whenever you see this symbol 🌿 after King Arthur Unbleached All-Purpose Flour in the ingredient list, feel free to substitute King Arthur Stone Ground Whole Wheat Flour. It will add a nutty flavor and hearty texture to whatever you bake in the oven or on the griddle.

• To test for correct pancake cooking temperature, sprinkle a few drops of water onto your griddle. The water should "dance."

• Using a ¼-cup measure or an ice cream scoop, pour your batter onto the griddle leaving enough space for each pancake to expand. Turn them when the bubbles on the top surface pop and don't fill in. The second side takes only half the amount of time needed to cook the first.

• If you are using a well-seasoned cast iron frying pan or "spider," a teflon -coated griddle, or if the batter has butter or vegetable oil in it, it probably won't be necessary to grease the pan after the first batch of pancakes.

• You can keep a batch of pancakes hot by piling them on a cookie sheet. To keep them from getting soggy and sticking together, place a clean cloth napkin or dish towel (not terry cloth) between each layer and on top of the piles to absorb steam. Put the cookie sheet in your oven set at the lowest temperature. Or you can be less elaborate and just stack the pancakes on a plate!

• Leftover batter can be a real gift. You can store it in the refrigerator where it will keep for several days. If it should thicken, you can resurrect it by adding a tablespoon of milk mixed with ¾ teaspoon of baking powder for each cup of batter you have on hand. Or if you find your batter has thinned while waiting for you to get back to it, add ½ to 1 cup of King Arthur Flour mixed with ¾ to ½ teaspoon of baking powder to revive it.

• To freeze pancakes, waffles or crêpes, place them side by side on a slightly greased cookie sheet. As soon as they are frozen, place them in a plastic bag to keep them from drying out. They will keep for about two weeks in a self-defrosting freezer and up to 6 months in a chest or upright freezer. To reheat, use a griddle, toaster or toaster oven.

PANCAKES & POPOVERS
WAFFLES & CRÊPES
II

Based on how small this section is, you might assume that there are not very many pancakes in the world. But that's just an illusion. Pancakes are one of the most ancient, basic and ubiquitous of shapes and there are recipes for them scattered throughout this book: Drop Scones and Scotch Pancakes are in Chapter III; Crumpets and English Muffins are in Chapter IV; Nan, Tortillas and Fratbraud are in Chapter VI; and "Whole Meal" Pancakes are in Chapter IX. The best pancake story of all is in the Sourdough chapter.

Because of all the ways they can be leavened, pancakes are found in almost every baking category. They can be leavened just with the steam produced by the moisture in them, just with eggs, with both wild and domestic yeasts, and, most familiarly in New England, with baking soda or baking powder. The one thing they all have in common is that they are flat. So when you get through exploring the recipes in this chapter, don't stop here; it's just a beginning.

Crêpes and waffles are specialized kinds of pancakes. Crêpes are made with a thin batter so they are flexible and can be wrapped around something delicious. Waffles are most often made with a traditional pancake batter and cooked in a special iron which makes them crisp and airy traps for butter and maple syrup.

Popovers are a closely related, but slightly different, branch of this family. Like crêpes, they are made with a very thin batter and leavened just with air and eggs, but rather than being cooked on a griddle, popovers are baked in the oven which performs a great magic on them. You'll find them and some of their interesting cousins at the end of the chapter.

• A PANCAKE & WAFFLE PRIMER •

BASIC PANCAKES OR WAFFLES

Pancakes or waffles make the basis for many great meals because they go to-gether so quickly and they're so versatile. This basic recipe makes enough for a good-sized hungry family (two or three adolescents with leftovers to freeze if you are lucky) but can easily be cut in half to accommodate smaller or fewer appetites.

As with muffins you can actually leave the butter or oil out of the batter. (Just make sure your griddle or waffle iron is well greased though.) The total calorie count is, of course, dependent on what you put on top. You can use butter and maple syrup which is traditional in the Northeast. For a low-calorie, calcium- and vitamin-rich meal, try them with unsweetened yogurt and sliced, slightly sweetened fresh fruit.

4 cups King Arthur Unbleached All-Purpose Flour 🪶
2 to 4 tablespoons sugar
1 tablespoon baking powder
1 teaspoon salt
1 teaspoon baking soda
4 eggs
1 quart buttermilk, yogurt or sour milk (or 1 quart sweet milk with ¼ cup
     vinegar or lemon juice plus 5 minutes to clabber)
½ cup (1 stick) melted butter or vegetable oil (optional)

Mixing: In a large bowl, mix the dry ingredients thoroughly.

In a second bowl, beat the eggs and buttermilk together until they are light and fluffy. Add the butter or oil. Take about 20 seconds and blend this mixture into the dry ingredients. Don't overdo it. Pancake and waffle batter is like muffin batter; a light hand in mixing means a light pancake on the plate.

Cooking: For successful pancakes, use a griddle that heats evenly. Cast iron is particularly good. Preheat and grease your griddle or waffle iron.

• **Pancakes:** To test for correct pancake cooking temperature, sprinkle a few drops of water onto your griddle. The water should "dance." Using a quarter-cup measure or an ice cream scoop, pour your batter onto the griddle leaving enough space for each pancake to expand. Turn them when the bubbles on the top surface pop and don't fill in. The second side takes only half the amount of time needed to cook the first.

If you are using a well-seasoned cast iron frying pan or "spider" (see page 67), or a non-stick griddle, and if the batter has butter or vegetable oil in it, it probably won't be necessary to grease the pan after the first batch. Pancakes can be stockpiled in the oven on "low."

- **Waffles:** Most waffle irons come with directions, but here are some general guidelines if you don't happen to have any.

Preheat the iron until it's just beginning to "smoke" and grease it just before you put the batter on. (A pastry brush is a good tool for this job.) Unlike a pancake griddle, a waffle iron usually needs to be greased each time you cook a waffle. To get the batter from the bowl to the iron, an ice cream scoop again is useful. Place a scoopful of batter in the middle of the iron. When you close it, the top will force the batter out to the edges.

Although waffle irons differ, a waffle usually cooks in 2 to 4 minutes. When steam stops pouring out from under the lid, check to see if it's done. If the top doesn't want to lift up, it probably needs another minute or two. A well-seasoned iron will "let go" of the waffle when it's done.

Waffles are best eaten right from the iron if you like them crisp. Even in a warm oven, wrapped in a clean dish towel, they are apt to soften if you stockpile them like pancakes.

Variations

These are written for pancakes but can be applied to waffle batter as well.

Light Pancakes: Separate the eggs and add only the yolks to the liquid ingredients. Beat the whites until they form stiff peaks and fold them in last.

Cinnamon Pancakes: For added zip, sprinkle a little cinnamon on the pancake before you flip it (or on the waffle before you close the lid).

Banana Pancakes: Fold 1 or 2 cups of mashed or chopped ripe bananas (2 to 4) into the batter.

Fruit or Berry Pancakes: Fold 1 to 2 cups of washed berries or sliced fruit into the batter. (Try a combination of sliced apples and grated Cheddar cheese.)

Pumpkin Pancakes: Add 1 teaspoon each of cinnamon, nutmeg and ginger to the dry ingredients. Fold $1/2$ to 1 cup mashed pumpkin into the batter and reduce the other liquid by the same amount.

Hearty Pancakes: Substitute $1/2$ to 1 cup of cornmeal, rye meal, oatmeal, wheat germ or bran for an equal amount of unbleached flour, and/or add $1/4$ to $1/2$ cup sunflower, sesame or poppy seeds.

Ice cream sandwiches made with fresh waffles are a treat. Frozen yogurt in place of ice cream minimizes the calories but offers the same combination of textures.

King Arthur Flour
Pancake "Mix"

To be prepared for those rushed mornings, or the lazy ones, you can either measure out just the dry ingredients ahead of time or go one step further and make this all-natural King Arthur Pancake "Mix." (You could even take this on your next camping trip.) Use any of the variations listed on the preceding page.

6 cups King Arthur Unbleached All-Purpose Flour
3 cups King Arthur Stone Ground Whole Wheat Flour
$\frac{1}{2}$ cup wheat germ or bran (optional)
1$\frac{1}{2}$ cups non-fat dry milk or 1$\frac{1}{2}$ cups dry buttermilk powder
1 tablespoon salt
$\frac{1}{4}$ to $\frac{1}{2}$ cup sugar, white or brown
$\frac{1}{4}$ cup baking powder
1 cup vegetable shortening

In a large bowl, combine flours, wheat germ or bran, dry milk, salt, sugar and baking powder, and mix well. Cut in the shortening until it is evenly distributed. (It is important to use shortening rather than butter because it remains stable at room temperature.)

To store this "Mix," place it in a large, airtight container, or put it up in premeasured (don't pack it), 2-cup portions. It will make approximately seven.

Using Your King Arthur Flour Pancake "Mix"

Each 2-cup batch of "Mix" makes about a dozen 5-inch pancakes.

1 egg, slightly beaten
1 to 1$\frac{1}{4}$ cups water (depending on how thick or thin you like pancakes)
2 cups King Arthur Flour Pancake "Mix" from above, not packed

Combine the egg and water in a bowl. Stir in the "Mix" until it's just moistened. Cook the pancakes according to the directions on the preceding page.

• SWEET PANCAKES & WAFFLES •

GINGERBREAD PANCAKES

This spicy pancake recipe is from our spicy Public Relations Director, Ellen Davies. Ellen and her husband, Bill, eat these almost every weekend. Ellen eats hers plain; Bill eats them with maple syrup. We thought we might eat them with some whipped cream laced with finely minced candied ginger.

The amount of ginger in this recipe is variable. Since ginger is an aroma and a sensation as well as a flavor, you'll have to decide how intense an experience you want.

1 cup King Arthur Stone Ground Whole Wheat Flour
1 cup King Arthur Unbleached All-Purpose Flour
1 tablespoon baking powder
½ teaspoon salt
2 to 3 teaspoons ground ginger
1 teaspoon cinnamon
½ teaspoon allspice
¼ teaspoon ground cloves and/or nutmeg
2 eggs
2 to 2¼ cups milk
¼ cup molasses
2 tablespoons vegetable oil or melted butter

Combine the dry ingredients in a large bowl. (This dry mixture can be stored in an airtight plastic bag to use as a mix in the future.)

Beat the eggs and 2 cups of the milk together in a smaller bowl until they're light. Whisk in the molasses and oil or butter.

Blend the wet ingredients with the dry adding the remainder of the milk to lighten the batter if you wish. Since pancake batter can be thick or thin to make pancakes that are thick or thin, the choice is up to you.

Cook according to the directions on page 32.

Apple Pancakes

You can always add apples or blueberries or other fruits to the Basic Pancake or Waffle batter, or the King Arthur Flour Pancake "Mix" if you have some of that made up. These sweet and spicy pancakes are delicious served with yogurt sweetened with brown sugar or maple syrup, or just sprinkled with cinnamon sugar. These pancakes and the following two are leavened just with eggs.

> 2 cups King Arthur Unbleached All-Purpose Flour
> 1 to 2 teaspoons cinnamon (depending on fruit and taste)
> 1/3 cup sugar
> 1/2 teaspoon salt
> 3 eggs
> 1 1/2 cups milk
> 4 apples, peeled, chopped and sprinkled with lemon juice (to prevent browning)
> butter or oil to grease griddle

Blend the dry ingredients together. Beat the eggs until they are light and mix in the milk. Blend the wet ingredients with the dry mixture. Gently fold in the sliced apple.

Melt butter in a griddle and drop the batter by the tablespoonful, allowing room for the batter to spread. Cook the pancakes on both sides until they are golden.

Guinevere's Pancakes

This batter, mixed in a blender, is ready in just the amount of time it takes you to get the ingredients out of the refrigerator and cupboard, plus one minute. (It makes great waffles too.) It will make about twenty 4-inch pancakes that are reminiscent of crêpes.

> 1 cup cottage cheese, plain, with pineapple or with chives
> 6 eggs
> 1/2 cup King Arthur Unbleached All-Purpose Flour
> 1/4 teaspoon salt
> 1/4 cup vegetable oil
> 1/4 cup milk
> 1/2 teaspoon vanilla

Blend all of the above ingredients together until they are smooth. Cook on a griddle as you would Basic Pancakes (page 32). You can eat the ones made with plain cottage cheese with traditional maple syrup for breakfast, the pineapple version with yogurt and fruit for lunch, and the chive variation with chicken and a light cream sauce for dinner.

Sunday Crêpes

Crêpes are thin French pancakes that can be varied to accommodate main meal or dessert fillings. They can be served wrapped around chicken with a cream sauce, or spread with jam and topped with whipped cream and fresh fruit. These thin, delicate pancakes rely on a high-protein flour to keep them flexible and intact.

1 cup King Arthur Unbleached All-Purpose Flour
a pinch of salt
2 eggs, separated
1 1/4 cups milk
2 tablespoons sugar (optional, for sweet crêpes)
2 teaspoons grated lemon rind (optional, for sweet crêpes)

Combine the flour and salt in a mixing bowl.

In a separate bowl, beat the egg yolks into 1/2 cup milk. Stir this into the flour and add 3/4 cup more milk. Beat thoroughly to incorporate air into the mixture. Beat the egg whites until stiff. (Add the sugar and lemon rind.) Fold this gently into the batter.

At this point, it is advisable to let the batter sit out for an hour or so before you cook it. You can even make up the batter the night before and refrigerate it overnight.

Heat your lightly buttered crêpe pan or frying pan until a drop of water dances on the surface. Pour in only enough batter to coat the pan, and tilt the pan so that it covers the entire bottom. For a 6-inch pan you only need only about 1 tablespoon of batter.

When the batter turns yellow and is no longer runny, loosen the edge and flip the crêpe. Cook the second side for 15 to 20 seconds.

- **Savory Crêpes:** Fill with your choice of meats, seafood or vegetables, roll and place on platter. Cover with a Béchamel (page 486) or other light sauce, warm and serve.

- **Sweet Crêpes:** Fill with lightly spiced, cooked sliced apples or other fruits, or spread with jam or jelly. Roll, place in a greased casserole or on a warm plate and place briefly in a low oven. They may be served sprinkled with confectioners' sugar or warmed maple syrup.

BUCKWHEAT CAKES

We've said that pancakes can be leavened with almost anything. These old-fashioned buckwheat cakes are leavened with that old-fashioned leaven, yeast. Buckwheat has a unique flavor so you may want to try these on yourself before you serve them to a crowd. This recipe makes enough for 8 hungry people.

3 tablespoons sugar
1 packet or tablespoon active dry yeast
1 cup water
3 cups of buttermilk, lukewarm
2 large eggs
2 cups buckwheat flour
2 cups King Arthur Unbleached All-Purpose Flour 🌾
1 1/2 teaspoons salt
1/4 cup (1/2 stick) butter, melted, or vegetable oil
1 teaspoon baking soda

In a glass or pottery mixing bowl, dissolve 1 teaspoon of the sugar and then the yeast in 1/2 cup of the water. When it's bubbling and active, add the balance of the sugar, the buttermilk and beat in the eggs. Add the buckwheat flour, the unbleached flour, the salt and the butter or oil. Blend thoroughly. Cover and let this sponge work for at least 2 hours or overnight.

After the rising period, stir in the baking soda, which you've dissolved in the remaining 1/2 cup of water, and watch what happens. Cook on a hot griddle as you do baking powder pancakes (page 32).

SWEET FRENCH TOAST

This is quick, easy and full of nutrition. It makes 1 large or 2 moderate servings, enough to get your own day started, or, in multiples, a whole family's.

2 eggs
1/2 cup milk
a pinch of salt
1 teaspoon (or less) vanilla or other extract
4 slices bread (preferably homemade with King Arthur Flour, and stale)
cinnamon (or other spice) for sprinkling

Beat the eggs, milk, salt and vanilla until they are light. Soak the bread in this mixture and place on a lightly buttered, moderately hot griddle. Sprinkle with cinnamon. Cook until brown and crisp, flip over and do the same on the other side. Serve with traditional butter and maple syrup, or for a slimmer track, slightly sweetened yogurt and fresh fruit. (Or just sprinkle with confectioners' sugar.)

• SAVORY TYPES •

SAVORY FRENCH TOAST

French toast doesn't need to be sweet. This version would make an equally good breakfast. This is enough for 2 large servings or 4 moderate ones. Multiply for more.

2 eggs
1/2 cup milk
a pinch of salt
4 slices homemade bread (preferably stale): white, whole wheat, rye, etc.
paprika (or parsley, etc.) for sprinkling
4 thin slices onion (optional)
4 slices cheese
4 slices tomato (optional)
basil, fresh and minced for sprinkling, or dried (optional)

Preheat your oven to 450°F.

Make the French toast (page 38), substituting the paprika for the cinnamon. When the toast is done, place the onion, cheese and tomato on top. Sprinkle on the basil. Place it on a baking sheet in the oven for about 5 minutes, until the cheese has melted. (The tomato can be placed on after baking if you prefer it fresh.)

NORWEGIAN RICE WAFFLES

Marilyn Magnus, who lives in a log cabin she and her husband, David, built from trees cut from their own land, shared this unusual recipe. In David's family these are served as an alternative to baked potato or rice with thin slices of yellow cheese or butter.

2 cups King Arthur Unbleached All-Purpose Flour 🌾
4 teaspoons baking powder
1 teaspoon salt
3 cups cooked rice
15 cardamom seeds, finely ground (1 teaspoon, rounded)
1/2 cup sugar
2 cups milk
6 eggs, beaten
4 tablespoons (1/2 stick) butter or margarine, melted

Mix together the dry ingredients. Beat the milk and eggs together and add the melted butter or margarine. Blend this mixture into the dry. Cook as you would the Basic Waffles (page 33).

ZUCCHINI PANCAKES

These pancakes will brighten a late summer, evening meal and are just as good served cold for lunch the next day.

    2 cups grated zucchini
    2 eggs, beaten
    1 teaspoon salt
    1/4 teaspoon freshly grated pepper
    2 tablespoons chopped chives or onions
    1/2 cup freshly grated Parmesan cheese
    1/2 teaspoon fresh minced basil
    1/2 teaspoon oregano
    3/4 to 1 cup King Arthur Unbleached All-Purpose Flour 🌾
    1/4 cup olive oil or vegetable oil

In a bowl, mix the grated zucchini, eggs, salt, pepper, chives or onions, cheese and herbs. Blend in enough flour to hold the mixture together when dropped from a spoon.

Heat a griddle until it is moderately hot. Add and heat the oil. Drop the batter by the tablespoonful and brown the pancakes on both sides. Drain them on a paper towel and serve immediately, or keep them warm in the oven.

POTATO PANCAKES

Here is another vegetable-based pancake that can be served for brunch or supper. Serve them hot with applesauce which complements the flavor of the potato.

    4 medium-sized raw potatoes
    2 eggs, separated
    1 teaspoon salt
    1/4 teaspoon fresh grated pepper
    1/4 to 1/2 cup chopped onion or chives
    approximately 2 tablespoons King Arthur Unbleached All-Purpose Flour 🌾
    1/4 cup (or less) vegetable oil

Grate the potatoes. Beat the egg yolks and add them to the potatoes. Blend in the salt, pepper, onions or chives, and flour. Beat the egg whites until they form stiff peaks and gently fold them into the potato mixture.

Heat the oil in a griddle. Drop the batter by large tablespoonfuls onto the griddle and brown both sides of the pancakes.

BASIC FRITTERS

This basic recipe can be used for about 2 cups of fruit (blueberries, chopped apples, etc.) or, by omitting the sugar, 2 cups of chopped meat or vegetables. Depending on size, you'll make between six and a dozen fritters. (See page 505 for other fritters.)

1 cup King Arthur Unbleached All-Purpose Flour 🌾
½ teaspoon salt
1 teaspoon sugar (optional)
1 teaspoon baking powder
2 eggs, separated
⅔ cup milk
1 tablespoon butter, melted
2 cups fruit, meat or vegetables, chopped (if necessary)

Mix together the dry ingredients. In a separate bowl, beat the egg yolks and add the milk. Combine this with the dry ingredients, stirring only to blend. Add the melted butter and mix it in gently. Beat the egg whites until stiff and fold them into the batter. Fold in whatever fruit, meat or vegetables you choose.

Place a few inches of frying fat in a saucepan and heat it to 375°F (or whatever will cook a 1-inch cube of bread to a golden brown in about 40 seconds). Dip a spoon or ice cream scoop into the hot fat, then take a spoonful of the batter and drop it into the hot fat.

Fry the fritters until they are browned, about 3 to 5 minutes, turning as one side cooks. Remove them from the fat and drain on absorbent paper.

SALMON FRITTERS

These are lightly seasoned to complement the flavor of the fish. Serve them with a Béchamel (white) sauce (page 486). This recipe makes about eight fritters.

2 eggs, separated
2 tablespoons King Arthur Unbleached All-Purpose Flour 🌾
½ teaspoon salt
⅛ teaspoon pepper
1 teaspoon chopped parsley
½ pound cooked or canned salmon

Beat the egg yolks in a large bowl until they are thick. Add the flour and the seasonings. Break the salmon into very small pieces and stir into the flour mixture. Beat the egg whites in a separate bowl until they are stiff and fold them into the fritter batter. Cook as for Basic Fritters above.

• BAKED "PANCAKES" & POPOVERS •

As we've seen, there are lots of ways to leaven pancakes. The oldest leavening agent, which is neither biological nor chemical, is simply the air one can incorporate into a batter or dough by beating it. The second oldest is probably the "barm" that makes beer ferment, which is better known as brewers' yeast. More recently, a brewers' yeast has been "domesticated" specifically for baking, resulting in bakers' yeast. And even more recently than yeast, chemical leavening agents appeared about the middle of the last century.

To end this chapter, we're going to give you some recipes that use none of the leavenings mentioned above. They use the simple and versatile egg which blows up those tasty baked balloons we know as popovers, along with some of their not-so-familiar cousins.

Monster Pie

For a hot meal that is easy, quick and nourishing, Monster Pie is a winner. Flavors and textures are varied by your choice of cheese and vegetables. It is impressive like a quiche, but much simpler because the egg mixture makes its own crust. Local legend has it that it originally called for Muenster cheese and was named Muenster Pie. But Rhea McKay, Liza Bernard's dear friend who shared it with us, preferred to use Cheddar cheese, and the name evolved.

Notice the similarities to the "Whole Meal" Pancakes on page 503. Like them, this pie is best if you make up the batter first and let it sit covered on your counter for an hour or so, or even in the refrigerator all day. (But when you can't wait, let it sit just while you cut up the vegetables.) And like "Whole Meal" Pancakes, it pays to make enough to have some left over because this pie is wonderful cold.

> 2 eggs
> ½ cup King Arthur Unbleached All-Purpose Flour
> ¼ cup King Arthur Stone Ground Whole Wheat Flour
> 1 cup milk
> 1 cup Cheddar cheese, cubed
> 1 small onion
> 2 cups chopped or shredded broccoli, carrots, green peppers,
>   cauliflower, spinach, zucchini or a combination of vegetables in
>   season (or leftovers)
> 1 teaspoon parsley
> 1 teaspoon basil
> Parmesan cheese (optional)

Preheat your oven to 425°F.

Beat the eggs well. Mix in the flour, add ½ cup of milk and blend well. (It is important for the finished texture of the pie to add the milk in two stages, so hold off on adding the remainder until you have prepared the vegetables and cheese.)

If you have time, let this batter sit for an hour or more. If you don't, just let it wait while you cut up the vegetables.

Chop the vegetables into big bite-sized pieces and cube the cheese. Place these in a greased cast iron skillet to produce a good crust. (These come in a range of sizes to handle multiples of this recipe.) If you haven't a skillet, a 9-inch square baking pan or its equivalent will do. A glass pan will also create a nice crust.

evermore!!

Add the herbs to the egg mixture and stir in the remaining milk. Pour this over the vegetables and cheese. Sprinkle some Parmesan cheese on top.

Bake for about 25 minutes or until golden. Remove the pie from the oven and let it set for a few minutes before serving.

Apple Monster Pie

This variation makes a savory (not sweet) confection, a perfect pick-me-up for tea time or after school. The first five ingredients are the same as those in Monster Pie. In place of the vegetables, herbs and Parmesan cheese, use the ingredients below.

2 to 2½ cups cubed or sliced apple; a pie or tart variety tastes best
a few drops of rosewater (see Appendix)

Preheat your oven to 425°F.

Prepare the batter as above. Place the apples and cheese in a greased skillet. Add the rose water to the egg mixture and stir in the remaining milk. Pour this over the apples and cheese. Bake as above.

POPOVERS

These crisp and airy creations, hot from the oven, accompanied by a bowl of chilled summer soup, or a steaming winter stew, are guaranteed to lift your spirits.

> 2 large eggs
> 1 cup milk
> ½ teaspoon salt
> 1 cup King Arthur Unbleached All-Purpose Flour

Beat the eggs into the milk until frothy. Add the salt and flour. Beat the mixture about one minute or until you begin to see large bubbles develop.

If you have time, let it sit for 30 to 45 minutes at room temperature and then beat again.

Fifteen minutes or so before the second beating, preheat your oven to 400°F and liberally grease an 8-cup muffin tin with butter.

To bake, fill the cups two-thirds full of batter and place in the hot oven. Bake for 35 to 40 minutes until the popovers are blown up and lightly browned. Make sure not to open the oven to look while they're baking. Until they're completely done, the airy structure of the popover will collapse without much provocation.

After they're done, remove them from the oven and prick them with a knife to let the steam escape. Make sure you time your baking so you can eat them while they're still warm. A cold popover loses much of its charm.

After you've mastered the basic popovers, try a variation or the Whole Wheat Popovers on page 505.

CHEESE POPOVERS

Add a few shakes of paprika, cayenne pepper or dry mustard and ½ cup of grated cheese to your batter. Fresh Parmesan would be wonderful, or equally good would be Asiago, Romano, plain or smoked Cheddar.

BACON POPOVERS

For Sunday breakfast put a bit of crisp, crumbled bacon in the bottom of each cup before you pour in the batter.

Or combine the two for Cheese & Bacon Popovers.

The Newcastle Inn
Baked Pancakes

Ted and Chris Sprague bought the Newcastle Inn in Newcastle, Maine, a little over two years ago. In the intervening time they have turned it into a four-star establishment. Since it's a way station for the Sands, they've gotten to know the Spragues and have had occasion to sample the Inn's most popular breakfast. If the Spragues' energy and enthusiasm are any indication, the Newcastle Inn will be a treasured haunt for travelers for a long time. Chris has been gracious enough to share her recipe for these simple but absolutely delicious baked pancakes, a very special breakfast for two.

The Batter

3 eggs
½ cup milk
½ cup King Arthur Unbleached All-Purpose Flour
a pinch of salt
2 tablespoons unsalted butter, melted

Preheat your oven to 450°F.

Whisk the eggs with the milk until well blended and light. Add the flour and salt and whisk until they're well incorporated. Blend in the melted butter and continue whisking until the batter is smooth.

Pour the batter into two lightly greased, 6-inch cake pans. Bake for 15 minutes. This is when the magic happens. The batter will rise right up the sides of the pans like giant open popovers to form a delicate open bowl.

They should be turned out as soon as they're done, set right side up and served immediately while the sides are still crisp and high.

Garnishes

We usually serve these pancakes with lemon zest and lemon juice sprinkled over the bottom with confectioners' sugar dusted over that and up the sides. Guests top this off with our Maine maple syrup.

These pancakes can also be a foil for the unfolding growing season. Try serving them in the early summer with sliced strawberries dusted with confectioners' sugar.

Later in the summer sprinkle blueberries with a little lemon juice and dust them with confectioners' sugar. Raspberries and blackberries come next.

And for the fall, use sautéed apple slices sprinkled with cinnamon and a little brown sugar.

YORKSHIRE PUDDING

Yorkshire Pudding is an English concoction that isn't really a pudding, and it is not sweet. It was developed in the north country of England during the Middle Ages to be eaten with mutton. Today, it is traditionally eaten with roast beef.

The first written recipes for Yorkshire pudding called for water as the liquid rather than milk. The resulting thin batter, similar to popover batter, was placed in a pan under a roasting meat to collect the drippings. It was then served as a first course to take the edge off one's hunger before eating what was probably a meager amount of meat. Yorkshire pudding was so good, however, that it is now an accompaniment to many a grand meal or feast.

The recipe itself is very simple. These directions are for a 10 x 14-inch roasting pan. If your roast is large and your pan much bigger, you can double or triple the recipe and allow a longer cooking time.

> 1 cup King Arthur Unbleached All-Purpose Flour
> ½ teaspoon salt
> 2 large eggs
> 1 cup water (or ½ cup water and ½ cup milk)

It is a good idea to have all your ingredients at room temperature, so take them out of the refrigerator when you begin roasting your meat. Put this pudding batter together about an hour and a half before you want to serve dinner.

Mix together the flour and the salt in a medium-sized mixing bowl.

In a smaller bowl, beat the eggs until they are light and lemon colored, and add either the water or the water/milk mixture. Whisk this mixture into the flour and beat until the batter is smooth and bubbly. Let this stand at room temperature for about an hour. Just before you're ready to bake the pudding, beat it again until it's bubbly.

When the roast is done, remove it from the roasting pan to a platter and put it somewhere to keep warm.

Turn the oven heat up to 400°F, place the roasting pan with the drippings back in the oven to heat up until they're just barely smoking. Pour the batter in the pan and bake for 25 minutes. If the pudding begins to brown too much, turn the temperature down to 350°F to finish baking.

The pudding will be puffed and browned on the top and crusty and moist on the bottom when done. It should be served immediately, either as a first course, as they do traditionally in Yorkshire, or alongside your roast.

QUICK BREADS
& MUFFINS
III

QUICK BREADS & MUFFINS
BISCUITS & SCONES

• For heartier quick breads and tastier scones, substitute one or more cups of King Arthur Stone Ground Whole Wheat Flour for the same number of cups of King Arthur Unbleached All-Purpose Flour.

• Buy baking powder in small containers since it loses its "oomph" after a while. If you want to test its potency, heat a teaspoon of baking powder in ½ cup of water. It should begin to froth and foam and look a bit like "proofing" yeast. In fact it is doing the same thing yeast does, making carbon dioxide bubbles. Baking powder does it chemically; yeast does it biochemically. If your baking powder doesn't seem to have what it takes, you can make a homemade version by mixing 2 teaspoons of cream of tartar with 1 teaspoon of baking soda (3 teaspoons in all) to make the equivalent of three teaspoons (1 tablespoon) of baking powder.

• If you find that you're out of baking powder and that you don't have any cream of tartar on hand either, here's another trick you can try. If your recipe calls for 2 cups of milk, add 2 tablespoons of vinegar to it and let it sit for 5 minutes. Then blend 1 teaspoon of baking soda with your dry ingredients in place of the baking powder. The soda and sour milk combination will produce carbon dioxide bubbles to leaven your muffins or bread.

• To make quick breads even quicker, or to adapt your King Arthur Unbleached All-Purpose Flour for a recipe calling for "Self-Rising" Flour, you can make up your own unbleached King Arthur "Self-Rising" Flour. To make a moderate quantity to keep on hand, start with 9 cups of King Arthur Unbleached All-Purpose Flour. Blend in 1 tablespoon of salt and 5 tablespoons of double acting baking powder. Store what you don't use in an air-tight container and be sure to label it. It's best not to make much more than this at a time since baking powder tends to lose its potency after a while. To make just one cup of King Arthur "Self-Rising" Flour, simply add 1½ teaspoons of baking powder and ½ teaspoon of salt to 1 cup of King Arthur Unbleached All-Purpose Flour. (Conversely, you can use "Self-Rising" Flour in a recipe calling for regular All-Purpose Flour; just leave out the baking powder and salt.)

• To make light and tender quick breads and muffins, mix the liquid and dry ingredients together for only 20 seconds!

• For light and tender biscuits and scones, knead the dough only 10 times after you've combined the ingredients. Roll out gently on a floured surface and cut with a cookie cutter or other cutter by pressing straight down without twisting or turning.

• Loaves may be made from most muffin formulas if you would rather minimize labor. Conversely, you can make muffins out of most quick bread recipes.

Quick Breads & Muffins
Biscuits & Scones
III

• A QUICK BREAD PRIMER •

Quick breads are a phenomenon of the last century and a half, beginning with the introduction of baking powder. When baking powder was fairly new, a lot of people felt that it was going to replace yeast for all bread baking. It produced the same gas that yeast did (carbon dioxide) and its action was indeed "quick" compared to that of yeast. It has in fact replaced yeast as a leavening agent for cakes almost entirely. But rather than replacing yeast to leaven bread doughs, yeast breads have continued in their own tradition and quick breads have evolved as a distinctly different one.

Quick breads cover a wide range, from biscuits and scones, which are made from a dough, to muffins and loaves that are made from a batter. They can be large or small, savory (salty) or sweet. The major thing that identifies them is the fact that they are, as their name implies, quick to make.

QUICK LEAVENS

So with that minimal definition, we'll start with some history about the "quick" leavening agents that our inventive ancestors used, followed by some information about the one we use most often today.

THINGS THAT MADE QUICK BREADS RISE

Salt of Hartshorn (Ammonium Carbonate)

Hartshorn is one of the oldest of "chemical" leavens. It was actually in use for many centuries before the predecessor of modern baking powder was developed in the middle of the nineteenth century.

The original hartshorn, as its name implies, was ground from deer antler and used primarily in Scandinavian countries. Today it is almost unknown, although there is a chemical version of the original, better known as "baker's ammonia," available from some pharmaceutical and baking supply companies.

A dough that contains hartshorn produces a strong smell of ammonia when it's in the oven, but the ammonia dissipates completely during the cooking process leaving no aftertaste or odor. Its unique action makes extremely crisp cookies and crackers.

Pearlash (Potassium Carbonate)

On this side of the Atlantic the early colonists were blessed with hardwood forests as far as the eye could see. Aside from being a logical building material and fuel, hardwoods provided another important resource, ashes. Ashes were a major export two hundred years ago, both to Canada and Britain. They were valuable for sweetening gardens and providing lye for making soap. They were also a source of potash and its derivative, pearlash, another creative leavening agent.

To make pearlash, you first have to make potash which itself is made from lye. To make lye, you pass water through a barrel of hardwood ashes over and over until an egg can float on the residue. (To make soap you boil this "lye water" with lard or other fat until it is thick, pour it into molds and harden it into cakes.) To make potash, you evaporate lye water until you have a solid.

Pearlash is a purified version of potash. It is an alkaline compound which will react with an acidic ingredient such as sour milk, buttermilk or molasses to produce carbon dioxide bubbles, the very same thing that yeast produces. Pearlash was used primarily in the seventeenth and eighteenth centuries but because of its bitter aftertaste, it not only did not replace yeast but was eventually replaced by "saleratus."

Saleratus (Potassium Bicarbonate or Sodium Bicarbonate)

Saleratus (aerated salt) is an old word for modern baking soda. It actually was used as a name for both of the above compounds, but, like pearlash, potassium bicarbonate had an unpleasant aftertaste and fell out of use early in the nineteenth century. So "saleratus" came to mean just sodium bicarbonate (bicarbonate of soda) itself. You'll find it in nineteenth-century recipe books used just as baking soda is used today.

Saleratus was first sold on this side of the Atlantic by John Dwight, who, with his brother-in-law, Dr. Austin Church, started manufacturing it in their kitchens. It was called "Dwight's Saleratus" with a cow as a trademark because of the necessity of using sour milk to activate it in baking.

Things That Make Quick Breads Rise Today

We have more choices for "quick" leavening agents today than ever before. (There may even be better ones on the horizon.)

Baking Soda (Sodium Acid Carbonate)

In the same year that Sands, Taylor & Wood Co. introduced King Arthur Flour at the Boston Food Fair, the descendants of Austin Church and John Dwight formed Church & Dwight, Co., introducing their old saleratus as Arm & Hammer Baking Soda. Today that company produces almost all the baking soda that is used in this country.

Baking soda comes from several sources, but the bulk of it is derived from an ore called "trona" which is mined in the Green River Basin in Wyoming. (Technology is being developed now to produce baking soda from sea water.)

When baking soda is heated, it slowly breaks down into sodium carbonate, water and those magic leavening bubbles, carbon dioxide. When mixed with something acidic and wet, it starts producing carbon dioxide right away without waiting to be heated. Below we'll explain when to use it and how much to use.

Single Acting Baking Powder

The next logical step after developing baking soda (which only worked when there was something acidic in a batter) was to create a "combination" powder which just needed to get wet to become active. To do this, baking soda was combined with a powdered acid along with a little cornstarch to keep the two dry and inactive. This second magic powder was "cream of tartar," a fruit acid that accumulates on the inside of wine casks as a wine matures.

When baking soda and cream of tartar are moistened in a batter or dough, they begin to react to each other right away producing (you guessed it) lots of carbon dioxide bubbles.

This combination powder is still a very effective leaven although it has a couple of drawbacks. As its name indicates, it is "single acting." When it's mixed into a batter or dough, it starts and finishes its reaction then and there. When you bake with it, you must get whatever you're making into a preheated oven as quickly as possible before the bubbles begin to disappear. The second drawback is that, no matter how dry these combination powders are kept, they lose their potency after awhile.

In spite of these limitations, there are people who still prefer the flavor of this old blend and value the fact that it is composed entirely of naturally occurring ingredients.

Double Acting Baking Powder

This is the leaven that our recipes are written for unless something else is specified. Double acting baking powder is single acting baking powder taken one step further. The baking soda is still there but the cream of tartar has been replaced by two acids, one like cream of tartar that reacts to the baking soda as soon as it's wet, the other that doesn't begin to react until it's heated. This means you can be more leisurely about getting a dough or batter into the oven.

Like single acting baking powder, double acting baking powder contains a little cornstarch to prevent the soda and acids from reacting. And it too will lose its leavening ability after a while. If you want to see if it still has its "get-up-and-go," put a little in a cup of hot water. It should start fizzing and bubbling right away.

The acids you find most frequently in double acting baking powder are calcium acid phosphate and sodium aluminum sulfate. Both of these substances are considered by the Food & Drug Administration to be "GRAS," or "generally regarded as safe." There have been some reports recently about potential neurological problems associated with aluminum. There are so many sources for aluminum around us that baking powder is probably a minimal one. If it is of concern to you, choose a powder that doesn't contain aluminum or use the old baking soda/cream of tartar standby.

Homemade Baking Powder

Since baking powder does tend to lose its leavening power after a while, rather than being caught empty handed, it's useful to have baking soda and cream of tartar around in separate containers. Then you can make your own baking powder in an emergency. These are both available separately at your grocery and, separated, have an indefinite shelf life.

To make the equivalent of 1 teaspoon of double acting baking powder, mix 1/2 teaspoon of cream of tartar with 1/4 teaspoon baking soda (two parts of cream of tartar to one of baking soda). This single acting baking powder will work very successfully but you must remember that when you use it, get whatever you're baking into the oven right away.

Baking Soda & Baking Powder

How To Know Which One To Use & How Much

First, acquaint yourself with a quick bread's structural ingredients (the things that hold it up) and then its "decorative" ingredients (the things that weigh it down).

Structural Ingredients

- flour and a liquid
- eggs

"Decorative" Ingredients

- any non-wheat flour or grain
- sugar
- fat
- "optional extras:" raisins, nuts, chocolate chips, cheese, diced fruit, etc.

In a quick bread (or any other baked good), structural ingredients form the skeleton and help it keep its shape. Decorative ingredients give it its personality but weigh it down. If a quick bread doesn't contain any decorative ingredients, it won't need much leavening power to lift or expand it. (You don't need much strength to walk around in summer clothes, but you do need lots of muscle to wear a suit of armor.) A quick bread that has lots of decorations or "optional extras" needs extra muscle or lifting power too.

When & How to Use Baking Powder

- First count the cups of flour your recipe calls for. You want to include at least 1 teaspoon of baking powder per cup.

- If your recipe contains a cup or more of decorative ingredients, add another $1/2$ teaspoon of baking powder per cup of flour.

Example: Let's say your recipe calls for 3 cups of flour and 1 cup of raisins. First you'll need 1 teaspoon of baking powder for each cup of flour. That makes 3 teaspoons. To help lift those raisins, you'll want an extra $1/2$ teaspoon of baking powder per cup of flour. This makes $1 1/2$ teaspoons or $4 1/2$ teaspoons of baking powder altogether.

When & How To Use Baking Soda

Baking soda is used generally when there is an ingredient in a batter that is particularly acidic, such as buttermilk or molasses, anything that can take the place of the acid in the baking powder.

Example: If our recipe contains 3 cups of flour plus 1 cup of raisins and we want to use 1 cup of sweet milk, we blend 4½ teaspoons of baking powder into the flour. If we want to substitute 1 cup of buttermilk for the sweet milk, we'll blend ½ teaspoon of baking soda into the flour and use only 2½ teaspoons of baking powder. In other words, ½ teaspoon of baking soda plus 1 cup of buttermilk (or an equivalent) can replace about 2 teaspoons of baking powder.

Here are some other ingredients that will react with ½ teaspoon of baking soda and can replace 2 teaspoons of baking powder. This list is by no means complete but it may give you a sense of what ingredients can be used.

- 1 cup sour milk
- 1 cup sweet milk soured with 1 tablespoon vinegar or lemon juice
- 1 cup sour cream
- 1 cup yogurt
- 1 cup fruit or vegetable sauces or juice
- ¾ cup brown sugar
- ¾ cup honey
- ¾ cup molasses
- 1 tablespoon vinegar or lemon juice (see King Arthur Flour's "Cake-Pan" Cake on page 281)
- ½ cup cocoa (not Dutch cocoa, which has been "de-acidified")

A Final Note

There is no situation where you must use baking soda, even when you have an acidic ingredient in your dough or batter. Because baking powder contains both baking soda and an acid, it will create carbon dioxide bubbles even when there's extra acid present, such as the buttermilk in our Basic Scone recipe (page 57).

You can choose to use baking powder completely. If you do, the flavor of the acidic ingredient (buttermilk, etc.) will be slightly more pronounced since there is no baking soda to react with or neutralize it. The texture will also be a bit finer than the coarse or "shaggy" texture that is characteristically caused by the action of baking soda.

You may find you like the flavor and texture of things leavened with baking soda or you may prefer baking powder. Try a recipe both ways. Just remember that you can't use baking soda in place of baking powder without something acidic to react to it. Without something to neutralize it, it will leave a bitter, salty taste. And always blend either one thoroughly into your dry ingredients first so it will be evenly distributed throughout the dough or batter.

SCONES: THE OLDEST QUICK BREAD

Scones are one of the oldest and most basic of quick breads. The name "scone" probably comes from the old Scottish or Gaelic word "sgonn," which rhymes with "gone," hence its favored British pronunciation, "skon." When you don't cut your dough into scones, but leave it intact, you have made a "bannock." This is another ancient Scottish term from the Latin word "panicum," for bread, which probably arrived in Britain with the Romans two thousand years ago. You'll find it still used in the west country of Britain today as well as in some parts of the United States and Canada.

Since wheat doesn't grow well in Scotland, scones and bannocks, or their ancestors, were originally made of local oat or barley flour mixed into a dough with a little water and no leavening. They were cooked on a "girdle," or griddle, which was (and still is in some places) a wonderful cooking implement. It's a large, round, flat cast iron pan which either stands on a tripod or is suspended over the coals of a fire. It's sprinkled with flour or wiped with a bit of grease before the dough or batter is "baked" on it.

Because wheat was imported and expensive, scones or bannocks baked with wheat flour were consumed just on special occasions. They were daily fare only for people who could afford them, which may explain the "elegant" aura that seems to surround them today. It's similar to the residual feelings we have about white flour and white sugar which, in centuries past, were also enjoyed only by the wealthy and noble.

With the introduction of leavening and the improvement and greater availability of ingredients, the scone has evolved into a light and delicious biscuit. Today in Scotland, you might eat a freshly baked scone with fresh butter and heather honey. In Britain, for a proper "Cream Tea," simple scones are split and served with raspberry or strawberry jam laced with whipped or "clotted" cream.

In this primer we'll take apart a basic recipe for scones and put it back together with lots of suggestions for substitutions and additions. When you understand how they go together, you'll more easily understand what makes quick breads tick.

King Arthur Flour's
Basic Scones

The only difference between scones and other quick breads is that scones are made with a dough rather than a batter. All this means is that they contain less liquid. If you learn to handle a quick bread dough, a quick bread batter will be a piece of cake.

All you need to make these delightful biscuits is a mixing bowl, some measuring utensils, a cookie sheet and half an hour, fifteen minutes of which you can spend doing something else. This is indeed "quick."

Since scones are an "old" quick bread, it makes sense that they are leavened with an "old" leaven, the reaction of buttermilk with baking soda. This creates their characteristic flavor and shaggy texture. We'll start with this combination and give you variations below.

You'll see that there is quite a lot of latitude in this recipe for the quantity of butter and sugar. For your first try, use 4 tablespoons of each and then decide which way you want to go from there. All scones are delicious hot from the oven but when they are made with a larger amount of butter they will keep a little longer, will reheat nicely and are delicious without being buttered after they're baked.

```
2 cups King Arthur Unbleached All-Purpose Flour
1 cup King Arthur Stone Ground Whole Wheat Flour
1 tablespoon baking powder
½ teaspoon baking soda
½ to 1 teaspoon salt
2 to 8 tablespoons butter, at room temperature (each end of the
     spectrum is fine; 8 tablespoons makes a richer scone)
0 to 8 tablespoons of sugar (depending on taste and type of scone)
1 to 1¼ cups buttermilk (more in the winter, less in the summer)
```

First: Preheat your oven to 500°F if you choose to bake your scones in the oven. (See page 59 for baking them on a griddle.)

Mixing: In a large mixing bowl, blend the dry ingredients together thoroughly. With a pastry blender, two knives, or, most easily, your fingertips, cut or rub in the butter until the mixture looks like bread crumbs.

Take about 20 seconds (really) to stir in the buttermilk.

Turn the dough out onto a well-floured board and, with well-floured hands, knead the dough very gently 8 to 10 times, just enough to bring it together. Sprinkle on more flour as you need it to keep the dough from sticking.

Shaping: Here's another place where you have a lot of latitude. You can shape this dough a number of different ways depending on when and how you want to serve it.

Bannocks: When you bake this dough intact and uncut in either one large dinner-sized round or two tea-sized rounds, you've made a "bannock." This is the oldest and most basic shape.

• **Large:** On a well-floured board, with a well-floured rolling pin, roll the dough into a circle about 8 inches in diameter and $^3/_4$ inch thick. Don't be afraid to throw some flour around to prevent sticking. Once it's rolled out you can tidy up the edges with the palms of your hands if you want, but do it gently. Half the charm of bannocks (and scones) is their "shagginess." You can leave it as is, or score it into 8 pie-shaped sections by pressing your spatula or bowl scraper into the dough about $^1/_4$ inch.

Sprinkle your baking sheet with flour. (A large round pizza pan is a perfect baking sheet for bannocks or scones.) Use your spatula or bowl scraper to transfer the bannock to the baking sheet.

• **Small:** Cut the dough into two circles and roll them out until they are about $^1/_2$ inch thick and 5 to 6 inches in diameter. Score as above.

Traditional Scones: Like the bannock, these can be made either large or small.

• **Main Meal Scones:** Roll the dough with a well-floured rolling pin into a circle about 8 inches in diameter and $^3/_4$ inch thick.

Cut 8 pie-shaped pieces with a spatula or bowl scraper, pressing down firmly without sawing. By cutting them this way, you shear the dough rather than squeeze it together which can happen when you "saw" it. A clean cut allows scones or biscuits to rise higher. Another way to help you get through the dough more cleanly is to dip the scraper in flour after each cut.

Sprinkle your baking sheet with flour. Use your spatula or scraper as a "shovel" to transfer each piece, gently, to the baking sheet leaving an inch or so between them.

• **Tea Scones:** Divide the dough in half and roll into two circles about $^1/_2$ inch thick and 5 to 6 inches in diameter. Cut these into 8 pie-shaped pieces as well.

Drop Scones: This is another traditional way to shape biscuits or scones. Use ¼ to ½ cup more liquid than the basic recipe calls for, which makes a batter rather than a dough. This you blend for 20 seconds, without kneading, the same way you would a quick bread or muffin batter.

After blending, drop large spoonfuls onto a floured or lightly greased cookie sheet (or into a greased muffin tin), and bake for 12 to 15 minutes. This method can rescue you if you wind up with a dough that is too wet when making traditional scones. (Better to bake them this way than to try and knead in more flour which will only make them tough.)

Cut Out Scones: After you roll out your dough, use a cookie or other cutter to cut the dough into shapes. You can make them typically round like biscuits or, for fun, tailor them to a specific occasion (hearts, clovers, pumpkins, etc.). Make sure you press your cutter into the dough quickly and firmly without twisting or sawing.

Filled Scones: Divide the dough in half and roll out two thinner circles, each about 8 inches in diameter. Spread fruit conserves, mincemeat, cranberry sauce, apple butter, anything that will stay put, on one layer.

Place the other on top, cut into pieces and bake. (You can also make a tea-sized version by cutting the dough into quarters and making two 5- or 6-inch filled circles.) If you have a suspicion that your filling might ooze, bake the dough in one piece as a filled bannock.

Rolled Scones: Roll out the dough until it's about ¼ inch thick (with care and a good sprinkling of flour). Spread a filling on top, gently roll up the dough and slice off pieces about 1 inch thick.

Place these on their sides in a well-greased muffin tin or next to each other in a cake pan. With this technique you can make "quick" baking powder sticky buns. (You can also roll up something quite different, such as herbs and grated cheese.)

Baking: Again, a couple of options.

- **Oven:** Turn the heat down to 450°F and bake the Bannock for about 25 minutes, Main Meal Scones for about 20 minutes and Tea Scones for 15 minutes, or until they are just beginning to brown.

- **Griddle:** Since bannocks or scones were originally "baked" on a "girdle" or griddle, you can use this method too. Heat a griddle to medium low, dust it with flour, or grease it lightly, and cook them for about 6 minutes or so on a side.

Ingredient Alternatives for Interesting Scones

Here are some ways to make additions and substitutions to the basic recipe so you can create a scone of your own. Most of these changes you can apply as well to our Basic "P. D. Q." Muffins (page 74) and Basic Quick Bread (page 90).

Substitutions

Dry Ingredients: Use our King Arthur Flours in any combination you want. Whole wheat scones are robust and hearty. Scones made completely with unbleached white flour are light and delicate. The combination we've suggested is one we like, but you can create your own.

Substitute other grains; oatmeal, the Scottish national grain, is an obvious one but try some non-traditional grains as well (cornmeal, rye, buckwheat, etc.). Substituting a bit of wheat germ or bran will also change a scone or quickbread's personality plus give you a nutritional bonus. Start with small amounts, 1/2 cup or so, until you find a combination you like.

When you decide to add a grain that contains no gluten (essentially everything but wheat), include an egg as part of your liquid. The egg will help to create structure to contain the gas bubbles. (See information on eggs, under "Liquids," below.)

Leavening Agents: This is covered fairly thoroughly at the beginning of the chapter.

Sweeteners: Although British scones are traditionally sweetened very little, the amount of sweetening you use is up to you. You'll find that if you're eating your scones alone, you might need more; if you're eating them with jam or honey, you won't need as much.

For a slightly different flavor sustitute brown sugar, molasses, maple syrup or honey for white sugar. If you do use a liquid sweetener, you'll want to hold back on your other liquid a bit. Add it slowly and only enough to make a dough you can gently knead. Or you can increase your baking time. If you use honey, bake your scones at 375°F for an extra five minutes as honey tends to scorch at high temperatures.

If you like your scones sweet, include an egg as part of your liquid. Sugar tends to make baked goods "spread." An egg will give the scone more structure.

Other quick breads generally contain more sweetening than you'll find in scones or biscuits. You can also substitute sweeteners there. If you substitute a liquid sweetener, you may want to hold back a bit on your other liquids or increase your baking time by 5 minutes.

Fats: To make a richer scone, increase the amount of butter up to 8 tablespoons (1 stick), if you want. By baking a bit more butter into a scone, you'll find you won't need to use any on it after it's baked.

You can use other fats such as vegetable shortening or lard, or even an oil in some cases. But the flavor of butter is hard to beat. In most quick breads the new butter/vegetable oil combinations are a good flavor/nutrition compromise.

Liquids: If you don't have buttermilk, you can substitute yogurt, sour cream or sour milk. To make sour milk out of sweet, add 1 tablespoon vinegar to 1 cup of milk and let it sit for 5 minutes to clabber.

You can also use sweet milk by itself, but omit the baking soda. If the soda doesn't have anything to react with, it adds an unpleasant taste.

For richer scones, use 1/2 to 1 cup cream as part or all of your liquid. If you use only 1/2 cup, the balance should be sweet milk. Omit the baking soda in this case.

Another substitution, which will create a richer scone and will give them more structure as well, is 1 extra large egg for 1/4 cup of liquid. (It takes 4 extra large and 5 large eggs to make 1 cup.) Break the egg into a two-cup liquid measure. Add your other liquid up to the one cup mark. (With this measuring method you can use whatever size egg you have on hand.) Beat the two together right in the cup with a whisk or egg beater.

When you're making fruit scones or quick breads, try using fruit juices or fruit sauces (apple, cranberry, etc.) as your liquid. Because fruits are acidic, like buttermilk, you can use 1/2 teaspoon of baking soda (blended with the dry ingredients) for every cup of juice or sauce you use.

Additions

When you add any of these "optional extras" to the basic scone recipe, you'll give them a distinctly different personality.

Fruit: A traditional British scone contains an added cup of currants or raisins, either purple or gold. An American counterpart might be 1 cup of blueberries, halved cranberries, chopped apple or peaches. Mix any of these in with the dry ingredients after you've rubbed in the butter or shortening but before you add your liquid.

Spices: To use alone or to vary the flavor of a fruit scone, you can add up to a tablespoon of spice (cinnamon, ginger, nutmeg, allspice, cloves or a bit of each) to your dry ingredients.

Nuts: A cup of halved or chopped pecans, walnuts, hazelnuts or almonds, either alone or with fruit, adds great flavor and texture. So will sunflower or pumpkin seeds or even pine nuts or pistachios. Add these before you add your liquid as you would currants or raisins.

Lemon or Orange Zest: Add a teaspoon of grated lemon or orange peel (zest) to your dry ingredients. This can be done alone or to enhance a fruit scone.

Cheese: A cup of grated cheese, such as Cheddar or Parmesan, can be added to the dry ingredients after you rub in the butter. (A teaspoon of dry mustard blended with the dry ingredients, or a prepared mustard beaten into the liquid, adds to and intensifies the flavor.) Try this with chopped chives or even apple. Use just a teaspoon or so of sugar with this combination.

Herbs: Two teaspoons of dry or a tablespoon of fresh herbs alone or in combination with cheese makes a wonderful variation as well as a great topping for a meat pie. When you make this variety, use just a teaspoon or so of sugar.

Savory Combinations: Add ½ to 1 cup of chopped ham, hard sausage, or crumbled bacon to your dry ingredients as you would fruit or nuts. You can even put together a whole meal combination. Try bacon, cheese and chopped apple. Again, just a little sugar will enhance the flavor without adding sweetness.

Chocolate or Other Chips: Perhaps the most unlikely variation that has emerged during the current fascination with scones is the addition of chocolate chips. This will seem a travesty to traditionalists, but if you are tempted by this idea, use ½ cup sugar with the dry ingredients, rub in 8 tablespoons of butter, toss in 1 cup of regular or mini chocolate chips, and include 1 teaspoon of vanilla and 1 beaten egg as part of your liquid. (Actually, these scones are very good, especially if you add a cup of pecans, hazelnuts or walnuts.)

For confirmed chocoholics, substitute ⅓ cup cocoa powder for ⅓ cup unbleached all-purpose flour. This variation may send your mind spinning on a very non-traditional tangent, but that's the fun of it.

One of our favorite scones was an experimental combination of cranberries, cut in half, golden raisins, walnuts and some spices (mostly cinnamon) with 6 tablespoons of sugar and a stick of butter worked into the basic recipe. Needless to say, the results stood on their own with no additional butter or jam necessary.

• QUICK BREAD DOUGHS •

Since we keep talking about them together, you may have guessed that scones, baking powder biscuits and even Irish soda breads are very much alike. Although they evolved in different places, they really are almost identical. All three are made from a dough (unlike other quick breads, which are made from a batter). Their differences lie in their names and some assumptions about where and when they should be eaten.

In America, baking powder biscuits are usually associated with savory foods. When they're sweetened and shaped a little differently, we're inclined to call them scones. Whatever you decide they are, scones, biscuits and soda breads are unbelievably easy to prepare, they bake in minutes, and, if we slow our lives down enough to enjoy them with a leisurely breakfast, a savory supper or with a cup of tea in the afternoon, we will have adopted a tradition worth keeping.

SCONES

MRS. HUMPHRIES' SCONES

Mrs. Humphries was an elderly English woman who lived in the little pink house across the street from Liza Bernard's parents. Her scones are rich and delicious.

1 cup King Arthur Unbleached All-Purpose Flour
$^1/_2$ cup sugar
2 teaspoons baking powder
3 tablespoons butter or margarine
$^1/_2$ cup raisins (plumped in milk, and drained, if you have time)
1 egg
$^1/_2$ teaspoon lemon extract
less than $^1/_4$ cup milk
sugar to sprinkle on top (optional)

Preheat your oven to 425°F.

Combine the flour, sugar and baking powder. Rub in the butter or margarine with your fingertips. Add the raisins, egg and lemon extract. "Mush it up and add just enough milk to make it soft, but not too sticky," were Mrs. Humphries' original directions.

Drop BIG tablespoons of the batter onto a greased cookie sheet. Sprinkle the top with sugar if you want a sweet finished scone. Bake for 12 to 15 minutes, depending on size.

MINCEMEAT SCONES

If you're a mincemeat fan, you'll love these; if you're not, you'll still like them.

2 cups King Arthur Unbleached All-Purpose Flour
1 cup King Arthur Stone Ground Whole Wheat Flour
1 tablespoon baking powder
1/2 teaspoon baking soda
1 teaspoon salt
3 tablespoons sugar
6 tablespoons (3/4 stick) butter, at room temperature
1 cup buttermilk
1 cup mincemeat (for our Mincemeat recipe see page 414)

Preheat your oven to 450°F and sprinkle a bit of flour on a baking sheet.

Thoroughly blend the dry ingredients in a large mixing bowl. Drop the butter in the center, cover it with the flour mixture, and quickly rub it in with your fingertips until the mixture looks like bread crumbs.

Pour in the cup of buttermilk and blend for 20 seconds. Turn out onto a floured surface and knead about 10 times, until it holds together.

Cut the dough in half and, with a well-floured rolling pin, gently roll each half into a circle about 8 inches in diameter. (Or make four smaller circles, 5 to 6 inches in diameter.)

Spread the mincemeat on one layer and, with a spatula or bowl scraper, lift the other layer on top. Cut the dough into 8 pie-shaped pieces. Lift them onto a lightly greased or floured baking sheet allowing space for them to expand.

Bake for 15 (small scones) to 20 (large scones) minutes.

SOUR CREAM SCONES

This recipe came, via a friend of the Sands, from an English war bride whose husband flew for the Royal Air Force during World War II. They are light and delicious, the perfect Cream Tea scone.

1 1/2 cups King Arthur Unbleached All-Purpose Flour
2 teaspoons baking powder
1/2 teaspoon baking soda
1/2 teaspoon salt
1/4 cup sugar
1 cup sour cream

Preheat your oven to 450°F.

In a mixing bowl, blend the dry ingredients thoroughly. Scoop in the sour cream all at once and stir together for 20 seconds or until the dry ingredients are damp.

This dough is very light. Turn out onto a floured board and knead, very gently, 8 to 10 times. Roll into a round ¹/₂ to ³/₄ inch thick. Flour a spatula or bowl scraper well and cut into quarters.

Flour your spatula again and gently lift each scone onto a lightly greased cookie sheet. Bake for 15 minutes.

Scottish Scones

This recipe is one of Gretchen McMullen's, our spokeswoman in the late 1920's and '30's. We've presented it as she wrote it, with notations to bring it into the 1990's.

¹/₂ cup raisins
4 cups King Arthur Unbleached All-Purpose Flour
3 teaspoons cream of tartar (see page 52)
1¹/₂ teaspoons baking soda
³/₄ teaspoon salt
2 tablespoons sugar
4 tablespoons (¹/₂ stick) butter
1 egg
1 cup milk

Preheat your oven to 400°F.

Cover the raisins with boiling water and let them stand five minutes.

Sift the dry ingredients three times (or just fluff the flour up and sprinkle it gently into a measuring cup). Rub in the butter (with your fingertips). Drain and add the raisins.

Beat the egg and milk together and cut it into the flour mixture with two knives (or mix it with a large spoon) for 20 seconds only.

Turn onto a floured board and knead lightly with a rolling motion for two minutes. (Kneading only 10 times will probably make lighter scones.) Divide the dough in four portions, pat each one into a circle about ³/₄ inch thick. Cut each circle in quarters and place on a floured baking sheet.

Bake about 20 minutes.

Scotch Pancakes Baird

We're including a "pancake" recipe in the scone section because it is actually not a pancake in the American sense. All Celtic countries have traditional "girdle cakes," made thick or thin and originally cooked on a Celtic girdle. The thin variety is known by several names, Scotch Pancakes, Tea Pancakes, or Scots Crumpets. They were, and are, enjoyed with a bit of butter and jam or honey for breakfast or tea.

This particular recipe came to us via Jim Baird, an ornithologist, antiquarian, Massachusetts Scot who is also Vice President of the Massachusetts Audubon Society. These pancakes are quite sweet and can be eaten unadorned with a cup of tea.

If your pancakes are about two inches in diameter you'll have enough batter for about forty. If you want to roll them, you can make them a bit larger and make between 2 and 3 dozen.

> 2 eggs
> $^3/_4$ to 1 cup sugar
> 2 cups King Arthur Unbleached All-Purpose Flour
> 1 tablespoon baking powder
> a pinch of salt
> 1 $^1/_2$ cups milk

Heat your griddle until it is moderately hot.

Beat the eggs into the sugar, one at a time, until the mixture resembles a soft meringue, very fluffy and light. In a separate bowl, mix the dry ingredients together. Blend them gently into the egg mixture alternately with the milk.

Because these pancakes contain no fat, you'll want to use a well-seasoned griddle or a non-stick pan. Grease the griddle lightly and drop the batter onto it by the spoonful.

When they're lightly browned on the first side, turn them and brown the second.

These pancakes can be served as is or, after they have cooled (covered with a tea towel), you can spread them with a bit of butter and jam and roll them up.

BAKING POWDER BISCUITS

Baking powder biscuits are eaten in a country where wheat grows in abundance so their mystique is quite different from the scones'. Biscuits make one think of farmhouse kitchens, enormous farm breakfasts and hot soups and stews, fare for the working man. Two centuries ago they were cooked over the coals on a "spider," a cast iron pan with legs and a long handle, very much like the scone's girdle on a tripod.

If you can imagine what this pan looked like, you can guess how its name came about. Occasionally, today, you'll hear someone refer to a cast iron frying pan as a "spider." You just have to remember that the original looked like its namesake.

ALL-AMERICAN BAKING POWDER BISCUITS

This is a basic baking powder biscuit recipe that makes approximately a dozen, depending on how you shape them.

> 3 cups King Arthur Unbleached All-Purpose Flour
> 1 teaspoon salt
> 1 tablespoon baking powder
> 1 to 4 tablespoons sugar
> 4 to 6 tablespoons ($^1/_2$ to $^3/_4$ stick) butter or shortening
> 1 cup milk (or buttermilk)

First: Preheat your oven to 425°F.

Making the Dough: Mix together the dry ingredients. With two knives, a pastry blender or your fingertips, cut or rub the butter or shortening in until the mixture looks like bread crumbs.

Add the milk, all at once, mixing quickly and gently for about 20 seconds until you have a soft dough.

Shaping: There are three ways to shape these biscuits.

- Drop them by the spoonful onto a lightly floured baking sheet.

- For tidier shapes, fill the cups of a greased muffin tin about two-thirds full.

- After kneading the dough gently on a floured surface 8 or 10 times, roll or pat it out until it's about ³/₄ inch thick and cut the biscuits with a round cookie cutter dipped in flour. You can also use a spatula or bowl scraper to cut out diamonds or squares so you don't have any dough scraps left over.

Baking: Bake the biscuits for 15 to 20 minutes or until they're lightly browned.

STRAWBERRY SHORTCAKE FOR SIX FOR TEA

In Britain, for a proper "Cream Tea," simple scones are split and served with raspberry or strawberry jam laced with whipped or "clotted" cream (see Appendix). In America, although one thinks of biscuits with soups and stews, Strawberry Shortcake is much like its British cousin. For an American version of the "Cream Tea," the biscuits are also split but we serve them with a generous helping of fresh strawberries and fresh whipped cream.

    12 All-American Baking Powder Biscuits, split
    2 quarts strawberries
    ¹/₂ to ³/₄ cup sugar
    2 cups (1 pint) heavy cream
    ¹/₄ to ¹/₂ cup confectioners' sugar
    2 teaspoons vanilla
    butter to top biscuits (optional)

A couple of hours ahead of time, clean and slice the strawberries. Sprinkle them with the sugar, mixing gently so the sugar draws out some of the juice.

Whip the heavy cream until it is fairly stiff. Blend in the confectioners' sugar and vanilla.

Put 4 freshly made biscuit halves on each plate, add a pat of butter to each and spoon on the strawberries. Top with whipped cream.

If you don't feel you could stand such an enormity of bliss, cut the servings in half and invite six more friends.

Food Processor Baking Powder Biscuits

Although making biscuits by hand is not a chore, here's a recipe that makes use of this device. Serve these biscuits with strawberries and whipped cream as described on the preceding page or with bowls of hot steaming soup or stew.

2 cups King Arthur Unbleached All-Purpose Flour
1/4 cup sugar
1 tablespoon baking powder
1/2 teaspoon salt
1/2 cup (1 stick) butter or margarine
3/4 cup milk

Preheat your oven to 350°F.

Put the dry ingredients in the food processor and pulse to mix them. Cut the stick of butter into thirds and add all at once to the dry ingredients. Pulse until this mixture resembles coarse cornmeal.

Add the milk through the feed tube all at once and pulse only until the mixture holds together. Avoid too much mixing. It is okay if the dough is lumpy.

Put into a greased, 9-inch round cake pan, patting the dough into place with greased fingers. Bake for 15 to 20 minutes.

Bert's Buttermilk Biscuits

This recipe comes from Bert Porter who was King Arthur Flour's most excellent spokesman during the 1960's and '70's. While he has retired to bake just for the fun of it, he still appears from time to time to cheer us on.

Bert's biscuits are an old cream of tartar variation. They're made with vegetable shortening so they're cholesterol free. (We include the instructions in his words.)

2 cups King Arthur Unbleached All-Purpose Flour
2 tablespoons sugar
1/2 teaspoon salt
2 teaspoons cream of tartar
1 teaspoon baking soda
1/3 cup shortening
3/4 cup buttermilk

"Preheat your oven to 425°F.

"Put the dry ingredients in a bowl and mix. Cut in the shortening with the side of a fork until the mixture resembles coarse crumbs. Add the buttermilk, stirring lightly with your fork until all the flour has been absorbed. Do NOT overmix and do NOT knead because you do not want to strengthen the gluten in the flour.

"Sprinkle a tablespoon of flour on your board, and gently roll the dough in it. With your fingertips, press out the dough into an oblong, approximately 4 x 10 inches. Cut this into 10 pieces, about 2 inches square, and gently round the corners of each piece.

"Bake on an ungreased cookie sheet (to prevent sticking you can sprinkle a bit of flour on it) for 12 to 14 minutes. These biscuits are done when the bottoms are a light golden brown."

Biscuits with Herbs

Whether these are baking powder biscuits or scones, who's to say? This variation contains no sugar at all. Whatever you call them, they are great all by themselves or as a topping for a pot pie.

3 cups King Arthur Unbleached All-Purpose Flour
1 tablespoon baking powder
1/2 teaspoon baking soda
1 teaspoon salt
1/3 teaspoon dry mustard
3/4 teaspoon dry sage
3/4 teaspoon celery seed
6 tablespoons (3/4 stick) butter
1 cup buttermilk

Preheat the oven to 425°F.

Mix the flour, baking powder, soda, salt and herbs. Cut or rub in the butter until the mixture resembles coarse crumbs. Add the buttermilk, stirring just enough to combine the ingredients.

Lightly flour your work surface. Work the dough with your fingertips into a 4 x 10-inch rectangle. Cut into 10 or 12 pieces and place on a lightly floured ungreased cookie sheet.

Bake for about 12 minutes.

SODA BREADS

Most of us associate soda breads with Ireland which has made them famous. These breads were originally "baked" in an iron pot over a peat fire, very much like their Scottish and American cousins.

IRISH SODA (OR DAIRY) BREAD

This is Ireland's version of the bannock. To our American way of thinking, Irish soda bread usually includes raisins and caraway seeds. But that is not the soda bread you find most often in its home country.

This recipe is for a traditional soda bread or dairy bread as it used to be called. It is round like a bannock and contains about 25% white flour and 75% whole wheat flour. Irish flour is much softer (meaning lower in protein) than King Arthur Stone Ground Whole Wheat Flour, and is more coarsely ground. With a few adjustments to our King Arthur Flours we can come fairly close to an authentic version.

1/2 cup cornstarch
3/4 cup King Arthur Unbleached All-Purpose Flour
1 3/4 cups King Arthur Stone Ground Whole Wheat Flour
1/2 teaspoon baking soda
1 teaspoon salt
4 tablespoons (1/2 stick) butter
1 cup buttermilk

Preheat your oven to 375°F.

Blend the dry ingredients together in a mixing bowl. Rub in the butter with your fingertips until it resembles bread crumbs.

Add the buttermilk and stir with a spoon until it just holds together (20 seconds). Turn it out onto a lightly floured surface and knead it gently 8 to 10 times.

You can bake this as a single loaf or cut the dough in half and bake two. Whichever you choose, form each loaf into a slightly flattened round and place on a floured baking sheet.

With a knife, cut about 3/4 inch into the dough in the form of a cross as if you were going to quarter it. Dust a bit of flour over the top and place the bread in your oven to bake for 30 minutes for 2 small loaves or 40 minutes for one large one.

Remove the bread from the oven and lay a damp cloth over it until it's cool. Or don't wait; eat some warm with butter and jam and a cup of tea.

AMERICAN IRISH SODA BREAD

On this side of the Atlantic, some additions have found their way into the soda bread tradition. Here we have the more familiar caraway seed and raisin variety.

This particular recipe, equally Irish, comes by way of Brinna Sands' sister-in-law, Margaret Mullins Baird. It was her grandmother's recipe and, of course, was never written down. It was passed on orally in phrases like "pinches" and "butter the size of a walnut." After many tries, Margaret's sister, Carol McLaughlin, has come very close to what the two sisters remember of the original. It's great, they say, plain or toasted and better when it's a couple of days old. If you have never tried raisins and caraway seeds before, you should. It is a compelling combination.

3 cups King Arthur Unbleached All-Purpose Flour 🌾
1 teaspoon baking soda
1/2 teaspoon salt
1/4 cup sugar
2 tablespoons butter, at room temperature
1 to 1 1/2 cups raisins
3 tablespoons caraway seeds
1 egg
2 cups buttermilk

Preheat your oven to 400°F.

Blend the dry ingredients together in a large mixing bowl. With your fingertips, quickly rub in the butter. Stir in the raisins and caraway seeds.

In a smaller bowl beat together the egg and buttermilk. Add to the flour mixture and mix only until just blended. (Note that although soda breads are usually made from a dough, this is a batter.)

Pour into a lightly greased 5 x 9-inch loaf pan. Bake for 10 minutes. Lower the temperature to 375°F and bake for a further 35 to 40 minutes.

Irish Whiskey Soda Bread

Here's another American version from Michael Jubinsky. This one contains baking powder to help with the leavening and is flavored with Irish whiskey.

4 cups King Arthur Unbleached All-Purpose Flour
3 tablespoons sugar
1 teaspoon salt
1 teaspoon baking powder
1/2 teaspoon baking soda
4 tablespoons (1/2 stick) butter
1 1/2 cups raisins
1 teaspoon caraway seeds (optional)
1 tablespoon Irish whiskey (or water)
2 eggs
1 cup buttermilk

Preheat your oven to 400°F.

Combine and blend thoroughly the flour, sugar, salt, baking powder and soda in a bowl. Cut or rub in with your fingers, the butter until the mixture resembles bread crumbs.

In another bowl, mix the raisins with the whiskey or water. Blend these and the caraway seeds (if you choose to add them) with the flour mixture.

Beat the eggs and stir all but one tablespoon (reserve in a small bowl) into the buttermilk. Add the wet ingredients to the dry and stir only enough to combine the two.

Place the dough on a lightly floured surface. Knead it 8 to 10 times until it comes together as a whole.

Form the dough into a round ball and place it in a well-greased, 8-inch round cake pan or casserole dish.

Brush the top with the reserved egg. Cut a 4-inch cross in the top of the dough with a sharp, floured knife.

Bake for 45 to 50 minutes or until a toothpick inserted in the center comes out clean. Remove the loaf from the pan and cool on a wire rack. Slice thin and serve with butter and jam.

• SMALL QUICK BREADS FROM BATTERS •

Quick bread batters are easier to make than quick bread doughs since the kneading and shaping steps are eliminated. In a quick bread dough the ratio of flour to liquid is about 3 to 1. In a quick bread batter, it's closer to 3 to 2, creating a mixture that will "pour." If you started with the quick bread doughs, these will be a cinch.

MUFFINS

Muffins are easier to put together than scones or biscuits and are richer, sweeter cousins. Because they have more moisture in them than scones or biscuits, and because they are leavened more frequently with baking powder, their texture is moister, finer and more cake-like.

KING ARTHUR FLOUR'S
BASIC "P. D. Q."* MUFFINS
"Pretty Darn Quick!"

As elsewhere in our 200th Anniversary Cookbook, we'll give you a basic ratio of ingredients for muffins. While you're putting together your first batch, try to memorize or make a picture of the process in your head. The ingredients are so few and they are so quickly combined that you won't find this part hard at all. Knowing how it's done, without having to look it up every time, gives you the freedom to make every muffin an inspiration of your own.

2 cups King Arthur Unbleached All-Purpose Flour
½ cup sugar
½ teaspoon salt
1 tablespoon baking powder
1 cup milk
¼ cup vegetable oil or softened butter (optional)
2 eggs

We are using 3 teaspoons or 1 tablespoon of baking powder because of the sugar and oil "decorations" which need an added lift. (See page 54.)

In place of the vegetable oil, you can use an equivalent amount of butter (which contains cholesterol but unsurpassed flavor), margarine or a blend. If you leave the oil out altogether, you can reduce the calories in your muffins by about 30%; the flavor will still be excellent but they won't keep as well should you happen to have any left over.

First: Preheat your oven to 500°F.

Mixing the Dry Ingredients: Blend together the dry ingredients as long and vigorously as you want. If you use a little whole wheat flour in your mixture, it's easy to tell when everything is thoroughly mixed.

Mixing the Liquid Ingredients: If you have a two-cup liquid measure (one with a lip above the two-cup mark) it makes mixing the liquid ingredients very easy. Most egg beaters will fit right in the cup so you can use it both as a measure and as a small bowl. Beat the liquid ingredients together (the milk, vegetable oil and eggs) until they are light.

Mixing the Liquid & the Dry: Pour the wet ingredients into the dry. Here's where you have to restrain yourself. Take a fork or wire whisk and blend the two for 20 seconds and no more. The secret to light and tender muffins lies in this final blending. It's okay if you've left some lumps that look as if they want more stirring. They really don't. So, no matter how hard it is, resist the impulse.

Baking: Fill the cups of a lightly greased, 12-cup muffin tin two-thirds full. As soon as the muffins are in the oven, drop the temperature to 400°F. Bake for about 20 minutes or until they're a lovely, golden brown.

When you put muffins in a very hot oven initially and then immediately drop the temperature, you help create the peaks that make them so appealing.

VARIOUS & SUNDRY "P. D. Q." MUFFINS

While each of the following recipes makes a unique version of the original, none is written in stone; they're written rather to inspire you to experiment. Turn to Ingredient Alternatives (page 60) for more ideas. Mix and bake as you did the basic recipe. You'll find that some batters are wetter than others. Not to worry; they'll all make muffins.

"P. D. Q." MUFFINS WITH BAKING SODA

Because this recipe contains buttermilk, we use baking soda which will react with it to create carbon dioxide bubbles. (See page 54 for more information.)

> 2 cups King Arthur Unbleached All-Purpose Flour
> 1/2 cup sugar
> 1/2 teaspoon salt
> 1 teaspoon baking powder
> 1/2 teaspoon baking soda
> 1 cup buttermilk
> 1/4 cup (1/2 stick) butter, softened (optional)
> 2 eggs

If you use butter, cut or rub it into the dry ingredients before you add the liquids.

"P. D. Q." Whole Wheat Muffins

$\frac{1}{2}$ cup King Arthur Unbleached All-Purpose Flour
1$\frac{1}{2}$ cups King Arthur Stone Ground Whole Wheat Flour
$\frac{1}{2}$ cup honey or brown sugar
$\frac{1}{2}$ teaspoon salt
1 tablespoon baking powder
1 cup milk
$\frac{1}{4}$ cup vegetable oil (optional)
2 eggs

Since honey tends to scorch, bake honey-sweetened muffins at 325°F for 20 to 25 minutes. You might also try substituting maple syrup or molasses.

"P. D. Q." Wheat Germ Muffins

In this one we're eliminating an egg and increasing the milk. (See page 61.)

1 cup King Arthur Unbleached All-Purpose Flour
1 cup King Arthur Stone Ground Whole Wheat Flour
$\frac{1}{2}$ cup wheat germ
1 tablespoon baking powder
$\frac{1}{2}$ teaspoon salt
2 tablespoons sugar
1$\frac{1}{4}$ cups milk
1 egg
3 tablespoons melted butter (optional)

"P. D. Q." Ginger Muffins

2 cups King Arthur Unbleached All-Purpose Flour
$\frac{1}{2}$ teaspoon salt
1 tablespoon baking powder
$\frac{1}{2}$ teaspoon cinnamon
$\frac{1}{2}$ teaspoon nutmeg
$\frac{1}{2}$ teaspoon ginger
1 cup milk
$\frac{1}{2}$ cup molasses
$\frac{1}{4}$ cup vegetable oil (optional)
2 eggs

Or, for truly gingery muffins, sauté 3 tablespoons of fresh grated ginger in about 2 tablespoons of butter and eliminate the ground dried ginger and vegetable oil.

"P. D. Q." CORNMEAL MUFFINS

1 cup King Arthur Unbleached All-Purpose Flour 🌾
1 cup yellow or blue cornmeal
1/2 cup sugar
1/2 teaspoon salt
1 tablespoon baking powder
1 cup milk or buttermilk
1/4 cup vegetable oil (optional)
2 eggs

Tom Fiddaman, a young friend of the Sands', discovered something interesting about combining blue cornmeal, which is often available in the specialty section of your grocery store, with something acidic such as buttermilk. We won't tell you what happens except to say that those of you who remember litmus paper experiments in chemistry may not need to make these muffins to figure it out.

"P. D. Q." FRUIT & NUT MUFFINS

2 cups King Arthur Unbleached All-Purpose Flour 🌾
1/2 teaspoon salt
1 tablespoon baking powder
1/2 cup chopped nuts (or sunflower or other seeds)
1/2 to 1 cup grated Cheddar cheese (optional)
1/2 cup honey or maple syrup
1 cup applesauce (or other fruit)
1/4 cup vegetable oil (optional)
2 eggs

After you blend the dry ingredients, stir in the nuts (and the cheese). Then add your blended liquids.

For a crunch with a different flavor, substitute 1/2 cup of bacon for the nuts and try maple syrup instead of brown sugar for the sweetener.

For the applesauce, try substituting mashed banana, cranberry sauce, crushed pineapple, cooked and mashed carrot or winter squash.

When you use mashed fruits and vegetables as the "liquid," your muffin batter will be stiffer than the original Basic "P. D. Q." Muffins made with milk. You can compensate for this difference by using a liquid sweetener like honey or maple syrup. Choose whichever seems most appropriate to accent the fruit or vegetable you're using.

"P. D. Q." Berry Muffins

2 cups King Arthur Unbleached All-Purpose Flour
1/2 cup sugar
1/2 teaspoon salt
1 tablespoon baking powder
1 1/2 cups blueberries, raspberries, blackberries or any other berries
1 cup sour cream, yogurt or milk
1/4 cup (1/2 stick) butter or margarine, melted
2 eggs

To make sure the berries stay evenly distributed throughout the batter, add the cup of berries to the dry ingredients and mix until coated before adding the liquid ingredients. This prevents them from sinking once the liquids are blended in. The same technique can be used for any other chopped fruit: apples, peaches, even pineapple, as well as nuts, seeds, etc.

"P. D. Q." Filled Muffins

2 cups King Arthur Unbleached All-Purpose Flour
1/4 cup sugar
1/2 teaspoon salt
1 tablespoon baking powder
1 cup milk or yogurt
1/4 cup vegetable oil (optional)
2 eggs

For a surprise, place a spoonful of batter in your muffin cup, then a spoonful of jam, and then batter to the two-thirds mark.

Once you've made all these, or variations of same, you'll have a foundation for making muffins for the rest of your life.

Following are more muffin recipes from our King Arthur Flour archives, our spokesmen and women, our fans, and ourselves. The Basic "P. D. Q." Muffin is still there, just dressed up.

ELEGANT MAPLE BRAN MUFFINS

This recipe from Barbara Lauterbach makes a dozen elegant muffins. Leavening comes from the reaction of the baking soda with the sour cream or yogurt.

1 cup King Arthur Unbleached All-Purpose Flour
1 cup bran flakes
1 teaspoon baking soda
1/3 cup raisins
1/3 cup chopped walnuts
1 cup sour cream or yogurt
1 cup maple syrup
2 eggs

Preheat oven to 400°F.

Combine the flour, bran, and baking soda. Stir in the raisins and nuts. In a separate bowl, beat together the sour cream or yogurt, maple syrup and eggs. Add the wet ingredients to the dry and mix for 20 seconds only.

Fill your greased muffin tin two-thirds full. Bake for 20 minutes.

CRUMBLE STATION BLUEBERRY MUFFINS

This recipe was sent by a "K. A." fan whose name and whereabouts are known only to Merlin. The note on our copy says these are "the world's best," though there was no location for "Crumble Station." The recipe will make a dozen muffins.

1 1/2 cups King Arthur Unbleached All-Purpose Flour
1/2 cup sugar
2 teaspoons baking powder
1/4 teaspoon salt
1 egg
1/2 cup milk
1/4 cup unsalted butter, melted
1 1/2 cups Maine blueberries (the tiny wild ones)

Preheat your oven to 400°F.

Mix the dry ingredients together. In a separate bowl, beat the egg, milk and butter together. Fold them into the flour mixture, stirring only until combined. Fold in the blueberries.

Fill your lightly greased muffin tin two-thirds full. Bake for 20 minutes.

BAGLEY HOUSE
ZUCCHINI LEMON MUFFINS

Bagley House, the oldest house in Durham, Maine, was originally built as an inn in 1772. Today, it is a Bed & Breakfast owned by Sigurd A. Knudsen, Jr., who tells his guests that they "can say they slept in the inn that George Washington would have slept in if he'd ever come to Durham." He tells us that these muffins, which he makes in the old inn kitchen with its beehive oven, "are by far the favorites."

They are wonderful at breakfast but can be a great accompaniment to a summer soup at dinner. This recipe will make about a dozen.

2 cups King Arthur Unbleached All-Purpose Flour
1/2 cup sugar
1 tablespoon baking powder
1 teaspoon salt
grated peel of 1/2 lemon
1/2 cup (or more) chopped walnuts
1/2 cup (or more) raisins
2 eggs, beaten
1/2 cup milk
1/3 cup vegetable oil
1 cup (packed) shredded zucchini

Preheat the oven to 400°F.

Combine the flour, sugar, baking powder, salt and lemon peel in a large bowl. Stir in the walnuts and raisins.

In a smaller bowl (or a two-cup liquid measure), combine the eggs, milk and oil.

Make a well in the center of the dry ingredients and add the wet ingredients. Stir just until barely combined and then gently fold in the zucchini.

Spoon the batter into a greased, 12-cup muffin tin. Bake for 20 to 25 minutes or until the muffins spring back when you press them with your fingertips.

Banana Pecan Muffins

This recipe from Michael Jubinsky makes 12 large muffins.

2 cups King Arthur Unbleached All-Purpose Flour
1 tablespoon baking powder
$1/2$ teaspoon salt
$1/2$ cup chopped pecans (or walnuts)
$1/2$ cup vegetable shortening
1 cup sugar
2 eggs
$1\frac{1}{3}$ to $1\frac{1}{2}$ cups mashed ripe bananas (about 3)

Preheat your oven to 400°F.

Blend the flour, baking powder and salt together in a mixing bowl. Mix in the chopped nuts.

In a second bowl, cream the shortening and sugar together until light and fluffy. Add the eggs one at a time and beat well. Blend in the mashed banana.

Add the wet ingredients to the dry, stirring just enough to moisten, about 20 seconds. Spoon the muffin batter into a greased muffin tin and bake for 20 to 25 minutes until the muffins are golden brown and the tops spring back when touched.

Fancy Department Store Muffins

Part of the current muffin mania is due to those enormous beauties you can buy in various commercial establishments. Their ingredients put them almost in the cake category since they contain such a high ratio of fat and sugar. They are lovely, but loaded with calories. Below you'll find a tasty example. This recipe will make 12 large muffins.

2 cups King Arthur Unbleached All-Purpose Flour
1 tablespoon baking powder
$1/4$ teaspoon salt
6 tablespoons ($3/4$ stick) butter or margarine
$1\frac{1}{4}$ cups sugar
2 eggs
$1/2$ cup milk
2 cups fresh blueberries, chopped apple or peach, etc. (optional)
1 cup chopped nuts: almonds, walnuts, pecans, etc. (optional)
$1/2$ teaspoon cinnamon or nutmeg mixed with 1 tablespoon sugar (for top)

Preheat your oven to 400°F.

Combine the flour, baking powder and salt.

In a separate bowl, cream the butter or margarine with the sugar until light and fluffy. Add the eggs and beat well. Blend this mixture with the dry ingredients alternately with the milk. Fold the blueberries and nuts (etc.) in quickly.

Because these muffins will rise up and over the edge of your muffin tin, you'll want to grease the top of the pan as well as the cups. Fill the cups nearly three-quarters full and sprinkle with the spiced sugar.

Bake for 25 to 30 minutes, or until golden brown.

CHOCOLATE CHOCOLATE CHIP MUFFINS

This muffin recipe is in the same high-calorie league as the previous one with very few redeeming qualities except that they're full of carbohydrates (quick energy) and they taste good. It will make a dozen muffins for a dedicated sweet tooth.

1¾ cups King Arthur Unbleached All-Purpose Flour
⅓ cup cocoa
½ cup sugar
1 tablespoon baking powder
1 teaspoon baking soda
½ teaspoon salt
1 cup chocolate chips
2 eggs
½ cup vegetable oil
¾ cup milk
1 teaspoon vanilla

Preheat the oven to 400°F.

Blend together thoroughly the first six ingredients and mix in the chocolate chips. In another bowl, beat the eggs, oil, milk and vanilla together. Add the wet ingredients to the dry, all at once, and mix together until just blended, about 20 seconds. Don't overmix.

Spoon the mixture into your greased muffin cups. Bake for about 20 minutes.

✺ *To make this an easy recipe for kids, substitute 1¾ cups of King Arthur "Self-Rising" Flour for the unbleached all-purpose flour, baking powder and salt. You'll find directions for making self-rising flour on page 597.*

Zella Lane's
Bran Muffins

Some of you may remember hearing the voice of Betty Crocker over the radio a number of years ago. The voice actually belonged to Zella Lane who is a real person who really does love to bake. She lives in Virginia and has her daughter ship King Arthur Flour to her since it is not available in that region.

This is one of Zella's favorite recipes, "a whale-of-a-big-one which will keep for 6 weeks in the refrigerator." This means with one effort, you'll have enough batter to use judiciously for a month and a half.

Zella says she's been working on a banana, coconut, pecan muffin made with both whole wheat and unbleached flours, and sweetened with maple syrup. She says she'll share it once she gets it perfected. We're waiting eagerly!

This recipe needs to be put together the night before baking so the bran can soften and the batter thicken.

> 1 cup boiling water
> 1 cup bran cereal (not flakes)
> 1/2 cup vegetable oil
> 2 1/2 cups King Arthur Unbleached All-Purpose Flour
> 2 1/2 teaspoons baking soda
> 1 teaspoon salt
> 2 large (or 3 medium or small) eggs
> 2 cups buttermilk
> 1 1/4 cups sugar
> 2 cups all-bran cereal
> 1 cup raisins

In a small mixing bowl, pour the boiling water over the cup of cereal. When this has cooled, add the vegetable oil.

While the water/bran mixture cools, blend together the flour, soda and salt in a large mixing bowl. Stir in the raisins if you wish to add them.

In a medium-sized bowl, beat the eggs until light. Continue beating while you add the buttermilk and then the sugar. Add this to the dry ingredients. Stir in the remainder of the cereal and then the water/bran/oil mixture.

Place this mixture in an airtight container and refrigerate overnight.

The next morning, preheat your oven to 375°F for 15 minutes. Fill the lightly greased cups of a muffin tin two-thirds full and bake for 20 to 25 minutes. If you only want 1 or 2 muffins, you can use lightly greased custard cups.

GARY'S MOTHER'S MUFFINS

The next couple of muffin recipes are made with self-rising flour which is a Southern phenomenon. Self-rising flour is simply flour to which baking powder and a little salt are added. You'll find our not-very-complicated instructions for making your own King Arthur Unbleached and/or Stone Ground Whole Wheat "Self-Rising" Flour on page 597.

This recipe comes from attorney Gary Brooks, one of the directors of our small company, whose parents live in Florida. It's an "instant" kind of recipe consisting of only three ingredients: self-rising flour, milk and mayonnaise. What magic turns these three ingredients into muffins?

As we explained above, self-rising flour is really three ingredients on its own, flour, baking powder and salt. Milk is straightforward enough so some of the magic must be in the mayonnaise. Mayonnaise is composed of eggs, vegetable oil, a little lemon juice or vinegar, sugar and flavorings.

A basic muffin recipe is composed of flour, baking powder, salt, some milk and eggs, butter or oil and a little sugar. It looks as if our three-ingredient recipe actually contains everything you need to make a dozen muffins.

> 1 cup milk
> 4 heaping tablespoons mayonnaise
> 2 cups King Arthur "Self-Rising" Flour

Preheat your oven to 425°F.

Thoroughly beat together the milk and mayonnaise. Put the flour in a mixing bowl, make a "well" in it and pour in the wet ingredients. With a fork, blend the wet and dry ingredients together, taking only 20 seconds.

Fill the cups of a greased muffin tin two-thirds full and bake for 10 to 12 minutes.

For variations, you might start with a homemade mayonnaise flavored with chives, dill or other herbs. Or you might try adding a few tablespoons of sugar and a handful of blueberries to the original recipe, or perhaps some grated cheese. The basic recipe is so easy, it asks for an experiment.

JACK-O-LANTERN MUFFINS

Self-rising flour is simple to make, simple to store, and makes a lot of baking a snap. (See page 597.) It's a great way to introduce kids to baking, because with very little coaching, they can do it from scratch all by themselves. These muffins are not only good, but making them is a good way to recycle a collapsing jack-o-lantern.

Cook the pumpkin first (it's best if it's a sugar or baking pumpkin) so you will have 1 cup mashed and ready to use. This recipe will make a dozen muffins.

2 cups King Arthur "Self-Rising" Flour
½ cup sugar
2 eggs
1 cup cooked pumpkin, mashed
¼ cup vegetable oil

Preheat the oven to 400°F and lightly grease your muffin tin.

The baker can mix the "self-rising" flour and sugar together to his or her heart's content. In another bowl the eggs, pumpkin and the vegetable oil, too, can be beaten as long as the inspiration lasts.

When the wet ingredients are stirred into the dry, you may have to urge gentle restraint. It should be done for 20 seconds and no longer. The mixing can be vigorous to make sure most of the ingredients are blended, but the batter need not be smooth. It should be a little lumpy.

With a couple of spoons, fill the lightly greased muffin cups two-thirds full. Bake for 20 minutes. That's all!

After this try, your baker can add a little cinnamon or nutmeg to the dry ingredients, but it's best to start simple. Understanding comes in small bites.

DOUGHNUTS

The batter for baking powder doughnuts is, actually, almost a dough because it has enough body to be rolled and cut.

DOUGHNUTS FOR "SUGARING"

The sun was warm, but the wind was chill.
You know how it is with an April day.
When the sun is out and the wind is still,
You're one month on in the middle of May
But if you so much as dare to speak,
A cloud comes over the sunlit arch,
A wind comes off a frozen peak,
And you're two months back in the middle of March.

There are no better words than Robert Frost's in Two Tramps in Mud Time, for conjuring up that sharp, sweet and temperamental season of early April in Vermont. One of the most exciting changes of this quickening season happens both unheard and unseen. With longer, warmer days but still freezing nights, those lifeless looking maple trees that dot the northeastern landscape turn into gigantic pumps, pulling gallons of water out of the thawing ground, mixing them with nutrients and sugars and sending them up and out to nourish buds that have been waiting patiently in a dormant state through the long New England winter.

Along with the new life pulsing throughout the North, you'll see "sugar houses" punctuating the hills, steaming away and transforming the precious spring sap of the Sugar Maple into maple syrup.

For those of you who have ever tapped a maple tree, you know what an exciting event this is. To drill a hole, hammer in a tap and watch those first drops of sap well up and spill out into your bucket make one look in wonder at all the trees in the landscape, knowing that, even though you can't see it, something quite miraculous is going on.

The taste of the first syrup is sweet and exciting. The traditional way to prolong this pleasure is to make and eat "sugar on snow." To create this once-a-year indulgence, we boil down a pan of fresh syrup until two or three drops form a ball when dropped in a cup of cold water. Then we pour it over fresh snow or crushed ice and watch it stiffen like taffy. We eat this chewy sweet with sour pickles (put up from last summer's garden) and homemade doughnuts while sitting and savouring the early spring sunshine.

Cake, or baking powder, doughnuts were developed in New England many years ago. They were originally shaped like nuts, hence their name. (The Pennsylvania Dutch added the holes.) Combining these with pickles and "sugar on snow" is probably one of the oldest traditions in America and a sweet finale to this section.

2 eggs
1 cup buttermilk
1 cup brown sugar
2 to 4 tablespoons butter, melted
1 cup King Arthur Stone Ground Whole Wheat Flour
3 cups King Arthur Unbleached All-Purpose Flour
1 teaspoon baking soda
1 teaspoon baking powder
$\frac{1}{2}$ teaspoon salt
$\frac{1}{4}$ teaspoon cinnamon
$\frac{1}{4}$ teaspoon nutmeg

Beat the eggs with the buttermilk until light. Add and beat in the sugar and melted butter. Mix the flours, baking soda, baking powder, salt and spices together. Blend with the liquid ingredients, mixing as little as possible.

The dough will be sticky so turn it out onto a well-floured board. With a rolling pin, also well floured, roll out the dough until it is between $\frac{1}{4}$ and $\frac{1}{2}$ inch thick.

Cut the doughnuts with a doughnut cutter and allow them to rest while you heat a frying pan of lard (traditional), vegetable oil or shortening to 365°F. It should be deep enough so the doughnuts will float.

Fry the doughnuts, giving them enough room to expand, until they're a golden brown on both sides. Remove them to a paper towel to drain.

While it's bliss to eat the stiffened maple syrup after you've poured it on some snow, for those who can't wait, try dipping a doughnut in the syrup while it's still warm. Follow this with a bite of pickle and you'll be ready for more.

For a southwestern version of this northeastern doughnut, see Navajo Fry Bread in the Flatbread Section of Chapter VI.

• LARGE QUICK BREADS FROM BATTERS •

Like the preceding muffins and doughnuts, these quick loaves are made with a batter. They are very much like muffins, just bigger. In fact you can use these quick bread batters to make muffins if you want and you can certainly cook muffin batter in a loaf pan.

Most of these recipes are sweet but a few are savory and all are good. Many of them taste even better the day after they're made. All of them can be frozen and reheated (either sliced or whole). If any last long enough to stale, you can quickly revive them in the toaster or oven.

Baking & Storing Quick Bread Loaves & Coffeecakes

Most of the loaves and coffeecakes in this section are made from recipes that make either 4½ to 5 cups of batter (2 cups of flour) or 6½ to 7 cups of batter (3 cups of flour). The ratio of ingredients in both groups is essentially the same. You can enlarge the smaller recipe by one-third and use the larger pan sizes below or you can reduce the larger recipe by one-third and use the smaller pan sizes. We'll give you an assortment of pan sizes and baking times so you have as many options as possible.

The baking times are only approximate because they are affected by a number of variables: the actual amount of batter in the pan, the temperature of the batter when it goes in the oven, how many "decorations" (see page 54) are added to it, and, equally important, the idiosyncrasies of the oven itself.

Preparing the Pans: Grease well whatever pan you use. If you use butter, you'll need to flour the pan to absorb the water that is present in butter. This isn't necessary if you use vegetable shortening or a mixture of two-thirds liquid lecithin and one-third vegetable oil (see Appendix, page 587).

Pan Sizes for 4½ to 5 Cups of Batter

You'll find recipes for this amount of batter in the sections on Sweet and Savory Quick Breads. It can most easily be baked in the following pans.

- One 5 x 9-inch loaf pan for about 1 hour

- One 9-inch round cake pan for about 40 minutes

- One 8-inch square cake pan for about 40 minutes

- Two small 3½ x 7½-inch loaf pans for about 40 minutes

Pan Sizes for 6¹/₂ to 7¹/₂ Cups of Batter

You'll find recipes for this amount of batter mostly in the section on Coffeecakes.

• One 9-inch springform pan for 60 to 70 minutes

• One 10-inch tube pan, ring mold or Bundt pan for 50 to 60 minutes

• Two 4¹/₂ x 8¹/₂-inch loaf pans for 40 to 50 minutes

• Two 8-inch round cake pans for 30 to 35 minutes

Baking: When you bake a loaf or coffeecake, start checking at the early end of the time range.

Checking to See if Your Bread is Done: Use all three checks below. Occasionally you'll find a bread that doesn't pull away from the sides of the pan (which doesn't necessarily mean that it isn't done). If the bread is browning too quickly, but doesn't seem to be done, lower the temperature 25°F and continue baking another 5 to 10 minutes.

• The top will spring back when you press it gently with your fingertips.

• The loaf will begin to shrink away from the sides of the pan.

• A toothpick or knife, inserted in the center, will come out without any batter sticking to it.

Cooling: After your bread has baked, let it cool for about 10 minutes in the pan. This allows the bread to "set" and contract a bit which makes it easier to get out of the pan.

Finishing Touches: If the bread has a topping or glaze and you're going to serve it right away, place the bread on a serving plate and sprinkle or drizzle the topping over the top.

If your bread doesn't have a topping or glaze, you can certainly add one to dress it up (see page 207). Flavor it with a teaspoon of whatever extract you used in the bread itself.

Storing: If you plan to store your time and effort away in the freezer, wrap the bread in plastic wrap or an airtight plastic bag after it has thoroughly cooled. Freeze the topping separately or make a fresh one when you want to serve the bread. Allow several hours for the bread to thaw.

SWEET QUICK BREADS

KING ARTHUR FLOUR'S
BASIC QUICK BREAD

This first recipe is from our archives. It's basic, good and waiting for embellishments. Two of the following variations can only be called "quick breads for kids."

1 cup King Arthur Unbleached All-Purpose Flour
1 cup King Arthur Stone Ground Whole Wheat Flour
2 teaspoons baking powder
1/2 teaspoon baking soda
1/2 teaspoon salt
1/4 to 1/2 cup vegetable oil
3/4 to 1 cup brown sugar
2 eggs
1 cup milk
1 teaspoon vanilla (or other extract)

Preheat your oven to 350°F.

Mix the flours, baking powder, soda and salt together in a medium-sized bowl. In a separate bowl, beat the oil, sugar and eggs together for 1 or 2 minutes until you've incorporated as much air as you can. Blend in the milk and vanilla.

Add the wet ingredients to the dry mixture, and stir just enough to blend. This will make a very wet batter. Pour into a lightly greased, 9 x 5-inch loaf pan.

Bake for about an hour or until the top of the loaf springs back when you press it with your fingertips. Let the loaf cool on a rack for 10 to 15 minutes before turning it out of the pan.

PEANUT BUTTER & JELLY BREAD

For the milk and vanilla, substitute 1/2 cup milk, 3/4 cup crunchy peanut butter and 1/2 cup strawberry preserves.

Beat the milk and peanut butter into the oil, sugar and eggs. Blend with the dry ingredients and pour into a greased loaf pan.

Pour the strawberry preserves onto the batter. With a knife or spatula, cut them into the batter to marble it.

Bake and cool as for the Basic Quick Bread.

LEMONADE ALMOND BREAD

Use only $1/2$ cup of milk in combination with $1/2$ cup partially thawed lemonade concentrate.

Add the lemonade concentrate and milk to the oil, sugar, and egg mixure. Beat these well and add to the dry ingredients stirring just enough to blend. Fold in $1/2$ cup of sliced almonds. Bake as for the Basic Quick Bread.

When the bread is done, loosen the sides from the edge of the pan with a knife or spatula and spread the top with 1 tablespoon lemonade concentrate. Cool for 10 to 15 minutes and turn out on a wire rack.

SHERRY PUMPKIN BREAD

This variation is for grownups.

Omit the milk. To the vegetable oil and eggs, add 1 cup of cooked pumpkin, 1 teaspoon cinnamon, $1/2$ teaspoon nutmeg and $1/3$ cup sherry. Fold $1/2$ to 1 cup of chopped nuts into the batter. Bake as for the Basic Quick Bread.

SPICY APPLESAUCE BREAD

And this one is for everybody to eat together.

Omit the milk. To the vegetable oil and eggs, add 1 cup of applesauce, 1 teaspoon each of cinnamon, ginger and allspice. Fold $1/2$ cup of chopped nuts and $1/2$ cup raisins into the batter. Bake as for the Basic Quick Bread.

WHEAT GERM ORANGE LOAF

This recipe was developed back in the 1940's when Sands, Taylor & Wood Co. was selling wheat germ along with our King Arthur Flour.

2 cups King Arthur Unbleached All-Purpose Flour
1 cup wheat germ
4 teaspoons baking powder
$1/2$ teaspoon salt
$1/2$ cup brown sugar
$1\,1/2$ cups milk
2 tablespoons grated orange rind
2 tablespoons orange juice
2 tablespoons butter, melted

Preheat your oven to 350°F.

Combine the flour, wheat germ, baking powder, salt and sugar. Add the milk slowly and stir well. Blend in the orange rind, juice and the melted butter. Pour into two greased, 4½ x 8½-inch loaf pans.

Bake the loaves for 50 to 60 minutes and cool them thoroughly before slicing.

The original directions say that this bread is best made a day ahead of time as a 24-hour rest mellows the flavor and texture. Many quick breads are better after a mellowing period, particularly when orange or lemon rind is included, since their flavors need time to permeate the bread.

CRANBERRY NUT BREAD

This recipe is from Barbara Lauterbach, who owns and runs Watch Hill, a Bed & Breakfast in Centre Harbor that caters to people who love antiques and the lovely hills and lakes of New Hampshire.

2 cups King Arthur Unbleached All-Purpose Flour
½ teaspoon salt
1½ teaspoons baking powder
½ teaspoon baking soda
1 cup sugar
juice of 1 orange
2 tablespoons vegetable oil
boiling water to make up 1 cup
1 egg, beaten
1 cup chopped pecans or walnuts
grated rind of 1 orange
1 cup chopped raw cranberries

Preheat your oven to 325°F.

Combine the flour, salt, baking powder, soda and sugar.

Squeeze the orange juice into a one-cup measure. Add the oil and then fill the rest of the cup with boiling water. Add this mixture to the beaten egg.

Stir the liquids into the dry ingredients. Fold in the nuts, orange rind and cranberries.

Pour into a greased, 9 x 5-inch loaf pan. Bake for 60 to 75 minutes. Allow the bread to cool completely before slicing. The flavor is best after maturing for 24 hours.

THE GOVERNOR'S INN
VERMONT PEAR BREAD

This recipe comes to us from Deedy and Charlie Marble, the duo who run The Governor's Inn, in Ludlow, Vermont, which won the Best Inn of the Year Award for 1988 and 1989. Deedy, who does much of the cooking at the Inn herself, was named one of four (and the only woman) "Outstanding Innovative Chefs in Vermont" last year and was featured as one of Yankee Magazine's *Great New England Cooks in July as well. This recipe attests to her inventive and creative abilities in the kitchen.*

About this recipe Deedy said, "When we first moved to Ludlow, our handsome high school–aged son caused quite a flutter among the young women at school. Each dreamed up a scheme to come by the Inn to attract his attention. One young, very inventive cutie went out in her back yard and gathered up all the pears she could find, put them in an enormous basket and brought them to me. (What she didn't know was that she could have gained access just by knocking on the door!) Well, there I was with a bushel of beautiful, ripe Vermont pears. The following recipe once again proves that 'necessity is the mother of invention.'" It is best made (and then refrigerated) the night before you serve it.

> 9 tablespoons (1 stick plus 1 tablespoon) unsalted butter, at room temperature
> 1 cup sugar
> 2 large eggs
> 2 cups King Arthur Unbleached All-Purpose Flour
> $\frac{1}{2}$ teaspoon salt
> $\frac{1}{2}$ teaspoon baking soda
> 1 teaspoon baking powder
> $\frac{1}{4}$ teaspoon nutmeg
> $\frac{1}{4}$ cup buttermilk
> 1 cup coarsely chopped pears (or puréed, for a smoother texture)
> 1 teaspoon vanilla
> $\frac{1}{2}$ cup chopped walnuts

Preheat your oven to 350°F.

Cream the butter until light. Slowly add the sugar, beating constantly. Add the eggs one at a time, beating thoroughly after each addition.

Combine the dry ingredients thoroughly. Add them to the egg mixture alternately with the buttermilk. Fold in the pears and vanilla. Pour into two lightly greased, $4\frac{1}{2}$ x $8\frac{1}{2}$-inch loaf pans or one large tube pan.

Bake for 35 to 40 minutes (loaf pans) or 1 hour (tube pan). Cool to room temperature and chill for several hours. Slice and serve with apple (or pear) butter.

LEMON BREAD

This is another of Barbara's wonderful breads. As with the Wheat Germ Orange and Cranberry Nut Loaves, waiting 24 hours before serving improves the texture and flavor of this bread. It will keep for two or three months in the refrigerator.

Batter

1 cup sugar
$^1/_3$ cup butter, melted
1 teaspoon lemon or orange extract
$^1/_4$ cup fresh lemon juice
2 eggs
$1^1/_2$ cups King Arthur Unbleached All-Purpose Flour
1 teaspoon baking powder
1 teaspoon salt
$^1/_2$ cup milk
grated rind of 1 large lemon
$^1/_2$ cup chopped pecans (optional)

Topping

$^1/_2$ cup confectioners' sugar
$^1/_4$ cup fresh lemon juice

First: Preheat your oven to 350°F.

Mixing the Batter: Combine the sugar, butter, extract and juice. Beat in the eggs, one at a time, until smooth.

In a separate bowl, mix together the flour, baking powder, and salt. Stir in the wet ingredients alternately with the milk. Add the lemon rind (and the pecans if you decide to use them).

Baking: Pour into a greased, $4^1/_2$ x $8^1/_2$-inch loaf pan. Bake for about 1 hour, or until a toothpick comes out clean.

Making the Topping: Dissolve the sugar in the lemon juice over low heat.

Finishing: When the bread is done, and still hot from the oven, pierce the top in several places with a sharp knife. Pour the topping over the cuts.

Let the loaf cool in the pan for an hour. Then remove it from the pan, wrap in foil and let stand for 24 hours for the flavors to mature.

RHUBARB BREAD

This recipe comes from Ellen Davies' aunts Rose and Millie Saco who also shared their recipe for Swedish Rhubarb Pie (page 405).

As you look through these quick breads, you can see how easily they might be adapted to use whatever you have on hand. Because this and the preceding one have a topping, they could be called coffeecakes as well.

Topping

2 tablespoons granulated sugar
2 teaspoons butter or margarine, melted

Batter

$2^3/_4$ cups King Arthur Unbleached All-Purpose Flour
$1^1/_2$ teaspoons baking powder
$^1/_2$ teaspoon baking soda
1 teaspoon salt
$1^1/_2$ cups diced rhubarb
$^1/_2$ cup chopped walnuts
$^2/_3$ cup vegetable oil
1 cup brown sugar
2 eggs
$^1/_2$ cup granulated sugar
1 cup milk
1 teaspoon vanilla

Preheat your oven to 350°F.

Blend the topping ingredients and set aside.

To make the batter, blend the flour, baking powder, soda and salt. Stir in the rhubarb and nuts.

In a separate bowl, beat the oil, sugar and eggs together until light, and blend in the milk. Mix the wet ingredients with the dry, stirring just enough to blend. Stir in the vanilla.

Pour the batter into two $4^1/_2$ x $8^1/_2$-inch loaf pans and drizzle the butter/sugar topping over them.

Bake for 40 minutes to 1 hour or until a toothpick inserted into the center comes out clean.

GARDEN VEGETABLE BREAD

This recipe will accommodate a variety of garden vegetables. You can substitute 2 cups of cooked winter squash, cooked sweet potato, grated summer squash or carrots, and probably even cooked grated beets. You might try some in combination.

Note that this bread is leavened completely with baking soda to react with the brown sugar, vegetables and vegetable juice or coffee.

> 2 cups King Arthur Unbleached All-Purpose Flour
> 1 cup King Arthur Stone Ground Whole Wheat Flour
> 1 cup white sugar
> 1 cup brown sugar
> 2 teaspoons cinnamon (or whatever herbs and spices you feel
>   complement your vegetable choice)
> 2 teaspoons baking soda
> 1 teaspoon salt
> ½ cup raisins (optional)
> ½ cup chopped nuts (optional)
> 1 cup vegetable oil
> 4 eggs
> ½ to ¾ cup water, tomato or vegetable blend juice, or even coffee
> 2 cups vegetable(s) of your choice (see note above)

Preheat your oven to 350°F.

In a large mixing bowl, combine the flours, sugars, spices, baking soda, salt and optional raisins and/or nuts.

In a separate bowl, beat together the oil, eggs and water (or other liquid). Blend or beat in the vegetable you've chosen.

Blend the wet ingredients with the dry, pour into 2 greased, 5 x 9-inch loaf pans and bake for about an hour.

Cool for 10 to 15 minutes and remove from the pans to a rack.

These loaves freeze beautifully and will bring back some summer sun when you thaw them out and warm them up for a winter meal.

Johnny Cake

This recipe came from Mary Baird, Brinna Sands' mother, who served it frequently because it was put together and baked so quickly, and it really tasted good.

3/4 cup cornmeal
1 cup King Arthur Unbleached All-Purpose Flour
1/3 cup sugar
1 tablespoon baking powder
3/4 teaspoon salt
1 cup milk
1 egg, well beaten
2 tablespoons butter or margarine, melted

Preheat your oven to 425°F.

Mix together the cornmeal, flour, sugar, baking powder and salt. Add the milk, egg and butter and stir just to blend.

Pour the batter into a greased, 8-inch square baking pan. Bake about 20 minutes.

Molasses Corn Bread

Marilyn Magnus, our friend from Peacham, Vermont, developed this hearty corn bread with lots of extra nutrition. It is leavened entirely with baking soda as it contains several acidic ingredients: molasses, honey and buttermilk.

1 cup cornmeal
1 cup King Arthur Unbleached All-Purpose Flour
1/4 cup King Arthur Stone Ground Whole Wheat Flour
1/4 cup non-fat dry milk
2 teaspoons baking soda
2 teaspoons salt
3 eggs
2 tablespoons blackstrap molasses
1/3 cup honey
2 cups buttermilk or sour milk

Preheat your oven to 350°F.

Mix the dry ingredients in a large bowl. In a separate bowl, beat the eggs and add the molasses, honey and buttermilk. Add this to the dry ingredients and stir just to combine. Pour into a greased, 9-inch round cake pan or iron skillet.

Bake about 40 minutes.

SAVORY QUICK BREADS

The breads in this next group are savory rather than sweet. This twist just opens up more experiment possibilities in the quick bread department.

CHEDDAR CHEESE BREAD

This cheese bread recipe comes from Brinna Sands' sister, Anne Baird, who makes it annually for the gathering of the clan at Thanksgiving. Following are variations with increasing embellishments.

1 cup King Arthur Unbleached All-Purpose Flour
1 cup King Arthur Stone Ground Whole Wheat Flour
1 tablespoon baking powder
$1/2$ teaspoon baking soda
$1/2$ teaspoon salt
1 cup grated Cheddar cheese
1 tablespoon caraway or dill seed
2 eggs
1 cup sour cream, buttermilk or yogurt
2 tablespoons butter, melted, or vegetable oil (optional)

Preheat your oven to 350°F.

Combine the dry ingredients, the cheese and caraway or dill. Beat the eggs until thick and light. Add and beat in the sour cream, buttermilk or yogurt. Add this mixture to the dry ingredients, mixing just enough to blend.

Depending on what you are serving this bread with, or your time frame, either:

• Bake in a lightly greased, 5 x 9-inch loaf pan for 50 to 60 minutes.

• Or bake in a lightly greased, 9-inch round cake pan or iron skillet for 30 to 45 minutes.

HEARTY CORN & CHEESE BREAD

This is a great addition to a summer meal when there's an abundance of fresh sweet corn on hand. And if you've tucked some corn in your freezer, this bread, with its added zip of chopped hot pepper, will warm a winter meal.

Substitute 1 cup of cornmeal for the whole wheat flour. In addition to the cheese, fold in 1 cup of corn, freshly cut from the cob, and $1/2$ cup chopped fresh hot pepper (optional). Bake as above.

Sausage, Cheese & Onion (or Apple!) Bread

This one has every food group in it, from grains to dairy, to fruit or vegetables, to protein. You can't get heartier than this.

In addition to the cheese, fold in 1 cup of diced hard sausage (or ham, crumbled bacon, etc.) and 1 cup of chopped onion or apple (or both!). Bake as above.

Shaker Cheese Bread

Because this bread contains sweet milk, it is leavened with baking powder rather than baking soda.

    2 cups King Arthur Unbleached All-Purpose Flour
    1 tablespoon baking powder
    $^3/_4$ teaspoon salt
    1$^1/_2$ teaspoons sugar
    1 cup grated cheese (sharp Cheddar is a good choice)
    $^1/_2$ cup chopped onion
    1 egg
    $^3/_4$ cup milk
    2 tablespoons melted butter

Preheat your oven to 350°F.

Blend the dry ingredients and mix in the
cheese and onion. Beat the egg, milk
and butter together and add to the dry
ingredients. Stir just enough to blend.

Let the batter stand for about 20 minutes.

Pour into a greased, 5 x 9-inch loaf pan.
Bake for 45 minutes to 1 hour.

STEAMED BREADS

The next quick breads aren't baked at all but steamed, a method of cooking that was used for centuries before ovens were found in every home. Although it takes longer to cook breads by steaming, the cooking time is quite flexible. A steamed bread can cook long past its finishing time without substantially changing, unlike an oven-baked bread which will pass from done to scorched in a matter of minutes. This is because steamed breads cook at the temperature at which water boils (212°F) rather than the 350°F at which quick breads are commonly baked in an oven.

BOSTON PLUM BROWN BREAD

This first bread, an old classic from Gretchen McMullen's "Testing Kitchen," contains absolutely no fat, but it is incredibly rich and moist because the liquid in the batter is locked in during the steaming process. Its name harks back to the time when raisins were known as "plums" (as in plum pudding).

Brown bread is traditionally eaten with baked beans, another of those clever combinations that create a complete protein out of foods that contain only incomplete ones. With or without beans, this bread is a nutritional winner.

1 cup cornmeal
1 cup rye flour
1 cup King Arthur Stone Ground Whole Wheat Flour
1 teaspoon baking soda
1 teaspoon salt
1 cup raisins
2 cups buttermilk, yogurt or sour milk
3/4 cup dark, unsulphured molasses

Mix the cornmeal, flours, baking soda, salt and raisins together. In a separate bowl, combine the buttermilk and molasses and add them to the dry ingredients.

Place the mixture in 2 greased, one-pound coffee cans or 1 two-quart pudding mold, filling them about two-thirds full. Cover these loosely with foil that has been greased on the inside, and secure with rubber bands.

Place the cans, or mold, in a kettle or saucepan on top of something (crinkled aluminum foil will do) to keep the cans off the bottom of the pan. The kettle should be deep enough so its lid can cover the pudding containers.

Fill the kettle with boiling water two-thirds of the way up the cans. Cover, bring the water back to a boil and lower the heat to a simmer. Steam your pudding for about 2 hours, adding water if necessary.

STEAMED HARVEST BREAD

Next we give you a formula for steamed breads which will make use of pumpkins, squash, apples and other autumn abundance. Again, it contains no fat, so for all of you who are looking for a filling, high-energy, vitamin-rich snack with a minimum of calories, this is it.

The spices can by varied to enhance the flavor of the vegetable or fruit used. Cinnamon, allspice and nutmeg are always good and, strangely enough, so is a bit of white or black pepper.

> 1½ cups King Arthur Unbleached All-Purpose Flour
> 1½ cups King Arthur Stone Ground Whole Wheat Flour
> 2 teaspoons baking powder
> 1 teaspoon baking soda
> 1 teaspoon salt
> 1 teaspoon cinnamon
> 1 teaspoon ginger
> 1 teaspoon cloves
> 1 cup yogurt, buttermilk or sour milk
> 3 eggs
> 1 to 1½ cups brown sugar
> 1½ cups cooked mashed pumpkin, carrot, squash, cranberry sauce, etc.
>   OR
> 2 or more cups grated raw carrot, chopped apple, etc.

Mix the flours, baking powder, soda, salt and spices together.

In another bowl, mix the yogurt, eggs, sugar and vegetable or fruit. Blend this mixture into the dry ingredients.

Place the batter in 2 greased, one-pound coffee cans or 1 two-pound pudding mold, filling them about two-thirds full. Cover these loosely with tin foil that has been greased on the inside, and secure with rubber bands.

Place the cans, or mold, in a kettle or saucepan that is tall enough to put a lid on over the top of everything. Fill the pot with boiling water about two-thirds of the way up the cans. Cover, bring the water back to a boil and lower the heat to a simmer. Steam for 2 or more hours, adding water if necessary.

If the batter seems too much for the mold, grease a custard cup and bake the remainder in the oven, or preview the finished product as a pancake.

Chocolate Steamed Pudding

Our last steamed bread recipe comes from Martha Douple, close friend of the Sands family, an invaluable part of the Sands, Taylor & Wood team and an occasionally possessed baker.

Martha's family takes the ingredients for this pudding on cross-country skiing treks. When they arrive at their destination, her mother, Ila, sets up a steamer: a one-pound coffee can, a piece of string to secure the aluminum foil that covers the pudding, and a tuna-sized can to keep the coffee can off the bottom of the lobster pot they steam the pudding in.

An hour and a half and a few snow ball fights later, Martha, her sister Jann, and parents Evan and Ila sit down to this hot, moist, ethereally light and altogether blissful delight. Over the top of it goes "Ope," a rich sauce whose name is of mysterious origin. (Any ideas anyone?)

This steamed pudding probably belongs in the Cake Chapter, but we're including it here because of the way it's cooked and to show you how varied steamed breads can be. Note that, even though it can almost be classified as a cake, it, like our other steamed breads, has little fat in it. This recipe may be easily doubled and cooked in two cans.

2 ounces (squares) unsweetened baking chocolate
1 teaspoon melted butter
1 teaspoon vanilla
1 egg
³/₄ cup sugar
1 cup King Arthur Unbleached All-Purpose Flour
¹/₂ teaspoon salt
1 ¹/₂ teaspoons baking powder
¹/₂ cup milk

Melt the chocolate with the butter in a small saucepan over low heat and add the vanilla.

In a mixing bowl, beat the egg until light and lemon colored. Add the sugar and beat until fluffy.

Combine the flour with the salt and baking powder. Add this, alternately with the milk, to the egg mixture. Then add the chocolate mixture and stir just enough to blend.

Place this batter in a greased, one-pound coffee can. Cover with aluminum foil and secure it with string or a rubber band. Steam over simmering water in a covered kettle for 1 ¹/₂ hours.

OPE

Although this pudding is delightful as is, the investment of a few more calories turns it into ambrosia (especially when you're out in the woods).

This sauce should be made just before the pudding is served as it is somewhat fragile. Or it can be made ahead of time and reheated and "refrothed." (For information about eating uncooked eggs, see Appendix.)

2 eggs
$^1/_2$ cup sugar
$^1/_4$ cup ($^1/_2$ stick) butter, melted
$^1/_2$ teaspoon vanilla

Beat the eggs until they are very light and lemon colored. Add the sugar very slowly while you continue to beat. (This may take two people.) Add the butter, beating furiously all the while. Beat in the vanilla.

Serve before it sags and loses its frothy consistency.

COFFEECAKES

Coffeecakes are the sweetest and richest of the quick breads. They are made with a larger amount of batter (6½ to 7 cups) than our loaves. (See Baking & Storing on page 88.) You will find coffeecakes with yeast in Chapter IV.

APPLE CHEESE COFFEECAKE

Topping

 1 cup King Arthur Unbleached All-Purpose Flour
 1 cup brown sugar, packed
 2 teaspoons cinnamon
 ½ cup (1 stick) butter, softened

Batter

 2 cups King Arthur Unbleached All-Purpose Flour
 1 cup King Arthur Stone Ground Whole Wheat Flour
 1 tablespoon baking powder
 ½ teaspoon baking soda
 1 teaspoon salt
 ¼ cup vegetable oil
 1½ cups sugar
 3 eggs
 1 cup buttermilk
 1½ cups diced Cheddar cheese
 1½ cups chopped apple
 1 cup chopped pecans (optional)

First: Preheat your oven to 350°F.

Preparing the Topping: Blend the dry ingredients. Rub in the butter with your fingertips or a pastry blender until the mixture resembles coarse crumbs.

Making the Batter: Mix together in a large bowl the flour, baking powder, baking soda and salt. In a separate bowl, beat the oil, sugar and eggs together for 2 to 3 minutes, until they are very light. Mix the buttermilk and the dry ingredients into the oil/sugar/egg mixture alternately, a half at a time. Stir only until blended. Fold in the diced cheese and chopped apple.

Assembling & Baking: Pour half the batter in whatever baking pan you've chosen (see page 89). Sprinkle one-third of the topping mixture over this, swirl it in with a fork and pour in the rest of the batter. Put a second third of topping over the second layer of batter and swirl that in.

Bake according to the directions for your pan. After the coffeecake is baked, let it cool for about 10 minutes and then turn it out onto a serving plate. Sprinkle the last third of the topping over the coffeecake while it is still warm.

SOUR CREAM OR BUTTERMILK COFFEECAKE

The original version of this coffeecake appeared in an old King Arthur Flour baking pamphlet. We've revised it a bit so it can be made either fat, with sour cream, or thin, with buttermilk or yogurt. Either way, it is a rich, moist, very satisfying cake.

Topping

1 cup almonds, pecans or walnuts, chopped or ground
1/2 cup packed brown sugar
2 teaspoons cinnamon (or whatever combination of spices you like)

Batter

3 cups King Arthur Unbleached All-Purpose Flour
1 tablespoon baking powder
1 teaspoon baking soda
1 teaspoon salt
3/4 cup (1 1/2 sticks) butter or margarine, softened
1 cup sugar
1/2 cup packed brown sugar
3 eggs
1 1/2 cups sour cream (fat) or buttermilk or yogurt (thin)
2 teaspoons vanilla (or almond extract)

First: Preheat your oven to 350°F.

Making the Topping: The topping is made first since some of it is incorporated into the cake itself. If you have a blender, you can easily chop your nuts in it. Mix the nuts with the brown sugar and spice.

Making the Batter: Mix together the flour, baking powder, soda and salt in a large bowl. In another bowl, cream the butter or margarine. Then add the sugars and eggs, one by one, beating until the mixture is light and fluffy.

Blend the sour cream or buttermilk into the creamed butter/sugar mixture alternately with the dry ingredients, a half at a time. Blend gently until smooth. Add and blend in the vanilla.

Assembling & Baking: Follow the directions for Apple Cheese Coffeecake (on preceding page).

Great Grandfather Frederick Pfander's
German Apple Cake

Nonnie Barnes is a Philadelphia friend who agreed to share this recipe which came from Germany with her great-grandfather. It is a delicious coffeecake with a wonderful history.

About it she wrote, "My great-grandfather, Frederick Pfander, devastated by the untimely death of both parents taken in an epidemic in Felbach, Germany, arrived in the United States as a tourist just after the end of the Civil War. While visiting a former family employee living in Philadelphia, he fell in love with their adopted daughter Christiana Elwanger. Wishing to stay and marry, my great-grandfather hired a journeyman baker and entered the baking business." Natalie Otter Barnes

Apple Filling

> 3 large apples
> lemon juice (optional, to sprinkle over apple slices)
> 5 tablespoons sugar
> 2 teaspoons cinnamon

Batter

> 3 cups King Arthur Unbleached All-Purpose Flour
> 1 tablespoon baking powder
> 1 teaspoon salt
> 1 cup vegetable oil
> 2 cups sugar
> 4 eggs
> $1/4$ cup apple juice (milk can be substituted)
> $2^1/_2$ teaspoons vanilla

First: Preheat your oven to 350°F.

Preparing the Filling: This filling is made before the batter as it is layered into the cake. Pare and thinly slice the apples. You can sprinkle them with a bit of lemon juice, if you like, to keep them from turning brown. Mix the sugar with the cinnamon. Set these aside.

Making the Batter: Mix the flour, baking powder and salt together in a large mixing bowl. In another bowl, beat the oil and sugar for 2 or 3 minutes until creamy.

In a separate small bowl beat the eggs until light. Add the juice and the vanilla, mix well and add to the sugar and oil, beating thoroughly. Add the liquid ingredients to the dry ingredients and gently fold together.

Assembling & Baking: You can use any of the pans described on page 89. Pour one-third of the batter into whatever pan or pans you choose, then add a thick layer of apples sprinkled generously with the cinnamon sugar; repeat ending with batter sprinkled with cinnamon. Bake this according to the directions for the pan or pans you've chosen.

BLUEBERRY BUCKLE

Our spokesman, Bert Porter, was originally taught to bake by his talented wife Ruth. Ruth is Swedish and this recipe came from her mother who, Ruth is certain, learned it from her mother in Sweden. "It's a very, very old recipe and it's been in the family for many years." It's interesting to see how closely this recipe is related to the previous two although the ingredients in this one are cut by about a third. Our American baking heritage is diverse and universal at the same time.

Topping

 ⅓ cup sugar
 ⅓ cup King Arthur Unbleached All-Purpose Flour
 1 teaspoon cinnamon
 ¼ cup (½ stick) butter or margarine

Batter

 2 cups King Arthur Unbleached All-Purpose Flour
 2 teaspoons baking powder
 ½ teaspoon salt
 ¾ cup sugar
 ¼ cup (½ stick) butter or margarine
 1 egg
 1 teaspoon vanilla
 ½ cup milk
 2 cups fresh or frozen blueberries, well drained

First: Preheat your oven to 375°F.

Making the Topping: Mix the sugar, flour and cinnamon in a small bowl. Cut or rub in the butter or margarine with the side of a fork, two knives or your fingertips until crumbly. Set aside.

Making the Batter: Blend the flour, baking powder and salt together in a medium-sized mixing bowl. In a large bowl cream together the sugar, butter or margarine, egg and vanilla. Alternately add the milk and the flour mixture to the creamed mixture, ending with flour. Stir only enough to blend. Fold in the blueberries.

Assembling & Baking: Pour the batter into a well-greased and floured, 9-inch cake pan. Sprinkle the topping over the batter and bake for 40 to 45 minutes or until a cake tester or knife comes out clean.

Let the buckle cool for 10 minutes. Loosen the sides with a knife or spatula. Holding the cake pan in your left hand, gently tip the cake out onto your right hand, remove the pan, and gently right the cake onto a serving dish.

BARBARA LAUTERBACH'S
HOLIDAY BREAD

This holiday bread from Barbara Lauterbach falls somewhere between a fruit cake and stollen so has arbitrarily become this chapter's grand finale. Before she serves it, Barbara runs it under the broiler for a minute or two and covers it with a lashing of sweet butter. Wrapped in foil and tied with red ribbons, these loaves are an ideal holiday gift.

3¼ cups King Arthur Unbleached All-Purpose Flour
1 cup sugar
¼ teaspoon salt
3½ teaspoons baking powder
2 teaspoons ground cinnamon
2 eggs, beaten well
1½ cups milk
3 tablespoons butter, melted
4 tablespoons dark rum
1½ cups broken pecans
1 cup golden raisins, plumped in dark rum and drained
¾ cup chopped dates
¾ cup chopped dried figs
¼ cup currants

Preheat your oven to 350°F.

Combine 3 cups of the flour with the sugar, salt, baking powder and cinnamon in a large bowl. Beat in the eggs and milk and then the butter and rum.

In another bowl, combine the pecans, raisins, dates, figs and currants and toss with the remaining ¼ cup of flour. (This helps prevent the fruit from settling to the bottom of your bread.) Gently stir the nuts and fruit into the batter.

Turn into two lightly greased, 4½ x 8½-inch loaf pans (for gifts) or one large tube or springform pan (to serve at home). Let the batter sit for about 20 minutes.

Bake according to the directions on page 89. Cool the bread on wire racks before slicing or wrapping.

YEASTED BREADS & ROLLS

IV

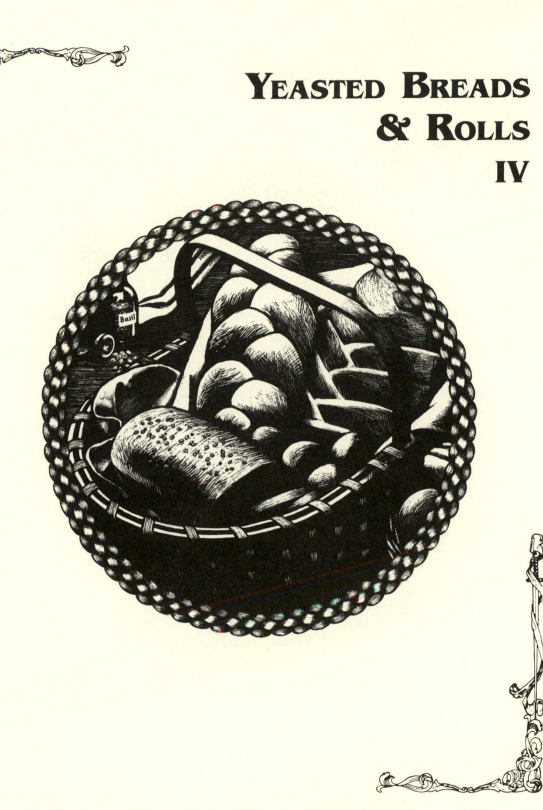

Yeasted Breads & Rolls
& Coffeecakes

• To cure any "yeast anxiety" you might be prone to, use regular active dry yeast and "proof" it. To do this, dissolve a bit of sugar (about 1 tablespoon for each 2 cups of liquid) or other sweetener in warm water (about 95°F, "baby bottle warm") and add the yeast. Wait about 10 minutes for it to dissolve and begin to "work," or develop tiny bubbles. When you see those bubbles, you'll be reassured and over the first (and worst!) hurdle in baking with yeast. Sugar substitutes won't provide any nourishment for a growing yeast so don't use it for "proofing."

• Yeast doesn't like salt so add any salt your recipe calls for **after** you've added 1 or 2 cups of flour.

• The second (and last) hurdle in baking with yeast is not adding too much flour. This is also easily dealt with simply by measuring correctly. Check the directions on the top of our bag of King Arthur Unbleached Flour or on page 597. If a flexible amount of flour is given in a recipe, start with the least amount and add only enough to keep the dough from sticking to you or your kneading board.

• Another reason to start with the smaller amount in recipes calling for flexible flour measures is that flour already contains some moisture. The amount of moisture varies according to the temperature and humidity of the air. You'll find that during cold, dry months you'll often need a bit less flour when making dough, and a bit more in hot, humid months. Add flour as you "knead" it.

• The 🌾 symbol after King Arthur Unbleached All-Purpose Flour in the ingredient list is a reminder that we encourage you to substitute some King Arthur Stone Ground Whole Wheat Flour for an equal amount of Unbleached All-Purpose Flour.

• Rest when you "knead" it! After 3 or 4 minutes of kneading dough, let it rest for a few minutes. The rest relaxes the dough, makes the remaining kneading easier, and gives you a break as well.

• It's possible to freeze bread dough, but because this is hard on activated yeast, double the amount of yeast that the recipe calls for to make sure the thawed dough will be vigorous.

• Baked bread freezes beautifully in a traditional deep freeze. (See page 592 for information on freezers.) Allow your bread to cool completely and then store it in an airtight plastic bag. It will taste oven fresh when you thaw it out.

YEASTED BREADS & ROLLS & COFFEECAKES
IV

• A BREAD BAKING PRIMER •

Making a loaf of bread, turning a sticky, lumpy mess into a loaf of real bread, feels different from buying a loaf that someone else or some mystery machine has made. If you haven't made bread yet, we won't tell you what that feeling is, or try to describe it.

When you are holding a slice of warm bread in your hand, one that you made yourself, you'll know that feeling, plus, from that slice of bread, you will get more energy than you can from any other kind of food. It can help you lose weight. It can be packed with things that are good for you, and things that are not so good when you're in the mood for a break.

Like your fingerprints, the bread you bake will be completely your own. It will reflect your personality and no one else's because of the infinite number of variables you affect, either consciously or unconsciously, as you bake. Whether your hand is light or generous when measuring and adding ingredients, the length of time you spend kneading, the aromas in your kitchen, its temperature and the rate the air flows through it, the color and shape of your bread pans, the size and age of your oven, even the mood you're in at the time you bake (whatever it is, making a loaf of bread will probably improve it!), all these and more imprint your bread so that it can be no one's but yours.

Baking with yeast lets the artist in you come out. It's somewhere between making mud pies and sculpting, the earthy mixed with the sublime. Your first loaf may not be beautiful, but baking can succeed on more than one level. Even if it doesn't look pretty, its smell and taste alone are enough to transport you.

THE EASIEST BREAD YOU'LL EVER MAKE

Our basic formula consists of only five ingredients, and only three of those are critical. This will make the simplest but most useful dough there is. Below we'll use it to make a basic hearth bread, but by shaping and cooking it differently, you can transform it into pizza, pita bread, bagels, English muffins, sticky buns, variations ad infinitum. Part of the lure and magic of baking is imagining and creating something that no one has ever tried before.

The key to being an intuitive baker lies in knowing what the key ingredients are in whatever you're baking, and the ratio they have to each other. In yeast baking, there are just the three alluded to above: the flour, the liquid and the yeast. In most breads you'll use three parts of flour to one of liquid, by volume, not weight. Our recipe for hearth bread, which will make 2 loaves, calls for 2 cups of water and three times that, or 6 cups, of flour. For this much flour and water, we'll use 1 packet, or a scant tablespoon of yeast.

There are only two other ingredients to worry about, sugar and salt. You can actually make bread without either but we include them because the sugar gives the yeast an easy first course, and both bring out flavor. You can adjust either to suit your taste or diet. In this recipe, a tablespoon of each is good place to start. So altogether we have 2 cups of liquid, 6 cups of flour and a tablespoon each of yeast, sugar and salt. When you've memorized this short list your life as an intuitive baker will have begun.

The following guidelines will take you through the process of making a loaf of bread with these five ingredients. Along the way you'll discover some of the mysteries and magic that yeast contains.

KING ARTHUR FLOUR'S HEARTH BREAD

Hearth breads were originally baked just where their name implies, at the hearth. Before the modern stove was invented, if you were well enough off, you had an oven built into the brick or stone work which contained the central fireplace or heating system of your house. This way, all the cooking and baking could be done in the same area and both could share the same chimney. These baking chambers, which may be familiar to some as beehive ovens, were used to bake almost everything that couldn't be cooked in a kettle over coals or an open fire.

If you didn't have a built-in oven, you would have used a Dutch oven, a portable cast iron kettle with a lid, which stood on legs right in the coals of the fireplace. To produce an all-around heat, more coals were shoveled directly on the lid. Dutch ovens are still made today and are very useful, since they are completely portable.

To preheat a built-in brick oven, a fire was built right in the oven chamber itself. About two hours later, most of the coals and ashes were removed and the baking began. A hearth bread was baked directly on the oven floor and was deposited there and removed with a long wooden paddle or "peel." The whole baking process was done "by feel" as there were no thermometers to let you know when the oven was the right temperature or when the bread was done.

To make a hearth bread with a crackly crust, it was necessary to expose the dough to steam for 8 or 10 minutes after it went into the oven. This technique, used today so successfully by the French, gelatinized the starch on the surface of the dough. As the bread continued to bake after the steaming period, this gelatinized surface baked into the characteristic crunchy crust of a hearth bread. In old ovens, steam was created by wiping the whole interior with a very wet cloth on the end of a pole, much like a mop. Today, most commercial hearth breads are baked in ovens that have steam injected into them mechanically at 2- or 3-minute intervals during this first 8- or 10-minute baking period. Later in the chapter, you'll find ideas for making your own oven bake like the old hearth ovens.

Hearth Bread the Traditional Way

This recipe is a typical one with two rising periods. We'll give you some alternative methods farther along. This one will take somewhere between 3½ and 5 hours from start to finish, depending partly on whether you work quickly or leisurely. But no matter how fast you work, most of this time it's the yeast, not you, that's busy. Where you put the dough to rise is the most important factor in determining the time frame.

2 cups water
1 tablespoon sugar
1 tablespoon or packet active dry yeast
6 cups King Arthur Unbleached All-Purpose Flour
1 tablespoon salt
(cornmeal to sprinkle on baking sheet)

There are only two hurdles to get over in putting these ingredients together and neither is a very big one. The first is activating or "proofing" the yeast at a temperature that will make it want to grow. This part of bread baking probably causes the most anxiety. To alleviate it, just remember that yeast likes and dislikes the same temperatures you do. Knowing what is comfortable for you means you know what's comfortable for the yeast.

Activating or Proofing the Yeast: Pour the water, hot from the tap, into a mixing bowl. Add the sugar and stir until it dissolves. As the water dissolves the sugar and warms the bowl, it cools somewhat and should be just right for dissolving and activating the yeast. Somewhere between 95°F and 115°F is fine. With such a wide temperature range, you know that yeast is really quite accommodating. Try a few drops of water on your wrist. If it feels warm and comfortable to you, it will feel the same way to the yeast. Add the tablespoon or packet of yeast and stir it in.

The temperature has to be 120°F, which feels hot, before it begins to kill the yeast. It has to get all the way to 140°F before all the yeast is completely done in. 140°F feels really hot. If you don't want to trust yourself the first time around, use a candy thermometer to see if you and the thermometer agree on what is "hot" and what's just right.

Let the yeast mixture sit for 5 or 6 minutes, 2 to 3 for it to become thoroughly dissolved and 2 or 3 more for it to begin to grow and show signs of life. Tiny bubbles should begin to appear on the surface. Some varieties will cause the whole mixture to expand rather dramatically.

If none of this happens (which is very unlikely), and you're sure that the water you used was not too hot, it may be that you have some "tired" yeast. (This is why activating the yeast is called "proofing." It proves that the yeast is alive and ready to go before you get too far into a recipe.) If you suspect your yeast might be too old, your best bet is to get a new batch and start again.

Don't add the salt yet. Yeast doesn't like salt and will be happier if you add it after you stir in the first cup of flour. The flour acts as a buffer and prevents the salt from making a direct "assault" on the newly growing yeast.

The second hurdle in making your dough is not to add too much flour. This, too, is easily avoided.

Measuring & Adding the Flour: All flour is sifted through many layers of silk screening (i.e., it is "pre-sifted") before it is packaged at the flour mill. During shipment it settles and becomes compressed. Our mothers and grandmothers used a flour sifter to return compacted flour to its original light and airy state. Since sifted flour weighs 4 ounces rather than the 5 or so ounces a compacted or "scooped" cup of flour weighs, you can see where it might be easy to inadvertently add more flour than a recipe calls for.

All of the recipes in this *200th Anniversary Cookbook* are written for 4-ounce cups of flour but you don't need a flour sifter to make sure your cups weigh that much. When you measure flour the following way, it will weigh 4 ounces a cup, you won't add too much to your dough and you'll have flour that is already full of lots of little air pockets, the first step to a light loaf of bread.

• First fluff up the flour in the bag or cannister with a spoon until it's light.

• Then sprinkle it lightly into a dry cup measure (the kind that measures exactly a cup at the rim).

• Scrape any excess off with the back of a knife.

Stir your first cup of flour into the yeast mixure and add the salt Then stir in 4¹/₂ cups more flour. When the dough begins to hold together and pull away from the sides of the bowl, it is ready to knead.

Kneading: This part of bread making is one of the most pleasurable, especially if you're kneading on a surface that is a comfortable height for you. Traditional counter height, 36 inches, is fine for someone who is quite tall. If you aren't, it's important to find a surface low enough so you can use your whole body when you're kneading, and not just your arms. Table height (29 or 30 inches) may be much better for you, or somewhere in between. Experiment to find what is comfortable and effective.

If you ever enjoyed rocking in a rocking chair, or rocking a baby, this is what kneading can be like, but only if you're doing it at an optimum height. Find a little music so you and the dough can have a dance all by yourselves.

Turn your dough out onto your kneading surface which you've sprinkled lightly with the remaining ½ cup of flour. Before you start, flour your hands well, too. When you first begin, it will be a bit messy, but don't be faint of heart.

Fold the outside edge of the dough over onto itself toward you and push the dough away gently with the heels of your hands. After every push, turn the dough a quarter of the way around and fold it toward you again. Keep repeating this sequence. You'll find that you'll begin to rock back and forth and relax as you do it.

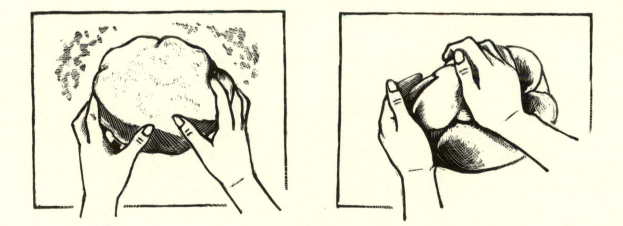

As you knead, sprinkle just enough more flour about to keep the dough from sticking to the board or to you. Depending on the humidity in the air, this can mean more or less than the original 6 cups.

Flour is porous like a sponge. When the air around it is dry, flour will be dry. When the air is humid, flour will absorb the moisture in it. Just as a dry sponge can soak up more water than a wet sponge, so can dry flour. You'll find that during cold, dry months you'll often need less flour when making a dough, and in hot, humid months, a bit more.

After you've kneaded for 3 to 4 minutes, let the dough take a little rest while you clean out and grease the bowl. When you return to your dough, you'll find that the little rest has changed it. It will feel more "together" and easier to work.

Continue kneading another 3 to 4 minutes, a few minutes more if you have time and are enjoying yourself, less if you don't. When the dough is smooth, elastic, and no longer sticky, it has been kneaded enough.

First Rising: Form the dough into a nice, round ball and place it in your greased bowl, turning it over so the top has a thin film of grease on it as well. This helps keep it soft so that, as the yeast begins to grow and produce carbon dioxide bubbles, it can expand.

Cover the bowl with a damp towel or a piece of plastic wrap. It's a good idea to grease the underside of the plastic so that it won't stick if the dough comes in contact with it.

Put the bowl somewhere cozy to let the yeast grow and multiply until it has doubled the size of the dough. This will take anywhere from 1 to 2 hours depending on warmth and humidity. If your kitchen is warm, that is probably cozy enough. If you have a pilot light in your oven, put it in there, or on top of your refrigerator, or on a heating pad (even on your water bed). Somewhere between 75°F and 85°F is ideal.

If you put your dough somewhere cooler, it will still rise, but more slowly.

You'll find that on rainy or stormy days (great days for baking anyway), when the barometric pressure is low, your bread will rise more quickly than it does ordinarily. This is because the dough doesn't have as much air to "push" against; the air is not as dense or heavy as it is on clear days. This is the same reason you don't need as much yeast or baking powder at high altitudes where the air is thinner and lighter.

Knocking or Punching Down the Dough: When you can poke your finger in the dough without it springing back, it has "doubled in bulk."

Make a fist and give it a good knock or punch. If anyone is passing through the room, it doesn't take much to entice them into assisting with this step. A few punches will knock most of the gas out.

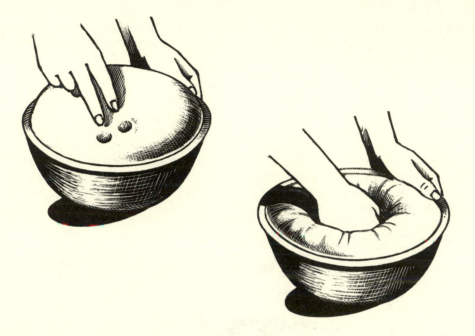

Turn the dough out onto your lightly floured kneading surface and knead out any stray bubbles.

Second Rising (optional): A traditional hearth bread usually has a coarse grain so if that's what you're aiming for, skip this step. (But it's good to know about for making rolls and other breads where you want a finer grain.)

By the end of the first rising the dough will contain almost twice as much yeast as it did when it started. If you wish, or a change in schedule necessitates it, you can let the dough rise a second time in the bowl after you've knocked it down. Because there is twice as much yeast working, the second rising will take about half as much time as the first. And because each of those little single-celled organisms is producing its own bubble of carbon dioxide, you'll have twice as many little carbon dioxide bubbles in the dough. (It's all these extra bubbles that make the grain finer.)

After the dough has doubled, knock it down again.

Traditional Shaping: Let the dough rest for several minutes after you've kneaded all the bubbles out. This will relax the gluten and make it much easier to shape. The directions may sound complicated, but don't let them intimidate you; the dough will tell you what to do.

Cut the dough in half to shape it into two loaves, either French style (long and narrow), Italian style (shorter and more oval), or round. Tuck the cut edge of each piece into the center of the dough so it is no longer exposed.

Gently, so you don't break the surface, roll it out with the flat of your hands like a fat play dough "snake." It may take two or three relaxing periods (of a few minutes each) and more light sprinklings of flour to make it the length you want.

Put the the smoothest side (which you'll want to make the top surface of the bread) DOWN on your kneading surface. Make sure it's lightly floured so it can move without sticking.

To shape the loaf, think about wrapping up something in a towel, bringing it around whatever you're wrapping and tucking the ends underneath. Imagine the surface of your dough is the towel. Bring it around, stretching it gently to expand the (bottom) surface and tuck all the edges into the center (at the top). Since this will be the bottom of your loaf, it doesn't matter what it looks like. Turn the loaf over and tidy it up if necessary.

Place the loaf on a baking sheet that has been sprinkled generously with cornmeal. Repeat with the second piece of dough.

Final Rising: Cover them both with a damp towel and let them rise until they have doubled, somewhere around an hour. Since you don't want to leave a big fingerprint in the dough when you check it this time, poke it gently on the side. If the dough doesn't immediately spring back at you, and your finger has left a slight impression, you can probably assume it is ready to go in the oven.

Dough can overrise. When it has, it looks billowy, as though it was pumped full of air. Don't be tempted to let your dough rise to this point hoping that the baked loaves will be lighter. Overrisen dough tends to collapse on itself either before or while it's baking. As a result, the bread will be dense and sour tasting, the opposite of what you intended.

If your dough should overrise after it's shaped, just knock it down and quickly reshape it (and pretend you meant to have it rise again all along).

Because King Arthur Flour has a greater tolerance than other all-purpose flours, it can stand more risings before the gluten begins to break down. What this really means is that a King Arthur dough is very accommodating and forgiving and will give you more chances to succeed.

Preparing the Oven: Although it's difficult to recreate the original hearth loaves in our modern ovens, we can come fairly close.

Every oven is unique, not like any other. Newer ovens are better insulated and tighter which means less fluctuation in temperature, though even in the newer ovens temperatures can vary. Check yours with an oven thermometer for any discrepancies that could account for under- or overdone bread. Getting to know your oven will keep it from surprising you and will help you work with it more effectively.

Using Baking Tiles: Although baking tiles aren't critical to making a successful hearth bread, they can help approximate a hearth oven. Baking stones or tiles are available at most kitchen supply or tile stores. Lay them directly on your oven bottom or, if that's not possible, on the first rack. The tiles will absorb moisture and release it slowly as well as act as a "heat sink" to even out any temperature fluctuations. You can leave baking tiles in the oven permanently. If you want to bake something at the level the tiles are on, cover them with a large cake rack. This will allow air to circulate underneath a cake pan or cookie sheet. Just remove the rack when you're making hearth bread.

Creating Steam: First, preheat your oven to 475°F about 15 minutes before you want to bake your bread. To create steam, you have several options.

• **Water:** Place a roasting pan directly on the oven bottom (on the baking tiles if you have them) or lower rack and let it preheat with your oven. Just before you're ready to put your loaves in the oven, pour 2 to 3 cups of water in it. Use something with a handle long enough to prevent you from getting burned. Steam is deadly. And keep a pan just for this purpose as this steaming business won't be kind to a pan you love.

• **Ice Cubes:** Our friend Rebecca Cunningham (whose fruit tartlets appear in Chapter VII) throws a tray of ice cubes in the preheated roasting pan. She says it creates a time-released steam that lasts just about as long as it should (8 to 10 minutes) and creates some pretty dramatic hissing and crackling in the process. Who said baking can't be exciting?

• **Mist:** Use a mister to spray your loaves with water every 2 minutes for the first 8 or 10 minutes of baking. This is fun too but you tend to lose heat every time you open your oven. (We have another friend who throws 1/4 cup of water on her tiles every 2 minutes. This we don't recommend, even though it, too, is pretty dramatic.)

Finishing Touches: Here are several options for dressing up your bread now that it has risen and is ready to bake.

Slashing the Top: Just before you put the loaves in the oven, slash the oval loaves diagonally three or four times about $1/4$ inch deep. To make an attractive pattern on the top of a round loaf, cut twice one way and twice at right angles across the first cuts. A good serrated knife does this easily. By making these cuts, you create places for the bread to expand where you want it to which can prevent (horrors!) a bread "blowout."

Washing: Each kind of wash has its own merits. You can use whichever appeals to you.

• **Water Wash:** This helps the steaming process and makes a crunchier crust. Just before you put your loaves in the oven, brush the tops with cold water. You can use your fingertips if you're gentle, a pastry brush, or even a mister which will spray on an even, fine film of water. Another alternative is a goose feather brush which will spread water (or any wash) over the surface of the dough with almost no pressure at all.

• **Whole Egg Wash:** To make your loaves "fancy for company," make a wash with a whole egg beaten with a tablespoon of water. Brush this gently over the exposed surface of the dough before it goes in the oven. This will give the loaves a shiny bronzed surface.

• **Egg White Wash:** This does essentially the same thing as the whole egg wash but the color is transparent. With 1 egg white, use 2 teaspoons of water.

• **Egg Yolk Wash:** This makes a very golden crust. With 1 egg yolk, use 2 teaspoons of water.

• **Milk Wash:** Like egg, milk makes a bronzed crust, but it will be softer and less shiny.

• **Butter:** A little melted butter can be brushed on, either before or after baking, for a softer, richer flavored crust.

Sprinklings: To dress up your loaves even more, make an egg wash "glue" by beating a whole egg with just 2 teaspoons of water. Brush this over the exposed surface of your dough and sprinkle on one or more of the following: kosher or coarse sea salt; one of the herbal salt substitutes or some chopped herbs themselves; sesame, poppy or sunflower seeds; minced garlic or onion; grated hard cheese; chopped nuts; or anything that will complement the meal your bread will be served with.

Baking: This is where the magic happens.

After your oven is thoroughly preheated, pour 2 or 3 cups of water (or throw a tray of ice cubes) into the preheated roasting pan. (Keep your hands well back so you don't get steamed.)

With pot holders, or preferably oven mitts, quickly place the loaves on a rack above the pan. Bake for 20 minutes. Check the bread after 15 minutes. If the crust is getting too brown, turn the temperature down to 450°F and finish baking.

Tap the bottom of a loaf after you take it out of the oven. If it sounds hollow, it should be done. If it isn't, the moisture in the interior will deaden the tap sound. If there's any question, put the bread back into the oven for an extra five minutes.

> • If you want a softer crust, remove the bread after the 20-minute baking period. As it cools, moisture will evaporate through the crust and soften it.

> • To keep the crust crunchy, turn the oven off after the bread has finished baking and leave the loaves inside with the door closed for 5 to 10 minutes.

> *It is in this simplest of breads that the marriage of wheat flour and yeast becomes sublime. The smell of it as it comes out of the oven, the first taste before it's even cool, that feeling of complete satisfaction after eating the first piece, all these combine to put the world right for at least a little while.*

Freezing Dough & Bread: For information about different types of freezers and how they perform see the Appendix.

> • Bread dough can be frozen prior to baking, either before or after it has been shaped. Freezing won't kill the yeast, but it does subdue it somewhat, so double the amount called for in the recipe.

> • Finished breads can be frozen very successfully in heavy, airtight plastic bags in a non-self-defrosting freezer. If you get them into the freezer as soon as they are completely cool, they will taste just as if they had come right out of the oven when they're thawed.

Fancy Shapes for Hearth Bread

Here are some elegant ways to shape this simple bread. Even though the ingredients remain the same, a different shape will change the bread's character and personality a lot. After shaping, follow the directions for Traditional Hearth Bread starting with Final Rising (page 119).

Three-Stranded Braid: Braiding takes a little time but besides looking quite elegant, it creates perfect-sized pieces to tear off. In tearing it you also release the bread's texture and aroma to the fullest. There's no better way to eat and appreciate it than this.

> **• Braiding from the End:** Divide the dough for each loaf into 3 pieces. Roll out the pieces until they're between $^3/_4$ and 1 inch in diameter. Each time the dough gets "baulky," give it a rest to relax the gluten. After you've rolled them until they're about 1$^1/_2$ times longer than your bread will be, pinch the ends together and braid the dough just the way you would braid someone's hair.

> To do this, take the outside strands and alternately place them over the middle strand. Each time you move an outside strand over the middle one, it becomes the middle strand.

> **• Braiding from the Center:** You can also braid the dough by laying the pieces over each other's middles and working from the center to each end as illustrated on page 156. To finish off, pinch the ends together as neatly as you can. The rising and baking process covers many awkward tracks. (For four- and six-stranded braids, see Shaping the Dough on page 210 in the Sweet Dough Primer.)

One Large Loaf: One recipe of Hearth Bread, baked in a traditional shape or braided as a single loaf, makes an impressive presentation.

You'll need an extra-large baking sheet and access to a large oven. Follow the shaping directions for 2 loaves (page 119) but make a single loaf. To get an extra few inches out of your pan, place the loaf on it diagonally. Let the dough rise and bake it as for the Traditional Hearth Bread (page 122), but turn the heat down to 375°F after the first 20 minutes and bake this large loaf 10 or 15 minutes longer.

Traditional "Pan" Loaves: Although this is not a fancy option, you can always bake bread in a loaf pan. Its texture will be somewhat different. It won't have the crunchy crust of free-form or braided breads, but it will be great for sandwiches.

This recipe will make 2 high, well-rounded loaves in 4$^1/_2$ x 8$^1/_2$-inch bread pans. You can use 5 x 9-inch pans, but the loaves will be shorter and wider.

Divide the dough in half, shape as described on page 119, and place it in your lightly greased bread pans. Here are a couple of baking options.

- **Full Rise:** This makes the lightest loaves. Let the dough double in bulk, which will take about an hour. Fifteen minutes before you want to bake your bread, preheat the oven to 400°F. Bake for 15 minutes at this temperature. Turn the heat down to 350°F and bake for a further 20 to 25 minutes.

- **Partial Rise:** This method avoids the possibility of overrising, takes a bit less time, and makes loaves that are not quite as light. Let the dough rise for about 30 minutes. Place your loaves in a COLD oven. Turn the heat to 400°F and bake for 15 minutes. Turn the heat down to 350°F and continue baking for another 25 to 30 minutes.

Hearth Bread Short Cuts

The traditional method of baking Hearth Bread will produce two of the easiest, tastiest loaves you will ever make. But there are ways to get homemade bread on the table more quickly.

Hearth Bread in a Hurry: By eliminating the rising period after shaping the loaves, you can make bread from start to finish in about 2½ hours. This bread will be a bit heavier than the traditional variety but very good.

After the dough has risen in a bowl once, shape the loaves, put them on a cornmeal-sprinkled baking sheet and let them rest for about 10 minutes. Slash the tops as above, brush with cold water and put them in a COLD oven. Set the oven temperature to 400°F and bake for 35 to 40 minutes.

Hearth Bread Even Faster: You can shorten the time even more by substituting a 10- to 15-minute rest period for the first rising period as well. Shape and bake as you would Hearth Bread in a Hurry. When time is more important than taste and texture, this is the method to use.

"Short-time Dough": The English have developed another trick to speed up the rising process. To make what they call a "short-time dough," the Flour Advisory Bureau in London suggests adding 25 to 50 milligrams of vitamin C (¼ to ½ of a 100 milligram tablet) to the water in which you proof your yeast. Since yeast likes an acidic environment, it will grow and divide somewhat faster when you provide one. (The vitamin C is destroyed in the baking process so adds nothing nutritionally to the bread.)

Hearth Bread "Slow Doughs"

In making bread quickly, there is a trade-off. What you gain in time, you lose in flavor. In fact, the bread that has the best flavor spends anywhere from 8 to 24 hours rising and maturing. Here are some ways to accomplish that without taking any more of your time.

The Sponge: If you want bread in the evening, mix up your dough in the morning, but use only a teaspoon of yeast and half the flour. This creates a "sponge" which can be mixed up very quickly. Cover and place it in a cool (50°F to 60°F), draft-free place. Because you use so little yeast, it will slowly bubble away all day creating an "armada" of yeast for the evening and lots of old-fashioned flavor. Add the remainder of the flour at that point, give the dough a short rest, form your loaves, and proceed with whichever baking method you wish.

Slow-Rise: Use the reduced amount of yeast, as above, but knead in all the flour. To insure a very slow rising process, put your covered bowl in a cool place. When you're ready to use the dough, knock it down, shape it and proceed with whatever baking method you want. If you want rolls or sticky buns in the morning, mix it up before you go to bed and let it work while you sleep.

Refrigerator Rise: This is useful when you want to make bread in loaf pans. Use the correct amount of yeast that the recipe calls for, make your dough and form it into loaves. Place the loaves in bread pans that have been lightly greased and lightly grease the top of your loaves also. Cover loosely with plastic wrap and refrigerate anywhere from 2 to 24 hours.

When you want to bake the bread, remove it from the refrigerator and let it stand while you preheat your oven to 350°F (at least 15 minutes). Bake for 30 to 40 minutes.

Playing with Ingredients

As with all things classic and fundamental, we can take this basic hearth bread apart and play with each ingredient to create breads with completely different textures, flavors, colors and characters.

Liquids

Water & Variations: When bread is made simply with flour and yeast with water as the liquid, the flavor of the grain is very apparent. Because there is nothing to interfere with the development of the gluten in the wheat, the texture is chewy. This simplest of breads is best eaten fresh or within a day of baking as it dries out or stales quickly.

Although we tend to think of water as "water," it has different characteristics depending on where it comes from. Soft water may make your dough a bit sticky. Hard water may toughen the dough and make the rising period longer. Chlorinated water may add an objectional flavor. Water that is heavily chlorinated (as it is in some parts of Australia) may inhibit the yeast. (Try leaving water out overnight to let the chlorine dissipate.)

Instead of plain tap water, you can use juices or the vitamin-rich water in which you've cooked vegetables. You can even mash up and use some of the vegetables themselves. (Beets and beet water make a dramatic dough.) Mashed potato and/or potato water create an exceptionally nutritious broth for the yeast and they produce a coarse-textured bread that butter and jam (or just your teeth) love to sink into.

Milk & Variations: When you use milk or milk derivatives as your liquid, the milk solids make the gluten connections in the dough a bit weaker. This creates bread with a more tender crumb and a mellower taste. Cultured milk products, such as buttermilk, yogurt and sour cream produce moist breads with flavor reminiscent of sourdoughs. As an added bonus, the proteins in milk complement the proteins in wheat to create a combined protein which is as complete and nutritionally valuable as that in meat or eggs but without the fat or cholesterol, just one of the reasons bread is so good for you.

Yeast is reluctant to dissolve in whole milk; it doesn't like the fat. See the information under Yeast (page 129) for some options to deal with this problem.

Eggs: Another "liquid" that can be used is the egg. Eggs add extra protein, color, richness and, like the gluten in our flour, structure. One extra large egg supplies about 1/4 cup liquid so when you add one or more, subtract an equal amount from your other liquids.

To make a loaf that is extra light, more like traditional French bread, substitute 2 egg whites for 1/4 cup of water in our Hearth Bread recipe. Beat the egg whites into peaks and fold them into the dissolved and bubbling yeast mixture before you add the flour. Beaten egg whites contain lots of tiny air bubbles which expand in the heat of the oven to help leaven and lighten the loaves.

Other Liquids: For those of you who are on salt-free diets, in addition to substituting one of the excellent "low or no-salt" herb mixtures which you can find in many grocery stores, try substituting a tablespoon or two of vinegar or lemon juice for the salt in your Hearth (or other) Bread recipe. Either will intensify the flavor of your bread.

Another trick with vinegar or lemon juice is to substitute 2 tablespoons for an equal amount of water in our recipe. This time don't eliminate the salt. This acidic addition mellows the gluten in the dough which also helps make the texture of a Hearth Bread more like a true French bread.

You can even use beer to help create a light texture and robust flavor. Beer has some other characteristics that take us to the next ingredient.

Yeast

Yeast has an almost mystical aura about it, probably because we know it is a living organism and nothing that we humans have ever produced in a lab, not even baking powder, can do the same job. We are fortunate in having more than one kind to play with. In the Sourdough chapter, you'll find out how to set a trap for the elusive wild yeast. In this chapter, we're dealing with its domesticated cousin.

Characteristics & History: There are many varieties of yeast present in the air around us all the time. Some create yogurt and cheese out of milk; others make beer and wine from the juices of grains and fruit. As long as six thousand years ago, the Egyptians began to use this microscopic biological activity, without knowing what it really was, both to make beer and to leaven bread. In doing so, they changed the nature of bread and bread baking forever.

In the presence of air, the by-product of growing and multiplying yeast, as it feeds on the natural sugars in a dough, is carbon dioxide. When no air is present, yeast keeps right on growing as long as it has a food source, but the by-product is alcohol. This biochemical process is called fermentation.

Although (in most cases) leavened bread has generally been preferred to un-leavened bread, there has been some concern, over the centuries, about the leavening agent itself. Fermentation was long associated with decay and decay with disease. The implication was that bread leavened through fermentation must consequently be unhealthy. As a result, there were periods when making leavened bread was actually illegal. This never completely stopped people from doing it but the healthfulness of the resulting bread was always a question of debate.

Finally, and fortunately for us, in the mid-1800's Louis Pasteur discovered that fermentation is really the busy activity of a tiny one-celled plant we now call yeast. He also discovered that this tiny plant, in addition to producing breads that had better texture and taste, created and added a nutritional bonus, contrary to all those centuries of thinking otherwise.

One tablespoon of active dry yeast contains 3 grams each of protein and carbohydrates, about 3½ milligrams of B vitamins and some minerals to boot.

Types of Yeast

• Cake or Compressed Yeast: The kind of yeast that we use for bread baking originated from brewer's yeast. (This shouldn't be confused with the nutritional brewers' yeast which isn't alive and won't leaven bread.) In the nineteenth century, a strain of this yeast, with flavor and aroma particularly suited for bread rather than beer, was finally "domesticated."

Our mothers and grandmothers used an early form of this domesticated yeast. If you grew up in a baking household, you probably remember it. It came in little moist, yeasty-smelling cakes and could be kept fresh for about two weeks in the refrigerator before the edges began to turn brown and crack.

Cake yeast can still be found in some supermarkets. There are some people who still feel that this compressed yeast produces breads with the best flavor and they may be right.

One cake of compressed yeast, which weighs a bit more than 1/2 ounce, can be used in place of 1 scant tablespoon or 1 packet of active dry yeast. (Cake yeast will keep for a few months in the freezer. Defrost it over a period of hours in the refrigerator.)

• Active Dry Yeast: Today we most commonly use yeast that has had the moisture removed. This dormant, dry yeast can be kept several months at room temperature or in the refrigerator, and almost indefinitely in the freezer. (Because it contains no moisture, there is no need to thaw it before adding it to your liquid.) It becomes active only when dissolved in a liquid that contains a bit of sugar or flour. This yeast is available in individual packets or by the jar at your grocer's. Some specialty or health food stores carry it in bulk.

One packet of active dry yeast is equivalent to 1 scant tablespoon of bulk active dry yeast or 1 cake of compressed yeast.

• Quick-Rising Yeast: Recently a new, higher protein strain of yeast has been developed. Like other dry yeast it will keep for a long time if kept dry and cool. It is blended with the dry ingredients and activated with very hot (125°F to 130°F) water. This eliminates the "proofing" process and, because of the warmer initial temperature, makes the rising process speedier.

One packet of quick-rising yeast can be used in place of 1 packet of active dry yeast. Because this yeast speeds up the rising process, it is perhaps not the best choice if you want a long leavening period to develop flavor.

Using Yeast: Yeast is reluctant to dissolve in whole milk because of the presence of fat. To deal with this, you have several options.

• Use warmed skim milk which contains no fat.

• Dissolve your yeast in ¼ cup water, adding the balance of the liquid as milk, slightly warmed.

• Add ¾ cup of non-fat dry milk (or more for added protein) to your dry ingredients.

• Dissolve your yeast in 1 cup warm water and then add 1 cup of evaporated milk.

• Use 2 cups of liquid whole milk and add the new quick-rising yeast directly to your dry ingredients.

Whichever type of yeast you choose to use and whatever method you activate it with, remember that it is composed of tiny, living, growing plants which have just about the same feelings about being warm and cold as you do.

Salt

You don't need salt to make bread. For those of you who are trying to lower your sodium intake, cut the amount the recipe calls for in half or leave it out altogether. Another option is to use one of the excellent herbal salt substitutes that are available.

As we mentioned above, yeast doesn't like salt. When there's none around to impede it, your bread dough will rise more quickly. You can counteract this by using a bit less yeast or by putting your bread dough in a cooler place to slow the rising process.

Sweeteners

Although no sweetening is needed to provide food for the yeast (flour provides all it needs), a little bit helps get it started, and it will intensify the flavor of the bread. Sweeteners also can provide flavor of their own; table sugar the least, through the increasingly stronger flavors of brown sugar, honey, maple syrup, light, dark and blackstrap (preferably unsulphured) molasses. Molasses contains some nutrients not found in other sweeteners (see Appendix). Using any sweetener will help your bread stay moist longer.

If you decide to use honey in a recipe that calls for one of the other sweeteners, lower your oven temperature 25°F, as it tends to scorch, and extend your baking period 5 to 10 minutes.

Sweet dough recipes call for a much larger proportion of sugar than our basic Hearth Bread formula calls for. In the presence of all this "food" one would assume that the yeast would grow wildly. But the reverse actually happens. The yeast overdoses on the sugar, its chemical balance becomes upset and it takes a significantly longer time to double the bulk of the dough. (Is there a message here for us?) Most sweet dough recipes specify twice the "normal" amount of yeast to compensate for this.

Fats

There is no oil or fat in our Hearth Bread recipe as neither is necessary to make bread. For those of you who are calorie conscious, this means that in one slice of bread made with this recipe, there are only 55 to 60 calories. They are calories that will make you feel full, as well as giving you that energy which only carbohydrates can provide.

As usual, there is a trade-off. Bread made without fat is wonderful and chewy when it's fresh, but it stales very quickly. If you add a couple of tablespoons of butter or vegetable oil, you'll add 12 to 15 calories per slice, but your bread will be more tender and will stay fresh for a longer period.

Dry Ingredients

Wheat: This is the only grain whose protein produces significant amounts of gluten when it comes in contact with liquid. Gluten is a substance that forms a complex interlocking network of elastic strands when it is kneaded in a dough. These strands capture the carbon dioxide bubbles created by the growing yeast, which makes the dough expand or "rise." For more information on King Arthur Flours and why they are uniquely suited for yeast baking see page 9 in the Introduction.

Throughout the recipes in our *200th Anniversary Cookbook* we are using this symbol ✒ to let you know that you can substitute some of our King Arthur Stone Ground Whole Wheat Flour for an equal amount of our King Arthur All-Purpose Flour. Actually, in almost every situation you can use a combination of the two which gives you the best of both, the lightness of the unbleached all-purpose and the heartiness and good nutrition of the whole wheat.

If whole wheat flour is new to you, a good ratio to begin with is 1 cup of whole wheat to 3 of unbleached. You can try this combination in almost anything, from breads to brownies and cakes to cookies. Look for recipes dedicated primarily to whole wheat flour in Chapter IX.

Other Grains: To alter the flavor or texture of your breads, substitute one or more of the following for some of your King Arthur Flours: other flours such as rye, buckwheat, triticale, barley, amaranth and soy; partially processed grains such as cornmeal, oatmeal, steel-cut oats, cracked wheat, wheat germ or bran, barley flakes or even cooked rice or millet.

When you substitute a grain that doesn't contain gluten, your bread dough won't be able to trap as many carbon dioxide bubbles and so won't rise as high. You'll want to use enough wheat flour, 2 or 3 parts for each part of non-wheat flour, to make sure your dough has adequate carbon dioxide catching ability.

Start with 1 part non-wheat flour or grain to 3 or 4 parts of wheat flour, either unbleached all-purpose or whole wheat. The recipe for Super Bread on page 151 will describe how to use these more fully.

Seeds & Sprouts: For extra nutrition, texture and/or flavor in the basic Hearth Bread recipe, you can add $1/2$ to $3/4$ cup of seeds such as sunflower or sesame, and sprouted seeds, such as alfalfa, mung bean, sunflower and wheat berry.

Fruits & Vegetables: You can add up to $1 1/2$ cups dried fruits (raisins, currants, apricots, etc.), or even vegetables (onions, garlic, potatoes, beets or squash) that have been chopped, sautéed or mashed.

Herbs & Spices: Try 3 tablespoons of freshly minced herbs (chives, parsley, basil, tarragon, etc.) or one of dried, either singly or in combination. You can also add 1 or 2 tablespoons of herb seeds (poppy, caraway, dill, fennel, etc.).

For spicy breads, add 1 to 3 tablespoons cinnamon, allspice, nutmeg, ginger, cloves, curry, mace, black pepper (!) or a combination.

Grated Cheeses: Add up to 3 cups of grated semi-hard or hard cheese (Cheddar, Parmesan, etc.) to the basic recipe to create a bread that is wonderful alone, especially toasted, and for sandwiches.

Liza Bernard's "signature bread" is flavored with a savory combination of Parmesan cheese, ground rosemary, thyme and marjoram. Once you've gotten the feel of a dough, create a signature bread of your own.

• LARGE BREADS •

To get you started, we'll give you some recipes people have already thought up. Some are classics, variations of which have been around as long as our company has, and longer. Some are inspirations from early in the twentieth century right up to and into this last decade. As we move through this chapter, we'll make reference to our basic Hearth Bread dough and show you how everything, in some way, is just a variation on its basic theme, one on which you, too, can create amazing compositions.

BATTER BREADS

These first recipes take some liberties with our Hearth Bread recipe but it's a way to start experimenting with yeast that's so easy you won't even know you're using it. It's also a good way to make bread if kneading is a problem for you.

Take the Hearth Bread recipe, or any bread recipe for that matter, and use about $1/3$ less flour than is called for (2 parts flour to 1 part liquid, rather than the 3 to 1 ratio you would ordinarily use). Stir it up like a muffin batter, pour it into a greased casserole dish and bake it without any kneading at all. The result is called a batter bread. The texture is coarser than that of a kneaded bread, but it's incredibly moist; it tastes great by itself, as an addition to a meal or as part of a sandwich.

CHIVE & DILL BATTER BREAD

There are particular batter breads that have become very popular over the years and this first recipe is one of them. It's full of dill, chives and low-fat cottage cheese, and contains no other fat at all. But it's so moist and chewy, you'd never think of eating it with butter.

In this recipe we still have essentially 2 cups of liquid: ½ cup is water; the eggs provide the rest of that cup. The second cup is in the cottage cheese. To make a batter bread, we cut the flour back by a third, so, rather than the 6 cups of flour we'd use in a kneaded bread, we'll use 4.

½ cup warm water
2 tablespoons sugar
1 tablespoon or packet active dry yeast
2 cups (1 pint) low-fat cottage cheese
½ cup chopped chives (or chopped onion or scallions)
1 heaping tablespoon dill weed or seeds
2 eggs
2 teaspoons salt
½ teaspoon baking soda
1 cup King Arthur Stone Ground Whole Wheat Flour
3 cups King Arthur Unbleached All-Purpose Flour

Pour the warm water into a large mixing bowl and dissolve in it the sugar and the yeast. While they dissolve, heat the cottage cheese in a large saucepan until the chill is off. When it has warmed slightly, add the chives, dill, eggs, salt, baking soda and flour. Mix this all up and add it to the yeast mixture, making sure it is all well blended.

The next part, the rising or proofing, takes time, but it's the yeast that's doing all the work. You can determine how long it will take by where you put the dough. If you want the yeast to work quickly, say in 1½ hours, put your bowl somewhere warm and cozy (75°F to 85°F). If you want the yeast to work slowly, say all day while you're at work, put the dough somewhere cool (55°F to 65°F) or in the refrigerator. Make sure your dough is covered so it doesn't dry out, and then go away and do whatever you have to do.

About an hour before you want to serve your bread, stir it down and pour it into two small, lightly greased casserole dishes or 4½ x 8½-inch bread pans. Cover and let them rise again, this time for ¾ to 1 hour. (If the dough is cold, the loaves may take a bit more time to rise.)

About 15 minutes before you want to bake your bread, preheat your oven to 350°F. Bake the loaves for 30 to 35 minutes or until they're brown and crusty.

Onion Oregano Batter Bread

2 cups water
2 tablespoons sugar
1 tablespoon or packet active dry yeast
2 teaspoons salt
2 tablespoons vegetable oil
1/2 cup minced onion
2 teaspoons dried oregano
4 cups King Arthur Unbleached All-Purpose Flour
1 medium-sized onion, peeled, sliced and separated into rings
2 tablespoons butter, melted

Activate the yeast as in the preceding recipe. Add the salt, oil, minced onion, oregano and 2 cups of the flour. Beat for 2 or 3 minutes by hand. Stir in the remaining flour and let rise as above.

When the dough has doubled, stir it down for about a half a minute and pour it into two 4 1/2 x 8 1/2-inch bread pans. Let the dough rise until it's about 1/2 inch from the top of the pans.

While you do the next step, preheat your oven to 350°F. Dip the onion rings into melted butter and place on top of the loaves. Bake for 30 to 35 minutes.

Whole Wheat Molasses Batter Bread

1 1/2 cups buttermilk
1/2 cup molasses
3 tablespoons butter
3 cups King Arthur Stone Ground Whole Wheat Flour
1 cup rolled oats
1 tablespoon or package active dry yeast
2 teaspoons salt

Heat the buttermilk, molasses and butter in a saucepan until the butter has melted and the mixture is warm but not hot. Mix the dry ingredients, including the yeast, in a mixing bowl. Add the buttermilk mixture to the dry ingredients and beat with a large spoon for 2 or 3 minutes.

Let rise as above. Beat the risen dough down with a spoon and pour into two lightly greased, 4 1/2 x 8 1/2-inch bread pans. Let rise for about 40 minutes.

Fifteen minutes before you want to bake your bread, preheat your oven to 350°F. Bake for 30 to 35 minutes.

CLASSIC BREADS

These classics, or their variations, have been baked and loved for generations. They are almost as basic as our Hearth Bread but in each case someone fiddled with the ingredients to give the resulting bread a personality all its own. Just because they are classics doesn't mean that you can't do some fiddling with them yourself.

WALTER SANDS'
BASIC WHITE BREAD

This is the bread that Frank Sands' father, Walter, President of Sands, Taylor & Wood Co., from 1941 to 1968, made faithfully once a week for years. Because of his arthritic hands, he used a bread bucket with a crank which kneaded hundreds of loaves of this fragrant bread with all its happy associations.

It's a classic white bread, very similar to our Hearth Bread but, because it has some fat and milk solids in it, it has a fuller, mellower flavor and it won't stale as quickly. For a classic whole wheat version, see page 506 in the Whole Wheat Chapter.

    2 cups warm water
    2 tablespoons sugar or honey
    1 tablespoon or packet active dry yeast
    ½ cup dry milk (optional)
    2 tablespoons butter, softened, or vegetable oil (or a combination)
    6 cups King Arthur Unbleached All-Purpose Flour
    1 tablespoon salt (or less if desired)

Making the Dough: Pour the warm water into a large mixing bowl. Add and let dissolve the sugar or honey and yeast. When the yeast is bubbling, add the dry milk, softened butter, 5½ cups of flour and the salt. With a large spoon, stir this mixture until it begins to hold together. Pour the remaining ½ cup of flour on the surface you intend to use for kneading.

Kneading: Turn the dough out onto the floured board and knead until it begins to feel as if it belongs together, about 3 or 4 minutes, adding only enough flour to keep it from sticking to the board or you. Let it rest while you clean and grease your bowl. Continue kneading the relaxed dough until it feels smooth and springy, another 3 or 4 minutes.

Rising: Form the dough into a nice ball, place it in the greased bowl, turning it so the top is lightly greased also. Cover it and put it where it will be warm and cozy (no drafts). Let this rise until it has doubled (when you can poke your finger in it and the dough doesn't spring back at you).

Shaping: Punch or knock the dough down, turn it out onto your floured board and knead out any stray bubbles.

Cut it in half, form 2 loaves and place them in two lightly greased bread pans (page 123).

Baking: With either of the following options, the longer baking time produces a crustier bread with a slightly drier interior.

• **Full Rise:** Let the loaves rise until they are doubled (about an hour). About 15 minutes before you want to bake the bread, preheat the oven to 350°F. Place the loaves in the preheated oven and bake 35 to 40 minutes. This method makes the lightest loaves.

• **Partial Rise:** Let the loaves rise for only 30 to 40 minutes. Place them in a cold oven, set the temperature to 400°F for 15 minutes and lower it to 350°F for a further 20 to 25 minutes.

This second method takes a little less time from beginning to end and avoids the possibility of the bread dough rising too far and then collapsing. The bread itself won't be quite as light but it will still be very good.

BERT PORTER'S "NATURALLY GREAT LOAF OF BREAD"

This recipe for white bread appeared on our King Arthur Unbleached All-Purpose Flour bags in the 1970's and early '80's. It was developed by Bert Porter, our spokesman during those years. Because Bert and his wife, Ruth, are the only ones at home now, he has a unique way of shaping this bread so they can eat half of one loaf and freeze the rest.

This recipe is about 1½ times larger than our Hearth Bread recipe and, consequently, makes three 4½ x 8½-inch loaves.

2 cups warm water
1 (5⅓-ounce) can evaporated milk
⅓ cup vegetable oil or margarine
¼ cup honey or sugar
2 tablespoons or packets active dry yeast
7 to 8 cups King Arthur Unbleached All-Purpose Flour 🌾
1 tablespoon salt

Mixing: Combine the water, milk and oil or margarine in a saucepan and heat until lukewarm. Pour into a mixing bowl and add the honey or sugar, yeast, 2 cups of the flour and then the salt.

Beat the mixture for 2 minutes by hand or with an electric mixer. Stirring with a large spoon, gradually add flour until the dough pulls away cleanly from the sides of the bowl.

Kneading & Rising: Knead until the dough is smooth and springy. Form the dough into a ball, place in a lightly greased bowl and turn the dough over so the top is greased. Cover and let rise 1 to 1½ hours or until doubled in bulk.

Shaping: Punch the dough down with your fist to break up the pockets of gas. Divide the dough into 6 pieces.

Form each piece into a round ball and place two, side by side, in each of three greased, 4½ x 8½-inch bread pans.

Cover and let these rise until doubled. Be sure not to let the dough rise more than double, for it can cause the loaf to fall or "flatten out" while baking.

Baking: Fifteen minutes before you want to bake the bread, preheat the oven to 375°F. Bake for 30 to 35 minutes. To make sure it's done, tap the bottom with your fingertips. If it sounds hollow, it's done.

Cooling & Storing: Remove the bread from the pans immediately and place on cooling racks. When the loaves are thoroughly cool, break them all in half. Save one-half to enjoy immediately. Individually wrap the others in airtight plastic bags and freeze them. Thaw them out as needed and you will have a supply of bread that is "oven fresh."

Oatmeal Bread

Oats, which like a cool, damp, northern climate, grow happily in Scotland and find their way into most every Scottish meal. Homemade oatmeal bread, sweetened with a little honey, has a special flavor and chewy texture that makes us glad that the Scots brought their oats to New England. Oats can be had either rolled or steel-cut.

The oats we are most familiar with are rolled. Steel-cut oats have been steamed as have rolled oats, but they have been cut in half rather than flattened, so are somewhat like cracked wheat. If you make your bread with steel-cut oats, it will have the texture of cracked wheat bread but the flavor of oats. You can often find steel-cut oats in the natural food section of your grocery store.

This recipe probably looks a bit different from our Hearth Bread. But as you read through it and understand how and why it's put together, you'll find the basic recipe again. We've combined the oats with unbleached and whole wheat flour. You can use whatever flour combination you like.

Oat Mixture

1 1/2 cups boiling water
1 cup rolled or steel-cut oats
1/2 cup honey
1/4 cup (1/2 stick or 4 tablespoons) butter
1 tablespoon salt

Dough

1 tablespoon or packet active dry yeast
1/2 cup warm water
1 teaspoon honey
2 cups King Arthur Stone Ground Whole Wheat Flour
3 1/2 to 4 1/2 cups King Arthur Unbleached All-Purpose Flour

Preparing the Oats: Pour the boiling water into a large mixing bowl and add the oats. Stir in the honey, butter and salt. While it's still warm, put your head over the bowl and take a deep breath! Then let it cool to room temperature.

Proofing the Yeast: Dissolve and activate the yeast in the 1/2 cup of water and honey. When it's frothy and bubbling, add it to the oat mixture and blend it in. Stir in the whole wheat flour and 3 1/2 cups of the unbleached flour.

Mixing the Dough: Mix the flour into the dough until it begins to hold together and pull away from the sides of the bowl. Turn it out onto a kneading surface where you've sprinkled some of the last cup of flour.

Kneading & Rising: Knead the dough until it feels together. Add only enough flour to keep it from sticking. Give the dough a rest while you clean out and grease your bowl. Continue kneading until the dough is elastic and springy and doesn't stick to you or the board anymore.

Form it into a nice ball and place it in the greased bowl to rise, turning it to grease the top. Cover it with a damp towel or plastic wrap and put it somewhere cozy. It will take about 1 1/2 hours to rise fully.

Shaping: When you can poke your finger into the dough without it springing back at you, punch it down, turn it out onto your kneading board again and divide it in two. Shape it into loaves and place in whatever bread pans you have, but 4 1/2 x 8 1/2 inches is a good size for this amount of dough. Cover the pans and let the dough rise for about 45 minutes.

Baking: Place the loaves in a cold oven, set the temperature to 400°F for 15 minutes and then down to 350°F for a further 25 minutes.

ANADAMA BREAD

As the Scots replaced some of the wheat in their breads with their local oats, early settlers here in New England responded in kind with "Indian meal," or cornmeal. The name Anadama, as the story goes, was originally an oath bestowed upon Anna by her hungry fisherman husband. It seems that she had abandoned him to a meal of cornmeal mush (hasty pudding) and molasses. He, in a burst of frustration and creativity, added flour, salt, butter and yeast and produced this now familiar and traditional New England bread.

> 2 cups boiling water
> 1/2 cup cornmeal
> 1/2 cup dark unsulphured or blackstrap molasses
> 1 tablespoon or packet active dry yeast
> 1/4 cup (1/2 stick) butter or vegetable oil
> 1/2 cup dry milk (optional)
> 2 cups King Arthur Stone Ground Whole Wheat Flour
> 1 tablespoon (or less) salt
> 3 1/2 to 4 1/2 cups King Arthur Unbleached All-Purpose Flour

Mixing: Pour the boiling water into a large mixing bowl and add the cornmeal. Stir in the molasses and keep stirring off and on while the mixture cools to lukewarm so the cornmeal doesn't get lumpy.

When the mixture has cooled, add the yeast and let the mixture sit for 5 to 10 minutes until the yeast has dissolved and begun to work.

Add the butter or oil, dry milk, whole wheat flour and salt. Stir in the unbleached flour gradually, mixing thoroughly until the dough pulls away from the side of the bowl. Turn out onto a flour-sprinkled kneading surface.

Kneading & Rising: From here, follow the directions for Oatmeal Bread on page 138.

JENNIFER SAWYER'S
ANADAMA OATMEAL BREAD

Our bread sculptress, Jennifer Sawyer, developed this dough to make her edible creations. You'll find her hints about sculpting bread dough on page 557 in the Fun! chapter. As well as creating healthy, bronze-colored sculptures, this bread is a very successful marriage of anadama and oatmeal breads, which just shows you what a little fiddling can accomplish.

$\frac{1}{2}$ cup old-fashioned oatmeal (not quick)
$\frac{1}{4}$ cup yellow cornmeal
2 cups boiling water
$\frac{1}{4}$ cup molasses
1 tablespoon or packet active dry yeast
$\frac{1}{2}$ cup non-fat dry milk
$\frac{1}{4}$ cup butter, melted, or vegetable oil
2 cups King Arthur Stone Ground Whole Wheat Flour
1 tablespoon salt
4 cups King Arthur Unbleached All-Purpose Flour

Mixing: Put the oatmeal and cornmeal in a large mixing bowl. Pour the boiling water over them and stir in the molasses. Let cool to lukewarm, stirring occasionally so the cornmeal doesn't lump.

When the mixture is lukewarm, stir in the yeast and let the mixture rest for 5 to 10 minutes while the yeast dissolves and begins to work.

Add the dry milk, butter or oil, whole wheat flour and salt. Blend together.

If you have time, let this sponge work for two or more hours, to develop more flavor. If not, slowly stir in the unbleached flour until it pulls cleanly away from the sides of the bowl. Turn out onto a floured kneading surface.

Kneading & Rising: From this point, follow the directions for Oatmeal Bread on page 138.

HEARTH BREAD
AS
"FRENCH BREAD"

To make a loaf of bread that is like a classic French Bread, you need to start with a dough that is slacker (wetter) than our Hearth Bread dough and you should allow 5 or more hours from start to finish to develop the flavor. In addition, because this wet dough tends to spread, you'll find it easier to bake it in baguette pans that are designed especially for French Bread.

While this method means a fairly long commitment of time on your part, it will produce a bread with flavor and texture that just can't be had any other way. Most of this time you can spend doing something else. The dough needs only occasional attention.

Use this same dough and technique to make exceptional Hard Rolls. (See the next section on Rolls & Small Breads on page 159.)

1³/₄ cups water
1 tablespoon sugar
1 tablespoon or packet active dry yeast
2 egg whites
5 to 5¹/₂ cups King Arthur Unbleached All-Purpose Flour
1 tablespoon salt

You can also use some vinegar or lemon juice as suggested under Other Liquids on page 126 to help make the texture even lighter.

Mixing & Resting: Dissolve the sugar and yeast in the warm water. Beat the egg whites until stiff and fold them into the yeast mixture. Blend in a cup of the flour and then the salt. Add 4 more cups of flour.

This dough will be quite soft and sticky so, after you've stirred the flour in as thoroughly as you can, cover the bowl with a damp towel or plastic wrap and place it in a draft-free place where it's not too warm (somewhere between 60°F and 70°F).

Let the dough develop for half an hour or so. This gives the flour a chance to absorb the moisture and will make the dough easier to handle and knead.

Kneading: Turn the dough out onto a floured surface and, with well-floured hands, knead for 8 to 10 minutes.

Working this sticky dough may be a bit frustrating. If you find you can't keep it from sticking to your hands, use a dough scraper to pick it up and slap it down on the counter in rhythm for as long as you would ordinarily knead it. Use just enough flour to minimize sticking. (This same technique is used in making a Brioche dough which you'll find on page 241.)

Rising: Place it in a greased bowl, turning it to grease the top. Cover and let it rise in the same cool place for 2 to 3 hours.

Knock the dough down and let it rise again. These long rising periods develop a flavor in the finished product that makes all this effort worthwhile. Our "hurry-up" lives shortchange us of those things that only time can accomplish.

Shaping & Rising: After the second rising period, knock the dough down again, turn it out onto a floured board, knead out any stray bubbles and let the dough rest for 5 minutes.

Lightly grease 2 baguette pans and sprinkle them with cornmeal if you wish. Divide the dough in half and shape into loaves to fit your pans. Gently lay the loaves in the pans and cover them so they'll stay moist. Allow these loaves to rise in the same cool place for another 1 1/2 to 2 hours.

Baking: Fifteen minutes before you want to bake your bread, preheat your oven to a hot 475°F.

Just before the loaves go in, slash the tops diagonally 2 or 3 times, about 1/4 inch deep. Use a sharp serrated knife and "saw" back and forth gently, without exerting any downward pressure. Brush the tops with cold water. A goose feather brush or water mister can do this without deflating these light-as-air loaves. Place them in the oven.

After 2 minutes, spray or brush them with cold water again. Repeat this 2 more times at 2-minute intervals and finish baking them for a total or 20 to 25 minutes. (For other steaming options, see page 120.)

At the end of the baking period, turn the oven off and leave the bread inside (with the door closed) for 5 minutes, or longer if you like a crust with real crunch. Like most French breads, this bread is best served immediately after it has cooled.

RYE BREADS

While rye breads are classics as well, there are so many varieties they merit a section of their own. Whole rye flour contains more minerals (iron, phosphorous and potassium) than wheat flour, but almost no gluten-producing protein. To make a loaf of rye bread with any cohesiveness and loft, you must incorporate a blend of both rye and wheat flours.

Rye is an interesting grain. It grows in colder, damper climates than wheat does and consequently plays a large role in northern European baking. It can be obtained as "flour," "meal" or "chops."

Rye flour is ground from the endosperm of the rye berry and, like "white" wheat flour, does not contain the germ or the bran. Unlike "white" wheat flour, rye flour comes in a whole array of colors depending on the amount of ash it contains. (Ash is what's leftover after a flour sample is burned. See Appendix for more information.) The amount of ash in a flour is dependent on what part of the endosperm the flour is ground from. The concentration of ash is greatest just inside the seed coat or bran layer of a rye or wheat berry.

Flour ground from the center of the endosperm where the percentage of ash is lowest, is "white rye." Flour ground from a large percentage of the endosperm nearer the seed coat is called "cream rye." Flour ground from the outside of the endosperm, which is left over after the white or cream ryes have been taken out, is "dark rye." Medium rye is ground from the entire endosperm.

The second category is rye meal. This is "flour" ground from the entire rye berry and is equivalent to whole wheat flour. Rye meal can also be had several ways, this time determined by the grind: fine, medium or coarse. Coarse rye meal is commonly called "pumpernickel flour," an affectionate German name given in fun, both to it and the hearty German breads made with it, to describe their effect on the digestive system. ("Pumpern" is the German word for "intestinal wind" and "nickel" is a word for demon or sprite.)

Rye "chops" is the equivalent of cracked wheat and can add the same crunch to bread. You may have to look in a health food or specialty store for dark and pumpernickel ryes or rye chops. If you can't find them, you can substitute a medium rye which you should be able to find in most grocery stores.

Rye breads are traditionally seasoned with such herbs and spices as caraway, grated orange peel, anise and fennel seed. Check the Sourdough chapter for some hearty sourdough ryes.

BASIC RYE BREAD

This recipe is designed for active dry "domestic" yeast with some suggestions for substitutions and additions. Use your own intuition and feeling for flavor blends to create a rye bread of your own.

2 cups warm liquid (water, potato water, yogurt, sour milk, etc.)
¼ cup brown sugar or dark, unsulphured molasses
1 tablespoon or packet active dry yeast
2 tablespoons (¼ stick) butter, softened, or vegetable oil
1 tablespoon salt
1 cup medium rye flour or pumpernickel (coarse rye meal)
3 cups King Arthur Stone Ground Whole Wheat Flour
1½ to 2 cups King Arthur Unbleached All-Purpose Flour

Optional Additions

2 tablespoons caraway or dill seed
1 cup chopped onion
1 tablespoon grated orange peel
2 teaspoons crushed fennel seed
1 cup raisins
2 tablespoons instant coffee and/or unsweetened cocoa

Mixing: To your warm liquid, add and dissolve the brown sugar or molasses and yeast. (If you are using a whole milk product as the liquid, this may take 10 minutes or so.) When the yeast is working, add the softened butter or vegetable oil, rye flour and then the salt. Add any "optional additions" to this mixture before you add the rest of the flour. Stir in the whole wheat flour and 1½ cups of the unbleached. When the dough begins to hold together and pull away from the sides of the bowl, turn it out onto your kneading surface where you've poured the last ½ cup of flour.

Kneading: Since rye dough tends to be sticky, keep your hands and the board well floured while you knead it. Even when it's thoroughly kneaded, it will still be a bit sticky. Don't try to get rid of the stickiness by continuing to add flour. (You can't, and if you try you'll have a rye doorstop!) When it's thoroughly kneaded, put it in a greased bowl, cover and let it rise until doubled in bulk.

Shaping: After the first rising, divide the dough into 2 pieces and either shape them to fit your bread pans or make 2 round, free-form loaves (page 119) and place them on baking sheets sprinkled with cornmeal. Cover them with a damp cloth or plastic wrap and let them rise for about an 1 hour.

Baking: Put the loaves in a cold oven. Set the oven temperature to 400°F for 15 minutes, lower it to 350°F and continue baking for 25 to 30 minutes.

Onion Rye Bread

This hearty rye bread is redolent of onion and caraway.

2 cups warm water
2 tablespoons sugar
1 tablespoon or packet active dry yeast
$\frac{1}{2}$ cup non-fat dry milk (optional)
2 cups medium rye flour
1 tablespoon salt
$\frac{1}{4}$ cup vegetable oil
1 cup chopped onion
2 tablespoons caraway seed (or dill)
1 cup King Arthur Stone Ground Whole Wheat Flour
3 to $3\frac{1}{2}$ cups King Arthur Unbleached All-Purpose Flour

Mixing: Pour the water into a mixing bowl and dissolve the sugar, yeast and dry milk in it. Blend in the rye flour and salt and then add the oil, onion and caraway. Stir in the balance of the flour until you have a stiff but kneadable dough.

Kneading: From this point, follow the preceding Basic Rye Bread recipe.

Pumpernickel Bread

This old King Arthur Flour recipe is a classic "pumpernickel" rye flavored with molasses and anise.

1$\frac{1}{2}$ cups water
1 cup pumpernickel (coarse rye meal)
$\frac{1}{2}$ cup warm water
$\frac{1}{3}$ cup molasses
1 tablespoon or packet active dry yeast
1 tablespoon salt
$\frac{1}{4}$ cup vegetable oil
1 tablespoon ground anise
2 teaspoons cocoa (optional, for a darker, traditional pumpernickel color)
4 to 5 cups King Arthur Unbleached All-Purpose Flour

Preparing the Rye: In a saucepan, bring 1$\frac{1}{2}$ cups water to a boil. Turn off the heat and stir in the pumpernickel. Let this sit until it's lukewarm.

Mixing the Dough: Pour the $\frac{1}{2}$ cup warm water into a large mixing bowl. Stir in the molasses and the yeast. Let this sit for a few minutes until it's working.

Add and blend in the the cooled pumpernickel mixture. Stir in the salt, vegetable oil, anise and cocoa. Gradually add the balance of the flour, stirring until the dough no longer sticks to the side of the bowl.

Kneading: From here follow the directions for Basic Rye Bread (page 144).

Vört Limpa

"Limpas" are typically Scandinavian rye breads. This particular one comes to us from Sandy Jubinsky, the distaff half of the Jubinsky bread baking and demonstrating team which is an extension of the larger King Arthur Flour team. Sandy wears many hats. Her hand-painted china is exquisite and so is this bread.

About this particular recipe Sandy said, "Several years ago a woman asked me if I could convert a 'rather large' recipe to family size. I quickly assured her that it would be 'no problem.' After more tries than I bothered to count, I finally reduced the original recipe, which called for twenty-five pounds of flour, into this wonderfully fragrant, and very manageable, two-loaf size." Lucky for us.

Proofing Sponge

> 2 tablespoons or packets active dry yeast
> ½ cup warm water
> a pinch of sugar
> ½ cup King Arthur Unbleached All-Purpose Flour

Setting up the Sponge: Dissolve the yeast in the warm water. Add the pinch of sugar and the flour. Cover with plastic wrap and/or a clean towel and set aside until bubbly, 5 or 10 minutes.

The Dough

> 1 cup very warm water
> 1 cup dark beer, warmed
> ¼ cup dark brown sugar
> ¼ cup molasses
> 2 tablespoons fresh grated orange peel or 1 tablespoon dried peel
> ¼ cup butter, melted
> 1 tablespoon salt
> ½ teaspoon ginger
> 1 teaspoon fennel or anise seed (or a combination)
> 2 cups medium rye flour
> 1 cup raisins (optional)
> 5 to 6 cups King Arthur Unbleached All-Purpose Flour
> melted butter or egg white for the top crust

Making the Dough: In a large bowl, combine the water, the warmed beer, brown sugar, molasses, orange peel, butter, salt, ginger and fennel or anise seeds. Add the sponge and stir in the rye flour and raisins, if desired.

Add the unbleached flour, one cup at a time, until the dough comes cleanly away from the sides of the bowl.

Turn the dough out onto a lightly floured board. Scrape the bowl and add the bits to the dough. Lightly oil the bowl and set aside. (This is a Jubinsky technique. It avoids washing the bowl, which they'd just as soon skip.)

Kneading & Rising: Knead the dough, adding only enough flour to prevent sticking. When it's thoroughly kneaded, after about 8 minutes, it should be moderately soft, smooth and elastic.

When baking with honey or molasses and rye flour, the dough never completely loses its tacky feel. "Tacky" is when your hand hesitates slightly before pulling cleanly away from the dough. "Sticky" is when bits of the dough actually stick to your hand or the board. Don't try to work enough flour into the dough to eliminate the "tacky" feel or you'll end up with a dry, tough loaf of bread.

Place the dough in the oiled bowl, turn to oil the top surface and cover with plastic wrap and/or a clean towel. Put the bowl in a warm, draft-free place to rise until doubled in bulk, 1 to $1\frac{1}{2}$ hours.

Shaping: Punch the dough down and divide it in half. Form into round loaves (page 119) and place on baking sheets that have been sprinkled with cornmeal.

Cover with plastic wrap and/or a clean towel and let rise until doubled, about an hour.

Baking: About 15 minutes before you want to bake the bread, preheat the oven to 375°F.

Brush tops of the loaves with melted butter or a beaten egg white. Bake the loaves for about one hour or until they sound hollow when tapped on the bottom. Cool on wire racks before slicing.

They say you shouldn't cut bread right after it comes out of the oven because you'll crush it. But we've found that if you cut very, very gently with a good serrated knife, you can do it without any damage. And why deprive yourself of one of life's greatest pleasures?

NEO-CLASSIC BREADS

These breads are all variations of our classic recipes, just a sampling of the ways you can play with ingredients to create some that are entirely new (which might become classics themselves someday).

CINNAMON RAISIN BREAD

This recipe is from King Arthur Flour's senior spokesman, Michael Jubinsky. It is egg-rich and will make three absolutely delicious loaves.

Fruit

    1 cup raisins
    apple juice (or water), warmed

Preparing the Fruit: Cover the raisins with warm water or warmed apple juice and set aside to plump while you proceed with the following.

Proofing Sponge

    2 tablespoons or packets active dry yeast
    $\frac{1}{2}$ cup warm water
    1 teaspoon sugar
    $\frac{1}{2}$ cup King Arthur Unbleached All-Purpose Flour

Making the Sponge: Dissolve the yeast in the warm water. Add the sugar and flour. Stir to combine, cover and set aside until bubbly, about 15 minutes.

Dough

    $1\frac{1}{2}$ cups milk, scalded (heated just to a boil)
    $\frac{1}{2}$ cup sugar, brown or white (or honey)
    $\frac{1}{2}$ cup (1 stick) butter
    2 teaspoons salt
    3 tablespoons cinnamon
    3 eggs, beaten
    3 cups King Arthur Stone Ground Whole Wheat Flour
    5 to 6 cups King Arthur Unbleached All-Purpose Flour
    1 egg yolk beaten with 1 tablespoon water (for wash)

Mixing the Dough: In a large bowl, combine the milk, sweetener, butter, salt and cinnamon. Stir and let cool to lukewarm. Add the beaten eggs, the sponge and the whole wheat flour. Combine well. Drain and add the raisins. Stir in 5 to $5\frac{1}{2}$ cups of flour until the dough comes cleanly away from the sides of the bowl.

Kneading & Rising: Turn the dough out onto a board where you've sprinkled the remainder of the flour. Scrape the bowl and add the bits to the dough. Lightly oil the bowl and set aside.

Knead the dough, adding only enough flour to keep it from sticking to the board. When it's smooth and elastic, after about 10 minutes, place it in the oiled bowl. Turn to oil all surfaces, cover with plastic wrap and a clean towel and set aside in a warm place to rise until doubled, 1 to 1½ hours.

Shaping & Rising: Punch down the dough, divide in thirds and let it rest for 10 minutes. Shape into loaves and place into greased bread pans. Cover with plastic wrap and a clean towel and let rise until doubled in bulk, 45 minutes to 1 hour.

Baking: About 15 minutes before you want to bake your bread, preheat the oven to 375°F. Brush tops of the loaves with the egg wash.

Bake 35 to 40 minutes or until the loaves are a rich brown color. They should sound hollow when tapped on the bottom.

Cinnamon Raisin Roll-Ups

Rather than mixing the raisins into the dough, save them to roll up in it.

> 6 to 8 tablespoons honey or brown sugar
> 1 tablespoon cinnamon
> melted butter for top

The honey can sometimes leak out into the baking pans, giving the bread a sticky bun effect. If you want to avoid that, instead of using honey, brush the 8 x 14-inch rectangle liberally with melted butter and sprinkle it with 2 to 3 tablespoons of brown sugar and 1 teaspoon of cinnamon.

Mixing, Shaping & Rising: Prepare the dough as directed above. Cut it into thirds and roll each into an 8 x 14-inch rectangle. Spread with a thin layer of honey, leaving a 1-inch clear space around the edges. Sprinkle with the raisins and cinnamon.

Roll up the dough starting with the short edge. Pinch the seams and ends together tightly to seal them and place, seam side down, in well-greased loaf pans. Cover the loaves and let them rise in a warm place until doubled in bulk, about 45 minutes to an hour.

Baking: About 15 minutes before you want to bake your bread, preheat the oven to 375°F. Brush the tops of the loaves with the melted butter and bake until done, about 45 minutes. Remove from pans and cool on a wire rack.

WHEAT GERM YOGURT BREAD

This is an especially nutritious bread with tremendous flavor. It comes to us from Frank and Brinna Sands' sister-in-law, Linda Weingarten, who bakes it with King Arthur Flour shipped all the way to South Carolina.

Although this is not written for a quick-rising yeast, Linda uses regular, active dry yeast in the same way (which you can do in most recipes). This gives you the ease of using a quick yeast with the flavor developed through a slower, more traditional rising period. Linda uses an electric mixer to combine her ingredients, which is an interesting and easy alternative. About this bread, she says, "I used half unbleached white and half whole wheat in this one. It's a 'toothy' but medium-weight bread—very yummy!"

6 cups King Arthur Unbleached All-Purpose Flour
¹/₂ cup non-fat dry milk
1 tablespoon salt
1 tablespoon or package active dry yeast
1 cup water
1 cup yogurt
¹/₄ cup honey
2 tablespoons butter
¹/₂ cup wheat germ
egg wash made with 1 egg beaten with 2 teaspoons water
extra wheat germ to sprinkle on top

Mixing: Mix 2 cups of the flour, the dry milk, salt and yeast in a large bowl. Combine the water, yogurt, honey and butter in a saucepan. Heat until the liquids are very warm. Gradually add to the dry ingredients and beat for 2 minutes at medium speed with an electric mixer. Add a further cup of flour and beat at high speed for 2 minutes. Stir in the wheat germ and enough additional flour to make a stiff dough.

Kneading & Rising: Turn the dough out onto a lightly floured board and knead until smooth and elastic. Clean out and grease your bowl, put the dough in, turning it so the top is slightly greased, cover with a damp towel or plastic wrap, and allow to rise for 1 to 1¹/₂ hours.

Shaping: Punch the dough down and divide in half. You can form this dough into 2 standard loaves to be baked in lightly greased bread pans, or you can divide each piece into 3 smaller pieces and braid them. (See page 123.) Place the braids on a lightly greased baking sheet. Whichever you use, cover the shaped loaves and let rise for 45 minutes to an hour.

Baking: Fifteen minutes before you want to bake your bread, preheat your oven to 350°F. Just before the loaves go in the oven, brush them with the egg wash and sprinkle with wheat germ. Bake for 30 to 35 minutes.

SUPER BREAD

When days have begun to shrink and you're up and off before the dark and chill have really let go, you begin to think of how to pack some warmth into breakfast and lunch, something that will fire your engines and keep them running all day. Here's how to pack all this into a loaf of Super Bread. (This recipe was developed by Brinna Sands when she was in her "bread as the ONLY staff of life" phase.)

When you make bread with milk as the liquid, you will create something that gives you two kinds of energy. The first is protein. Whole proteins are divided up into lots of little parts. Wheat has some of those parts and milk has others. When you put them together, you make a protein as complete as any you find in meat but with vegetable fiber replacing the fat. Everyone needs some protein. If you are growing you need a lot. Protein helps you develop a healthy body as you grow and it also provides a form of energy that burns long and slow.

The second kind of energy comes from carbohydrates in the wheat itself. Carbohydrates burn hotter and faster than protein and provide you with a "jump start" and the "overdrive" you need to breeze through a busy day. We all need more of this second kind of energy, especially when we're very active.

What else can you add to make this a really SUPER bread? An egg or two will boost the protein. Stone ground whole wheat flour substituted for some unbleached white, adds extra vitamins, fiber and heartiness. Soy flour, oatmeal, cornmeal, wheat germ and bran, available at your local market or health food store, create variety and an extra nutritional wallop. Dark, unsulphured or blackstrap molasses as the sweetener adds iron and an irresistable flavor, and helps the bread retain moisture or freshness.

Because this bread contains essentially no fat, you will find that it gives you a maximum amount of energy with minimum number of calories; it will satisfy your hunger, provide excellent nutrition, plus, if you've ever made a loaf of bread, you know what that will do for you. No wonder bread is called the staff of life. The flavor of this bread is developed by making a sponge, so read through the recipe first to plan your timing.

2 cups liquid (this can include 2 eggs which count as a liquid, page 126)
1 to 4 tablespoons sugar (white or brown), honey or molasses
1 tablespoon or packet active dry yeast (page 129)
$3/4$ cup non-fat dry milk (optional, but increases the protein)
1 to $1\frac{1}{2}$ cups of the following, your choice: cracked wheat; oatmeal, steel-cut oats; triticale; wheat, barley, rye or other flakes; cornmeal; wheat germ; wheat or oat bran, soy flour, etc. You can also use a blend of these. (If you're using soy flour, start with $1/2$ cup and increase the amount next time if you like the flavor.)
2 cups King Arthur Stone Ground Whole Wheat Flour
1 tablespoon salt (or less if desired)
3 cups King Arthur Unbleached All-Purpose Flour

The total amount of flour you need will vary. To produce a loaf with good volume, use at least 4½ to 5 cups of wheat flour, either unbleached or stone ground whole wheat. Wheat is the only grain that contains gluten, the amazing protein that causes a dough to capture carbon dioxide bubbles produced by the yeast, which creates the "rise." The other 1 to 1½ cups can be a combination of any of the other dry ingredients mentioned.

Making the Sponge: Dissolve the sweetener and yeast in your liquid. (When measuring your liquid, keep in mind that if you're planning on adding eggs, each one counts as about ¼ cup, so subtract that amount from the total liquid. Don't add the eggs to the sponge.) Stir in the dry milk, any whole grains and the whole wheat flour.

Cover your sponge with plastic wrap and let it sit in a cool spot for anywhere from 2 to 12 hours.

Making the Dough: Stir down the sponge, add the salt and beat in the eggs if you choose to add them.

Stir in the remainder of your flour, except for half a cup which you'll sprinkle on your kneading board. (If you use a liquid sweetener, such as honey or molasses, you will need to use a slightly smaller percentage of liquid or a bit more flour.)

When your dough begins to hold together and pull away from the sides of the bowl, turn the dough out onto the floured kneading board.

Kneading, Rising, Shaping & Baking: From this point on, follow the same procedure as for Basic White Bread beginning with Kneading on page 135.

Storing: Once the bread is out of the oven and cool, wrap it in an airtight plastic bag. You can freeze it at this point and it will be "oven fresh" when you thaw it to fire up another day.

There isn't much you can buy commercially that can compare with a loaf of the Super Bread you make at home. Once you've experimented a few times, you'll find combinations that you or your family particularly like and maybe some they don't. (The rather large amount of brewers' yeast added to one batch several years ago didn't get past the kids.) You will discover that you can get an amazing amount of nutrition into an amazingly tasty loaf of bread.

New Mother Bread

Brinna Sands wrote this recipe back in 1986 for a "Radio New England Magazine" segment called "King Arthur's Kitchen" which she has done weekly for several years. This bread, again, is based on the Hearth Bread recipe. By incorporating special ingredients you can tailor your bread to your own needs which no commercial bread can ever completely meet.

"I don't know whether it's because it's that time of the year when so many things have reached the peak of productivity and have borne fruit in infinite shapes and sizes, or whether it's because we've spent this summer watching our daughter Ellen and her husband, Christopher, as well as our Vice President, Scott Berry, and his wife, Ann, lovingly prepare for the births of their first children, both of whom made their appearances at the end of August. At any rate, my mind has been on mothers, fathers and babies of late. They seem to be popping out all over the place, with daddies being involved and creating 'bonds' with their babies in lots of non-traditional ways, which can only give us reason for optimism about the future of the species.

"New mothers have particular nutritional needs and it's been fun devising a loaf of bread that meets a good many of them as well as having that comforting taste and aroma which only homemade bread can have. New mothers need lots of protein, vitamins and minerals (particularly calcium and iron), and lots of fiber. Here's how to pack a lot of that in a loaf of bread."

    1 1/2 cups warm water
    1 tablespoon sugar
    1 tablespoon or packet active dry yeast
    2 eggs
    1 cup non-fat dry milk
    1 to 2 teaspoons salt (less than usual to help minimize fluid retention)
    1/2 cup dark, unsulphured or blackstrap molasses
    1/2 cup wheat germ
    1/2 cup wheat bran
    1/4 cup vegetable oil
    4 cups King Arthur Stone Ground Whole Wheat Flour
    2 to 3 cups (more or less) King Arthur Unbleached All-Purpose Flour
    1 to 2 cups raisins, chopped apricots or prunes (optional)

Making the Sponge: Measure the water into a large mixing bowl. Add and dissolve the sugar and yeast. Add and blend in the eggs, dry milk, whole wheat flour, salt, molasses, wheat germ, bran, and vegetable oil. If the mother you're thinking about is partial to raisins, apricots or prunes, now is the time to add them also. At this point, you'll have a relatively sticky dough, or "sponge."

Cover and let it work for at least 2 (and if you have the time, up to 12) hours. This will soften the bran which will allow the finished loaves to rise higher.

Making the Dough: After you've allowed this sponge to work, add about 2 cups of the unbleached flour, stirring vigorously until the dough holds together and begins to come away from the sides of the bowl.

Kneading: Turn the dough out onto a floured surface and knead for 5 to 10 minutes, until it no longer feels sticky. You can add a bit more flour if necessary. At this point you can let the dough rise a second time, which will develop a finer texture and more flavor, or you can proceed with shaping.

Shaping & Rising: Cut the dough into 2 pieces, shape to fit two lightly greased $4^{1}/_{2}$ x $8^{1}/_{2}$-inch bread pans. Cover and allow the dough to rise for 45 minutes to an hour.

Baking: Place the loaves in a cold oven, set the temperature to 400°F for 15 minutes and then down to 350°F for another 20 to 30 minutes. The shorter baking time will produce a softer loaf, the longer one a loaf that is firmer and dryer with a more defined crust. Turn out and cool.

Brinna's postscript: "Our granddaughter, Hillary, and Scott and Ann's daughter, Emily, are both now three years old. Hillary is making her own tiny loaves of bread which she calls 'Matassa loaves' after her imaginary friend who is 'very small.' And Emily, not very long ago, surprised all of us at the office with a 'Cake-Pan' Cake which she'd mixed together all 'byself'!"

KOCHEN COQ'S
LIGURIAN OLIVE BRAID

This bread was developed by Robin Voight who runs a fledgling baking business in Greenwich, Connecticut, called Kochen Coq, Inc. Robin's company makes "breads by hand" which are exciting enough to be in demand not only in Connecticut, but also in New York City and as far away as the nation's capital. Robin is a King Arthur niece so is naturally imbued with the King Arthur tradition. We are very pleased that she has graciously agreed to share with us Kochen Coq's "heretofore secret recipe for Ligurian Olive Braid." For those of you who love olives, this bread is ambrosia.

Liguria, whose capital is Genoa, is located on the northwestern coast of Italy. This region grows some of the finest olives in the world. One of its oldest families produces olive "pestos" from both black and green olives. Olive pesto is a combination of olives (either black or green), extra virgin olive oil, fresh lemon juice, wine vinegar, salt, sugar and herbs. You can find olive pestos in the specialty section of many supermarkets.

This recipe will make 4 small loaves, 3 larger loaves, or one giant wreath. If you make small loaves, you can freeze at least 3 of them to wait for an appropriate occasion. Each slice of this bread has its own individual configuration of colors. Robin says, "It tastes wonderful sliced thin, brushed with garlic and herb olive oil and toasted until crispy."

Green Olive Pesto Dough

This first dough you make with green olive "pesto."

1 cup warm water
3³/₄ cups (approximately) King Arthur Unbleached All-Purpose Flour
1 tablespoon or packet active dry yeast
2 tablespoons extra virgin olive oil
¹/₂ cup olive pesto
1 teaspoon salt

Mixing: Pour the warm water into a mixing bowl. Stir in (as well as you can) 1 cup of flour and the yeast. Let this sit until the yeast has dissolved and the whole mixture has expanded.

Stir in the olive oil, pesto and salt. Add the balance of the flour gradually until it begins to pull away from the sides of the bowl as you stir it with a spoon.

Kneading & Rising: Turn the dough out onto a lightly floured board and knead for three or four minutes or until it becomes cohesive.

Give the dough a rest while you clean out and grease your bowl. When you return to the dough it will be more pliable and "together." Continue kneading until it's soft, smooth and elastic.

Put the dough in a lightly greased bowl, turning it to grease the top. Cover and put aside to let it double in bulk.

Black Olive Pesto Dough

Make this second dough just as you did the first but use black olive pesto rather than the green. Put this aside to rise while you make the third dough.

Olive Oil Dough

This dough you make only once.

1¹/₄ cups warm water
4 cups King Arthur Unbleached All-Purpose Flour
1 tablespoon or packet active dry yeast
1 tablespoon butter
¹/₄ cup extra virgin olive oil
1 teaspoon salt
wash made of 1 egg white beaten with 1 teaspoon water
kosher or pretzel salt (to sprinkle on top)

Mixing: Pour the warm water in a mixing bowl. Stir in as well as you can 1 cup of flour and the yeast. Let this sit until the yeast has dissolved and the whole mixture has expanded. Stir in the butter, olive oil and salt. Add the balance of the flour gradually until it begins to pull away from the sides of the bowl as you stir it with a spoon.

Kneading & Rising: Follow the same directions as for the pesto doughs.

Catching Up: You may have to knock down the first two doughs and let them begin to rise a second time in order to give the third dough enough time for a complete rise.

Braiding & Rising: After all the doughs have doubled at least once, divide each into four equal-sized pieces. Roll each of the pieces into a rope about 15 inches long.

Robin braids her breads from the middle to the end. Take three strands of dough, one of each color, and lay them across each other at their midpoints so they look like a 6-pointed star.

Starting with the strand on the bottom, weave each side alternately over the center strand until you get to the end. Pinch the ends together.

Repeat with the other strands until you have 4 loaves. (If you want to divide this dough differently, you can make 3 larger loaves or even 1 huge wreath.)

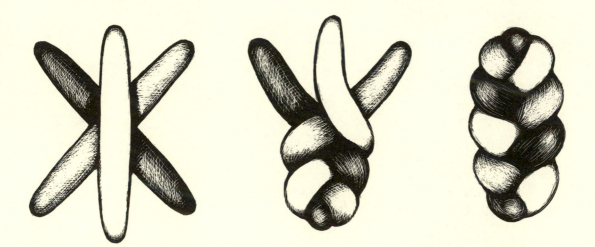

Place the loaves on a lightly greased baking sheet allowing at least three inches between them for expansion. Cover with a damp towel and let them rise for 1 to 1 1/2 hours.

Baking: Fifteen minutes before you want to bake the loaves, preheat your oven to 425°F. Brush the braids with the wash and sprinkle kosher salt on the white part of the braid.

Bake for 15 minutes at 425°F. Turn the oven down to 375°F and bake for a further 20 to 25 minutes. (If you're baking larger loaves, after 20 minutes at 375°F, turn the heat down once more to 350°F and bake a further 10 to 15 minutes depending on size.)

The braids are done when they are golden brown and sound hollow when thumped on the bottom. Cool on a rack. When they are thoroughly cool, seal the ones you want to freeze in airtight plastic bags.

Betsy Oppenneer's Sesame Cheddar Bread

This bread comes to us from Betsy Oppenneer whose love of bread baking has taken her all over the world, both to learn and to teach.

This particular recipe is from a collection called Betsy's Breads *which is available through King Arthur Flour. About this bread she says, "Without a doubt this is one of my family's favorites. By toasting the sesame seeds you intensify their flavor which goes beautifully with the flavor of sharp Cheddar. The cheese is added in two stages so that you have a cheese dough plus large shreds of cheese marbled throughout. It's braided so it can be pulled apart to release its heavenly aroma to the fullest."*

2 cups warm water
¼ cup sugar
2 tablespoons or packets active dry yeast
6 cups King Arthur Unbleached All-Purpose Flour
2 teaspoons salt
2 eggs, slightly beaten
2 tablespoons butter, softened
½ cup sesame seeds, toasted
3 cups shredded sharp Cheddar cheese

To toast sesame seeds, put them in a small saucepan over medium heat. Cook, stirring occasionally, until the seeds turn a golden color, about 5 to 7 minutes. Cool before adding them to the dough.

Mixing: Dissolve the sugar and yeast in the water in that order. Stir in 2 cups of flour and then the salt. Add the eggs, butter, sesame seeds and 2 cups of the cheese. Beat this mixture vigorously for 2 minutes. Gradually add the remaining flour until you have a dough stiff enough to knead.

Kneading & Rising: Turn the dough out of the bowl onto a flour-sprinkled kneading surface and knead until the dough is smooth and elastic.

Put the dough into a greased bowl, turn once to grease the top surface, cover with a damp towel and let rise until doubled, 1 to 1½ hours.

Marbling the Cheese into the Dough: Turn the dough out onto your kneading surface which you've dusted with flour. Flatten it with the heels of your hands until it's about a 15-inch square. Sprinkle with the remaining cheese, roll the dough up and knead a few times so the cheese is marbled throughout the dough. Cover with a damp towel and let rest for 5 minutes.

Braiding & Rising: Divide the dough into thirds. Roll each third into a rope about 18 inches long. Lay the ropes side by side on a lightly greased, 10 x 14-inch baking sheet. Braid according to Robin's directions on page 156. Cover and let rise until doubled, about 45 minutes.

Baking: About 15 minutes before you want to bake your bread, preheat your oven to 375°F. Bake for 35 to 45 minutes.

SHAPING VARIATIONS

Other Braids: If you are feeling ambitious, divide your dough into quarters, to make a four-stranded braid (page 210) or sixths, to make a six-stranded braid (page 212).

Pan Loaves: Divide the dough into 2 pieces. Shape and place in two lightly greased, 4½ x 8½-inch bread pans. Bake for 30 to 35 minutes.

Dinner Rolls: Divide the dough into 36 pieces, shape into balls and place in well-greased muffin tins. Bake at 400°F for 15 to 20 minutes.

• ROLLS & SMALL BREADS •

With a little more deft manipulating, your Hearth Bread dough can become a whole spectrum of small breads.

DINNER & OTHER INTERESTING ROLLS

There are countless ways you can vary both the basic dough and the way you shape it to make rolls in all sizes, shapes and flavors. Whatever your inspiration is, homemade rolls can turn a humdrum meal into an elegant dinner and a dinner into a banquet.

KING ARTHUR FLOUR'S
BASIC DINNER ROLLS

We start with the basic Hearth Bread dough, but see page 162 for ingredients to substitute and/or add.

Making the Dough: Make up a recipe of Hearth Bread dough which you'll find on page 114.

Rising Twice: Allow your dough to rise, preferably twice, before you shape it. This creates a finer grain which will make a "refined" roll. After it's risen, knock it down, turn it out on a floured kneading surface and knead out any stray bubbles.

Shaping: These shapes are traditional ones, but don't let tradition stop you.

• **Simple Round Rolls:** Flour your hands and break off Ping-Pong ball–sized pieces of dough. Form these into balls and place them on a greased baking sheet.

• **Cloverleaf Rolls:** Make large, marble-sized pieces of dough into balls, and place three in each cup of a greased muffin tin.

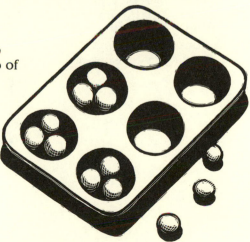

• **Parker House Rolls:** Roll out the dough until it's about ¼ inch thick, making sure your rolling surface and pin are well floured. Cut into 2½-inch squares and brush with melted butter.

Separate the squares and ease them into a rounded shape with your fingers. Crease the piece of dough just off center with the back of a knife or ruler. Fold the larger half over the smaller half, and place, barely touching, on a greased cookie sheet.

• **Crescent Rolls:** Roll the dough into a circle ⅛ inch thick. Brush the entire surface with melted butter and cut into 8 pie-shaped wedges.

(If you feel like being adventurous, sprinkle on some chopped chives, grated cheese, your favorite herbs, strawberry jam or some cinnamon sugar, making sure you leave about ½ inch around the outside edges to keep the filling mostly on the inside.)

Start at the outside of the circle and roll up the dough toward the tip of the wedge. Pinch the tip tightly to the layer of dough just inside it, to seal. Place on a greased cookie sheet with the tip on the bottom. Bend the ends away from the tip to make the rolls crescent shaped.

• **Fan-Shaped Roll:** Take ½ of your Hearth Bread dough and roll it out until it's a very thin rectangle, about 10 x 22 inches. Brush the dough with melted butter. The tips of your fingers will do this nicely if you don't have a pastry or goose feather brush.

Using your dough scraper or a knife, and a ruler (or just your intuition), cut the dough into 1½ x 2-inch pieces (in fifths the long way and in fourteenths the short way).

To shape the rolls, take 5 or 6 pieces and lay them on top of each other. Place the short end in the bottom of a muffin cup. (Repeat with the rest of your dough.)

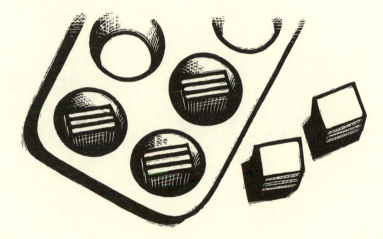

As these rise and bake, they will "fan out" to make layered and buttery dinner rolls.

Rising & Baking: You have a several choices here. The longer rising period will make much lighter rolls but, if you're in a hurry, the short resting period does pretty well.

• **Partial Rise:** Give your shaped rolls a short, 15-minute rest period covered with a damp cloth. Place them in a COLD oven, turn the heat to 400°F and bake for 20 to 25 minutes. For a crisper crust allow the rolls to remain in the oven for 5 minutes after you've turned the oven off.

• **Full Rise:** Let the formed dough rise for an hour. Fifteen minutes before you want to bake your rolls, preheat your oven to 400°F. Bake the rolls 15 to 20 minutes. For a crisper crust allow the rolls to remain in the oven for 5 minutes after you've turned the oven off.

Freezing: Rolls (and other small breads) can be frozen before or after they are shaped or baked. (See page 122.)

> • **Shaped Rolls:** To freeze dough, shape the rolls. Cover the pan lightly with plastic wrap and freeze until firm. Once they're frozen, remove them from the pan, put them in plastic bags and seal tightly.
>
> To bake, put the frozen rolls back in (or on) their pans, cover with a damp cloth and let them thaw and rise for about $1/2$ hour. Bake (or cook) according to the specific recipe directions.
>
> • **Brown & Serve Rolls:** To put a little labor in the freezer, let your shaped dough either rest or rise as above. Then bake any of these rolls for 15 minutes at 325°F. Remove them from the oven before they start to brown. Let them cool thoroughly before putting them in an airtight plastic bag and freezing.
>
> When you want rolls for dinner, preheat your oven to 350°F and pop the frozen, partially baked rolls in the oven leaving plenty of space between them. Bake for 15 to 20 minutes or until they are hot and golden brown.
>
> • **Baked Rolls:** To freeze finished rolls, bake and cool them thoroughly and then store them in your freezer in an airtight plastic bag.

INGREDIENT VARIATIONS

Here are some ways to substitute or add ingredients to make rolls that are truly your own.

> • Substitute milk for the water.
>
> • Substitute an extra-large egg for $1/4$ cup liquid; it will add richness and color.
>
> • Add 3 cups of grated Cheddar cheese to the dough, knead it in thoroughly. (You'll need to bake the rolls for an extra 5 minutes.)
>
> • Add $3/4$ cup chopped chives, scallions or onions to the dough.
>
> • Add any or a combination of the following: 1 to 2 tablespoons dried dill weed or seed, savory, marjoram, caraway, oregano, thyme or basil.
>
> • Or make rolls out of any of the doughs you've made into large loaves: Anadama, Oatmeal, Rye, Sesame Cheddar, etc. (Conversely, you can make large loaves out of any of these variations or some rolls and a single loaf.)

No-Knead Dinner Rolls

These rolls are almost as easy to make as muffins. Although they take more time, they take somewhat less time than traditionally kneaded rolls. Their flavor is a bit sweeter than our Hearth Bread rolls and their texture, like other no-knead breads, is coarser and just waiting for a bit of butter.

This recipe is a bit smaller than our Hearth Bread recipe, 1½ cups of liquid (1 cup water, 1 egg and ¼ cup vegetable oil) to 3 cups of flour, but for a no-knead recipe the ratio is still what it should be, 1 part liquid to 2 parts flour.

> 1 cup warm water
> 4 tablespoons sugar
> 1 tablespoon or packet active dry yeast
> 1 egg, beaten
> ¼ cup (4 tablespoons) vegetable oil
> 3 cups King Arthur Unbleached All-Purpose Flour
> 1 teaspoon salt

Pour the water into a mixing bowl. Add and dissolve the sugar and yeast. Beat in the egg and the vegetable oil.

Add the flour and salt. With a large spoon, beat this spongy dough until it is elastic and smooth. Cover it with a damp towel or plastic wrap and put it somewhere warm to rise for 45 minutes to 1 hour.

Drop the dough into a greased muffin tin, filling each cup ½ full. There should be enough dough to fill 12 large or 18 medium cups.

Cover it loosely with plastic wrap (which you've greased so the dough won't stick to it if it comes in contact with it). Let this dough rise again, until almost doubled, 30 to 45 minutes.

Fifteen minutes before you want to bake your rolls, preheat the oven to 400°F.

Bake the rolls for 18 to 20 minutes or until they are golden brown. When done, remove them from the muffin tin and cool.

HARD ROLLS

These hard rolls, with a crackling crust and a soft, moist interior, are best eaten fresh and hot from the oven.

1 recipe Hearth Bread as "French Bread" dough (page 141)

Making the Dough: Make up your dough as described on page 141 and allow it to rise twice. Turn the dough out onto a floured board, knead out any stray bubbles and let the dough rest for 5 minutes.

Shaping: Take Ping-Pong ball–sized pieces of dough and shape them into round rolls. Place each into a greased muffin tin, cover them with a damp cloth and let them rise for 1 to 1½ hours, in a cool place.

Baking: Fifteen minutes before you want to bake your rolls, preheat your oven to a hot 450°F. Just before the rolls are ready to go in, slash the tops, brush with cold water and pop them in. After 2 minutes, brush them with cold water again. Repeat this 2 more times at 2-minute intervals and finish baking them for a total of 20 to 25 minutes. (See page 120 for other steaming options.)

At the end of the baking period, turn the oven off, remove the rolls from the muffin tin, place them directly on the oven rack and let them sit in the oven with the door closed for another 5 minutes or longer.

RICH & TENDER DINNER ROLLS

Here's a way to alter your Hearth Bread dough to make softer, richer rolls.

1½ cups warm water
3 to 4 tablespoons sugar
1 tablespoon or packet active dry yeast
¼ cup vegetable oil or butter
1 large egg
½ to 1 cup King Arthur Stone Ground Whole Wheat Flour
1 tablespoon salt
½ cup non-fat dry milk (optional)
4½ to 5 cups King Arthur Unbleached All-Purpose Flour

Follow the directions for making up the Hearth Bread dough (page 114), beating in the butter and egg after you've activated the yeast. Add the salt and dry milk after you mix in the whole wheat flour. To make these rolls softer, it's best to use the lesser amount of flour.

Shape and bake them according to the directions which start on page 159.

REFRIGERATOR ROLLS

Refrigerator rolls have been around for a long time and for some pretty good reasons. The advantage of making refrigerator rolls is that, with one initial investment of time, you can have enough dough on hand to make rolls every night for about a week. Another advantage is that the longer and slower a dough has to mature, the better flavor it has.

The dough for these rolls is about the same as the dough for the preceding Rich & Tender Dinner Rolls. Dough made with water should keep about a week in the refrigerator; dough made with milk is richer but will not keep as long. If you have a large family, double the recipe.

1 1/2 cups warm water
1/4 cup white or brown sugar (less or more as desired)
1 1/2 tablespoons or 2 packets active dry yeast
1/4 cup vegetable oil (no cholesterol and mostly unsaturated fat) or
      softened butter (cholesterol and saturated fat, but wonderful
      flavor, one of those trade-offs we have to make)
1 egg, which you can beat into the liquid ingredients
1/2 cup dry milk (optional, see note above)
2 cups King Arthur Stone Ground Whole Wheat Flour
1 tablespoon salt (or less if preferred)
3 1/2 to 4 cups King Arthur Unbleached All-Purpose Flour

Mixing & Chilling: Pour water into a mixing bowl. Add and dissolve 1 tablespoon of the sugar and the yeast. When this mixture is bubbly, add the balance of the sugar, the oil or butter, egg and dry milk. Beat this mixture with an egg beater or whisk. Stir in the whole wheat flour and then the salt. Stir in the remaining flour and mix as well as you can. Cover this soft dough with plastic wrap and chill it in the refrigerator for at least 2 hours.

Shaping: After the 2-hour chilling period, the dough has relaxed and begun to develop. Now you can remove whatever portion you like to make rolls. The reason that rolls work so successfully this way is that when you handle such small amounts of dough, they return to room temperature quickly and are ready to bake anywhere from 1/2 hour to 1 1/2 hours after you shape them.

You can shape these rolls any way you wish. Check shape variations under the Basic Dinner Roll recipe (page 159). By shaping them differently each time you can offer something unique with each meal.

Rising & Baking: Rise and bake as for Basic Dinner Rolls (page 161), but for either method, allow an additional 15 minutes for the dough to warm to room temperature.

SANDWICH ROLLS

By using the same Hearth Bread dough, you can make outstanding rolls for hamburgers, hot dogs, submarine sandwiches, or even French Bread Pizza.

1 recipe Hearth Bread dough, or one of the variations (page 114)
1 egg, beaten with 1 tablespoon of water (optional)
poppy or sesame seeds, or minced onion (optional, for top)

Making the Dough: Follow the recipe for Hearth Bread to the point where you've punched the dough down and kneaded out any stray bubbles. Let the dough rest for 5 to 10 minutes to relax the gluten.

Shaping: With a rolling pin, roll out the dough to about ³/₄ inch in thickness. With a large cookie cutter, or a clean tin can (large tuna-sized works well) with a hole punched in the opposite side to relieve pressure, cut out large round rolls. You can either reroll the dough or use the remainder of the dough for hot dog rolls. To make those, form short, fat "snakes," about ¹/₂ to ³/₄ inch in diameter and 5 to 6 inches long.

Place all of these rolls on a greased cookie sheet and let them rest for at least 20 minutes and up to 1 hour if you have time.

Baking: While they're resting, preheat your oven to 475°F. Just before you pop them in, brush them with cold water or egg beaten with a teaspoon or so of water and sprinkle on poppy or sesame seeds.

Bake for 15 minutes. For a crunchier crust, turn the oven off and let the rolls remain inside with the door closed for an additional 5 minutes.

Storing: When the rolls are done, cool them on a rack and either split them to use right away, or store them in an airtight plastic bag in your freezer.

HOT SUBMARINE SANDWICHES

The Sands' son-in-law, Christopher Smith, has devised a sandwich that's as big a hit with the big-appetite crowd as pizza.

After your dough has risen once, divide it into 4 to 6 pieces. Shape these into small, elongated loaves and let rise, covered, on a cookie sheet, for 20 minutes (if you can't wait) to an hour (if you can). Bake as above.

While the dough rises, get out all the things you want to put in your sandwiches: cheese, onion, lettuce, sliced meats, pickles, mustard, mayonnaise, etc. After the tiny loaves are done, wait 2 minutes (if you can), slice them lengthwise (gently) with a serrated knife and build the sandwiches while the bread is hot.

SMALL BREADS THAT AREN'T ROLLS

ENGLISH MUFFINS

To make English Muffins, we make another variation of our basic Hearth Bread dough and cook it on a griddle or skillet instead of in the oven. (For Sourdough English Muffins, see page 538.)

   1/4 cup warm water
   1 tablespoon sugar
   1 tablespoon or packet active dry yeast
   1 3/4 cups buttermilk, sour milk or yogurt, slightly warmed
   6 cups King Arthur Unbleached All-Purpose Flour
   (cornmeal to sprinkle on baking sheet and griddle)

Mixing, Kneading & Rising: Since yeast is reluctant to dissolve in milk, dissolve it in the small amount of water into which you put the sugar. Once it's bubbly and active, add the balance of the liquid.

Continue making the dough as for Hearth Bread (page 115).

Shaping: After the dough has doubled in bulk, knock it down, turn it out onto your floured board, knead out any bubbles, and let it rest for 5 minutes. This rest relaxes the gluten so you can more easily roll it out.

Using a flour-dusted rolling pin, roll out the dough until it is 1/4 to 1/2 inch thick. With a large cookie cutter (a large tuna-sized can, cleaned and with both ends removed, works well), cut out the muffins and place them on a baking sheet sprinkled with cornmeal.

Let these rest for about 1/2 hour but don't be too worried about exact timing.

Cooking: Heat your skillet to very low, grease it lightly with butter and gently place 3 or 4 muffins on it, cornmeal side down, allowing space for them to expand.

Cook for about 10 minutes, turn them over and cook 10 minutes more.

Splitting: Cool the finished muffins on a rack. When you're ready to eat them, split them with a fork and toast. When you use a fork rather than a knife you create the shaggy surface which so effectively traps butter and jam.

CRUMPETS

The crumpet is a cakelet or muffin that conjures up visions of English teas and open fires. Like the English muffin, it is leavened with yeast and cooked in a skillet or griddle on top of the stove. But rather than being made from a dough stiff enough to roll out, a crumpet is made from a batter that is poured into a metal ring that is set on the griddle. As the batter cooks, it rises up in the ring rather than out like a pancake. But, like the English muffin, the crumpet develops holes for butter and jam.

Like our batter breads (whose flour-to-liquid ratio is almost the same), crumpets are easier to make than almost anything else made with yeast. If you like English muffins, butter and jam, you'll like crumpets.

> 2 cups warm water
> 2 cups King Arthur Unbleached All-Purpose Flour
> 1 tablespoon or packet active dry yeast
> 1 teaspoon salt

Mixing & Rising: Pour the water in a mixing bowl. Blend in 1 cup of the flour and the yeast. Allow this mixture to grow and develop for 10 to 15 minutes before you add the balance of flour and the salt.

Mix this batter thoroughly, cover with a damp towel or plastic wrap, and let rise for 1 to 2 hours.

Shaping: After the batter has doubled in size, stir it down and let it rest for 5 minutes while you heat up your griddle.

In England you can buy rings to cook crumpets in, but we can approximate them by using large tuna-sized cans with the tops and bottoms cut out. Clean them thoroughly and grease with butter.

Cooking: Lightly grease and then heat your griddle over medium low heat. Place as many rings on it as you have room for. Fill each ring with about 1/4 inch of batter. (The batter should be thin enough so that holes develop.)

Cook until the batter is beginning to dry on top and brown on the bottom, about 6 to 7 minutes. Remove the rings, flip the crumpets and finish cooking. This will take 1 to 2 minutes.

It's traditional to toast crumpets on a brass fork over an open fire, but in lieu of that, a toaster will do.

Bread Sticks

Bread sticks, especially ones seasoned with herbs rather than salt, are a great low-fat, carbohydrate-rich snack, so don't wait for company to have some around. Any of the doughs for rolls can be made into bread sticks. This recipe is one which, again, is closely related to our versatile Hearth Bread dough.

    2 cups warm water
    1 tablespoon sugar
    1 tablespoon or packet active dry yeast
    1 tablespoon salt
    2 tablespoons olive oil or butter, barely melted (optional)
    2 egg whites, beaten until stiff
    1 cup King Arthur Stone Ground Whole Wheat Flour
    5 to 5½ cups King Arthur Unbleached All-Purpose Flour
    1 egg beaten with 2 teaspoons water (optional, for wash)
    pretzel salt, sesame seeds, poppy seeds, herb mixtures (optional, to
           sprinkle on top)

Mixing: Pour the water into a large mixing bowl. Add and dissolve the sugar and yeast. Mix in the olive oil or butter and then the beaten egg whites.

Add the whole wheat flour and then the salt. Stir in the balance of the flour until the dough begins to pull away from the sides of the bowl.

Kneading: Turn out onto well-floured board and knead until the dough is smooth and springy. Divide the dough in half and give it a 10-minute rest to relax the gluten. (You can use this dough to make one large loaf of bread and one batch of bread sticks or you can make 2 batches of bread sticks, one to eat and one to freeze.)

Shaping: Cut one half of the dough into 16 equal pieces. Roll each piece into a rope, 18 inches long. If you want long bread sticks, leave them as they are or cut them in halves or thirds for a variety of lengths. If you make them a bit fatter than usual, they'll be chewy as well as crunchy. Repeat with the remaining dough.

Topping & Baking: Place these on lightly greased baking sheets, cover and let rest for 15 to 20 minutes while you preheat your oven to 450°F.

For simple bread sticks, you can brush the tops with cold water just before they go in the oven and bake as is. Or brush them with the egg wash and sprinkle on pretzel salt or whatever inspires you. There are a variety of herb and seed mixtures that are excellent salt substitutes.

Bake for 12 to 15 minutes.

BAGELS

It's amazing how many different ways you can cook our Hearth Bread dough. This time we're going to boil it first and then bake it.

>   1 recipe Hearth Bread dough (page 114) or a variation
>   1 egg beaten with 2 teaspoons water
>   sesame seeds, poppy seeds or other topping

First: Make up a recipe of the Hearth Bread dough and allow it to double in bulk.

Shaping: After the first rising, punch down the dough and, on a well-floured board, with a well-floured rolling pin, roll it out to about ¹/₂ inch in thickness. There are several ways to form bagels. Experiment and pick whatever method suits your fancy.

> • Cut strips about ³/₄ inch wide by 6 or 7 inches long. Pinch the two ends together, moistening the ends with water to help them stick. Unless you seal them well, they tend to come apart as you cook them.

> • Cut them out with large and small cookie cutters. If you don't have the appropriate sizes, small coffee or large tuna sized cans will work for the outside and a small juice or other can (even a film cannister with a hole punched in the end to relieve pressure) will work for the inside.

> • Take a piece of dough slightly larger than a golf ball, poke a hole through it with your finger, enlarge it a bit, and twirl the dough around your finger on your floured surface until the hole is an inch or so in diameter.

Boiling: Let the formed bagels rest for 15 minutes or longer while you preheat your oven to 450°F.

After 10 minutes or so, begin heating a large saucepan containing about 3 inches of water. Add a tablespoon of sugar if you want a shiny shell or add a tablespoon of salt if you want a slightly salty surface.

Just before the bagels are ready to cook, bring the water to a full boil and then turn it down so it's still bubbling gently but not rolling. This keeps the action of the boil from deflating the bagel dough.

Carefully slip the bagels into the water making sure you give them enough room to expand. Keep the water at a simmer.

After 1 minute, flip them over and continue cooking them 3 more minutes. While the bagels are simmering, grease a baking sheet.

Baking: At the end of 3 minutes, lift the bagels carefully out of the water with a slotted spatula or spoon and place them on the greased cookie sheet very gently to keep them from deflating.

Slide them into the oven and bake them for 10 minutes. At this point you can safely brush them with the egg wash and sprinkle sesame or poppy seeds on them.

Bake the bagels 8 to 10 minutes more (18 to 20 minutes altogether), turning them over 4 to 5 minutes before they're done. Cool them on a wire rack.

Serving: Unlike English muffins, bagels are best split carefully with a knife, or just break them apart.

VARIATIONS

Egg Bagels: For a classic and delicious bagel, make up a batch of Hearth Bread Dough, using for the 2 cups of liquid 2 extra large eggs (equals 1/2 cup liquid) and 1 1/2 cups water in which you've boiled potatoes.

Any Bread Dough Bagels: Use any yeasted bread dough flavored any way you want for a whole variety of bagels. Sprinkle on chopped onion or garlic, or caraway or dill seeds, or whatever you want to bring out or add to the flavor of the dough.

"Bagins": These are just bagels with the holes left in. The Sands' son, Davis, devised this English muffin/bagel hybrid to maximize the surface that cream cheese can be spread on.

Li-Xi's
Steamed Dumplings

This time we're going to take the dough and steam it. This recipe is a very special one which comes to us from Li-Xi (Lee Shee), a young man whose home is in the great Chinese mainland city of Shanghai. He is here in the United States doing graduate study in radiobiological cancer research, to bring new techniques in cancer treatment to China.

Li-Xi loves to cook. It is one of the ways in which he communicates his enthusiasm for life, which is enormous and infectious. The energy and the time he devotes to preparing these steamed buns is quite incredible. While our interpretation of his recipe may not be quite authentic, we can come fairly close.

These dumplings, or buns, are best cooked in a Chinese bamboo steamer, although it's possible to rig up a makeshift steamer with a large kettle and something on which to place the buns to keep them above the water in the bottom. You might try a small, lightly greased cake rack or a piece of screening set on three empty tin cans (with both lids removed).

1 ½ cups of water hot from the tap
1 teaspoon sugar
1 tablespoon or packet active dry yeast
1 teaspoon salt
3 ½ to 4 cups King Arthur Unbleached All-Purpose Flour

Mixing: Pour the water into a mixing bowl and dissolve in it the sugar and then the yeast. When the yeast mixture has begun to grow and is frothy, add the salt and 3 ½ cups of flour. Mix this together thoroughly in the bowl until it pulls away from the sides.

Kneading & Rising: Turn the dough, which will be quite soft, onto a lightly floured surface and knead it until smooth and elastic. Clean out and grease the bowl and return the dough to rise for 1 to 1 ½ hours.

Shaping & Rising: When the dough has doubled in bulk, knock it down, turn it out onto a floured kneading surface and break off large marble-sized pieces of dough. Shape these into small balls and place them on the table, covered, to rise for about 20 minutes.

Steaming: Bring water to a boil in the bottom of your steamer, place the buns on the rack over the water, cover, and when the water has come to a boil again, turn the heat down and let the buns steam for about 30 minutes.

These are delicious when served with a Chinese meal, especially when you use them to soak up all those delicious juices.

FILLED DUMPLINGS

Savory Dumplings: The fillings for these dumplings can be anything you wish but Li-Xi's was a simple dice of raw pork or chicken. They are very tasty as is, but added to a clear soup they are exquisite.

    1 recipe Li-Xi's Steamed Dumpling dough
    1 to 1 1/2 pounds pork or chicken, diced
    2 large eggs
    3/4 teaspoon monosodium glutamate (optional)
    2 tablespoons soy sauce
    1 teaspoon salt
    1/4 cup peanut oil
    2 tablespoons minced fresh ginger
    "perhaps a little wine to taste"

Monosodium glutamate is a salt used traditionally in Chinese cooking as a flavor intensifier. Although the Food and Drug Administration considers it to be GRAS, or "generally regarded as safe," some people experience a reaction to it. If there is any question, this ingredient may be left out.

Make up the dough the same way you did above. Again, break off large marble-sized pieces of dough but this time shape them into a round flat cake with your hand.

Blend the filling ingredients together. Dab a small spoonful in the middle and fold the cake over it, like a turnover, pinching the edges together firmly.

These should be steamed a bit longer, 35 to 40 minutes, to make sure the meat is thoroughly cooked.

Sweet Dumplings: By using diced apple sprinkled with cinnamon and sugar for the fillings, Li-Xi has made dessert dumplings which are lovely with a cup of Chinese green tea. Shape as for the Savory Dumplings but steam for only 30 minutes. You might give them a sprinkling of cinnamon sugar after they come out of the steamer.

PITA BREAD

Flat breads are probably the oldest form of bread in the world and not much changed from their unleavened ancestors. These yeasted varieties of flat bread come from around the Mediterranean which is where leavening with yeast originally began. It was probably a dough for breads just like these that was the first to "catch" a wild yeast and rise. Ancient though flat breads may be, they continue to be appealing, perhaps because of their classic simplicity.

1 recipe Hearth Bread dough (page 114)

Mixing & Rising: Make up your dough and allow it to rise once.

Shaping: Knock the dough down and divide it into 8 pieces. Flatten and roll each piece into a circle about 6 inches in diameter and $1/8$ inch thick. Let them rest occasionally to relax the dough.

Sprinkle baking sheets with cornmeal, and place two circles on each. Let the dough circles rest here for at least 15 minutes while you preheat your oven to 500°F.

Baking: When the pita circles have finished resting, place the baking sheet on the oven bottom or, if this is not possible, on the lowest rack. Close the oven door and keep it shut for 1 minute. Don't peek.

At the end of the minute, place the sheet on a rack higher in the oven and continue cooking anywhere from 3 to 7 minutes until the pitas have blown up into balloons and are lightly browned. Remove them from the oven and cool. The bread will deflate somewhat after cooling. Once they're thoroughly cool you can press more air out of them so they take up less storage room.

After experimenting with Hearth Bread dough, we tried an egg-rich bagel dough. Bagel dough makes lovely pitas. With that discovery, we started experimenting in earnest.

PITA BREAD WITH HERBS

1 recipe Hearth Bread dough (with the following changes)
$1/4$ cup olive oil
2 tablespoons fresh basil (or 2 teaspoons dried)
2 tablespoons fresh oregano (or 2 teaspoons dried)

Substitute $1/4$ cup of olive oil for an equal amount of the liquid in the basic recipe. Blend the herbs in after you've added 2 cups of flour.

Follow the pita bread directions above for shaping and baking. (This might also make an interesting pizza dough.)

Pita Bread with Yogurt & Dill

This next variation involved a bit more daring in terms of the liquid ingredients. Although it is a variation on our basic Hearth Bread, we'll give you the whole thing, variations, additions and all. It, too, made successful pitas.

    1 cup warm water
    1 tablespoon sugar
    1 tablespoon or packet active dry yeast
    1 cup yogurt, plain
    2 cups King Arthur Stone Ground Whole Wheat Flour
    1 tablespoon salt
    2 tablespoons fresh dill weed (or seeds)
    4 cups King Arthur Unbleached All-Purpose Flour

Put the water into a mixing bowl and dissolve the sugar and yeast. When the yeast is working, blend in the yogurt, whole wheat flour and salt. Stir in the dill and add the remainder of the flour.

Knead and let this dough rise as your regular Hearth Bread dough. After it's doubled in bulk, knock it down and proceed with the directions for pita bread.

Pita Bread with Cheese

This variety was very heavy so was only 80% successful (a couple of the pitas didn't want to blow up so they were eaten flat; they tasted just as good).

    1 recipe Hearth Bread dough (page 114)
    3 cups grated Cheddar cheese
    3 tablespoons chopped chives

Add the cheese and chives to the dough after about half of the flour.

These heavier pitas needed to be baked a bit longer, but flavor-wise they were a great success.

To do your own experimenting, cut our basic Hearth Bread recipe in half, keep the liquid-to-flour ratio in mind, and let your creative impulses go. You'll soon be making pita breads that you'll never find in a store.

• A PIZZA PRIMER •

The format of a pizza is a wonderful thing, a lovely large circle of crispy, crunchy dough decorated with any number of toppings that taste good and are, for the most part, good for you. However, there's a war brewing in Naples over what constitutes a true pizza. Neapolitan purists contend that the only real pizza is the variety that has been served in Naples for the last hundred years: a crust made from a dough that has matured for at least half a day, a little olive oil, some chopped plum tomatoes, a sprinkle of grated mozzarella cheese with a touch of fresh basil and oregano, all baked to perfection in a wood-fired oven.

But these purists may be fighting a losing battle. The format of a pizza is so appealing, people can't help but embellish it with their latest inspirations. Like a successful life form, the pizza is evolving and changing. We hope, after you've tried some of the traditional as well as the more unorthodox versions, that you will help continue the pizza evolution (or revolution). Buon Appetito!

CLASSIC PIZZA

If you want to have fun, invite a group over to help make this pizza from scratch. All you do is make up some Hearth Bread Pizza Dough and provide enough toppings to inspire your guests. You can even ask them to bring their own secret ingredients. It's amazing what the word "pizza" conjures up.

Before you embark on this adventure, read through the recipes for both the Traditional and the Light Pizza dough variations because there are so many options for shaping, decorating and baking your creations.

HEARTH BREAD PIZZA

To begin we'll cover some basic information on building a more-or-less traditional pizza. This dough is simply a variation of our basic Hearth Bread dough. One batch will make 3 thin, or 2 thick, 12-inch shells. One pizza will serve 1 hungry adolescent or 2 people with average appetites.

TRADITIONAL PIZZA DOUGH

1 3/4 cups warm water
1 tablespoon sugar
1 packet or tablespoon active dry yeast
6 cups King Arthur Unbleached All-Purpose Flour 🌾
1/4 cup olive oil
1 tablespoon salt

Preparing the Dough: Pour the water into a mixing bowl and dissolve in it the sugar and the yeast. When the yeast is active, add your first cup of flour, then the oil and salt. Add another $4^{1}/_{2}$ cups of flour, mixing with a large spoon until the dough comes away from the sides of the bowl and holds together.

Kneading: Sprinkle the last $^{1}/_{2}$ cup of flour onto your kneading surface. Turn out the dough and knead until it begins to feel as if it really belongs together, adding only enough flour to keep it from sticking to the board or you. Let it rest while you clean and grease your bowl. Continue kneading the relaxed dough until it feels smooth and springy.

Rising: You have three options here.

> • **Full Rise:** Form the dough into a nice ball, place it in the greased bowl, turning it so the top is lightly greased also. Cover it and put it where it will be warm and cozy (no drafts). Let this rise until it is doubled (when you can poke your finger in it and the dough doesn't spring back at you).

> • **Slow Rise:** If you want to make up your dough ahead of time (a slow-rising dough has the best flavor), make it up, with about half the yeast, the morning of your gathering. Cover it with greased plastic wrap and put it in the refrigerator. It will rise happily all day. About 15 minutes after you take it out, it will be ready to roll out and decorate.

> • **No-Rise:** If this is a spur-of-the-moment party, just give your dough a 5- to 10-minute rest. It won't have quite the flavor or be as light as a fully risen dough, but it will still be "better than bought."

Preparing the Toppings: These toppings are only possibilities. They'll all make great pizza but if you think of something that's not here, add it to the list. You'll want to have them ready before you shape your dough.

> • pizza, spaghetti or marinara sauce for a red pizza
> • pesto for a green pizza
> • a blend of cheeses for a white pizza
> • oregano, basil, red pepper flakes
> • sliced or chopped onions, scallions, chives, peppers, mushrooms, olives, minced garlic
> • broccoli tops or asparagus tips, raw or steamed to the "tender but crunchy" stage
> • sliced or diced ham, pepperoni, salami, prosciutto, smoked turkey
> • anchovies, sardines, smoked oysters or clams or other fish
> • cooked and crumbled hamburger or sausage (hot or sweet)
> • capers, sun-dried tomatoes in olive oil, artichoke hearts, pineapple chunks (great with ham)
> • lots of grated cheese: mozzarella, Monterey Jack, Cheddar, provolone

Shaping the Dough: After the dough has risen (if you have time to let it), punch it down, turn it out onto a floured board and knead out any stray bubbles. Cut it into the number of pieces you need depending on whether you're a thick- or thin-crust devotee.

Flatten each piece with your hand and, with a rolling pin you've dusted with flour, roll out each piece like pie dough, from the center to the outside. If you don't have a rolling pin, use a wine bottle or pat and stretch it out right on the pan with your hands. If the dough isn't being cooperative, let it rest for 2 or 3 minutes to relax the gluten.

If you like a softer crust, lightly wipe your pan with olive or vegetable oil. If you like a dryer, crunchier crust, sprinkle it with cornmeal. If you don't have a pizza pan, a pie plate, cake pan, roasting pan or baking sheet with a lip will do just fine. Pizzas don't have to be round.

When the dough is about the size you want, slide it onto the prepared pan. Brush it lightly with olive oil to keep the topping from soaking in and making it soggy. You can eliminate this step if you want to avoid using any more fat.

Preheating your Oven: Again, you have some choices, depending on how quickly you want pizza on the table.

- **Before:** For added crispness, you can prebake your crust at 475°F for 10 to 12 minutes before you decorate it. If it puffs up while baking, just press the air out of it before adding toppings. This method works well but adds an extra step to the pizza-making process.

- **Now:** If you don't want to wait, preheat your oven to 475°F before you start decorating your dough. Bake your pizza right after you've decorated it. It won't be as light but, again, it will still be "better than bought."

- **Later:** For the lightest, crunchiest crust, this is the best choice. Let your pizza rise for 15 to 30 minutes after you've decorated it. Preheat your oven to 475°F for at least 15 minutes before you bake.

Decorating the Dough: Spread the pizza crust (baked or unbaked) with sauce, commercial or homemade. Add some additional herbs, etc., if you want.

Some people feel the grated cheese should go on before the toppings. Some feel it should cook down through the toppings. You can put it wherever you feel it will look and/or taste best.

Scatter on, or artistically arrange, any combination of toppings you desire. This is when creative juices really begin to flow and you can see how differently people express themselves.

The longer you let the pizza rest after decorating, the lighter and crunchier the crust will be.

Baking the Pizza: The best way to bake pizza is on a pizza stone or quarry tiles set on the lowest rack of your oven or on the oven bottom itself. This makes the crust crisp and brown. If you don't have either of these, place the pizza on the lowest rack of your oven to bake. Check it after 5 or 10 minutes of baking and lower the temperature to 450°F if it is browning too quickly.

If you've prebaked the shell, your pizza will only need 5 to 10 minutes. If not, bake it for 15 to 20 minutes (depending on thickness) or until the crust is golden brown.

After taking your masterpiece out of the oven, let it cool to solidify the cheese a bit. This also makes cutting easier and sometimes prevents burned tongues.

One of the nicest tools to come along is a pair of pizza shears, which not only makes neat, clean slices, but the wide, flat blades can even be used to serve your pizza.

LIGHT PIZZA DOUGH

Because pizza and its relatives are flat (they don't need to stand up), you can make them with a much lighter, or "slacker," dough. This produces a light, airy (and very crunchy when baked) structure. One recipe will make 2 medium-thick shells which are more easily pushed than rolled into shape right on the pizza pans.

> 1³/₄ cups warm water
> 1 tablespoon sugar
> 1 packet or tablespoon active dry yeast
> 5 cups King Arthur Unbleached All-Purpose Flour
> ¹/₄ cup olive oil
> 1 tablespoon salt

Preparing the Dough: Mix the ingredients as for the Traditional Pizza dough.

Kneading: This slack dough is kneadable if you keep your hands and kneading surface well floured. Use your bowl scraper to help you knead if the dough insists on sticking to your hands.

Rising, Shaping, Decorating & Baking: You will find directions on the preceding pages. Use whichever options fit your mood and time frame.

• PIZZA & CALZONE •

NEO-CLASSIC PIZZA

This collection of pizzas is definitely not traditional, but they might be in time. To make these, we've taken some fairly large liberties with our Hearth Bread-turned-Pizza dough, but if you look closely, you'll see it hiding underneath.

KING ARTHUR FLOUR'S REUBEN PIZZA

This pizza "nouvelle" appeared at a pizza party we had with our Board of Directors. It would certainly turn the hair of a Neapolitan purist white. Whether you choose to call it a pizza or not, it tastes good. For better or worse, we've named this culinary collision of countries and cultures King Arthur Flour's Reuben Pizza.

The Dough

> 2 cups warm water
> 2 tablespoons sugar
> 1 tablespoon or packet active dry yeast
> 2 cups medium rye flour or pumpernickel (coarse rye meal)
> 1 tablespoon salt
> 2 tablespoons olive or other vegetable oil (optional)
> 2 cups King Arthur Stone Ground Whole Wheat Flour
> 2 cups King Arthur Unbleached All-Purpose Flour

Rye flour does not contain gluten, that magic substance you find in wheat flour which enables a dough to rise. A dough made completely with rye flour will have great flavor but will be too flat, even for a flat bread. So to have the best of both worlds, we use a combination of rye and wheat. (For more information about rye flour, see page 143.)

Mixing: Pour the water into a large mixing bowl and dissolve the sugar and yeast in it.

Add the rye flour, salt, vegetable oil, whole wheat and unbleached flours, in that order. Stir, and turn out onto a floured surface as for the Hearth Bread.

Kneading & Rising: A rye flour dough will be "tacky," so when you knead this, keep your hands, and the surface you're kneading on, covered with a thin layer of flour.

As you knead, add only enough flour to keep the dough from sticking. When you finish kneading, place it in a bowl to rise until doubled.

The Topping

> Russian dressing laced with horseradish
> sliced corned beef
> sharp mustard
> chopped onion, scallions or chives
> sauerkraut that has been rinsed and squeezed fairly dry
> grated Swiss cheese
> capers (optional)

As in our other pizza recipes we're being purposely vague about amounts as each individual's taste is unique. Use your best judgment and if you have ingredients left over, turn to the Sourdough chapter and make a good sourdough rye bread for traditional Reuben sandwiches.

Shaping & Decorating: Knock the dough down, divide it into 3 pieces, roll out each to fit a 12-inch pizza pan.

Spread a thin layer of Russian dressing on the crust. Then layer on several slices of corned beef spread with a sharp mustard. Spread the mustard fairly liberally as it really adds some punch. Next, sprinkle on some chopped onion, scallions or chives. Arrange a layer of sauerkraut over this as thickly as you wish depending on how strongly you feel about sauerkraut. Finish it off with several handfuls of grated Swiss cheese. For a bit more flavor and color, sprinkle a few capers on top.

Baking: Let this rest for 15 to 30 minutes while you preheat your oven to 450°F. Bake for 15 to 20 minutes.

MEXICAN PIZZA

This pizza should warm your taste buds. Serve with bowls of salsa, sour cream and guacamole.

> 1 recipe Hearth Bread Pizza dough, Traditional (page 176) or
>   Light (page 179)
> taco sauce, plain or mixed with cooked and crumbled hamburger
> chopped onion
> chopped peppers, sweet and/or hot
> grated Monterey Jack cheese
> a sprinkling of crushed red pepper
> salsa, sour cream and guacamole

Shape, decorate and bake as described in the Pizza Primer (page 178). Serve with bowls of salsa, sour cream and guacamole.

CURRY PIZZA

With a fruit salad, this next pizza makes a great evening meal. It also makes an unorthodox breakfast which the Sands' departing son, Davy, found not only portable, but good enough to request a second piece of before the door slammed behind him.

The dough for this pizza, still related to our Hearth Bread, contains a couple of interesting ingredients, a little honey and some curry powder.

Dough

2 cups warm water
1 heaping tablespoon honey
1 tablespoon or packet active dry yeast
2 cups King Arthur Stone Ground Whole Wheat Flour
1 tablespoon salt
1 1/2 teaspoons curry powder
1/4 cup vegetable oil
4 to 4 1/2 cups King Arthur Unbleached All-Purpose Flour

Making the Dough: Pour the water into a large mixing bowl. Add and dissolve the honey and yeast. Stir in the whole wheat flour, salt, curry, vegetable oil, and then the unbleached flour.

Turn out onto a floured surface and knead until it's smooth and springy. Clean and grease your bowl, and put the dough in it to rise for about an hour.

Topping

2 cups grated Cheddar and/or other cheese
2 cups chopped black olives
2 cups chopped onion, scallions or chives
2 cups chopped mushrooms and/or eggplant
1 cup chopped artichoke hearts
1/2 cup sun-dried tomatoes, chopped
1/2 cup roasted peppers, chopped
1 (3-ounce) jar capers
1 teaspoon salt
1 teaspoon curry powder
1 tablespoon regular or white wine Worcestershire sauce
1 cup mayonnaise

Making the Topping: While the dough rises in a warm spot, you can prepare the topping. It isn't necessary to use all of the listed ingredients, but the more the merrier. You can probably think of some things to add yourself.

Blend all of the topping ingredients together in a large mixing bowl and set aside.

Shaping & Decorating: When the dough has doubled in bulk, knock it down, turn it out on your floured board and divide into 3 pieces. Roll each piece out to fit a 12-inch pizza pan, lightly oil the pan, and place the dough on it. Spread one third of the mixture on each circle of dough.

The longer this has to rise, the better it will be. Give it at least 15 minutes and try to hold out for 30. Fifteen minutes before you want to bake the pizza, preheat your oven to 450°F.

Baking: Bake for 15 to 20 minutes. If the pizza seems to be browning too quickly, turn the temperature down to 425°F for the final few minutes.

A Honey of a Heart-Healthy Pizza

This next pizza has a "heartwarming" story. The pizza itself won the "Quintessential Pizza Contest," sponsored by the Convention and Tourism Bureau of Greater Providence in the winter of 1989. Out of a field of one hundred fifty, five pizzas were chosen. All five finalists made their dough from scratch, and the flour that they used was King Arthur! (We discovered this bit of information through the grapevine as we had no connection with the contest in any way.) We subsequently made friends of the couple whose pizza prompted this story and who graciously agreed to share it with us.

Joe and Barbara Feeley of Cranston, Rhode Island, weren't even living in Rhode Island when they began making pizza in earnest. They were in California near a medical center where Joe had had a heart transplant. Barbara said, "During the four months that Joe was recuperating after his surgery, we had little money on hand but lots of time."

It was during these months that they began the attempt to recreate the pizza that Barbara's grandmother had imprinted her young life with. Since there were seven children in her family, pizza was a usual hearty, healthy lunchtime meal. As a little girl, Barbara learned to make dough by watching her grandmother Gulla, which left her with wonderful memories of baking and, intertwined with it, stories of the old country.

After the grandchildren had grown and had children of their own, Grandma Gulla traveled from house to house with her treasured pizza pans, blackened with use and age. During these visits she helped with the housework and baked pizza for the next generation. Barbara said, "We loved that single day a week that she would spend with us and the memories she created for my children, that wonderful smell of fresh pizza and the joy of the first bite!"

After Grandma Gulla died, Barbara's family tried to duplicate her pizza. But like so many intuitive cooks, she'd never measured anything. So Joe's recuperation time in California gave them the opportunity and time to recreate Grandma Gulla's original.

"While we were there," said Barbara, *"Joe really perfected the art of dough making; we have friends there who still talk of his pizza."* The pizza that actually won the contest is an inspiration of Joe's. The topping is vegetarian. It's high on flavor and nutrition, low on saturated fats, cholesterol and sodium, and "heart healthy" from anyone's point of view. The dough may seem to vary from the Hearth Bread dough but if you look closely, it's still there, divided in half and sporting honey as the sweetener.

The last six years have created new meaning in the lives of the Feeleys. That they are profoundly grateful for these years hardly need be said. The only thing they hope that all of us are aware of is that by just checking that little organ donor box on your license, you might help someone like Joe live out a healthy and creative life.

Dough

> 1 cup water, hot from the tap
> 2 tablespoons honey
> 1 tablespoon or packet active dry yeast
> 1/2 teaspoon salt
> 1 1/2 cups King Arthur Stone Ground Whole Wheat Flour
> 1 1/2 cups King Arthur Unbleached All-Purpose Flour (or try 3 cups King Arthur Stone Ground Whole Wheat Flour)

Making the Dough: Prepare the dough as you would for the Hearth Bread Pizza (page 176). Knead and let it rise until doubled in bulk. While the dough rises, make the topping.

Topping

> 2 to 3 cloves garlic, minced
> 1/4 to 1/3 cup olive oil
> 1 1/2 cups sliced fresh mushrooms
> 10 ounces spinach, steamed or frozen and squeezed free of excess water
> 4 ounces sliced black olives
> salt to taste
> 3 to 4 tablespoons grated Parmesan or Romano cheese
> shredded mozzarella or provolone

Preparing the Topping: Sauté the garlic in oil. Add the mushrooms and cook until just done. Add spinach to pan, with olives, salt (if desired), and the Parmesan or Romano cheese. Mix and taste for seasoning.

Decorating & Baking: Spread the mixture on the pizza dough. Sprinkle mozzarella or provolone on top.

Let your pizza rest for 15 to 20 minutes while you preheat your oven to 400°F. Bake for 15 to 20 minutes or until done.

PIZZA UNDER COVER

Although traditional pizza is like a baked, open-faced sandwich, here are some close relatives that are "closed."

CHICAGO-STYLE PIZZA

This recipe is from the King Arthur Flour archives and makes one family-sized pizza. It is made entirely from scratch, sauce and all, so you should allow about 3 hours from start to finish (some of which time you can be doing something else). It should be baked in a 12-inch, deep-dish pizza pan. If you don't have such a thing, a large cake pan or small roasting pan will work.

Dough

1 cup warm water
1 teaspoon sugar
1 tablespoon or packet active dry yeast
3 cups King Arthur Unbleached All-Purpose Flour
2 tablespoons olive oil
1 teaspoon salt

Making & Rising the Dough: Pour the water into a mixing bowl and dissolve the sugar and yeast. Stir in 1 cup of the flour and then add the oil and salt. Add the rest of the flour. Although this is about ½ of the Hearth Bread Pizza dough, you turn it out, knead and let rise the same way (page 177).

Sauce

1 medium onion, chopped (about ½ cup)
1 small green pepper, chopped
1 large clove of garlic, finely chopped
2 tablespoons olive oil
2 cups (16-ounce can) whole tomatoes, undrained
1 cup tomato paste
1 teaspoon dried basil
½ teaspoon salt
½ teaspoon dried oregano
¼ teaspoon fennel seed
⅛ teaspoon pepper

Preparing the Sauce: Combine all of the ingredients in a saucepan, breaking up the tomatoes with a fork. Heat to the boiling point and then reduce heat. Cover and simmer for about 45 minutes.

Rolling & Shaping the Dough: When your dough has doubled, punch it down and divide into 2 pieces. One should be a bit larger to cover the bottom and sides of your pan. The other should to be large enough to cover the top. Roll the dough into circles (or whatever shape your pan is) and let them rest while you prepare the meat and vegetables for the filling.

Filling

> 6 cups (about 1 pound) mushrooms, cleaned and sliced
> 2 green peppers, sliced
> 2 tablespoons olive oil
> 1 pound Italian sweet sausage
> 1½ to 2 cups mozzarella cheese, shredded
> minced garlic
> oregano
> freshly grated Parmesan cheese

Preparing the Filling: Sauté the mushrooms and green peppers in 2 tablespoons of olive oil. Remove the sausage from its casing, crumble it into the frying pan, cook well and drain.

Constructing the Pizza: Lightly grease your pizza (or other) pan with olive oil and sprinkle on some cornmeal if you like. Place the larger circle of dough in the pan and spread the filling over it. Sprinkle with mozzarella, minced garlic and oregano. Place the smaller circle of dough on top of the filling. Pinch both crusts together, sealing the edges. Prick the top crust and drizzle olive oil over it. Sprinkle on Parmesan cheese and minced garlic and oregano. Spread with the sauce and sprinkle on more cheese. Let the pizza rest for 15 to 30 minutes.

Baking: Fifteen minutes before you are ready to bake, preheat your oven to 400°F. Bake for 25 to 30 minutes. Let the pizza stand 10 minutes before cutting.

CALZONE

For centuries, pastries and doughs have served as containers for foods of all types. Here's a way to use our Hearth Bread Pizza dough to make another kind of "pizza under cover." It's a robust Italian bread with meat, cheese and vegetables baked right inside, a portable meal. One variety is rolled and the other is folded like a giant tart.

Dough

> 1 recipe Hearth Bread Pizza dough (page 176)
> 1 egg beaten with 1 tablespoon water for wash (optional)
> poppy or sesame seeds, or chopped garlic or onion (optional)
> (cornmeal for baking sheet)

Preparing the Dough: Make up your dough as described in the Primer, beginning on page 177. While it rises, get the fillings together.

Filling

> sliced meat: ham, pepperoni, prosciutto, salami, etc.
> sliced cheese: provolone, mozzarella, etc.
> herbs: minced oregano, basil, marjoram, thyme, parsley, crushed red
> > pepper, etc.
> vegetables, minced and/or sautéed: green pepper, mushrooms, onion,
> > garlic, olives, etc.

The fillings for a calzone can be as varied and wild as your imagination. When choosing them there are only three things to keep in mind. Don't make the filling too juicy (choose spaghetti or marinara sauce rather than sliced tomatoes). Feel free to use ingredients with strong flavors; they won't overwhelm the bread. And finally, leave enough room around the outside edge of the dough to seal it. You don't want all those yummy things leaking out while the calzone bakes.

Shaping: There are two ways to shape a calzone.

• Rolled Calzone: This first method is the older and more traditional one. It creates a calzone that looks like a loaf of Italian bread but with the filling as a surprise inside.

Cut the dough into 2 pieces. Roll out each piece into a rectangle about 10 x 14 inches. Layer each rectangle with your choice of filling ingredients.

Starting with the long edge, roll the dough around your filling jelly-roll style. Pinch the ends and seam together very tightly and place the roll on a greased baking sheet sprinkled with cornmeal.

• Folded Calzone: Cut your Hearth Bread dough into 3 pieces and roll them out into 10- or 12-inch circles as if you were going to make pizza. Layer the ham, pepperoni, and sliced cheese in the center of the dough. Sprinkle oregano, basil, and a touch of crushed red pepper on top. Add sautéed, chopped green pepper, mushrooms, onion and garlic if you like.

Fold one side over the other like a giant tart. Seal the edges thoroughly (moistening the edges with a bit of water helps) and place the calzone on a lightly greased and cornmeal-sprinkled baking sheet. (Greasing helps prevent sticking, as does the cornmeal which also adds a nice bite.)

Rising: Cover it with a damp towel or plastic wrap (grease the underside of the wrap so it won't stick to the dough).

Baking: Like our other pizza, there is more than one way to bake a calzone.

> • **Quick:** Let the calzone rest for 20 to 30 minutes. While it's resting, beat the egg together with a tablespoon of water until it's light.
>
> After the resting period, slash the top diagonally 3 times, cutting through to the filling. This gives the calzone a place to let off steam and expand so it (hopefully) won't break through somewhere else. Brush the tops with the egg wash and sprinkle with poppy or sesame seeds or even chopped onion or garlic. Put the calzone in a cold oven, set the temperature to 450°F for 15 minutes and then down to 400°F for 20 to 25 minutes until the crust is a golden brown.
>
> • **Traditional:** Let the calzone rise for 45 minutes to an hour. Fifteen minutes before you want to bake it, preheat your oven to 450°F.
>
> To make the crust crunchy like our Hearth Bread, preheat a roasting pan on the oven bottom along with the oven. Just before the calzone goes in, pour in 3 or 4 cups of water. (We don't recommend doing this with the first baking method. Since that one begins with a cold oven you can't create enough steam during the first 10 minutes of baking to produce the same kind of crust you can in a preheated oven.) Slash the tops of the loaves, brush with the egg wash and sprinkle with sesame or poppy seeds.
>
> Bake for 15 minutes at 450°F, turn the heat down to 400°F and bake for a further 15 minutes until the crust is golden brown.

Calzone Bianca or Rolled Herb Bread

Here is a variation of rolled calzone that relates to the traditional variety as Pizza Bianca relates to the traditional pizza.

Shaping & Filling: Roll out your dough as you did for the rolled variety of calzone. Spread lightly with melted butter. Sprinkle with chopped onion, garlic, mustard and/or a mixture of herbs of your choice. Roll up and seal the seams very tightly.

Rising & Baking: Place them on a lightly greased cookie sheet or in two greased bread pans. Let rise for 45 minutes to an hour. Slash the tops and brush with an egg wash. Sprinkle on herbs or chopped onion, if you like. Fifteen minutes before baking, preheat your oven to 350°F. Bake for 35 to 40 minutes.

"ANTIPASTO" PIZZA

These pizzas make excellent appetizers. They are usually made with a variety of cheeses and herbs without the traditional tomato-based sauce.

FOCACCIA

The predecessor of Pizza in Italy was a flat bread called "Focaccia" which is used both as an appetizer (an antipasto, the course before the pasta) or as an accompaniment to a main meal.

Making the Dough: Mix up, knead and let rise a batch of Light Hearth Bread Pizza dough which you'll find on page 179.

Shaping: Cut the dough in half and, after a couple of minutes' rest to relax the gluten, push the dough out with your fingers to fit two 12-inch pizza pans. Let it rest for about 15 minutes.

Decorating Options: Make indentations in the surface of the dough with your fingertips, little places to catch and soak up the flavorings you put on top.

> • Spread the surface liberally with a good olive oil that has been flavored with garlic, and then sprinkle it with chopped onion and crushed rosemary.

> • Or, add a tablespoon of basil and oregano to the dough and, after it is shaped and relaxed, press a liberal amount of chopped onion or scallion into the surface.

Baking: Preheat your oven to 475°F for at least 15 minutes while you let the focaccia rest. Bake for 15 to 20 minutes.

PIZZA BIANCA

This second version, which is quite plain, is eaten in and around Rome.

Making the Dough: Make the Light Hearth Bread Pizza dough (page 179) and allow it to rise once.

Shaping: Cut the dough in half and let it rest for a couple of minutes to relax the gluten. Push the dough out with your fingers to fit two 12-inch pizza pans lightly greased with olive oil. Let these pizza shells rest for about 15 minutes.

Decorating: Brush the surface liberally with olive oil and sprinkle with pretzel or kosher salt.

Baking: Preheat your oven to 475°F while you let the pizza rest for 15 to 20 minutes. Bake for 15 to 20 minutes.

GORGONZOLA & SCALLION PIZZA

This non-traditional version is the inspiration of the Sands' daughter, Jennifer, who has found that being irreverant with tradition can produce some quite wonderful results. For lovers of blue cheese, this is absolutely delicious.

Making the Dough: Make the Light Hearth Bread Pizza dough (page 179) and allow it to rise once.

Shaping: Divide the dough in half, let it rest for a couple of minutes and push it out gently with your hands to fit two 12-inch pizza pans lightly greased with olive oil.

Let the dough rest again for about 15 minutes

Decorating: Brush the shell with olive oil, then sprinkle it heavily with chopped scallions or onions and pieces of Gorgonzola cheese. You can substitute a domestic blue cheese for the Gorgonzola, or, for an incredibly rich variation, use a triple-cream blue cheese which you can find in the gourmet cheese section of your market.

Baking: Preheat your oven to 475°F while you let the pizza rest for 15 to 20 minutes. Bake for 15 to 20 minutes.

Try these variations and take it from here.

PIZZA FOR DESSERT

We've had "antipasto" pizza and pizza for a main meal. Here's pizza for dessert (or maybe breakfast).

APPLE PIZZA

Whether you serve this for dessert or breakfast, or just eat it as a snack, apple on a pizza is a great new twist for two old friends. This dough is still related to our Hearth Bread dough (every dough is) but we've sweetened and spiced it for this recipe.

Dough

1 1/2 cups warm water
1/2 cup brown sugar
1 tablespoon or packet active dry yeast
2 eggs, slightly beaten
2 tablespoons vegetable oil
1/2 cup non-fat dry milk
1 tablespoon salt
2 teaspoons cinnamon
1 cup King Arthur Stone Ground Whole Wheat Flour
5 cups King Arthur Unbleached All-Purpose Flour

Making the Dough: Prepare your dough as you would for the Light Hearth Bread Pizza (page 179) by dissolving 1 tablespoon of the sugar and yeast in the warm water. Beat in the eggs, oil and dry milk. Add the balance of the brown sugar, the salt and the cinnamon. Mix in the flour, a cup at a time. This will make a very slack or light dough.

Kneading & Rising: Turn it onto a floured board, keep well floured and knead until it is smooth and elastic. If you have trouble kneading it, use your bowl scraper to lift and slap it down on the board until it is well kneaded. Let it rise in a greased and covered bowl while you make the topping.

Topping

3 or 4 apples
1 cup pecans, walnuts or sunflower seeds
2 teaspoons cinnamon
1/2 cup brown sugar
1 cup raisins (optional)
melted butter (optional)

Preparing the Topping: Peel and slice the apples.

With a knife or blender, grind or chop the nuts or seeds you choose. Mix in the cinnamon, brown sugar and the raisins, if you like them. Set this mixture aside while you shape the dough.

Shaping: Divide the dough into 2 pieces. Push it out to fit two lightly greased, 12-inch pizza pans or reasonable facsimiles.

Decorating & Baking: Place the apple slices close together in a single layer on top of the dough, sprinkle liberally with the sugar/nut/raisin mixture, cover and allow to rest for 15 to 30 minutes.

Preheat your oven to 400°F for at least 15 minutes before you want to bake the pizza.

If you want to throw all dietary caution to the winds, sprinkle a bit of melted butter over the surface just before you pop it in the oven. After 10 minutes at 400°F, turn the heat down to 350°F and bake a further 15 minutes.

A "Pizza" Tart

In every chapter we have a maverick, and this pizza (which is probably closer to a tart) is a complete bit of serendipity. It comes to us from Ann Berry whose daughter, Emily, takes it to her play school for special occasions. You can serve it for dessert or maybe even breakfast (if you have an insatiable sweet tooth). For a special birthday, make up the crust beforehand and let the birthday child do the decorating.

The dough is best made ahead of time so it can chill for a couple of hours (or a couple of days). It will make enough for three 12-inch pizzas or for 1 pizza and 4 dozen 2½-inch sugar cookies. (See page 328.)

The "Crust"

> 1 cup (2 sticks) butter
> ³⁄₄ cup white sugar
> ³⁄₄ cup packed brown sugar
> 2 eggs
> 3 cups King Arthur Unbleached All-Purpose Flour
> 1 cup King Arthur Stone Ground Whole Wheat Flour
> 1 teaspoon salt
> 1 teaspoon baking powder
> ¹⁄₂ teaspoon baking soda
> ¹⁄₄ cup milk
> 1 teaspoon vanilla

Mixing & Chilling the Dough: Cream the butter and sugar together. Drop in the eggs and beat until the mixture is light.

Thoroughly combine the flours, salt, baking powder and baking soda. Add about 1 cup to the butter mixture. Blend in the milk and vanilla and then the remaining dry ingredients.

Chill the dough until you're ready to make the pizza.

Shaping: When you're ready to put your pizza together, take the dough out of the refrigerator and cut it into 3 pieces. If the dough is too hard to shape with your hands, let it soften for 10 or 15 minutes.

At this point, preheat your oven to 325°F and lightly grease your pizza pan.

You can either roll out the dough like pie dough to fit the pan or you can put it on your pan in several pieces and push it into place with floured fingers (best in hot weather). Once it's fairly evenly distributed, tidy up or flute the edges.

Baking the "Crust:" Bake this crust for about 12 minutes. Let it cool to room temperature before you fill it.

The "Filling"

> 1 pound cream cheese, softened
> 1 tablespoon sugar
> 3 to 4 cups fruit and/or nuts in bite-sized pieces: pineapple, strawberries, kiwi fruit, bananas, etc. and/or walnuts, pecans, etc.
> shredded coconut (optional)
>
> *These ingredients are for 1 pizza. If you're planning to make three, triple them.*

Assembling the Pizza: Blend the cream cheese with the sugar and spread over the cooled crust as evenly as you can.

Decorate with pieces of fruit and nuts and sprinkle with coconut.

• A PUFF DOUGH PRIMER •

If bread is the staff of life on earth for us, confections made with puff dough must be the staff of life for the gods in heaven. Puff dough is yeast baking at one of its pinnacles, the wonder child of puff pastry and yeasted dough. On this side of the Atlantic, we are most familiar with it in Danish pastry and French croissants.

The dough is, again, just a variation of our Hearth Bread dough. Although it contains the addition of some sugar, you'll still see the same ratio of flour to liquid. Its unique and characteristic flakiness comes from the way the dough is put together and the amount and method of folding and rolling a large quantity of butter into it.

The richest of puff doughs contain equal amounts, in weight, of flour and butter. This amount of butter is almost more than the dough can hold when it bakes, so to achieve the same flaky, buttery effect without overwhelming the dough, we're using a ratio of 1½ pounds of flour to only a pound of butter. (Even this reduction won't put our dough in a low-calorie league.)

Puff dough takes a bit longer to make than a typical yeast dough but each step of the way is easy. It will keep for several days in the refrigerator, and you can even freeze it until the right occasion arrives. Then all you need to do is warm it up, roll it out and fill it. Because you can make it well ahead of time, it's the perfect thing to have on hand when you have a house full of weekend company or when you want to make one or two of something special just for yourself. With directions for rolling and filling, a package of puff dough will make a gift that truly shares the joys of baking.

PASTRY

Danish Pastry

Danish Pastry is not called "Danish" in Denmark. In its homeland it is called "Vienerbrod," or Vienna bread. During the nineteenth century, the bakers in Copenhagen went on strike. Up to that point they had never baked anything resembling modern Danish pastry. Owners of Danish baking establishments, rather than negotiating with their own bakers, went abroad for replacements. Soon there was an influx of Austrian bakers who brought with them the Viennese technique of making a yeasted dough behave like a puff pastry.

The striking Danes, with their unique talent and love for baking, couldn't stay away from their craft for long. They soon reentered the marketplace and began to use this new Viennese dough to create the heavenly breakfast rolls, with their exquisite fillings, that we in America now call Danish pastries.

1 pound (2 cups) sweet (unsalted) butter, chilled
$^1/_2$ cup water, warm from the tap
4 to 6 tablespoons sugar
1 well-rounded tablespoon or 2 packets active dry yeast
5$^1/_2$ to 6 cups King Arthur Unbleached All-Purpose Flour
1 scant tablespoon salt
$^1/_2$ to 1 teaspoon ground cardamom (optional but used in traditional
      Danish pastry)
1 cup cold milk
2 large eggs
1 teaspoon vanilla

First: Remove the butter from the refrigerator to allow it to soften slightly.

Making the Sponge: Pour the warm water in a small mixing bowl and dissolve 1 tablespoon of the sugar in it. Next, add the yeast and allow it to dissolve. When the yeast mixture is bubbly, stir in $^1/_2$ cup of the flour and let this sponge go to work while you prepare the dry ingredients and the butter. Because you keep this dough chilled, this tiny sponge will help get the yeast off to a good start.

Preparing the Dry Ingredients: Put 5 cups of flour into a large mixing bowl. Blend in the balance of the sugar, the salt and the optional cardamom.

Remove the sticks of butter from their paper wrappers. With a knife cut about $^1/_4$ inch of butter off the end of each stick (you'll have about 2 tablespoons altogether) and put it in the flour mixture. With your fingertips, rub the butter into the dry ingredients.

By rubbing in the butter you give the flour particles the barest of coatings, which helps tenderize the dough. (You can melt the butter over low heat and add it later to the milk/egg mixture if you prefer, or, to make it very simple, you can leave the butter out of the dough altogether.)

Preparing the Butter: Roll the remainder of the butter into two 6 x 9-inch (approximately) rectangles. To do this most easily, cut half the butter (two sticks) in half lengthwise. Place them side by side on a well-floured piece of waxed paper or plastic wrap. Sprinkle the top of the butter with flour, place another piece of paper or wrap on top and roll the butter out until it's about the dimension you want. Repeat the process with the remaining two sticks of butter.

If the butter has softened a great deal (i.e., if you can easily make a dent in it with your fingertip), put both the waxed paper and butter in the refrigerator to chill while you prepare the dough. If the butter is still quite hard, leave it out to soften a bit more. When you roll it into the dough you don't want it so hard that it "shatters," or so soft that it combines with the dough. (Even if either of the possibilities occurs, you'll still have a dough that has ethereal qualities so don't be overly worried about it.)

Making the Dough: The sponge should be quite bubbly by now.

Measure the cup of cold milk in a two-cup liquid measure. Break the eggs directly into it and beat them into the milk along with the vanilla. (If you opt to melt the 2 tablespoons of butter, add and blend it in at this point.)

Make a well in the middle of the dry ingredients and pour in the yeast and the milk mixture. Blend the dough with a large spoon until it holds together and begins to come away from the sides of the bowl.

Kneading: Sprinkle flour on your kneading surface, turn out the dough and begin to knead. Add only enough flour to keep it from sticking to the board or you. When the dough is smooth and elastic, after 4 or 5 minutes, cover it with a damp towel and let it rest for about 10 minutes.

Making the "Turns" or Layers of Butter: Now that the gluten is relaxed, sprinkle the table and the surface of the dough with flour. With a floured rolling pin, begin to roll out the dough. Turn it over from time to time and give it a bit of a rest if it becomes reluctant. Sprinkle flour around lightly if the dough begins to stick.

First Turn: When the dough is about 12 inches wide and almost 24 inches long, dust its surface with flour.

Take one of the pieces of rolled out butter, place it in the middle third of the dough and fold the top third over it so it's completely covered.

Take the second piece of butter and place it on the dough that covers the first piece and fold the bottom third of dough up and over that. Pinch the edges together to seal the butter inside.

Second Turn: Turn the dough 90° so one of the edges is facing you. Roll it out again so it's about 10 x 24 inches. This time fold the top and bottom edges to the middle until they meet.

Take the top half of the dough and fold it over the bottom half like a book (8 layers of butter). Your book should be about 6 x 10 inches.

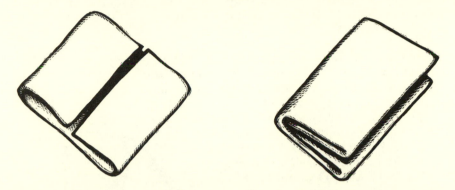

Dust the surface with flour and wrap it in plastic wrap. Place it in the refrigerator to chill for about 20 minutes, long enough to relax the gluten in the dough but not so long that the butter becomes too hard.

Third Turn: Take the dough out of its wrap and place it on your kneading/rolling surface again. With the short edge facing you, roll the dough again into a 10 x 24-inch rectangle. Fold the top and bottom edge into the middle until they meet and then the top half over the bottom. Cover the dough with a cool, damp towel or refrigerate it again, and let it rest for 10 or 15 minutes to relax the gluten.

Fourth Turn: Turn the dough 90° and repeat the same procedure for 1 final time.

Chilling the Dough: At this point, flour the dough lightly, wrap it and return it to the refrigerator for at least 2 hours but preferably overnight. During this time the flavor and texture of the dough matures and mellows and the whole mass, butter included, reaches the same temperature.

We've rolled and folded the dough only 4 times but every time it's done, the number of layers of butter is multiplied by four. We started with 2 layers, turned it and made 4 more layers to make 8 altogether. After chilling it for 20 minutes, we rolled it and folded it again to make 32 layers of butter. The final rolling and folding makes an amazing 128 layers. Some people like to turn and fold it a fifth time making 512 layers, but at this point the layers are so thin they're difficult to distinguish and the dough is more like an incredibly rich sweet dough. If you want your dough to be puffy because of the yeast and flaky because of the layers of butter, stick with 4 turns and 128 layers.

Making the Fillings & Glazes: While the dough chills you can get ready for the next step by making fillings and glazes (page 203). This also takes a little time but most of the fillings will keep for several weeks in the refrigerator and/or can be frozen.

Shaping & Filling: Almost anything goes when it comes to shaping Danish pastry. There are several traditional shapes but this dough invites experimentation. You can make pastries in individual serving sizes, in miniature sizes, or in one grand coffeecake size.

• **Envelopes:** These are the simplest. Take one-third of the dough and roll it into an 8 x 16-inch rectangle. With your bowl scraper, cut the dough in half lengthwise and in quarters widthwise so you have 8 squares. Spread a bit of filling on the center of each square (or just inside the corners). Take the two opposite corners (or all 4 corners), and bring them to the middle of the square and press them into place. Place a dollop of filling on top. Place on a lightly greased cookie sheet and cover with a damp cloth.

To make miniature pastries, cut each square into quarters so you have 4 squares that are 2 inches on a side. Lots of tiny pastries make it possible to do lots of sampling.

• **Pinwheels:** These are shaped just like a child's pinwheel. Cut the dough into 4-inch squares as you did above. With a spatula or a bowl scraper, make 4 cuts in each square starting at each corner and stopping about $1/2$ inch from the center. Spread a bit of filling in each corner. Take the left (or right) side of each corner and press it to the center of the square. Place another dollop of filling on top.

• **Cockscombs or Bear Claws:** Roll and cut the dough into eight squares as you did for envelopes. Spread a filling lightly down the middle of each square. Fold the square in half over the filling. With a knife (or your bowl scraper), make cuts through the dough perpendicular to and through the side where the edges of the square come together. Stop the cut about where the dough begins to bulge out around the filling. Place on a lightly greased cookie sheet. By shaping the uncut edge (the fold) into a crescent, you will open the cuts you made in the opposite edge to form the cockscomb.

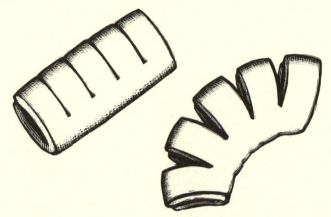

• **Snails, Small & Large:** Roll and cut the dough into squares as you did above. Cover the top of the square with a filling, leaving about $1/2$ inch clear around the outside edge. If you are using nuts, press them into the dough. Roll the dough into a tube. With your bowl scraper, make cuts in the dough almost through to the other side but not quite. Place on a lightly greased cookie sheet. Again shape the uncut edge into a crescent to spread apart the cut sections. Twist each section so the cut edges lie flat on the cookie sheet.

This technique can be used with a whole piece of dough. In order to turn each cut section flat, the whole dough will wind up in the shape of a snail. (If you find it easier, cut right through the dough and place the circles of dough, cut side flat, in a greased cake pan. This is a Danish variation of the American sticky bun.)

Rising & Baking: After shaping your pastries, cover with a damp towel and let them rise for up to 2 hours. You can also bake them after a 20-minute rest, but by giving them longer, the yeast will have a chance to do its work and the pastries will be ethereally light.

Preheat your oven to 400°F fifteen minutes before you want to bake them.

- Bake miniature pastries for 15 minutes.

- Bake individual-sized pastries for 18 to 20 minutes.

- Bake large coffeecake-sized pastries for 25 to 30 minutes. Reduce the heat to 350°F for the last 10 to 15 minutes.

Finishing: When the pastries are still hot, you can brush them with one of the glazes you'll find on page 207. If you do this while they're hot, the glaze will melt and create a shiny, transparent coating. If you wait until they're cool, you can drizzle the glaze, which will stay put and remain opaque, into a lacy pattern over the pastries.

If you allow these airy wonders to cool (sometimes difficult), their structure becomes set. This makes it possible for you to bite through them without mashing them flat. While they cool, warm up your coffee or tea and then sit down and enjoy some of the world's most basic ingredients in one of their finest forms.

Croissants de Boulanger

The same magic dough we used to make Danish pastry can be used, with minor and optional modifications, to make that other familiar continental breakfast bread, the rich, and equally ethereal, French croissant. A single batch of our Danish Pastry dough will make about 16 croissants.

The croissant has its own story as well. The Sands' son Frank has long had a fascination with the origins of Germanic and Old Norse languages. Over the years, he has provided his parents with a continuous flow of continental lore. According to his sources, the croissant evolved when the Turks and their Ottoman empire were posing a threat to western Europe. To raise funds to fight the enemy, the bakers in the west sold a crescent roll for the price of a larger, round one. The money they saved was contributed to the cause. It was said that if you bought one of these croissants, you were "taking a bite out of the Turk" (whose symbol was, in fact, the crescent).

This crescent roll, or croissant, has now outlived the memory of its origins and has become a familiar hallmark of the French baker or "boulanger." You can find another kind of croissant, Croissants de Patissier, made without yeast, on page 445.

1 pound (2 cups) sweet (unsalted) butter, chilled
1/2 cup warm water
4 tablespoons sugar
1 well-rounded tablespoon or 2 packets active dry yeast
5 1/2 cups King Arthur Unbleached All-Purpose Flour
1 scant tablespoon salt
1/2 to 1 teaspoon ground cardamom (optional, used in traditional Danish
        pastry)
1 cup cold milk
2 large eggs (optional)
1 teaspoon vanilla

Traditionally when making croissants, eggs are not used. You can substitute 1/2 cup of milk, but croissants made with an egg-rich dough are quite splendid.

Making the Dough: Prepare the dough, make the turns and chill the dough as for Danish Pastry (page 195).

Shaping (& Optional Filling): Remove the dough from the refrigerator and cut off one-third. Rewrap and refrigerate the remainder.

Flour your work surface and rolling pin. Roll out the dough until it's about 10 x 20 inches. While rolling, turn it over and let it relax from time to time. Use the rolling pin to help push it into the rectangular shape.

With a knife or your bowl scraper, cut the dough in half lengthwise and into quarters widthwise. You should have 8 squares which are about 5 inches on a side.

Trim the dough to make your shapes more exact and to remove any folded edges; this will allow the dough to rise higher. (The trimmings are fair game for the cook. See page 401.)

Cut each square diagonally so you have 16 triangles. Roll each triangle up from the long side toward the point. To form the traditional crescent shape, bend the ends away from the point.

Place them on a lightly greased baking sheet. If you wish, put a bit of sweet filling on the dough before you roll it up, or, for a totally different sort of croissant, roll up a bit of ham and/or cheese (or perhaps some cream cheese and caviar).

Baking: After the croissants are shaped, cover them with a damp towel and let them rise for up to 2 hours (or as long as you can hold off your family or company; croissants will still be very good, but not as heavenly, with just a 20-minute rest). About 20 minutes before you want to bake them, preheat your oven to a hot 475°F.

Just before they go in the oven, brush them with an egg beaten with a couple of teaspoons of water or milk. Bake for about 12 minutes.

Croissants, like Danish pastries, are better if you let them cool a little before you eat them. This allows their structure to set and will accentuate their flaky texture.

DANISH PASTRY FILLINGS & GLAZES

These are some of the traditional fillings for Danish pastry (remember you can fill croissants too), but the beauty of this dough is that each pastry can be an experiment, a new combination of delights for both the eye and the tongue. Don't feel you need to stop here. Look over the other fillings listed in the index, or use one or your own favorites. Just as you can use any of these in other recipes, you can use any of the Sweet Dough Fillings (page 218) or Pie Fillings (page 402) in Danish pastry.

REMONCE

This is a classic Danish filling and is made simply with equal amounts of butter and either white or brown sugar flavored with vanilla and/or cinnamon to taste. Blend and refrigerate. It will keep almost indefinitely.

FRESH & DRIED FRUIT FILLINGS

Any fruit conserve or preserve makes a great filling. You can add ground nuts or seeds to them to make them more interesting. Add a flavoring extract as well: vanilla, almond, lemon, rum, etc.

Apple, or other fresh fruit, stewed in a bit of water and sugar with added flavoring or nuts, makes a good filling.

Dried fruits make delicious fillings. Take 2 cups of any of the following: raisins, currants, prunes, dates, apricots or figs, cook them in about 1 cup of water (flavored with a bit of rum if you like), ½ cup white or brown sugar and 2 teaspoons of lemon and/or orange rind until they're soft. You can either purée or chop this mixture until it suits your taste.

NUT FILLING

3 cups walnuts, pecans, hazelnuts, etc.
½ to 1 cup sugar
½ teaspoon salt
2 eggs
1 to 2 teaspoons vanilla or other flavoring

Grind the nuts in a blender or hand-cranked grinder. Blend in the remaining ingredients (a food processor does this second mixing nicely but it can be done by hand). Remove and store.

CHEESE FILLING

1 cup cottage, ricotta, or cream cheese (or a mixture)
2 to 4 tablespoons sugar
1/4 teaspoon salt
1 egg
1 to 2 teaspoons grated lemon rind (optional but adds some zip)
1/4 cup raisins, currants, chopped apricot or other dried fruit (optional, to create a completely different but delicious filling)

Blend thoroughly. (Again, a food processor does a great job.)

THE TRIPLET

The next three fillings, Almond, Poppy Seed, and Lemon are written to be made one after the other because they share some ingredients. The recipe makes 12 to 14 ounces of each (about the equivalent of a 13-ounce commercial can). They will keep for at least a month if they're refrigerated, so one batch of fillings will last you through several batches of pastry. Directions for making each alone (without the other two) follow.

Unfortunately to make the almond and poppy seed fillings, you need a blender or a food processor (or a hand-cranked grinder). We've tried to keep most of our recipes simple enough to be made without a lot of fancy equipment but it's difficult to grind nuts and seeds without some sort of mechanical help. There are commercial fillings available, but you can't beat the ones you make from scratch.

ALMOND FILLING WITH A BASE FOR POPPY SEED FILLING

3 cups sliced almonds (about 10 ounces), skins and all if you wish
1 cup granulated sugar
1/2 teaspoon salt
1 egg
6 tablespoons butter, softened
1 teaspoon freshly grated lemon rind (any leftover rind can be used in a confectioners' sugar glaze, page 207)
1 teaspoon juice from 1 lemon (you'll use the rest in the Lemon Filling)
1/2 to 1 teaspoon almond extract (start with the lesser amount and add to taste)

Grind the almonds in your blender in two batches and dump them into your food processor. Add the sugar and salt and blend. Add the egg and butter and blend. Remove 1 cup of the mixture and set it aside. Add the lemon rind, juice and almond extract and blend thoroughly. Remove this to a storage container.

POPPY SEED FILLING FROM THE ALMOND FILLING BASE

The flavor of this filling is very good as is; the addition of the raisins creates something brand new and will add 3 to 6 ounces.

1 cup almond mixture from above
$\frac{1}{2}$ cup poppy seeds
$\frac{1}{4}$ cup sugar
$\frac{1}{8}$ teaspoon salt
1 egg white (yolk will go in the Lemon Filling which follows)
1 teaspoon vanilla
1 teaspoon freshly grated lemon rind (optional, but adds zip)
$\frac{1}{2}$ to 1 cup raisins (optional)

Return the cup of almond mixture, which you removed above, to the processor. Add the rest of the ingredients and blend thoroughly. Remove and place in a storage container.

LEMON FILLING OR CURD

$\frac{1}{4}$ cup ($\frac{1}{2}$ stick) butter
grated rind from 1 lemon
$\frac{1}{4}$ cup lemon juice (the juice of one to two lemons; use the one you
      squeezed above plus whatever you need of the one you grated for
      this recipe)
$\frac{3}{4}$ cup sugar
2 eggs
1 egg yolk (from the Poppy Seed Filling above)

Melt the butter over low heat in a small saucepan and add the grated lemon, lemon juice and sugar. Cook gently until the sugar has dissolved and the mixture is clear.

While the sugar mixture is dissolving, beat the eggs and egg yolk together until they're light. Add this slowly to the saucepan stirring constantly with a wire whisk to blend them in thoroughly. (A double boiler is safer in this operation but, if you're careful and stir constantly, you'll be all right with a saucepan over direct heat.)

After the mixture has begun to bubble gently and is thick, remove it from the heat, let it cool and place it in a storage container.

ALMOND FILLING MADE ALONE

The following recipe can be made without the preceding Poppy Seed or Lemon Fillings. It makes the equivalent of a generous can of commercial filling.

2 cups sliced almonds
2/3 cup sugar
1/4 teaspoon salt
1 egg
4 tablespoons (1/2 stick) butter
grated rind from 1 lemon
1/2 teaspoon lemon juice
1/4 to 1/2 teaspoon almond extract

Follow the same directions as in the Triplet Almond Filling recipe but don't remove any of the mixture before you add the lemon and almond flavorings.

POPPY SEED FILLING MADE ALONE

This recipe can be made without the Triplet Almond or Lemon Fillings. It makes about the equivalent of a can of poppy seed filling.

1 cup sliced almonds
1/2 cup poppy seeds
1/2 cup sugar
1/4 teaspoon salt
1 egg
1 teaspoon vanilla
4 tablespoons (1/2 stick) butter
1/2 to 1 teaspoon freshly grated lemon rind (optional, but good)
2/3 cup raisins (optional)

Grind the almonds in your blender in one batch and dump them into your food processor. Add the rest of the ingredients and blend thoroughly.

GLAZES & WASHES

EGG WASH

Before baking, gently brush the surface of the pastry with an egg wash made of a whole egg, or the white or yolk separately, beaten with 2 to 3 teaspoons of water or milk.

The wash can be left as is, or you can sprinkle on some sugar, cinnamon sugar and/or chopped nuts. This wash gives the pastry a shiny, bronzed surface. The egg white creates a transparent surface, the whole egg and egg yolk deeper shades of bronze.

CLEAR SUGAR GLAZE

After baking, drizzle on a glaze made of 1 cup confectioners' sugar mixed with 2 tablespoons liquid (water, milk, a few drops of flavor extract, rum, brandy, grated lemon or orange peel, etc.).

If you drizzle it on right after the pastries come out of the oven, it will spread and create a clear, shiny glaze over the whole surface. For more crunch, sprinkle nuts over this before it hardens.

WHITE SUGAR GLAZE

Wait until the pastries are cool and use the Clear Sugar Glaze to create a white, lacy pattern over the surface. If the glaze doesn't behave the way you'd like, add either more liquid or more sugar.

JELLY GLAZE

In a small saucepan, over low heat, melt a clear fruit jelly to brush on as a glaze. You can leave it as is or add flavoring and/or grated lemon or orange peel and a sprinkling of chopped nuts.

• A SWEET DOUGH PRIMER •

Sweet doughs can be divided into two groups, those which are made for that most ordinary of meals (breakfast) and those which are made to celebrate the most extraordinary of events, births, marriages, deaths, coronations, those festive occasions which occur only once in a while. All of them can be made from a basic sweet dough with just a few simple alterations.

THE VERSATILE SWEET DOUGH

As we did with our Hearth Bread dough, we'll start by giving you a formula for a basic sweet dough that can be the foundation for an infinite variety of sumptuous things. It can be used as is for rolls, sticky buns, coffeecakes, or as the basis for a festival bread. We'll use it as a guide and reference point for the variations that follow.

King Arthur Flour's Simple Sweet Dough

As we mentioned in the Bread Baking Primer at the beginning of this chapter, recipes for sweet doughs often call for a much larger ratio of sugar, fat and eggs than our basic Hearth Bread formula calls for. All of these things tend to dampen the enthusiasm of the yeast. To compensate, many recipes for sweet doughs call for double the "normal" amount of yeast or indicate that the rising periods will take somewhat longer.

Another way to deal with this is to give the yeast a head start in a "proofing sponge" which is an environment designed just for it. This initial meal gives it enough energy to deal with all those rich ingredients. (You'll find that some sweet doughs are made this way and some are not. There are lots of ways to make a loaf of bread.) Once you're comfortable with either process, you can decide which method works best for you.

Proofing Sponge

½ cup warm water
1 teaspoon sugar
1 tablespoon or packet active dry yeast
½ cup King Arthur Unbleached All-Purpose Flour

Proofing the Yeast: Pour the water into a large mixing bowl. Stir in the sugar, yeast and flour.

Let this mixture sit for 10 to 15 minutes until it begins to foam and expand.

The Dough

> 1½ cups warm water
> 1 tablespoon salt
> ½ cup (1 stick) softened butter or vegetable oil (or a combination)
> ¼ cup sugar
> 4½ to 5½ cups King Arthur Unbleached All-Purpose Flour

Customizing Your Sweet Dough

By flavoring your dough with a tablespoon or two of your favorite spices, some grated orange or lemon peel or a flavor extract, you can completely alter the personality of our Simple Sweet Dough. By adding 2 or 3 cups of diced fruit, chopped nuts, etc., you can turn what looks like a simple loaf of bread into a banquet of hidden flavors and textures. Here's how to incorporate some of these.

- Replace the water with milk (see page 129) or add ½ cup dry milk to the dry ingredients.

- Add up to ½ cup more sweetener (see page 129) after the yeast has been proofed.

- Add 1 extra large egg (up to 4) for ¼ cup water or milk. Beat these in after the yeast has been proofed.

- Add 1 to 2 tablespoons spice of your choice (allspice, cinnamon, cloves, ginger, mace, nutmeg, pepper, etc.) to the dry ingredients.

- Add to the sponge 2 to 3 teaspoons flavoring extract (vanilla, almond, lemon, rum, etc.) after the yeast has proofed.

- Toss 2 to 3 cups of diced fruit or chopped nuts in the last cup of flour before you add it.

Making the Dough: After the yeast is really working, stir in the balance of the water, the salt, butter and sugar. Add 4½ cups of flour stirring until you've formed a dough that begins to pull away from the sides of the bowl.

Make any substitutions and/or additions according to the directions that accompany them above.

Kneading, Rising & Punching Down the Dough: Refer back to the directions for our basic Hearth Bread dough (starting on page 116).

Shaping the Dough: This dough makes enough for 2 medium-sized loaves or 1 very large loaf.

Free-form Loaves: This is the simplest shape of all. Cut the dough in half and shape it into two round or oval loaves and place them on a lightly greased baking sheet, allowing them enough room to expand. (This dough can also be placed in two bread pans.)

Braided Loaves: Braids can be straight or, if you make them long enough (perhaps by using the entire recipe), they can be twisted to form a wreath. After braiding, place your loaves on a lightly greased baking sheet.

• **Three-Stranded Braid:** Directions for making a braid with three strands are in the Bread Baking Primer on page 123.

• **Four-Stranded Braid:** To braid four strands, divide the dough into 4 or 8 parts (depending on whether you want two smaller loaves or one huge one). Form the dough into ropes or strands. Lay four strands so the ends are pointed toward you and pinch the farthest ends together. Start the braid with the ends that are farthest away and braid toward you.

*Take the left-hand strand and move it to the right over 2 strands and to the left under 1 strand.

Take the right-hand strand and move it to the left over 2 strands and to the right under 1 strand.

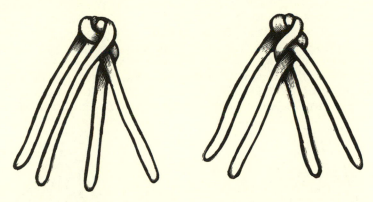

Repeat from * until the loaf is done. Pinch the ends together.

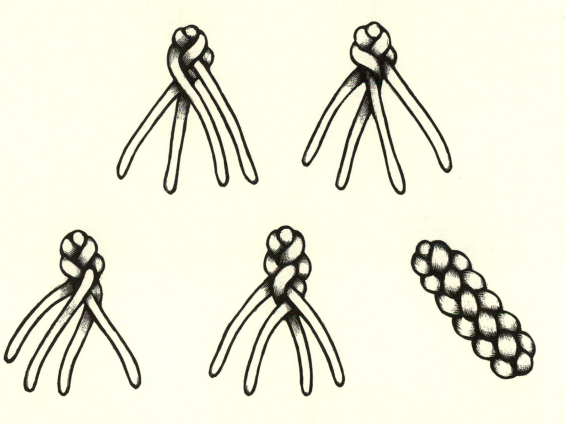

• Six-Stranded Braid: To braid six strands, lay them side by side so the ends are pointing toward you. Start the braid with the ends that are farthest away and braid toward you. First, pinch those ends together. The most important thing to remember about braiding with so many strands is that the only ones that you're going to be doing anything with will be the two on the outside, the one on the right and the one on the left.

To begin, take those two strands, one in your left hand and and one in your right, and cross the left strand over the right, switching them to the opposite hands as you do so, as close to the top of the braid as you can.

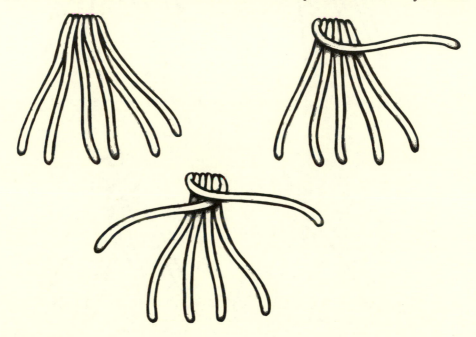

Take the strand on top, bring it down and place it in the center of the 4 strands that are left on the board. You should now have 1 strand remaining in your left hand with 5 strands down on the table.

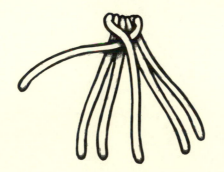

*With your right hand, take the strand that is farthest to the left on the board, and bring it up and over to the right. Lay the strand in your left hand in the center of the 4 strands remaining on the board.

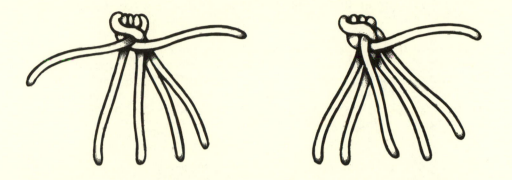

With your left hand, take the strand that is farthest to the right on the board, and bring it up and over to the left. Lay the strand in your right hand in the center of the 4 strands remaining on the board. Repeat the pattern from the * until you come to the end and pinch those ends together. That's all there is to it!

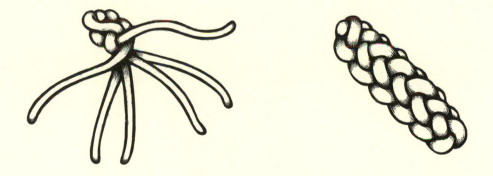

If, in spite of these directions, a six-stranded braid seems a bit much, the following technique is a slightly easier way to create a braided effect that looks much more complicated than it is.

• A Braid on a Braid: Take your dough and cut off about one-third. First, make a three-stranded braid out of the larger piece of dough. Then make a three-stranded braid out of the smaller piece and lay it on top of the larger one. This simple technique creates quite an elegant braided loaf.

Filled Loaves: Rather than blending sugar, fruit and nuts into the dough, braid or roll them up in it. While this requires a little more time, it's still relatively simple.

• Mock Braid: Cut the dough in half and roll it into a rectangle about 10 x 18 inches. Spread your filling lengthwise down the center third of the rectangle. Cut strips about ³/₄ to 1 inch wide from each side of the filling out to the edges of the dough. Fold about an inch of dough at each end over the filling to contain it. Then fold the strips, at an angle, across the filling, alternating from side to side.

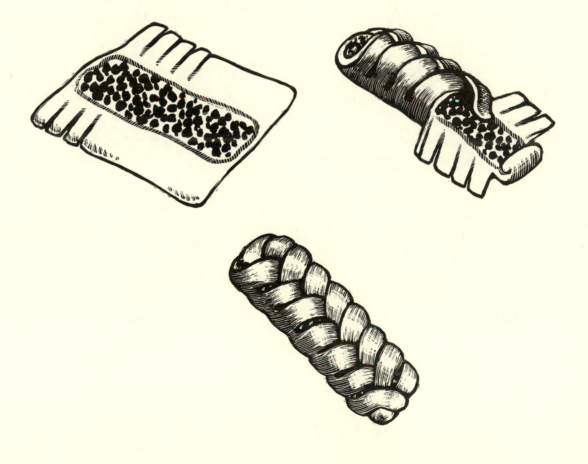

• **Rolled Loaf:** Cut the dough in half and roll out one half until it's about a 10 x 14-inch rectangle. Spread your filling on the dough leaving about an inch around the outside free.

Roll the dough up starting with the long side. Pinch the sides and seam along the length of the loaf tightly closed. Don't worry about how it looks. Place the loaves on a greased baking sheet or in two $4^1/_2$ x $8^1/_2$-inch bread pans.

• **Tea Ring or Snails:** Shape as for the rolled loaf. Make incisions about three-quarters of the way into the roll, spaced about 1 inch apart. Twist the slices until they are lying on their sides. As you do this, coil the dough into a circle. This is most easily done on the lightly greased baking sheet that you intend to bake it on.

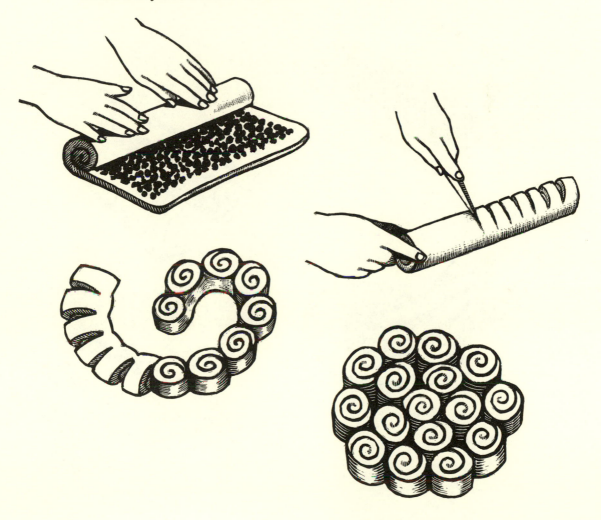

• **Sticky Bun Circles:** Shape as for the rolled loaf. Cut all the way through the loaf at 1-inch intervals. Lay each separated slice in a lightly greased cake or roasting pan (depending on the size of your dough). Leave space between each for the dough to expand.

• **Coffeecake Twist:** Roll out and shape as for the rolled loaf, but this time, slice through the roll lengthwise leaving one end intact. Twisting the dough slightly so the cut edges are facing up, cross one piece over the other, as you would cross your legs. Tuck the end that you cut apart back together. This is most easily done on the sheet, lightly greased, that you intend to bake it on.

• **Stollen:** Roll the dough into a 9 x 12-inch oval. Without stretching the dough, fold the long side to within 1 inch of the opposite edge.

Rising & Baking: Here are two methods that can be used for most sweet doughs. Try both and see what is most comfortable and successful for you.

• **Full Rise:** This method makes the lightest loaves.

Let the dough rise until it has almost doubled, usually between 1 and 1½ hours.

About 15 minutes before you want to put the bread in the oven, preheat it to 350°F. Bake the bread for 35 to 40 minutes.

• **Partial Rise:** This method saves a bit of time and can prevent the dough from overrising and then collapsing in the oven.

Let the dough rise for about 40 minutes or until it's about two-thirds doubled. (Don't feel that you've got to get out a ruler and be precise.) If the dough looks full but it still springs back a bit when you press it gently with your finger, it's probably about where you want it.

Place it in a cold oven, set the temperature to 400°F and bake for 15 minutes. Turn the temperature down to 350°F and continue baking for another 25 to 30 minutes.

SWEET DOUGH FILLINGS

Here are recipes for fillings to put in your dough as well as icings to paint on it. Mix and match with the Danish Pastry Fillings & Glazes on page 203.

CRANBERRY DATE-NUT FILLING

$3/4$ cup sugar
$3/4$ cup water
$1 1/2$ cups whole cranberries
$1/2$ cup chopped dates
$1/2$ cup chopped walnuts
1 tablespoon lemon juice

Heat the sugar and water to boiling in a medium-sized saucepan over medium-high heat. Boil for 5 minutes. Add the cranberries, cover and cook over medium heat for 4 minutes, stirring occasionally. Add the dates and cook for 1 minute. Remove from heat and stir in nuts and lemon juice. Cool completely. This filling is enough for 4 loaves.

PINEAPPLE FILLING

$1/2$ cup sugar
2 tablespoons cornstarch
2 cups crushed pineapple (juice and fruit)
2 teaspoons lemon juice

Blend the sugar with the cornstarch. Add it and the lemon juice to the pineapple which you've put in a small saucepan. Cook over low heat until the mixture thickens and clears. This makes enough for 2 loaves.

POPPY SEED FILLING WITH NUTS & FRUIT

2 recipes Poppy Seed Filling (page 206), made without the raisins
1 egg (additional), beaten
1 teaspoon cinnamon
$2/3$ cup walnuts, chopped
$2/3$ cup candied lemon peel

Combine poppy seed filling, egg, cinnamon and walnuts in a saucepan over medium heat. Stir constantly to prevent sticking. Heat until mixture is thickened. Remove from heat, add candied peel and set aside to cool. This is enough filling for 4 loaves.

Butter Walnut (or Pecan) Filling

4 egg whites
1¾ cups sugar
2 tablespoons butter, melted
5 cups (1¼ pounds) walnuts or pecans, ground
1 teaspoon vanilla
1 to 2 tablespoons milk

Beat the egg whites until thick. Slowly add the rest of the filling ingredients except the milk. Stir in the milk. Chill in the refrigerator as the dough is being made. This recipe makes enough for 4 loaves.

Cottage Cheese Filling

2 cups cottage cheese
½ cup sugar
2 tablespoons King Arthur Unbleached All-Purpose Flour
2 egg yolks
2 tablespoons butter, softened
1 teaspoon vanilla or other flavoring or extract (rum, ginger, almond, lemon, orange, etc.)

Cream together the cottage cheese, sugar and flour. When smooth, add the egg yolks, butter and flavor extract. Beat until smooth. This makes enough to fill 2 loaves.

Cream Cheese Filling

8 ounces cream cheese, at room temperature
½ cup sugar
½ cup King Arthur Unbleached All-Purpose Flour
1 egg, beaten
1 tablespoon vanilla or other flavoring or extract (rum, ginger, almond, lemon, orange, etc.)

Mix the cheese, sugar, flour, egg and flavor extract together until very smooth. Refrigerate until chilled. This makes enough filling for 2 loaves.

• BREAKFAST BREADS •

In this section you'll find recipes for yeast-raised coffeecakes, sweet rolls, doughnuts, etc., all of which we are fortunate to have access to on a daily basis. For the sake of our waistlines and wardrobes, they should probably be saved for special occasions like their festival bread counterparts. Since these recipes have come from several different people, the procedures will vary. (There are lots of routes to the same destination.) We hope they will inspire you to engineer a never-before-created bread of your own.

BÁBA KALÁCS
TRANSYLVANIAN COFFEECAKE

Our first coffeecake, from the central province of Romania, is made with an egg yolk-rich, no-knead batter, an easy way to begin this section. It comes from the archives of Michael and Sandy Jubinsky who have a vast storehouse of ethnic European treasures.

Dough

2 tablespoons warm water
1 teaspoon or ½ packet active dry yeast
¼ cup sugar
⅔ cup milk
¼ cup (½ stick) butter
6 egg yolks
2 cups King Arthur Unbleached All-Purpose Flour
½ teaspoon salt

Filling & Topping

½ cup coarsely chopped walnuts
½ cup packed brown sugar
1 teaspoon vanilla

Making a Sponge: Dissolve the yeast in the warm water with a pinch of the sugar. Let it work until it is bubbly, 3 or 4 minutes.

Scald the milk, remove from the heat and add the balance of the sugar and the butter. Cool to lukewarm.

In a mixing bowl, beat the egg yolks until well blended. Add and blend in the cooled milk mixture and the yeast. Add 1 cup of the flour and beat until smooth.

Cover and let this sponge stand in a warm, draft-free place for about ½ hour.

Preparing the Filling: Combine and thoroughly mix the filling ingredients and set aside.

Making the Dough: Stir the salt and the remaining flour into the batter, making a soft, spongy dough that can be dropped from a spoon. Beat it vigorously until it becomes elastic and "blisters."

Constructing the Coffeecake: Spoon half the dough into a well-greased Bundt pan or ring mold. Sprinkle half the nut mixture over the dough, taking care not to get it too close to the edges. Spoon the remaining dough over that, and top with the rest of the nut mixture.

Cover and let the coffeecake rest for 30 to 45 minutes.

Baking: While the dough rests, preheat your oven to 350°F. Bake the coffeecake for 45 minutes or until golden brown.

Cool the cake in the pan for 10 minutes and remove. It can either be served warm on a plate or allowed to cool thoroughly on a rack.

CzECHOSLOVAKIAN WALNUT ROLLS

This recipe is a treasure from the King Arthur Flour archives. The five individual rolls, made of an extremely butter-rich dough, are very much like French brioche. Since the dough must be chilled for several hours (also like the brioche), it's best to make this one day and bake it the next.

The filling for this bread needs to be made first since it should chill while you prepare the dough. The egg yolks that aren't used in the filling are used in the dough.

> 1 recipe Butter Walnut Filling (page 219), chilled
> 1 rounded tablespoon or 2 packets active dry yeast
> 1/2 cup warm water
> 1/2 cup sugar
> 1 1/2 cups milk
> 1 teaspoon vinegar
> 1 cup (2 sticks) butter
> 4 egg yolks
> 1 teaspoon vanilla
> 6 to 7 cups King Arthur Unbleached All-Purpose Flour
> 1 teaspoon salt
> 1 egg beaten with 1 tablespoon water (for wash)

Making the Dough: Dissolve the yeast in water with a pinch of the sugar. Let this sit until the mixture is bubbly.

Scald the milk and pour into a large mixing bowl. Stir in the vinegar, butter and the remainder of the sugar. Let this mixture cool to lukewarm.

Beat the egg yolks into the yeast mixture. Add the vanilla, 1 cup of the flour and the salt and stir to combine. Blend in 5 more cups of the flour, a cup at a time, mixing well after each cup.

Kneading: When the dough holds together (it will be quite soft) and begins to pull away from the sides of the bowl, turn it out onto your kneading surface where you've sprinkled part of the last cup of flour.

Knead with well-floured hands for 3 to 4 minutes. Add only enough flour to keep it from sticking (though you may need the whole extra cup).

Shaping: Divide the dough into 5 parts. Cover with a damp towel and let rest for 15 minutes.

Roll out the dough, 1 part at a time, into a rectangular shape a little thicker than pie crust (¹/₈ inch). Spread the surface with filling leaving 1 inch clear on 2 short sides and 1 long side.

Starting with the side where the filling comes all the way to the edge, roll the dough up. Pinch the seam as well as the ends together with your fingertips. Place the seam down on greased baking sheets, allowing room for the dough to expand.

Chilling: Cover loosely with plastic wrap that you've greased lightly so the dough won't stick to it. Refrigerate for 4 to 5 hours or overnight.

Baking: Thirty minutes before baking, remove the rolls from the refrigerator. Preheat the oven to 375°F.

Just before you put the rolls in the oven, brush them gently with an egg beaten with a couple of teaspoons of water.

Bake for 30 to 35 minutes or until they are golden. Cool on a wire rack.

SWEDISH COFFEE BREAD

This coffee bread comes from Ruth Porter's Swedish forebears. Ruth, with her great knowledge of baking, taught and inspired her husband, Bert, who was King Arthur Flour's chief spokesman for many years. (Bert and Ruth are currently enjoying a peaceful retirement and although we continue to consult with them from time to time, we miss them.)

1 cup milk, lukewarm
1 rounded tablespoon or 2 packages active dry yeast
4$^1/_2$ to 5 cups King Arthur Unbleached All-Purpose Flour
2 eggs
$^1/_2$ cup sugar
6 tablespoons butter, softened
1$^1/_2$ teaspoons salt
1 teaspoon crushed cardamom or 6 whole cardamom seeds crushed
melted butter
cinnamon mixed with sugar to sprinkle on top

Making the Dough: Blend the milk, yeast and 1 cup of the flour together in a mixing bowl. Let this stand for 12 to 15 minutes while the yeast dissolves and becomes active. When the yeast mixture is bubbling and expanded, beat in the eggs, sugar, butter, salt and cardamom. Don't worry about lumps.

Gradually add the balance of the flour stirring until the dough begins to hold together and pull away from the sides of the bowl.

Kneading & Rising: Turn this soft dough out onto a lightly floured kneading surface and knead for 3 to 4 minutes. Let the dough rest while you clean out and grease the bowl. Continue kneading for another 3 or 4 minutes. When the dough is smooth and elastic, place it in the bowl, turning it so the top is greased. Cover and let it rise until doubled, 1$^1/_2$ to 2 hours.

Shaping & Rising: When you can poke a finger in the dough without it springing back, punch it down, turn it out and knead out any stray bubbles.

Cut the dough in half and then each half into 3 pieces. Roll each of the pieces into a long rope and then braid so you have two braided loaves (see page 123). If you want to form the loaves without braiding that's all right too.

Place the loaves, braided or unbraided, in two 4$^1/_2$ x 8$^1/_2$-inch, greased bread pans. Brush the tops with melted butter and sprinkle with cinnamon sugar. Cover and let rise until doubled, about an hour.

Baking: About 15 minutes before you want to bake your loaves, preheat the oven to 350°F. Bake them for about 30 minutes. Turn out and cool on a rack.

Ricotta Sweet Bread

This is an old King Arthur Flour recipe redesigned by Michael Jubinsky to include ricotta cheese, making a lovely, rich loaf which can be baked in a traditional loaf pan or filled and made into a mock braid or twist.

Proofing Sponge

2 tablespoons or packets active dry yeast
1/2 cup warm water
pinch of sugar
1/2 cup King Arthur Unbleached All-Purpose Flour

Proofing the Yeast: Dissolve the yeast in the warm water with the sugar and the flour. Stir and set aside until bubbly and expanded, about 15 minutes.

Dough

1 cup milk
1 cup sugar
1/2 cup (1 stick) butter
2 teaspoons salt
1 cup ricotta cheese
1 tablespoon vanilla
3 eggs
7 1/2 to 8 1/2 cups King Arthur Unbleached All-Purpose Flour
1 cup golden raisins (optional)
1/2 cup candied fruit and peel (optional)
wash made of 1 egg yolk beaten with 1 tablespoon water

Making the Dough: Scald the milk. Stir in the the sugar, butter, salt and ricotta cheese. Allow this to cool to lukewarm and then add the vanilla.

In a large bowl, beat the eggs and add the milk and yeast mixtures. Stir in 7 1/2 cups of flour, one cup at a time, until the dough comes cleanly away from the sides of the bowl. (If you are using golden raisins and/or candied fruit and peel, add them to the recipe after 4 or 5 cups of flour have been added.)

Turn the dough out onto your kneading surface which you've sprinkled with the remainder of the flour. Scrape the bowl and add the extra bits to the dough. Wash out and lightly oil (or just oil) the bowl and set it aside.

Kneading & Rising: Knead the dough until it is smooth and elastic, adding only enough flour to prevent sticking. The dough will be moderately soft.

Place it in the oiled bowl and turn it over to oil all surfaces. Cover the bowl with plastic wrap and/or a clean towel and set in a warm, draft-free place until doubled in bulk, 1 to 1½ hours. Punch down the dough, divide into thirds (for 3 loaves) and let rest, covered, for 10 minutes.

Shaping & Rising: Divide the dough into thirds, shape and place in lightly greased baking pans. Cover with plastic wrap and a clean towel and let rise in a warm, draft-free place for about 45 minutes.

Baking: About fifteen minutes before you want to bake your bread, preheat your oven to 350°F. Just before the loaves go in, brush the tops of the loaves with the egg wash.

Bake for 30 to 40 minutes, or until the loaves are a deep golden brown. If the tops appear to be browning too rapidly, loosely tent them with foil.

When done, immediately remove the loaves from their pans and cool on wire racks.

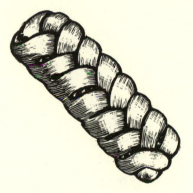

FILLED RICOTTA SWEET BRAID, ROLL OR TWIST

Prepare the Cream Cheese Filling flavored with orange extract, which you'll find with the Sweet Dough Fillings on page 219.

Divide the dough into thirds, and shape into a Mock Braid (page 214), Rolled Loaf (page 215), or Twist (page 216). Let it rise for 45 minutes to an hour before baking as above.

BABKA

"Babka" is a Polish word for grandmother. This rich bread, laced with rum syrup, derives its name from its shape. It is baked in a tube or (preferably) a Bundt pan so, when it's served, it looks like a grandmother's wide, fluted skirt. Although it's traditionally shaped that way, Babka, like other sweet doughs, can be shaped any way you please.

Proofing Sponge

> 1/2 cup warm milk, preferably fat free
> 1 teaspoon sugar
> 2 teaspoons or 1 packet active dry yeast
> 1/2 cup King Arthur Unbleached All-Purpose Flour

Making the Sponge: Pour the warmed milk into a medium-sized mixing bowl. Add and dissolve the sugar and the yeast. Blend in the flour and let this work for 10 to 15 minutes until the mixture is bubbly and expanded.

Dough

> 3 eggs, at room temperature
> 1/2 teaspoon salt
> 1/4 cup sugar
> 1/4 cup (1/2 stick) butter, softened
> 1/4 cup mixed candied fruit or peel
> 1/4 cup currants or raisins
> 1 1/2 cups King Arthur Unbleached All-Purpose Flour

Making the Dough: When the yeast mixture has doubled, add and beat in the eggs. Stir in the salt, sugar and butter. Add the fruit to the flour and blend into the yeast mixture. Beat this spongy dough with a large spoon until it is smooth and elastic.

Rising: Cover the bowl with a damp towel or plastic wrap and place it somewhere warm to rise for about an hour.

Shaping & Rising: Stir in the fruit. Turn the dough into a greased, two-quart Bundt or tube pan, cover, and let rise again for 1/2 hour.

Baking: Fifteen minutes before baking, preheat your oven to 350°F. Bake for 35 to 40 minutes.

Rum Syrup

$^1/_2$ cup sugar
$^1/_4$ cup water
1 tablespoon rum

Preparing the Rum Syrup: Combine the ingredients in a small saucepan and bring to a boil.

Immediately after the cake comes out of the oven and before removing it from the pan, prick the surface with a fork. Pour the syrup over the cake. After the syrup is absorbed, remove the cake from the pan and cool on a wire rack.

When the Babka is cool you can drizzle on the White Sugar Glaze (page 207), if you wish.

CHEESE BABKA

This is a Babka of a completely different sort.

Proofing Sponge

$^1/_2$ cup warm water
1 teaspoon sugar
1 rounded tablespoon or two packets active dry yeast
$^1/_2$ cup King Arthur Unbleached All-Purpose Flour

Activating the Yeast: Pour the warm water into a large mixing bowl and dissolve in it the sugar and the yeast. Stir in the $^1/_2$ cup of flour and let this small sponge work for about 10 to 15 minutes, or until the mixture is bubbly and expanded.

Dough

$^1/_2$ cup milk
$^1/_2$ cup (1 stick) butter
$^1/_2$ cup sugar
2 eggs plus 1 egg yolk
$3^1/_2$ to $4^1/_2$ cups King Arthur Unbleached All-Purpose Flour
1 teaspoon salt
$^3/_4$ cup golden raisins
1 tablespoon grated lemon peel
1 recipe Cottage Cheese Filling (page 219)
1 egg white beaten with 2 teaspoons water, for wash (the yolk is in the filling)

Making the Dough: Scald the milk in a small saucepan. Remove from the heat and add the butter and sugar. Stir to melt the butter and dissolve the sugar.

When the milk mixture has cooled, beat it and the eggs (and the extra yolk) into the active yeast. Add 2 cups of flour and the salt and mix thoroughly. Add the raisins and lemon peel and enough of the remaining flour to make a soft dough. Stir until this holds together and comes away from the sides of the bowl.

Kneading: Turn the dough out onto a lightly floured kneading surface. Flour your hands and knead for 3 or 4 minutes.

Let the dough rest while you clean out and grease your bowl. Knead the dough another 3 or 4 minutes or until it is smooth and elastic. Add only enough flour to keep it from sticking to the board or to you.

Rising: Place the kneaded dough in the bowl, turning it so the top is also greased. Cover it with a damp towel or plastic wrap and let it rise until it has doubled in bulk, 1 1/2 to 2 hours.

While the dough is rising, make up the Cottage Cheese Filling.

Shaping & Rising: When you can poke your finger in the dough without it springing back, turn it out onto your floured kneading board, cut it in half and shape each into a ball. Cover with a damp towel and let the dough rest for 15 minutes.

With a rolling pin, roll each piece of dough into a rectangle 10 x 18 inches. Spread cheese filling down the center third of each rectangle and form a Mock Braid (page 214).

Place the shaped loaves on a lightly greased baking sheet, cover with a damp towel or greased plastic wrap and let rise for 45 minutes to 1 hour.

Baking: Fifteen minutes before you want to bake your loaves, preheat the oven to 350°F. Just before they go in the oven, brush the tops with the egg wash. Bake for 30 to 35 minutes.

Remove from the baking sheet and cool on a wire rack.

PORTUGUESE SWEET BREAD

If you've spent any time in southeastern Massachusetts or northern Rhode Island, you have discovered one of New England's secrets. This recipe was collected by the Jubinsky bread baking team which has an affinity for this part of the world. Some versions of this cake-like bread contain a hint of lemon flavoring which you can add if you wish.

Proofing Sponge

> ½ cup warm water
> 1 teaspoon sugar
> 2 tablespoons or packets active dry yeast
> ½ cup King Arthur Unbleached All-Purpose Flour

Making the Sponge: Pour the water into a large bowl and in it dissolve the sugar and yeast. Stir in the flour and set aside until bubbly and expanded, about 15 minutes. Don't worry about lumps.

Dough

> 1 cup milk
> ½ cup (1 stick) butter
> 1 cup sugar
> 1 teaspoon salt
> 1 tablespoon grated lemon peel (optional)
> 7½ to 8½ cups King Arthur Unbleached All-Purpose Flour
> 4 eggs plus 1 egg yolk
> wash made of 1 egg white beaten with 1 tablespoon water

Making the Dough: Scald the milk. Remove from heat and add butter, sugar, salt, and lemon peel. Stir to dissolve and then let the mixture cool to lukewarm.

Beat the eggs and yolk together until frothy. Add them and the milk mixture to the proofing sponge. Stir in 6 to 7 cups of flour, one cup at a time, until the dough comes cleanly away from the sides of the bowl.

Turn the dough out onto a lightly floured board. Scrape the bowl and add the bits of dough. There is no need to wash the bowl at this time; just lightly oil and set it aside.

Kneading & Rising: Knead the dough, adding only enough flour to keep the dough from sticking to your hands and the board. When the dough is smooth and satiny, place in the oiled bowl. Turn to lightly oil the entire surface of the dough. Cover the bowl with greased plastic wrap and a clean towel. Let the dough rise in a warm place until doubled in bulk, 1½ to 2 hours.

Shaping & Rising: Punch the dough down and divide in two equal pieces. Shape into two round loaves and place in two greased, 9-inch round cake pans.

Cover loosely with plastic wrap (which you've greased so that it won't stick to the dough) and a clean towel and let the loaves rise in a warm place until doubled in bulk, about one hour.

Baking: Preheat your oven to 375°F for at least 15 minutes. Brush the loaves with the egg white and water mixture.

Bake 35 to 40 minutes or until the loaves sound hollow when tapped on the bottom with a finger. If the tops appear to be browning too rapidly, loosely tent with foil. When the bread is done, remove it from the oven and cool it on a wire rack.

MONKEY BREAD

This is certainly a coffeecake, but its name is Monkey Bread. No one knows quite where that name came from although it might be its resemblance to a bunch of coconuts after it's baked. It's a favorite of former President and Mrs. Reagan who use it as a festival or holiday bread. Nancy's explanation of the name is that you have to "monkey around" with it when you make it.

With a few minor adjustments, we can turn a basic sweet dough into Monkey Bread. A savory variation follows.

Dough

> 2 eggs
> warm water (to make 2 cups)
> ½ cup brown sugar, packed
> 2 tablespoons or packets active dry yeast
> ½ cup non-fat dry milk
> ¼ cup (½ stick) butter, softened
> 5½ to 6½ cups King Arthur Unbleached All-Purpose Flour 🌾
> 1 tablespoon salt

Making the Dough: Break two eggs into a two-cup liquid measure and fill the balance with warm water. Pour this into a mixing bowl and beat it together. Add 1 tablespoon of the brown sugar and when it has dissolved, add the yeast.

After the yeast has dissolved, stir in the dry milk, the balance of the sugar and butter. Mix in a cup of the flour and then the salt. Add about 5½ cups more flour, a cup at a time, and mix until it begins to hold together.

Kneading & Rising: Turn the dough out onto a floured surface and, with floured hands, knead until the dough begins to feel smooth and less sticky. Add only enough flour to keep it from sticking to you or the board.

Give the dough a little rest while you clean out and grease your bowl. Knead the dough a little longer until it's really smooth and silky. Place it in the greased bowl, turning it so it is greased all over. Cover it with plastic wrap or a damp towel and put in in a cozy, draft-free place to double in bulk. This will take 1 1/2 to 2 hours depending on how warm it is. When you can stick your finger in it without it bouncing back, the dough has doubled.

Glaze

> 1 cup maple syrup or brown sugar
> 1/2 cup (1 stick) butter
> 1/2 cup currants (optional)
> 1/2 cup chopped nuts (optional)

Monkeying Around: Knock the dough down and let it rest for 5 minutes or so. While it's resting, grease two monkey bread pans (see Appendix) or one 9- or 10-inch tube pan, and prepare the glaze. On the stove, over low heat, combine the maple syrup or brown sugar, butter, currants and nuts. You can leave these last two ingredients out, but they add flavor and texture. Let the mixture cool so you won't burn yourself.

Take the dough and pull off small pieces to make balls that are about 1 inch in diameter. Roll them in the glaze and place them in the monkey bread (or tube) pans. If there is any glaze left over, pour it over the top.

Cover the tube pan and let the dough rise for about an hour.

Baking: About 15 minutes before you want to bake the bread, preheat the oven to 350°F. Bake this delectable concoction for 30 to 35 minutes (45 to 50 minutes for the tube pan). If the top appears to be browning too fast, turn the heat down to 325°F for the last 15 minutes.

Turning Out & Serving: After the bread has cooled for about 5 minutes, turn it out onto a platter large enough to accommodate it. When it has cooled enough to handle, break off pieces to enjoy with a cup of tea or coffee, or a big glass of milk.

SAVORY MONKEY BREAD

Use this same monkeying around technique to make a savory bread as well.

Make up your basic Hearth Bread dough (page 114) and, as you did with the preceding dough, pull off and shape 1-inch balls of dough.

Roll the balls in melted butter that has been seasoned with an herb mixture and perhaps some minced scallions or onions. Roll them once more in some grated cheese if that appeals to you.

Bake as you would the preceding Monkey Bread.

JACK-O-LANTERN BREAD

If you make jack-o-lanterns at Halloween, you'll probably have plenty of pumpkin on hand. Usually the old, sad faces get made into quick breads or pumpkin pies, or, dreariest for them, tossed back into the garden. But here's a new twist, a yeasted bread flavored with all those things that go into quick breads or pumpkin pies. (Make sure your pumpkins are the small, sweet variety known as "pie pumpkins.")

1 1/2 cups warm water
1 tablespoon sugar
2 tablespoons or packets active dry yeast
1/4 cup (1/2 stick or 4 tablespoons) butter or margarine, softened
1/2 cup brown sugar, packed
2 eggs
1 cup cooked, mashed pumpkin
2 teaspoons cinnamon
1 teaspoon nutmeg
1 cup raisins
2 cups King Arthur Stone Ground Whole Wheat Flour
1 tablespoon salt
3 1/2 to 4 1/2 cups King Arthur Unbleached All-Purpose Flour

Making the Dough: Pour the water into a large mixing bowl. Stir in the sugar and yeast. Let this sit until the mixture is bubbly.

Add the butter, brown sugar (you can get rid of lumps by pressing the sugar through a coarse sieve), eggs, pumpkin, spices, and raisins. Mix this slurry together and then blend in the whole wheat flour and salt.

Slowly add the unbleached flour, stirring with a spoon until the dough begins to hold together and pull away from the sides of the bowl.

Kneading: Turn it out onto a floured board and knead for 3 or 4 minutes adding only enough flour to keep it from sticking to you or the board.

Give the dough a rest while you clean and grease your bowl. When you return to the dough, it will have relaxed somewhat.

Continue kneading another 3 or 4 minutes until it's smooth and doesn't stick to you or the board. When it's smooth and springy, form it into a nice ball and place it in the bowl, turning it so the top of the dough is greased.

Rising: Cover and let it rise until you can poke your finger in it without it springing back. This should take 1 to 2 hours depending on how warm it is.

For a finer grain, or if you have something else to do once it's fully risen, knock the dough down a second time and let it rise again.

Shaping: When you're ready to put the dough into your bread pans, knock it down a final time and cut it into 2 or 3 pieces depending on whether you want 2 large or 3 medium-sized loaves.

Shape it, put it in greased pans and let it rise a final time for 35 to 45 minutes.

Baking: Put the loaves in a cold oven, set the temperature to 400°F and bake for 15 minutes. Turn the temperature down to 350°F and bake a further 20 minutes (or more).

After the bread is done, cool the loaves completely (they slice much more easily) and put one in the freezer (in an airtight plastic bag) to save for Thanksgiving day.

STICKY BUNS

The aroma of sticky buns in a cozy kitchen creates one of the loveliest of childhood memories. With a few adjustments to your basic sweet dough, you can create a few memories yourself. Here is our basic recipe, followed by several variations. Don't hesitate to dream up your own using any dough or filling.

The Dough

2 eggs
warm water (to make 2 cups)
2 tablespoons sugar
1 tablespoon or packet active dry yeast
2 tablespoons butter, softened, or vegetable oil
1/2 cup non-fat dry milk
2 cups King Arthur Stone Ground Whole Wheat Flour
1 tablespoon salt
3 to 3 1/2 cups King Arthur Unbleached All-Purpose Flour

A Traditional Filling

8 tablespoons (1 stick) butter, at room temperature
3/4 to 1 cup packed brown sugar
1 teaspoon cinnamon
1 cup chopped or ground nuts or 1/2 cup each chopped or ground nuts
    and currants or raisins (optional; leave out, or add even more)

Making the Dough: Break the eggs into a two-cup liquid measure and fill the balance with warm water. Pour this into a mixing bowl and beat until thoroughly blended.

Add and dissolve the sugar and yeast. Let this mixture work until it's bubbly and expanded, 5 to 10 minutes. Then beat in the butter or oil and the dry milk.

When all of this is thoroughly blended, add the whole wheat flour and salt. Stir in 3 cups of unbleached flour until the mixture holds together and pulls away from the side of the bowl.

Kneading & Rising: Turn the dough out onto a well-floured board. This dough will be sticky, so keep your hands well floured. Knead for 3 to 4 minutes, adding only enough flour to keep it from sticking to the board or you. Use a dough scraper to help if you need to.

Give the dough a rest while you clean and grease your bowl. Continue kneading until the dough is smooth, elastic and no longer sticky. (This will happen, even with a soft dough such as this.)

Place it in the greased bowl, cover, put it somewhere cozy, and let it rise until you can poke your finger in it without it springing back, between 1½ and 2 hours.

Preparing the Filling: While the dough is rising, gather your ingredients for the filling. (Be sure to see the Other Sticky Bun Fillings on the following page.) Put aside about one-quarter of the filling for later.

Shaping & Rising: Punch the dough down and roll it out into a large rectangle, about 12 x 24 inches (or, if you haven't the room, two smaller ones, 9 x 18 inches). The dough should be somewhere between ¼ to ½ inch thick.

Spread the softened butter on the rectangle(s), leaving an inch around the outside edge. Sprinkle on the brown sugar and cinnamon. (Add the nuts and currants or raisins, if you're so inclined.) This is where children can help.

Half of this dough will fill a 9-inch cake pan. The whole recipe needs a medium-sized roasting pan. If you brush your pans with a thin film of shortening (even before buttering it), it will help prevent sticking.

Butter, sugar and "cinnamon" your pan with the ingredients you had set aside. (You can even throw some nuts in as well.)

Starting with the long edge, roll the dough up like a jelly roll. Pinch the outside edge to the main body of the dough.

Cut the roll into ¾- to 1-inch slices. Place the slices in the prepared pans with a bit of space between them so they have room to expand. Cover the buns and let them rise for 45 minutes to an hour.

Baking: Place the pan in a cold oven and set the temperature to 400°F for 15 minutes. During this 15 minutes, the buns will finish rising and assume their final, wonderful, expanded shape.

After this 15-minute period, turn the temperature down to 350°F for a further 20 to 30 minutes. Check after 20 minutes. If there's the slightest aroma of browning sugar, turn the temperature down to 325°F for the final 10 minutes.

Turning Out: While these buns are still hot, loosen the sides a bit with a knife. Then find a plate or platter that will accommodate them.

Invert the platter over the baking pan, flip them both over and allow the baking pan to stay in place for a few minutes to allow everything to come out. (Anything left in the bottom of the pan is fair game for the cook and the helpers.)

ORANGE RAISIN STICKY BUNS

    6 tablespoons (1 stick) butter
    ½ cup sugar
    1 to 2 tablespoons freshly grated orange peel (rind of 1 orange)
    ½ to 1 cup raisins

If you haven't a sharp grater or don't want to risk your knuckles, use a sharp vegetable peeler. This will take off just the outside layer of orange peel, which is what you want. This can be minced as finely as you wish.

Prepare and shape the dough as directed on the preceding page. In this case just grease the bottom of your pan without sprinkling on any filling ingredients.

Orange Glaze

    2 cups confectioners' sugar
    3 tablespoons orange juice

Combine the sugar and juice to make the glaze.

When the buns are done, turn them out as described on the preceding page and drizzle the glaze over them.

CRANBERRY STICKY BUNS

Cranberries, brown sugar and butter, cooked until the cranberries burst and release their lovely color, flavor and tiny crunchy seeds, create a flavor that even a child will love. It doesn't need anything else; it is sublime just as it is. For a special ray of sunshine during dark winter days, make some sticky buns with this sunny little fruit.

    2 cups cranberries, cleaned
    1 cup light brown sugar, packed
    8 tablespoons (1 stick) butter
    1 to 2 tablespoons freshly grated orange rind (optional)

Simmer these ingredients together in a large saucepan and then chill them. This filling may be rather oozy and some of the cranberry mixture will escape from the slices, but that's fine since it becomes the glaze when the pan is inverted.

Make the dough, shape and bake as for the Sticky Buns on the preceding page.

English Chelsea Buns

The antecedent of the sticky bun is probably the Chelsea Bun. Chelsea Buns were made famous more than 200 years ago when they were baked and sold at the Chelsea Bun House, not far from the River Thames, in London. In those years this was a magnetic place where many Londoners walked on a Sunday morning to sit and indulge themselves with a treat we can only imagine today. They were a favorite of the Royal family who often visited the Bun House by way of the river.

Dough

> 1 recipe Sticky Bun dough (page 234)
> 1 tablespoon freshly grated lemon peel

Filling

> 6 tablespoons butter, at room temperature
> ½ cup sugar
> 1 cup currants, plumped in fruit juice or tea

Glaze

> 1 cup confectioners' sugar
> 4 to 5 teaspoons water
> 1 teaspoon freshly grated lemon peel

Make up the same dough but add the tablespoon of freshly grated lemon peel.

Shape and bake as for Sticky Buns without putting any filling on the bottom of the pan.

Mix the glaze ingredients together. Right after the buns come out of the oven, drizzle the glaze over them. Let them cool and "set" for a few minutes before you try to remove and separate them.

Raised Doughnuts

Unlike cake doughnuts which are leavened with baking powder, raised doughnuts are leavened with yeast and have a lighter, spongier texture. These take some time, but the yeast will do a lot of the work for you while you go about other things.

The Sponge

> 1 cup warm water
> 1 tablespoon sugar
> 1 tablespoon or packet of yeast
> ½ cup non-fat dry milk
> 1½ cups King Arthur Stone Ground Whole Wheat Flour

Making the Sponge: Pour the warm water into a mixing bowl. Dissolve in it the sugar, yeast and dry milk. Blend in the whole wheat flour. This makes a sponge which you cover and let work for 15 or 20 minutes, until it is bubbly and expanded.

The Rest

> 2 tablespoons butter, softened
> ½ cup sugar
> 1 egg, well beaten
> 1 teaspoon salt
> 2 cups King Arthur Unbleached All-Purpose Flour

Making the Dough: After the sponge is bubbling, blend in the butter, sugar, and egg. Add the salt and unbleached flour. This should make a dough just barely firm enough to knead, but don't be afraid to add a bit more flour to make it manageable.

Kneading & Rising: Turn the dough out onto a floured board and knead with floured hands for 3 to 4 minutes. Let it rest while you clean and grease your bowl. Knead the dough another 3 to 4 minutes until it's smooth and elastic. Then place it in the bowl turning it to grease the top. Let it rise for 1½ to 2 hours, until doubled.

Shaping: Turn the dough out onto your floured board and roll it out to about ½ inch in thickness. Cut out doughnuts with a doughnut cutter and let the doughnuts and holes rest about 20 minutes.

Frying: While they rest, prepare a heavy skillet with enough vegetable oil or shortening in which to submerge them. It should be heated to about 375°F or whatever will cook one of the doughnut holes to a golden brown in about 40 seconds.

Drop the doughnuts gently into the heated oil with the raised side down. As soon as they come to the surface, flip them over so they'll expand evenly without cracking. When they're golden brown, remove them with a slotted spoon and drain them on absorbent paper.

Finishing Touches: Enjoy your doughnuts plain or all dressed up.

- **Confectioners' Sugar Glaze:** Blend 4 teaspoons of water or milk with 1 cup of confectioners' sugar. For extra zip, you can add a teaspoon of grated lemon peel. Brush on this glaze while the doughnuts are hot.

- **Honey Glaze:** Blend 1/2 cup of honey with 2 tablespoons of water and 1 or 2 teaspoons of lemon juice. Brush on while the doughnuts are hot.

- **Confectioners' Sugar:** When the doughnuts are cool, shake them, 2 or 3 at a time, in a paper bag with 1/2 cup of confectioners' sugar.

- **Cinnamon Sugar:** When the doughnuts are cool, shake them in a paper bag with 1/2 cup sugar mixed with 2 to 4 teaspoons of cinnamon.

ANNIE DAVIS'S FRIED BREAD

This next recipe is not so much a recipe as a joyful way of using up some leftover bread dough. When Brinna Sands was a little girl, her Grandmother Davis always saved some dough from the week's baking to make this treat. Even today, the anticipation of fried bread for a weekend breakfast (now created for different little grandchildren) creates for her that same old anticipation as well as myriad memories. Any bread dough will do although Anadama is a particular favorite.

Making & Rising your Dough: Make up Anadama dough according to the directions on page 139 and allow it to rise once (at least). Don't knock it down.

Frying: Heat a small kettle of vegetable oil as for the raised doughnuts. Drop in golf ball–sized pieces of dough. If they're a bit ragged, all the better for soaking up butter and maple syrup. You can even flatten them out to look more like those you can buy at county fairs. Turn them over when they float to the top and flip them back and forth occasionally until they look done. Peek inside one (two forks help prevent burns) to make sure they really are. Drain them on paper towels and serve while still hot with butter and maple syrup.

The Sands' younger son, Davis, a next-generation aficionado of fried bread, has taken this idea in another direction. Instead of frying a blob of empty dough, he opens it up, tucks in some chopped ham and cheese, closes it up tight, and then drops it in the oil to cook. The cheese melts around the ham, and the fried bread is transformed into a hot ham & cheese fritter "sandwich."

KEES WILLEMSEN'S
OLIE BOLLEN

An olie bol is reminiscent of a yeast-raised doughnut or fried bread, but different. The Dutch celebrate New Year's Eve with them, but they are so good, you may want to practice making them several times so at year's end, you'll be an expert. This recipe came from the Sands' Dutch, American Field Service son who has spent many a New Year's Eve cooking these on the sidewalk outside his father's bakery in Haarlem, Holland. Since they are made especially for New Year's they really belong in the Festival Bread section, but they are irresistible for breakfast any time of year.

1 tablespoon sugar
1 tablespoon or packet active dry yeast
½ cup non-fat dry milk
2 cups warm water
2 eggs
1 teaspoon lemon juice
1 teaspoon salt
½ cup currants
½ cup golden raisins
2 apples peeled, cored and chopped
4 cups King Arthur Flour Unbleached All-Purpose Flour

Mixing: Dissolve the sugar, yeast and dry milk successively in the warm water. Let sit until bubbly, about 5 minutes. Beat in the eggs and lemon juice. Add the salt and fruit to the flour and stir into the yeast mixture. This will produce a very wet dough which you'll want to cover with plastic wrap or a damp towel so it can bubble away and expand for 1 to 2 hours. If you want to mix this together in the evening for brunch the next day, put the bowl in the refrigerator where it will rise but at a pace designed to give you a good night's sleep.

Cooking: About half an hour before you want to cook the Olie Bollen, stir down the dough and let it rest. After 20 minutes, heat 3 to 4 inches of vegetable oil in a large saucepan until it reaches 375°F or whatever will cook a 1-inch cube of bread to a golden brown in about 40 seconds.

With a large spoon or ice cream scoop (dipped first in the hot oil), transfer a glob of dough to the hot fat. Cook several at a time, but allow enough room for them to expand. To help them expand somewhat uniformly, flip them over after they've first risen to the surface. Continue cooking them until they're a warm golden brown on both sides, flipping them back and forth as needed. Remove with a slotted spoon and drain them on paper towels.

The Dutch eat these wonderful things by tearing them apart and dipping them in powdered sugar, but the Sands know from experience that maple syrup is an acceptable alternative, even to a Dutchman.

French Brioche

Brioche dough contains many eggs, lots of butter and just a touch of sugar to produce an incredibly light, almost cake-like bread. With its own traditional shape, it's the perfect thing for a special occasion breakfast or brunch. It is best to start this the day before you want to serve it.

2 tablespoons or packets active dry yeast
1/4 cup sugar (or less)
1 cup warm water
4 to 6 eggs (to equal 1 cup)
1 cup (2 sticks) butter, at room temperature
5 1/2 cups King Arthur Unbleached All-Purpose Flour
1 tablespoon salt
1 egg beaten with 2 teaspoons of water for wash

Mixing: Dissolve the yeast and 1 tablespoon of the sugar in the water. Let this sit until bubbly. Beat in the eggs one at a time. Add the balance of the sugar and the butter, in pieces. Stir in your first cup of flour and then add the salt. Add the balance of the flour.

Kneading: Because this dough is so soft, it's almost impossible to knead on a board so the easiest way to handle it is right in the bowl. Pick it up with well-floured hands (or use your bowl scraper or even a large wooden spoon), fold it in half and throw it back in the bottom of the bowl. Do this for at least 10 minutes to develop the elasticity of the gluten sufficiently. You'll be able to tell when you've arrived at this point because the dough, although it will still be "gloppy," will have developed a resilience and sheen.

Rising: Cover the dough and let the yeast work at room temperature for at least two hours, like a sponge, although you won't be adding more flour later.

Chilling: After this 2-hour period, stir the dough down, cover it again and refrigerate it all day or overnight. This not only develops the flavor through a slow, cool rise, but it also solidifies the butter so the dough is more manageable.

Shaping & Rising: The traditional way to bake brioche is in a special pan shaped like a very large, fluted muffin cup (see Appendix). Our recipe will make two of these. (If you don't have a brioche pan see the variations that follow.) Remove the dough from the refrigerator and punch it down. Cut it in half and from each half cut a piece that is about the diameter of a golf ball. Take one of the larger pieces, shape and put it in the greased brioche pan. Make an indentation in the top. Shape the smaller piece into a ball and place it securely in the indentation in the larger piece. Let the brioche rise for 1 to 1 1/2 hours.

Baking: About 15 minutes before you want to bake them, preheat your oven to 350°F. Brush with the egg/water wash and bake for 30 to 40 minutes.

Shaping Variations

If you don't have a brioche pan, here are a couple of alternatives.

Bread Pan Brioche: Divide this dough in half and place in two 4½ x 8½-inch, greased bread pans. Let it rise for 1 to 1½ hours, brush with the egg/water wash and bake in a preheated 350°F oven for about 35 minutes.

Muffin Tin Brioche: Use a muffin tin to make smaller, individual brioche, with or without topknots. Allow these to rise for about an hour after they're shaped and bake them in a hotter 400°F oven for about 15 to 20 minutes.

Sally Lunn

A Sally Lunn is typical of seventeenth- and eighteenth-century English cakes or buns leavened with yeast. This particular one has long been associated with Bath, England, where the origin of the name has two traditions. The first is that they were made and "cried" in the streets by a woman name Sally Lunn to wealthy Britons who came to soak in the hot springs in the old Roman spa. The second involves a French connection which suggests that the name came from the French for "sun and moon," "soleil et lune," and was in fact originally a French bread similar to the French Brioche.

There is a strong Sally Lunn tradition in our own South where some families have handed down recipes through several generations. The cake itself, although light and sweet, contains much less sugar and fat than modern butter cakes.

Proofing Sponge

½ cup milk, lukewarm
3 or 4 threads of saffron (optional)
1 teaspoon sugar
1 teaspoon or packet active dry yeast
½ cup King Arthur Unbleached All-Purpose Flour

Saffron is made from the dried stigmas of a flower similar to a crocus which blooms in the fall. It takes tens of thousands of them to make a pound of saffron, which makes it extremely expensive. In medieval England, it was grown widely (Saffron Waldon in Essex was one the the largest centers of cultivation) and used to flavor both sweet and savory foods, as well as to give them its characteristic deep yellow color. It has now almost disappeared from use in sweet dishes although you will find it in a traditional "saffron" cake from Cornwall, and occasionally in a Sally Lunn.

Saffron has pungent flavor and odor which verge on the bitter if you use too much. With that admonition, if you're interested in giving it a try, heat the milk almost to boiling, drop in the threads and let them soak until they have released their color and aroma. Let the milk cool until it is lukewarm before you add the sugar and yeast.

Making the Sponge: Put the milk in a small mixing bowl and mix in the sugar, yeast and flour. Don't worry about lumps. Let this small sponge sit for 15 to 20 minutes until it is bubbly and expanded.

The Rest

> 2 eggs
> 2 cups King Arthur Unbleached All-Purpose Flour 🌾
> ¼ cup sugar
> ¼ cup (½ stick) butter, softened
> 1 teaspoon salt
> 1 teaspoon freshly grated lemon peel (optional)
> ½ recipe confectioners' sugar glaze (page 207)
> sweetened whipped cream (for filling)

Stirring & Rising: After the yeast mixture is happily bubbling away, beat in the eggs. Stir in 1 cup of flour and then the sugar, butter and salt (and lemon peel). Add a further cup of flour and beat this spongy dough thoroughly with a spoon until the mixture is smooth and elastic. Cover with a damp towel or plastic wrap and allow to rise for 1½ to 2 hours. After the dough has doubled, stir it down.

Shaping & Rising: Sally Lunns are traditionally baked in small, 5-inch cake pans (this recipe would take 3). In lieu of these, you can use most easily one 9-inch cake pan or a brioche pan. Or for smaller, individual versions this amount of batter will go nicely in a 12-cup muffin tin (medium sized) or one 6-cup muffin tin (giant size).

Lightly grease whatever pans you want to use. Divide the dough and put an equal amount in each. Cover loosely with greased plastic wrap and let rise for ¾ to 1 hour.

Baking: Fifteen minutes before you want to bake, preheat your oven.

> • **Cake or Brioche Pan:** Preheat oven to 375°F and bake for 30 minutes.

> • **Muffin Tins:** Preheat oven to 400°F. Bake for 15 to 20 minutes depending on size.

Finishing Touches: Brush on the glaze while the cakes are still hot.

A Sally Lunn is traditionally split in half horizontally once or twice (3 times for the brioche version) and filled with whipped cream. If you bake it as a cake, serve it cut in wedges.

It is completely delicious just as is, but you might garnish it with strawberries (or other fruit) in season.

• FESTIVAL BREADS •

Festival breads have long been a part of every culture's important days and events. They are usually embellished variations of daily fare, full of things that symbolize the richness of the occasions they are made to celebrate. These breads are important in that they are not just meant to be eaten and enjoyed, but are made and shared in ways that serve to bind people together.

Festival breads, made with yeast-leavened doughs, probably create more excitement that any other kind of baking. The magic of yeast, breathing life into a dough filled with symbolic ingredients, makes these breads the culinary symbols of the most important days in our lives. In making them you not only share the joys of baking but also the joys of living.

A FESTIVAL BREAD
FROM THE LAND OF KING ARTHUR
WITH A VERSION FOR NEW ENGLAND

All the Celtic countries with which the legendary King Arthur was associated have a colorful bread filled with fruits and spices, traditionally made to celebrate festivals and holidays. In Scotland it's called "Selkirk Bannock," in northern Wales "Bara Brith," in Ireland "Barm Brack," and across the channel in Brittany (or Little Britain) "Morlaix Brioche." It is simply our Simple Sweet Dough which has been loaded with those hard-to-get sweetmeats and spices which were saved for special occasions.

In addition to the old Celtic version, we've included variations to create a festival bread unique to New England.

  1 cup brown sugar
  2 cups warm water
  2 tablespoons or packets active dry yeast
  ½ cup non-fat dry milk
  2 cups King Arthur Stone Ground Whole Wheat Flour
  1 teaspoon cinnamon
  1 teaspoon allspice
  1 teaspoon nutmeg
  ½ cup (1 stick) butter or vegetable oil (or a combination)
  1 tablespoon salt (or less if you choose)
  4 to 5 cups King Arthur Unbleached All-Purpose Flour
  2 cups dried fruit: choose from either the Celtic or the New England
      version (or mix the two)

Celtic Version

> $^2/_3$ cup sultanas
> $^2/_3$ cup currants
> $^2/_3$ cup chopped peel (orange, lemon, citron, etc.)

New England Version

> $^2/_3$ cup cranberries chopped in half
> $^2/_3$ cup golden raisins
> $^2/_3$ cup currants

Mixing the Dough: Dissolve 1 tablespoon of the sugar in the water. Add and dissolve the yeast and dry milk. Stir in the whole wheat flour and spices. Cover and let this mixture work for 2 hours.

Preparing the Fruit: While the sponge bubbles away, melt the butter over very low heat. Remove it from the heat and add the balance of the sugar and the dried fruit of your choice. After 2 hours, blend this into the sponge.

Finishing & Kneading the Dough: Add the salt and then the unbleached flour a cup at a time, mixing thoroughly until the dough begins to pull away from the sides of the bowl. Turn out onto a floured surface and knead until it begins to feel as if it belongs together. Let it rest while you clean and grease your bowl. Continue kneading the relaxed dough until it feels smooth and springy.

Rising: Form it into a ball, place it in the greased bowl turning it so the top is greased, cover and place it where it will be warm and cozy. Because this is a sweet dough, we are using double the amount of yeast. Even so, the rising period may take longer than usual, $1^1/_2$ to 2 hours.

Shaping & Rising: When you can poke your finger in the dough without it bouncing back, knock it down, turn it out onto your floured board and knead out any stray bubbles.

You can divide this dough in two pieces and bake it in two bread pans or bake it as two round, free-form loaves. For a grander offering, bake it as one large, round loaf. Place the shaped dough in lightly greased bread pans or on a baking sheet. Let the dough rise until almost doubled again.

Baking: Fifteen minutes before you bake the bread, preheat your oven.

>   • **Two Loaves:** Preheat to 350°F and bake for 35 to 40 minutes.

>   • **One Large Loaf:** Preheat your oven to 400°F. Bake for 1 hour, lowering the temperature 25°F after the first 15 minutes and every 15 minutes thereafter.

CHALLAH

This bread is one whose origins lie deep in Jewish history. It is baked and eaten in many Jewish households on Friday night to welcome the Sabbath. The bread itself, while not overly sweet, is rich with eggs which make it golden in color and, like the French Brioche, almost cake-like in texture. Because it is contrary to Jewish dietary laws to eat milk and meat together, this bread is usually made with water and a vegetable oil or shortening so it may be eaten with any meal. It is traditionally braided and sometimes sprinkled with poppy seeds.

  1 cup warm water
  2 tablespoons sugar
  1 tablespoon or packet active dry yeast
  5$\frac{1}{2}$ to 6$\frac{1}{2}$ cups King Arthur Unbleached All-Purpose Flour
  4 eggs
  6 tablespoons vegetable oil
  1 tablespoon salt
  wash made of 1 egg mixed with 2 teaspoons water
  poppy seeds (optional)

Mixing: Pour the water into a mixing bowl, add and dissolve the sugar and then the yeast. Stir in one cup of the flour and let this work until bubbly and expanded, about 15 minutes.

In the meantime, beat the eggs until light. Beat the vegetable oil into the eggs and then add this to the yeast mixture. Blend in the salt and 4$\frac{1}{2}$ to 5 cups of flour and stir until the dough pulls away from the sides of the bowl.

Kneading & Rising: Turn out onto a floured kneading surface and knead for 3 or 4 minutes adding only enough flour to keep the dough from sticking. Give the dough a rest while you clean out and grease the bowl.

Knead the dough another 3 or 4 minutes, place it in the bowl, turning it so the top is greased. Cover and let it rise until it has doubled in bulk, 1$\frac{1}{2}$ to 2 hours.

Braiding & Rising: When you can poke your finger in the dough without it springing back, knock it down and turn it back out onto your floured kneading surface. Knead out any stray bubbles and let the dough rest for about 5 minutes.

Cut the dough in half and each half into 3 equal pieces. Roll these out until they're $\frac{3}{4}$ to 1 inch in diameter. You may need to let the dough relax from time to time.

Take 3 strands and braid them together and repeat for the second loaf. Pinch the ends together tightly. Place the braided loaves on a lightly greased baking sheet, cover and let rise for about 1 hour.

Baking: Fifteen minutes before you want to bake your bread, preheat the oven to 350°F.

Brush the surface of the loaves with the egg wash, sprinkle with poppy seeds if you wish, and bake for 35 to 40 minutes.

If you have a large enough baking sheet, it's fun to bake this as one large braided loaf. Increase your baking time by 10 to 15 minutes and reduce the heat to 325°F during the last 10 minutes of baking.

FOUR-IN-ONE HOLIDAY BREAD

When you want to make several loaves to freeze or to use as gifts, this large recipe is a good one. It was developed by Michael and Sandy Jubinsky who have given away more incredible loaves than most of us have ever baked.

This versatile dough, enough for 4 loaves, can be filled with the Cranberry Date-Nut Filling, the Butter Walnut Filling, the Poppy Seed Filling with Nuts and Fruit, etc., which you'll find with the Sweet Dough Fillings (page 218). This bread may be shaped as a Mock Braid, Rolled Loaf, Tea Ring, etc., instructions for which you'll find starting on page 214.

Proofing Sponge

3 tablespoons or packets active dry yeast
1/2 cup warm water
1/2 cup King Arthur Unbleached All-Purpose Flour
pinch of sugar

Proofing the Yeast: In a large bowl, dissolve the yeast in the water with the flour and pinch of sugar. Stir and set aside until bubbly, about 15 minutes.

Dough

2 cups milk
1 1/2 cups sugar
1/2 cup (1 stick) butter
1 tablespoon salt
6 eggs
1 tablespoon extract: vanilla, almond, lemon, etc. (optional)
9 1/2 to 11 1/2 cups King Arthur Unbleached All-Purpose Flour
1 egg beaten with 1 tablespoon water (for wash)

Making the Dough: Scald the milk, and add the sugar, butter and salt. Stir to dissolve and let this mixture cool to lukewarm. Add and beat in the eggs. Stir in flavoring if desired.

Add the milk mixture to the sponge. Stir in the flour, one cup at a time, until the dough comes cleanly away from the sides of the bowl.

Kneading & Rising: Turn the dough out onto a lightly floured board. Scrape the bowl and add these bits to the dough. Lightly oil the bowl and set it aside.

Knead the dough until it is smooth and elastic, adding only enough flour to prevent sticking. It will be moderately soft.

Place it into the oiled bowl, turning to oil all surfaces of the dough. Cover with plastic wrap and/or a damp towel, and set in a warm, draft-free place until doubled in bulk, 1½ to 2 hours.

Shaping: Punch down the dough, divide it into quarters and let it rest, covered, for 10 minutes.

Shape and fill your loaves in any way you wish and place on lightly greased baking pans. Cover with greased plastic wrap and a clean towel and let rise in a warm, draft-free place until doubled in bulk, about an hour.

Baking: About 15 minutes before you want to bake your bread, preheat your oven to 350°F. Just before the loaves go in the oven, brush their tops with the egg wash.

Bake at 350°F for 35 to 40 minutes or until a deep, golden brown. If the tops appear to be browning too rapidly, loosely tent with foil. When done, immediately remove the loaves from the pans and cool them on wire racks.

CHRISTMAS STOLLEN

This is an old recipe from the King Arthur Flour archives. It's a German festival bread closely related to the preceding Celtic bread. It is put together a bit differently but, as we've said before, there's more than one way to make bread.

1 ½ cups milk
½ cup (1 stick) butter
2 teaspoons salt
¼ cup sugar
¼ teaspoon mace
1 egg
grated rind of 1 orange
grated rind of 1 lemon
1 heaping tablespoon or 2 packets active dry yeast
5 to 6 cups King Arthur Unbleached All-Purpose Flour
½ cup purple raisins
½ cup golden raisins
½ cup chopped candied peel
½ cup chopped walnuts, pecans or sliced almonds
wash made by beating 1 egg with 2 teaspoons water (optional)

Making the Dough: Combine the milk and butter in a saucepan and heat until lukewarm. Pour into a large mixing bowl. Add the salt, sugar, mace, egg, orange and lemon rind, yeast and 1 ½ cups of the flour. Mix thoroughly and let stand for 15 to 20 minutes until the yeast has become active.

Add the fruit and nuts and about 5 cups of the flour, stirring until the dough begins to hold together and pull away from the sides of the bowl.

Kneading & Rising: Turn it out onto a floured kneading surface and knead for 7 to 8 minutes, adding only enough flour to keep the dough from sticking.

Clean out your mixing bowl, oil it lightly and place the dough inside, turning it over to grease the top. Cover and let rise until doubled (1 ½ to 2 hours).

Shaping & Rising: Punch the dough down and divide it into 3 pieces. Let it rest for about 5 minutes.

Take one piece and roll it into a 9 x 12-inch oval. Without stretching the dough, fold the long side over to within 1 inch of the opposite edge.

Repeat with the other pieces of dough. Place them on a greased baking sheet. Cover and let rise until doubled (about 1 hour).

Finishing & Baking: About 15 minutes before you want to bake the loaves, preheat your oven to 350°F. For a shiny crust, brush with an egg wash. Bake for about 25 minutes.

Instead of the egg wash, brush on melted butter just after you take the loaves from the oven. After they have cooled completely, dust with confectioners' sugar for a "snowy" crust.

ELFRIEDE FRANKLE'S HEFENKRANZ

Several years ago the Sands received a call from a woman in a neighboring town whose young son wanted to do a report on King Arthur. Since they've both had a long interest in matters Arthurian, both the mythical and the "real," they were delighted to share their accumulated materials with this young man. Todd Gunnerson's final presentation was excellent and it was gratifying to see the story of Arthur spark the excitement and imagination of another generation. Glimpses of a world fifteen hundred years in the past can be as exciting as contemplation of a world fifteen hundred years in the future.

As thanks, the mother of this young Arthurian scholar baked and presented them with a loaf of her mother's Christmas bread called Hefenkranz, which means "yeast wreath." It comes from the edge of the Black Forest in Germany, where Elfriede grew up.

2 eggs
warm water to make up 2 cups
1/4 cup sugar
1 tablespoon or packet active dry yeast
1/2 cup non-fat dry milk
1/2 cup (1 stick) butter, softened
5 to 6 cups King Arthur Unbleached All-Purpose Flour
1 teaspoon salt
grated rind of 1 lemon
1/2 to 1 cup golden raisins
1 egg beaten with 1 tablespoon of water for wash
sliced almonds for top

Mixing the Dough: Break the eggs into a two-cup measure and fill the balance with water. Pour these into a large mixing bowl and beat together. Add and dissolve 1 tablespoon of the sugar and the yeast.

When this mixture is active and bubbly, add the remaining sugar and dry milk. Blend the butter in as well as you can. It will be lumpy, but that's all right.

Blend in 3 cups of flour and the salt and again, don't worry about lumps. At this point add the lemon rind and the raisins. Work in between 2 and 3 more cups of flour until you have a soft but kneadable dough.

Kneading & Rising: Turn it out onto a floured surface and knead for 2 or 3 minutes. Let the dough rest while you clean and grease your bowl.

Continue kneading another 3 or 4 minutes. Put the dough in the bowl, cover, and let it rise somewhere cozy, until it's doubled.

Knock it down and let it rise again. This double rise creates a very fine grain which is appropriate for this bread.

Shaping & Rising: After this second rise, knock the dough down, turn it out onto your kneading board and divide into 3 pieces. Roll these out like snakes as far as you can. Let them rest for 3 or 4 minutes and continue rolling. You want 3 long strands about an inch in diameter which may involve several resting periods.

When the strands are the size you want them, braid them together gently and form a circle by weaving the two ends together as well as you can. Place the wreath on a large, well-greased baking sheet and let it rise, covered with a damp cloth, for 45 minutes to an hour.

Baking: Just before you place it in your oven, brush the surface with the egg and sprinkle on a generous handful of sliced almonds.

Place in a cold oven, turn the temperature to 400°F for 15 minutes and down to 350°F for a further 25 to 30 minutes.

Storing: After this glorious bread is thoroughly cooled, you can place it in an airtight plastic bag and freeze it until the morning of the day you serve it.

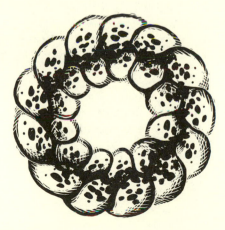

Italian Panettone

Panettone, once known only in the Milan area of Lombardy as a Christmas cake, has grown steadily into an all-season holiday bread. This is another from Michael and Sandy (Delano) Jubinsky's vast store of European festival breads.

Proofing Sponge

1 cup warm water
2 tablespoons or packets active dry yeast
1 teaspoon sugar
1 cup King Arthur Unbleached All-Purpose Flour

Making the Sponge: Dissolve the yeast in the warm water with the sugar. Stir in the flour and set aside until bubbly and expanded, about 10 minutes.

Dough

1 cup hot water
1 cup dry milk
1 cup sugar
$\frac{1}{2}$ cup (1 stick) butter
2 teaspoons salt
1 teaspoon vanilla
1 tablespoon orange rind
5 egg yolks, beaten
7 to 8 cups King Arthur Unbleached All-Purpose Flour
1 cup golden raisins, plumped in apple juice or warm water
$\frac{1}{2}$ cup candied citron
$\frac{1}{2}$ cup candied orange peel
fine bread crumbs (to sprinkle in pan)
wash made of 1 egg mixed with 1 tablespoon water

Making the Dough: In a large bowl, combine the hot water, dry milk, sugar, butter and salt. Stir to dissolve and let cool to lukewarm. Stir in the vanilla and orange rind.

Add the sponge, the beaten eggs yolks and 2 cups of the flour. Drain the raisins and add them. Stir in the candied fruit. Add the flour, one cup at a time, until the dough comes cleanly away from the sides of the bowl.

Kneading & Rising: Turn the dough out onto a lightly floured board. Scrape the bowl and add the bits to the dough. Lightly oil the bowl and set aside.

Knead the dough until it is smooth and elastic, adding only enough flour to prevent sticking. The dough should be moderately soft. Place it in your oiled bowl and turn to oil entire surface of the dough.

Cover with plastic wrap and a clean towel. Set in a warm, draft-free place until doubled in bulk, 1½ to 2 hours.

Shaping & Rising: Punch down the dough, divide it in half and let rest for 10 minutes.

Panettone is traditionally a tall, cylindrical loaf. Grease two large (26-ounce) coffee cans and sprinkle the insides with fine bread crumbs.

Shape each piece of dough into an "egg" and drop it into a can. Cover with plastic wrap and a clean towel and let rise until doubled in bulk.

Baking: About 15 minutes before you want to bake the bread, preheat your oven to 250°F.

Brush the tops with the egg wash and cut a cross into the top. (A serrated knife does this nicely.)

Bake at 250°F for 10 minutes. Raise the temperature to 350°F and bake for 35 to 45 minutes or until a deep, golden brown. If the tops appear to be browning too rapidly, loosely tent with foil.

Storing: When the loaves are done, take them out of the oven, remove them from the cans and let them cool on a wire rack.

This bread freezes very well and will keep for at least 3 months. Be sure that it has cooled thoroughly before you seal it in airtight plastic bags.

HOT CROSS BUNS

Hot Cross Buns are one of the small, spiced buns that became popular in fif- teenth- and sixteenth-century England, pre-dating even the Chelsea Bun (in the Breakfast Breads section). English folklore traces this bun, with its cross on top, all the way back to pagan Britain, before the arrival of Christianity, to the celebration of the vernal equinox and the return of the sun's dominance in the sky. The bun represented the earth and the four sections, delineated by the cross on top, represented the seasons of the year. In addition to its seasonal implications, for the medieval baker the cross also was a sign to ward off evil and to encourage the dough to rise.

During the reign of Elizabeth I, sweetened and spiced breads were allowed by law to be made and sold only on special occasions, Good Friday being one. While these laws were relaxed in the next century, Hot Cross Buns continued, even as they are today, to be associated with Good Friday. It is said that if the buns are made on Good Friday itself they will protect the baker, and those sharing them, from misfortune in the coming year.

The Proofing Sponge

$\frac{1}{2}$ cup warm milk
1 teaspoon sugar
2 tablespoons or packets active dry yeast
$\frac{1}{2}$ cup King Arthur Stone Ground Whole Wheat Flour

Starting the Sponge: Put the milk in a large mixing bowl and mix in the sugar, yeast and flour. Let this small sponge sit for 10 to 15 minutes until it is bubbly.

The Rest

1 cup milk
$\frac{1}{3}$ cup brown sugar
2 eggs
1 cup King Arthur Stone Ground Whole Wheat Flour
$\frac{1}{2}$ cup (1 stick) butter, at room temperature
$1\frac{1}{2}$ teaspoons salt
1 teaspoon cinnamon
$\frac{1}{2}$ teaspoon nutmeg
$\frac{1}{2}$ teaspoon allspice
$\frac{1}{2}$ to 1 cup raisins (optional)
$3\frac{1}{2}$ cups King Arthur Unbleached All-Purpose Flour
wash made from 1 egg mixed with 2 teaspoons milk

Making the Dough: Add the warm milk and brown sugar to the sponge. Beat in the eggs and add the whole wheat flour. Stir in the butter, salt, spices and raisins if you wish. Mix in the unbleached flour until the dough holds together and pulls away from the sides of the bowl. This will make a soft but kneadable dough.

Kneading: Turn the dough out onto a lightly floured surface and knead 3 to 4 minutes. Give it a rest while you clean and grease the mixing bowl. Knead the dough another 3 to 4 minutes or until it's smooth and satiny. Add only enough flour to keep it from sticking to you or the board.

Rising: Place the kneaded dough in the mixing bowl turning it so the top is greased. Cover and place it somewhere cozy and let it rise until it has doubled or until you can leave a deep fingerprint in it, 1½ to 2 hours.

Shaping & Rising: Punch it down, return it to your floured board and divide it in half. Make a 16-inch-long "snake" from each half and cut each into 16 pieces. Grease two 9-inch square cake pans and place the 16 pieces, which you have rolled into balls, in each. Cover and let rise for 45 minutes to an hour.

Baking: About 15 minutes before you want to bake the buns, preheat your oven to 350°F. Just before they go in, cut a cross in each using a serrated knife or a sharp razor blade. Saw gently back and forth without exerting much downward pressure so you don't deflate them.

Brush the surface of the buns with the egg wash. Bake for 20 to 25 minutes or until they're golden brown.

The Glaze

> 1½ cups confectioners' sugar
> ½ teaspoon vanilla and/or 1 teaspoon lemon juice
> 1 to 2 tablespoons milk or whatever creates a "drizzleable" consistency

Making the Glaze: While the buns bake, make the glaze by mixing the sugar and vanilla and/or lemon juice. Gradually add the milk until you can drizzle the mixture in a fine line.

Decorating the Buns: You have two options here.

> • For a shiny, sweet surface, drizzle the glaze over the entire bun right after it comes out of the oven.

> • To make the cross more apparent, let the buns cool and drizzle the glaze just through the cross to leave a distinct white trail.

Russian Easter Kulich

Easter is truly a moveable feast. The general rule is that it is held on the first Sunday after the first full moon, which occurs on or after the vernal equinox.

But not all Christians agree to this formula. The Eastern Orthodox Church determines the date of Easter by additionally factoring in the Jewish festival of Passover which celebrates the exodus of the Jews from Egypt. Since Jesus celebrated Passover, the Eastern church has determined that Easter must never fall beforehand, which the western calculations don't preclude.

New England has sizeable Greek and Russian Orthodox communities. For them the Easter celebration is the end of a strict seven-week Lenten fast, a holiday deeply rooted in their Slavic past. When Christianity was brought to Russia in the tenth century, the celebration of Easter coincided with an ancient celebration marking the end of the severe Russian winter. Many of the customs and traditions of these ancient celebrations have become incorporated into their Easter observances.

Kulich is a Russian festival bread that symbolizes Easter and this season of rededication and hope. It tastes almost like a cake and, like panettone, is tall and cylindrical. This is another of the Jubinsky festival bread collection.

Dough

1 cup sugar
3 tablespoons or packets active dry yeast
1½ cups warm water
3 eggs
3 egg yolks
½ cup non-fat dry milk
1 teaspoon vanilla
grated peel from one lemon
¼ teaspoon nutmeg
8½ to 9½ cups King Arthur Unbleached All-Purpose Flour
1 teaspoon salt
1 cup (2 sticks) butter, softened
1 cup golden raisins
¼ cup slivered almonds
¼ cup candied peel
fine bread crumbs for lining cans

Making the Dough: Dissolve 1 tablespoon of the sugar and the yeast in the water. When it's bubbly and expanded, beat in the eggs, egg yolks, dry milk and remaining sugar. Add the vanilla, the grated lemon peel and nutmeg.

Stir in 1 cup of flour and then the salt. Add 2 more cups of flour and then blend in the softened butter as well as you can. This will be lumpy but, never fear, it will disappear as you work the dough.

Stir in the raisins, almonds and candied peel. Add the flour, one cup at a time, until it is well incorporated and the dough comes cleanly away from the sides of the bowl.

Kneading & Rising: Turn the dough out onto a lightly floured board and knead until it's smooth and satiny, adding only enough flour to keep the dough from sticking. After it's been kneaded it should be soft rather than stiff, so try to stay on the lighter side of the flour. Place the dough back in the bowl which you've cleaned and greased, turn it to grease the top and cover it with a damp towel or plastic wrap to rise.

Shaping & Rising: When the dough has doubled in bulk, punch it down, and divide into halves. Thoroughly grease the inside of two (26-ounce) coffee cans and sprinkle with fine bread crumbs.

Shape each piece of dough into an "egg" and carefully drop it into the coffee can. Cover the loaves and let them rise for an hour or until almost doubled.

Baking: Preheat your oven to 300°F. Bake the bread for 1 to 1¼ hours. When the loaves are done, remove them from the oven and let them stand in the cans for ten minutes. Gently remove them from the cans and cool them on their sides on a towel placed over a wire rack.

Glaze

> ½ cup confectioners' sugar
> 1½ teaspoons water
> ½ teaspoon lemon juice or grated lemon rind

Making the Glaze: Mix the sugar with the water and juice. Before the loaves have completely cooled spread the glaze over the top.

Traditionally Kulich has the letters "XV" formed on the top, which stands for "Christ is risen." If you wish, when the loaves have completely cooled, take the remainder of the glaze and form the letters XV over the clear glaze.

WEDDING BREAD

We end this section on a note of hope for the next generation with a festival bread designed for weddings. Traditionally in this country, we celebrate weddings with a lavish cake. But in other countries and other times, the "cake" has been an elaborate bread.

We applaud the idea of a wedding bread. Bread is the staff of life. To break bread together is a kind of communion, a sharing of oneself with another. As has been said, "bread is life itself." What could be a more fitting way to embark upon married life than for a new husband and wife to ceremonially break bread together, made especially for them by someone who can fill it with good omens, hope and love.

To embark upon an undertaking such as this, you'll first want to decide what shape you want the bread to take. Next, you'll want to determine how to flavor it. Sweet doughs are very basic and can be flavored in any number of ways. Let the bride and groom give you some ideas. Finally, you'll want to decide how to decorate it. It's fun to cover it with small shapes related to the bridal couple in some way. You can also add some of your own which symbolize your own feelings about them. After the bread is baked, you can add color with wild flowers or some special blooms from your own garden.

To help you get started, we'll give you the recipe for a wedding bread that the Sands made for their daughter Ellen and her husband, Christopher, several years ago. This recipe will make a fairly large bread. If you have access to a large oven, you could make it half again as large. Measurements for the larger size appear in parentheses after each ingredient.

Proofing Sponge (same for large loaf)

$\frac{1}{2}$ cup warm water
1 tablespoon sugar
2 tablespoons or packets active dry yeast
$\frac{1}{2}$ cup King Arthur Stone Ground Whole Wheat Flour

Dough

1 cup warm water ($1\frac{3}{4}$ cups)
4 tablespoons butter, softened, or vegetable oil (6 tablespoons)
3 eggs (4)
$\frac{3}{4}$ cup brown sugar (1 cup)
$\frac{1}{2}$ cup dry milk ($\frac{3}{4}$ cup)
1 tablespoon salt (1 rounded tablespoon)
2 tablespoons grated orange peel (3 tablespoons)
1 tablespoon almond extract ($1\frac{1}{2}$ tablespoons)
1 teaspoon vanilla ($1\frac{1}{2}$ teaspoons)
$5\frac{1}{2}$ to $6\frac{1}{2}$ cups King Arthur Unbleached All-Purpose Flour (9 to 11 cups)
1 egg beaten with 1 tablespoon water for a wash

Making the Sponge: Pour the warm water into a large bowl and mix in the sugar, yeast and flour. Let this sit for 10 to 15 minutes, until it is bubbly and expanded.

Making the Dough: Add the cup of water to the sponge. Beat in the butter or oil, eggs, sugar, dry milk, salt, orange peel and flavorings. Stir in the flour gradually, stirring with a large spoon, until it becomes cohesive and pulls away from the sides of the bowl.

Kneading & Rising: Turn the dough out onto a board sprinkled with the balance of the flour. Knead until the dough feels springy and elastic, adding only enough flour to keep it from sticking.

Clean your bowl, oil it, and place the kneaded dough in it, turning the dough so the top surface is covered with a light film of oil. Cover the bowl, put it somewhere cozy and let it rise until it has doubled, 1 1/2 to 2 hours.

Knock it down and let it rise once more if you want a finer grain.

Shaping & Rising: After the rising period(s), knock it down, turn it out onto a floured board, knead out any stray bubbles, and give it a 5-minute rest to relax the gluten.

If you are making the recipe with the smaller amount of dough, you may want to roll it out into a long cylinder and bring the two ends together to form a circle. (Don't forget to set aside some dough to form shapes for placing on the surface of the bread.)

If you have made the larger dough, you might form an infinity symbol, a figure eight lying on its side with one side representing the bride and the other, the groom.

After the dough is shaped, place it on a baking sheet and cover with a damp towel while you make the decorations.

Decorating: Roll out the dough you set aside until it is very thin (1/4 to 1/8 inch thick). Let it relax occasionally to make it more cooperative. Cut out appropriate shapes with a knife, a small pair of scissors or small cookie cutters.

Attach them to the bread dough with a little of the egg/water mixture you'll use for the wash.

Finishing Touches: When all the shapes are attached (make sure they are predominantly on the top so they don't fall off), brush the egg/water wash over the entire loaf. To make the decorations more apparent, give them a second coat of wash.

Carefully cover and let rest for 30 to 45 minutes. (The main body of the dough will have had a longer rising period because it will take you some time to make and attach the decorations.)

(You can brush on a shiny, sweet glaze after the loaf is baked if you'd prefer. See page 207.)

Baking: Place the bread dough in a cold oven, set the temperature to 400°F and bake for 10 minutes.

Lower the temperature to 350°F and bake for a further ten minutes.

Lower the temperature to 325°F and finally 300°F and bake 10 minutes more at each setting.

(For the larger amount of dough, bake 15 minutes at each temperature setting.)

If the bread looks as if it is browning too much toward the end of the baking period, tent it loosely with foil.

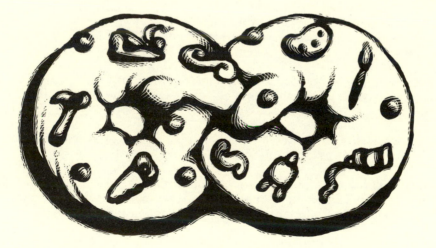

This bread can be frozen until the wedding day, but make sure you allow it plenty of time to thaw. Good luck and best wishes!

CAKES &
CRUMBLES
V

CAKES & CRUMBLES
CRISPS & PUDDINGS

• Follow the directions for measuring flour on page 597 and on the top of our bags. This will give you a 4-ounce cup of flour which contains many pockets of air, the first step to a light and tender cake.

• While mixing ingredients, it's helpful to remember that your goal is to incorporate as much air as possible. Although an electric mixer is a blessing here, you can do very well with a hand-held mixer, a wire whisk or, most simply, a spoon.

• You can blend dry ingredients together to your heart's content. The goal here is to have them well blended, free of lumps, and "light," (i.e., not compacted). You can rub lumps out of baking soda with your fingers. You can press lumpy white or brown sugar through a sieve. (Use a coarse sieve for brown sugar.)

• You can also blend wet or moist ingredients, in the order given in the recipe, without limit. You're only adding air bubbles as you do. One exception is egg whites which can be overbeaten. You want to stop when they're glossy and create stiff peaks that don't flop over when you lift your beater out of them. Beating beyond this begins to knock the air out of them! Add any alcohol-based flavoring, such as vanilla, last to retain as much flavor as possible.

• When you blend wet ingredients with dry, use restraint. Once flour is in contact with liquid, the elastic property in it called gluten will begin to develop. You want to minimize this to produce light and tender cakes, so blend thoroughly, but quickly.

• You only need to flour cake pans when you grease them with butter or solid shortening. Butter contains moisture and shortening contains air bubbles. In both cases, a batter can find its way through them to stick on a cake pan bottom. Flouring prevents this from happening. When you grease a pan with vegetable oil or a lecithin spray, flouring isn't necessary since both create an uninterrupted barrier between batter and pan.

• When you remove a cake from the oven, allow it to remain in the pan for several minutes. This allows time for its structure to stabilize and become less fragile. Loosen it from the sides with a knife, turn it out gently onto your hand and place it bottom down on a cake rack. When it's thoroughly cool, you may frost it if you wish.

• If you want to make a King Arthur "Cake" Flour, put 2 tablespoons of cornstarch into your measuring cup. Fill the remainder of the cup with King Arthur Flour and blend. Presto! You have cake flour with the unbleached goodness of King Arthur.

CAKES & CRUMBLES
CRISPS & PUDDINGS
V

• A CAKE PRIMER •

Cakes are the sweetest quick breads of all. About the only thing common to all cakes is the fact that they are called cakes. Although most of us might agree on what should go in a "cake," cakes can, literally, contain anything from soup to nuts. Conversely, every ingredient you might assume ought to be in a cake will be absent in some variation. The only two ingredients that you'll find in all of them are some kind of sweetener and a little salt to intensify flavor. (Some cakes don't even contain flour but those we'll leave for someone else's book.)

Cakes can be made with butter, margarine, lard, vegetable oil, or no fat at all. They can be made with one egg or a dozen, with just the whites or yolks, or with no eggs at all. They can be flavored simply with vanilla, or with other extracts, liqueurs, spices, fruits, vegetables or nuts. They can be enjoyed straightforward, light and simple; they can be a vehicle for elegant toppings or icings; they can be the binding for a profusion of fruits and nuts. All these and more can be called cakes. So with this rather broad spectrum, we'll try to find a way to organize them.

CAKE CONSIDERATIONS

A "traditional" cake contains flour and an equal amount or more, by weight, not volume, of sugar with a little salt to intensify flavor. From there, the variation in ingredients is infinite.

KING ARTHUR "CAKE" FLOUR

According to some, the best flour for cakes is heavily bleached with chlorine which, among other things, toughens the protein so that it can hold more of those ingredients (sugar and fat) which put stress on a cake's structure. King Arthur Flour does not pretend to be a "cake flour." Not only are we opposed to adding chemical bleaches to our flour, but because King Arthur is milled from hard wheats, it contains more protein than cake flour. It will, however, produce cakes that have excellent flavor and texture. But they are characteristically "King Arthur Cakes" with a fuller body and greater "substance." Here are a couple of ways to make King Arthur Cakes as light as possible.

Aerating the Flour: The first is to incorporate as much air into the flour as possible at the outstart. All flour is pre-sifted through many layers of silk screening before it is bagged and shipped from the mill. During shipment, all flour settles and compacts. Our mothers and grandmothers used a sifter to restore flour to its original sifted state. Today it is still desirable to accomplish this even when flour is labeled "pre-sifted," but here's a simpler way to do it.

Before you measure, fluff up the flour in the bag with a spoon. Then sprinkle it into a "dry" cup measure, and scrape off the excess with the back of a knife. Flour measured this way weighs 4 ounces per cup. Flour scooped from a bag will weigh as much as 5 ounces per cup. Our recipes, unless otherwise specified, are written for 4-ounce cups of flour. If you used the scoop and sweep method in one of our recipes, your cake might better be used as a door stop! Four-ounce cups of flour also contain significantly more air which is the first leavening agent in a cake and where a "light" cake begins.

Adding Cornstarch: A second way to lighten a cake made with King Arthur Flour is to approximate the characteristics of "cake flour" more closely. To do this, spoon 2 to 4 tablespoons of cornstarch into a one cup "dry" measure. Sprinkle in your King Arthur Flour until it is full and scrape off the excess with the back side of a knife. Blend this thoroughly and you'll have pure, golden, never bleached, never bromated King Arthur "Cake" Flour. While this technique will produce lighter cakes, many King Arthur fans use our flour straight because they prefer "King Arthur Cakes." And many of us who prefer robust cakes use some whole wheat flour in place of unbleached all-purpose. (See Chapter IX for other hearty cakes.)

CAKE LEAVENS

Baking Powder: Cakes used to be leavened by yeast or by the air that was beaten into the eggs and/or butter in them. (The electric mixer has taken most of the drudgery out of this part of cake making.) Although getting air into cakes manually is still important, most cakes today depend on the leavening power of baking powder which is a combination of baking soda (alkaline or "sweet") and an acid ("sour") in powder form. When this magic powder is mixed with a liquid and exposed to heat, it begins to bubble and foam. It's producing carbon dioxide, just as we do when we exhale and just as yeast does when it's making bread rise. Cakes that contain an acid in another form, such as sour milk, buttermilk, or fruit juice, need only the "sweet" half of baking powder, the baking soda. (For more information about "quick" leavening agents, see page 50.)

Yeast: "Chemical" leavening has been used for over a century now in most cake baking, replacing yeast. We have included a couple of recipes for old yeast-leavened cakes in this section. They take longer to make but are unique in texture and flavor. In the same mode, you will find recipes in the Sourdough chapter for an incredibly dark, moist chocolate cake as well as a "Friendship Cake" leavened with its own special sourdough starter.

CAKE TYPES

There are several classic cakes which we have organized according to their density, the lightest to the most compact. A cake's density is determined by several factors: the way it's leavened, the absence or presence of a fat and its type, and those ingredients which contribute to its structure as opposed to those which are held in the structure. The two basic ingredients that create a cake's structure, or skeleton, are the flour and the eggs. Everything else determines its "body type" and "personality."

Although there are other ways of differentiating between cake types, density is a readily observable one. In this section you'll find examples of each, some suggestions for variations, and a few of King Arthur's favorites. As you make them, you'll discover what creates the unique characteristics of each. There are many, many more cakes in the world and many that won't fit into any of the categories here. But if you keep this "density scale" in mind, it will give you a starting place and some perspective with which to understand these and other cakes in your life.

ANGEL FOOD CAKES

An angel food cake, as the name suggests, is the lightest cake of all. It contains no fat (!) and only the whites of up to a dozen eggs. These egg whites are beaten until they are stiff with air bubbles and then gently folded into the other ingredients. As the batter heats up in the oven, those bubbles expand like a million little balloons, creating a cake that almost floats in the air.

TRADITIONAL ANGEL FOOD CAKE

This is definitely the "cake you can have and eat too." Its lighter-than-air, melt-in-your-mouth texture hints at its secret. Unlike any other cake, it contains no butter, no oil, no egg yolks, nothing that cholesterol or fat can hide in. Since fat is the greatest calorie culprit, this is the cake for people who are counting them. But this cake is exciting not for caloric reasons; it's because there is just nothing else like it. For those of you who are afraid you could never create anything so ethereal, just follow our easy directions. Something this heavenly is within anyone's reach.

1 cup King Arthur Unbleached All-Purpose Flour
1 1/2 cups sugar
12 large eggs at room temperature
1/2 teaspoon salt
1 teaspoon flavoring: vanilla or almond extract or a combination
1 1/2 teaspoons cream of tartar

Preheat your oven to 325°F.

Blend the flour and 3/4 cup of sugar in a mixing bowl. You can use a wire whisk to really whip these two together.

Separate the eggs. Try not to get any yolk in the whites because it tends to keep them from getting as stiff and glossy as they should be. (It is okay to get a little white in the yolks.)

Add the salt and flavoring to the egg whites and beat with a whisk or electric beater until they are just frothy. Sprinkle the cream of tartar on top and continue beating until they form stiff glossy peaks.

Cream of tartar is not a mysterious chemical from a lab, but a natural by-product of wine making, a fruit acid that accumulates on the sides of the wine casks. It contains no alcohol. Cream of tartar is often used as a leavening agent in combination with baking soda. When the acidic cream of tartar and the alkaline baking soda are mixed with a liquid, they produce carbon dioxide bubbles. In this Angel Food Cake, the acid in the cream of tartar coagulates (or sort of "cooks") the protein in the egg whites. This "sets" or stabilizes them and keeps them from collapsing when you add the other ingredients.

Once the egg whites are stiff, add the remaining sugar, ¼ cup at a time. Then fold in the dry ingredients gradually.

Scoop the batter into your ungreased angel food cake pan (see Appendix) and bake for 40 to 45 minutes. The cake is done when it springs back if lightly touched and the top is golden brown.

Place the cake (still in the pan) upside down on a bottle or metal funnel to keep from crushing the top; or, if your pan has legs, set it directly on them. Let the cake cool thoroughly for about 1½ hours. This cooling-off period "sets" the structure and keeps the cake from collapsing. Loosen the edges with a knife if necessary and remove it from the pan. Rather than slicing this cake, use two forks to pull it apart.

HEAVENLY VARIATIONS

Lemon, Orange or Peppermint Angel Food Cake: Substitute lemon, orange or peppermint extracts for the vanilla and/or almond. To intensify these flavors and make the cake more interesting visually, add 1 or 2 tablespoons of grated lemon or orange peel or ½ cup of crushed peppermint candy.

Chocolate Angel Food Cake: Substitute ¼ cup of cocoa for ¼ cup of unbleached all-purpose flour. You might try this with a peppermint or orange extract as well.

To use up those leftover egg yolks, try the Golden Angel Food Cake which you'll find on page 511 in the Whole Wheat chapter. Because it's made with whole wheat flour, that angel food cake has more earthly associations.

SPONGE CAKES

Sponge cakes, too, are light and supple. They are leavened by the air that is beaten into the egg whites, but they contain the egg yolks as well which give them a richer, fuller flavor and texture. These cakes are lovely alone, sprinkled with confectioners' sugar, or rolled up with something wonderful inside.

MERLIN'S MAGIC SPONGE CAKE

Sponge cake can appear in many different forms, which is why we gave it this name.

6 large eggs, at room temperature
1/2 teaspoon salt
1 to 1 1/4 cups sugar
1/2 cup water or milk
2 teaspoons vanilla
1 teaspoon baking powder
1 1/2 cups King Arthur Unbleached All-Purpose Flour

Preheat your oven to 325°F.

Separate the eggs into two mixing bowls. Beat the egg whites with the salt until they have peaked. Gradually beat in half the sugar and then set this mixture aside.

In the other bowl, beat the egg yolks with the remaining sugar until the mixture is thick and yellow. Blend in the water or milk and vanilla.

Mix the baking powder into the flour. With a wire whisk, if you have one, or a large spoon, blend these dry ingredients into the egg yolk mixture. Then gently fold in the egg whites.

Bake in a 10-inch, ungreased angel food cake pan for 1 hour. When your cake is done, invert it over a bottle (to keep from crushing the top) until it is cool. Loosen the edges with a knife if necessary and remove it from the pan. Like the Angel Food Cake, use two forks to pull slices apart.

MAGIC VARIATIONS

Here are some ways to vary the flavor of this magic cake.

Orange Sponge Cake: Substitute orange juice for the water or milk and add grated rind from 1 orange.

Lemon Sponge Cake: Use water rather than milk, the grated rind from 1 lemon and 1 teaspoon lemon extract in place of 1 teaspoon vanilla.

Almond Sponge Cake: Substitute 1 teaspoon almond extract for 1 teaspoon of vanilla. To serve, sprinkle the top with confectioners' sugar and crushed or sliced almonds.

Chocolate Sponge Cake: Substitute 6 tablespoons of cocoa ($1/4$ cup plus 2 tablespoons) for 6 tablespoons of flour.

In a Jelly Roll Disguise

Sponge cake batter can also be baked thin in a sheet pan.

Preheat your oven to 350°F and line a 13 x 18-inch sheet pan (sometimes called a half-sheet or jelly roll pan) with parchment.

Make 1 recipe Merlin's Magic Sponge Cake batter.

Pour the batter directly on the paper without greasing it and spread it into all corners gently.

Bake for 20 to 25 minutes.

Let it cool completely after you take it out of the oven. Then loosen the edges with a knife and turn it out onto waxed paper or foil that has been liberally sprinkled with confectioners' sugar. Peel the paper off. To keep the edge from cracking when you roll it, trim about an eighth of an inch from around the outside.

Now comes the fun! First, try rolling it up once to get a feel for it. This cake will be happy to roll up and unroll without anything catastrophic happening.

Fillings: Now that you know that it will safely roll up let's consider some things to roll up inside it.

• There's always jelly. A jelly roll is a great way to use up several jars of odds and ends. After you spread the jelly on the cake, roll it up, and then roll the waxed paper or aluminum foil around the outside to keep it rolled and covered while you chill it. To serve, remove the paper wrapping, slice, and garnish with a dollop of flavored yogurt or lightly sweetened whipped cream.

• Or roll up the yogurt or whipped cream inside, and serve it with sliced fresh fruit on top.

• Roll up the cake with some of your favorite ice cream, slightly softened, freeze it, and then serve it with hot chocolate or butterscotch sauce.

• Or roll up some chocolate mousse or chocolate butter cream and serve it with plain or chocolate whipped cream on top.

Our low-calorie dessert seems to be slipping away. Actually, if you've been nibbling the trimmings, you'll know this cake is wonderful all by itself. It melts in your mouth in a chewy sort of way. So if you can't make up your mind what to do with it, don't do anything. Try eating it plain with a cup of tea or glass of milk and get yourself back on a slimmer track.

ENGLISH TRIFLE

English Trifle comes from the land of Arthur itself and its roots go back two or three hundred years, not quite to Arthur's time, but long enough to make it a venerable presentation.

What we hope is that you still have some of Merlin's Magic Sponge Cake, in any form, left over and that it has gotten a bit stale. English Trifle is so good, though, that you might want to make another Magic Sponge Cake just for it.

If you picked and put up some raspberries, strawberries or any other berries last summer, trifle is a wonderful foil for them. If you didn't, slightly sweetened frozen ones, available at your grocery, will do as well, as will a berry jam. The quantities given are approximate. Use whatever you have on hand and what tastes good to you. Trifle is a wonderful combination of textures and flavors and a fabulous finale for Merlin's Magic Sponge Cake.

> 1 recipe Custard, already made up and cooled (either Slim & Suave or
>   Thick & Rich, page 315)
> Merlin's Magic Sponge Cake, slightly stale (or fresh if you can't wait)
> 1/2 cup sherry or rum
> 2 cups fruit: raspberries, strawberries or whatever is in season
> 1 cup almonds or other nuts, chopped or sliced (optional)

Cut the sponge cake into two-inch squares and line the bottom of a large glass bowl with them. Sprinkle sherry or rum over the cake and spoon on some of your fruit. If you enjoy a bit of a crunch, sprinkle on some blanched, sliced almonds, or other chopped nuts.

Add another layer of cake and repeat the process with the sherry, fruit and nuts.

Pour your choice of custard over the cake and fruit mixture, sprinkle with sliced almonds, cover and chill.

STRAWBERRY SHORTCAKE JELLY ROLL
WITH GRAND MARNIER FILLING

Michael Jubinsky's daughter, Stavana, made the original Strawberry Shortcake Jelly Roll. With the addition of some Grand Marnier, Michael transformed it into this royal confection. Note that this cake batter and technique for baking are different from the previous sponge cake. This just demonstrates that no recipe is "the recipe."

      6 large eggs, preferably at room temperature
      2 egg yolks
      1/8 teaspoon salt
      1 teaspoon baking powder
      3/4 cup sugar
      2 teaspoons lemon juice
      1 teaspoon vanilla
      1 cup King Arthur Unbleached All-Purpose Flour
      confectioners' sugar
      1 recipe Strawberry Grand Marnier Filling (page 315)
      additional strawberries
      lightly sweetened whipped cream (optional)

Preheat your oven to 350°F and grease the bottom and sides of a 13 x 18-inch baking pan. Line the bottom with parchment paper and grease again.

Place the eggs, egg yolks, salt and baking powder into a mixing bowl and beat until they are light and lemon colored. Gradually add the sugar and continue beating for a minute or two until the mixture is thick, fluffy and light.

Add the lemon juice and vanilla. Gently fold the flour into the batter. Spread it in your prepared pan and bake for 20 to 25 minutes (until the cake is golden).

While the sponge cake is baking, spread a clean dish towel (not terry cloth) on the counter and generously sprinkle with confectioners' sugar.

Remove the sponge cake from the oven and loosen the edges with a knife. Invert the jelly roll pan over the prepared towel, lift the pan and remove the paper liner. Trim the crisp edges from the cake and loosely roll it up in the towel. Cool it on a wire rack with the seam on the bottom.

While the cake cools to room temperature, prepare the Strawberry Grand Marnier Filling.

Carefully unroll the cake and spread it with the filling. Re-roll, sprinkle heavily with confectioners' sugar and place on a serving plate. Slice and serve garnished with additional strawberries and a dollop of lightly sweetened whipped cream.

GÉNOISE

The génoise is like a sponge cake in that it contains many whole eggs. These are beaten until very light by themselves, and then in combination with sugar, to create the leavening. But a génoise also contains the addition of melted butter which is folded in at the end of the mixing period. This addition creates a cake that is both light and rich. (You'll note that with each variation, our cakes are getting richer.)

A GÉNOISE

A génoise makes a wonderful cake on its own or, like the sponge cake, can be filled and rolled, made into a superb trifle, or cut up to make lady fingers or petits fours.

> 6 eggs
> 1 cup granulated sugar
> 2 teaspoons vanilla or almond extract (or 1 teaspoon each)
> 1 cup King Arthur Unbleached Flour
> 6 tablespoons butter, melted and cooled but still liquid

Preheat your oven to 350°F.

Melt the butter in a small saucepan and leave it to cool while you prepare the other ingredients.

Beat the eggs in a mixing bowl with an electric beater until they are light and lemon colored. Add the sugar, $1/4$ cup at a time, and beat well after each addition.

After all the sugar is in, continue beating until you can dribble some of the mixture from the beater onto the remainder in the bowl and leave a "track" that doesn't sink in and disappear.

Add the vanilla and/or almond flavoring. With a wire whisk, gently fold in the flour and, finally, the butter.

Bake in a lightly greased, 9-inch cake pan for 30 to 40 minutes or until the cake has pulled away from the sides of the pan and the center of the cake springs back when you press on it gently with your finger.

Cool the cake for about 10 minutes in the pan and then turn it out on a wire rack.

When it is thoroughly cool, you can frost it or serve it with a sauce (see page 317), or cover it with fruit and a lightly sweetened, vanilla-laced whipped cream.

VARIATIONS

Baba au Rhum: Flavor the batter with almond extract. Sprinkle sliced almonds on top after it has baked and drizzle it with Rum Syrup (page 227) while it is still warm. Serve with sweetened whipped cream.

Lady Fingers: Cover a baking sheet with ungreased parchment cut to fit. Spoon batter on in long ovals about 1 x 4 inches. Bake in a preheated 350°F oven for 12 to 15 minutes. When cool, dust with confectioners' sugar and serve with fruit or sherbet.

Jelly Roll: Cover a baking sheet with ungreased parchment cut to fit. Spread the batter to cover the entire surface. Bake for 15 to 20 minutes. When the cake is fully baked, the top should spring back when you touch it but it should be just barely golden. Let it cool thoroughly before you use it. See page 270 for rolling options.

Trifle: Use this cake as the basis for an especially rich and delicious Trifle (see page 271).

Baked Alaska: Bake as for the Jelly Roll above. Preheat your oven to 500°F. Cut pieces of cake to completely surround a 1-quart block of ice cream (the flavor is your choice).

Make a double recipe of Meringue (page 420). Cover the entire cake surface with meringue and bake for 3 to 5 minutes or until the meringue is slightly golden. Serve immediately with or without an accompanying sauce (page 321).

BUTTER CAKES

These cakes are heavier and richer still, the kind that most of us probably first learned to bake. A butter cake contains all those ingredients that we generally associate with cakes: butter, eggs, sugar and flour. These are the versatile cakes that are found most often at birthday parties and bake sales.

King Arthur Flour's Original Pound Cake

At the heavy end of the butter cake spectrum is the pound cake, the original or "grandmother" of all butter cakes. This cake is incredibly rich, but fortunately, a very thin slice goes a long, long way.

Traditionally a pound cake is leavened by creaming the butter for a long period to incorporate air, then slowly adding and beating in the sugar until the mixture is light. Finally, one by one, up to a dozen eggs are beaten in. By separating the eggs, even more air can be incorporated when folding in the egg whites, stiffly beaten, at the end.

Today, beating air into pound cake ingredients has been simplified by the electric beater. Some ingredient modifications have made modern versions less costly, more acceptable nutritionally and less dependent on lengthy beating for adequate leavening. Margarine or vegetable shortening can be substituted for the butter. Milk and baking powder are sometimes used in place of some of the eggs. But no version can surpass the original. It keeps wonderfully well and actually improves in flavor after two or three days.

1 pound butter
1 pound sugar
1 pound eggs
1 pound King Arthur Unbleached All-Purpose Flour

In reading the first list of ingredients, it's obvious where the pound cake got its name and it's certainly not the weight of the finished product. Translated into the volume measurements we are accustomed to, the ingredients are as follows:

2 cups (4 sticks) butter
2 to 2¼ cups sugar
8 extra large or 9 large eggs
4 cups King Arthur Unbleached All-Purpose Flour

A cup of sugar weighs 7 ounces so a pound of sugar is closer to 2¼ cups. You can use your own discretion and inclination here.

A traditional pound cake has no leavening other than air and eggs. Our recipe, while egg rich, has some baking powder in it as well to lighten it a little. In addition to the pound of each of the four ingredients above, you will need:

> 1 tablespoon baking powder
> 1 teaspoon salt
> 1 cup milk
> 3 tablespoons brandy or sherry
> 2 teaspoons vanilla, almond or other flavoring

To lighten it even more, separate the eggs before you begin. After creaming the butter and adding the sugar, beat in just the egg yolks. Beat the whites separately until they form stiff peaks, and fold them in after all the other ingredients have been combined.

Preheat your oven to 350°F.

In a large mixing bowl, cream the butter until very light. Add the sugar gradually and then the eggs, one by one, and continue beating until the mixture is very light and fluffy. (An electric mixer can be most helpful and effective here.)

When you cream butter, it may seem at the beginning as if you're just mashing it flat. But if you persevere, you'll begin to see it get "fluffy." What you're really doing is adding air. When you beat the butter with sugar, it becomes even fluffier, evidence of more air. And when the eggs are beaten in, the fluffiness is at its peak. That's why this part of mixing is so important. The more air bubbles you can beat in at this stage, the more air bubbles there are to expand in the heat of the oven. Baking powder or soda can do part of the work of leavening, but the more air bubbles you can get into a batter manually, the finer and lighter the texture of the finished cake.

In a separate bowl, blend together the flour, baking powder and salt.

Pour the milk into a third small bowl, mix in the brandy and vanilla, or whatever flavoring you're partial to.

Alternately add the wet and dry ingredients to the butter/sugar/egg mixture. Pour into a lightly greased tube pan, or two 5 x 9-inch bread pans, and bake for about 1 hour or until the top surface of the cake springs back when you press on it gently with your fingers.

Let the cake cool thoroughly after it is done, cover and store for a couple of days to allow the flavor to mature. A pound cake is usually sliced thin and served unadorned.

King Arthur Flour's
Basic Butter Cake

Our basic butter cake contains half as much butter and egg, in relation to the rest of the ingredients, as our pound cake, so it is clearly not as rich. But these cakes are ordinarily served with a frosting (page 317) which puts them in the same caloric league.

In going through our King Arthur Flour archives to gather baking history for our cookbook, we've discovered a number of gems. One of them is a method of combining the ingredients of a basic butter cake that flies in the face of the traditional method most of us grew up with. It makes the whole process almost as easy as a mix, and certainly, in view of the control we have over what goes into the cake, infinitely better.

½ cup (1 stick) butter (or vegetable shortening) at room temperature
1 cup sugar
2 eggs
2 cups King Arthur Unbleached All-Purpose Flour
1 tablespoon baking powder
1 teaspoon salt
1 cup milk
1 teaspoon vanilla

The Traditional Method

Preheat your oven to 350°F.

First, cream the butter by mashing it against the side of a mixing bowl with a large, preferably wooden, spoon. When the butter is light and fluffy, slowly add the sugar, creaming it with the butter until the two are soft and light. Add the eggs, one at a time, beating them in thoroughly until the mixture is smooth, light and fluffy. (Today, all of this can be done quickly and easily with an electric mixer, but appreciate our grandmothers who did it by hand.)

In a separate bowl, thoroughly mix together the flour, baking powder and salt. Pour the milk into a one-cup measure and add the vanilla.

Alternately add the wet and dry ingredients to the butter/sugar mixture, a third at a time, stirring just enough to blend the ingredients after each addition. Over-beating, once the flour is in, will toughen the cake.

Pour the batter into two lightly greased, 8 x 8-inch round or square cake pans and bake for 30 to 35 minutes. The cake is done when it shrinks slightly from the sides of the pans, springs back when pressed lightly with a finger, or when a toothpick comes out clean from the center. Let it cool for 5 minutes or so before turning it out onto a wire rack. (Frost it after it is thoroughly cool, if you wish.)

The "Quick" Method

Preheat the oven to 350°F as above.

Put the flour, baking powder, salt and sugar into the mixing bowl and mix thoroughly. (A wire whisk will do this nicely.)

Add the butter, milk and vanilla directly to the dry ingredients. Stir the whole mixture until it's smooth. (If you're using an electric mixer, mix at slow to medium speed for about a minute and a half.) Add the unbeaten eggs and beat for another 2 minutes. That's all there is to it.

Pour the batter into lightly greased pans and bake as for the traditional version.

Sometimes it's worth being a bit irreverent with tradition. In doing so you may discover something new or you may decide that tradition has its merits.

Devil's Food Cake

This cake is from our cookbook Easy Home Baking, *published in the late 1940's, now out of print. It's a chocolate variation of the butter or shortening cake.*

½ cup boiling water
½ cup cocoa
⅔ cup shortening
1½ cups sugar
3 eggs
1 teaspoon vanilla
2¼ cups King Arthur Unbleached All-Purpose Flour
¾ teaspoon baking soda
1 teaspoon baking powder
1 teaspoon salt
¾ cup buttermilk or sour milk

Preheat your oven to 350°F.

In a small bowl, pour the boiling water over the cocoa, blend and allow to cool.

To easily measure ⅔ cup of shortening, put 1⅓ cups of cold water into a two-cup "liquid" measuring cup, one that has a lip above the two-cup mark. Push pieces of shortening into and under the surface of the water until the water level comes up to the two-cup mark. Pour out the water and you are left with exactly ⅔ cup of shortening.

In a large bowl, cream the shortening and then add the sugar and beat until light and fluffy. Add the eggs and vanilla and beat well.

Blend the flour, baking soda, baking powder and salt together.

Alternately add the dry ingredients and the buttermilk to the shortening/sugar mixture stirring just enough to combine them. Gently blend in the cooled cocoa and water.

Bake in a greased, 9 x 11-inch baking pan for 40 to 50 minutes.

When the cake is thoroughly cool, turn to our Frostings & Sauces, page 317, for inspiration. Red Velvet Cake Frosting is a favorite with any chocolate cake.

GRANDMA DODGE'S
SPICE CAKE

The "receipt" for this spice cake came from Brinna Sands' great grandmother Dodge whose husband plied the seas as captain of the clipper ship "Surprise" in search of spices from the East.

Vegetable shortening is a good alternative here because this cake is flavored with molasses and spice so the flavor of butter would be hidden. Vegetable shortening is already aerated, so by nature makes cakes that are light and finely grained.

2 cups buttermilk or sour milk
½ cup vegetable shortening
2 cups sugar
¼ cup molasses
2 eggs
4 cups King Arthur Unbleached All-Purpose Flour 🌾 (this is the original
        amount called for; 3½ cups of flour will create a lighter cake)
2 teaspoons baking soda
1 teaspoon salt
1 teaspoon cinnamon
½ teaspoon cloves
½ teaspoon nutmeg
1 cup raisins or currants (optional)

Preheat your oven to 350°F.

Measure 2 cups of buttermilk or sour milk into a mixing bowl. If you don't have sour milk, it can be made easily by adding 1 tablespoon of vinegar or lemon juice to 1 cup of milk. Let it stand for about 5 minutes to "clabber" or curdle.

In a large mixing bowl cream the shortening and then add the sugar and molasses and beat thoroughly until light. Add the eggs, one at a time, beating until thick and light after each.

In a separate bowl, blend the dry ingredients and mix in the fruit if you choose to add it.

Alternately add the liquid and dry ingredients to the shortening/sugar mixture. Pour into two lightly greased, 9-inch cake pans and bake for 40 to 45 minutes.

This cake will taste wonderful with a plain butter frosting, a light lemon sauce or a cream cheese frosting, all of which you'll find with the Cake Fillings & Frostings (starting on page 313) at the end of this chapter.

ALMOND CREAM CAKE

This cake is a butter cake maverick. The "butter" is here, but it's in liquid form. This recipe is unbelievably easy and quick to put together and has a wonderful "creamy" texture and flavor.

As a single layer, it is delicious warm with hot chocolate or other sauce (see page 321), or simply garnished with slightly sweetened crushed fruit.

2 eggs
3/4 cup sugar
2/3 cup heavy cream
1 teaspoon vanilla
1 teaspoon almond extract
1 1/2 cups King Arthur Unbleached All-Purpose Flour
2 teaspoons baking powder
1/2 teaspoon salt

Preheat your oven to 350°F.

Beat the eggs in a mixing bowl until light and fluffy. Slowly add the sugar, cream, vanilla and almond extracts. Beat this mixture for 2 or 3 minutes until it is very light and full of tiny air bubbles.

In another bowl, thoroughly mix the dry ingredients. Add the wet ingredients to the dry and stir only enough to blend.

Pour into a greased, 9-inch square or round cake pan and bake for 30 to 35 minutes. Cool for 10 minutes before removing from the pan to cool on a wire rack.

You can double the recipe to create two layers. Try serving it with slightly sweetened whipped cream (flavored with vanilla and almond extracts) between the layers and sliced, sweetened strawberries on the top. This is even better the next day after the whipped cream and strawberry juice have soaked into the cake.

VEGETABLE OIL CAKES

The vegetable oil cake is relatively new to the cake spectrum. Many were devised during World War II when all those things that make pound cakes rich (butter, sugar and eggs) were rationed. But since then, these cakes have become increasingly popular both for dietary reasons and because they are incredibly moist and delicious in their own right.

This type of cake is the basis for the wonderful "vegetable" cakes that we all love nowadays (carrot, zucchini, etc.) as well as King Arthur Flour's quick-as-a-mix "Cake-Pan" Cake and all its variations.

King Arthur Flour's Original "Cake-Pan" Cake

This wartime cake has survived the intervening years for several reasons: it contains no cholesterol, it can be put together right in the pan it's baked in and it is a dark, moist and delicious chocolate cake.

Once you've learned the knack of putting this cake together, you'll never think of buying a mix. It's so easy to experiment with, you'll find you can substitute ingredients and add little extras to create your own "Cake-Pan" Cake tradition.

A "Cake-Pan" Cake does not like to part from its pan. Either plan to serve it right in the pan or grease the pan before putting in your dry ingredients. Shortening (not butter) will usually do the trick. The grease doesn't seem to be disturbed when you mix the ingredients. If you use a non-stick pan, it will also be easier to coax the cake out.

1 1/2 cups King Arthur Unbleached All-Purpose Flour
1 cup sugar
1/4 cup cocoa
1/2 teaspoon salt
1 teaspoon baking soda (rub between fingers to remove lumps)
1 teaspoon vanilla
1 tablespoon vinegar
1/3 cup vegetable oil
1 cup cold water (original recipe), coffee (next inspiration), milk (later inspiration), or 3/4 cup water and 1/4 cup rum (latest inspiration)

Preheat your oven to 350°F.

Measure all the dry ingredients into an 8- or 9-inch square or round cake pan.

Blend these together thoroughly with a fork and scoop out 3 holes or indentations.

Pour the vanilla into the first hole, the vinegar into the second, and the vegetable oil into the third.

Take the cup of cold liquid (water, coffee or milk, etc.) and pour it directly over everything in the pan. Stir all the ingredients together with your fork until they are well blended.

Bake for 35 to 40 minutes. Warm from the oven, this "Cake-Pan" Cake is wonderful with ice cream or just by itself with a big glass of milk.

If you want a layer cake, double the recipe, use two cake pans and frost with your favorite frosting.

"CAKE-PAN" CAKE VARIATIONS

We have had fun experimenting with our "Cake-Pan" Cake and have developed a number of variations. They go together the same easy way as the original recipe but each is unique.

"Cake-Pan" Cakes are leavened through the reaction of baking soda, which is alkaline, and vinegar, which is acidic. The reaction, which is quite dramatic, creates carbon dioxide bubbles which expand like hot air balloons when they're exposed to the heat of an oven. This causes the cake to expand or rise. In some of our other "Cake-Pan" Cake variations, we use other ingredients, such as buttermilk or fruit juice, to provide the acid.

In these, as with most of our recipes, you can use King Arthur Unbleached All-Purpose Flour and King Arthur Stone Ground Whole Wheat Flour together. The ratio suggested in the recipes below is a good place to start but you can use any combination you choose.

"Cake-Pan" Cottage Pudding

Cottage Pudding is wonderful with hot Dark Semi-Sweet Chocolate Sauce (page 321) or the Lemon Sauce (page 322).

1 cup King Arthur Unbleached All-Purpose Flour
1/2 cup King Arthur Stone Ground Whole Wheat Flour
1 cup sugar, white or brown
1/2 teaspoon salt
1 teaspoon baking soda
2 teaspoons vanilla (or 1 teaspoon each vanilla and almond extracts)
1/3 cup vegetable oil
1 cup yogurt, sour cream, buttermilk or sour milk (add 1 tablespoon
     vinegar to 1 cup milk and let it sit for 5 minutes to "clabber")

"Cake-Pan" Cake with a Citrus Twist

1 1/2 cups King Arthur Unbleached All-Purpose Flour
1 cup sugar (or 2/3 cup honey mixed with wet ingredients)
1/2 teaspoon salt
1 teaspoon baking soda
1 tablespoon grated orange or lemon rind (fresh is best)
1 teaspoon vanilla
1 tablespoon vinegar
1/3 cup vegetable oil
1 cup orange juice or lemonade (if you use lemonade, don't use the
     tablespoon of vinegar)

Tipsy Sherry "Cake-Pan" Cake

This cake gets even better if you wait a day before you serve it.

1 cup King Arthur Unbleached All-Purpose Flour
1/2 cup King Arthur Stone Ground Whole Wheat Flour
1/2 teaspoon salt
1 teaspoon baking soda
1 teaspoon baking powder
3/4 cup sugar
2 teaspoons vanilla
1/3 cup vegetable oil
3/4 cup inexpensive cream sherry (no vinegar this time)
1/4 cup water

Spicy "Cake-Pan" Cake

Tomato juice sounds a bit far out but actually makes one of the best variations we've tried. It gives the cake depth and accentuates its spiciness.

1 ½ cups King Arthur Stone Ground Whole Wheat Flour
1 cup brown sugar, packed (this will mix better with the wet rather than the dry ingredients)
½ teaspoon salt
1 teaspoon soda
1 teaspoon cinnamon
½ teaspoon cloves
½ teaspoon nutmeg (or your choice of other spices)
1 teaspoon vanilla
⅓ cup vegetable oil
1 cup buttermilk or tomato juice (no vinegar this time; buttermilk or tomato juice does the same job)
1 cup grated carrot, raisins, chopped apple, nuts, or whatever strikes your fancy for a final wallop of vitamins and fiber

Maple Walnut "Cake-Pan" Cake

This is delicious with a maple walnut ice cream and a little warm maple syrup on top. Note the lesser amount of vinegar because of the presence of the buttermilk.

1 cup King Arthur Stone Ground Whole Wheat Flour
½ cup King Arthur Unbleached All-Purpose Flour
½ teaspoon salt
1 teaspoon soda
2 teaspoons vanilla
1 teaspoon vinegar
⅓ cup vegetable oil
¾ cup maple syrup
¾ cup buttermilk
1 cup chopped walnuts

Sybil Kitchel's
Carrot Cake

This recipe comes from one of the Northeast Kingdom's great cooks. This region is located in the northeastern corner of Vermont, a rugged, hilly country containing some of the last wilderness areas in New England. It's a bastion of that independent spirit which has made Vermont a touchstone for the rest of the country.

Many years ago, Sybil and her husband, Doug, moved to one of the oldest hill farms in the state and over the years turned it into one of the loveliest places in the world. Sybil's touch in her vegetable garden just hints at her expertise in the kitchen. In this cake, she combines both.

> 1 1/2 cups vegetable oil
> 4 eggs
> 2 cups sugar
> 2 teaspoons vanilla
> 2 cups King Arthur Unbleached All-Purpose Flour
> 3 teaspoons cinnamon
> 2 teaspoons baking soda
> 1 teaspoon salt
> 3 cups carrots, finely grated
> 1 1/2 cups chopped pecans or walnuts (optional)

Preheat oven to 350°F.

Cream together the oil and eggs until they are light and full of air bubbles. Beat in the sugar 1/2 cup at a time and then add the vanilla.

In a separate bowl, blend together the flour, cinnamon, baking soda and salt. Mix these gently into the oil/egg/sugar mixture.

Fold in the carrots and nuts.

Pour into a lightly greased, 10 x 14-inch cake pan and bake for 35 to 40 minutes, or a 9 x 13-inch cake pan and bake for 45 to 50 minutes.

Let the cake cool thoroughly before you frost it.

This Carrot Cake is wonderful as is, but is elegant with Cream Cheese Frosting, which you'll find on page 317. The minced candied ginger, which is an optional ingredient in this frosting, was Sybil's inspiration.

SALLY THOMPSON'S
PINEAPPLE COCONUT CARROT CAKE

This embellished variation of the familiar carrot cake is the inspiration of Sally Thompson whose cheerful voice you hear on the telephone when you call King Arthur Flour's Headquarters in Norwich, Vermont. Along with successfully managing our increasingly busy office, Sally also juggles an increasingly busy household and still has enough energy to create a winner like this.

1 1/2 cups vegetable oil
4 eggs
2 teaspoons vanilla
1 1/2 cups sugar
2 cups King Arthur Unbleached All-Purpose Flour
1 1/2 teaspoons baking powder
2 teaspoons baking soda
1 teaspoon salt
1 tablespoon cinnamon
1/2 teaspoon nutmeg
2 1/2 cups finely grated carrots
1 cup shredded or flaked coconut
1 can (8 ounces) crushed pineapple drained
1/2 cup chopped nuts

Preheat your oven to 350°F.

Beat together for at least two minutes the oil, eggs, vanilla and sugar. Blend the flour, baking powder, baking soda, salt and spices together.

Add the liquid ingredients and stir just enough to blend them. Gently fold in the grated carrots, coconut, pineapple and nuts.

Pour this batter into a lightly greased, 10 x 14-inch cake pan and bake for 35 to 40 minutes, or a 9 x 13-inch cake pan and bake for 45 to 50 minutes. After the cake is done, cool it completely.

This moist cake, with the added flavor of coconut and pineapple, is an orchestra of flavor on its own, but to dress it up, spread it with the Cream Cheese Frosting you'll find on page 317. (Sally sometimes bakes this in three 8-inch round or square cake pans and puts it together as a layer cake.)

THE ORIGINAL CARPENTER STREET RESTAURANT
POPPY SEED CAKE

Our first office/headquarters in Norwich, Vermont, was located upstairs at the back of the 1820 House at 1 Carpenter Street, just off Main Street. The Carpenter Street Restaurant, a favorite place for business lunches as well as elegant dinners, was located downstairs in the front of the building. We've moved and the restaurant has changed hands, but we are including this recipe in remembrance of our original Norwich headquarters and the original restaurant.

This cake contains a smaller percentage of sugar than most so it could almost be called a quick bread, but it has a particularly delicate flavor and texture, so we decided it belonged right here.

2 cups King Arthur Unbleached All-Purpose Flour
2½ teaspoons baking powder
1 teaspoon salt
¼ to ½ cup poppy seeds
⅔ cup light vegetable oil
¾ cup granulated sugar
2 large eggs, at room temperature
¾ cup milk or evaporated milk
¼ cup orange juice (or milk)
2 teaspoons vanilla extract (almond is delicious as well)

Preheat your oven to 350°F and grease a 9-inch cake pan or a 5 x 9-inch loaf pan.

In a mixing bowl, blend the first three ingredients thoroughly. Mix in the poppy seeds.

In a separate bowl, with an electric mixer, whip the oil and sugar together for about a minute. Add the eggs and beat at high speed for three minutes until the mixture is very light. On low speed, mix in the evaporated milk, juice and vanilla.

Blend the wet ingredients with the dry very gently until they are just mixed.

Pour the batter into the cake pan and bake about 40 minutes or a loaf pan for about an hour. The cake is done when it begins to pull away from the sides of the pan, or a toothpick comes out clean from the center.

• "PUDDINGS" •

We have included several puddings in this chapter: pudding cakes, summer pudding, bread pudding and plum pudding (with Festival Fare). They are all soft, friendly confections (with the exception of plum pudding, although that too was soft until three hundred years ago). Beyond their common names and friendly associations, they are not very much alike at all.

PUDDING CAKES

Pudding Cakes, in just one act of creativity, are both cake and sauce at the same time. If you have all your ingredients close at hand, these cakes will take only 2 or 3 minutes to put together. You can either mix the ingredients in a bowl (this makes the blending fairly easy) and pour them in a greased cake pan, or, to avoid cleaning a bowl, grease the cake pan and mix the ingredients directly in it (like our "Cake-Pan" Cakes).

CHOCOLATE PUDDING CAKE

This is a devastatingly rich version, and, if you choose to use the vegetable oil, cholesterol free. It's great hot from the oven when the "sauce" is a sauce. (After it has cooled, the "sauce" becomes a pudding.) For an added flourish, serve it with a bit of whipped cream or ice cream.

> 1 cup King Arthur Unbleached All-Purpose Flour 🌾
> 2 teaspoons baking powder
> ½ teaspoon salt
> 1¼ to 1½ cups sugar
> 6 to 8 tablespoons cocoa powder (depending on how serious
>   a chocoholic you are)
> ½ to ¾ cup chopped pecans or walnuts
> 2 cups water
> 1 teaspoon vanilla
> ¼ cup (½ stick) butter or vegetable oil

First, preheat your oven to 350°F.

Measure the dry ingredients and put them in a mixing bowl (or right in a greased, 8-inch cake pan) and blend. Add, but don't blend (yet), the vanilla and butter or oil. Pour the water over everything, blend thoroughly and fold in the nuts.

Pour into a lightly greased, 8-inch square cake pan and bake for about 45 minutes. That is all there is to it.

PUDDING CAKE VARIATIONS

The next three cakes are all variations of the chocolate version. Each contains the same amount of flour, baking powder, salt, sugar, water, vanilla and butter or vegetable oil. We will list only the divergent ingredients and any special instructions that go with them. Otherwise, they are put together and baked the same way as the Chocolate Pudding Cake and for the same length of time.

VANILLA PUDDING CAKE

This one eliminates the cocoa to intensify the vanilla flavor. It's a great foil for fresh fruit.

1 tablespoon vanilla

The batter is a bit "wetter" so may take an extra five minutes of baking.

RUM RAISIN PUDDING CAKE

For added flavor and a lovely aroma, sprinkle a tablespoon of rum over the top right after it comes out of the oven. Serve alone or with ice cream.

1 to 1½ cups brown sugar (for the white sugar)
1 teaspoon nutmeg or other spice
½ cup chopped nuts
½ cup raisins
¼ cup dark rum in a two-cup measure
water, hot from the tap, to fill the two-cup measure

To get rid of lumps in brown sugar, push it through a coarse sieve after you measure it.

MAPLE WALNUT PUDDING CAKE

A bit of maple walnut ice cream will accentuate the flavors in this cake.

½ cup chopped walnuts
1¾ cups water, hot from the tap
1 cup maple syrup (for the sugar)

Pour the maple syrup in after the water and then mix and bake as for the Chocolate Pudding Cake.

LEMON PUDDING CAKE

This pudding cake is a bit different. It contains eggs, which make it light and feathery, with a sauce that is tart and sweet at the same time. As a wintertime cake, try it hot from the oven with a cup of tea or a glass of milk. As a summertime cake, serve it at room temperature, or chilled, with fresh berries or a little fruit sherbet or sorbet.

```
3 eggs
1 cup King Arthur Unbleached All-Purpose Flour
2 teaspoons baking powder
1/2 teaspoon salt
1 cup sugar
zest (grated rind) from 2 lemons
juice from these 2 lemons squeezed into a two-cup measure
water to fill the two-cup measure
2 tablespoons vegetable oil
```

Eggs separate more easily when they are cold but will incorporate more air when you beat them at room temperature. After you separate them, let them sit and warm up a bit while you deal with the other ingredients.

To get the most juice out of the lemons, first hold them under hot water from the tap. Then, with the palm of your hand, roll them around on the counter top, using a fair amount of pressure. This helps break up the cells of lemon juice inside so they will burst easily when you squeeze them. You should get about half a cup of juice from 2 lemons.

Preheat your oven to 350°F.

Separate the eggs into two small bowls.

Measure the dry ingredients into a mixing bowl and blend. Grate and add the rind from 2 lemons. Squeeze the lemon juice into a two-cup measure. Fill the remainder of the cup with lukewarm water from the tap and set aside.

Beat the egg whites until they're stiff and form peaks. Without rinsing your beater, beat the yolks until they're light and lemon colored.

Slowly pour the lemon juice/water mixture into the dry ingredients, using a wire whisk to blend everything together. It will make a pretty soupy batter. Blend in the vegetable oil and egg yolks. Fold in the egg whites.

Pour the batter into a greased, 8 x 8-inch cake pan. It will almost fill it up, but in this case the cake won't rise up and flow out of the pan.

Bake for about 50 minutes. The cake is done when it has pulled away from the sides of the pan.

BREAD PUDDINGS

Here are a few other friendly puddings which most of us will remember from our childhood or will want to become acquainted with now. They were originally made to use up stale bread, but these puddings are so good that you might want to make some "stale" bread just to make them.

SUMMER PUDDING

Summer pudding was devised by the English in the nineteenth century for people who wanted something that tasted richer than it actually was. This pudding, also designed to use up stale bread, is chilled rather than baked. In the summer you can use whatever berries are in season. Because of the invention of the freezer, this Summer Pudding can now be a Winter Pudding, as frozen berries will also do very nicely.

> bread made with King Arthur Flour, enough to line your baking dish and to make a "lid" (with crusts removed)
> 4 cups strawberries, blackberries, blueberries or whatever berries are on hand (or a combination)
> 1 cup sugar (with fresh berries only)

Line the bottom and sides of a 1½-quart bowl (it doesn't need to be oven proof) with the bread. Fill in any gaps with small pieces of bread cut to fit.

Heat the berries with the sugar over low heat until the sugar is dissolved and the juice of the berries starts to flow. (If you're using sweetened frozen berries, you can skip this part. Just make sure they are thoroughly thawed before you use them.)

Pour the fruit mixture over the bread. Place another layer of bread on top of the fruit, making a "lid" with these slices.

Cover with plastic wrap, and then a place a small plate that will fit inside the rim of the bowl on top. Weigh this down with something heavy (a jar of fruit, a can of beans...) to force the juices up into the top layer of bread.

Refrigerate the pudding for 6 to 8 hours. The juices will seep into the bread turning it a lovely rose color and the fruit will set somewhat.

To serve, remove the weighted plate and plastic wrap. Put a serving plate upside down on top of the bowl and flip the whole thing over.

To serve, cut in wedges and top with whipped cream or yogurt sweetened with a bit of maple syrup or brown sugar.

Cinnamon Bread Pudding

While bread puddings are traditionally eaten for dessert, the ingredients in this first pudding suggest that it might be a sweet way to begin a day, served hot with a little cream or warmed maple syrup. If you decide to serve it for dessert add a dollop of ice cream or whipped cream.

    3 tablespoons butter
    Cinnamon Raisin Bread (page 148), to make 2 cups cubed
    2 cups milk
    2 eggs
    1 teaspoon vanilla
    1/2 cup maple syrup
    1/2 teaspoon salt

Butter the slices of bread and then cut into cubes. Place in a buttered baking dish. In a mixing bowl, beat the rest of the ingredients together. Pour this mixture over the bread cubes.

Let it soak for 15 to 20 minutes while you preheat your oven to 350°F. Bake for 30 to 45 minutes (depending on the shape of your baking dish).

Chocolate Bread Pudding

This old friend is ambrosial served hot with chilled whipped cream or ice cream.

    1/2 to 1 cup sugar
    2 cups milk
    4 to 6 tablespoons cocoa
    2 cups cubed stale (or toasted) bread made with good King Arthur Flour
    2 tablespoons butter
    2 large eggs
    1/4 teaspoon salt
    1 teaspoon vanilla

In a double boiler, mix the sugar into 1/2 cup of the milk. Add the cocoa, heating enough to melt and dissolve them.

Place the bread cubes into a greased baking dish.

When the sugar has dissolved and the milk mixture is hot, stir in the butter. Add the remainder of the milk. Beat in the eggs and stir in the salt and vanilla.

Pour this mixture over the bread in the baking dish and proceed as above.

• FESTIVAL FARE •

The festival foods we have in this section are mostly from the "land of Arthur" and are based on recipes that are hundreds of years old. They were imbued with symbolism relating to the harvest, the changing of the seasons, religious ceremonies, and the most important of human events, births, deaths, marriages, coronations. The rituals involved in their preparation were a focus of excitement themselves, giving the finished products an aura of power and magic.

Compared to what we enjoy today, resources were extremely limited when Arthur was King and for the next thousand years after that to the days when Elizabeth was Queen of England and Mary, Queen of the Scots. Cooking facilities were primitive and produce was predominantly local. Trade routes were established but the foodstuffs that came from any distance were available only sporadically. So these special occasions were celebrated with variations of everyday fare embellished by those hard-to-get fruits and spices.

As advances in trade and technology allowed, traditional recipes evolved and changed. Each cook interpreted basic guidelines differently as well, so each recipe had as many variations as there were cooks.

As soon as you set hand to pot and spoon, you become part of this fascinating history yourself. When you make some of this festival fare, we hope you will feel some of the magic that it represents, and will want to experiment and add some of your own. It is exciting to join the long culinary history that connects us to the people who lived when Arthur was King.

FESTIVAL CAKES

CHRISTMAS PUDDING
STEAMED PLUM PUDDING

The ancestor of this Plum Pudding was first served in the dim, pre-Christian Celtic past of Britain, as the climax of a feast at the winter solstice, when the sun was at its lowest arc in the sky. It was served flaming, to entice the sun to return, and with a sprig of holly in its center, to ward off witches and misfortune. It is an ancient "cake," layered with centuries of history.

Plum pudding was originally more like a porridge in texture, and the "plums" were actually raisins. Sometime at the beginning of the 1700's it became the firm cake we know today, but retained its original name. As befits an ancient cake, it is steamed rather than baked, as only the lord of the manor had an oven.

It's best to make your pudding several weeks in advance so the flavors have time to mellow and mature. But don't despair if the inspiration to make it comes the day before you want to serve it. It will still be rich and festive, and it will certainly help you light up the dark season of the year.

1 cup King Arthur Unbleached All-Purpose Flour
2 cups fresh crumbs from bread made with King Arthur Flour
1 cup (firmly packed) grated suet
1 cup currants soaked overnight in tea (if you have time)
2 cups golden raisins (also plumped in tea)
½ cup grated carrot
½ cup chopped, candied peel
1 teaspoon salt
½ cup firmly packed brown sugar
¼ teaspoon nutmeg
¼ teaspoon cinnamon
¼ teaspoon allspice
¼ teaspoon cloves
¼ teaspoon ginger
1 cup milk
3 eggs
juice and grated peel (zest) from one lemon (or 1 teaspoon dried lemon
       peel and 1 tablespoon lemon juice)
¼ cup brandy or rum

Grease a two-quart pudding mold or any two-quart container that can be tightly covered.

In a large bowl, mix the flour, bread crumbs, suet, fruit, carrots, candied peel, salt, sugar and spices together thoroughly.

In a smaller bowl, beat the milk, eggs, lemon juice and zest together until light.

Mix the liquids into the dry ingredients. (The easiest way to do this is with your hands.)

Put the combined ingredients into the mold, making sure it is filled only two-thirds full. Cover tightly. (Aluminum foil and a large rubber band will do as a lid.)

You'll need a kettle or pot that is large enough to cover with a lid with the pudding mold in it. You will also need something to keep the mold off of the bottom of the kettle; a vegetable steamer or even a crinkled-up piece of aluminum foil will do.

When you're ready to steam the pudding, place the mold in the kettle and pour boiling water around it until it comes about two-thirds up the side of the mold.

Cover the kettle and, when the water is boiling vigorously, turn the heat as low as you can and steam for 5 hours, adding water when necessary.

When the pudding is done, remove the lid and sprinkle with the rum or brandy. Let it cool a bit to allow the pudding to set before removing it from the mold. When it is thoroughly cool, wrap it in plastic and store it in a cool place.

To reheat it for serving, place the pudding back into the mold and steam it for about 2 hours. Turn it out onto a serving dish with a lip.

Heat ¼ cup brandy in a small saucepan on the stove until it is close to a boil. Pour it over the pudding, carefully (!) ignite it with a match and carry the flaming pudding to the table. (It has the most impact with all the lights turned off, but watch your step as you carry it to the table.)

Plum Pudding should be served with the Hard Sauce you'll find on page 322.

LIGHT OLD-FASHIONED FRUIT CAKE

If you think you don't like fruit cake, try this one from our Peacham friend, Marilyn Magnus. A fruit cake is a close relative of plum pudding, although a much younger cousin as it's baked in that "modern convenience," the oven. Fruit cakes are either "light" or "dark." Dark variations are more heavily spiced and contain a darker, stronger flavored sweetener.

This cake is of the "light" variety, but light in color only for it is very dense and meant to be eaten in very thin slices. (On our "cake density" scale, this is at the heavy end.) Spices are added with a "light" touch and it is sweetened with white sugar so the predominant flavor is that of the fruit and nuts all bound together with a token amount of flour.

Like plum puddings, fruit cakes should be made several weeks ahead of time so all the flavors have time to blend, mellow and mature. If your inspiration to make them comes late, they are still excellent fresh from the oven. Because these taste so good, they are welcome holiday gifts as well.

4 cups King Arthur Unbleached All-Purpose Flour
$^1/_2$ teaspoon baking powder
1 teaspoon nutmeg
$1^1/_2$ teaspoons cinnamon
$1^1/_2$ teaspoons salt
4 cups ($1^1/_2$ pounds) pecan halves
3 cups ($1^1/_2$ pounds) whole candied cherries or $1^1/_2$ cups each cherries
      and chopped candied pineapple
2 cups (1 pound) golden or purple raisins (optional)
1 cup (2 sticks or $^1/_2$ pound) butter
$2^1/_4$ cups sugar
6 large eggs
3 tablespoons brandy or rum
more brandy or rum for the maturing period

Preheat your oven to 275°F.

In a very large mixing bowl, mix together the flour, baking powder, spices and salt. Add the nuts and fruit, mixing until they are well coated.

In a second bowl, cream the butter until it is light. Add the sugar, a quarter at a time, beating until the mixture is light and lemon colored. Add the eggs, one at a time, beating the mixture thoroughly after each addition until it is fluffy. Blend in the brandy or rum.

Stir the wet ingredients into the dry and mix only until they are combined.

Lightly grease a 10-inch tube pan, two 9 x 5-inch loaf pans or four 1-pound coffee cans (the wide, short kind). Fill two-thirds full and bake for about 2½ hours (the tube pan or loaf pan) or 2 hours (the coffee cans).

As soon as you remove the cakes from the oven, sprinkle brandy or rum over them. After it has soaked in, remove the cakes from their pans and let them cool completely.

Wrap them in plastic and then aluminum foil. Store them in a cool place to mature. Every few days during the maturing period, sprinkle a few drops of brandy or rum over them if you wish. The alcohol will evaporate and leave only flavor.

LARDY CAKE

Wiltshire, England, is the ancestral home of another festival cake. Lardy cakes were generally made from a simple bread dough left over (or saved out) from the week's baking and enriched by adding milk and lard. Milk made the bread tender and more nutritious. Lard also made made the bread tender and increased the length of time it would stay fresh. These things were important in the days when a cook had to take her dough to be baked in the manorial oven of the lord whose lands her family worked.

In our recipe we use a combination of King Arthur Flours to create a blend similar to the flour used by farming people in England two or three hundred years ago. The brown sugar used in the filling was available to common people in old England although it was considered less desirable than white.

Currants and raisins were imported from the Mediterranean. They were available only occasionally and saved to be included in festival fare. Spices were equally cherished and though there are recipes for lardy cakes that don't include them, we have, since they improved the flavor of the cake and were used when possible.

Dough

> ¼ cup warm water
> ½ teaspoon sugar
> 1 tablespoon or packet yeast
> ¾ cup warm milk
> 1 tablespoon fresh lard (or butter), softened
> 1 cup King Arthur Stone Ground Whole Wheat Flour
> 1 teaspoon salt
> 1½ cups King Arthur Unbleached All-Purpose Flour

Butter or vegetable shortening can be substituted for the lard if you wish, as can white sugar for the brown. (See Appendix for nutritional information about lard.)

Preparing the Dough: Dissolve the sugar and yeast in the water. Add and blend in the warm milk and lard.

Add the whole wheat flour, salt and unbleached flour. Stir with a large spoon until the dough begins to hold together and pull away from the sides of the bowl. This is a very soft dough so make sure you and your kneading surface are well floured when you turn it out to knead.

Knead until it is smooth and elastic, adding only enough flour to keep it from sticking to you or the board.

Let the dough rise in a warm, draft-free place until doubled in bulk, 1 to 1 $\frac{1}{2}$ hours. Knock it down and knead out any stray bubbles. Let it rest while you prepare the filling.

Filling

> $\frac{1}{2}$ cup brown sugar
> $\frac{3}{4}$ cup currants
> $\frac{3}{4}$ cup golden raisins
> $\frac{1}{2}$ teaspoon cinnamon
> $\frac{1}{2}$ teaspoon allspice
> $\frac{1}{8}$ teaspoon nutmeg
> $\frac{1}{2}$ cup lard (or butter) at room temperature

Making the Filling: In one bowl, mix together the brown sugar, currants, raisins and spices.

Forming the Cake: Roll the dough into a 10 x 14-inch rectangle (roughly) with the short side next to you. Dab one-third of the lard onto the bottom two-thirds of the dough making sure you leave at least an inch clear on the edges so you can seal them. Sprinkle with one-third of the brown sugar mixture.

Fold the top third of the dough over the middle third and then the bottom third up over that, the way you would fold a letter. Pinch the edges firmly and turn the dough one-quarter of the way around so the short edge is again next to you.

Roll out again into roughly the same dimensions (10 x 14 inches), and repeat the process with another third of the lard and sugar mixture.

Turn the dough one-quarter of the way around once more and repeat the process again. Roll out a final time into a square which will fit an 8 x 8-inch cake pan.

Grease the pan well. Score the dough diagonally about every half inch and place the scored side down in the pan. Cover and let rise until doubled.

About 15 minutes before you want to bake your cake, preheat the oven to 350°F. Gently score the top side of the dough (as you did the bottom), brush with melted lard and bake for 35 to 40 minutes.

Glaze

> 2 tablespoons lard (or butter)
> 2 tablespoons brown sugar
> ¼ teaspoon cinnamon (optional)

Making the Glaze: When the lardy cake is almost done, melt the lard or butter.

After you remove the cake from the oven, invert it onto a serving plate.

> • If you are being authentic and using lard, sprinkle the cake with the brown sugar and cinnamon and drizzle the melted lard over it. (Brown sugar does not combine well with lard.)

> • If you are using butter, you can blend the brown sugar and cinnamon with it and drizzle this mixture over the cake.

This cake is obviously tremendously rich and, despite current feelings about lard and butter, tastes absolutely heavenly. It should probably, however, be relegated to celebration days as was intended.

Shaping Variation

You can also shape a lardy cake as you would sticky buns. Instead of rolling the dough out into a square the final time, roll it again into a 10 x 14-inch rectangle.

This time roll it up starting with a long side. Pinch the seam closed and cut off slices about ¾ inch thick.

Place these on their sides in a greased, 8 x 8-inch cake pan or one that's large enough to give them room to expand. Bake, invert onto a serving plate and glaze as above.

As you might have gathered, this recipe uses the same ingredients found in our other festival fare and ingeniously combines them in a different way. Where resources are few, imagination flourishes.

A Twelfth Night Cake

Think what a turmoil there would be if we were told that we had to drop eleven days from our calendar in order to correct an astronomical error made by astronomers centuries earlier. Could there ever be a consensus on which days to choose?

This actually happened in Britain in 1752. The events that led up to this decision began back in the first century A.D. when Rome invaded Britain and made her a colony. Not long after the Romans arrived, the early Roman Britons adopted the Roman calendar as their own. When the Roman empire began to crumble four hundred years later, the Romans left England and its people to fend for themselves. Despite their departure, their calendar, with its little imperfection, continued to be used for more than a thousand years.

In 1582, Pope Gregory XIII decided that it was necessary to remedy the time creep caused by the calendar. But the Britons dug in their heels and wouldn't accept the recalculations until almost two hundred years later. When it was finally agreed it had to be done, the decision created general havoc. A particularly difficult issue was the placement of important festivals around Christmas and the New Year.

The timing of Twelfth Night, which marks the end of the Christmas season (originally the most revelrous festival of all), has never really been resolved, or it has been resolved in two different ways. In most of England, it is celebrated on January 6, twelve nights after Christmas. But in the West country, land of those ancient Britons where Arthur sprang from, it is held January 17th, eleven days later.

An important part of this festival was the appearance of the Twelfth Night cake. Whichever man and woman found a bean and pea baked inside the cake were declared the "King and Queen of Misrule." They were then granted the right to determine the course of events for the rest of this evening of celebration and revelry.

A Twelfth Night cake is a variation of a pound cake, rich in butter, honey and eggs. Traditionally it contained a substantial quantity of nuts and dried fruit. This version eliminates the fruit to focus on honey and almonds. However (and whenever) you decide to celebrate Twelfth Night, this cake will add a final flourish to your festivities.

1 1/2 cups (3 sticks) good quality butter
6 large eggs
1 cup honey
1 teaspoon vanilla
1 teaspoon almond extract
1 cup King Arthur Stone Ground Whole Wheat Flour
2 cups King Arthur Unbleached All-Purpose Flour
1 tablespoon baking powder
1/2 teaspoon baking soda (to neutralize the acidity of the honey)
1/2 teaspoon salt
3/4 cup buttermilk
1 1/4 cups sliced almonds

Preheat your oven to 300°F. Because honey tends to scorch at high temperatures, this cake is baked more slowly and at a lower temperature than most.

In a large bowl, cream the butter until it is light. Add and beat in the eggs one by one until the mixture is fluffy. Add the honey ¼ cup at a time, beating thoroughly after each addition. (Since this is a variation on a pound cake, it is important to incorporate as much air into it as possible.) Blend in the vanilla and almond extracts.

In another bowl, measure and blend thoroughly the dry ingredients.

Mix the dry ingredients into the butter/honey mixture alternately with the buttermilk, a third at a time. Finally, fold in 1 cup of almonds.

Pour the batter into a 12-cup Bundt pan and then press a dried pea and bean into it, carefully covering your tracks. Bake for 45 to 50 minutes or until done.

After you remove the cake from the oven let it cool for 10 minutes before turning out onto a serving dish.

Try glazing the cake with ¼ cup honey flavored with 1 teaspoon lemon juice. (To make the honey more spreadable, heat it gently.) Coarsely chop or grind the remaining ¼ cup of almonds (a blender does this nicely) and sprinkle over the surface of the cake.

RED VELVET CAKE

This cake, with its deep, red color, hearty texture and delicate flavor, is fun to make for Valentine's Day. The real origin of this cake is misty, but everyone who has made it has heard some fascinating "first-hand" version.

To make the heart shape, you'll need both an 8-inch round and an 8-inch square cake pan. If you don't want to shape your cake like a heart, or if you want to use this cake for another celebration day, bake it in two 8-inch round pans, cut each cake horizontally, and create an elegant four-layer torte. If you don't want to be so elegant, a two-layer cake will taste just as good.

We don't ordinarily like the idea of using food coloring, especially in this amount, but as with all those "good" things that are "bad" for you, an occasional transgression probably won't hurt much. If you're uncomfortable with it, leave it out and increase the buttermilk to 1¼ cups.

The only leavening in this cake comes from the air you cream into the shortening and sugar, and the reaction of the buttermilk, soda and vinegar.

½ cup shortening
1½ cups sugar, less 2 tablespoons
2 eggs
¼ cup (2 ounces) red food coloring
2 tablespoons cocoa
1 teaspoon salt
1 teaspoon baking soda
1 teaspoon vinegar
1 cup buttermilk
2¼ cups King Arthur Unbleached All-Purpose Flour
1 recipe Red Velvet Cake Frosting (page 319)

Preheat your oven to 350°F.

Cream the shortening, sugar and eggs until light. Blend in the food coloring and cocoa. Add the salt, soda and vinegar to the buttermilk and mix thoroughly. (Watch what happens.) Add this mixture in thirds, alternately with the flour, to the shortening mixture, beating thoroughly after each addition.

Pour half the batter into the 8-inch round cake pan and half into the 8-inch square cake pan. Bake for 30 minutes or until done. While the cake bakes, make the Red Velvet Cake Frosting. When done, remove the layers from the pans and cool them on a wire rack.

After they have cooled, cut both layers in half horizontally (with the blade of your knife parallel to the table) and then cut the round layer in half vertically (with the blade of your knife at right angles to the table). Take the bottom layers of all three pieces and place them on a large serving platter.

Frost the bottom layer and place the remaining pieces on top. Frost the top and decorate in any way your heart desires.

SIMNEL CAKE

For several hundred years in England, the fourth Sunday of Lent has been known as "Mothering Sunday." Mothering Sunday originated when young girls, who had gone into the service of another household, were allowed to come home midway through Lent to visit their mothers. For many of these young women, who began their service when they were just beyond childhood, this was a very important day. Their work was long and hard, and a good dose of mothering was very much needed. When they came home, they brought a sample of what they had learned, made of the finest ingredients, traditionally a Simnel Cake.

The name of this cake comes from the Middle English word "simenel," probably derived from the Latin word, "simila," meaning fine flour. This particular cake has long been associated with Mothering Sunday, but in recent years, as this practice of servitude has disappeared, the association has been extended through the whole Lenten Season to Easter itself.

There are two types of Simnel Cake. The original, before the appearance of baking powder, was leavened with yeast and contained a mixture of spices and dried fruit with a layer of almond paste (or marzipan) in the middle. Later the yeast was replaced by baking powder and the marzipan became a frosting on top of the cake. Our version is the original yeast-leavened variety with marzipan layers in the middle and on top, a truly festive cake. It keeps well and improves with age.

> 1 cup warm water
> 1 tablespoon brown sugar
> 1 tablespoon or packet active dry yeast
> 3 eggs
> 4 tablespoons dry milk (optional)
> 4 tablespoons ($\frac{1}{2}$ stick) butter, softened
> $\frac{1}{2}$ cup brown sugar
> 1 teaspoon cinnamon
> $\frac{1}{2}$ teaspoon nutmeg
> $\frac{1}{2}$ teaspoon allspice
> 1 cup currants (plumped in hot spiced tea if you have time)
> $\frac{1}{2}$ cup candied lemon peel
> 1 cup King Arthur Stone Ground Whole Wheat Flour
> 1 teaspoon salt
> 2 cups King Arthur Unbleached All-Purpose Flour
> 3 (7-ounce) packages almond paste, or marzipan; enough to roll out into two 8- or 9-inch circles and to sculpt into tiny Easter eggs or other appropriate decorations (or, to make marzipan, see page 590)

Making the Dough: Measure the water into a mixing bowl and dissolve in it the tablespoon of brown sugar and yeast.

Beat in the eggs and dry milk and then stir in the butter which can be either soft or barely melted. Add the balance of the sugar, the spices and fruit.

When this is well blended, stir in the whole wheat flour and the salt. Add the unbleached flour to make a very slack dough. Beat the dough thoroughly for 2 or 3 minutes.

Rising: Place the dough in a warm, draft-free spot to rise until doubled. This will take anywhere from 1 to 2 hours depending on conditions. If you cover it with plastic wrap, you may want to wipe the bottom of the wrap with vegetable oil to prevent the dough from sticking.

Preparing the Marzipan Layers: While the dough rises, take one package of the marzipan and cut it in half and reserve one of the halves (3½ ounces) for sculpting.

Take the remaining marzipan (17½ ounces) and divide it into 2 portions. Work each portion with your fingers or a rolling pin into a round to cover each layer of the cake. You may need to dust the rolling pin and table with a bit of flour to help keep it from sticking. (The bottom layer doesn't need to be too elegant since it will be hidden.)

Assembling the Cake: After the rising period, stir the dough down. Put half of it in the bottom of an 8- or 9-inch springform cake pan, spreading it out so it covers the bottom of the pan. Put the most ragged round of marzipan on top. Put the remainder of the dough on top of the marzipan.

Rising & Baking: Cover the dough again, and let it rise for another hour.

About 15 minutes before you want to bake the cake, preheat your oven to 350°F. Bake the cake for 35 to 40 minutes.

Preparing the Marzipan Sculptures: Take the 3½ ounces of marzipan and mold it, like clay, into tiny eggs, chicks, rabbits or whatever inspires you. You can knead food or vegetable coloring into it to make it more festive if you wish. A child might like to make this part of the Mothering Sunday cake. (If no one's interested in sculpting marzipan, a sprinkling of jelly beans would be equally festive.)

Decorating the Cake: After the cake is thoroughly done and before it cools, place the second marzipan round on the top. (This one will have to be fairly presentable since that's the part of the cake that will be visible.)

To finish, place the marzipan sculptures around the outer rim of the cake.

GINGERBREAD

Gingerbread has a venerable history. It is the "sweetmeat" that has had the longest association with festivals and holidays for the last thousand years. Back in thirteenth-century England, ginger and pepper were often the only spices available for general use. Around these grew a tradition of baking that has passed from generation to generation to us in the twentieth century.

In medieval England, gingerbread was even more popular than chocolate cake is today. It was the sweet that children looked for at the fairs, which were the most exciting social events of the year. It was an important part of every festival and holiday. Rather than the ice cream man in his truck, it was the gingerbread man who wandered through crowded streets and markets calling to children to buy his hot, spiced cakes, irresistibly shaped as animals and people, and iced or gilded.

Gingerbread ultimately became so important that making it evolved into a separate profession. If you have an old cookbook that belonged to your grandmother or great grandmother, look under "gingerbread." A hundred years ago, cookbooks contained whole sections dedicated to this popular sweet.

The rest of Europe had its own affair with gingerbread too. Each town, and even each baker, had individual specialties. When these gingerbread-loving colonists crossed the Atlantic to America, they brought their recipes with them weaving them into the culinary traditions of this country. This holiday season, join hands over the centuries and continue the gingerbread tradition.

AMERICAN GINGERBREAD

On this side of the Atlantic, gingerbread, sweetened with molasses or maple syrup, developed its own identity. Here is a typical American version which is moist and mild. It is delightful as is or can be served with hard sauce, lemon sauce, plain cream, whipped cream, or ice cream.

6 tablespoons ($^3/_4$ stick) butter or margarine
1 cup brown sugar
$^1/_2$ cup molasses
1 egg
$2^1/_2$ cups King Arthur Unbleached All-Purpose Flour
1 teaspoon baking soda
1 teaspoon ginger
1 teaspoon cinnamon
$^1/_2$ teaspoon salt
$^3/_4$ cup buttermilk

Preheat your oven to 350°F.

Cream the butter until it is light. Add the sweeteners, ½ cup at a time, and continue beating until light. Add the egg and beat until fluffy.

Blend the dry ingredients together. Add them to the butter mixture alternately with the buttermilk.

Pour into a lightly greased, 9-inch cake pan, or more traditionally, a 10½-inch iron skillet, or "spider" as they were called, and bake for 40 to 45 minutes.

GINGERBREAD GALORE

Here are some ways to vary this basic gingerbread.

Molasses Gingerbread: For a more pronounced molasses flavor, use 1 cup of molasses and ½ cup brown sugar as the sweetener.

New England Gingerbread: For a gingerbread with a typically New England flavor, use 1 cup of maple syrup and ½ cup brown sugar as the sweetener.

English Gingerbread: For a traditional English gingerbread, use a cup of dark corn syrup or molasses and ½ cup of sugar as the sweetener, and add a heaping tablespoon of fresh grated orange peel.

Whole Wheat Gingerbread: For a heartier gingerbread, substitute any amount of King Arthur Stone Ground Whole Wheat Flour for an equal amount of King Arthur Unbleached All-Purpose Flour.

Low-Calorie Gingerbread: For a "low-cal," low-cholesterol version, leave out the butter and egg.

Rich Gingerbread: For a richer version, substitute sour milk or sour cream for the buttermilk.

Upside-Down Gingerbread: For an "upside-down" version, place peeled, sliced apples, peaches, pears or pineapple you've sprinkled liberally with cinnamon sugar, on the bottom of a well-buttered cake pan or iron skillet. Pour the batter over the fruit and bake as indicated above.

After removing this from the oven, invert a serving plate onto the cake pan. Flip them over (carefully, using pot holders) and allow them to sit a minute with the pan in place so the fruit loosens and winds up on the cake (instead of the pan).

For Gingersnaps, see page 342 in the next chapter. Gingerbread people and houses are included in Chapter XI, Fun! (page 563).

• FRUIT SOMETHINGS •

This section contains recipes for those things which, like our puddings, aren't quite cakes and aren't quite pies. They fall somewhere in between, each almost in a category of its own. They are similar in that fruit is their focus but good King Arthur Flour appears in a different way in each to provide the setting.

PINEAPPLE UPSIDE-DOWN CAKE

In this cake, the fruit starts out on the bottom, is baked with a cake batter on top and is served upside-down. Because it's made with King Arthur "Self-Rising" Flour it's an easy, quick "from scratch" cake either for you or an eager child who loves to play baker. You can bake it in an iron skillet or "spider" (see p. 67), if you have one, or a large (10- to 12-inch) pie plate, if you don't.

Topping that Starts on the Bottom

¼ cup (½ stick) butter
½ cup brown sugar
1 can (20 ounces) pineapple rings (you'll need 6 to 7)
maraschino cherries (optional)
½ cup pecan halves (optional)

Cake Batter

2 eggs
⅓ cup vegetable oil
1 cup sugar, white or brown
½ cup milk or buttermilk
2 teaspoons vanilla
1½ cups pre-mixed King Arthur "Self-Rising" Flour (see page 597 for
     directions)

You can substitute 1½ cups of King Arthur Unbleached All-Purpose Flour, 2 teaspoons of baking powder and ½ teaspoon of salt for the "self-rising" flour.

First: Preheat your oven to 350°F.

Preparing the Topping: Make a slurry of the butter and brown sugar in your skillet over low heat.

After the sugar has dissolved, remove the skillet from the heat. (If you're going to bake your cake in a pie plate make the slurry in a small saucepan and then pour it into the pie plate.)

Place a layer of pineapple rings in the butter/sugar mixture so the sides are just touching. If you have them and/or feel like using them, place the maraschino cherries and pecan halves in the center of each ring. Put this aside while you mix up the cake batter.

Making the Batter: In a mixing bowl, beat the eggs until light and, while still beating, slowly add the vegetable oil. Mix in the sugar, milk and vanilla. Blend in your King Arthur "Self-Rising" Flour or blended dry ingredients.

Gently spoon this batter over the pineapple slices and slide the skillet (or pie plate) into your oven and bake for about 30 minutes. Make sure the cake is done by pressing gently on the center surface. If it's done, it will spring back.

Flipping the Cake: Now comes the exciting part. Take the cake out of the oven. Invert a serving plate over the top of the skillet. Holding the plate and the skillet very firmly with a couple of pot holders or folded towels, quickly flip them over and set them back down on the counter. Leave the skillet upside down for a couple of minutes to make sure everything drops out of it and onto the cake. Take the skillet off and rearrange anything that has slipped out of place.

An upside-down cake is particularly fun to make. There is something a little racy about flipping a cake over after it comes out of the oven, perhaps because you're supposed to treat cakes gently, or perhaps because a successful flip creates an added sense of victory.

Easy One Bowl No-Knead Apple Cake

In this recipe, which came from a collection of King Arthur recipes that was circulating in the 1950's, the fruit is baked on the top of a yeast-raised batter. On reading its name, the first thing that comes to mind is an apparent contradiction. "No-knead" suggests the presence of yeast and yeast doesn't usually show up in cakes, or hasn't since the development of baking powder in the middle of the 1800's. So the original version of this cake presumably has roots deep in the last century.

But the way the yeast is handled in this recipe brings it right up to date even though our version is at least twenty-five years old. Like the new quick-rising varieties, the yeast is mixed right into the dry ingredients. There is just nothing new under the sun.

This is a "good morning" cake to serve at a brunch or for a lazy weekend break-fast. The apple topping can be prepared ahead of time and the batter can be put together as quickly as muffin batter. If you've never worked with yeast before, it's a good place to start. It takes a little over two hours from start to finish, but most of the time, it's the yeast that's doing the work.

Fruit

2 cups tart, firm apples, peeled, cored and sliced
2 to 3 tablespoons water
2 heaping tablespoons brown sugar
1/4 teaspoon cinnamon
1/4 teaspoon nutmeg
2 tablespoons butter

Batter

1/2 cup King Arthur Stone Ground Whole Wheat Flour
1/2 cup sugar, white or brown
1/4 cup non-fat dry milk
1/2 teaspoon salt
1/2 teaspoon cinnamon
1/2 teaspoon nutmeg
1 tablespoon or packet active dry yeast
2 tablespoons butter
1/2 cup water, hot from the tap
1 egg
1 cup King Arthur Unbleached All-Purpose Flour
1/2 cup raisins, currants or halved cranberries (optional)

Preparing the Fruit: Put the apples in a saucepan with the water, brown sugar, cinnamon and nutmeg (everything except the butter). Cook gently 4 or 5 minutes until the apples are just barely soft. Remove from heat, blend in the butter and let this mixture cool while you prepare the batter.

Making the Batter: In a large mixing bowl, thoroughly blend the whole wheat flour, sugar, dry milk, salt, cinnamon, nutmeg and yeast. (Note that the yeast is not proofed in the traditional way but added directly to the dry ingredients.) Drop the butter on top of the blended dry ingredients. Pour the hot water on top to melt the butter. Blend this mixture well and let it rest for a couple of minutes.

Add the egg and $^1/_2$ cup of unbleached flour. Beat this mixture for a couple of minutes. Stir in the remainder of the flour or enough to make a fairly stiff batter, not a dough. Add the raisins, currants or cranberries at this point, if you choose.

Assembling the Cake: Spread the batter evenly into a greased, 9-inch square or round cake pan or a 10-inch pie plate.

Take the cooled apple slices and lay them artfully on top of the batter. Pour any juices over the top, cover with plastic wrap and let the yeast do its work for the next hour or hour and a half.

Preheat your oven to 350°F. When the batter looks as if it's trying to come up through the apples, remove the plastic wrap, pop the baking dish into the oven and bake for 25 minutes. When the cake is done it will be gently browned and the center will spring back when you press it with your fingers.

The cake can be removed from the pan after it has cooled for about 10 minutes and served as is, or, for a special occasion, you can "drizzle" a confectioners' sugar glaze (page 207) over the top.

APPLE CRISP
(OR RASPBERRY, BLUEBERRY, PEACH...)

In our crisp, the fruit is baked under a crumbly topping of flour, oatmeal, sugar, butter and spices. It's quick, easy and good. In the Whole Wheat Chapter you'll find Rhubarb Crumble, a close cousin of this crisp.

4 cups (approximately 8) apples, or other fruit, peeled and sliced
$^3/_4$ cup King Arthur Unbleached All-Purpose Flour
1 cup brown sugar
$^3/_4$ cup oatmeal
$^1/_2$ teaspoon salt
$^3/_4$ teaspoon cinnamon
$^1/_4$ teaspoon allspice
$^1/_2$ cup (1 stick) butter or margarine, softened

Preheat your oven to 375°F.

Place peeled, cored and sliced apples or other fruit into a lightly greased 8 x 8-inch baking dish.

Blend the dry ingredients. Rub in the butter with your fingertips until the mixture is crumbly. Sprinkle this crumb mixture over the fruit.

Bake for 35 to 40 minutes. Serve warm with cream or ice cream or just as is.

Fresh Fruit Cobbler

In a cobbler, the fruit is again baked under a topping but this time it's a biscuit dough. For an example of a similar biscuit with the fruit on top, see our recipe for Strawberry Shortcake (page 68). This recipe will serve about 6 people.

Fruit

> 3 cups sliced fruit (almost anything goes here: strawberries, blueberries, peaches, apples, rhubarb or a combination)
> 1/2 to 1 cup sugar (use more or less depending on sweetness of fruit)
> 2 tablespoons butter or margarine

Crust

> 2 cups King Arthur Unbleached All-Purpose Flour 🌾
> 1/2 teaspoon salt
> 1 tablespoon sugar
> 1 tablespoon baking powder
> 1/3 cup butter, margarine or shortening, at room temperature
> 1 egg
> 3/4 cup milk

First: Preheat oven to 450°F.

Preparing the Fruit: Line a lightly greased, 8 x 8-inch baking dish with the sliced fruit. Cover with the sugar and dot with butter.

Making the Crust: Combine flour, salt, sugar and baking powder. With your fingertips rub in the butter until the mixture resembles bread crumbs.

Beat the egg, add the milk and mix quickly into the dry ingredients.

Turn the dough onto lightly floured surface and with floured hands, knead about 10 times until the dough holds together. It will be quite wet so keep well floured.

Pat your dough out to fit the baking pan. Place it over fruit and make slits as you would for pie crust.

Baking & Serving: Bake for 15 minutes at 450°F and then lower the temperature to 350°F and bake an additional 30 minutes.

Serve hot from the oven all by itself or dressed up with cream or ice cream.

SUPERFAST STRAWBERRY COBBLER
(OR APPLE, RASPBERRY, BLUEBERRY, PEACH...)

In our Pineapple Upside-Down Cake, the fruit was baked on the bottom but served on top. In this Superfast Cobbler variation, the topping starts out as a batter on the bottom but becomes a buttery crust on top. Serves 4 to 6.

Batter

> $1/2$ cup butter or margarine
> 1 cup King Arthur Unbleached All-Purpose Flour
> $1 1/2$ teaspoons baking powder
> $1/2$ teaspoon salt
> $1/4$ cup sugar
> $3/4$ cup milk

Fruit

> 2 cups fresh strawberries, washed, hulled and halved
> $1/3$ cup sugar
> $1/2$ cup water

Preheat your oven to 350°F.

Melt the butter in a shallow, $1 1/2$-quart baking dish. In a mixing bowl, combine the flour, baking powder, salt, sugar and milk. Pour evenly over the butter.

Combine the berries, sugar and water and spoon evenly over the batter, but don't stir. Bake for 40 to 45 minutes.

As we've mentioned, it's hard to know where one category should end and another begin. We have not included pies in this section, because pies and pastry go beyond fruit into other dimensions, and merit a chapter all their own. So to end this short section on fruit desserts, we have to say it's only a beginning.

• CAKE FILLINGS & FROSTINGS •

Before you add anything to your cake, think of its "body type" and "personality." Fillings and frostings can enhance, embellish or act as a counterpoint. Some cakes just ask for a sprinkle of confectioners' sugar, nuts, shredded coconut or some slices of fruit. Others want to be drenched with a creamy custard or a rich, soaking sauce. Ask your cake what it wants and listen carefully.

FILLINGS & CUSTARDS

VANILLA (OR BUTTERSCOTCH) FILLING

1/4 cup (1/2 stick) butter
2/3 cup sugar (or brown sugar, packed)
2 eggs
2 cups milk
1/3 cup King Arthur Unbleached All-Purpose Flour
1/4 teaspoon salt
1/2 teaspoon vanilla

For Butterscotch Filling, substitute brown sugar for the white.

In a saucepan over very low heat, or in a double boiler, mix the butter and sugar and cook for 3 minutes. Beat the eggs into 1 3/4 cups of milk and slowly add to the butter/sugar mixture, stirring all the time.

Blend the flour with 1/4 cup of milk, add to the hot mixture and cook until thick. Let cool, and add salt and vanilla. When cold, use as a filling for cake or in cream puffs.

LEMON FILLING

1 cup sugar
2 1/2 tablespoons King Arthur Unbleached All-Purpose Flour
rind of 2 lemons, grated
1/4 cup lemon juice
1 teaspoon butter
1 egg, slightly beaten

Beat the sugar, flour, lemon rind and juice together. Melt the butter and add the lemon mixture, stirring constantly until it just reaches a boil. Remove from the heat and stir in the egg. Cool and spread between layers of cake.

LEMON CURD

This richer version of the preceding filling is enough for a 9-inch pie as well.

1/2 cup butter
1/2 cup lemon juice
2 teaspoons grated lemon rind
1 1/2 cups sugar
4 whole eggs
2 egg yolks

Melt the butter in the top of a saucepan or double boiler. Add the juice, rind and sugar. Stir until the sugar is dissolved. Beat the eggs and egg yolks together until thick and blend into the butter/sugar mixture. Cook, stirring constantly, until quite thick. Cool and refrigerate.

RAISIN FILLING

1 1/2 cups sugar
1/3 cup water
1/8 teaspoon cream of tartar
2 egg whites
1 teaspoon vanilla
1/8 teaspoon salt
1 cup raisins

"Spinning a thread" is a confectioners' term that means a sugar syrup has reached a temperature where it will form, or "spin," a coarse thread that stays intact for 2 or 3 inches after it's dropped from a spoon. The temperature of the syrup is about 230°F. This is just below the "soft ball" stage which starts at 234°F.

Boil sugar, water and cream of tartar until it "spins a thread." Beat the egg whites until they are stiff. Pour the sugar/water syrup slowly over the egg whites, stirring the mixture until it is cool enough to hold its shape (the cream of tartar at work on the egg whites, see page 267). Blend in the vanilla, salt and raisins.

SOUR CREAM FILLING

2 tablespoons King Arthur Unbleached All-Purpose Flour
1/4 cup sugar
2 eggs
1 1/2 tablespoons butter
1/2 cup sour cream
1/3 cup nuts, chopped

Mix together the flour and sugar. Add the eggs and beat well. Add the butter and cream and cook over low heat until thickened. Cool, add the nuts, and spread on the bottom layer of a two-layer cake.

STRAWBERRY GRAND MARNIER FILLING

1 quart strawberries
1/2 cup sugar
3 tablespoons cornstarch
1/4 cup orange juice
1/8 teaspoon orange peel
2 tablespoons Grand Marnier

Wash and hull the strawberries and slice into a medium saucepan, saving a few berries for garnish. Combine the sugar, cornstarch and orange peel and add, with the orange juice, to the strawberries. Bring the mixture to a gentle boil over medium heat. Stir constantly, mashing the berries with a fork or the back of a mixing spoon. Cook until the mixture thickens and clears. Remove from the heat and let cool slightly. Add the Grand Marnier and mix thoroughly. Cool to room temperature before using.

STIRRED CUSTARDS

Custard, like cake, can be made either fat or thin. Below are recipes for both.

SLIM & SUAVE CUSTARD

This recipe resembles a thick white sauce and will make about 3 cups.

3 large eggs (or 2 whole eggs and 2 yolks)
1/4 cup sugar
a pinch of salt
2 cups milk
1 teaspoon vanilla, almond or lemon extract, or other flavoring
1 tablespoon sherry or rum (optional, but good with Trifle)

Beat the eggs (and yolks), sugar and salt together. In a double boiler, or very carefully in a saucepan, barely heat the milk. Pour a little into the egg mixture, blend it together and pour this back into the saucepan. Cook slowly, stirring with a wire whisk without letting it come to a boil or it will curdle. When it begins to thicken, remove the pan from heat and stir occasionally to cool it and prevent it from developing a skin. When it's almost cool, add your choice of flavoring. (If it should curdle, you can whirl it in a blender and fool just about everyone.)

THICK & RICH CUSTARD

This richer version has the consistency of thick whipped cream and will make about 4 cups.

2 whole eggs and 4 egg yolks (or 1 egg and 6 egg yolks, or 8 egg yolks)
¼ to ½ cup sugar (start with the lesser amount and add to taste)
a pinch of salt
1 cup milk
1 cup cream
1 teaspoon vanilla, almond or lemon extract, or other flavoring
1 teaspoon sherry or rum (again, optional)
1 cup cream, whipped

Beat the eggs, yolks, sugar and salt together. In a double boiler, or very carefully in a saucepan, barely heat the milk. Pour a little into the egg mixture, blend it together and pour this back into the saucepan. Cook slowly, stirring with a wire whisk without letting it come to a boil or it will curdle. When it begins to thicken, remove the pan from heat and stir occasionally to cool it and prevent it from developing a skin. When it's almost cool, add your choice of flavoring. (If it should curdle, the blender can come to your rescue.) When it's completely cool, fold in the whipped cream.

FLAVOR VARIATIONS

Mix and match these flavors as you are inspired or think up your own.

Chocolate Custard: Melt ½ square of bitter chocolate in the double boiler. Mix it into the egg mixture before you combine it with the milk. If you are making the Thick & Rich Custard, add 2 tablespoons of cocoa to the cream after it is whipped.

Coffee Custard: Use ½ cup strong coffee in place of an equal amount of milk. If you are making the Thick & Rich Custard, flavor the whipped cream with a tablespoon or so of coffee liqueur.

Mocha Custard: Do both of the above (!).

Maple Custard: Use half the sugar, and substitute an equal amount of maple syrup.

Lemon or Orange Custard: Add 1 to 2 teaspoons grated rind of lemon or orange (and leave out the vanilla if you wish).

Rum Custard: Substitute 2 or 3 tablespoons of dark rum for an equal amount of milk. (Try using rum in the Chocolate variation above.)

FROSTINGS & SAUCES

Frostings can match and intensify the flavor of a cake or act as a foil or counterpoint. Any of these sauces, with the exception of Hard Sauce, can be drizzled over a cake in place of a frosting (or over the ice cream that goes with the cake). Hard sauce is traditionally eaten with plum pudding but is also good with any bread pudding or "fruit something" that is served hot.

BUTTER CREAM FROSTING

4 tablespoons ($^1\!/_2$ stick) butter
2 cups confectioners' sugar, scooped
a pinch of salt
$^1\!/_4$ cup cream
1 teaspoon vanilla

Melt the butter in a saucepan or double boiler. Add the sugar, salt and cream, bring just to a boil and remove from the heat. Add the vanilla and beat until cool and of spreading consistency. This makes enough for one 8- or 9-inch double-layer cake.

CREAMY VARIATIONS

Try these and then experiment on your own.

Chocolate Butter Cream Frosting: Use 1 square of chocolate and melt it with the butter. Proceed as above.

Mocha Butter Cream Frosting: Use 1 square of chocolate and melt it with the butter. Replace the cream with $^1\!/_4$ cup of strong coffee.

Orange Butter Cream Frosting: Omit the vanilla, use orange juice instead of the cream and add 1 teaspoon of grated orange rind.

CREAM CHEESE FROSTING

$^1\!/_4$ to $^1\!/_2$ cup ($^1\!/_2$ to 1 stick) butter, at room temperature
8 ounces cream cheese, softened
1 teaspoon vanilla
$3^1\!/_2$ cups (1-pound box) confectioners' sugar
1 cup chopped nuts
$^1\!/_2$ cup minced candied ginger or 1 teaspoon ground ginger (optional)
milk, to make the frosting spreadable

Combine the butter, cream cheese and vanilla. Beat until light and fluffy. Add the sugar gradually, beating well. Stir in the nuts and/or ginger if desired. Add milk, a very little at a time, until the frosting is a spreadable consistency. This makes enough for a large 10 x14-inch cake.

CHOCOLATE CREAM CHEESE FROSTING

2 ounces (squares) unsweetened baking chocolate
1 (3-ounce) package cream cheese
3 tablespoons cream (or a bit more, for thinning)
2 cups confectioners' sugar, scooped
$1/4$ teaspoon salt

Melt the chocolate and set it aside. Beat the cheese and cream together. Add the sugar gradually and then the cooled chocolate and salt. Beat until smooth. Thin with more cream, if necessary. (Enough for an 8- or 9-inch double-layer cake.)

CREAMY CHOCOLATE FROSTING

3 cups confectioners' sugar
$1/3$ cup butter, softened
$1/4$ teaspoon salt
1 egg
1 teaspoon vanilla
3 squares unsweetened chocolate, melted
2 to 3 tablespoons milk

Beat together confectioners' sugar, butter and salt. Add egg, vanilla and melted chocolate and blend well. Add only enough milk to make it spreadable.

FUDGE FROSTING

1 cup sugar
1 tablespoon King Arthur Unbleached All-Purpose Flour
a pinch of salt (or less)
2 ounces (squares) unsweetened baking chocolate
$1/3$ cup milk
2 tablespoons butter
$1/2$ teaspoon vanilla

Combine the first five ingredients in a saucepan. Heat this until it reaches the boiling point, stirring to help melt and blend the chocolate.

Simmer the mixture until a few drops of it form a "soft ball" when dropped in cold water. Add the butter and cool. When the mixture has reached room temperature, add the vanilla and beat until it's stiff enough to spread. If it becomes too thick, add a bit of cream until it has reached a spreadable consistency.

RED VELVET CAKE FROSTING

Developed and named for the Red Velvet Cake (page 301), this vanilla frosting is also great on chocolate cakes.

1 1/2 cups milk
1/4 cup King Arthur Unbleached All-Purpose Flour
1 1/2 cups (3 sticks) butter (it must be of good quality with most of the
         whey washed out or the frosting may separate)
1 1/2 cups granulated sugar
1 1/2 teaspoons vanilla

Cook the milk and flour together until thick, stirring constantly. Cool to room temperature. Cream the butter with the sugar and add the vanilla. Add this to the cooled milk mixture and beat until light and fluffy.

SOUR CREAM FUDGE FROSTING

1 cup granulated sugar
1 cup brown sugar
1 cup sour cream
2 ounces (squares) unsweetened baking chocolate
1/8 teaspoon cream of tartar
1/4 teaspoon salt

Combine all the ingredients in a saucepan. Cook, stirring constantly, until the mixture reaches a boil. Turn the heat down and simmer until a few drops of it form a "soft ball" when dropped in cold water. Remove from the heat and cool without stirring. When cool, add the salt and beat until creamy and spreadable.

MAPLE FROSTING

1/2 cup (1 stick) butter
3/4 cup dark maple syrup
1 teaspoon vanilla
3 1/2 cups (1-pound box) confectioners' sugar

Soften butter and stir in maple syrup and vanilla. Add sugar until spreadable.

WHIPPED CREAM FROSTING

1 tablespoon butter, melted
1 cup brown sugar
1 cup heavy cream, whipped
1 teaspoon vanilla
a pinch of salt

Combine the melted butter with the sugar and add it to the whipped cream. Add the vanilla and salt and beat until well blended.

CHOCOLATE WHIPPED CREAM FROSTING

1 cup heavy cream
1/2 cup confectioners' sugar
1 teaspoon vanilla
3 tablespoons cocoa powder

Whip the cream until thick. Beat in the sugar, vanilla and cocoa.

ORNAMENTAL ICING

You can use vegetable coloring and flavor extracts to customize this basic Ornamental Icing any way you wish.

Without investing in a lot of cake decorating gear, you can be pretty artistic with this icing. Cut off the corner of a small plastic bag, or roll a piece of sturdy, plain paper into a cone and squeeze the icing through in whatever design or shape suits the occasion. Adjust the size and shape of the "nozzle" with your scissors.

2 egg whites
1/4 teaspoon salt
3 cups confectioners' sugar
1/4 teaspoon cream of tartar or 2 teaspoons lemon juice

Beat the egg whites with the salt and 1/2 cup of confectioners' sugar for about 10 minutes. Gradually add another 2 cups of sugar and continue beating. Add the cream of tartar or lemon juice and only enough additional sugar for the mixture to hold its shape.

Cream of tartar is used both here and in our angel food cakes to "stabilize" the egg white after it's beaten. The acid of the cream of tartar or lemon juice coagulates the protein in the egg white. This sets it in its airy state, which keeps the frosting light and fluffy. (See page 267.)

Butterscotch Sauce

8 tablespoons (1 stick) butter
1 cup brown sugar, packed
$\frac{1}{2}$ cup heavy cream or evaporated milk
$\frac{1}{4}$ teaspoon salt

Cook the ingredients together in a double boiler or small saucepan over low heat until smooth and well blended.

Maple Syrup Sauce

8 tablespoons (1 stick) butter
1 cup maple syrup
$\frac{1}{2}$ cup heavy cream or evaporated milk
$\frac{1}{4}$ teaspoon salt

Cook the ingredients together in a double boiler or small saucepan over low heat until smooth and well blended.

Dark Semi-Sweet Chocolate Sauce

2 ounces (squares) unsweetened baking chocolate
2 tablespoons butter
$\frac{1}{2}$ cup hot water
$\frac{2}{3}$ cup brown sugar, packed
$\frac{1}{4}$ teaspoon salt
1 teaspoon vanilla (and/or 2 tablespoons brandy or rum)

Melt the chocolate and butter together in a double boiler or (carefully) in a small saucepan. Mix in the hot water stirring until it's well blended. Blend in the brown sugar and salt. Cook for 3 or 4 minutes. (If you want the kind of sauce that hardens on ice cream, let it continue to cook for a further 8 to 10 minutes but keep an eye on it and give it an occasional stir.) Remove from the heat and blend in the vanilla.

Lemon or Orange Sauce

¹/₂ cup sugar
1 tablespoon cornstarch
1 cup boiling water (or orange juice)
1 tablespoon grated lemon peel (or orange peel)
2 tablespoons lemon juice (omit if you are making orange sauce)
a pinch of salt
2 tablespoons (¹/₄ stick) butter

Mix the sugar and cornstarch together in a small saucepan. Slowly drizzle in the hot water or orange juice. Put the pan over a low heat stirring until the mixture is smooth and thickened. Add the grated peel, lemon juice if that's your sauce, salt, and swirl in the butter.

Rum Sauce

1 cup sugar, white or brown
1 cup water
2 tablespoons butter
¹/₄ to ¹/₂ cup dark rum (depending on how strong a flavor you want)

Simmer the sugar and water together for 8 to 10 minutes. Remove from the heat. Blend in the butter and the rum.

Hard Sauce

Although this is called a sauce, it is hard when served.

8 tablespoons (1 stick) butter, softened
¹/₂ cup packed brown sugar or 1¹/₂ cups confectioners' sugar
1 teaspoon vanilla
2 or 3 tablespoons brandy or rum (or to taste)

With an electric mixer, beat the butter and sugar together until it is light and fluffy. Beat in the vanilla and brandy or rum. To adjust the consistency, add either sugar or liquid. Cover and chill.

COOKIES & BARS VI

COOKIES & BARS
CRACKERS & FLATBREADS

• *The most successful cookies are made from the highest quality ingredients, from grade A butter to the freshest of eggs, to your good King Arthur Flour. To make sure you're using your flour to the best advantage, measure it so you have 4-ounce cups. Refer to the directions on page 597 or on the top of a King Arthur Unbleached All-Purpose Flour bag.*

• *Remember to try substituting King Arthur Stone Ground Whole Wheat Flour for King Arthur Unbleached All-Purpose Flour in your cookies and brownies and especially in crackers.*

• *When you bake, it's optimum to have your ingredients at room temperature before you begin, but because cookie making is apt to be a spontaneous sort of creativity, don't let a less-than-ideal temperature stop you!*

• *Cookies made with Unbleached Flour tend to spread more than with other flours because this gluten is naturally tender and relaxed. Most professional bakers prefer this characteristic. Cookies with a high sugar-to-fat ratio also tend to spread more. In both situations, you can create a higher, "thicker" cookie by reducing the amount of sugar in the recipe and by using vegetable shortening rather than butter.*

• *Remove cookies and crackers from the baking sheets as soon as you can do it without mutilating them! To make them crisp, cool them on a wire rack, if you have one.*

• *If you are short on time, you can spread your cookie dough in a brownie pan and bake it as you would bars. Cut into squares and serve. This gives you the flavor of your favorite cookie with a different texture and time investment.*

• *Cookies and crackers don't like hot weather and they especially don't like humidity. Store them in the freezer during this kind of weather if you aren't planning to eat them soon after baking. After they're thoroughly cooled, seal them in a plastic bag before freezing.*

• *Cookies and crackers can both be made in bulk and frozen to be popped out when company pops in. Crackers can be quickly crisped, if need be, by heating them on a cookie sheet in a preheated, slow (275°F to 300°F) oven for a few minutes.*

COOKIES & BARS
CRACKERS & FLATBREADS
VI

• A COOKIE PRIMER •

Our good friend Stan Bornstein told us that his son thinks that cookies are one of the four basic food groups. While this may be a bit of misinformation, Daniel has certainly made it clear how important cookies are in his life. If you look at America's love affair with cookies, his view on the subject is very much in the mainstream. Cookies are certainly in a category all by themselves.

Although cookies are now big business in this country, it's interesting to note that they are advertised to be "as close to homemade as homemade itself." This seems to be an admission that homemade cookies can't be outdone, which, we would have to agree, is true. When you make cookies at home, you can not only make them much less expensively, but you know what all your ingredients are and, most important, you can pack lots of extra nutrition in them that you'll never find in the commercial varieties.

The American name "cookie" probably comes from the Dutch word "koeckje." Many of our original colonists, having been driven out of England for religious reasons, took refuge in Holland before coming to America, which exposed them to Dutch ways and words. The Dutch themselves came as well, peppering New York State all the way south to Virginia with their wonderful Dutch names. Whether through the Dutch-influenced English, or through the Dutch themselves, the "koeckje" seed found fertile ground in America. As our country grew and developed its many-faceted personality, so has the cookie.

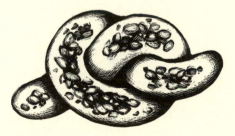

We begin with a basic, all-purpose sugar cookie, one created for us back in the 1930's by Gretchen McMullen, our first spokeswoman. Sugar cookies are, simply, unadorned, plain cookies. We have made a few minor changes in her recipe so it can be used for both the Basic Drop Cookie and, by adding another cup of flour, the Basic Refrigerator Cookie. Once you've mastered these you can go on and substitute ingredients, or embellish the dough with "optional extras," to create cookies that are truly your own.

BASIC DROP COOKIES

Drop cookies (the kind you can mix up, drop from a spoon onto a cookie sheet and bake right away) are an instant gratification kind of cookie, the kind kids are most likely to make themselves when the spirit moves them. These require the least fussing and can be dropped in traditional small blobs or in giant ones to make those huge creations that are the current rage.

As we mentioned in the introduction, the difference between a drop cookie and a refrigerator cookie recipe is in the amount of flour in the dough. This drop cookie version will make three dozen 3½- to 4-inch large cookies or five dozen 2½- to 3-inch smaller cookies.

    1 cup (2 sticks) butter
    ³/₄ cup white sugar
    ³/₄ cup brown sugar, packed
    1 teaspoon vanilla
    2 eggs
    2 cups King Arthur Unbleached All-Purpose Flour
    1 cup King Arthur Stone Ground Whole Wheat Flour
    1 teaspoon salt
    1 teaspoon baking powder
    ¹/₂ teaspoon baking soda
    ¹/₄ cup milk

First: Preheat your oven to 375°F.

Mixing the Dough: Cream the butter and sugar together until light. Add the vanilla and eggs and beat until the mixture becomes fluffy.

When you cream butter for cookies (or cakes, for that matter), it may seem at the beginning as if you're just mashing it flat. But if you persevere, you'll notice that it begins to get fluffy. What you're really doing is beating air into it. As you add the sugar, the mixture will become even fluffier, evidence of more air. And when the eggs are finally beaten in, the fluffiness created by those air bubbles is at its peak. That's why this part of baking is so important. The more air bubbles you can beat in at this stage of baking, the more air bubbles there are to expand in the heat of the oven. Baking powder or soda can do part of the work of leavening, but the air bubbles you can get into a dough manually make the difference between a good and superlative final product.

Thoroughly combine the flours, salt, baking powder and baking soda. Add about 1 cup of this mixture to the butter mixture. Blend in the milk and then the remaining dry ingredients.

Baking: Drop the dough from a teaspoon or tablespoon (depending on whether you want small or large cookies) onto a lightly greased cookie sheet and bake from 10 minutes (small cookies) to 14 minutes (large cookies) or until the edges are beginning to brown.

Storing: In cool, dry weather, cookies will keep for several days (if they aren't eaten) in a cookie jar or crock. Hot and humid weather will make any cookies wilt so if you're not going to eat them immediately, put them in an airtight plastic bag after they've cooled. You can even pop them in the freezer since they freeze beautifully. To thaw frozen cookies, remove them from their wrapping so moisture won't condense on them as they come back to room temperature.

Basic Refrigerator Cookies

To make refrigerator cookies, you make the same dough but add more flour to make it fairly stiff. Then you chill it for 2 or 3 hours (or even overnight) just as you do a good pie dough. Chilling cookie dough "ripens" or "matures" it, which means that it changes its nature to make cookies that can be baked thin and crisp rather than thick and chewy. You can roll out this dough like pie dough and cut it into fanciful shapes with cookie cutters or a knife. Or you can roll the dough into "logs" to chill (like the ones in the grocery store) and then slice off and bake a batch at a time. Cookie dough will keep several days in the refrigerator or it can be put in the freezer to wait for an appropriate "occasion."

Refrigerator cookies are best baked small. This recipe will make 8 dozen 1½-inch cookies and 6 dozen 2½-inch cookies. To make 3 or 4 dozen, cut the recipe in half.

1 cup (2 sticks) butter
¾ cup white sugar
¾ cup brown sugar, packed
1 teaspoon vanilla
2 eggs
3 cups King Arthur Unbleached All-Purpose Flour
1 cup King Arthur Stone Ground Whole Wheat Flour
1 teaspoon salt
1 teaspoon baking powder
½ teaspoon baking soda
¼ cup milk

Mixing the Dough: Cream the butter and sugar together until light. Add the vanilla and eggs and beat until the mixture becomes fluffy.

Thoroughly combine the flours, salt, baking powder and baking soda. Add about 1 cup to the butter mixture. Blend in the milk and then the remaining dry ingredients. Chill according to the directions for each shaping technique below.

Shaping the Dough: After the dough has chilled but before you start shaping it, preheat your oven to 400°F.

• **Rolling Pin Cookies:** Chill the dough for 2 or 3 hours until it is firm but still malleable. Dust your rolling surface lightly with flour and, with a flour-dusted rolling pin, roll the cookie dough out like pie dough until it's about $1/8$ inch thick. Slide a spatula or bowl scraper under the dough from time to time to keep it from sticking to the table. (Some people use the "wide" setting on their pasta machine to roll out the dough.) Cut out shapes with cookie cutters or a knife.

• **Sliced Cookies:** Roll the dough into a "log," $1 1/2$ to 2 inches in diameter, and then wrap and chill it. If it doesn't want to cooperate and roll easily into a log right after you've made the dough, chill it for an hour or so first. You can also chill it in a cleaned, lightly greased juice can.

Before chilling, try rolling the dough log in chopped nuts, seeds or shaved chocolate for more flavor and texture. Let the dough chill for several hours until it is quite hard. To bake, slice the log into $1/8$- to $1/4$-inch-thick rounds.

• **Hand-Rolled Cookies:** An easy way for children to handle this dough after it has been chilled is to roll nickel- or quarter-sized balls of dough between their hands. Then they can put them on a cookie sheet and press them flat with a fork or the bottom of a glass or cup. (This technique doesn't need to be confined to children!)

• **Pinwheel Cookies:** Make 2 half-batches of the basic recipe but blend $1/4$ cup of cocoa with the dry ingredients in one half-batch. Roll out each half into similar shaped rectangles somewhere between $1/8$ and $1/4$ inch in thickness. Place one on top of the other and roll up into a "log." Chill for 2 or 3 hours. To bake, cut the dough into $1/8$- to $1/4$-inch slices.

Baking: Refrigerator cookies are generally thinner than drop cookies, which is part of the reason for their crisp texture. They are also baked at a hotter temperature for a shorter time.

Place your cookies on a lightly greased cookie sheet and bake for 6 to 8 minutes for very thin cookies and 10 to 12 minutes for thicker ones. They are done when the center is "delicately tinted" and the edges are crisp and brown. As soon as you can, remove them from the cookie sheet to a cooling rack. This ensures their crispness.

See the Basic Drop Cookie (page 328) for information about storing cookies.

SUBSTITUTIONS, ADDITIONS & FINISHING TOUCHES

When you substitute ingredients or embellish the dough with "optional extras," you can completely alter the personality and appearance of the finished cookies. We have already taken the liberty of using some whole wheat flour in our cookies as well as some brown sugar because we think a basic cookie is more interesting with those flavors.

Substitutions

Dry Ingredients

• For sugar cookies with a traditional sugar/butter flavor, or to emphasize another flavor, you can certainly use unbleached all-purpose flour in place of the whole wheat. (See information under sweeteners below.)

• To make Oatmeal Drop Cookies, reduce the amount of flour to 2 cups and add 2 cups of rolled oats (regular or quick).

• You can decrease the amount of salt as much as your taste or nutritional needs merit. It is there merely to intensify flavor.

Sweeteners

• Although we like the flavor of brown sugar, for a traditional sugar cookie you can use white sugar entirely. If you do, eliminate the baking soda and substitute 1 teaspoon of baking powder so you have a total of 2 teaspoons. (You can read more about the "whys and when-tos" of baking powder and baking soda in the Quick Bread Primer, page 54.)

• We have used a relatively "small" amount of sugar in our cookie dough. These cookies are sweet but not so sweet that the flavor of the other ingredients is masked. The more sugar a cookie contains, the more it will spread. You can accentuate or minimize this phenomenon by increasing or decreasing the amount of sugar the recipe calls for. Start with $\frac{1}{4}$ cup in either direction and adjust from there.

• You can also use a "wet" sweetener such as honey, maple syrup or molasses. If you do, eliminate the milk and bake at 350°F. Because these sweeteners are slightly acidic like brown sugar, use $\frac{1}{2}$ teaspoon baking soda and 1 teaspoon baking powder.

Fats

All fats have about the same number of calories per equivalent amount, but some have nutritional advantages and others have flavor/texture advantages. (For more information about fats, see the Appendix.)

• Gretchen's recipe called for lard which was much more commonly used in the first half of this century. In spite of its bad name, lard contains less than half the cholesterol of butter, almost half the saturated fat (the bad kind) and more than twice as much unsaturated fat (the good kind). Lard and butter contain about the same number of calories per tablespoon (about 115) but butter has unbeatable flavor and the added bonus of vitamin A.

• Cookies made completely with butter have the best flavor but tend to be hard because butter contains some milk solids in addition to the fat.

• In cookies where the flavor of butter might be overwhelmed by other ingredients, you can substitute margarine or a solid vegetable shortening. Gary Brooks (one of our Board of Directors, and Sands, Taylor & Wood Co.'s valued counsel) and his designer/dancer wife, Barbara Duncan, spend one evening a week baking for the rest of the week. After innumerable experiments with cookies, they've found that a combination of $\frac{1}{2}$ cup of butter (or margarine) and $\frac{1}{2}$ cup of vegetable shortening makes cookies that have great flavor because of the butter, and are light and crisp because of the shortening. The nutritional advantage of using all vegetable fats is that they are less saturated and contain no cholesterol. (To measure vegetable shortening, see page 278.)

• Although there are many recipes for baked goods where you can substitute vegetable oils for solid shortening, the cookie department is one place where you shouldn't. The new butter/vegetable oil combinations are an acceptable substitute although they're best used in drop cookies rather than the refrigerator variety. Vegetable oils have their own merits as they are not hydrogenated. But don't use them alone. Because they don't or can't contain any air, they'll make a dense, oily cookie if you use them without an equal amount of a solid shortening.

Liquids

• The small amount of milk in this recipe is a magic ingredient. It creates cookies that are light and crisp. For denser, chewier cookies, you can leave it out.

• Eggs are considered to be a liquid although their protein creates structure as well. To include eggs but exclude cholesterol, you can substitute 3 egg whites for 2 whole eggs in most cookie recipes. But since most recipes that include 2 eggs make between 3 and 5 dozen cookies (depending on how large they are), the egg issue may not be terribly important. If you ate 2 small cookies, you would be eating one-fifteenth of an egg yolk, which is where the cholesterol is. This probably isn't much cause for concern.

• Vanilla extract is traditionally used to flavor sugar cookies. You can use whatever you like: almond, lemon, peppermint, rum, etc.

Additions

• Adding a second extract gives you the basic flavor of vanilla with highlights of whatever else you use.

• Two or three teaspoons of grated lemon or orange peel add great flavor, especially in refrigerator cookies where the flavor has a chance to permeate the dough before it bakes.

• Add 1 to 3 teaspoons of ground spices or herbs, or even a tablespoon of whole dried herbs or seeds such as caraway, dill, poppy or sesame, etc.

• To make chocolate cookies, add $1/2$ to $3/4$ cup cocoa to the dry ingredients. (For a triple treat, add $3/4$ cup of cocoa, $1 1/2$ cups chocolate chips and $1 1/2$ cups chopped pecan, or peanuts.) For a little more texture, try this combination with oats (page 330).

• Pack in lots of extra flavor, texture and nutrition by adding some "optional extras" to the Basic Drop Cookie dough. A cup or two of one (or more) of the following will completely change the basic cookie: raisins; currants; chopped apricots; dates; chopped almonds, pecans, walnuts or hulled sunflower seeds; chocolate, butterscotch or peanut butter chips; chopped candy bar, etc. If you want a nutrition vacation, just add some chocolate chips all by themselves.

For the Basic Refrigerator Cookie dough, keep the size of any of these "optional extras" fairly small. Since they are rolled out fairly thin, a raisin or chocolate chip might hinder the rolling process. It's better to decorate their tops.

• If you are making rolled cookies, you can coat the outside of the log roll with finely chopped nuts or shaved chocolate. When you slice and bake them, the "optional extras" will decorate the outside edge of the finished cookies.

Finishing Touches

• Sprinkle sugar or place a nut on the cookie just before baking.

• Spread an icing on top after the cookies have cooled. (See page 317, Frostings & Sauces.)

• Before baking your cookies, try "painting" them with the Cookie Paint found on page 562.

• After your cookies are cool, gently shake them in a small bag of confectioners' sugar.

• COOKIES FOR ANY OCCASION •

Cookies come in all sizes, shapes, textures and flavors, which is what makes experimenting with them such an adventure. Cookies can be candy-sweet or they can be packed with healthy nuts, fruits and grains.

There are also cookie doughs that, rather than going into the oven or the refrigerator, are dropped directly into hot fat which creates the crispest cookies of all. There is a cookie or bar for every phase of your personality. They can be simple and quick to make when you have the urge but not the time, and complicated and creative when you do have time. There are additional cookie recipes in the Whole Wheat chapter.

EVERYDAY COOKIES

DORIS SANDS' OATMEAL CRISPIES

Up until the early 1980's, the extended Sands family gathered together around the 4th of July with parents (and grandparents) Walter and Doris Sands at their home in Duxbury, Massachusetts. For several days, there were exploratory trips by foot onto the mudflats of Duxbury Bay when the tide was out and an equal number by Sailfish when the tide was in. There were games of kick-the-can and tennis, swims by moonlight and much sharing of the joys of being together. There was also much feasting. This recipe was one that Grandma Sands made in abundance when grandchildren were around. It's a perfect example of how our basic drop cookie recipe can be changed to create something unique and, in this case, to become one of the memories of Duxbury. This will make three dozen 3½- to 4-inch large cookies or five dozen 2½-inch small cookies.

½ cup (1 stick) butter
½ cup vegetable shortening
¾ cup white sugar
¾ cup brown sugar, packed
1 teaspoon vanilla
2 eggs
1 cup King Arthur Unbleached All-Purpose Flour
1 cup King Arthur Stone Ground Whole Wheat Flour
2 cups quick oatmeal
1 teaspoon salt
1 teaspoon baking powder
½ teaspoon baking soda
¼ cup milk
1 cup chopped walnuts

Preheat your oven to 375°F.

Cream the butter, shortening and sugars together until they are light and fluffy. Add the vanilla and eggs and beat until the mixture is light.

Thoroughly combine the flours, salt, baking powder and baking soda. Add about 1 cup to the butter mixture. Blend in the milk and then the remaining dry ingredients. Fold in the nuts.

Drop the dough from a teaspoon or tablespoon (depending on whether you want small or large cookies) onto a lightly greased cookie sheet and bake from 10 minutes (small cookies) to 14 minutes (large cookies), or until the edges and tops are beginning to brown.

GRANOLA CHIP COOKIES

This drop cookie recipe comes from the Sands' daughter, Ellen Smith, who makes them with her daughter, Hillary. These cookies can almost go in the "healthy food" department so are great for lunch boxes and snacks. This recipe makes between 2 and 3 dozen cookies, depending on size, and can easily be doubled.

1/3 cup butter
1/2 cup honey
1 egg
1 teaspoon vanilla
1 1/4 cups King Arthur Stone Ground Whole Wheat Flour
1/2 teaspoon baking powder
3/4 teaspoon salt
1 teaspoon cinnamon
1 cup chocolate chips
1 cup granola

Preheat your oven to 350°F.

Cream the butter and honey. Add the egg and vanilla. Combine the flour, baking powder, salt and cinnamon and gradually blend them into the butter mixture. Stir in the chocolate chips and granola last.

Drop from a teaspoon (or tablespoon) onto lightly greased cookie sheets and bake for 10 to 14 minutes.

RECIPROCAL COOKIES

These cookies can be made separately or in tandem. They're mirror images of each other, each great on its own, but fun to serve at the same time. Both recipes make between 2 and 3 dozen cookies.

PEANUT BUTTER CHOCOLATE CHIP COOKIES

This recipe is from The Wellesley Cookie Exchange Cookbook, *edited by Susan Peery. Susan, King Arthur Flour's friend and collaborator, mentor of many a Great New England Cook at* Yankee Magazine, *mother of Molly and Spencer, is an eminently qualified peanut butter cookie expert.*

1/2 cup (1 stick) butter
1/2 cup chunky peanut butter
1/2 cup sugar
1/2 cup brown sugar, firmly packed
1 egg
1 1/4 cups King Arthur Unbleached All-Purpose Flour
1/2 teaspoon baking powder
1/2 teaspoon baking soda
1/4 teaspoon salt
1 cup chocolate chips (optional, but part of our two-recipe plan)
granulated sugar to sprinkle on top (optional)

Preheat your oven to 375°F.

Cream the butter, peanut butter and sugars until light. Add the egg and mix until fluffy.

Blend the flour, baking powder, soda and salt together well. Add these dry ingredients to the butter mixture. Add the chocolate chips, if you choose, and mix well. Cover and chill for an hour to make the dough easier to handle.

You have a couple of options for shaping these cookies:

• For the "reciprocal cookies," drop by teaspoonfuls onto a greased cookie sheet. (Don't press these with a fork.)

• For traditional peanut butter cookies, roll the dough into 1-inch balls between the palms of your hands and place 2 inches apart on a lightly greased cookie sheet. Use a fork to flatten with a crisscross pattern. Sprinkle with a bit of granulated sugar if you are so inclined.

Bake either shape for 10 to 12 minutes.

CHOCOLATE PEANUT BUTTER CHIP COOKIES

    $\frac{1}{2}$ cup (1 stick) butter
    $\frac{1}{2}$ cup sugar
    $\frac{1}{2}$ cup brown sugar
    1 egg
    2 squares (2 ounces) unsweetened baking chocolate, melted
    1 teaspoon vanilla
    1$\frac{1}{4}$ cups King Arthur Unbleached All-Purpose Flour
    $\frac{1}{2}$ teaspoon baking soda
    $\frac{1}{4}$ teaspoon salt
    1 cup peanut butter chips (optional, but part of the two-recipe plan)

Preheat your oven to 375°F.

Cream the butter and sugars until light. Beat in the egg, melted chocolate and vanilla. Mix the flour, baking soda and salt together and add to the butter mixture. Blend in the peanut butter chips if you decide to use them. Cover the dough and chill for an hour.

Drop by teaspoonfuls on a lightly greased cookie sheet and bake for 10 to 12 minutes.

ALMOND CRISPS

In its original form this recipe stood out from the midden of King Arthur possibilities on the strength of its tantalizing ingredients. It was finally reworked into this delicious, crisp cookie, redolent with almond and a hint of lemon. These are best made in dry weather. This recipe makes between 3 and 4 dozen cookies.

    unbeaten egg white from 5 large eggs (about $\frac{3}{4}$ cup)
    1$\frac{1}{2}$ cups sugar
    $\frac{1}{4}$ teaspoon salt
    1 cup (2 sticks) butter, melted and cooled
    1$\frac{1}{2}$ cups King Arthur Unbleached All-Purpose Flour
    $\frac{3}{4}$ cup finely ground or chopped blanched almonds (a blender does
         this nicely)
    1 tablespoon lemon juice
    1 teaspoon freshly grated lemon peel (optional)

To get a maximum amount of juice out of a lemon, first run it under hot water. Then roll it around on your counter with your hand putting on a fair amount of pressure. This helps to release all those tiny cells of juice inside. If you're going to grate it for peel, do that before you warm and soften it.

Preheat your oven to 350°F.

Beat the egg whites with the sugar and salt for 2 or 3 minutes until the sugar is dissolved and the egg whites are thick and white. Blend in the melted butter and then gently fold in the flour, almonds, lemon juice and peel.

Using two teaspoons, drop blobs of dough, well apart, onto a lightly greased non-stick cookie sheet. Bake them for 10 to 12 minutes.

With a spatula, lift them off the cookie sheet to a cooling rack soon after they come out of the oven. They are somewhat reluctant to part company with the sheet once they have thoroughly cooled.

GUMDROP COOKIES

This recipe came out of the original King Arthur Flour Cookbook, Easy Home Baking, *which appeared almost 50 years ago. In the original recipe the gumdrops were mixed into the cookie dough. While experimenting, we found that a few gumdrop slices (easily cut with clean, sharp scissors), placed on top of the cookie before it goes into the oven, look more festive. Jelly beans could be used just as effectively here. The original recipe included a mysterious cup of coconut in the ingredient list, but never mentioned it in the directions. You can include it, adding it in any way you wish, or leave it out altogether. This recipe makes 5 to 6 dozen cookies.*

    1 cup (2 sticks) butter
    1 cup white sugar
    1 cup brown sugar
    2 eggs
    $^1/_2$ teaspoon salt
    2 teaspoons vanilla
    2 cups oatmeal
    1 teaspoon baking soda
    1 teaspoon baking powder
    2 cups King Arthur Unbleached All-Purpose Flour
    1 cup gumdrops cut in slices (or less if you only decorate the tops)

Preheat your oven to 375°F.

Cream the butter and sugars together well. Add the eggs, salt and vanilla and mix well. Stir in the oatmeal. Mix the baking soda and baking powder into the flour. If you want to put some gumdrops and/or coconut into the cookies, add them to the flour and stir gradually into the batter.

Drop by spoonfuls onto a lightly greased cookie sheet and place gumdrop slices on top, either in a pattern or randomly. Bake for 8 to 10 minutes.

LACE COOKIES

These gossamer cookies have just enough flour in them to keep them from flowing off the cookie sheet. They spread enormously to become "cookies made of lace." Like snowflakes, they should be a winter phenomenon as they will become totally limp in any but the dryest of weather.

While we have tried to stay away from kitchen equipment that you wouldn't already have on hand, baking parchment is one thing that you might treat yourself to sometime. Whenever you run into a recipe that seems to have a desire to stay on a cookie sheet after it's been baked, a sheet of baking parchment can change its mind.

An added advantage is that you can pick up the parchment, with the cookies on it, and place it on a cooling rack right after it comes out of the oven. While the first batch bakes, drop cookie dough on a second piece and have it ready to go on the cookie pan as soon as the first batch is off. Each piece can be used several times. Parchment can be found at most kitchen supply stores.

Lace Cookies can be baked on a lightly greased, non-stick cookie sheet, but by using parchment, you may save some cookies and a certain amount of teeth-gnashing. This recipe makes between 3 and 5 dozen cookies depending on size.

3 tablespoons King Arthur Unbleached All-Purpose Flour
2¼ cups regular rolled oats
2¼ cups light brown sugar
1 teaspoon salt
1 cup (2 sticks) butter (not margarine)
1 egg
1 teaspoon vanilla

Preheat your oven to 375°F.

In a large mixing bowl, mix together the flour, oats, sugar and salt. In a small saucepan, warm the butter until it's just melted. Mix this into the dry ingredients. In a small bowl, beat the egg with the vanilla and blend it with the rest of the ingredients.

Drop this dough in small spoonfuls on a lightly greased, non-stick cookie sheet allowing plenty of room for them to spread. Bake for 5 to 7 minutes depending on how large your cookies are.

Let the cookies cool just enough on the cookie sheet so you can get a spatula under them without tearing them. If you wait any longer, your love affair with these Lace Cookies might go sour, as they will stick tenaciously. Cool them thoroughly on a wire rack.

VARIATIONS

• If you don't mind risking a few broken cookies, try rolling them loosely around the end of a wooden spoon into tubes after they're off the cookie sheet but before they have completely cooled and stiffened. They look quite elegant served this way.

• If you want to go one step further, melt a couple of squares of bittersweet chocolate in a small saucepan and dip the ends of the rolled cookies in it. Place them on a piece of waxed paper or aluminum foil while the chocolate hardens.

• For a heavenly variation in flavor, use ½ teaspoon each almond and vanilla extracts and add ½ cup sliced almonds to the dough.

• Substitute ½ cup of sesame or hulled sunflower seeds for an equal amount of oatmeal to vary the flavor and create different patterns of "lace."

CHINESE CHEWS

Liza Bernard, co-creator of this 200th Anniversary Cookbook, *inherited this recipe from her paternal grandmother, Madeline. The origin of and reason for their name is an enigma, but whatever the answer, these Chinese Chews are truly wonderful. They are also a truly all-weather cookie, crisp and chewy at the same time in dry weather and "chewy and chewy" in damp. Eggs aside, they are also fat free. This recipe makes about 2 dozen cookies.*

> ¾ cup King Arthur Unbleached All-Purpose Flour
> 1 teaspoon baking powder
> 1 cup sugar
> ¼ teaspoon salt
> 2 eggs
> 1 (8-ounce) package dates, chopped
> 1 cup walnuts, chopped

Preheat your oven to 325°F.

Combine the flour, baking powder, sugar and salt. Beat the eggs until light. Fold the wet ingredients into the dry. Gently blend in the dates and nuts.

Drop by the spoonful onto a greased, non-stick cookie sheet. Bake for 20 minutes and remove from the sheet to cool.

Even though the only liquid in this dough is beaten egg, it is moist and rich with the nuts and dates.

GRANDMA SWIFT'S
MOLASSES COOKIES

Here's a recipe for a traditional molasses cookie by way of Clint Swift and Bonnie Allard. Clint is one of Sands, Taylor & Wood Co.'s outside Directors, a former lawyer who now dispenses financial expertise. The recipe itself comes from his grandmother, Mrs. Archie Dean Swift, who had a very extensive collection which she carefully recorded in several books, a bit of culinary history caught in print. Although the recipe came from Clint's family, these cookies are now one of Bonnie's specialties.

Since this is a refrigerator cookie dough, it's best made the day before baking. It's a large recipe and will make between 6 and 8 dozen cookies.

    1 cup (2 sticks) butter
    1 teaspoon salt
    1 cup brown sugar
    1 1/2 cups molasses
    2 eggs
    1 cup water
    1 teaspoon ginger
    1 teaspoon cinnamon
    1 tablespoon baking soda
    5 cups King Arthur Unbleached All-Purpose Flour
    1 cup King Arthur Stone Ground Whole Wheat Flour
    1 tablespoon vegetable oil
    small bowl of granulated sugar

Put the butter, salt, sugar and molasses into a saucepan and bring to a boil. Remove the pan from the heat and let cool. Transfer the mixture into a large bowl.

Add and blend in the eggs and water. Blend in the spices and baking soda. Stir in the flour until all the ingredients are thoroughly blended. Cover and refrigerate overnight.

Preheat your oven to 375°F.

With a tablespoon, scoop out dough the size of a small egg and drop onto a lightly greased cookie sheet. Dip the bottom of a drinking glass into the vegetable oil, then in the bowl of granulated sugar and use it to flatten each cookie until it's about 1/4 inch thick.

Bake approximately 10 minutes. Cool on a wire rack. These will store for quite some time in an airtight container with sheets of waxed paper between layers to prevent them from sticking together.

GINGERSNAPS

Because this recipe and its variations contain a greater amount of sweetener and butter than the basic recipe, these cookies will spread more during baking, making thin, crunchy "snaps." This recipe will make between 10 and 12 dozen cookies, though you can easily cut it in half.

1 1/2 cups (3 sticks) butter
2 cups sugar
2 eggs
1/2 cup dark unsulphured molasses
4 cups King Arthur Unbleached All-Purpose Flour
1 teaspoon baking soda
2 teaspoons salt
4 to 6 teaspoons ginger (depending on how gingery you like gingersnaps)
1 teaspoon cinnamon

Preheat your oven to 350°F.

Put these ingredients together according to the basic recipe. (If you have time, let the dough chill for several hours or overnight in the refrigerator. The cookies will still be crisp and gingery without chilling.)

Roll nickel-sized pieces of dough into balls between the palms of your hands. Then roll them in granulated sugar and place them on a lightly greased cookie sheet (a non-stick coating helps with this recipe). In this case don't press them down with a glass. They spread very nicely by themselves.

Bake for 10 to 12 minutes.

ROSEMARY SNAPS

This rosemary variation is a serendipitous and delicious evolution of the Gingersnap, graciously shared with us by Happy Griffiths. For another version see page 513.

Substitute 4 to 6 teaspoons of rosemary, crushed or powdered, for the ginger and add 1 teaspoon ground ginger and 1/2 teaspoon ground cloves.

HONEY CURRY SNAPS

For the sweetening, use 1/2 cup honey and 1 1/4 cups sugar. Substitute 1 tablespoon of curry powder for the spices. For a more subtle curry flavor, use only 2 teaspoons. Because honey tends to scorch, bake this variation at 325°F for 12 to 14 minutes.

FESTIVAL COOKIES

These cookies are particularly appropriate for festivals or holidays.

SCOTTISH SHORTBREAD

Scottish shortbread was originally made from oatmeal and was served on the Winter Solstice, the shortest day of the year. The edges of the round "cake" were notched, symbolizing the sun which was being entreated to return. Nowadays in Scotland, short-bread is mostly made with wheat flour but the edges are still marked with those symbolic notches. It is served on Hogmanay (New Year's Eve) and New Year's morning to "first-footers," those revelers who have stayed up all night to see the New Year in and are the first to go from house to house, visiting and celebrating.

The amount of flour in a shortbread recipe can vary anywhere from 1½ to 3 cups. The Scots generally prefer their shortbread with the lesser amount of sugar and the greater amount of flour.

> 1 cup (2 sticks) butter at room temperature
> ½ to ¾ cup confectioners' sugar (depending on taste)
> ½ teaspoon salt, rounded
> 1½ to 3 cups King Arthur Unbleached All-Purpose Flour 🌾

Preheat your oven to 350°F

Cream the softened butter with the sugar. Add salt and flour, working these ingredients into a soft dough by hand (or with a food processor if you have one). Press the dough into a round 9- or 10-inch pie plate and score (or notch) the dough by cutting halfway through it to divide the shortbread into 6 or 8 pie-shaped pieces.

Bake until firm and barely golden. Depending on the amount of your ingredients, this can vary from ½ to 1 hour. After removing from the oven, dust with confectioners' sugar and cool before removing from the pan.

VARIATIONS

• To create a texture that is fine but not as "tight" as the previous version, substitute ⅓ cup rice flour for ⅓ cup King Arthur Unbleached All-Purpose Flour.

• The addition of 1 cup ground almonds or hazelnuts to the lesser amount of flour (1½ cups) makes a delicious flavor variation.

• A slightly heretical but flavorful addition to shortbread dough is 1 cup of tiny chocolate chips.

BETSY'S
SHORTBREAD BITES

These delicate cookies are tiny mouthfuls of melt-in-your-mouth shortbread. The recipe comes from Betsy Comstock Vontobel, a dear Canadian-American friend of the Sands'. It has traveled many a mile and has come to life in many a kitchen. This recipe will make about 4 dozen bites.

    2 cups King Arthur Unbleached All-Purpose Flour
    1 cup (2 sticks) butter
    1/4 cup sugar
    1/2 teaspoon salt
    2 teaspoons vanilla
    confectioners' sugar

Cream the flour, sugar, butter and salt with a pastry blender or two knives. Add the vanilla and mix with a fork. Cover this dough and let it chill until it is firm, 3 or 4 hours or overnight.

Preheat your oven to 350°F.

Roll small pieces of dough between the palms of your hands into little balls about 1/2 inch in diameter and place them on a greased cookie sheet. Bake for about 12 minutes or until golden.

Remove from the oven, cool thoroughly and shake them gently in a bag of confectioners' sugar. (If they're not totally cool, the sugar won't stick.)

ALMOND NUGGETS

This recipe comes from Liza Bernard's mother, Kathleen, and will make 3 to 4 dozen nuggets. Her recipe card is marked "A Christmas cookie must!!!"

    3/4 cup vegetable shortening
    1/2 cup (1 stick) butter (or, for richer cookies, use 1 1/4 cups butter and
        omit the vegetable shortening)
    1/2 cup confectioners' sugar
    1 teaspoon vanilla
    1 teaspoon almond extract
    1/2 cup finely chopped walnuts or almonds
    2 cups King Arthur Unbleached All-Purpose Flour
    1 teaspoon salt
    confectioners' sugar

Preheat oven to 325°F.

Cream the shortening, butter and sugar well. Blend in the vanilla and nuts. Combine the salt with the flour and add gradually to the butter mixture. Blend well.

Drop by the teaspoonful onto an ungreased cookie sheet. They are rich, so make them small.

Bake for 20 to 25 minutes.

When the cookies have cooled, roll them in confectioners' sugar.

PECAN CRESCENTS

This is another recipe from our original King Arthur Flour cookbook, Easy Home Baking. *It is similar to a shortbread but fragrant with the aroma and flavor of pecans. Like the Almond Nuggets, they are wonderful holiday cookies.*

This recipe will make about 4 dozen crescents.

> 1 cup (2 sticks) butter
> 1/4 cup confectioners' sugar
> 1 teaspoon vanilla
> 1/4 teaspoon salt
> 1 tablespoon water
> 2 cups King Arthur Unbleached All-Purpose Flour
> 2 cups pecans, ground
> more confectioners' sugar

Preheat your oven to 300°F.

Cream the butter until light. Beat in the sugar, vanilla, salt and water and beat until fluffy. Fold in the flour and ground nuts.

Cover and chill for at least an hour.

Form the dough into small rolls, about the size of a finger, and bend into crescents. Place on a lightly greased cookie sheet and bake for 50 minutes.

Shake them in a bag of confectioners' sugar when they are thoroughly cooled.

Mincemeat Cookies

These make wonderful holiday cookies. You can substitute whole cranberry sauce (not the jellied kind) to make Thanksgiving cookies or use an inspiration of your own for some other time of year. You can certainly use other fillings (strawberry jam is one suggestion); just make sure they aren't too runny. This will make about 3 dozen cookies.

1 recipe Basic Refrigerator Cookie dough (page 328)
1 recipe Mincemeat (page 414)

Make the dough as described in the Cookie Primer (page 328).

After the dough has chilled, preheat your oven to 350°F.

Roll the dough on a flour-dusted surface with a flour-dusted rolling pin until it's about ⅛ inch thick. Use a cookie cutter (or a scrubbed soup or other can with a hole punched in the opposite end to relieve pressure) and cut out twice as many circles as will easily fit on your cookie sheet.

Place small spoonfuls of mincemeat on half of the circles and cover with the rest of the circles. You can crimp the edges with a fork or just press the two halves together gently with your fingers. Make small slits in the dough on the top of the cookies as if they were the tops of tiny pie crusts.

Transfer them to a cookie sheet and bake for 12 to 15 minutes.

Lebkuchen
Honey Cakes

This German recipe comes from Berlin relatives (by marriage) of Anne Baird, Brinna's sister. It makes about 2 dozen and can be easily doubled.

1 egg
¾ cup brown sugar, packed firmly
½ cup honey
½ cup dark unsulphured molasses
3 cups King Arthur Unbleached All-Purpose Flour
1¼ teaspoon each cinnamon and nutmeg
½ teaspoon each ground cloves and allspice
½ teaspoon baking soda
½ cup chopped mixed candied fruits and peels
½ cup slivered almonds

In a mixing bowl, beat the egg until light. Add the sugar and beat until fluffy. Stir in the honey and molasses.

Blend the dry ingredients and stir in the fruit and nuts. Combine the wet with the dry ingredients, cover and chill several hours or overnight.

Preheat your oven to 350°F.

Roll out this fruit-and-nut-filled dough on a floured surface until it's ¼ inch thick. Cut the dough into rectangles about 1 x 1½ inches. Bake on a lightly greased cookie sheet for about 12 minutes. Cool slightly before you remove them from the pan.

Mary Baird's
Christmas Cookies

When Brinna Sands was young, her mother, Mary Baird, would start making these cookies several weeks before Christmas. For Brinna, they are full of memories, both warm and loving as well as furtive and guilty. After they were baked, they were stored in an enormous cannister to "mature" before they were served. A certain person found it impossible not to filch a few every day or so and then artfully rearrange the cookies on top to hide her tracks. Here they are lovingly remembered. This recipe makes 7 to 8 dozen cookies, some to keep and some for artful removal.

> 1 cup (2 sticks) butter
> 2 cups sugar
> 4 eggs
> 4 ounces bitter chocolate
> 4 cups King Arthur Unbleached All-Purpose Flour
> 1 teaspoon baking powder
> 1 teaspoon salt
> 3½ cups (1 pound) walnuts or pecans

Preheat your oven to 325°F.

Cream the butter and sugar together until light. Beat in the eggs. Melt the chocolate and let it cool slightly before adding it to the butter/sugar mixture.

In a separate bowl combine the flour, baking powder and salt. Add this flour mixture to the wet ingredients in three stages, mixing thoroughly after each.

Grind the nutmeats in a blender or food processor, or chop them very finely. Stir them into the dough.

Roll walnut-sized pieces into balls and place on a greased cookie sheet. Bake for about 13 minutes.

After they have cooled, store them somewhere (maybe not quite out of reach) to "mature."

THUMB PRINTS

These cookies are a bit like tiny fruit tarts. The directions we've given you below are fairly specific. Don't let them stop you from devising your own flavor combinations. After you've become acquainted with how these go together, have a Thumb Print party and provide your guests, both small and large, with a variety of things to roll cookie dough in and a variety of fillings. They are fun to make with children but elegant enough to serve for tea. This recipe will make between 5 and 6 dozen cookies.

1 cup (2 sticks) butter
½ cup sugar
½ cup brown sugar, firmly packed
2 eggs, separated
1 teaspoon vanilla
½ teaspoon salt
2½ to 3 cups King Arthur Unbleached All-Purpose Flour
½ cup finely chopped nuts
½ cup shredded coconut
raspberry preserves
pineapple preserves

In a large bowl, beat the butter and sugars until very light. Beat in the egg yolks and vanilla. Blend the salt into the lesser amount of flour and mix into the butter mixture. If the dough seems too sticky, add just enough flour to make it workable.

Cover and chill the dough for about an hour or more. While the dough chills, cover the egg whites and leave them out of the refrigerator to warm up to room temperature.

Preheat your oven to 325°F.

Beat the egg whites until they're foamy. Break off pieces of dough and roll them between your palms to form 1-inch balls. Dip the balls into the egg whites and roll them in chopped nuts or coconut.

Place about 2 inches apart on lightly greased cookie sheets. Make a thumb print in the center of each cookie (hence their name).

Bake for 8 to 10 minutes, remove from pan and allow to cool. Fill the indentation with jam or preserves, raspberry for the nut cookie and pineapple for the coconut.

Cookies rolled in ground almonds might be wonderful with Lemon Curd (page 314) or strawberry jam. Or, for a "healthy version," try rolling some in sesame seeds and filling them with rose hip jam.

FATTIGMANDS BAKKELSE
NORWEGIAN COOKIES

We promised a cookie that is deep-fat fried and here it is. This comes to us from Dolores Plyer, a dear friend of Norwegian extraction from Chicago. These festive cookies are really quite easy and a lot of fun to make. Since you need to chill this dough it's best to make it several hours ahead of time or the day before. This recipe will make about 9 dozen bakkelse.

3 eggs
1 cup sugar
1/4 cup cream
1/2 cup (1 stick) butter, melted
1 1/2 teaspoons vanilla
3 1/2 cups King Arthur Unbleached All-Purpose Flour
1/2 teaspoon salt
1 teaspoon baking powder
confectioners' sugar, for sprinkling

Beat the eggs until light and fluffy. Gradually add the sugar, beating constantly until the mixture is thick and light. Beat in the cream, butter and vanilla.

In a second bowl, thoroughly blend the flour, salt and baking powder. Blend the dry ingredients with the wet. Cover the dough and chill for several hours or overnight.

When you're ready to make your cookies, heat 3 or 4 inches of shortening or vegetable oil in a large saucepan on your stove until it's about 365°F. While the fat heats, flour your rolling surface and rolling pin well and roll the dough out until it's about 1/16 inch thick. The crispness of the cookie depends on the thinness of the dough. Dust lightly with flour wherever the dough seems to stick.

Cut the dough into elongated diamond shapes, about 1 1/2 inches on a side. A spatula or King Arthur bowl scraper will do a nice job here. Just press it straight down through the dough to cut it. Then use a sharp paring knife to cut a vertical slit about 3/4 inch long just above the center of each diamond.

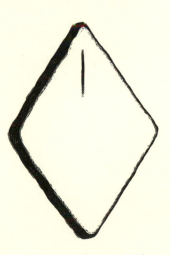

With floured hands, pull the opposite end of the diamond-shaped dough through the slit. A dusting of flour seems to help wherever anything sticks.

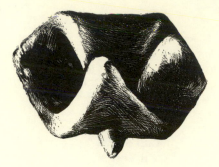

Test the fat with a piece of dough trimming. The fat should not be so hot that it smokes but the dough should cook to a golden brown in 1 to 2 minutes.

Fry the cookies, turning them once or twice, and drain them on absorbent paper.

When they're almost cool, sprinkle them (or shake them in a paper bag) with confectioners' sugar.

NANA ROSA'S BISCOTTI

The next two recipes are Italian versions of cookies or "biscuits," as they are called on the Continent. The root of the word biscuit actually means "twice baked." Although most cookies or biscuits are only baked once nowadays, this first version is an example of the old twice-baked biscuits, or, as they call them in Italy, "biscotti."

Our Public Relations Director at King Arthur Flour is Ellen Davies whose grandmother, Palmina Rosa, was born over a hundred years ago in Italy in 1886. In Palmina Rosa's village in those days, only the boys were sent to school so Nana Rosa never learned to read or write. When she grew up all of her baking was done from the memories of baking with her mother and grandmother. Nana Rosa made wonderful biscotti. Ellen always loved them and finally asked her for the recipe. Nana Rosa replied, "Elna, I trada you onea for one." So Ellen taught her how to make brownies and Nana Rosa gave Ellen the recipe for her biscotti.

Somehow, though, Ellen's biscotti never quite tasted as good as Nana Rosa's. Many years later, after her grandmother had died, she learned that she had left out one important detail. She had instructed Ellen to use ½ teaspoon of anise extract, when in fact, an entire bottle, or 2 tablespoons, was the correct amount. Ellen was initially bemused by what seemed like a small betrayal, but by understanding her grandmother's background, she realized how in that era when women were not educated, a recipe was an essential part of a woman's identity, her special claim to fame, and was thus not easily given away.

Fortunately for us, Ellen discovered the secret through an aunt. Nana Rosa might not mind that her secret is out if she knew that it makes us think warmly of her now. From her basic recipe several types of cookies can be made.

1 1/3 cups sugar
2 teaspoons baking powder
2 tablespoons margarine
1 (1-ounce) bottle (equals 2 tablespoons) anise extract
3 eggs
2 1/4 cups King Arthur Unbleached All-Purpose Flour
1 egg plus 1 teaspoon water (beaten together for egg wash)

Preheat your oven to 325°F.

Combine the sugar, baking powder, margarine and eggs. Blend in the entire bottle of extract and then the flour, one cup at a time.

Remember that flour is a bit like a sponge. It absorbs whatever moisture is in the air around it. So, on a humid day (not the best day for cookie making, but don't let that stop you), you'll have a "wetter" flour. As a result, you'll need to add more to your dough or batter to absorb the moisture in it. But always start with a lesser amount. It's easy to add flour to a dough or batter but once it's in there, you can't get it out.

Spoon the dough onto a greased cookie sheet to form two logs 1 1/2 inches wide by 1 inch high. To shape the logs, wet your hands and pat the top and sides of the dough. Brush the logs with egg wash and bake for 20 minutes.

Remove them from the oven and cut the logs diagonally into slices 1 inch thick to produce cookies. Turn each cookie on its side and rebake at the same temperature for 15 minutes.

BISCOTTI VARIATIONS

• Instead of forming the dough into logs, shape the dough into balls the size of a 50¢ piece (with wet hands). Roll each ball in sesame seeds or sliced almonds. Bake at 325°F for 20 minutes. (Do not rebake.)

• Substitute 1 ounce (2 tablespoons) of vanilla, almond, orange or rum extract for the anise.

• For the holidays you can divide the dough in half and use food color to color one half red, the other half green. Shape each into a log and continue as above.

THERESA DELREGNO'S
ORANGE BLOSSOM BISCOTTI

Theresa DelRegno is the wife of Victor DelRegno, President of our outstanding food broker, Morris Alper & Sons, Inc. Theresa, an exceptional baker, has agreed to share this biscotti recipe, which has been in her family for at least four generations. "Orange Blossoms always bring back memories of big family gatherings during the holidays. Our family loves them so much that I break tradition and serve them all year round."

Theresa also notes, "It's important to use King Arthur Flour for these cookies because they need a flour of high gluten content; otherwise the cookies will be of poor quality."

This large recipe will make between 10 and 15 dozen biscotti. Theresa says, "Don't let the quantities in the recipe scare you; they disappear quickly. I bet they'd freeze beautifully; we just never have any left to freeze!" It's also possible to cut this recipe in half.

Dough

12 eggs
2 cups sugar
1 cup (2 sticks) margarine or shortening (melted)
2 (1-ounce) bottles orange extract
2¹/₂ pounds (about 10 cups) King Arthur Unbleached All-Purpose Flour
2 tablespoons baking powder
a pinch of salt

First: Preheat your oven to 350°F.

Making the Dough: Beat the eggs and sugar together in a large bowl for 3 to 4 minutes. Stir in the margarine and orange extract.

Mix the dry ingredients together and slowly add to the egg mixture. Because of the difference in the size of eggs, you may or may not need all the flour. You want a kneadable dough that isn't too stiff.

When the dough holds together, turn it out onto a kneading surface and knead until it's smooth adding only enough flour to make it workable and to keep it from sticking. Let the dough rest for about 30 minutes.

Take a small piece of dough and roll by hand until it's about the diameter of your little finger and between 6 and 8 inches long. (Little kids love to pretend these are snakes or worms!) Theresa ties these in a simple knot, as if you were going to tie your shoe but just the first turn (see page 326). She says you can shape them any way you want but this shape has been traditional in her family.

Place them on a lightly greased cookie sheet and bake for 15 to 18 minutes until they are golden brown. While they bake, prepare the icing.

Icing

> 1 (1-pound) box confectioners' sugar
> 1 (1-ounce) bottle orange extract
> cold water

Stir the sugar, extract and enough cold water (a little at a time) to make the icing thick but spreadable. If it's too thin, it will run off the cookie.

Cool the biscotti on waxed paper (this makes cleaning up easy). While they are still warm, spread with the icing.

ZAND KOECKJES

From America, where the Dutch koeckje found fertile ground so long ago, we go back full circle to Holland, the source of the original. This recipe comes from the Sands' Dutch "son," Kees Willemsen, who came to them through the American Field Service. (Kees's father is a baker in Haarlem, Holland.) This recipe will make about 5 dozen koeckjes. We give it to you as Kees gave it to us, with translations.

> 200 grams (14 tablespoons or 1¾ sticks) butter
> 150 grams (¾ cup) sugar
> 1 egg
> 1 teaspoon vanilla
> ½ teaspoon salt
> 1 teaspoon grated lemon rind
> 300 grams (2½ cups) King Arthur Unbleached All-Purpose Flour
> confectioners' sugar (optional, to dust on top)

"Mix together the butter, sugar, egg, salt and lemon rind in a mixing bowl. Then mix in the flour. Cover and chill this dough overnight.

"Preheat your oven to 180°C (350°F).

"With your hands roll little biscuits, about 1 inch in diameter. Put them on a lightly greased cookie sheet and bake them for 15 to 20 minutes.

"When the koeckjes are completely cool, shake them gently in a paper bag of confectioners' sugar if you want."

• BARS •

Bars fall into a category somewhere between cookies and cakes and have a unique character of their own. Some can be made from cookie dough itself. Many are concoctions which could only be made in a cake pan. Here is a selection, some old favorites and some that are elegant and new.

GRANDMOTHER'S BROWNIES

We have all been called upon at some point (usually at the last minute) to produce a contribution for a bake sale, the baked goods table for this year's fair, or an offspring's athletic banquet or cast party. What is easier and quicker to make (and faster to disappear) than the good old chocolate brownie? The wonderful thing about brownies is that they can be made with a certain amount of abandon without committing any more utensils to the effort than you would with a mix. The ingredients are ones you're apt to have at home, making a trip to the store unnecessary.

This is a "receipt" that Brinna Sands inherited from her grandmother. Annie Davis's brownies are the dense fudgy kind. Over the years this recipe has put on many different faces depending on what was on hand or what seemed to be an interesting addition at the time. It is simple, flexible and accommodating, a "never fail" recipe. In fact it's so easy that if you have been "volunteered" by your children to provide the baked goods, you could choose to delegate that opportunity right back to them.

This recipe can be easily doubled (or even tripled) so you have some to give away and some to keep.

4 ounces (squares) unsweetened chocolate
½ cup (1 stick) butter or margarine, or a combination
2 cups sugar or brown sugar (don't use confectioners' sugar which
      contains cornstarch and will create a dry and board-like brownie)
2 to 4 eggs (the more eggs you use, the "cakier" the brownie will be;
      if you like dense, chewy brownies, use fewer eggs)
½ teaspoon salt
2 teaspoons vanilla
1 cup King Arthur Stone Ground Whole Wheat Flour

This is a recipe in which you can use whole wheat flour totally and no one will be the wiser.

Preheat your oven to 350°F.

Melt the chocolate and butter in a large saucepan over very low heat (or use a double boiler to be safe), stirring to blend.

Remove the pan from the heat; add and blend in the sugar, and then the rest of the ingredients. Mix this all together with a large spoon and put it into a greased, 9 x 9-inch cake pan.

Bake for 35 to 45 minutes or until they just begin to pull away from the sides of the pan. Remove the brownies from the oven.

Let them cool enough so you can cut them in squares, remove them from the pan with a spatula and (before you pack them up) enjoy at least one with a glass of cold milk.

Depending on the baker and/or the recipient, you might try adding 1 cup of any of the following:

- raisins, chopped apricots or other dried fruit
- chocolate, butterscotch or peanut butter chips (or all three)
- coconut
- chopped nuts, sunflower or sesame seeds
- chopped candy bar
- or anything else that looks interesting

BLOND BROWNIES

These have the flavor of butterscotch with bursts of pecan and chocolate. Along with brownies, these are the bars that always sell at bake sales. (Try a Blond Sundae with vanilla ice cream, butterscotch sauce, and a sprinkling of chopped pecans on top.)

2/3 cup butter or margarine
2¼ cups (1 pound) light brown sugar
3 eggs
2 teaspoons vanilla
2½ cups King Arthur Unbleached All-Purpose Flour 🌾
2½ teaspoons baking powder
½ teaspoon salt
1 to 2 cups of chocolate, butterscotch or peanut butter chips (optional)
1 cup chopped nuts (optional)

Preheat your oven to 350°F.

Cream the butter and sugar together until they're very light. Add the eggs and beat in thoroughly one at a time. Blend in the vanilla.

Mix the dry ingredients together. Blend the butter mixture with the flour mixture. Fold in the chocolate, butterscotch or peanut butter chips (or a mixture) and the nuts.

Spoon the dough into a lightly greased, 9 x 13-inch baking pan (or use two 8 x 8-inch cake pans).

Bake for 25 to 30 minutes. Cool, cut into squares and serve.

"TOLL HOUSE" COOKIES

It is said with some authority that the original "Toll House" Cookies were made with good King Arthur Flour.

To make "Toll House" Cookies, drop rounded spoonfuls of the Blond Brownie dough onto a lightly greased cookie sheet and bake at 350°F for 10 to 12 minutes. There should be enough dough for 80 to 100 cookies.

BROWN BAG BANANA BARS

A customer included this recipe with her order for one of our premiums. (Her name was lost, so if it's yours, we'd love to hear from you.) She called it a "brown-bagger's delight." The combination of sweetness and heartiness, along with the unexpected texture of the poppy seeds makes this an unusual treat. We are fortunate to have so many in our vast King Arthur family who are willing to share their treasures with us. We, in turn, share this one with you. Quid pro quo.

$\frac{1}{2}$ cup (1 stick) butter or margarine
$\frac{2}{3}$ cup brown sugar, packed
1 egg
1 teaspoon vanilla
$1\frac{1}{2}$ cups coarsely mashed ripe bananas (about 3 medium)
$1\frac{1}{4}$ cups King Arthur Unbleached All-Purpose Flour
$\frac{1}{2}$ cup King Arthur Stone Ground Whole Wheat Flour
$\frac{1}{4}$ cup cornmeal
2 teaspoons baking powder
$\frac{1}{2}$ teaspoon salt
2 tablespoons poppy seeds
$\frac{3}{4}$ cup golden raisins

Preheat your oven to 350°F.

Cream the butter, sugar and egg together. Add the vanilla and bananas and mix just to blend. Combine the dry ingredients and stir into the creamed mixture. Do not overmix. Stir in the raisins.

Spread into a greased, 10 x 14-inch baking pan. Bake for 20 to 25 minutes, or until the edges are golden. Cool on a rack and cut into bars.

HERMITS
COOKIES OR BARS

Hermits have a lot in common with good King Arthur Flour. They evolved in New England, they've been a classic for many years and they have great keeping qualities. Back in the day of the clipper ship, tins of long-keeping hermits accompanied many a sailor as he set out for the Orient or other exotic parts of the world.

In comparing old and new variations of hermit recipes, there are very few differences, so as a recipe, it appears to have worn well. Hermits themselves also improve with age, so make enough to weather and warm your winter.

1/2 cup (1 stick) butter
1 cup sugar, white or brown or a combination
1 teaspoon salt
2 fresh eggs, well beaten
1 cup buttermilk
1 cup dark, unsulphured molasses
4 cups King Arthur Unbleached All-Purpose Flour
1 teaspoon baking soda
2 teaspoons baking powder
1 teaspoon cinnamon
1/2 teaspoon allspice
1/2 teaspoon nutmeg
1 cup dried fruit such as raisins, currants or chopped apricots, which
     you've plumped in a cup of tea (or water)
1/2 cup chopped nuts or sunflower seeds or whatever you like that's
     crunchy and good for you (optional)

Preheat your oven according to the way you plan to shape the hermits: 375°F for cookies or 350°F for bars or squares.

In a large mixing bowl, cream the butter and sugar. Add the salt, eggs, buttermilk and molasses.

In a separate bowl, mix the flour, baking soda, baking powder and spices. Stir in the fruit and nuts. Blend the dry ingredients into the wet.

   • **Hermit Cookies:** Drop the dough by the spoonful onto a greased cookie sheet. Bake for 12 to 15 minutes. This will make about 6 dozen.

   • **Hermit Bars or Squares:** Spread the dough in a large (13 x 18-inch), greased baking pan. Bake for 25 to 30 minutes or until the top is firm. Cut into squares while still warm.

Lemon Squares

The recipe for these "melt-in-your-mouth" squares comes from Peg Hurley, an old Lexington, Massachusetts, friend of the Sands'. She says they are even better sprinkled with confectioners' sugar after they have cooled.

Bottom

> 1/2 cup (1 stick) butter
> 1 cup King Arthur Unbleached All-Purpose Flour
> 1/4 cup confectioners' sugar

Topping

> 2 eggs
> 1 cup sugar
> 2 tablespoons lemon juice
> 2 tablespoons flour
> a pinch of salt

Preheat your oven to 350°F.

Cut the butter into the flour and confectioners' sugar and press into a 9-inch square pan. Bake for 20 minutes or until light brown.

Combine the topping ingredients. When the bottom is done, and still hot, pour the topping over it and continue baking for about 25 minutes.

Edinburgh Tea Squares

Dough

> 1/2 cup (1 stick) soft butter or margarine
> 1 cup brown sugar, packed
> 1/2 cup oatmeal
> 1/2 teaspoon salt
> 1 cup King Arthur Unbleached All-Purpose Flour

Filling

> 1 cup dates
> 1 cup water
> a pinch of salt
> 1 tablespoon lemon juice
> grated rind (zest) from one lemon

Preheat your oven to 350°F.

Cream the butter until light. Add the brown sugar and continue beating until fluffy. Mix in the oatmeal, salt and flour. Pat half of this dough evenly in a lightly greased, 9-inch square pan.

Cook the dates in the water until soft. Mix in the salt, lemon juice and rind. Spread the filling over the bottom layer of dough in your baking pan. Sprinkle the remaining dry mixture over the filling.

Bake for 30 to 40 minutes. Cool and cut into squares.

MERINGUE BARS

Dough

> ⅓ cup butter
> 1 cup sugar
> 2 eggs (1 egg plus 1 yolk; you use the white in the Meringue)
> 1⅓ cups King Arthur Unbleached All-Purpose Flour
> 1 teaspoon baking powder
> ½ teaspoon salt
> 2 tablespoons milk
> ½ teaspoon vanilla
> 1 teaspoon grated lemon or orange rind (or a combination)

Meringue

> 1 egg white (from above)
> 1 cup brown sugar
> ½ teaspoon vanilla
> ¾ cup shredded coconut

Preheat your oven to 300°F.

Cream the butter and sugar until light. Blend in one whole egg and the yolk. In a separate bowl, combine the flour, baking powder and salt. Add ⅓ of these dry ingredients to the butter/sugar mixture. Add the milk, vanilla and grated rind. Gradually stir in the remainder of the flour mixture. Spread this in a well-greased, 9 x 9-inch cake pan to make a layer about ⅓ inch thick.

Beat the remaining egg white until it is light. Add the brown sugar, vanilla and coconut. Spread this over the top of the dough.

Bake for 25 to 30 minutes. Cut into bars, and allow them to cool before you try to remove them from the pan.

• CRACKERS •

Crackers have been around for a long time. Because they are dry and will keep for many weeks if they are stored properly, they have been the mainstay of many a sea voyage and land expedition. Two hundred years ago, the ancestors of the modern cracker, "hard tack" and "sea biscuits," were an important part of a voyager's diet, providing him with one of the four basic food groups, that of cereals or grains. As we know today, the carbohydrates in grain products provide our main source of energy, so those early crackers provided much of the energy for discovering and colonizing the New World.

Today, most of us aren't pioneering any more and crackers have been relegated to "snack food." But as a snack food, they're one of the best. They contain very little sugar, if any; you can make them almost salt free; and they're still a great source of carbohydrates. If you eat them with a glass of low-fat milk and a piece of fruit or some raw vegetables, you have the makings of a low-calorie balanced meal.

Once they're baked and thoroughly cooled, crackers can be stored in an airtight container on the shelf or in the freezer. If they ever get limp or stale, they can be quickly brought back to life by spending a few minutes in a moderate oven.

CRACKERS THAT ARE ALMOST COOKIES

ENGLISH DIGESTIVE BISCUITS

Digestive biscuits are as English as Peter Pan. They're in the "never-never-land" between cookies and crackers, a perfect "in-between" sort of biscuit for an "in-between" sort of meal. Developed during the latter part of the nineteenth century to increase fiber in Victorian diets, they are best described as "sophisticated graham crackers." This recipe makes between 3 and 4 dozen biscuits.

$1/2$ cup King Arthur Unbleached All-Purpose Flour
$1 1/2$ cups King Arthur Stone Ground Whole Wheat Flour
1 teaspoon baking powder
$1/2$ cup (1 stick) butter, at room temperature
$3/4$ cup confectioners' sugar
$1/4$ cup cold milk

Place the dry ingredients in a mixing bowl. Cut or rub in the butter with a pastry blender, two knives or your fingertips. Add the sugar and enough milk to make a stiff dough. Knead this mixture on a floured surface until smooth. (All this can be done almost instantly in a food processor.)

If you have time, return the dough to your bowl, cover and chill for an hour. This resting time will make the biscuits more tender and crisp. After the dough has chilled, preheat your oven to 350°F.

Roll out the dough until it is a bit more than $1/8$ inch thick, and cut into any desired shape. (Traditionally, digestive biscuits are about $2 1/2$ inches round.)

Place on greased cookie sheets, prick evenly with a fork and bake until pale gold, between 15 and 20 minutes.

GRAHAM CRACKERS

Sylvester Graham, the originator of graham flour, lived and preached in the first half of the nineteenth century. He was a minister of rather overwhelming, although per-suasive, zeal. When he was in his mid-thirties, he began a dietary crusade the echoes of which are still reverberating today. He preached fervently about the benefits of the flour that was named after him, arguing that to separate the bran from the rest of the wheat berry was against the will of God.

The original graham flour was, essentially, whole wheat flour with fairly large particles of bran, making it quite coarse. The coarseness or fineness of the grind has nothing to do with the amount of bran in the flour or the resulting amount of fiber. You can use whole wheat flour anywhere graham flour is specified.

Although Sylvester Graham would be considered somewhat of a zealot or fanatic if he were alive today, he was nutritionally on the right track. His legacy is our awareness of the importance of bran in our diets, and the following cracker. This recipe will make about 2 dozen crackers.

1 cup King Arthur Stone Ground Whole Wheat Flour (instead of graham)
1 cup King Arthur Unbleached All-Purpose Flour
$1/4$ cup sugar
$1/2$ teaspoon salt
1 teaspoon cinnamon
1 teaspoon baking powder
1 egg
$1/4$ cup vegetable oil
$1/4$ cup honey
2 to 3 tablespoons milk (approximately)

Preheat your oven to 350°F.

In a mixing bowl, combine the dry ingredients. Beat the egg until light, adding the vegetable oil, honey and 2 tablespoons of the milk. Stir into the dry ingredients until you have a fairly stiff dough.

Turn the dough onto a floured surface and knead gently until it holds together. Roll it out until it is about $1/8$ inch thick. Cut into 2-inch squares, prick with a fork and place on a barely greased cookie sheet. Brush the tops with milk (and cinnamon sugar if you are so inclined) and bake for 15 to 20 minutes.

TEETHING CRACKERS

Since it's not a good idea to feed honey to babies who are less than a year old (see note about honey in following recipe), substitute some maple syrup or iron-rich molasses. Roll the dough a bit thicker ($1/4$ inch or more) and cut it into 1 x 3-inch rectangles. Bake for 30 to 35 minutes at 300°F. If they're browning too quickly after 20 minutes, reduce the heat 25°F. Let them cool and dry.

TEETHING BISCUITS
FOR BABIES

These teething biscuits might not taste good to you. There's no leavening in them so they will be hard. Those baby teeth that are coming in need something to work on. There is no salt in these cookies either. Babies haven't developed a taste for it.

Our biscuits are made with whole milk and they do have some vegetable oil in them. Babies don't usually need to be on diets. They need those fats to absorb fat-soluble vitamins which help them grow up bright eyed and healthy.

These biscuits also have some molasses in them because molasses tastes interesting and is full of iron. If you don't want the flavor of these cookies to be too strong, you can substitute 2 tablespoons of sugar for 2 of the molasses. Don't substitute honey if your baby is less than a year old. Honey can contain dormant botulism spores which are a concern until babies are beyond that sensitive first year. (See Appendix.)

Our teething biscuits have lots of pure King Arthur Flour in them, both all-purpose and whole wheat. Alone, flour provides lots of carbohydrates, which babies need when they are busy. In combination with milk, our flour provides lots of protein, which babies need while they grow. Although we have used an equal amount of both flours in our recipe, you can vary it any way you wish. Some babies have sensitive tummies so whole wheat flour may need to be introduced slowly. If you want to add a bit of soy flour or wheat germ to boost the nutritional value of these cookies, by all means do. That's the beauty of something homemade.

If you don't happen to have a baby at home at the moment, these biscuits, along with the recipe, make a wonderful present for parents of a toddler. This will make 3 to 4 dozen teething biscuits.

> 1/2 cup whole milk
> 1/4 cup vegetable oil
> 1/4 cup dark, unsulphured molasses
> 1 1/2 cups King Arthur Unbleached All-Purpose Flour
> 1 1/2 cups King Arthur Stone Ground Whole Wheat Flour

Mixing: Blend the liquid ingredients together as best you can. Stir in the flours, turn out onto a floured surface and knead for 3 or 4 minutes until the dough is well blended and smooth.

Cover it and let it rest for at least 20 minutes.

Preheat your oven to 350°F.

Shaping: Roll the dough out until it's about 1/4 inch thick. Cut into rectangular pieces about 1 x 2 1/2 inches.

These biscuits won't expand much so you can place them close together on a lightly greased cookie sheet. Prick them with a fork several times for no other reason than to give you a gauge to check your baby's progress as he or she works down the biscuit.

If you let the biscuits rest for 15 or 20 minutes before they go into the oven, the gluten will relax and they'll keep their shape.

Baking: Bake for about 30 minutes until the biscuits are quite firm. If they seem to be browning too fast, top or bottom, turn the heat down to 325°F for the last 10 minutes. Let them cool and harden before you wrap them.

CRACKERS FROM SCRATCH

The first two recipes are basic, simple and quick to make, and offer much latitude for experimenting.

KING ARTHUR FLOUR'S
BASIC CRACKERS

This recipe makes about 3 dozen crackers.

2 cups King Arthur Unbleached All-Purpose Flour
$\frac{1}{2}$ teaspoon salt
$\frac{1}{4}$ teaspoon baking powder
1 teaspoon sugar
4 tablespoons butter
1 egg, beaten into $\frac{1}{2}$ cup milk (or $\frac{3}{4}$ cup milk and no egg)
coarse salt, herbs or herbal salt substitute to sprinkle on top

First: Preheat your oven to 400°F.

Making the Dough: Mix the flour, salt, baking powder and sugar together. With a pastry blender or your fingertips, rub the butter quickly into the flour until it resembles cornmeal. Beat the egg into the milk and, with a fork, stir half of it into the flour/butter mixture. Add the rest, stirring it in quickly with your fork.

Shaping: Turn the cracker dough out onto a floured surface and knead gently a few times with floured hands until it holds together. (Let the dough rest for an hour if you have time.) With a floured rolling pin, roll the dough out until it is very thin. Aim for $\frac{1}{16}$ inch. Every once in a while, slide a spatula or bowl scraper under the dough to keep it from sticking. Sprinkle a little flour about to help.

Once your dough is rolled thin, you can shape your crackers a couple of different ways. You can make circles with a floured cookie cutter, or, to eliminate the need of rolling out the leftover dough, you can cut it into squares.

After the crackers are shaped, separate them and lift them onto a greased cookie sheet. Let the crackers rest for about 5 minutes. With a fork, prick each several times, and then sprinkle with salt, herbs or herbal salt substitute.

Baking & Storing: Bake for 5 to 6 minutes on one side and then turn them over and bake another 5 minutes or until they are golden brown and crisp. Because they're so thin, they can go from gold to dark brown very quickly, so keep an eye on them.

Remove the crackers from the oven, cool and store in an airtight container.

BUTTERMILK CRACKERS

This recipe makes use of the reaction between baking soda and the acid in buttermilk for leavening. It will make about 3 dozen crackers.

1¼ cups King Arthur Stone Ground Whole Wheat Flour
¾ cup other grains of your choice, whole or ground: cracked wheat,
      wheat berries, wheat germ or bran; oatmeal or oat flour; medium
      rye flour or pumpernickel; sunflower or sesame seeds, etc. (use
      them individually or in combination)
½ teaspoon baking powder
½ teaspoon baking soda
½ teaspoon salt
1 teaspoon whole dill, caraway, cumin, poppy, sesame or other seed
3 tablespoons butter or margarine
up to ½ cup buttermilk (sour milk or yogurt can also be used)
coarse salt, herbs or herbal salt substitute, to sprinkle on top

Mixing: Combine all of the dry ingredients and cut in the butter. Mix in only enough liquid to make the dough hold together. If you have time to let the dough rest for an hour or so, it will relax the gluten and the dough will be more receptive to being rolled out.

Preheat your oven to 350°F.

Shaping: Roll out the dough on a floured surface until it's very thin. Try for ¹⁄₁₆ inch thick. You can cut this into circles with a floured cookie cutter (or cut it into 2½-inch squares to save rolling it out a second time).

After they are shaped, lift them gently onto a lightly greased cookie sheet.

Let the crackers rest for about 5 minutes. Prick them with a fork and sprinkle on salt, herbs or herbal salt substitute.

Baking: Bake them for 5 to 6 minutes on one side, flip them over and bake them another 5 to 6 minutes or until they're crisp and lightly browned. Cool on a rack to maximize crispness.

TWICE-BAKED CRACKERS

Like "brown & serve" rolls and the original biscotti, these crackers are baked in two stages. You can even freeze them after the first baking, then take them from the freezer and pop them in the oven to serve them freshly baked at a moment's notice. This recipe makes between 4 and 5 dozen crackers.

3 eggs
²/₃ cup milk
¹/₂ cup safflower oil
2¹/₄ cups King Arthur Stone Ground Whole Wheat Flour
¹/₂ cup yellow cornmeal (plus a little more for dusting the baking sheet)
3¹/₂ teaspoons baking powder
4 teaspoons salt
¹/₂ cup oats
4 tablespoons butter, melted
¹/₂ cup sunflower seeds

First: Preheat your oven to 325°F.

Mixing: Beat the eggs in a large bowl. Add the milk, then the oil and blend. Mix the flour, cornmeal, baking powder and salt together and add gradually to the liquid ingredients. Add the oats and sunflower seeds and mix thoroughly.

Shaping: Dust a baking sheet with cornmeal and roll out half of the dough directly on it as thinly as possible, covering the sheet. If the dough sticks, dust it with more cornmeal. Trim off the dough at the edge of the sheet. Cut it into 2-inch squares, and leave them in place on the pan.

Baking Once: Prick the tops of each cracker with a fork and brush with melted butter. Bake for 10 minutes only. Although the crackers will still be pale, remove them from the oven.

At this point, if you want to freeze them, you can let them cool, dust them with a bit of cornmeal to keep them separate from each other and put them in the freezer in an airtight plastic bag.

Baking Twice: If you are not planning to freeze them, while they're still hot and flexible, separate them and place them on another (ungreased) baking sheet. Bake them again at 325°F for about 10 minutes or until golden brown.

CHEESE BITES

Because they are so easy, these Cheese Bites could be a great first-time cracker for kids to make. This recipe makes about 3 dozen bites. (Try sprinkling a little paprika on their tops before they go in the oven.)

1 cup King Arthur Unbleached All-Purpose Flour
2 cups grated Cheddar cheese
¹/₂ cup (1 stick) softened butter

Preheat your oven to 375°F.

Mix all of the ingredients together with your hands. Knead a few times (or squish around a little bit!) and form into small, bite-sized balls. Place on an ungreased cookie sheet and bake for about 12 minutes. Lift off and cool on a piece of absorbent paper.

CORNMEAL CHEDDAR CRACKERS

This recipe is from Ken Haedrich, an enthusiastic baker, teacher, food writer, husband and father. Ken's philosophy about the joys of baking are very much in concert with our own. His enthusiasm has found its way into a number of magazines and books, as well as in everything he bakes. As he said in an article he wrote about crackers several years ago, "I enjoy my small role as a cracker revivalist. I see myself as helping to preserve an all-but-forgotten kitchen craft.... Making crackers is just good fun, a nice way to unwind after a hectic day, a nice way to spend time with your kids." Ken and his family play and bake in their kitchen across the river in New Hampshire. This recipe makes about 3 dozen crackers.

1 cup King Arthur Unbleached All-Purpose Flour
³/₄ cup cornmeal
¹/₄ cup King Arthur Stone Ground Whole Wheat Flour
¹/₄ teaspoon baking powder
¹/₂ teaspoon salt
¹/₄ teaspoon cayenne (or maybe a teaspoon or two of Dijon mustard)
1 cup finely grated Cheddar cheese (or Monterey Jack, Swiss
    or Parmesan)
1 egg
¹/₄ cup oil
¹/₄ cup water

Preheat your oven to 375°F.

Combine the flours, cornmeal, baking powder, salt and cayenne and "toss with your hands." Add the grated cheese and toss again to mix. In a separate bowl, lightly beat together the remaining ingredients.

Make a well in the dry ingredients and add the liquids, mixing with your hands until the dough sticks together.

Dust your work surface with flour and roll the dough out to between ¹/₁₆ and ¹/₈ inch thick. Cut and transfer to an ungreased baking sheet. Ken says his kids like to cut out "zany shapes or teddy bears, and we like giving our crackers to appreciative friends."

Bake for about 15 minutes, depending on thickness. They should be crisp and golden when done.

• FLATBREADS •

Flatbreads are the ancestors of modern leavened breads, so every culture has its own variety. Here is an assortment from all over the world, from the equatorial country of India to the northern latitudes of Iceland.

In addition to providing a major source of carbohydrates, almost every culture has discovered that the grains in flatbreads (such as wheat), eaten with beans, cheese or another milk product, make a meal that will stick with you longer and give you more energy than either eaten alone. The Mexicans have their tortillas and refried beans; in the Middle East, you'll find pita bread and hummus. Scandinavian flatbreads are often made with a dairy product baked right in.

What nutritionists have confirmed about these combinations, which our ancestors knew intuitively, is that each of these food groups contains certain proteins, but not all the ones we need. By combining wheat with these other foods, you put different parts of a whole protein together and produce something worth more than the sum of its parts, a case of one plus one equalling more than two.

So flatbreads are in vogue again and probably for the same reasons they were important in the first place. They're a high-energy, low-fat bread and, when eaten with the right food companions, a source of protein that is as valuable as that found in any meat or fish. They can be eaten as snacks between meals, or in place of bread or rolls at a main meal.

Many kinds of flatbreads are available commercially, but, like crackers, they are easy to put together and, because they're so "flat," cook in minutes. Give them a try and discover one more way to liberate yourself from the limitations of the grocery store.

SCOTTISH OAT CAKES

This recipe is somewhere between a cracker and a flatbread. It comes from Margaret and Lillian Sticht of Norwich, Connecticut, via the Jubinskys. The Stichts say, "These Oat Cakes don't look like much but are truly love at first bite!"

3 cups King Arthur Unbleached All-Purpose Flour
3 cups quick rolled oats
1 cup (2 sticks) butter
1 cup vegetable shortening
1 cup sugar
1/2 teaspoon salt
1/4 cup water (scant)

Preheat your oven to 350°F.

Mix together flour, oats, butter, shortening, sugar and salt. Gradually add the water and form the dough into a ball.

Divide the dough into 4 pieces. Roll out each one between two sheets of waxed paper until it is about 1/4 inch thick. With a spatula, or your bowl scraper, cut the dough into rectangles, approximately 2 x 3 inches, and place them on an ungreased cookie sheet.

Bake for 15 to 20 minutes until they're golden brown. Remove to wire racks to cool.

SCANDINAVIAN CRISP BREAD

These crisp breads, variations of which have been made traditionally in Scandinavia for hundreds of years, are retaking Europe by storm, and beginning an invasion on this side of the Atlantic. They are like grown-up crackers, large, hearty and perfect to break apart and eat warm with butter, cheese, meat or fruit. They are a great accompaniment to any meal but are a good low-calorie, high-energy snack by themselves.

1 1/2 cups King Arthur Unbleached All-Purpose Flour
1 1/2 cups pumpernickel or medium rye flour
1 teaspoon salt
1 teaspoon sugar
2 teaspoons baking powder
1/2 teaspoon baking soda
2 tablespoons dill or caraway seeds (optional but a nice variation)
4 tablespoons (1/2 stick) butter (or lard, which is traditional)
1 1/4 cups buttermilk or yogurt

Preheat your oven to 400°F.

In a mixing bowl, blend the dry ingredients and stir in the seeds if you opt to use them. Cut the butter into pieces and rub them into the dry ingredients with your fingertips until the mixture looks like bread crumbs.

Add the buttermilk or yogurt and stir until the mixture holds together and pulls away from the sides of the bowl. This should make a kneadable but fairly soft dough. Turn the dough out onto a floured surface and knead gently for a minute or so until it is smooth. Cut the dough into 2 pieces, cover and let rest for 10 minutes (or up to an hour if you have time).

Roll each piece out until it is ¼ to ½ inch thick and 10 or so inches in diameter. Place on a lightly greased baking sheet (a 12-inch pizza pan is perfect), cover and let rest for 5 minutes.

Prick the surface all over with a fork and bake for about 20 minutes or until the bread is just beginning brown. Remove and cool on a rack so the bottom crisps as well.

Although the buttermilk or yogurt combined with the grains makes a complete protein which is a nutritional advantage, you can eliminate some calories (along with some nutrition) by substituting water. Water also will intensify the flavor of the grains. If you decide to try this, use 1 more teaspoon of baking powder in place of the ½ teaspoon of baking soda.

Indian Nan

This flatbread from India is baked by sticking the dough on the side of a clay oven called a tandoor. Although most of us don't have access to a clay oven, we can do fairly well with a griddle on top of the stove. We'll just have to imagine the earthy aroma that a real tandoor would give this bread. Nan has a wonderful chewy texture and should be eaten unadorned with a main meal.

Most bread in India is made from a very finely ground whole wheat flour called "aata." King Arthur Stone Ground Whole Wheat Flour is also finely ground and will do in place of the traditional Indian whole wheat flour.

1¼ cups King Arthur Unbleached All-Purpose Flour
1¼ cups King Arthur Stone Ground Whole Wheat Flour
1 teaspoon salt
1 teaspoon sugar
½ cup milk
4 tablespoons plain yogurt
1 egg
1 tablespoon vegetable oil

Blend the flours, salt and sugar in a mixing bowl. Mix the yogurt with the milk and heat in a small saucepan until it's just lukewarm. Remove it from the heat and beat in the egg. Add this to the dry ingredients along with the oil and mix into a soft dough.

Knead for about 5 minutes, like a bread dough, until it's smooth and elastic.

Cover the bowl with a damp cloth or plastic wrap and let it sit for several hours or overnight. This allows the dough to "ripen" and develop wonderful flavor and a tender texture.

Divide the dough into 12 pieces, shape into balls and roll out on a floured surface into 4- or 5-inch circles. Cover these with a damp cloth while you heat your griddle. Cook with the damp side up until it puffs up and is crisp underneath. Flip it over gently and brown on the other side. The nan should be brown only in patches. Keep them warm on a low heat in your oven until the rest are cooked.

Navajo Fry Bread

This flatbread comes out of the American Southwest. It was collected by anthropologist Natalie Pattison and conveyed to us via friend and Dartmouth College geologist Charles Drake.

> 2 cups King Arthur Unbleached All-Purpose Flour
> 2 teaspoons baking powder
> $\frac{1}{2}$ cup powdered milk
> $\frac{1}{2}$ teaspoon salt
> $\frac{3}{4}$ cup warm water, more or less

In a large skillet or griddle, melt shortening $\frac{1}{2}$ to 1 inch deep.

Mix the dry ingredients together. Add the warm water slowly and only until you have a dough that is soft but not sticky.

Divide the dough into 3 or 4 pieces. On a lightly floured surface, with a floured rolling pin, roll each piece into a circle between $\frac{1}{8}$ and $\frac{1}{4}$ inch thick. You can also pull the dough out with your hands or pat it back and forth to form circles.

Test the fat by putting a pinch of dough in the skillet. If it browns quickly but does not burn, the shortening is ready. Place the circles of dough, one at a time, into the skillet. Brown on both sides and drain on paper towels. Serve hot.

Brinna Davis Dworsky (Frank and Brinna Sands' niece), whose mother grew up in Navajo country, makes a similar version of fry bread and serves it hot with honey or jelly.

TORTILLAS DE HARINA

Like Navajo fry bread, you will find this flatbread in the Southwest, but its real home is south of the Mexican border. Although a traditional tortilla is made of "masa harina," or corn flour, this version is made simply "de harina," or of wheat flour. These are usually larger and lighter in texture than the masa harina variety.

1 1/2 cups King Arthur Unbleached All Purpose Flour 🌾
1 teaspoon baking powder
1/2 teaspoon salt
2 tablespoons lard (traditional) or butter
1/2 cup warm water

Mixing: Mix the dry ingredients together in a large mixing bowl. With a pastry blender, two knives or your fingertips, cut or rub in the shortening until the mixture looks like cornmeal. Blend in the water and when the dough seems to be holding together, turn it out onto a floured surface.

Kneading & Resting: Knead for 4 or 5 minutes or until it's smooth, adding only enough flour to keep it from sticking to you or the board. Cover with plastic wrap and let mature for several hours if you have the time.

Shaping & Cooking: Heat a griddle on the stove until it's moderately hot.

While it's heating, divide the dough into 6 pieces. Shape each into a ball and press it down on your floured kneading surface. With a floured rolling pin, roll it out until it's very thin, 8 or 9 inches in diameter. Cook each tortilla on the griddle, either ungreased or with a bit of butter, for 2 or 3 minutes, or until the bubbles that have formed on the surface begin to brown.

Serving & Storing: You can stack these on a plate, covered with a damp towel in a warm oven, if you're planning to eat them right away. Tortillas de Harina can be served several ways:

• Cut them in wedges and deep-fat fry them to make your own tortilla chips.

• Deep-fat fry them whole, sprinkle them with Monterey Jack cheese and green chillies and, while they're still hot, serve them as an appetizer.

• Sauté them lightly on a griddle, fill with a combination of refried beans, spiced beef or chicken, and melted cheese. Serve them hot with a dollop of guacamole, sour cream, chopped onions, tomato and a wedge of fresh chilled lettuce.

Or you can cool them and wrap them in an airtight plastic bag. They will keep for several days stored in the refrigerator, or for several weeks in the freezer.

ICELANDIC FLATBRAUD

This flatbread comes from a land of glaciers and volcanos. Icelandic flatbraud is traditionally eaten cold with a little butter. It is also excellent with paté, cheese, smoked fish or smoked lamb (hangikjöt) which is unique to this northern country and utterly delicious.

Auby Haldorsdóttir, a close friend of the younger Frank Sands' from Reykjavík, graciously shared this family recipe.

a pinch of salt
1 to 1¼ cups boiling water
2 cups King Arthur Unbleached All-Purpose Flour 🌾
2 cups medium rye flour or pumpernickel

Dissolve the salt in the smaller amount of boiling water. Mix with the flours and add only enough water to make a dough that is soft enough to knead.

Knead for several minutes. Doughs made with rye flour are sticky so flour your hands and kneading surface just enough to keep the dough from sticking. Unlike other doughs, a rye dough will be sticky even when it's kneaded enough.

Divide the dough into 4 parts and roll each one until it is very thin and about the size of a dessert plate. Let these rest for about 5 minutes.

Cook on a lightly greased, very hot cast iron griddle, turning frequently.

ICELANDIC LAUFABRAUD

This is another fascinating flatbread from Auby who says, "'Laufabraud,' or 'leafcutting,' is an old Icelandic tradition. For many families it was, and still is, one of the most festive days of the year when everybody gets together to cut out the 'laufabraud' and fry it.

"Laufabraud is always made right before Christmas and is usually served with hangikjöt (smoked lamb) or just eaten separately with a little butter.

"The style of the cut ought to be left up to the individual's imagination, but traditional ones are all kinds of little stars, leaves, Christmas trees, suns or small houses.

"When fried, the 'cakes' should slightly change color. When they are taken out of the oil, they will get darker still but they should not be too dark. As soon as they've been taken out of the oil, press the cakes lightly to flatten them."

Although Laufabraud is eaten with most of the same things as the previous bread, this one is clearly a festive variety.

2 cups King Arthur Unbleached All-Purpose Flour 🌾
1/2 teaspoon salt
1 teaspoon baking powder
1 teaspoon sugar
3/4 cup milk
1 teaspoon butter

Mixing: Mix the dry ingredients together in a medium-sized mixing bowl.

Heat the milk in a small saucepan until it just reaches a boil. Add and melt the butter. Pour this over the dry ingredients and mix until you have a soft dough. Turn the dough out onto a lightly floured surface and knead until it is smooth. Cover the bowl and refrigerate the dough for 2 hours, or more if you have time. This relaxes the gluten and mellows the dough so the finished bread will be more tender.

Rolling: Divide the dough into 12 small pieces and roll each out, keeping everything lightly floured so nothing sticks, until the rounds are about 5 inches in diameter and 1/16 inch thick. (You can make them bigger if you wish. Just make sure you have a pan large enough in which to cook them comfortably.)

Stack the rounds on a plate with lightly greased waxed paper separating them. Refrigerate them again for at least 1/2 hour.

In a frying pan, heat an inch or so of vegetable oil to about 360°F.

"Leafcutting": While the oil heats, gather people around to cut a design in each round of dough with sharp knives or small scissors. (You can also leave them as is if you wish.)

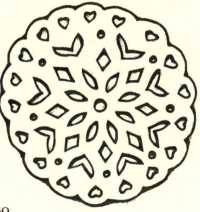

Cooking & Serving: Fry each round until it is golden. Using a fork, flip it over once to brown the other side. You want it to be crisp on the outside but chewy on the inside, tricky for something so thin.

Drain the laufabraud on absorbent paper and serve warm with smoked lamb if you happen to have any. A tasty alternative might be some smoked salmon and chopped onion. You can also just eat them as is to make any meal festive.

PIES & PASTRY VII

PIES & PASTRY
SWEET & SAVORY

• To make tender pie crusts, use King Arthur Flour! Our flour has never been treated with bleach. As the best pastry chefs will attest, the bleaching process toughens the gluten in flour before you even set hand to it.

• Another trick for making tender pie crust is one our grandmothers used. Include a teaspoon of vinegar or lemon juice in the liquid ingredients for each cup of King Arthur Flour in your recipe. This tempers the gluten and tenderizes the dough.

• Lard produces the flakiest crust; butter has the best flavor; and vegetable shortening makes a tender crust with no cholesterol. Try them all or a combination to produce just the mix you want.

• A secret to flaky pastry is to cut half the shortening in at a time and to make sure it's chilled. When you roll out this dough, you produce layers of flour and shortening which bake into tender flakes. Chilling the finished dough makes it much easier to roll out and much less likely to stick. It also resolidifies the shortening to ensure flakiness.

• When rolling out your dough, roll from the center to the outside edge. Loosen it occasionally with your bowl scraper and turn it over. Use just enough flour on the rolling surface and rolling pin to keep the dough from sticking.

• To bake a "blind," or unfilled crust, first chill it for 20 minutes and then fit a piece of aluminum foil on the inside surface. Prick both the crust and the foil, to allow steam to escape and (hopefully) keep the crust from developing a bubble. Fill the foil with something which will mimic a filling to help the crust keep its shape while it bakes. You can use anything from dried beans to small stones which you've washed free of grit, or special aluminum pellets that are made just for this purpose, available at most kitchen supply stores. Keep this filling in a jar to use over and over.

• To store up some labor in the freezer, make several pie shells at a time and freeze them in airtight plastic bags. They'll keep for a few weeks to several months depending on your freezer.

PIES & PASTRY
SWEET & SAVORY
VII

"Sing a song of sixpence, a pocket full of rye.
Four and twenty blackbirds baked in a pie.
When the pie was opened, the birds began to sing.
Wasn't that a dainty dish to set before the king!"

When we were children, most of us sang this nursery rhyme without thinking too much about the words. Upon remembering it as adults, we probably assumed it was written just to please a child's sense of the fantastic.

But, at one time, pies were actually made like this to please an adult sense of the fantastic. In the late Middle Ages in England, it was briefly fashionable to present a large pie of this sort to the host of a gala dinner, whether he was a king or a high ranking nobleman. When the pie was cut open, many small birds, very much alive, would fly out into the great hall eliciting cries of astonishment and delight from the guests.

To accomplish this, a very sturdy pie crust was made ahead of time. After it was cooled, the bottom was cut out and into it went as many small birds as could be fit without doing them in. Such a "happening" almost half a millennium ago gave rise to that familiar nursery rhyme of our childhood.

• A PIE CRUST PRIMER •

PASTRY YESTERDAY

As we mentioned in the chapter on yeasted breads, doughs and pastries have acted as containers for food for centuries. As baking with yeast seems to have originated somewhere around the Mediterranean, so, too, did the art of baking with pastry. The earliest pastries from Greece sound a bit like modern baklava, vehicles for carrying a concoction of nuts and honey. Romans used pastry to enclose and cook meat, rather like cooking in a pastry "Dutch oven."

In fact, it was as containers for cooking and serving food that pastry was primarily used until sometime in the fifteenth or sixteenth centuries. At that point, when types of grain and the process of milling them improved, the quality of the pastry also improved. People discovered that a pastry could be an edible addition to a filling rather than just a container.

But even then, pastries contained fillings that were basically savory (salty) rather than sweet, although most savory, or meat, pies contained fruit as well. This was a combination of flavors that was dear to medieval tastes. We still have remnants of this culinary inclination around today in the form of plum puddings and mince pies whose roots are centuries old. It wasn't until the end of the eighteenth century (about the time that the parent company of King Arthur Flour was formed) that pastries filled just with spiced and sweetened fruit appeared.

As it takes many decades for eating habits to change and evolve, those early fruit pies, like their meat-filled predecessors, were still eaten as part of a main meal, often breakfast. There are families today whose "fit breakfast" includes a chunk of cheese and a big piece of pie, which together are a great source of energy for anyone who is very active physically.

PASTRY TODAY

Pastry itself is a fairly simple combination of ingredients: flour, salt, sometimes a bit of sugar, fat and a little liquid. But, as with all types of baking, there are a number of pastry types or traditions that have evolved over the years. These are determined by the ratio of those ingredients to each other and the way in which they are combined.

Today, there are five basic types of classic pastry: mealy or short flake, medium flake, long flake, puff and "choux," with variations that may have characteristics of more than one type. Some, like their pastry ancestors, are relatively durable since they need to stand up by themselves; some are tender and flaky since they are baked in containers that provide the structure; some are ethereally light puff pastries that can act as containers for fillings but can stand on their own as well. In this chapter we'll explain and explore most of these, give you some old and new recipes to try, and provide enough information so you can set off to experiment on your own.

In this primer we will focus on a traditional American pie crust made with a medium flake pastry. After describing it and explaining how to make it, we'll use it as a standard to measure other types of pastry by. This isn't because it's better, but because, for most of us who have had any experience with pies at all, either making or eating, it's friendly and familiar.

King Arthur Unbleached "Pastry" Flour

Because the bleaching process chemically toughens the gluten in wheat flour and destroys some of the flavor and nutrition, an unbleached flour is preferable for making pastry and pie dough. King Arthur Flour is unbleached but it is a strong flour, which means it has more protein than other pastry flour. When it's handled gently, it can make a superior pie crust.

To make King Arthur Unbleached "Pastry" Flour, substitute 2 tablespoons of cornstarch for an equal amount of flour in each cup. This lowers the percentage of gluten in the flour. (For another way of tempering the gluten, read about lemon juice or vinegar under Liquids on page 391.)

BASIC MEDIUM FLAKE PASTRY

Medium flake pie crusts can be used for main course dishes or, by adding the optional sugar, for sweet fillings and tart shells. They contain the same ingredients as other pie crusts, but it's the way the shortening is incorporated into the flour that gives these crusts their name and characteristics.

When you break a medium flake pie crust with your fingers, it separates into flakes rather than breaking "clean." A crust that breaks clean is made with short flake pastry. To make a crust "short," the ingredients are put together a little differently. Short crusts are equally good and used just about as universally.

A TRADITIONAL AMERICAN PIE CRUST

Our Generous Version makes more than enough dough for one 9- or 10-inch double-crust pie, two or three 9-inch single crust shells or about a dozen tart shells. We've made it very generous to give you lots of dough for patches and trimmings and some to share when you have "helpers." (See Trimmings & Tail Ends on page 401.) When you have become a very efficient pie crust maker, or don't have someone to share your dough with, you can cut this recipe by a third and still have enough for a double crust 9-inch pie. The resulting, smaller, Economy Version follows.

Although instructions are neat and tidy, the first (and maybe every) pie crust you make won't necessarily be. But don't ever let that discourage you. Just undertake pie making as a new and exciting adventure.

GENEROUS VERSION

3 cups King Arthur Unbleached All-Purpose Flour
1 to 1½ teaspoons salt (depends on taste and whether you use salted or salt-free shortening)
1 tablespoon sugar (optional and not necessary even for a sweet filling)
¾ to 1 cup shortening, your choice; the larger amount will make a richer, flakier crust but add more calories (to measure see page 278)
6 to 9 tablespoons ice water

ECONOMY VERSION

2 cups King Arthur Unbleached All-Purpose Flour
½ to 1 teaspoon salt
2 teaspoons sugar (optional)
½ to ¾ cup shortening
4 to 7 tablespoons ice water

THE TWO-STEP METHOD OF INCORPORATING THE SHORTENING

When you blend shortening into flour to make pie dough, you want to break it into lots of medium-sized pieces which become coated with flour in the process. By doing this in two steps, incorporating half the shortening at a time, you will create a dough with multiple pieces or pockets of shortening. When you roll this mixture out with a rolling pin, you flatten out all those little pieces of shortening which will bake into layers, or "flakes," hence the name of the crust.

Combining the Ingredients: In a large bowl, combine the flour, salt and sugar, if you're using it.

Cutting or Rubbing in the Shortening: With a pastry blender, two knives, or your fingertips, cut or rub half of the shortening into the flour mixture until it resembles cornmeal.

Then take the remainder of the shortening and cut or rub it in until the largest pieces are the size of peas.

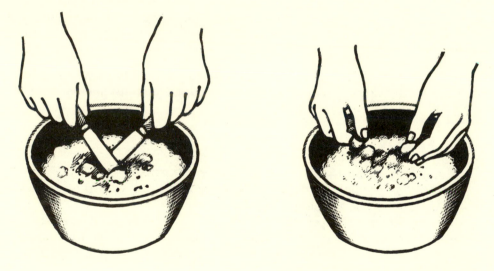

Although "rubbing in the shortening with your fingertips" may sound like just what you don't want to do, this is actually a very effective way to do this job. Your fingertips are usually quite cool so, if you work quickly, they won't really soften the butter much.

As you become more experienced, you will find that your fingertips will "know" when the shortening pieces are the right size. You can also lift and fluff the mixture with your fingertips to incorporate air, another ingredient in a flaky pie crust. The trick with this (or any) method is not to overdo it.

Adding the Water: By using ice water, you keep the shortening solid and minimize the development of the gluten.

You want to use just enough water so the dough will just stick together. Too little and your crust will be crumbly; too much will liberate the gluten in the flour, which can make the final pie crust tough. (Neither is a disaster. By experimenting with "too little" and "too much," you'll discover what's "just right," one of those things that experience will tell you.)

Sprinkle the ice water, one tablespoon at a time, over the flour/shortening mixture. With a fork, toss together the mixture you've just moistened and push it to one side. Continue until the dough is just moist enough to hold together when you press it.

Shaping the Dough: Gather the mixture together and cut it in two pieces. If you are making the dough for a double-crust pie, make one piece slightly larger than the other since it has to fit down into the pie plate. Gently press each piece into a round, flattened disk about 4 or 5 inches in diameter. This makes the dough easier to roll out later.

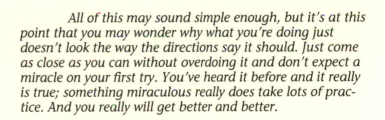

All of this may sound simple enough, but it's at this point that you may wonder why what you're doing just doesn't look the way the directions say it should. Just come as close as you can without overdoing it and don't expect a miracle on your first try. You've heard it before and it really is true; something miraculous really does take lots of practice. And you really will get better and better.

To Chill the Dough or Not to Chill: Now that you're this far along, you have several options.

> • **Overnight or Two-Hour Chill:** This will produce the most tender and flavorful crust. After you've divided and shaped your dough into disks, wrap them, separated, in plastic or waxed paper and put them in the refrigerator for about 2 hours or even overnight. This re-solidifies the shortening in the dough so it stays in its separate flaky state, it puts the gluten in the flour soundly to sleep, and it also matures the flavor of the dough. In addition to making a more tender crust, it will help keep it from shrinking as it bakes.

> • **Short Chill:** Another option is to chill the dough for a shorter period, from 30 minutes up to 2 hours, which will partially accomplish all of those things mentioned above.

> • **Chilling or Freezing after Shaping:** This time roll your crust out immediately after you finish mixing your ingredients (see next step) and chill the shaped crust, covered, right in the pie plate for 20 minutes to an hour before you fill and bake it. (You can also freeze pie crusts at this point so you always have one on hand.) Chilling the shaped crust before baking relaxes the gluten and minimizes shrinkage during baking. You can even chill a filled pie for 10 or 15 minutes, just enough to relax the gluten, which helps keep the crust from shrinking or pulling out of shape as it bakes.

> • **No Chill:** Roll out your crust and bake it (or fill and bake it) right away according to the directions below. As with many things, what you gain in time, you lose in flavor and texture but if you haven't overworked your dough during the mixing process, this method will still produce a pretty good pie crust.

Rolling Out & Shaping a Single or Bottom Crust: If your dough has been in the refrigerator for more than an hour, give it 10 or 15 minutes at room temperature to soften a bit.

The simplest way to roll out your dough is on a lightly floured surface with a floured rolling pin. (Give your rolling pin an occasional rubdown with a good-quality vegetable oil. It is not only good for the wood, it will help prevent it from sticking to a dough.)

Or roll your dough between two sheets of floured waxed paper, which gives you a bit more control and makes it easier to get the crust into a pie plate.

If you want to get a bit more "high-tech," you can buy a pastry cloth and sleeve for your rolling pin at most hardware stores. They are not critical to making a good pie crust, but they eliminate sticking and make it easier to get the dough into a pie plate.

Roll the dough from the center to the outside edge in all directions. Do it gently, without pushing down hard, because you don't want to squeeze out any air that is lurking in the dough. Use a spatula or bowl scraper to loosen it if it begins to stick, and throw a bit of flour underneath to keep it loose. Ditto with your rolling pin.

By rolling from the middle out to the edges, you enlarge the dough without making it "stretchy," which happens when you go back and forth over the whole thing. This helps keep it from shrinking when it bakes.

If the crust tears or splits, just patch it by moistening the edges and pressing some excess dough on the "wound." Dust it with a bit of flour, top and bottom, before you begin rolling again. If the wound is on the bottom crust, no one will see it; if it's on the top, only a grouch will care.

- **Single-Crust Shell:** Roll the crust until it is about $1/8$ inch thick and about 2 inches larger than the diameter of the pie plate. This gives you enough to make a good high rim. If you turn your pie plate upside down on the dough, you'll be able to figure out just about how big to roll it.

- **Double-Crust Bottom:** This one can be a little smaller, about $1 1/2$ inches larger than the diameter of the pie plate.

- **Latticed Crust Bottom:** Roll this out 2 inches larger than the diameter of your pie plate as this piece needs to come up and over the edges of the lattice.

Getting the Dough into the Pie Plate: If you've rolled the dough directly on the table, slide a spatula or bowl scraper under it and make sure it's completely loose from the rolling surface. Then fold it in half gently (or fold it over your rolling pin) and slide it onto your pie plate.

Unfold it and settle the dough down into the plate by lifting and pressing it. Don't stretch it to get it into place since that makes it want to pull into a funny shape while it bakes.

If you've used waxed paper or a pastry cloth, upend the plate onto the dough, slide your hand under the paper or cloth and turn the whole thing over, putting the dough, hopefully, right where it should be in the pie plate.

Trim the dough all around so it isn't too ragged and uneven, leaving yourself as much dough as possible to flute the edge.

Sealing the Bottom Crust: If you have a juicy filling, brush the bottom piece of dough with a little melted shortening or egg beaten with a bit of water. This keeps the juices from soaking into the crust and making it soggy. (Omit this step if you are prebaking the crust.)

Rolling Out & Shaping the Top Crust: A top crust is usually rolled a little thinner than the bottom crust, but don't be too concerned about this.

• **Double-Crust Top:** Since it needs to go over a filling and then under the edge of the bottom crust, you need to make it about 1¼ inches larger than the diameter of the plate. This size will give you a bit of leeway. You can always trim off what you don't need.

Pour in the filling and then moisten the edges of the crust with a little cold water. Cover the filling with the top crust. Again, trim anything that's too ragged.

• **Latticed Crust:** These are fun and often used on berry pies because the filling looks so appealing through the lattice, like roses through a picket fence. You can form them a couple of ways.

Simple Lattice: Roll out your second piece of dough, a little thinner than the first if you can manage it, and cut it into ½- to ¾-inch strips. After you fill the bottom shell, lay a row of strips one way across the pie and then a row at right angles to it. Trim the ends of the strips.

Woven Lattice: Roll out and cut your top crust into strips as for a simple lattice. Lay a row of strips across the filling as you did above. Fold back every other strip just to the middle of the pie. Lay another strip at right angles to these strips across the middle. Straighten out the strips you pulled back and cover the new strip. Then take the alternate strips and fold them back as far as you can (the strip running at right angles will determine how far that is). Lay down a second strip. Straighten out the strips you've folded back.

Repeat this until you get to the edge and then turn the pie around and follow the same pattern for the other side. Trim the ends of the strips.

Fluting & Finishing: Because a pie shell will always shrink a bit, flute the edge as near to the outside of the pie plate rim as you can. The trick is to make whatever you do look relatively uniform. This makes it look as if you know what you are doing, even if you have never done this before.

• **Single Crust:** Fold the extra dough underneath and then build up a rim by pressing or pinching the dough between the index finger of one hand and the thumb and index finger of the other. When you make an open pie, this forms a high edge which lets you be generous with the filling and helps keep it inside where it should be.

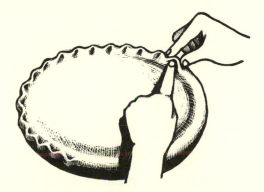

• **Double Crust:** It's not necessary to make this edge stand up as much since the filling will be contained by the top crust. Tuck the edge of the top layer of dough under the bottom edge.

To flute this lower profile edge you can use either the tines of a fork or your fingers. The fork is the easiest. Just work around the edge of the pie, pressing the dough onto the rim of the pie plate.

Although a fork does a good job of crimping, the pattern you make with your own fingertips makes the pie your own. Pinch the dough into ridges using your two index fingers or the index finger and thumb on one hand.

Before you put the pie in the oven, cut several slits through the top crust to allow steam to escape. This can be done as artistically as you want.

• **Latticed Crust:** Moisten the edge of the bottom crust. Bring the bottom crust up and over the ends of the lattice work. Pinch the bottom crust to the lattice and flute with your fingers. By bringing the bottom crust up and over the top, you will hide the edges of the lattice and help keep the pie juices in the pie shell where they belong.

Decorating & Glazing: Another way to be creative with your top crust, either solid or latticed, is to use some of the dough scraps to decorate it. Cut them into leaves, flowers, or something that is symbolic of what is in the pie or the occasion the pie is for. Stick these on with a bit of water, or egg beaten with a bit of water.

You can always bake a pie as is, but in some instances a wash or glaze makes it more attractive.

• Plain milk or cream will make a browner, shiny crust.

• An egg, white or yolk or both, beaten with 1 or 2 teaspoons of water will intensify the color and create a gloss; the egg white wash will be clear, the whole egg or egg yolk wash will be bronze.

A pastry brush does a fairly good job of painting on a wash but if you can get hold of one, a goose feather brush, available at many kitchen supply stores, does the best job. It spreads the wash evenly, doesn't exert any pressure on the dough and can be easily rinsed out and used many times. It's also reassuring to use something so primitive and know that modern technology can't improve on it.

If you have added pastry scrap decorations, an extra coating of wash will make them darker and more visible.

A sprinkle of sugar over an egg wash adds texture and makes the crust browner.

Baking: If, while a pie is baking, you find that the edge of the crust is browning too much and too fast, make a shield for it out of tin foil or turn down the heat.

• **A "Blind" Crust:** This crust is used for fillings that are not baked, or are baked for only a short time.

Fit a piece of aluminum foil on the inside surface of a single crust shell and fill it with something that will mimic a filling. This helps the crust keep its shape while baking. You can use anything from dried beans to small stones (washed free of grit) or special aluminum pellets that are specially made for this purpose. (Keep this "blind" filling in a jar to use again.)

Fifteen minutes before you want to bake the crust, preheat your oven to 425°F. Bake for 12 to 15 minutes. If the bottom begins to bubble up, give it a jab with a fork to make it go back where it belongs. Let it cool thoroughly before filling.

• **Single & Double Crusts for Filled Pies:** You will find baking directions for these with the pie fillings that begin on page 402.

Freezing Pie Crusts: Pie shells can be frozen both unbaked and baked.

If you freeze your pie shells unbaked, freeze them right in a pie plate. After they are solid, remove, stack and seal them in an airtight plastic bag. If you are going to bake a frozen crust blind (unfilled), bake it in a preheated 425°F oven right after it comes out of the freezer for about 15 minutes. If you're going to fill it, allow the shell to thaw first.

Baked crusts can also be frozen the same way unbaked crusts are, in the pan and then removed to an airtight plastic bag. Frozen pie crusts are great to have on hand, lots of hours of frozen labor.

Freezing expands and contracts the water in a pie crust, breaking down its structure. Those which freeze most successfully are made with a larger amount of fat which remains more stable when frozen.

INGREDIENT ALTERNATIVES FOR INTERESTING PIE CRUSTS

Before we give you recipes for specific pies, let's look at what ingredient choices you have and some ways to handle them. Some ingredients can be substituted for an equal amount of unbleached all-purpose flour. Others can be added to a dough to complement the flavors in the filling.

Dry Ingredients

King Arthur Stone Ground Whole Wheat Flour: You can substitute whole wheat flour for an equal amount of your unbleached white. Start with about ½ cup until you find a ratio you like. Whole wheat flour produces a crust with a "bite" and a hearty flavor that's great with savory fillings and is a wholesome alternative for sweet fillings too.

Grains & Nuts: You can always substitute extra bran or wheat germ. Rolled oats or oats that you've turned into "oat flour" in a blender or food processor can be substituted for an equal amount of your wheat flour, again starting with about ½ cup until you find a ratio you like. Try rye and buckwheat flours or cornmeal the same way. Ground or chopped nuts can be substituted as well.

When you substitute any of these non-wheat alternatives for wheat flour, don't use King Arthur Unbleached "Pastry" Flour (page 380). Because they don't contain gluten, they will reduce the percentage of gluten in your dough, just as cornstarch does.

Salt: A little salt brings out the flavor in a pie dough. If you are on a low- or no-salt diet, leave it out, try a salt substitute or, for a savory crust, substitute one of the herbal salt substitute mixtures.

Sugar: When you are making a dough for a sweet filling you can include a tablespoon of sugar with your dry ingredients but it's not necessary. The contrast of a slightly salty pie crust with a sweet filling is very appealing, much as it was to our medieval ancestors.

Herbs & Spices: A tablespoon of fresh or a teaspoon of dried herbs or spices can be added to the dry ingredients. Don't forget about paprika, curry powder, chili powder, dry mustard, poppy or sesame seeds, etc. You can also add 2 or 3 teaspoons of freshly grated lemon or orange peel or even candied ginger to complement the flavors of fruit pies.

Cheese: Add ½ to 1 cup of grated cheese to the flour before cutting in the lesser amount of shortening. This is great with savory pies, but it's fun with apple pies too.

Fats: Nutritional information about fats can be found in the Appendix.

Lard: On page 376, we briefly described some of the differences between the fats that are generally used to make pie crust. Fifty years ago, lard was the first choice of most pie makers. It was readily available, inexpensive and, because it physically breaks into larger flakes than vegetable shortening or butter, it produces the flakiest pie crust of all. There are people today who would use nothing else. If you decide to use lard, just make sure it is fresh.

Vegetable Shortening: Many good pie makers use vegetable shortening instead of lard these days, both for dietary reasons (since it's vegetable in origin, it contains no cholesterol) and its keeping qualities. It will stay stable at room temperature for unlimited periods and it's also best used at room temperature.

Vegetable shortening contains a certain amount of air so it's light by nature. When you cut it into your dry ingredients the way we've described above, it will produce a pie crust that is light as well as flaky. Some vegetable shortenings have less saturated fat than others but a small amount of saturated fat in a balanced diet is considered acceptable.

Butter: Butter has the best flavor, but because it contains some milk solids and water, a pie crust made solely with it tends to be harder. You might decide this is fine or you may choose to combine it with lard or vegetable shortening.

Butter contains significantly more cholesterol than lard and more saturated fat.

Vegetable Oil: It is also possible to use a vegetable oil, rather than a solid fat, to make pie crusts. (See page 397.)

Liquids: Although water is used traditionally in a pie crust, here are some other things to consider.

Milk Products: By using milk, or other milk products, you'll make a richer, mellower crust which browns very nicely.

Eggs: Eggs both leaven and create structure. By using an egg as part of the liquid in making pastry, you will create a dough that will puff up a bit and will hold together better. This is useful when making meat pies or "pasties" which you'll find later on in this chapter. It also makes the crust brown more quickly.

Lemon Juice or Vinegar: In many of the recipes (or "receipts") for pie crust you may have inherited from a grandmother or found in an old cookbook, you'll find one or two teaspoons of lemon juice or vinegar included in the ingredient list. The acid in either one tempers the gluten in the dough, helping to achieve that tenderness which is the sometimes elusive (but attainable) goal of the pie crust maker. As with the goose feather brush, old technology is often hard to beat.

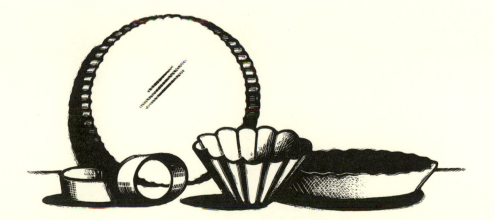

SIX MEDIUM FLAKE PIE CRUSTS

The next six recipes are all variations of the medium flake pie crust to give you some ideas about how to create a favorite of your own. Turn to Pie Fillings & Toppings, starting on page 402, for something delicious, savory or sweet to put inside.

GRANDMA DODGE'S
PIE CRUST WITH LARD

This is another medium flake crust, an old "receipt" handed down to Brinna Sands from her great-grandmother Dodge who was born before the Civil War. It's made with lard which makes the loveliest, flakiest, melt-in-your-mouth crust imaginable. We know that lard is on most people's lists of dietary "no-nos" for lots of good reasons, both real and imagined, but once in your lifetime, put your objections aside and try a pie made with this old-fashioned crust. (For nutritional information about lard, see the Appendix.)

Because it has an egg in it, this crust is particularly good with a very liquid filling. Grandma Dodge used it when she made her lemon pie which has graced Thanksgiving tables in Brinna's family for over a century. You'll find the filling for this on page 405. You can make a flakier version of this crust by eliminating the egg and using the larger amount of cold water.

> 2 cups King Arthur Unbleached All-Purpose Flour 🌾
> ½ teaspoon salt
> ½ to ¾ cup lard
> 1 teaspoon lemon juice
> 1 egg (optional, for a firmer, more golden crust)
> 1 to 4 tablespoons cold water (use the lesser amount if you include an
>   egg)

Blend the flour and salt together. With two knives, a pastry cutter or your fingertips, cut or rub half of the lard into the flour/salt mixture until it looks like bread crumbs. Cut in the remainder until the largest pieces are the size of peas.

Beat the lemon juice and egg into the cold water and sprinkle this over the flour/lard mixture blending it in lightly with a fork until the dough just holds together.

From this point you can either roll it out right away or chill it. Read about the merits of both on page 384.

BUTTERMILK PIE CRUST

This is a simple but rich crust that can be used for just about everything. (When Hillary and Althea, the Sands' grandchildren, are around, their Grandma makes this "generous version" so they can have Trimmings & Tail Ends, page 401.) For an "economy version," cut the ingredients by one-third.

2 1/2 cups King Arthur Unbleached All-Purpose Flour
1/2 cup King Arthur Stone Ground Whole Wheat Flour
1/2 to 1 teaspoon salt
1/2 cup vegetable shortening
1/2 cup (1 stick) butter, chilled
about 1/2 cup buttermilk

The buttermilk makes the crust mellow and full flavored. Like lemon juice or vinegar, its acidity helps temper the gluten.

Mix the dry ingredients together in a mixing bowl. With your fingertips, rub the vegetable shortening into the dry ingredients until it looks like bread crumbs.

Cut the butter into small pieces and rub them into the flour mixture until the largest pieces are about the size of peas and they are evenly distributed through-out the flour. Stir in the buttermilk lightly with a fork, one tablespoon at a time.

Divide the dough, press gently into two disks, wrap and chill. Proceed according to the directions on page 384.

A LOT OF PIE CRUST

This recipe is from Sally Thompson, who, when she bakes, does it in bulk. It will make 4 single-crust or 2 double-crust pies and contains an egg and some vinegar. Sally says this recipe browns faster than an eggless dough so "watch it!"

1 egg
1 tablespoon vinegar
1/2 cup ice water
4 cups King Arthur Unbleached All-Purpose Flour
1 tablespoon sugar
2 teaspoons salt
1 3/4 cups shortening

Beat the egg with the vinegar and water. Combine the ingredients as described in the Pie Crust Primer (page 382).

Refrigerate or freeze whatever dough you don't use (page 389).

Medium Flake Pie Crust "Mix"

Here's a way to save some time by making up your own pie crust mix. In doing this it's important to use a solid vegetable shortening which is stable at room temperature. If you want to make a double amount to have on hand, it will be easier to do it in two single batches. The amount of shortening is variable. Either end of the spectrum will make a good crust. A crust made with the larger amount will be obviously richer and fuller of calories. This much mix will also make about a dozen tart shells.

6 cups King Arthur Unbleached All-Purpose Flour
2 to 3 teaspoons salt
1 1/2 to 2 1/4 cups solid vegetable shortening

Put this mixture together as per directions in the Pie Crust Primer (page 382).

Storing & Using Your Pie Crust "Mix": Store what you don't use in an airtight container. Because all of the ingredients in this mix can be stored at room temperature, the mix can too. This makes it ideal to take on camping trips or anywhere you don't have refrigeration. Make sure you tuck in a piece of paper identifying what it is and how to use it.

• **For One 9-Inch Single Crust:** Measure about 1 1/2 cups of the mix into a mixing bowl without packing it. Add 3 to 5 tablespoons of cold water and proceed as you would for the Basic Medium Flake Crust. This much mix will also make about 6 tart shells.

• **For One 9-Inch Double Crust:** Measure about 3 cups of mix into a mixing bowl and use 6 to 8 tablespoons of water. Proceed as you would for the Basic Medium Flake Crust.

Ken Haedrich's
Three Grain Butter Pastry

Ken was clearly having fun in the kitchen when he developed this one. This recipe is a generous one, enough for one 9-inch, double-crust pie or 2 single-crust shells and can be used for both sweet and savory fillings.

1/2 cup yellow cornmeal (preferably stone ground)
1/2 cup old-fashioned rolled oats (or oat flour)
1 1/2 cups King Arthur Unbleached All-Purpose Flour
1 tablespoon sugar (omit if you're making a savory dinner pie or tart)
1/2 teaspoon salt
14 tablespoons (1 3/4 sticks) butter
1 egg yolk
3 1/2 to 4 1/2 tablespoons ice water

Put the cornmeal and rolled oats into a blender and pulse the machine, on and off, until the oat flakes are reduced to small flecks; a few remaining larger pieces are fine. (Do this only if you are using rolled oats rather than oat flour.)

Transfer to a large mixing bowl and stir in the flour, sugar and salt. Cut the butter into pieces and drop it into the dry ingredients. With two knives, a pastry cutter or your fingertips, cut or rub the butter into the dry ingredients until the mixture resembles coarse bread crumbs with the largest pieces about the size of small peas. (That means don't overdo it.)

Beat the egg yolk with 3 tablespoons of the cold water. Sprinkle this liquid over the dry mixture, mixing it in and lifting it gently with a fork. If the mixture is too dry, add more water, a tablespoon at a time until the dough holds together when you press it with your hands. It should be damp but not tacky.

Divide the dough in halves and flatten each into a disk about $1/2$ inch thick right onto a piece of waxed paper or plastic wrap. Wrap and refrigerate for at least 30 minutes before rolling. Proceed according to the directions on page 384.

Pastry with Baking Powder & Eggs

This crust is from the Jubinskys. The baking powder and eggs give it puffiness as well as flakiness. The addition of vanilla and lemon extracts intensifies the flavor of the Ricotta Orange filling (page 410) which is designed to go with it. After looking at these ingredients you can see how many liberties you can take with a pie dough.

2 cups King Arthur Unbleached All-Purpose Flour
$1/2$ cup sugar
2 teaspoons baking powder
$1/4$ teaspoon salt
$1/2$ cup lard or shortening (or half of each)
3 eggs, beaten
$1/2$ teaspoon lemon extract
$1/2$ teaspoon vanilla
1 egg yolk mixed with 1 tablespoon water (optional, for wash)

Combine the flour, sugar, baking powder and salt in a large bowl. Cut in $1/4$ cup lard or shortening until the mixture resembles cornmeal. Cut in the remaining fat until the mixture resembles small peas.

Combine the beaten eggs, lemon extract and vanilla and mix thoroughly. Tossing the flour mixture with a fork, add a small amount of the egg mixture at a time until the dough holds together without being either crumbly or sticky.

Form into a ball, wrap in waxed paper or plastic wrap and refrigerate for at least an hour (which gives you time to make the filling).

SIX SHORT FLAKE PIE CRUSTS

When you hear someone remark when tasting a pie, "My, that crust is short!," they are referring to our next kind of pie crust, "mealy" or "short flake." A short crust can be used interchangeably with a medium flake crust. The main difference is in their texture and the way they're put together. Many people swear by them. They're easy to make, they have great flavor and their texture is like that of a crisp butter cookie. A couple of them also have some important nutritional advantages.

BASIC SHORT FLAKE PIE CRUST

GENEROUS VERSION

3 cups King Arthur Unbleached All-Purpose Flour
1 to 1½ teaspoons salt (depends on taste and whether you use salted or salt-free shortening)
1 tablespoon sugar (optional and not necessary even for a sweet filling)
¾ to 1 cup shortening (your choice; the larger amount of shortening will make a richer crust but add more calories)
6 to 9 tablespoons ice water

ECONOMY VERSION

2 cups King Arthur Unbleached All-Purpose Flour
½ to 1 teaspoon salt
2 teaspoons sugar (optional)
½ to ¾ cup shortening
4 to 7 tablespoons ice water

To make a crust "short" rather than flaky when using a solid shortening, cut or rub the shortening into the flour in one stage until it's all like bread crumbs, no pea-sized pieces.

When you cut or rub in the shortening this way, the fat breaks into lots of very tiny, or short, pieces (this means there are no large pieces of fat which will create flakes). The resulting dough bakes into a crisp rather than a flaky crust.

From this point, you continue as in the Pie Crust Primer (page 383). That's all there is to it. Most people's crusts probably fall somewhere in between medium and short.

No-Roll Vegetable Oil Pie Crust

Here is another way to make a pie crust "short." This crust is made with vegetable oil so it contains little saturated fat and no cholesterol, and you don't even have to roll it out. Instead you mix it up right in a pie plate and push it into place with your fingertips. For those of you who are a bit daunted by the prospect of pie crust making, this one is so easy you will hardly know you've made a pie crust and the crust itself is amazingly tender and crisp. It's a great one for children to begin with because it is somewhat akin to the art of making mud pies!

This type of dough is best baked "blind" or without a filling (page 388) to make it as crisp and short as possible. The ingredients listed are for a single 9-inch pie shell, but you'll find measurements in parentheses for a larger amount, which gives you enough dough for a crumbled topping.

1 1/2 cups King Arthur Unbleached All-Purpose Flour 🖋 (2 cups)
1 1/2 teaspoons sugar, optional; use with a sweet filling (2 teaspoons)
1 teaspoon salt (1 1/4 teaspoons)
1/2 cup vegetable oil (1/2 cup vegetable oil plus 2 tablespoons)
2 tablespoons milk (3 tablespoons)

Stir the dry ingredients together thoroughly right in your pie plate. Add the milk to the vegetable oil and beat together with a fork until it blends together in a milky white emulsion. Through creating this emulsion you incorporate some air which makes the oil "less oily" and makes a lighter pie crust.

Make a well in the middle of the dry ingredients and pour in the oil/milk emulsion. Blend this together with a fork and then, with your fingertips, press the dough out to cover the bottom and sides of the pie plate. Make it as even as you can and push enough up the sides so you can pinch together a rim as you would a traditional pie crust.

Although in this case chilling the dough won't solidify the fat, it will relax the gluten in the flour which helps keep the pie shell from shrinking. So, if you have time, cover the formed pie shell with plastic wrap and chill it for about an hour.

Fifteen minutes before you want to bake your shell, preheat your oven to 425°F. Bake for 12 to 15 minutes.

(If you're making a crumbled topping for your pie with the larger measure of ingredients, use two-thirds of the dough for the bottom. Bake this blind, as above. Sprinkle the remaining one-third of the dough over the filling before baking.)

HOT WATER PIE CRUST

Although this particular recipe comes out of our old King Arthur Cookbook, Easy Home Baking, *now out of print, you'll find variations everywhere. Like crusts made with vegetable oil, the method used here flies in the face of traditional pie crust–making methods which demand that everything be kept as cold as possible.*

This is another variation of the short crust, one that is crisp but not flaky. The addition of baking powder lightens the texture and also means that the pie should be baked as soon as it is shaped so as not to lose the leavening power of the baking powder. This will make a 2-crust, 9-inch pie.

2 cups King Arthur Unbleached All-Purpose Flour
1 teaspoon salt
$^1/_2$ teaspoon baking powder
6 tablespoons of boiling water
$^3/_4$ cup shortening (all vegetable or half vegetable and half butter or lard)

In a mixing bowl, blend together the dry ingredients.

Pour the boiling water over the shortening and beat until it's creamy (another emulsion). Let this mixture stand until it has reached room temperature.

After the water/shortening mixture has cooled, add it to the dry ingredients. Mix it with a fork very lightly and only enough to allow the mixture to cling together.

Roll and shape as for the Medium Flake Pie Crust on page 384.

VIRGINIA BENTLEY'S "NEVER-FAIL PIE CRUST"

This recipe comes from an old King Arthur Flour friend who reveled in the joys of preparing and sharing food. Virginia's first "big" book, the Bentley Farm Cookbook, *in which this recipe first appeared, was inspired by an old cookbook of her grandmother's and dedicated to her granddaughter, "a torch-passing gesture across the generations." In Ginny's memory, we pass the torch to you.*

Her favorite pie crust is tender and crisp and breaks apart much the way a butter cookie does. It too is made with vegetable oil. Like the other crusts we've covered so far, it can be used for almost anything.

About this recipe Virginia said, "There are purists who disdain pastry made with oil. I can't imagine why. This is one sure-fire pie crust which never fails, and, if present research is correct, corn oil is better for one than animal fats. Another advantage is that there is no floury board to clean up after rolling the pastry. And most important, this pastry is tender and delicious."

Never-Fail Pie Crust

(Enough pastry for a 9-inch, one-crust pie)
Be sure to have waxed paper on hand!

2 cups all purpose flour*
1 teaspoon salt
½ cup corn oil
¼ cup cold milk

Stir ingredients together, lightly, in order given. Form into a ball. Flatten and shape into a circle on a piece of waxed paper. Cover with another piece of waxed paper and roll out, with a rolling pin, to desired size. Peel off the top piece of paper. Place pie plate, upside down, onto the pastry. Holding pastry and plate together, turn plate right side up. Gently peel waxed paper off pastry. If pastry tears, it is easily mended. Press pastry firmly onto plate with fingers and a fork. If you are going to bake shell with nothing in it, prick it all over with a fork so that pastry will not blister. Otherwise do not make holes in pastry, for the filling will hold it down. Make a nice, rippled, upstanding edge with your fingers, and then push edge inward a bit, so it is not stuck to rim of pie plate. This holds the filling in better, so it doesn't run over, and also keeps edge from browning too fast. A good pie should not be stuck to the pie plate anywhere after it is baked. Ideally, it should slide around in the plate. This makes for easy serving. This recipe is a little more than enough for one pie (see page 275), so you have plenty of pastry to play with to make a good high, thick collar.

Warning: Never chill this pastry before rolling. Chill it all you want after it is arranged in pie plate. In fact, I always place the pie plate in the refrigerator while preparing filling.

For baking pie shell alone: Bake in preheated 475° oven for about 10 minutes. Cool on rack for maximum crispness.

★ I use King Arthur unbleached flour.

FOOD PROCESSOR PIE CRUST I

The action of the food processor makes these crusts short. This recipe will make a enough pastry for an 8-inch, double-crust pie or a single crust for a 9- to 11-inch pie.

1¾ cups King Arthur Unbleached All-Purpose Flour
½ teaspoon salt
1 tablespoon sugar (optional)
½ cup (1 stick) unsalted butter, cold or frozen, cut into 4 pieces
2 tablespoons solid shortening
about 6 tablespoons ice water

Using the steel blade of the food processor, quickly blend flour, salt, sugar, butter and shortening.

Slowly pour in the ice water through the feed tube while pulsing the machine. Process only until a mass of dough has formed on the side of the bowl. Don't overdo it. Wrap the dough in plastic and chill for at least an hour. (You can also freeze the dough at this point.)

Roll out according to directions on page 384. This crust can be filled and baked at this point, or baked blind (page 388).

FOOD PROCESSOR PIE CRUST II

This recipe, from Ann Berry, goes together quite differently from the preceding dough but it is equally good and versatile. It makes enough for a double, 9-inch crust.

2 cups King Arthur Unbleached All-Purpose Flour
1 teaspoon salt
⅓ cup water
⅔ cup vegetable shortening

Put the flour and salt in the processor and pulse to mix them. Remove ⅓ cup of the flour mixture and add ⅓ cup water to make a paste. Add the shortening to the remaining flour mixture in the food processor and pulse 12 times until the mixture resembles large curds. Add the paste and pulse 3 to 4 times until it's just mixed.

Spoon out half the dough (it will be wet) onto waxed paper and shape into a round pancake. Cover with waxed paper. Repeat with the remaining dough and refrigerate at least 15 minutes, enough time to relax the gluten.

As in the above recipe, roll out according to directions on page 384. This crust can be filled and baked at this point, or baked blind.

TRIMMINGS & TAIL ENDS

When you're making pies with a "helper," and are using the Generous Version of our Basic Pie Crusts, here are some things to do with all the pastry that doesn't get used up.

Ingredients You'll Need

pieces of leftover pie dough
a little softened butter

Ingredients to Play With

- cinnamon sugar
- grated cheese
- leftover pie filling
- jam or jelly

Ideas to Play With

Cinnamon Sugar Crisps: This is the simplest option. Roll out the dough until it's thin, brush it with a little butter and sprinkle it with cinnamon sugar. Cut into any shape you like and bake on a lightly greased baking sheet at 425°F for about 10 minutes

Trimming Curls: If you have some pieces that are large enough, after they've been buttered and sprinkled with cinnamon sugar, they can be rolled up and sliced into half-inch pastry versions of tiny sticky buns.

Place them on their sides on a lightly greased baking sheet and bake at 425°F for 10 to 15 minutes depending on how large they are. This can also be done with a little jam or jelly or grated cheese, which needs to be pressed gently into the surface of the dough.

Tail End Tarts: You can always reroll the trimmings and cut tiny circles of dough, 5 or 6 inches in diameter, to let a helper make a tiny, tart-sized version of what you're making, in a (lightly greased) muffin tin or custard cup. Bake at 425°F for about 15 or 20 minutes depending on the size.

Pie Crust "Play Dough": Even if the dough gets rolled and rerolled and used generally like modeling clay while you go about your own baking, it can still be decorated and baked. A child's definition of success lies more in being with you and in "doing" than in results. If you catch some of the enthusiasm in the process, all the mess is worth it!

• PIE FILLINGS & TOPPINGS •

The fillings that follow can be baked in any of the pie crusts described at the beginning of the chapter. They can be used in tart shells as well, or in any way in which you're inspired to experiment.

Rolled crusts are better for double crust pies. Pressed crusts are best used for single crust pies. Almost all filled pies can be frozen before baking, except for the cream varieties.

Unless otherwise noted, these fillings are for a 9-inch, unbaked pie crust.

SWEET FILLINGS

APPLE OR BERRY PIE

You can use frozen berries if you thaw them enough to separate them.

1 double crust
4 cups firm, tart apples, pared and sliced, or 3 cups cleaned berries
1 tablespoon King Arthur Unbleached All-Purpose Flour
1/2 to 1 cup sugar, white or brown, the amount depending on the tartness
    of the apples and/or berries
juice and grated rind of half a lemon
1/4 teaspoon nutmeg or allspice (optional in the berry variety but good)
1/2 teaspoon cinnamon (optional in the berry variety)
2 tablespoons butter or margarine

Preheat your oven to 450°F.

Place the sliced apples or berries in the pie shell so they are slightly mounded in the middle. Sprinkle the lemon juice over them.

Mix the flour (and spices) with the sugar and sprinkle over the fruit. Place the butter in dots on the top.

Cover with the top crust, solid or latticed, and bake for 15 minutes. Turn the temperature down to 350°F for a further 15 minutes.

CRANBERRY APPLE PIE

This delicious combination comes from Dorothea Douple (Martha's grandmother) from that town in Pennsylvania which is a mecca for chocoholics, Hershey. The first time she made this pie, the fruit and nuts went in uncooked. The recipe arrived written that way with a note saying that the next time she made it, she was going to cook the berries, sugar and orange peel with flour to thicken it before pouring it over the apple. This, she felt, would make a better flavor. "I have a 'why-not' curiosity," she says. She's obviously a "can-do" person, much like her granddaughter Martha (whose nickname here in the office is "Martha Do"). She made the change and she was right. The flavor was better and the new version is the one you see here.

1 double crust
1 1/2 cups chopped cranberries
1 cup sugar
1/2 teaspoon grated orange peel (zest)
1 tablespoon King Arthur Unbleached All-Purpose Flour
1/3 cup orange or cranberry juice
6 tablespoons chopped pecans
3 firm, tart apples sliced 1/4 inch thick
1/2 teaspoon cinnamon
1 tablespoon butter

Preheat your oven to 425°F.

In a medium saucepan, cook the cranberries with the sugar, orange peel, flour and juice until the mixture is slightly thickened.

Sprinkle half the pecans on the bottom crust of an unbaked pie shell. Make 2 layers of apples on top of the nuts. Sprinkle these with cinnamon and dot with butter. Pour the cranberry mixture over the apples and sprinkle on the remaining pecans. Cover with a latticed top (directions on page 386).

Bake for 30 minutes or until the crust is golden and the berries are bubbly.

CRANBERRY PIE

1 double crust
1/2 cup raisins
1/2 cup water or cider
2 tablespoons King Arthur Unbleached All-Purpose Flour
1 cup sugar
1/4 teaspoon salt
1 1/2 cups cranberries
1 tablespoon butter

Preheat the oven to 450°F.

Heat the water or cider in a medium-sized saucepan, add the raisins and let them soak for 5 minutes.

In a small bowl, mix together the flour, sugar, salt and cranberries. Add this to the saucepan and simmer, covered, for 5 minutes. Stir in the butter. Remove from heat and allow to cool. Pour the cooled mixture into your pastry shell.

Cover with a latticed top crust (directions on page 386).

After the pie is in the oven, turn the heat down to 350°F and bake for 40 minutes.

RHUBARB PIE

> 1 double crust
> 2 eggs
> 1 cup sugar
> 2 tablespoons King Arthur Unbleached All-Purpose Flour
> 3 cups rhubarb cut into $1/2$-inch pieces
> 1 teaspoon grated or minced orange rind
> 1 tablespoon orange juice
> 1 tablespoon butter
> egg wash made by beating 1 egg with 1 tablespoon water
> sugar for sprinkling.

Preheat your oven to 450°F.

Beat the eggs very slightly. Beat the sugar and flour into the eggs and add the orange rind and juice. Combine with the rhubarb and put in your unbaked pie shell. Dot with butter.

Cover with a latticed top crust, following the directions on page 386. Brush the lattice with the egg wash and sprinkle with sugar.

Put the pie in the oven, turn the temperature down to 350°F and bake for 35 to 40 minutes.

STRAWBERRY RHUBARB PIE

Substitute $1^1/2$ cups fresh strawberries, sliced in halves or quarters, for $1^1/2$ cups of the rhubarb. Reduce the sugar to $3/4$ cup and use lemon rind and 1 teaspoon lemon juice in place of orange rind and orange juice.

SWEDISH RHUBARB PIE

This recipe is from our Public Relations Director, Ellen Davies' great-aunts, Millie and Rose Saco, who live in Arlington, Massachusetts.

1 double crust
3 cups diced rhubarb
1 1/2 cup sugar
1 teaspoon cinnamon
3/4 cup butter or margarine, melted
1 cup King Arthur Unbleached All-Purpose Flour
1 egg
1/2 cup chopped walnuts
a pinch of salt

Preheat your oven to 350°F.

Fill the bottom crust with the diced rhubarb. Sprinkle with 1/2 cup of the sugar and the cinnamon. In a separate bowl, combine the butter or margarine, the remaining cup of sugar, the flour, egg, nuts and salt. Spoon this mixture over the rhubarb.

Cover with the upper crust (page 386) and bake for 45 to 50 minutes or until golden brown.

LEMON PIE

This recipe came from Brinna Sands' great-grandmother Dodge. Although it can be baked in any pie crust, you'll find Grandma Dodge's original crust on page 392.

1 double crust
1 cup sugar
3 tablespoons King Arthur Unbleached All-Purpose Flour
generous pinch of salt (about 1/4 teaspoon)
grated (or minced) rind of 1 lemon
juice from 1 lemon (about 3 tablespoons)
scant 1/2 cup milk
1 egg, beaten
3 tablespoons butter, melted
1 egg, beaten with 1 tablespoon water for wash (optional)

Rather than grating the lemon, try cutting a very thin layer of rind off the entire lemon with a very sharp knife. Mince this finely. This produces slightly larger pieces of rind which, when you come upon them, give you a little burst of flavor and something to chew.

Preheat your oven to 400°F.

Mix the sugar, flour and salt in a medium-sized mixing bowl. Blend in the lemon rind and lemon juice.

Break the egg into the milk in a small bowl and beat until light. Blend this into the lemon mixture. Fold in the butter last.

Pour the filling into an unbaked pastry shell and cover with a top crust. Moisten the edge of the bottom crust, tuck the edge of the top crust underneath the bottom crust and flute the edges with a fork or with your fingers (page 387).

Prick holes or cut a design in the top piece of dough with a knife.

If you have any pastry trimmings left over, you can cut out small shapes (maybe lemons?) and attach them artistically to the top crust with a bit of water. To make them a bit more visible, brush them with a wash made of an egg beaten with a tablespoon of water.

Bake for 30 to 35 minutes.

LEMON MERINGUE PIE

This is another old classic from Easy Home Baking.

1 prebaked single pie crust
$^1/_3$ cup King Arthur Unbleached All-Purpose Flour
$^3/_4$ cup sugar
$^1/_4$ cup cold water
1 cup boiling water
3 egg yolks
$^1/_4$ teaspoon salt
1$^1/_2$ tablespoons butter
$^1/_4$ cup lemon juice
grated rind of 1 lemon
1 recipe Meringue Topping (page 420)

Mix the flour and sugar in a saucepan with the cold water. Gradually add the boiling water, stirring constantly. Cook over low heat (continue stirring) until thick and clear.

Beat the egg yolks until light and drizzle them slowly into the simmering flour/sugar/water mixture. (Keep stirring.) Remove from the heat and add the salt and butter.

When the mixture has cooled slightly (an occasional stir will help), add the lemon juice and rind. When it has cooled completely, pour the filling into the baked pie shell.

Preheat your oven to 325°F. While the oven is heating (and the filling is cooling), prepare the meringue.

Pile the meringue lightly on top of the lemon filling in the pie shell and bake for 20 minutes or until the meringue is delicately browned.

Fluffy Pumpkin Pecan Pie

This recipe is another inspiration of Dorothea Douple, who also gave us the recipe for Cranberry Apple Pie.

> 1 unbaked single crust with a "stand up" rim (page 387)
> 1/2 cup sugar
> 1/4 teaspoon salt
> 1 teaspoon cinnamon
> 1/2 teaspoon nutmeg
> 1/4 teaspoon ground cloves
> 1/4 teaspoon ginger
> 1 cup strained and drained freshly cooked pumpkin (or 1 cup canned)
> 1 cup milk
> 3 eggs, 1 separated and 2 whole
> 1/2 cup chopped pecans

Preheat your oven to 425°F.

Mix the sugar, salt and all the spices together and combine with the pumpkin. Blend in the milk.

Beat 2 of the eggs and 1 egg yolk until light and add to the pumpkin mixture. Beat the remaining egg white until soft peaks form and then fold into the pumpkin mixture.

Sprinkle half the pecans on the unbaked pie shell. Pour the pumpkin mixture over these. Sprinkle the remaining pecans on top.

Bake for 15 minutes and then reduce the heat to 400°F for 20 more minutes or until a knife inserted in the center comes out clean. The filling will be slightly puffed but will fall evenly on cooling.

SOUTHERN PECAN PIE
OR NORTHERN BUTTERNUT MAPLE PIE

Either version makes enough filling for a single 9-inch, partially baked (10 minutes at 425°F) pie crust.

SOUTHERN VERSION

> 3 large eggs
> 1/4 cup brown sugar, packed
> 1 cup dark corn syrup
> 1 teaspoon vanilla
> 1/2 teaspoon salt
> 1 cup pecan halves
> 2 tablespoons butter

NORTHERN VERSION

> 3 large eggs
> 1/4 cup brown sugar, packed
> 1 1/2 cups maple syrup (darker syrup has more flavor)
> 1 teaspoon vanilla
> 1/2 teaspoon salt
> 1 cup butternuts, shelled
> 2 tablespoons butter

If you're making the maple syrup variety, boil the syrup down to make about a cup and allow it to cool while you chill the pie dough. Make sure you use at least a 3-quart saucepan when you boil the syrup. If it looks as if it wants to overflow while it cooks, toss in a tiny piece of butter.

While the syrup cools, roll out and bake your pie shell. After the shell has baked, turn the oven temperature up to 450°F.

Beat the eggs until light. Add the sugar, syrup, vanilla and salt. Pour into the partially baked pie shell. Sprinkle the nuts over the top of the filling and dot with butter.

Bake for 10 minutes. Reduce the heat to 350°F and continue baking for a further 20 to 25 minutes.

You can always mix and match the ingredients of either variety or substitute some other nuts. Another "optional extra," which will completely change the character of either pie but will appeal to some people's tastes, is to add 1/2 to 1 cup of chocolate chips.

PUMPKIN PIE

1 single crust
1½ cups cooked pumpkin
¾ cup sugar (white or brown), honey or maple syrup
1 teaspoon cinnamon
½ teaspoon ginger
½ teaspoon nutmeg
½ teaspoon salt
3 eggs
1½ cups milk, evaporated milk or cream (or a combination)
1 tablespoon butter, melted

Preheat your oven to 450°F.

Put the cooked pumpkin in a mixing bowl. Stir in the sweetener of your choice, the spices and the salt.

Beat the eggs slightly and add the milk or cream. Combine the pumpkin and milk mixtures. Stir in the melted butter.

Pour into the pastry shell and bake for 10 minutes. Turn the heat down to 350°F and continue baking for 35 minutes.

MOTHER MAGNUS'S PINEAPPLE CHEESECAKE

This recipe is from Marilyn Magnus's Norwegian mother-in-law, which may or may not have a bearing on the origin of this delicious dessert.

1 unbaked 11-inch or 2 unbaked, 9-inch single pie crusts
1 can (20 ounces) crushed pineapple
¾ cup sugar
½ cup King Arthur Unbleached All-Purpose Flour
¼ teaspoon salt
2 tablespoons fresh lemon juice
2 eggs
1 teaspoon vanilla
½ cup milk
2 cups (1 pound) cottage cheese
1 cup (½ pint) sour cream

Preheat your oven to 350°F.

Place the prepared crust(s) in your pie plate(s) according to the directions in the Pie Crust Primer, page 385.

Drain the pineapple well. (Marilyn suggests that you drink the juice for a little mid-pie-making pick-me-up.) Spread the pineapple evenly over the pie crust.

Combine the rest of the ingredients and beat well with an egg beater. Pour this mixture over the pineapple.

Bake for about 1 hour or until the top(s) is(are) golden brown.

Ricotta Orange Pie

1 recipe Pastry with Baking Powder & Eggs, page 395 (a double crust)
¼ cup King Arthur Flour
¾ cup sugar
4 cups (2 pounds) whole milk ricotta
4 eggs, beaten
1 tablespoon orange extract
1 tablespoon grated orange peel
½ teaspoon vanilla

Hint from an Italian baker: "The day before baking, wrap the ricotta in cheese-cloth to drain for 24 hours in the refrigerator."

Combine the flour and sugar. Add the drained ricotta, eggs, flavorings and grated peel and blend until smooth. Chill this filling while you roll out the pie dough.

Preheat your oven to 375°F.

Divide dough in halves and roll one out slightly thicker than for regular pie crust. Line the pie plate with this half. Roll out a second circle.

Fill the shell with the slightly chilled ricotta filling. Top with the remaining circle of dough. Trim and flute the crust as described in the Pie Crust Primer starting on page 387.

Cut a vent hole in the center of the top crust and brush on the egg wash.

Bake for 45 minutes or until the filling is set and the top crust is golden brown. Remove from the oven and cool on a wire rack.

VANILLA CREAM PIE

This cream filling and its variations were designed for pies, but they can be used as fillings for tarts, puff pastry, cream puffs, etc. For additional variations on this classic custard filling, see Custards (page 315).

1 prebaked single crust
2 tablespoons King Arthur Unbleached All-Purpose Flour
3 tablespoons cornstarch
$1/2$ teaspoon salt
$1/2$ cup sugar
$2^1/2$ cups milk
3 egg yolks
1 tablespoon butter
1 teaspoon vanilla
sweetened whipped cream or Meringue (page 420) for top

Preheat your oven to 325°F if you are making meringue for the top.

Mix the dry ingredients together in a saucepan.

In a separate pan, scald the milk and then pour it over the dry ingredients, stirring constantly. Cook this mixture until it is smooth and thick.

Beat the egg yolks, and add some of the hot mixture to them. Combine the yolks with the custard and cook for 1 minute. Add the butter and the vanilla. Remove from the heat and allow to cool.

When the mixture is cool, pour it into the baked pastry shell. Top the pie with chilled whipped cream or cover it with meringue and bake for 20 minutes (or until the meringue is delicately browned).

CREAM FILLING VARIATIONS

Banana Cream: Prepare the Vanilla Cream Filling as above. Add 2 sliced bananas to the cooled custard before pouring it into a baked pastry shell. Top with whipped cream or meringue, as above.

Butterscotch Cream: Using the recipe for Vanilla Cream Filling, substitute brown sugar for the white sugar and use 4 tablespoons of butter rather than 1 tablespoon. Top with whipped cream or meringue, as above.

Cherry Cream: Add 1 cup of cooked, drained cherries to the Vanilla Cream Filling. (If the cherries are unsweetened, use $2/3$ cup sugar instead of $1/2$ cup sugar.) Top with whipped cream or meringue, as above.

Coconut Cream: Prepare the Vanilla Cream Filling. Add ½ cup shredded coconut before pouring it into the baked pastry shell. Cover with meringue. Sprinkle the meringue with ¼ cup of coconut. Bake for 20 minutes at 325°F.

Chocolate Cream: Prepare Vanilla Cream Filling adding 2 squares of baking chocolate to the hot milk. Top with whipped cream or meringue, as for Vanilla Cream Pie.

Pecan Butterscotch Cream: Add ½ cup pecan meats to the Butterscotch Cream recipe. Top with whipped cream or meringue, as above.

Pineapple Cream: Add 1 cup of drained, crushed pineapple to the cooled Vanilla Cream Filling before pouring it into the baked pastry shell. Top with whipped cream or meringue, as above.

Boiled Cider Pie

This next recipe is a special one that comes from Janice George, a friend of the Sands'. Janice remembers eating this pie as a child when it was made by her grandmother, Ida Pierce Godfrey. Ida, who was born the year the Civil War broke out, was part American Indian (probably Abenaki since her family, one of Vermont's oldest, has long lived in the northern Connecticut River Valley). Janice says this recipe did not originate with her grandmother so it could be over one hundred fifty years old.

> 1 double crust
> 3 eggs
> ½ teaspoon salt
> ⅓ cup sugar or maple syrup
> ¾ cup boiled cider
> ½ teaspoon cinnamon
> 2 large or 4 to 5 small common crackers, oyster crackers or other hard
>   biscuits, crushed (somewhere between ½ and ⅔ cup crumbs)

Boiled cider is made much the way you make maple syrup out of maple sap. It is available in some stores in New England but to make your own, boil 1 gallon of unpasteurized apple cider down until you have about 1 quart. This makes a thick fluid which is really a loose jelly because of all the pectin in the juice. It is tart and delicious. (If you boil off another 1½ cups, you'll have a true cider jelly.)

Preheat your oven to 400°F.

Beat the eggs together with the salt until light and lemon colored. Add and beat in the sugar or syrup, boiled cider and cinnamon.

Crush the crackers with a rolling pin (don't use a blender or food processor because the crumbs will be too fine) and stir into the cider mixture.

Pour into a pie shell. Cover with a latticed top crust (don't worry if it sinks into the filling) and bake for about 30 to 35 minutes. As the pie bakes, the crackers come to the top and sort of merge with the crust so the top of the pie has a different, lighter texture than the bottom.

The original directions called for a 325°F oven and a baking time of 45 minutes. But, as Janice says, the original oven that this pie was baked in was wood fired and it was difficult to be precise about temperatures and baking times. Try either way and if you're lucky enough to have a wood fired oven, you'll be getting pretty close to the original.

NUTTY VARIATION

Although this idea is not part of the original recipe, experimenting is half the fun.

Pour the boiled cider filling into a single unbaked shell. In place of the crackers, sprinkle on a cup of chopped butternuts (which are local to New England), pecans or walnuts for a crunchy, nutty alternative.

MINCEMEAT PIE(S)

Mince pies have been eaten at Christmas time for hundreds of years. Back in "Old England" they contained mutton and were in fact called "mutton pies" until the end of the sixteenth century. Medieval mincemeat was quite different from the mincemeat we're generally familiar with today. It contained as much meat and suet as fruit and only a touch of sugar. It was really a spiced, savory dish rather than a sweet one, very much like the original plum pudding.

Today traditional mincemeat still contains meat, but fruit is now the dominant ingredient and the sweetening has increased by a large measure (quite an evolution from its original form). Rather than mutton, it's usually made with beef. In the north country of New England you'll find it often made with venison and sweetened with maple syrup.

Our version is a typical New England mincemeat. We are giving you the whole process of making the pie even though the mincemeat is best when it's made several weeks ahead of time. Like a plum pudding, it needs time for the flavors to mellow and mature.

The ingredients for the mincepmeat are by no means written in stone. If some aren't available, substitute what you have on hand or what appeals to your own sense of taste. If you're a vegetarian, you can even leave out the meat.

The important thing when you make this is to surround it with a bit of ceremony. One legend says that everyone needs to stir it once clockwise while it cooks or while it's "ripening" to bring luck in the New Year.

The Mincemeat

    1 pound venison or lean beef
    1 quart apple cider (or 2 cups cider and 2 cups cranberry juice)
    1 cup maple syrup
    1 cup brown sugar, packed
    1 teaspoon cinnamon
    1 teaspoon mace
    $1/4$ teaspoon allspice
    $1/4$ teaspoon nutmeg
    $1/4$ teaspoon cloves
    $1/4$ pound ground suet or $1/4$ pound (1 stick) butter
    $1/2$ pound currants ($1 1/2$ cups firmly packed)
    $1/2$ pound golden raisins ($1 1/2$ cups firmly packed)
    $1/2$ pound cranberries, cut in half (about 1 cup)
    minced rind and juice of 1 lemon (or orange if you like it less tart)
    $1/4$ cup "spirits"
    1 cup blanched chopped almonds or other nuts (optional, for crunch)
    granulated sugar to sprinkle on top of small pies (optional)

Trim the meat if necessary and cut it into cubes. Pour the cider in a large saucepan or small kettle and add the sweeteners and spices. Add the meat and bring this mixture to a boil, then turn down and simmer for about 2 hours or until the meat is tender.

Remove the meat with a slotted spoon, turn off the heat and add the currants, raisins, cranberries and lemon rind and juice. Let these steep while you grind or mince the meat along with the suet, if you're using it. (Suet is added to deepen the flavor of the mixture.)

Return the meat (and suet) to the fruit mixture, bring back to a boil and then down to a simmer for about $1/2$ hour. Boil off enough liquid so the mixture is thick.

If you opted not to use suet, melt and blend in the butter at this point. Butter was used in place of suet in years past but was considered a luxury in a pie. Since these days we're more apt to have butter, it may not be quite such a luxury for us and may be more to our twentieth-century taste.

After the mixture has cooled, add $1/4$ cup of "spirits." This may be anything from a maple liqueur to brandy to rum to a hearty red wine. This adds flavor and helps preserve the mincemeat.

Cover and store it in a cool place for 2 or more weeks if you have time. This recipe makes 2 quarts of mincemeat, enough for $2 1/2$ to 3 dozen small pies (or tarts) or three 9-inch pies.

The Pie(s)

Although mincemeat has changed in character over the centuries, the spirit in which it's made and eaten has survived fairly intact. In medieval England, to eat a small mince pie on each of the twelve days of Christmas was to insure that each of the twelve coming months would be blessed. We may not want to eat quite so many mince pies, but this season of the year certainly demands at least one.

To make two double-crust 9-inch pies or 12 tiny pies for the 12 days of Christmas, you'll need to double our recipe for Traditional American Pie Crust (page 381), make A Lot of Crust (page 393) or double a favorite recipe of your own. You'll also need a wash made by beating an egg with a tablespoon of water.

Rolling & Shaping

• **Double Crust Pies:** Follow the directions for rolling and shaping in the Pie Crust Primer, page 384.

• **Tarts:** Roll out your dough and cut the pastry into rounds 5 or 6 inches in diameter or big enough to fill the cups of a muffin tin, with smaller circles for the tops. Carefully place the larger circles in your muffin tin.

Fill the shells about half full with mincemeat. Moisten the rim of the dough with cold water, place the slightly smaller rounds of the dough on top of the filling and, with a fork or your fingers, press them to the bottom crusts. If you wet the rim of the muffin tin before you press top to bottom, the little pies will come away from the tin more easily after they are baked.

Chilling: Cover and let these chill for about 15 or 20 minutes while you preheat your oven to 450°F.

Finishing & Washing: Before baking, make a slit, plain or fancy, in the top of the pies. Brush with the egg wash, and sprinkle the small pies with a little granulated sugar if you like.

Baking: After you put the pies in the oven, turn the heat down to 375°F and bake the 9-inch pies for about 35 minutes and the smaller ones for about 20 minutes. If they begin to brown too quickly, turn the heat down to 350°F for the final 5 to 10 minutes. Let the small pies cool for about 5 minutes before removing them from the muffin tin.

In this country, we often eat mince pie with vanilla ice cream. In England, it's customary to serve little Christmas pies with cream or Hard Sauce (page 322). When you sit down to eat it, think about all the other people over the ages who've sat down to eat a mince pie and who've joined you in hopes that the year ahead will be as rich as the pie itself.

SAVORY FILLINGS

MEAT PIE

This is a fairly basic formula for a savory, or meat pie, filling. It can be altered according to taste and what's in your garden or refrigerator. It is not highly seasoned because the flavors of the ingredients are all you need. This is enough filling for two 9-inch, double-crust pies (see A Lot of Pie Crust, page 393). You'll find directions for using this to make a good-sized pot pie with the Batter Crust recipe, page 454.

2 double crusts
3 tablespoons butter or drippings
2 pounds cubed or diced beef, turkey, chicken, lamb, etc. (uncooked)
1 large onion (1 to 1½ cups), chopped
½ to 1 cup chopped green pepper
½ to 1 cup chopped celery
1 to 1½ cups sliced carrots
1 to 1½ cups sliced mushrooms
2 to 2½ cups of stock or broth
4 tablespoons King Arthur Unbleached All-Purpose Flour
egg wash made by beating 1 egg with 1 tablespoon water

In a large, fairly hot skillet, melt the butter and then cook the cubes of beef, chicken, etc. until they are nicely browned. Remove them to a small bowl.

Sauté the onion, green pepper, celery, carrots and mushrooms until they begin to brown. Pour in the stock and return the meat to the skillet. Cook uncovered until the liquid is reduced and the meat is tender, about 15 or 20 minutes.

Remove some of the remaining liquid and allow it to cool slightly. Blend in the flour, mixing until it's smooth. Return this to the skillet and cook until the juices have thickened slightly. Remove from the heat.

While the filling cooks, roll out your 4 rounds of pie dough. Line two pie plates. Brush the bottoms with some of the egg wash to keep them from getting soggy while the pies bake.

Pour the filling into the pie shells. Cover with the remaining circles of dough and flute the edges (page 387). Cut vents in the tops and brush with the egg wash to give the crusts a bronzed appearance.

Fifteen minutes before you are ready to bake your pies, preheat your oven to 500°F. Bake for 10 minutes at 500°F, and then turn the heat down to 375°F and bake for 20 to 25 minutes more.

TOURTIÈRE

A tourtière is a Christmas pie from Quebec whose roots go back to medieval France. Back in the fifteen and sixteen hundreds, a French "tourt" was a very fashionable meat pie and the container it was baked in was (and still is) called a tourtière. On this side of the Atlantic the original tourte has taken the name of its container and is most often made with pork. It has maintained its original dignity with its Christmas associations. In northern New England, you will often hear it pronounced "toocheer." This pie is at its best served hot, but makes a tasty and hearty cold meal as well.

1 double crust of your choice (lard was used traditionally; see Grandma
      Dodge's Pie Crust and use the variation with egg, page 392)
1 1/2 pounds ground pork (traditional, but you could also substitute beef,
      chicken or turkey)
1/2 pound diced potato (optional)
1 large chopped onion (1 to 1 1/2 cups depending on inclination)
1 cup water
1/2 teaspoon salt (adjust after cooking)
1/4 teaspoon allspice
1/4 teaspoon nutmeg
1/4 teaspoon savory
1/4 teaspoon black pepper
egg wash made by beating 1 egg with 1 tablespoon water

Prepare whichever pie dough you choose and chill it while you make the filling.

Place the ground pork, onion, water and spices (the medieval influence) in a saucepan and bring to a boil. Turn down to a simmer and cook uncovered for 25 to 30 minutes. Stir it frequently to keep it from sticking. You want the liquid to cook down to prevent the filling from being too soupy.

While the filling cooks, roll out two rounds of pie dough. Line a 9-inch pie plate with one. Brush the bottom with some of the egg wash to keep it from getting soggy while it cooks.

Pour the filling into the pie shell. Cover with the second circle of dough and crimp the edges.

Cut vents in the top and brush with the egg wash to give the crust a bronzed appearance.

Fifteen minutes before you are ready to bake your pies, preheat your oven to 500°F. Bake for 10 minutes at 500°F; then turn the heat down to 375°F and bake for 20 to 25 minutes more.

INDIVIDUAL TOURTIÈRE

Cut rounds of pastry to fit the cups of a muffin tin. Fill about two-thirds full. Cover with small top rounds of dough and flute the edges. Make small artful slits in the top crust and brush with the egg wash.

Bake these for 10 minutes at 500°F and an additional 15 minutes at 375°F.

A FORMULA FOR QUICHE

Although the quiche swept through the culinary circles of America some years ago, it is still a great way to use up leftovers and provide an all-in-one-container meal. It's also a great medium for experimentation, since almost anything can go in a quiche if you follow this fairly basic formula of 1½ cups of vegetables and/or meat, 1½ cups cheese and 1½ cups custard. Even this can be tinkered with.

> 1 single crust (Try the No-Roll Vegetable Oil Crust on page 397, if
> you're in a hurry or, to make a unique crust, see page 389.)
> 3 to 4 eggs
> 3 tablespoons King Arthur Unbleached All-Purpose Flour
> 1 to 1½ cups liquid (milk, evaporated milk, buttermilk, yogurt, sour
> cream, cream, etc.)
> 1½ to 2 cups cooked, chopped vegetables and/or meat
> 1½ cups grated cheese (anything goes here: Cheddar, Swiss, Parmesan
> or a combination)

For a crisper crust (this step isn't necessary or critical), prebake whichever pie crust you choose for 10 minutes at 425°F. When you take the pie shell out of the oven, turn the heat down to 375°F.

Prepare the custard by combining the eggs, flour, and a liquid of your choice. Pour a bit of this mixture on the bottom of the crust to seal it and keep the juices from soaking in.

Strew your pie shell with the vegetables, meat, etc., and then sprinkle the cheese over all. Some vegetable suggestions are onions, peppers, carrots, broccoli, cauliflower, snow peas and/or mushrooms. Cooked turkey, bacon, fish, even tofu can be added.

Pour the remainder of the custard over the whole thing and bake for 35 to 40 minutes or until the custard is firm and a knife inserted in the middle comes out clean.

CLASSIC QUICHE LORRAINE

Although a quiche can contain almost any combination of ingredients, there are certain classics which are fairly specific. This is one.

1 single crust
4 strips of bacon
1 onion, thinly sliced
3 eggs
1 1/2 cups cream
1/4 teaspoon nutmeg
1/4 teaspoon white pepper
1/2 teaspoon salt
1 cup freshly grated Gruyere or other Swiss cheese
1/2 cup freshly grated Parmesan cheese

Preheat your oven to 450°F.

Cook the bacon until it is crisp. Remove it from the pan and sauté the onion very quickly until it is barely transparent.

In a mixing bowl beat together the eggs, cream, spices and salt. Pour a little of this custard into the bottom of the pie shell to seal it. Arrange the onion slices over this and sprinkle the bacon, crumbled, on top.

Mix the cheeses together. Sprinkle them over the bacon and pour the custard mixture over all.

Bake for 15 minutes and then reduce the heat to 350°F. Continue baking until a knife inserted in the center of the quiche comes out clean, a further 15 to 20 minutes.

TOPPINGS

These three sweet toppings are specifically called for by recipes in this chapter but can be used anywhere you want. (See the Appendix for information about foods containing uncooked egg whites.)

EASY CHOCOLATE SAUCE

3 ounces (squares) semi-sweet chocolate
2 tablespoons butter
1 tablespoon vanilla extract, brandy or rum

Melt the squares of semi-sweet chocolate in a small saucepan or double boiler. Fold in the butter and a tablespoon of brandy or rum.

MERINGUE

This recipe makes enough for one 9-inch pie.

3 egg whites
1 tablespoon cold water
6 tablespoons sugar

Preheat oven to 325°F.

Beat the egg whites with the tablespoon of water until stiff. Beat in the sugar. Pile the meringue on top of pie filling and swirl it to form peaks.

Bake for 20 minutes until delicately browned.

ROYAL ICING

1 egg white
1 1/2 cups confectioners' sugar
1/8 teaspoon salt
1 teaspoon lemon juice

Beat the egg white with the rest of the ingredients until it forms peaks.

• TARTS & TURNOVERS •

A tart is the European antecedent of the traditional American pie. The name "tart" is French in origin, so many tart pastries have French names. "Flan" is the English equivalent, "torte" and "kuchen" the Germanic. Our American single crust, open fruit pie is the closest thing to a European tart. The shape of a tart is a little different, however, as it is traditionally baked in a special pan with fluted, vertical sides.

Although we tend to associate fruit with tarts, a tart shell can be used for savory fillings as well. The shells themselves are most often made with a "short flake" pastry, which you've already met, or a "long flake" pastry, which you will be introduced to in the next recipe.

Turnovers are usually smaller, individual pastries made to be eaten by hand. Their names vary depending on their ethnic orgins, but all of them, sweet and savory, are delicious.

LONG FLAKE PASTRY

This variation of pastry is somewhere between medium flake, which is described in the Pie Crust Primer, and a true puff pastry, which is described further along.

REBECCA CUNNINGHAM'S
CARAMELIZED FRUIT TARTLETS

Up the road and across the river from our company headquarters, in Lyme, New Hampshire, is a restaurant called D'Artagnan. D'Artagnan has not only withstood the test of time here in the Upper Valley but it has never lost its original touch of magic. It is owned and run by Peter Gaylor and Rebecca Cunningham, a husband-and-wife team whose enthusiasm for their venture infuses everything they do. Each one orchestrates separate parts of each meal, but together they create a glorious symphony of flavor, color and design. For those on the receiving end, it is a total culinary experience that transcends all of its individual parts. You may find D'Artagnan's equal in other parts of the world, but you won't find better.

One of Rebecca's triumphs is her desserts, and in particular, her fruit tarts. She has happily agreed to share her knowledge with us so we can attempt to reach the same culinary heights in our own kitchens. The pastry for these tarts is "long flake," somewhere between medium flake and true puff pastry. As Rebecca explains, it is one of the most versatile pastries she uses.

FLORENCE MILLER'S PASTRY WITH CREAM

"The dough for these tartlets is the basic recipe that my grandmother, Florence Miller, taught me years ago which she uses for every sweet and savory pie, tart, and delicious pastry curl. For years I have used it at D'Artagnan. By making additional "turns" in the pastry, as one does with a true puff pastry, you can change this rich dough into a glorious tender pastry which closely resembles a true puff pastry. My favorite use for it is for Caramelized Fruit Tartlets. Here, I've outlined the details for the pastry making."

Although this dough can be refrigerated or frozen, you can cut the ingredients in half to make a smaller amount if you wish. The full recipe will make eight 5-inch tartlets.

4½ cups King Arthur Unbleached All-Purpose Flour
2 cups pastry flour
2 teaspoons salt
3 cups (6 sticks) unsalted butter, chilled
6 ounces heavy cream, chilled
6 ounces cold water

At this point in time, King Arthur does not have a pastry flour on the retail market. Pastry flour is lower in protein than our King Arthur Unbleached All-Purpose Flour, which means it will form a weaker gluten network when it's mixed with a liquid. Rebecca's recipe works best with a ratio of about 2 parts of King Arthur Unbleached All-Purpose Flour to 1 part pastry flour. If you haven't access to a pastry flour, for this recipe you can reduce the protein and temper the gluten by using ½ cup of cornstarch along with 6 cups of King Arthur Unbleached All-Purpose Flour. According to Rebecca who made the tarts both ways, this combination produces an excellent result, very close to the pastry flour version.

Making the Dough: Blend the dry ingredients together in a large mixing bowl. Cut the butter into small pieces and add them to the dry ingredients. With your fingertips press and re-press the pieces of butter into the flour until they are about the size of quarters.

What you are doing here is forming lots of layers and separations in the flour/ butter mixture. By using your fingertips, which are generally cool, you can create these layers and keep the mixture light and airy in the process.

Pour the chilled cream and water together into the center of the flour/butter mixture. Mix with a spatula (which presses the flour and fat together into flakes rather than blends them) until you are able to gather the dough in the center of the bowl.

Handle the dough lightly. Pressing too hard or kneading it will only make the mixture more homogeneous in content and tough in texture. What you want is a delicate, differentiated, or distinctly layered dough which creates steam and bubbles in the heat of the oven, resulting in "puff."

Divide the dough in fourths (in halves if you've made only half the recipe). Press each piece evenly flat between two sheets of plastic wrap. Don't form the dough into a ball. These flattened pieces of dough should be covered and chilled for at least 2 hours.

At this point the dough is similar to a medium flake pastry. After it has been chilled, it can be rolled out to be used for traditional pie crusts, tarts and all sorts of other pastry casings. To make delicious and flaky pastry fingers, roll out the dough until it's about ⅛ inch thick. Cut it into rectangles that are 1 x 5 inches and push sliced almonds into the surface vertically (and randomly). Bake in a preheated 375°F oven for 10 to 12 minutes. When they are cool, dust them with confectioners' sugar.

Rolling & Folding the Dough: To produce the layers which will create the "puff," you next roll and fold your dough. It is this process which creates long flake pastry.

Dust your surface with a scant amount of flour. Work with 1 piece of chilled dough at a time. With a lightly floured rolling pin, roll the pastry from the center, with a light and even pressure, away from and toward you. Do not roll toward either side or press down heavily. Keep rolling until the lengthened and thinned pastry is a rectangle about 8 x 30 inches and about ⅛ inch thick. Fold this in thirds so you have an 8 x 10-inch rectangle.

Cover and chill the dough for 20 to 30 minutes. With the short, or 8-inch side, facing you, roll out the dough one more time as you did above, to an 8 x 30-inch rectangle. Fold again and chill for at least 2 hours. (If you are making tartlets with poached fruit, this is a good time to prepare the fruit.)

Shaping the Dough for the Tartlets: Remove the dough from the refrigerator and allow it to come to 60°F to 65°F, just below room temperature.

Dust your rolling area lightly with flour again. From the center of the dough, begin rolling toward and away from you as well as toward each side this time. The desired thickness for the tartlets is ⅜ inch and they should be about 4½ to 5 inches in diameter. Each piece of dough will make 2 tartlets, or 8 for the entire recipe.

Cover the cut-out circles and refrigerate. While they chill, prepare the filling according to whichever of the following tartlet recipes you have chosen.

At D'Artagnan we use a 5-inch round plate for caramelized tartlets. There is no filling other than spiraled fresh or poached fruit on the top. The pastry gets the limelight with a special fruit garnish. It's the perfect finish to any meal and may go well with the last of your dinner wine.

APPLE TARTLETS

"For caramelized apple tartlets, we use Cortland, Northern Spy, Rome and Jonathan apples which are firm, crisp and tart. McIntosh apples tend to shrink too much during baking." This recipe makes enough filling for 4 tartlets.

½ recipe Florence Miller's Pastry, cut into circles and chilled
6 apples (1½ apples per tartlet)
butter
vanilla sugar

Vanilla sugar is made by burying a split vanilla bean in a jar of granulated sugar for at least 2 weeks. During this time, the bean infuses the sugar with its flavor. (Vanilla sugar is also great in morning coffee.)

Preheat your oven to 400°F.

Place the rounds of chilled pastry on a parchment-covered baking sheet. Prick the center in about 4 places to create a vent for steam. (This prevents the pastry from blowing up in the middle and tumbling the fruit off.)

Peel, slice and spiral the apples on top of the pastry, overlapping the pieces. Sprinkle the tops with vanilla sugar and dot them with cold butter. Place the tarts on the top rack of your oven.

Keep the oven at 400°F for the first 10 minutes, then turn it down to 350°F for 10 to 15 minutes longer. They should take about 20 to 25 minutes in all to cook but keep an eye on them and watch for the color you want. The apples will brown, especially on the edges, and the pastry will puff and triple in height.

"This pastry can be baked until it's darker than we are accustomed to seeing in the United States. This tends to bring out the wholesome flavor of the wheat. In Paris, I whispered across the table to my husband, 'That tart is burned!' the first time I encountered a truly caramelized apple tartlet. He laughed and exclaimed that I was accustomed to seeing and tasting the typically anemic-looking baked goods on the American side of the Atlantic. Truly the flavor of the wheat is intensified and matches the caramel flavor of the apple and the sugar in this tart when you dare to bake them longer."

POACHED PEAR, PEACH OR APRICOT TARTLETS

"If you use these poached fruits in the same manner as the apples, you can create an equally elegant and very intensely flavored glazed tartlet. The taste here is very smooth and delicious with dessert wines and brandies, many of which you can match with the fruit of the tart such as Pear William Brandy or Liqueur de Peche. Great fun!"

The Almond Honey Foil Gaylor on the next page is optional but lifts these tartlets from the heavenly to the sublime.

    1 recipe Florence Miller's Pastry, cut into circles and chilled
    simple syrup made of 3 cups water and 2 cups sugar
    grated rind of an orange (optional)
    vanilla bean (optional)
    juice of a lemon
    4 pears, peaches or apricots (½ fruit for each of the 8 tartlets)

Preheat your oven to 400°F.

Bring the water and sugar to a boil. If you wish, you can add orange rind and/or a vanilla bean to the simple syrup. They add a sweet and smooth flavor without added sugar. Cool and add the lemon juice.

Peel the pears, peaches or apricots. (Peaches and apricots can be peeled very easily if you first submerge them in boiling water for 20 or 30 seconds and then dip them in cold water.) Slice them from top to bottom around the center. So the fruit will maintain its shape during poaching, Rebecca suggests that you leave the peeled fruit pieces attached to the pit or core.

To poach, submerge the fruit with a slotted spoon in the simple syrup. Cover the pot with a paper towel and a plate that just fits into the circumference of the pot (or over it if that's as close as you can come). You want the mixture to be able to breathe a little bit.

Bring the fruit mixture to a low simmer. Check it after 5 minutes by piercing it with a knife and looking at the flesh. When fruit is properly poached, it can be easily pierced with a knife and will be bright yet firm. The total cooking time depends on the ripeness of the fruit as well as its texture, size and variety, so, again, keep an eye on it.

Cool the fruit while it is still submerged and covered. Rebecca does this quickly by plunging the pot into a larger pot filled with ice and water. Quick cooling is important so you stop the cooking process. If the fruit becomes mushy, it loses its appeal. A most wonderful aspect of poaching peaches and apricots is that they become very bright in color and, after they've absorbed the syrup, almost fluffy in texture.

Once the fruit is cooled, proceed as you would for the Apple Tartlets. If you are using the foil below, follow the baking instructions that accompany it. (The lower baking temperature prevents the honey from scorching.)

Almond Honey Foil Gaylor
(for Pear, Peach or Apricot Tartlets)

Although Rebecca and Peter have their own domains in the kitchen, each adds a dimension to the other's expertise. This foil is an inspiration of Peter's. In cooking, a foil is something that adds contrasting flavor to accentuate or intensify the flavor of the primary ingredient. Here, almonds and honey set the fruit off in a very different and utterly delicious way. This recipe makes enough for 8 tartlets.

1 cup blanched sliced almonds
3 tablespoons honey (clover, orange blossom or raspberry)
3 tablespoons vanilla sugar (page 424)

Preheat your oven to 375°F.

Blend these ingredients all at once in a food processor until the honey brings the almonds and sugar together in a crunchy looking paste. Don't overprocess; the particles of almond should not be too small or disappear.

Divide the foil into 8 pieces. Roll each piece into a small round ball. Place them, one at a time, between two layers of waxed paper or plastic wrap. With a rolling pin, roll each ball lightly into a flattened round approximately 4½ inches in diameter.

Take the pastry circles out of the refrigerator and place them on a parchment-covered baking sheet. Pierce them with a fork around the center about 4 times to allow steam to escape while they bake. Place a round of the almond honey foil over the pastry.

Spiral your choice of pear, peach or apricot over the top. Rebecca uses fairly large pieces of fruit which, as the tartlets bake, let the pastry puff up in between, allowing the exposed foil to bubble and the fruit to caramelize.

To bake them, place the tarts on the top rack of your oven. Keep the oven at 400°F for the first 10 minutes, then turn it down to 350°F for 10 to 15 minutes longer. They should take about 20 to 25 minutes but keep an eye on them and watch for the color you want.

"Voila! These are relatively low in fat compared to pastry cream filled tarts. They are crispy, crunchy, juicy and beautiful! What more could we want from fruit?"

A TROVE OF TARTS

Because tart shells can vary in so many ways, we are presenting the shells and the fillings that were designed to go with them together. This does not mean you can't use these shells with other tart fillings or vice versa. There are a number of pie fillings in the preceeding section that would make wonderful tart fillings as well. Mix and match as you please.

The basic dough for tarts has a French name, Pâte Brisée, or, literally, "pastry made of small broken pieces." This refers to the butter which is incorporated into the flour in very tiny pieces making this pastry short rather than flaky. Tart dough is richer than traditional pie dough and usually needs to be chilled to be rolled out. Some variations are so rich that you need to push them into place with your fingertips.

STRAWBERRY DEVONSHIRE TART

The dough for this tart is tender but sturdy and can be rolled out like a traditional pie crust. This recipe will make one large, 9-inch tart and is designed to be baked in a traditional tart pan with a removable bottom (see Appendix). If you do not have such a pan, use a 9-inch regular or springform cake pan.

Allow several hours to make this dessert, as the shell needs to be baked before you fill it and the finished tart should be chilled before serving.

Pâte Brisée (Tart Shell)

> 1 cup King Arthur Unbleached All-Purpose Flour
> 1 tablespoon sugar
> 6 tablespoons ($^3/_4$ stick) butter, at room temperature (soft but firm)
> 1 egg yolk
> ice water

Making the Shell: In a mixing bowl, combine the flour and sugar and rub in the butter with your fingertips. Work in the egg yolk and 1 tablespoon ice water with your fingers until dough holds together. (Don't overdo it.)

Pat the dough into a flat round. Roll it out between sheets of waxed paper or plastic wrap until it's 2 inches larger than the diameter of your pan.

Remove the top paper and turn the pastry over your pan, centering it. Let it slip down into the pan and gently pull off the bottom sheet of paper. Use your fingertips to press the pastry evenly onto the bottom and sides.

Trim the top edge, cover and chill for at least an hour.

About 15 minutes before you want to bake the shell, preheat your oven to 375°F. Prick the dough with a fork to prevent it from developing bubbles. Bake for 15 minutes or until it is lightly browned.

Filling

> 3 ounces cream cheese, softened
> 3 tablespoons sour cream
> 1 to 1½ quarts fresh strawberries
> 1 cup sugar
> 3 tablespoons cornstarch
> water

Making the Filling: Beat the cream cheese together with the sour cream until fluffy and smooth. After the tart shell has baked and cooled, spread this mixture on the bottom. Cover and refrigerate while you prepare the rest of the filling.

Wash and hull the strawberries. With a fork, mash approximately 1 cup of imperfect berries and then force them through a sieve. Return them to your measuring cup and add water, if necessary, to the one-cup mark.

Combine the sugar and cornstarch in a saucepan. Add ½ cup water and sieved berries. Cook over medium heat, stirring, until mixture is clear and thickened, then boil gently for about 1 minute. Stir to cool slightly.

Assembling the Tart: Cover the cream cheese/sour cream mixture with a single layer of fresh berries with their tips, or bottoms, up. Pour the strawberry/sugar mixture over them. Chill for at least an hour before serving.

LEMON CURD TART
WITH RASPBERRY SAUCE

This next variation of tart pastry, flavored with lemon peel and vanilla, is pressed into a tart or pie plate.

Pressed Short Crust Shell

> 1 cup King Arthur Unbleached All-Purpose Flour
> 1 tablespoon sugar
> ¼ teaspoon salt (omit if you use salted butter)
> ¼ teaspoon grated lemon peel
> ½ cup (1 stick) unsalted butter, not too cold
> 1 tablespoon water
> ½ teaspoon vanilla extract

Rather than grating the lemon for the filling, try cutting a very thin layer of rind off the entire lemon with a very sharp knife. Mince this finely. This produces pieces of rind slightly larger than the grated variety and, when you come upon one in the tart, it gives you a little burst of flavor.

Preparing the Crust: In a mixing bowl, combine the flour, sugar, salt and lemon peel.

Cut the butter into 2-inch slices and rub it into the flour mixture with your fingertips, two knives or a pastry blender until it is the texture of coarse bread crumbs or cornmeal.

Combine the water and vanilla and sprinkle it over the flour/butter mixture and blend lightly with a fork just until the pastry will hold together when you press it.

Gather it into a ball, wrap it and let it rest for 30 minutes. (You can either use it immediately or freeze it for up to a month.) If you plan to bake it immediately, preheat your oven to 375°F.

Press the pastry into a 9-inch pie or tart pan, distributing it as evenly as possible over the bottom and sides so it will bake evenly. Prick the shell in a few places with a fork.

Bake for about 25 minutes or until it's a light golden brown. While it bakes, prepare the filling.

Filling

>1 cup sugar
>1 tablespoon grated or minced lemon peel (zest)
>4 eggs
>½ cup lemon juice
>½ cup (1 stick) unsalted butter

Making the Filling: Beat the sugar, lemon peel and eggs together in a small saucepan. Stir in the lemon juice and butter. Cook over medium heat until the mixture comes to a simmer.

Turn down the heat and continue to simmer, stirring constantly, until the mixture thickens (about 7 minutes). Remove from the heat, cover and let this cool, stirring occasionally.

Fill the cooled tart shell with the lemon filling and refrigerate it while you prepare the sauce.

Sauce

  3 cups fresh raspberries or 1 (10-ounce) package frozen raspberries
  1 teaspoon kirsch or cassis

Making the Sauce: Purée and sieve the raspberries to remove the seeds. Sweeten to taste. (If you use frozen berries that are already sweetened, don't add more sugar.) Stir in the kirsch or cassis.

Drizzle the sauce in thin stripes across the tart in one direction. With a toothpick, draw lines across the stripes to create a pattern.

Chill thoroughly (about an hour) before serving.

SANDBAKKELSE

This is a Swedish version of tart pastry from our old Easy Home Baking. *It's a large recipe and will make at least 3 dozen small tarts. Although it is put together quite differently from the previous recipe it, too, is pressed with the fingertips into either traditional sandbakkelse pans (see Appendix) or, just as successfully, muffin tins.*

These tart shells are delicious filled with fresh fruit, any pie filling, mincemeat, chocolate or other mousse, lemon curd, etc. You can top them with whipped cream, toasted almonds, fruit pureé, etc.

  2 cups (4 sticks) unsalted butter
  2 cups sugar
  1 egg
  ½ teaspoon salt
  1 teaspoon vanilla
  5 cups King Arthur Unbleached All-Purpose Flour

Preheat your oven to 425°F.

Cream the butter and sugar together until very light. Beat in the egg, salt and vanilla until fluffy. Gradually stir in the flour.

Press a ¼ inch layer of the dough onto the bottom and sides of sandbakkelse pans or a regular muffin tin. Prick well with a fork.

Bake until delicately browned, about 12 minutes. Let them cool thoroughly before you fill them.

Puréed Peach & Lemon Curd Tart

This tart was developed by Mary Ann Esposito, the creative and energetic host of "Ciao Italia," a series on Italian cooking which made its premier appearance on many public television stations in the northeast in 1989. It has been so successful, it will be televised nationwide in the coming season.

The crust for this tart is a sweet variation of Pâte Brisée (page 427), the traditional butter-rich tart. It is easily made in a food processor. The tart itself will serve about 8 people.

Pâte Sucrée (Pastry Made With Sugar)

>   1 cup King Arthur Unbleached All-Purpose Flour
>   2 tablespoons sugar
>   1/8 teaspoon salt
>   6 tablespoons butter, frozen (for the food processor) or chilled (if you are making the dough by hand)
>   1 egg yolk
>   1 tablespoon cold water
>   1 tablespoon apple jelly

Making the Pastry: Mary Ann puts these ingredients together easily and quickly in a food processor. You can do it by hand almost as easily.

> **Food Processor:** Put the dry ingredients in the processor and pulse to blend. Cut the frozen butter into pieces and add to the dry ingredients with the egg yolk and water. Process for 5 to 10 seconds. Do not overprocess.

> **By Hand:** Blend the dry ingredients in a mixing bowl. Cut in the chilled butter with two knives, a pastry blender or your fingertips until the mixture resembles bread crumbs. Beat the egg yolk with the cold water and sprinkle this over the flour/butter mixture, blending quickly with a fork.

Form the dough into a ball, wrap and chill for 30 minutes.

Preheat your oven to 425°F.

Roll out the dough to fit a 9-inch, loose-bottom tart pan or a 9-inch cake pan. Prick the bottom of the shell and bake for 12 to 15 minutes. (If you wish, you can press aluminum foil over it and weigh it down with beans to keep it from bubbling.)

Let the shell cool completely before filling. While the tart shell cools, prepare the filling, starting with the lemon curd.

Lemon Curd

    grated rind and juice of 4 medium lemons
    ¼ cup (½ stick) sweet butter, cut up into pieces
    1¼ cups sugar
    4 eggs lightly beaten

Making the Curd: In a double boiler over simmering water, combine the lemon rind, juice, butter and sugar, stirring until the butter melts. Mix the eggs into the butter/sugar mixture. Stir constantly over medium-low heat until the mixture thickens enough to coat the back of a spoon. Don't let it curdle. Remove it from the heat and let it cool.

Peach Purée Filling

    2 cups (10-ounce package) dried peaches
    ½ cup water
    ⅓ cup sugar
    1 teaspoon almond extract

Making the Filling: While the lemon curd cools, cook the dried peaches in ½ cup of water (you may need to add more water). Add the sugar and cook until the peaches are soft. Put them in a food processor and purée. Add the almond extract and set this mixture aside.

Assembling the Tart: Brush your cooked tart shell with 1 tablespoon of apple jelly that has been warmed and melted. This will seal the crust. Next spoon in about 2 cups of the cooled lemon curd. (The lemon curd directions above will make 2 to 2½ cups.) Spread the curd to the edges of the tart shell.

Spread the peach purée over the lemon curd and refrigerate.

Topping

    1 cup heavy cream
    ⅓ cup confectioners' sugar
    canned mandarin orange slices, drained and patted dry
    fresh mint sprig (for garnish)

The Final Steps: Whip the heavy cream until it is fairly stiff. Beat in the confectioners' sugar, and spread over the tart.

Arrange mandarin oranges on the whipped cream. Place the fresh mint sprig in the center for garnish.

French Fruit Cake

Our next tart, with its interesting name, comes from Stephanie Random, whose husband is the graphic artist for our advertising agency, DiBona, Bornstein & Random. Stephanie acquired her baking talent from one of the best bakers around, her mother, Zella Lane, who for many years, was the radio voice of Betty Crocker.

Tart Shell

> 1 cup King Arthur Unbleached All-Purpose Flour
> 1 tablespoon sugar
> 1/4 teaspoon salt
> 1/2 cup (1 stick) butter
> 1 egg, beaten

Blueberry Cinnamon Filling

> 2 to 3 cups of fresh blueberries
> 1/2 to 1 cup sugar (this depends on your sweet tooth)
> 2 tablespoons cornstarch
> 1 teaspoon cinnamon

Making the Shell: Mix the dry ingredients. Cut in the butter until the mixture looks like bread crumbs. Drizzle in the beaten egg, using a fork to distribute it evenly.

Press the dough with your fingertips onto the bottom and sides of a 9-inch pie plate. Cover and refrigerate while you prepare the filling.

About 15 minutes before you are ready to bake your shell, preheat your oven to 400°F.

Making the Filling: Mix the filling ingredients gently in a mixing bowl and then spread evenly over the dough in the pie plate.

Baking: Bake for 20 minutes or until the tart shell is golden and crisp, or "a pretty color," says Stephanie. When the 20 minutes' cooking time is up, you may see undissolved grains of sugar, which is fine.

APFELKUCHEN

Apfelkuchen is a German tart. Literally translated it means "apple cake." The French Fruit Cake on the preceding page is a close cousin whose name may have been the result of a loose translation.

Dough

1 cup King Arthur Unbleached All-Purpose Flour
1 tablespoon sugar
a pinch of salt
8 tablespoons (1 stick) chilled butter
1 egg yolk
$\frac{1}{2}$ teaspoon milk

Apple Topping

4 tablespoons of sugar, white or brown
1 tablespoon cinnamon
4 or 5 apples
lemon juice, enough to sprinkle on the apples
1 egg yolk
3 tablespoons cream

Making the Crust: Measure the flour into a medium-sized mixing bowl. Stir in the sugar and salt. With a pastry cutter, two knives or your fingertips, cut or rub in the butter until it looks like coarse bread crumbs.

Beat the egg yolk with the milk and blend quickly into the flour/butter mixture. Handle the dough as little as possible to keep the dough tender. Pat this dough into an 8 x 8-inch cake pan or a pie plate.

Cover with plastic wrap and put it into your refrigerator to chill while you prepare the topping and preheat your oven to 400°F.

Preparing the Fruit: Blend the sugar with the cinnamon. Peel, core and cut the apples into eighths.

Assembing the Apfelkuchen: Lay the apple slices in rows on top of the chilled dough and sprinkle them with the lemon juice and then the sugar/cinnamon mixture. Beat the egg yolk with the cream and drizzle over everything.

Bake for 25 to 30 minutes until the apples are tender and the crust golden.

Hot from the oven, this wonderful concoction is elegant as is. To add an American touch, serve it with a piece of sharp Cheddar cheese or vanilla ice cream.

A SAMPLER OF SMALL PASTRIES

The next pastries are small ones. Some are rolled up like the crescents below, some are folded over to form turnovers. Many are specific to certain regions or cultures, some are pure serendipity. Feel free to be creative with any of them. The fillings for these can be used interchangeably with other pastry or pie doughs, so, again, mix and match.

RUGELACH

In the introduction to the recipe for croissants made with yeast (page 201), we told you a story about their origin. This recipe evolved as the second chapter of that story. The rugelach, or kipfel, is another crescent pastry. This one, it is said, was made by rejoicing Viennese bakers who were celebrating the decisive victory of the west over the invading Turks. It is clearly a celebration pastry, rich and overflowing with a joyous filling.

This recipe is from Barbara Asnes who inspired the recipe for Classic Puff Pastry (page 442). With it she included this note: "The dough needs to be made ahead of time so you can chill it for at least 2 hours or overnight. It can even be made and frozen several days ahead of when you want to serve it.

"Like anything made with preserves or wet fillings, these pastries tend to leak. The best solution is to use a non-stick pan or line your pan with parchment. If you are lazy like I am, just butter the cookie sheet and bake the pastries. When they're done, soak the pan in hot water and scrub the debris off later. This probably falls under the 'penny-wise and pound-foolish' mode of preparation but it works."

The Pastry

> 3 cups King Arthur Unbleached All-Purpose Flour
> 1 teaspoon salt
> 2 cups (4 sticks) unsalted butter
> 1 cup sour cream

Preparing the Pastry: Combine the flour and salt. Cut in the butter until the mixture is like coarse meal. The dough is more tender or flaky if it is not cut in too finely. Add the sour cream and blend until the dough holds together. Form into 4 balls and wrap in plastic wrap to chill. After the dough has chilled, get set up to fill the pastries.

The Apricot Filling

> ½ cup ground almonds or walnuts
> ¼ cup sugar
> 1 tablespoon (or more to taste) cinnamon
> 1 pound apricot preserves (about 1½ cups)

Preparing the Filling: Combine the sugar, nuts and cinnamon in a small bowl for dredging.

Assembling & Baking: Preheat your oven to 375°F.

Roll one of the dough balls out into a circle about ¼ inch thick. Spread preserves to within about an inch of the edge. Cut the circle into 8 to 12 wedges and roll into crescents.

Dredge these in the sugar mixture and place on a lightly greased baking sheet. Bake for 15 or 20 minutes until light brown.

CHEESE KNISHES

The pastry for this recipe is an old one from the King Arthur Flour archives. It is made in a slightly smaller quantity than the one for Rugelach but is essentially the same idea. It is a very delicate pastry with a tantalizing filling that is savory and sweet at the same time.

This pastry also needs to be chilled for 2 hours or overnight and can be frozen.

The Pastry

> 1 cup (2 sticks) butter
> 2 cups King Arthur Unbleached All-Purpose Flour
> 1 cup (½ pint) sour cream

The Cheese Filling

> 2 onions
> butter to sauté onions
> 1½ cups farmer cheese (or fresh cottage cheese)
> ½ cup (4 ounces) cream cheese
> 2 large eggs
> ½ teaspoon salt
> 1 tablespoon sugar
> 1 egg beaten with 1 tablespoon of water (for wash)

Preparing the Pastry: Cut the butter into the flour until it is like coarse meal. As noted in the previous recipe, the dough is more tender or flaky if it is not cut in too finely.

Add the sour cream and blend until the mixture holds together. Form into 2 balls and wrap in plastic to chill.

Preparing the Filling: Chop the onions and sauté them in butter until transparent. Combine with the cheeses, one of the eggs, the salt and the sugar, mixing well.

Assembling & Baking: Preheat your oven to 375°F.

Roll one of the dough balls out on a floured board until it's about ⅛ inch thick. Cut into desired shapes (circles, squares, etc.), anything that you can fold over the filling and seal.

Place a small amount of filling on each one, fold over and seal with your fingers or the tines of a fork. Place on a lightly greased (or parchment lined) baking sheet. Brush the tops of the pastries with the egg wash.

Bake for approximately 20 minutes or until lightly browned and puffy.

DEEP-FRIED FRUIT TURNOVERS

Here's an alternative way of cooking pastry turnovers to entice those of you who find yourselves hooked on those fried pies found at fast-food restaurants. If you make them at home you'll have a tastier and healthier alternative.

Make a recipe of any pie dough. A medium crust pastry with an egg in it will hold together well.

Roll out your dough until it's about ⅛ inch thick. With a large cookie cutter or a cleaned tin can (with a hole punched in the opposite end to relieve pressure), cut pastry circles 3 or 4 inches in diameter.

Place some fruit filling (see Pie Fillings & Toppings, page 402 or Danish Pastry Fillings, page 203) on a half of each circle. Moisten the edge with cold water, fold over and seal by crimping with your fingers or a fork.

Heat vegetable oil to 375°F and cook the turnovers, turning them as they brown, for about 4 minutes or until they're crisp and golden. Remove them with a slotted spoon and put them on absorbent paper to drain.

Serve these turnovers hot with ice cream, or wait until they've cooled and sprinkle them with confectioners' sugar.

North Country Turnovers

This is a hearty tart pastry from Ken Haedrich who is very much a "whole grain" sort of person. This pastry can be used for sweet turnovers but Ken's choice is the hearty, savory filling you'll find below.

Since this dough needs to chill you may want to make it the day before you plan to serve your turnovers. You will have enough dough and filling for 7 turnovers.

Cream Cheese Pastry

1 1/4 cups King Arthur Unbleached All-Purpose Flour
1/4 cup King Arthur Stone Ground Whole Wheat Flour
1/4 teaspoon salt
10 tablespoons (1 1/4 sticks) unsalted butter, cut into small pieces
4 ounces cold cream cheese, cut into small pieces
2 to 2 1/2 tablespoons ice water

Making the Pastry: Combine the dry ingredients in a large mixing bowl. With two knives, a pastry blender or your fingertips, cut or rub the butter and cream cheese into the dry ingredients until they are broken up into tiny, pea-sized pieces.

Sprinkle in the ice water, a tablespoon at a time, mixing and tossing with a fork until the dough is evenly moistened.

Turn the dough out onto a lightly floured work surface and knead once, flattening it into a 1/2-inch-thick disk. Wrap in waxed paper or plastic and refrigerate for (at least) 1 hour.

Rolling out the Dough: If you have refrigerated your dough for longer than 1 hour, let it sit at room temperature for 10 to 15 minutes before rolling.

On a lightly floured work surface, roll out the dough into a 14 x 21-inch rectangle slightly thinner than a regular pie crust, somewhere between 1/16 and 1/8 inch. Lightly dust the the board and the dough with flour if things begin to stick.

Using a bowl as a guide, cut out circles of dough about 6 inches in diameter with a sharp paring knife. Stack the pastry circles in between layers of waxed paper on a plate.

Dust off the excess flour from the dough trimmings and pack them into a ball. Roll this out and cut 1 more round. Add this to the stack, wrap the stack with plastic and refrigerate for at least 10 minutes and up to 24 hours before using.

North Country Filling

1 1/4 cups (about 9 ounces) rinsed and drained sauerkraut
1 tablespoon German-style mustard
4 ounces Canadian bacon or ham, cut into 1/4-inch dice
1 1/4 cups (about 4 ounces) grated sharp Cheddar cheese
1 tart green apple (preferably Granny Smith) peeled, cored and
     thinly sliced
1 egg beaten with 1 tablespoon milk for wash

Prepare the Filling: Mix the sauerkraut and mustard in a saucepan (preferably stainless steel or enamel). Cook over moderately high heat, stirring occasionally, until all the liquid evaporates, about 3 minutes. Immediately transfer the sauerkraut to a plate to cool. Divide into seven relatively equal piles.

Assembling the Turnovers: Preheat your oven to 400°F.

Arrange the meat, cheese and apple in separate bowls nearby.

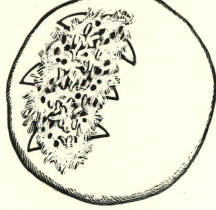

Place the rounds of pastry on a work surface. Working quickly so the dough doesn't get too soft, arrange 3 apple slices on one-half of each pastry round 1/4 inch from the outside edge.

Cover each group of apple slices with a pile of sauerkraut keeping it away from the pastry's edge as well.

Top the sauerkraut with about 2 tablespoons of bacon or ham and 2 1/2 tablespoons of cheese.

Lightly moisten the edge of each pastry round with water. Gently stretch and then fold the half of the pastry that has nothing on it over the filling. Press the edges of the turnovers with the tines of a fork or your fingers to make a decorative, tightly sealed edge.

Baking: Transfer the turnovers to a lightly greased baking sheet. Pierce the tops of the turnovers twice with a fork and brush them with the egg wash.

Bake in the middle of the oven for 10 minutes. Reduce the temperature to 375°F and continue baking to 15 to 20 minutes longer until the bottoms are browned and the tops are golden.

Let them cool on a rack for at least 15 minutes before serving.

CORNISH PASTIES

Cornwall is the west country of England where you'll find Bodmin Moor and Dozmary Pool. Dozmary Pool is one of the lakes into which, some legends say, the Lady of the Lake took King Arthur's sword, "Excalibur."

Just north of the moor is the rugged, beautiful Cornish coast and Tintagel Castle where, according to historian, Geoffrey of Monmouth, in his History of the King of Britain, King Arthur was born. Since the castle at Tintagel was built in the twelfth century, some seven hundred years after Arthur, this particular story is just a myth. Although Arthur is placed firmly in Celtic Britain, claims for his birthplace range from Cornwall all the way north to the western lowlands of Scotland.

Cornwall is rugged and hilly and the Cornish, who are Celtic in origin, are a tough and independent lot, much like Vermonters. In fact, just northwest of Norwich, Vermont, there are a number of old Cornish families who left the copper mines in Cornwall to work the copper mines in Strafford which, at one time, were the largest in the world.

It was for the Cornish miner that the "pasty" was originally developed. It was an edible lunch box, a meal enclosed in a rugged short crust pastry, equally good hot or cold. Traditionally the pasty was made from a circle of dough as big as a dinner plate. A filling of meat, potatoes onions, etc., was placed in the middle. Then the pasty was folded up around it and the edges were pinched together and fluted like the edge of a pie. The initials of the owner were cut into one corner enabling him to reclaim his own later on in the day.

Although a pasty usually contains a hearty stew, it can be used as a container for any appropriate leftover or for a filling of your own devising. With this recipe you can make four 5- or 6-inch pasties, a bit smaller than the traditional variety but enough for most of us these days.

Before you start making the dough, have your filling cooked and ready. You'll find a recipe for Meat Pie filling under Pie Fillings & Toppings.

1 recipe Meat Pie filling (page 416)
2 cups King Arthur Unbleached All-Purpose Flour
1/2 teaspoon salt
1/2 cup lard (traditional but you can substitute vegetable shortening
          and/or butter)
1 beaten egg (this makes a tighter, more durable crust)
1 tablespoon water
2 teaspoons vinegar
1 egg beaten with 1 tablespoon water for wash

First: Preheat your oven to 400°F.

Making the Dough: Combine the flour and salt. Cut the lard into small pieces and distribute evenly over the flour. With two knives, a pastry cutter or your fingertips, cut or rub the fat lightly into the flour lifting it up as you do to incorporate as much air as possible and to keep the mixture cool. Continue until the mixture resembles cracker crumbs.

Beat the egg, water and vinegar together. Sprinkle this lightly over the flour mixture using a fork to distribute it as evenly as possible.

Gather the dough together and divide it into four pieces. Roll each piece out on a floured surface into 5- or 6-inch circles.

Filling: Place the filling of your choice in the center. Dampen the edges, bring the edges up and over the filling and pinch them together. Flute the edge as you would the edge of a pie crust.

Cut a design (or initials) on one of the sides, as you would a pie crust, to release steam.

Baking: Place the pasties on their backs, with the seams up, on a greased baking sheet and brush with the egg wash. Bake at 400°F for 35 to 40 minutes or until the pasties are golden brown.

• A PUFF PASTRY PRIMER •

Puff pastry, or "pâte feuilletée," which means "pastry made leaf-like" is the ultimate of the French butter pastries. In fact, it has so many "leaves" that it is also called "millefeuille," meaning a thousand leaves. Each of these "leaves" consists of a layer of flour separated by a layer of butter. The expansion (puff) occurs because the butter layers create steam when exposed to the heat of an oven. This expands the space between the flour layers. Ultimately, in classic puff pastry, you want to create seven hundred twenty-nine layers of folded dough, not quite one thousand, but like the millipede which really doesn't have a thousand legs, the effect is there.

A great way to share the joy of baking, literally, is to give a friend a block of chilled puff pastry, with instructions for shaping and baking it.

Classic Puff Pastry
Pâte Feuilletée

The inspiration for this section comes from Barbara Asnes who is currently running her very successful "Good Taste Catering," just south of our company headquarters, in White River Junction. Barbara is a woman of many talents. Now that her catering business is solidly in the black, she's putting it on hold so she can go off to law school. She insists that her culinary expertise will still be available between courses and cases.

Before you embark on this adventure, here is something to keep in mind. Keep everything, including yourself, cool. If your goal is to create distinct layers of butter and flour, then you don't want the butter to melt. If you have any suspicion that the butter is too soft (oozing or breaking through the layers) refrigerate the dough for 30 minutes to firm it up.

1 pound (4 cups) King Arthur Unbleached All-Purpose Flour (or 3½ cups King Arthur Unbleached All-Purpose Flour and ½ cup cornstarch)
1 pound (4 sticks) unsalted butter, ½ stick chilled, the rest at room temperature
1 to 2 teaspoons salt (1 for sweet pastry, 2 for savory)
1¼ cups cold water (use more if necessary, a tablespoon at a time); you can also substitute 1 tablespoon of lemon juice for 1 of water if you wish to further temper the gluten in the flour

Cornstarch is the finely ground endosperm of a kernel of corn. It corresponds to the endosperm of a wheat berry which is what is ground into white flour. Unlike wheat flour, cornstarch (or corn flour) has no gluten in it. It can be used in combination with a strong (high-gluten) wheat flour like King Arthur Flour to reduce the percentage of gluten in the whole. When this is made into a dough or pastry, you'll have the integrity and strength of the original flour as well as the tenderness made possible by the cornstarch.

Making the Dough: Measure the flour into a mixing bowl. Remove ½ cup and set it aside in another bowl.

Take the half stick of chilled butter, cut it into small pieces and drop it into the flour. With two knives, a pastry blender or your fingertips, cut or rub the butter into the flour until it resembles cornmeal.

Add the salt (and optional lemon juice) to the water and add this to the flour. Mix gently with a fork until you have a rough dough that pulls away from the sides of the bowl. If you need to add more water, do it a tablespoon at a time until the dough holds together.

Turn the dough out onto a lightly floured surface and knead until it is smooth and the gluten has been somewhat developed, about 2 or 3 minutes. Wrap it in plastic and refrigerate for at least 30 minutes.

Preparing the Butter: Take the remainder of the butter and the reserved flour and mix the two together until they're well blended and smooth. You can do this with a mixer, a food processor or with a spoon, by hand.

Pat this butter/flour mixture into an 8-inch square on a lightly floured piece of waxed paper. Cover it with second sheet of waxed paper and refrigerate it for at least 30 minutes. By mixing the butter with flour, you stabilize it somewhat so it won't decide to "flow."

Rolling & Folding: Remove the dough from the refrigerator and put it on a lightly floured surface. Gently roll it into a square about 12 inches on a side. You don't have to be obsessive about the dimensions but be pretty close.

Put the butter square in the center of the dough square but turn it so that the corners of the butter square point toward the sides of the dough square. Fold the corners of the dough over the butter until they meet in the middle. Pinch and seal the edges of the dough together.

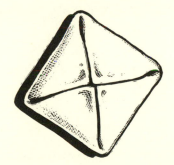

Turn the square over and tap it gently with your rolling pin or by hand into a rectangular shape. (Make sure everything is still completely, but lightly, floured.) Begin rolling the dough from the center, away from and toward you, into a larger rectangle 20 inches long and 10 inches wide.

As you work, keep the dough, the table and the rolling pin well dusted with flour. Although the dough will absorb some of the flour, it is relatively soft to begin with so the dusting flour isn't enough to worry about.

Turn the dough over from time to time. As you roll you tend to expand the top layers more than the bottom. By turning it, you'll even it out.

When the dough is the right size, fold the bottom third of the dough up to the center and the top third over (like a business letter) and turn the dough package ¼ turn to the right so it looks like a book ready to be opened. If the dough is still nice and cold and still relaxed, do another rolling and turning the same way. (If it begins to feel too soft or wants to resist being rolled, cover it, put it on a small baking sheet and refrigerate it for 15 minutes.)

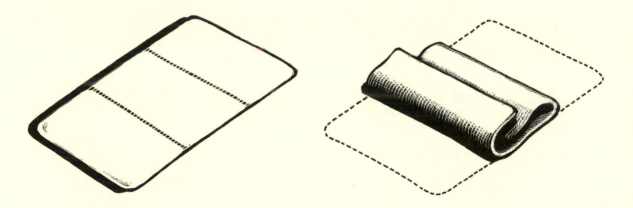

If you've successfully rolled it out and folded it twice, you've completed 2 turns. Classic puff pastry gets six. Continue refrigerating it after each 2 turns (or more often if necessary) until all 6 turns are completed.

Make sure you make a checklist somewhere so you know how many turns or layers you've made. Bakers commonly put fingerprints in a corner of the pastry to indicate the numbers of turns. If you try this, be careful you don't break through with your fingernails since the layers are very thin.

An alternate way of rolling and folding which is both more and less demanding is to make a turn every 15 minutes. This means that you will have to be more attentive to the dough, but the dough, because it has a chance to rest after each turn, will be nice and relaxed for the next one. This means each turn takes less time and the dough stays cool.

The Big Chill: When all 6 turns are done, put the dough in the refrigerator for at least an hour (and preferably overnight) before shaping.

Shaping: After being thoroughly chilled, the dough can be shaped into croissants, patty shells, twists, straws, etc. Specific recipes follow. Scraps can be chilled and rerolled. Pastry from rerolled dough won't be quite as flaky, but it will still be great. (See Trimmings & Tail Ends page 401.)

Freezing: Like other pastry doughs, you can freeze puff pastry in a non-self-defrosting freezer for up to a year if it's well wrapped. It can also be frozen at any time during the rolling, folding, turning process. Defrost it thoroughly before you use it, just make sure it doesn't get too soft.

Croissants de Pâtissier

Puff pastry croissants are called "croissants de pâtissier" because they are made by a pastry chef rather than a baker who makes "croissants de boulanger." A recipe for Croissants de Boulanger can be found on page 201 in the chapter on Yeasted Breads. Both varieties are incredibly light; Croissants de Boulanger, made with yeast, are flaky and earthy; Croissants de Pâtissier, made without yeast, are flaky and ethereal. As we suggested with our other croissants, you can fill these with jam or any savory filling. This recipe will make a dozen.

½ recipe Classic Puff Pastry (page 442)
1 egg beaten with 1 tablespoon water for wash

Shaping: On a lightly floured surface, roll out the dough until it's a rectangle about 12 x 18 inches. Trim the dough all the way around by pressing straight down with a very sharp knife or your King Arthur bowl scraper. This cuts off the folded edges which would inhibit the "puff."

Cut the dough in half lengthwise and in thirds widthwise. This should give you six 6 x 6-inch squares. Cut these squares in half diagonally.

Roll each triangle up starting with the long edge and working toward the tip. Form the crescent by bending the two ends in the opposite direction from that in which you rolled the dough.

Chilling: Place the croissants on a lightly greased baking sheet. Cover and chill for 30 minutes to an hour.

Baking: Fifteen minutes before you want to bake the croissants, preheat your oven to a hot 425°F. Just before they go in the oven, brush the tops with the egg wash. Bake for 15 minutes. Turn the heat down to 350°F and bake for another 10 to 15 minutes.

PUFF PASTRY TURNOVERS

This recipe will make 6 turnovers.

$^{1}/_{2}$ recipe Classic Puff Pastry (page 442)
filling, sweet or savory, your choice (page 203)
1 egg beaten with 1 tablespoon water for wash

Shaping: On a lightly floured surface, roll out the dough until it's about 12 x 18 inches. Trim the dough all the way around by pressing straight down with a very sharp knife or a bowl scraper. Cut the dough in half lengthwise and in thirds widthwise. This should give you six 6 x 6-inch squares.

Filling & Chilling: Put a dollop of whatever filling you choose in the center of the dough. Moisten the edges with a bit of water and fold the dough in half diagonally. Place them on a lightly greased baking sheet, cover and chill for 30 minutes to an hour.

Baking: Fifteen minutes before you want to bake them, preheat your oven to a hot 425°F. Just before they go in the oven, brush them with the egg wash. Bake for 15 minutes. Turn the heat down to 350°F and bake for another 15 to 20 minutes.

VOL-AU-VENT OR BOUCHÉE

The next pastries we are familiar with as patty shells. A large shell, which will serve 4 to 6 people, is known as a "Vol-au-Vent," literally, a "flight or gust of wind." The smaller variation is called a "Bouchée," or "mouthful." This recipe is for 1 large patty shell or 4 generous individual ones.

$^{1}/_{2}$ recipe Classic Puff Pastry (page 442)
egg wash made with 1 egg beaten with a tablespoon of water (optional)

Shaping: Roll out the dough until it's a little more than 8 x 16 inches. Trim the dough all the way around to 8 x 16 inches by pressing straight down with a very sharp knife. This eliminates any folded edges which would inhibit the "puff."

Although patty shells are traditionally round or scalloped, the most efficient way to use your dough is to make square ones. This eliminates trimmings and re-rollings and saves some time. They also taste just as good and are clearly made at home.

   • **Vol-au-Vent:** For 1 large shell, cut the dough in half so you have two pieces that are 8 inches on a side. Place one piece on a lightly greased or parchment lined baking sheet large enough for both the shell and a "lid."

Leaving a border of 1 to 1½ inches, cut a square out of the center of the remaining piece of dough. Place the square, with the smaller square cut out of it, on top of the one on the baking sheet. Put the smaller square, or "lid," on the baking sheet beside it.

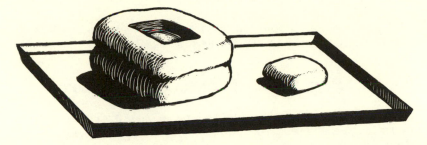

• **Bouchée:** For 4 small shells, cut the dough in half as you did above so you have two 8-inch squares. Cut each square in quarters so you have eight 4-inch squares altogether. Form the smaller shells as you did the large one using two 4-inch squares per shell.

Chilling: Cover the pastry and chill for ½ to 1 hour.

Baking: Fifteen minutes before you want to bake your patty shell(s), preheat the oven to 425°F. Just before it goes in the oven, brush the top surface with an egg wash if you wish. Bake for 15 minutes. Turn the heat down to 375°F and bake the large shell for a further 30 to 35 minutes. Bake the smaller shells for 20 to 25 minutes.

Serving: Cool completely and then fill with whatever inspires you: seafood Newburg, creamed chipped beef, or slightly crushed and sweetened strawberries with whipped cream on top, etc.

CHEESE TWISTS

This recipe will make 1½ dozen cheese twists.

½ recipe Classic Puff Pastry
egg wash made by beating 1 egg with 1 tablespoon water
½ cup freshly grated Parmesan cheese

Shaping: Roll the dough into a very thin rectangle, about 6 x 18 inches.

Brush the surface with the egg wash and sprinkle generously with grated cheese. Press the cheese gently into the surface of the dough. Fold the dough over so you have a rectangle that is 6 x 9 inches. Cut off the folded edge. With a sharp knife or bowl scraper, cut eighteen ½ x 6-inch strips.

Chilling: Place these on a lightly greased baking sheet, cover them and put them back into the refrigerator to chill and relax for about 10 minutes.

Remove the strips from the refrigerator and give each one a few twists. Cover and chill them again for about 30 minutes.

Baking: Fifteen minutes before you want to bake your cheese twists, preheat the oven to 400°F. Bake for 15 to 20 minutes.

Puff Pastry Éclairs or Napoleons

By using the same technique that you use to make Vol-au-Vent, but cutting the dough into rectangles, you can create puff pastry versions of the éclair, or its close cousin, the napoleon. This will make 6.

> ½ recipe Classic Puff Pastry
> 1 recipe Custard (page 315), either Slim & Suave or Thick & Rich
> 1 recipe Fudge Frosting (page 318)
> 1 recipe Royal Icing (page 420), for napoleons

Shaping & Chilling: Roll the dough very thin into a rectangle 12 x 18 inches. Trim the edges and cut the dough into thirds crosswise so you have three pieces that are 6 x 12 inches. Cut each of these into 2 x 6-inch rectangles. You should have 18 pieces altogether.

Place 6 pieces on a lightly greased baking sheet. Cut the center out of six more pieces leaving a rim of about ¼ inch. Place these on top of the pieces on the baking sheet. Take the remaining 6 pieces and place these on top of the cut out pieces. Cover and chill for about 30 minutes.

Baking: Preheat your oven to 425°F. Bake for 15 minutes. Turn the heat down and continue baking for a further 20 to 25 minutes.

Filling & Frosting: After the pastries have cooled, pry off the top, take out any excess dough on the inside with a fork. Fill with the custard of your choice. Replace the tops.

> • **Éclairs:** Spread the tops with Fudge Frosting.
>
> • **Napoleons:** Spread the tops with Royal Icing. Drizzle a thin line of Fudge (or other chocolate) Frosting in a pattern over the top.

• A CHOUX PASTE PRIMER •

The next recipes are made with "Pâte à Choux" (pat-a-shoo), or Cream Puff Pastry, also known as Choux Paste. The French name almost says in words what happens to this pastry in the oven. Whoever devised this concoction was clearly having fun experimenting. By putting together the ingredients, which are common enough, in a slightly startling manner, you create an almost magical dough.

But the magic is really quite simple. In the heat of the oven, this egg-rich mixture expands into something almost three times its original size. A strong and elastic flour (like King Arthur) makes this expansion even more dramatic. With it you can make any number of familiar things, such as cream puffs, éclairs, profiteroles but you can also use this pastry for some not-so-familiar things.

PÂTE À CHOUX

1 cup water (or milk)
$\frac{1}{2}$ teaspoon salt
2 to 3 teaspoons sugar (optional)
$\frac{1}{2}$ cup butter (1 stick)
1 cup King Arthur Unbleached All-Purpose Flour
4 large or 5 medium eggs, at room temperature

First: Preheat your oven to 425°F.

Making the Dough: Combine the water or milk, the salt and the sugar and bring to a boil in a medium saucepan. Add and melt the butter. When the liquid has almost returned to a boil again, take the saucepan off the heat and add the flour all at once.

Turn the heat way down and put the pan back on the burner. Stir the mixture until it holds together in one mass, the texture is smooth and you can easily pull it away from the sides of the pan with your spoon. This should happen within a minute or two.

Stop stirring at this point and remove the pan from the heat to cool for 5 or 10 minutes. This is important because you don't want to cook the eggs before they go in the oven.

With renewed vigor, add the eggs, one at a time, beating hard after each egg until all are fully mixed in and the dough is smooth and no longer slippery.

Shaping & Baking: Follow directions for the pastry of your choice.

CREAM PUFFS, PROFITEROLES & ÉCLAIRS

1 recipe Pâte à Choux (page 449)
1 recipe Custard, Slim & Suave or Thick & Rich (page 315) or whipped
    cream, sweetened
1 recipe Fudge Frosting (page 318)
    OR
1 recipe Dark Semi-Sweet Chocolate Sauce (page 321)

Shaping: Cream puffs and éclairs are about the same size but shaped differently. Profiteroles are just tiny cream puffs.

Cream Puffs & Profiteroles: To make large cream puffs or smaller profiteroles, drop rounded tablespoons (or teaspoons, respectively) onto an ungreased baking sheet (parchment paper is great here), 2 to 3 inches apart. (If you have a pastry bag, which is nice but not critical, use a ½- or ¾-inch tip for the cream puffs and a ¼-inch tip for the profiteroles.)

Éclairs: To form éclairs, drop the dough in an elongated shape, about ½ or ¾ inch by 4 inches, on your ungreased baking sheet. (If you have a pastry bag, you can do this with a ½- or ¾-inch tip)

Baking: Bake the pastries for about 10 minutes at 425°F and then turn the temperature down to 375°F and continue baking for 15 to 25 minutes (depending on size) or until the puffs are golden. Like well-baked bread, they should sound hollow when they're done.

After they've finished baking, make a tiny incision or slit with a sharp knife near the bottom of the puffs and put them back in the oven with the temperature turned off and the door ajar for 5 or 10 minutes so the steam can escape without softening the shells. Then take them out and put them on a wire rack to cool thoroughly before you fill them.

At this point, you can put them in an airtight plastic bag and freeze them to use later. When you take them out of the freezer, just put them in a moderately hot oven (375°F to 400°F) for 5 to 10 minutes to crisp them up again.

Filling the Pastry

Cream Puffs & Éclairs: Slice the puffs in half horizontally. You can fill them either with a custard or with slightly sweetened whipped cream flavored with a bit of vanilla. Cover the top with the Fudge Frosting.

Profiteroles: These smaller variations of cream puffs are filled with a thick and sweetened whipped cream flavored with vanilla. They are then stacked in a pyramid and topped with a sluice of rich chocolate sauce flavored with brandy or rum.

Pâte à Choux Swans

If you want to make something really elegant, try these. A pastry bag is almost a neccessity here, though you can make a close approximation. (See page 320.)

    1 recipe Pâte à Choux (page 449)
    1 recipe Easy Chocolate Sauce (page 420)
    1 recipe Custard, either Slim & Suave or Thick & Rich (page 315)
    confectioners' sugar

Shaping: The shaping needs to be done in two steps. First, using a pastry bag with a large star tube, make the body by squeezing an oval mound of choux paste about 3 inches long onto an ungreased cookie sheet. Raise the tube to create a ridged center and relax the pressure on the bag while pulling the tube to create a tail. Bake these bodies at 375°F for about 30 minutes.

Form the necks by fitting your pastry bag with a small, number 0, plain tube. Pipe an "S" on an ungreased baking sheet. These thin necks are very fragile so make a couple of extras in case one breaks. Bake at 350°F for 10 to 13 minutes.

When the teardrop-shaped puffs have cooled thoroughly, slice off the tops parallel to the base but leave the tail. Halve the tops lengthwise to make wings. Dip one end of the neck in the chocolate and set it into the body base.

Fill the swan body with custard. Place the wings artfully into the cream filling. With a toothpick, put a dot of chocolate on each side of the head to make the eyes. Sprinkle with confectioners' sugar.

Beignets Soufflés

To make a variety of confection you'll find in Louisiana, deep fry this dough. Because the same cavity is created when it is cooked, beignets can be filled with anything that seems appropriate: jam, sweetened yogurt, custard, etc.

Heat a pan of vegetable oil until it's about 375°F. Drop in blobs of Choux Paste and cook them until they are golden and crisp. Drain on absorbent paper. When they've cooled a bit, fill them and sprinkle them with confectioners' sugar or, for a New England touch, drizzle a little maple syrup over them.

ANNA'S FAMOUS CHEESE PUFFS

This variation of Pâte à Choux is savory rather than sweet. It was given to Walter Sands years ago by Anna Coombs, an old Swedish friend from Carlisle, Massachusetts.

These little puffs, reminiscent of tiny popovers, are fun to make, a great project for an aspiring young baker. They can be used as a savory rather than a sweet biscuit at tea time, as an hors d'oeuvre or as an addition to a meal. Try adding some minced green or white onion, ham, prosciutto, etc. Or, with these possibilities in mind, go off in a direction all your own. They can also be deep fried like the preceding Beignets Soufflés.

1 cup water
½ teaspoon salt
¼ cup (½ stick) butter
1 cup King Arthur Unbleached All-Purpose Flour
½ teaspoon chili powder, paprika or dry mustard (optional but good)
1 cup (about 4 ounces) sharp Cheddar (or Parmesan, etc.) cheese, grated
4 large eggs, at room temperature

First: Preheat your oven to 425°F.

Preparing the Dough: Bring the water and salt to a boil in a medium-sized saucepan. Add and melt the butter. When the butter is melted and the mixture is close to a boil again, take the pan off the heat and add the flour, spice (if you use it) and grated cheese, all at once.

Turn the heat way down and put the pan back on the burner. Stir the mixture until it holds together in one mass, the texture is smooth and you can easily pull it away from the sides of the pan with your spoon. This should happen within a minute or two. Stop stirring at this point and remove the pan from the heat to cool for 5 or 10 minutes. This is important because you don't want to cook the eggs before they go in the oven.

One at a time, beat in the eggs until the dough has completely incorporated them and doesn't look or feel slippery.

Baking: Drop the dough by small spoonfuls on a greased baking sheet. Bake the puffs for about 25 minutes or until they are puffed and golden brown.

To make them crisper, stab each one on the side with the tip of a sharp knife and leave them in the oven with the heat turned off and the door ajar for another 5 to 10 minutes. This allows the steam to escape without softening the shell of the puff.

These can be prepared ahead of time. Cover the baking sheet with a damp towel or plastic wrap, and store them at room temperature until you're ready to pop them in the oven.

• PASTRY MAVERICKS •

The next few recipes are all misfits. Although they are called pies, they are completely different branches of the pastry family and not even very closely related to each other. Some could just as well have been included elsewhere, but the fact that they're all called "pies" sealed their fate as far as this book is concerned.

DEEP-DISH FRUIT PIE

This pie is made with just a top crust which is more like a baking powder biscuit dough than a pie dough.

Fruit Filling

> 3 cups sliced fruit (peaches, apples, blueberries, etc.)
> 2 tablespoons butter
> 2 tablespoons King Arthur Unbleached All-Purpose Flour
> $1/2$ cup sugar
> 1 teaspoon cinnamon, or other spice (optional)
> $1/3$ cup water

Dough

> 1 cup King Arthur Unbleached All-Purpose Flour
> 2 teaspoons baking powder
> $1/2$ teaspoon salt
> 1 teaspoon cinnamon
> 3 tablespoons shortening or butter
> 1 egg
> $1/3$ cup milk

First: Preheat your oven to 400°F.

Preparing the Filling: Arrange the slices of fresh peaches, apples or other fruit in a deep, lightly greased, 9-inch pie plate. Dot them with butter.

In a mixing bowl, combine the flour, sugar and spice. Gradually stir in the water. Pour this mixture over the fruit and set aside while you prepare the dough.

Making the Dough: Blend the dry ingredients together in a mixing bowl. With two knives, a pastry cutter or your fingertips, cut or rub in the shortening until the mixture resembles bread crumbs.

Measure the milk into a small bowl and beat in the egg until light.

Make a well in the flour mixture, pour in the milk/egg mixture and stir together for about 15 seconds until it just holds together.

Place the dough on a floured board and pat or gently roll it out to fit the pie plate. Place it over the fruit and make several artistic slits in the dough.

Bake the "pie" for about 25 minutes.

BATTER CRUST FOR SAVORY PIES

This is an old King Arthur Flour recipe. It's closely related to the Deep-Dish Fruit Pie but it's designed for a savory, meat pie filling which you'll find with the Pie Fillings & Toppings.

1 cup King Arthur Unbleached All-Purpose Flour
1 teaspoon baking powder
1/2 teaspoon salt
1 teaspoon minced fresh parsley (or other herbs)
1 egg, separated
3/4 cup milk
2 tablespoons butter, melted
1 egg white
1 recipe Meat Pie filling (page 416)

Preheat your oven to 400°F.

Combine the flour, baking powder, salt and herbs.

In a separate bowl, beat the egg yolk with the milk and stir this into the flour mixture. Add the melted butter.

Place the egg white in a separate bowl, beat well and fold it into the batter.

Put the meat filling in a medium-sized casserole. Spread the batter by spoonfuls over the top of the filling. Bake for 20 to 25 minutes.

Boston Cream Pie

Boston Cream Pie isn't a pastry at all and is here purely because of its name. For other cream filling options see page 411.

Batter Base

> $^1/_3$ cup butter
> 1 cup sugar
> 2 eggs, separated
> $^1/_2$ teaspoon salt
> $^1/_2$ teaspoon vanilla
> 2 teaspoons baking powder
> $1^1/_2$ cups King Arthur Unbleached All-Purpose Flour
> $^1/_2$ cup milk
> 1 recipe chocolate frosting of your choice (starting on page 318)

First: Preheat your oven to 375°F.

Making the Batter Base: Cream the butter, add the sugar and cream until light. Add the egg yolks and beat until fluffy. Stir in the salt and the vanilla.

Combine the baking powder with the flour and add this to the batter alternately with the milk. Stir only as much as is necessary to blend the ingredients. Beat the egg whites until they are stiff and fold them into the batter.

Pour the batter into two greased, 8-inch cake pans. Bake for 30 minutes. While the batter bakes, prepare the filling.

Cream Filling (or Custard)

> $^1/_3$ to $^1/_2$ cup King Arthur Unbleached All-Purpose Flour
> $^2/_3$ cup sugar
> $^1/_8$ teaspoon salt
> 2 cups milk
> 2 eggs
> 1 teaspoon vanilla

Making the Filling: Combine the flour, sugar and salt. Scald the milk and pour it over the dry ingredients gradually. Cook until it has thickened.

Beat the eggs slightly and add them to the hot, thickened custard. Allow the custard to remain heating for 1 minute. Cool and add the vanilla flavoring.

Assembling the "Pie:" When the cake layers are cool, put the cooled cream filling between them and top with your choice of chocolate frosting.

APFEL STRUDEL

Europe has a wonderful way with fruit. Here's an apple specialty that many people are familiar with but probably few have made themselves. Strudel dough is more closely related to "noodle dough" than pie dough but somehow belongs in this Pastry chapter anyway. Making it requires a large table and cloth and a sense of adventure.

Strudel Dough

> 1 egg
> 1/3 cup warm water (or more if it's wintertime and the flour is very dry)
> 1 1/2 cups King Arthur Unbleached All-Purpose Flour
> 1/4 teaspoon salt

Making the Dough: Beat the egg lightly together with the water in a medium-sized mixing bowl. Blend in the flour and the salt. When the dough begins to hold together, turn it out onto a large floured board or table, and knead until it is smooth and elastic and no longer sticks to the board or to you.

Cover the kneaded dough with a warm, earthenware bowl, the warmer the better, for at least half an hour or, better, for an hour. While the dough rests, make the filling.

Apple Filling

> 8 cups firm, tart apples, peeled, cored and chopped
> 1 cup raisins
> 1/2 cup currants
> 1/2 cup blanched chopped or sliced almonds
> 1 tablespoon grated lemon rind
> 1 cup sugar
> 1 tablespoon cinnamon
> 1/2 cup (1 stick) butter

Making the Filling: Put the apples in a large mixing bowl. Mix in the remainder of the ingredients except for the butter.

Melt the butter in a small saucepan but don't mix this into the filling.

Before proceeding to the next step, preheat your oven to 400°F.

Shaping the Strudel: Place the dough on a large floured pastry cloth (or clean table cloth). With a floured rolling pin, begin rolling it out as thinly as possible, making sure you keep the cloth under it sprinkled with flour to keep it sliding smoothly.

If the dough seems to be reluctant to expand, give it a little rest to relax the gluten and begin again.

When you can't roll it any farther with the rolling pin, flour your hands and, putting them under the dough, coax it gently out, trying not to tear it, until it is about 3 feet in diameter. Try doing this with the backs of your hands or knuckles. This part is almost like a game, like trying to peel an entire apple without breaking the skin.

When you've stretched the dough as close to paper thin as you can, spread it thinly with a couple of tablespoons of the melted butter. Spread the filling in a line along one edge of the dough.

Sprinkle about ¼ cup of melted butter over the filling.

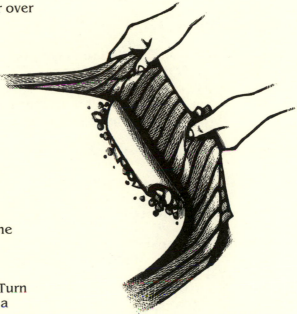

Using the cloth, pick up the edge of the dough where the filling is and roll it up like a jelly roll so the filling is wound up in many layers of dough.

Tuck the ends of the dough underneath and slide the roll onto a greased baking sheet, bending it into a crescent or horseshoe shape so it will fit.

Brush the roll with the remainder of the melted butter.

Baking: Slide the strudel into your preheated oven to bake 20 minutes. Turn the heat down to 350°F and bake for a further 15 minutes.

When the strudel is done, remove it from the oven and dust it with confectioners' sugar.

Baking Apfel Strudel is an art, taking the apple to its ultimate elegance. But even an imperfect strudel will seem exquisite, so take courage, some apples, and have fun!

Condensed Milk Lemon Pie

Brinna Sands and her sister Anne Baird learned how to make this lemon pie from their Grandmother Davis when they were little. It was always made with a graham cracker crust which is a great alternative to a traditional pie crust and is perfect for introducing kids to the arts and delights of pie making. Not only is the crust fun to make, but the reaction of the condensed milk as you stir the lemon juice into it is magic every time. It's unbelievably rich, tart and delicious, a very special pie for children.

This recipe makes enough crust for a 9-inch plate with lots to sprinkle on top of the pie (or a 10- or 11-inch pie plate with no topping), and filling for a 9-inch pie shell. To increase the amount of filling, add 1 can of condensed milk and 3/8 to 1/2 cup lemon juice for every inch larger in diameter (than 9 inches) your pie plate is.

Graham Cracker Crust

> 16 Graham Crackers or English Digestive Biscuits (page 361), about
>   2 cups of crumbs
> 1/2 cup sugar
> 3/4 cup (1 1/2 sticks) butter, softened
> 1 teaspoon cinnamon (optional)

Lemon Filling with Condensed Milk

> 2 (14-ounce) cans sweetened condensed milk (see Appendix)
> 3/4 to 1 cup lemon juice (add the lesser amount first and more to taste)
> grated or minced rind of 1 lemon

Preparing the Crust: The easiest way to crush the crackers is to put them inside a clean paper or plastic bag and roll them with a rolling pin until they're fine. After they're sufficiently squashed, put them in a mixing bowl and stir in the sugar. Cut the butter into pieces and drop them in.

For the fastidious, a pastry cutter will blend these ingredients very nicely. But one of the joys of childhood is to get right in with small (or large) hands and "moosh" everything together.

Save some of this mixture to sprinkle on top of your pie. Put the rest into a 9-inch pie plate and pat it into place.

Preparing the Filling: Pour the condensed milk into a mixing bowl. Add 3/4 cup lemon juice and the lemon rind and stir until the milk has undergone its magic reaction. Add more lemon juice if the filling is not tart enough for you.

Assembling & Chilling: Pour the filling into the crust, sprinkle on the remaining graham cracker mixture and chill for 2 hours, or overnight.

PASTA
VIII

PASTA
SHAPES & FILLINGS

• Pasta dough should be elastic enough to roll out without tearing, strong enough to hold together while it cooks and be firm but tender when it's served. King Arthur Unbleached All-Purpose Flour makes superior pasta because of its high-quality, naturally tender gluten.

• Whenever you see this symbol in the ingredient list after King Arthur Unbleached All-Purpose Flour 🌾, try substituting some King Arthur Stone Ground Whole Wheat Flour for the same amount of King Arthur Unbleached All-Purpose Flour. Pasta made with whole wheat is wonderful!

• When you roll your pasta by hand, keep a good dusting of flour on the rolling pin and the work surface. Roll it out until you can almost see through it!

• Letting the dough rest as you work with it allows the gluten to relax, making the pasta easier to roll out and shape.

• If you are working with the pasta dough in sections, be sure to wrap the portion that you are not using with plastic wrap, or cover it with a damp towel, so it doesn't dry out.

• When you cook pasta, use more water than you think you need. As pasta cooks, it sheds starch granules. If you don't cook it in enough water, this starch tends to reattach itself to the cooking pasta giving it a gummy surface.

• It's best to cook pasta in a stainless steel or enameled pot. If the only pot you have available is aluminum, add a tablespoon of lemon juice to the water so the pasta won't discolor.

• If you need to keep cooked pasta in a holding position while you stuff it or build a lasagna, keep it in a pot of luke warm water. It will remain pliable but won't get mushy.

PASTA
SHAPES & FILLINGS
VIII

Yankee Doodle went to town,
Riding on a pony.
He stuck a feather in his cap
And called it macaroni.

Yankee Doodle keep it up,
Yankee Doodle Dandy,
Mind the music and the step,
And with the girls be handy.

Fath'r and I went down to camp,
Along with Captain Goodin',
And there we saw the men and boys,
As thick as hasty puddin'.

Yankee Doodle keep it up,
Yankee Doodle Dandy,
Mind the music and the step,
And with the girls be handy.

Uncle Sam came there to change
Some pancakes and some onions,
For 'lasses cake to carry home
To give his wife and young ones.

• A PASTA PRIMER •

Although pasta has been available commercially for years, for the first two-thirds of the twentieth century it was only available dried and in a fairly limited number of sizes and shapes. Our early experience with pasta, for those of us who weren't fortunate enough to grow up in an Italian household, was probably confined to macaroni and cheese (more about that later) with an occasional foray into spaghetti with tomato sauce. That's about as far as most of us went. The diverse and colorful world of pasta wasn't really discovered by the rest of America until this last third of the twentieth century.

Pasta can be an appetizer, a simple accompaniment to a main meal or the centerpiece of a meal itself. As so many of the new, commercial "fresh" pastas attest, it can be shaped and flavored in ways most of us never dreamed of. And the sauces it can be served with are as limitless as are the fillings you can stuff it with.

Fortunately, we're discovering that we can make pasta by hand almost as quickly as going to the store to buy it, and that once we've made it successfully, no other kind quite measures up. So here are some guidelines for exploring this intriguing realm of wheat.

How "Macaroni" Came to America

When we think of pasta today, the first thing that comes to mind is Italy. There isn't any country that has taken to its culinary heart this unique product of wheat and eggs with as much gusto. So it's natural to assume that pasta might have had its origins there. But at the back of our minds is that story of Marco Polo bringing pasta back from China in the thirteenth century.

As we keep thinking, it begins to dawn on us that, actually, we can find pasta-like concoctions of wheat and eggs (or water) in many countries and cultures. They are found in other Mediterranean countries. Farther north, in Germany, you'll find "spaetzle," German noodles made with a batter rather than a dough. And, whether the Marco Polo myths are true or not, the Far East certainly has a long tradition of noodle or pasta making, and it's definitely not confined to China. You'll find noodles in Japan, Korea, Thailand, and so on.

When you think about it, there probably isn't an easier way to store wheat (except intact as the whole berry itself), than in a dried wheat/egg paste, or "maccherone" as it is called in Italy. So pasta, or its equivalent, has probably been made and used for centuries wherever people have been growing and storing grains. And you will find recipes for dishes that include pasta, or its equivalent, in a great many different cultures.

This is not to say that Italy wasn't the source of an original version. Since it lies on the Mediterranean where so many other products originated that included wheat (pastry and yeasted breads being two of the more significant), it is likely that a dried wheat product has been made there for as long as wheat has been in cultivation.

It took trade routes and commerce to bring a wheat-based pasta to countries where wheat didn't grow well. In wasn't common in Britain until the Middle Ages. In eighteenth- and nineteenth-century England, "macaroni," which is what the English called pasta in those days, became a fashionable ingredient in daily fare. It was there and then that "Macaroni & Cheese" became embedded in our culinary culture.

In fact, the English were so taken with Italian pasta, or macaroni, that the word came to mean something very upscale, stylish and elegant. The term "macaroni" was even extended to the Englishmen themselves who traveled in Italy and found pasta new and fascinating. So, in addition to meaning something stylish, it came to mean someone who was stylish as well, or, from another vantage point, a "dandy," someone who was quite taken with himself.

During this period when things "macaroni" were "in," a group of Englishmen even formed The London Macaroni Club to debunk English food and to espouse those things that were "macaroni." All of this begins to shed some light on the verse that opens this chapter.

"Yankee Doodle" with its "macaroni" feather, was a ditty developed by the British sometime after the middle of the eighteenth century to poke fun at the dowdy American colonists. When the elegantly attired English "Red Coats" marched from Boston to Lexington on the 19th of April in 1775, this was the tune they sang.

As that fateful day progressed, the "macaroni" English soldiers suffered a sound defeat at Concord thus marking the beginning of our American Revolution. As they retreated back to Boston, the dowdy colonists marched behind them, taunting them with the same song. From that point on, "Yankee Doodle Dandy" was the colonists' song of rebellion.

And that's how "macaroni" came to America.

KING ARTHUR FLOUR'S
HOMEMADE PASTA (BY HAND)

The important thing when you make pasta at home is to use a "strong" unbleached flour. This combination produces a pasta with a pure wheat flavor (the unbleached part) which can be cooked "al dente," or tender (again, the unbleached part) yet firm (the strong part). If you are fortunate enough to have access to eggs from free-ranging chickens, your pasta will be doubly blessed because those bright orange yolks will create an even more intense golden hue than unbleached flour can alone. (For an even brighter yellow, try a pinch of saffron.)

The following recipe, which can be easily doubled, will make about ½ pound of dough or 4 cups cooked. This amount of pasta, combined with a sauce, will serve two extremely generously and four more than adequately. It is based on approximately ⅔ cup flour to each large egg. Since eggs vary in size and thus in absorption ability (like flour), the flour measurement is a variable one.

Plan to make your sauce and/or filling while the pasta dough rests after kneading and then again after cutting (about 30 minutes each time).

1⅓ to 1½ cups King Arthur Unbleached All-Purpose Flour
¼ teaspoon salt (optional)
2 large eggs
2 teaspoons olive or other vegetable oil (optional)

To make "perfect" pasta, you really don't need the salt or the oil. They are in the ingredient list because some people do include them. Try making your pasta without them the first time (with the smaller amount of flour) and add them only if you feel that something's missing.

The traditional method for mixing these ingredients is to work directly on a kneading surface. If you'll feel more comfortable containing the ingredients, you can just as successfully mix the dough in a bowl.

Making the Dough: Pour the flour (and salt) into a mound on a kneading surface or board. Make a well in the center and break the eggs into it. (By making an indentation in the mound of flour, you'll keep the eggs where you want them, which is important if you are working on a flat surface.)

Gradually draw the flour into the eggs with a fork and beat lightly. You can add olive oil at this point, which some feel makes the pasta more tender. Continue until the flour has absorbed all the egg.

Work in a little additional flour if the mixture is exceptionally moist, but don't overdo it. If you are not sure about the amount of flour to add, push your finger into the ball of dough as far as its center. When you pull it out, it should feel somewhat sticky, but not moist. If it feels moist, work in a little more flour.

Kneading: Let the dough rest for a few minutes to give the flour a chance to really absorb the liquid. Sprinkle a bit more flour on the board and knead the dough until it's smooth and silky, usually between 6 and 8 minutes.

Since this is a much smaller amount of dough than you would ordinarily knead to make bread, its easier to fold the dough forward with one hand and push or roll it away with the other. Use only the barest dusting of flour while you're kneading to keep the dough from sticking to you or the board.

Resting: Cover the dough with a damp towel or plastic wrap (or invert a small bowl over it) and let it rest for at least 10 minutes but up to 30 minutes or more if you have time. This rest relaxes the gluten in the flour and mellows the dough, making it easier to roll out as well as giving you time to begin your sauce or filling.

Rolling: When you unwrap the dough, it will seem damper, but don't add more flour. Pick up the pasta, lightly dust the board (and your hands) with flour, place the pasta on the floured surface and flatten it out with your hands.

Now you want to move fairly quickly so the pasta doesn't dry out while you're rolling it. Roll as you would pie dough, from the center to the outside. Turn the pasta over from time to time and sprinkle on just enough flour to keep it from sticking.

If, as you're rolling, the dough isn't cooperating, put a damp towel over it and give it a little rest to relax the gluten. It will really pay to take the time to roll it thinner than you can imagine you want it.

When it's rolled out far enough, it should be about 24 inches in diameter (if you made a circle) about 21 inches on a side (if you made a square).

For long, flat noodles, like fettuccine or spaghetti, which will be served loose with a light sauce, roll the dough out until it is almost transparent (it will thicken a lot as it cooks).

For "structural" pasta, like lasagna or ravioli, which will contain or support a filling, you can roll the dough a little thicker, somewhere close to the thickness (or thinness) of a dime, but again, thinner than you think.

Resting: After you finish rolling out your dough, let it rest for about 10 minutes uncovered, long enough for it to begin to dry without the edges becoming brittle. When it's ready to cut, it should feel a bit like suede glove leather.

Making Flat Noodles: These are the simplest and quickest to make.

Cutting: Make sure your knife is good and sharp. Lightly dust the sheet of pasta with flour, roll it up loosely and cut. (You might find it easier to fold the sheet of pasta in half or thirds and use a ruler or other straight edge to guide your knife blade.)

- **Linguine, Fettuccine & Tagliatelle:** These range between $1/8$ and $1/2$ inch wide. Fettuccine, which is $1/4$ inch wide, is a good place to start.

- **Quadrucci or "Little Squares:"** These are excellent in a good clear meat or chicken broth. Cut the pasta into $1/2$ inch tagliatelle and then cut them at right angles into $1/2$ inch squares.

- **Bows:** These can be used in dishes that need a three-dimensional pasta to catch and hold a sauce, for pasta salads, Macaroni & Cheese (page 486) or just for fun. Cut rectangles about 1 x 2 inches. Pinch the middle together in a pleat with your thumb and forefinger, using a bit of water to help them stick.

- **Spaghetti & Cappellini:** For spaghetti, cut the dough about as wide as it is thick (i.e., very narrow). For cappellini, or very thin spaghetti, cut it even thinner. (Tricky but doable with patience, and worth trying once.)

Drying: Loosen the coils of pasta with your fingers. If you're going to cook them right away, let them rest and dry on a lightly floured towel for 30 minutes. You can also hang them on a clothes rack (or even a broom handle propped between two chairs). If you are going to store them, let them dry completely.

Cooking: A good Italian pasta maker calculates that you need 1 liter of water per 100 grams of pasta, which is about 4 quarts per pound. Our recipe makes ½ pound of dough or slightly more than 200 grams so we'll use 2½ to 3 quarts of water to cook it. You need enough so you won't lose your boil and, because pasta sheds a bit of its starchy surface as it cooks, enough to dilute the escaped starch. When you use too little water, the concentration of starch becomes so great it tends to restick itself to the surface of the pasta making it gummy.

• **The Watched Pot Method for Fresh Pasta:** Bring the water to a boil, preferably in a stainless steel or enamel kettle.

After it's boiling, add 2 teaspoons of salt (you want about 1 rounded tablespoon for every 4 quarts of water). Salt not only intensifies the flavor of the pasta but it raises the boiling point of the water, which helps create its "tender but firm" texture. If the sauce to be used is bland, you may want to use an additional teaspoon of salt or you may want to cook it in a broth or stock.

You can add a tablespoon of olive oil to the cooking water to help keep the pasta from sticking together, but this will also keep some toppings and sauces from sticking to it as well. So decide whether to add it or not based on your sauce.

Put the pasta in the water when it has come to a rapid boil. Add it all at once so that it cooks evenly. Give it an occasional stir to make sure it's not sticking together. When cooking a long pasta, such as spaghetti, bend it in the middle with a wooden spoon instead of breaking it.

Cover the pot after the pasta is in the water to bring it back to a boil more quickly but then uncover it and continue cooking at a brisk, but not fierce, boil. It will come to the surface fairly quickly after you put it in the water. Just push it back under with a wooden spoon so it is mostly submerged. It cooks quickly, so keep testing it (don't burn your tongue). Thin noodles may take only 2 or 3 minutes, thicker ones will take longer, but all fresh pasta cooks more quickly than dried. Cook until it is "al dente," or firm to the bite.

• **The Ignored Pot Method for Dried Pasta:** This is an acceptable (but second-choice) solution for cooking dried pasta when your mind and body need to be elsewhere.

Bring water to a boil in a large kettle and add the pasta. Leave uncovered and let the pot come back to a boil. Cook for about 2 minutes. Remove the kettle from the heat, cover and let it sit until you can get back to it.

Draining & Serving: When the pasta is done, immediately remove it from the heat and drain in a colander, gently shaking it to remove extra water. If it must wait, put it back in the pot after it has drained and stir in a bit of olive oil or butter to keep it from sticking. It's best to have your sauce piping hot so you can serve the pasta right away.

Making "Structural Pasta": A ruler can be a useful guide here.

• **Lasagna:** Cut strips about ¹/₂ inch shorter than the pan you'll bake it in, and whatever width you like. Traditionally lasagne is about 2 inches wide. Unless you're planning to dry these, you'll want to "build" your layers of lasagne without cooking the noodles. They'll cook as it bakes. (See page 487.)

• **Cannelloni & Manicotti:** Cut the sheet of dough into squares about 4 or 5 inches on a side. Dry for about 30 minutes and cook like flat noodles. Drain, fill, roll (cannelloni one edge to the other, manicotti, diagonally) and place seam side down in a baking pan. Cover with a sauce and bake. (See page 492.)

• **Ravioli:** Cut your sheet of dough in half. On one half make an imaginary grid of squares about 2 inches on a side. Place a bit of filling in the center of each "square." Moisten the "edges" of the squares, cover with the second sheet of dough and press the pieces together along the moistened edges around the filling. Cut into individual pieces. (A pizza wheel is useful here.)

Let the ravioli rest while you bring a pot of water (or broth) to a boil. Because they are thicker and take longer to cook than other pasta, put them in a few at a time (so you don't lose your boil) and cook for about 2 or 3 minutes after they come to the surface.

• **Tortellini:** Cut the dough into 3-inch circles with a cookie cutter or cleaned soup can (with a hole punched in the opposite end to relieve pressure).

Put a dot of filling in the center of each circle. Moisten the edges and fold them in half like a turnover, pressing the edges to seal them.

Turn the curved edge up like the cuff on a pair of pants and bend the straight edge around your finger and moisten and pinch the two ends together. It sounds complicated but your hands will learn to do this quickly so it won't take as much time as you think.

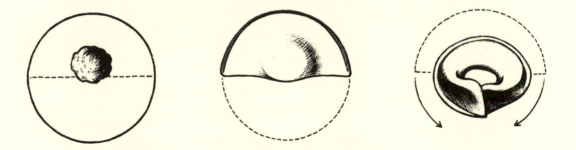

Let the tortellini rest while you bring a pot of water (or broth) to a boil. Drop them in slowly, a few at a time, so the liquid doesn't lose its boil. Cook for about a minute after they come to the surface. Remove them with a slotted spoon and then do another batch.

Filling Suggestions for Tortellini & Ravioli

Here are a few; you'll be able to come up with many more combinations of ingredients which, finely minced, can be wrapped in their own little pasta containers.

- pesto with minced pignoli (pine nuts)
- freshly grated Parmesan cheese and minced walnuts
- spinach, cooked, minced and squeezed dry with freshly grated Parmesan cheese
- mushrooms, sautéed until almost dry, with freshly grated Parmesan cheese
- chopped prosciutto and ricotta cheese

Storing Homemade Pasta

Storing Fresh: Without drying, any of the unstuffed pasta variations can be refrigerated in an airtight container for about a week.

Storing Dried: Pasta that has been dried thoroughly and sealed in airtight plastic bags will remain fresh for a month stored in a cool dry cupboard. (Be sure the pasta has dried completely or it will mold.) When you want to use it, cook it as you would fresh pasta, but allow more time. Handle it carefully as it is very brittle at this stage.

Storing Stuffed: Although stuffed pasta can be put in an airtight container and safely refrigerated for several days (how long depends on the ingredients in the stuffing), it ought to be frozen if you intend to keep it any length of time. Drying stuffed pasta at home is not recommended.

Freezing: If you want to store pasta for a longer period, it can be frozen successfully fresh, dried and/or stuffed. It can go directly from the freezer to a pot of boiling water.

Homemade Pasta (by Machine)

The Food Processor

Although combining pasta ingredients by hand isn't taxing, it's very quick and easy in this modern device.

1 1/3 to 1 1/2 cups King Arthur Unbleached All-Purpose Flour
1/4 teaspoon salt (optional)
2 large eggs
2 teaspoons olive oil (optional)

Mixing: Using the metal blade of your food processor, combine the flour and eggs and process for 20 to 30 seconds. The mixture should resemble small beads. If it appears too wet, add flour, one teaspoon at a time. If it appears too crumbly, add water, one teaspoon at a time.

Remove the dough from the processor, gather it together in a ball and knead it by hand for a minute or two to bring it together. Cover it with plastic wrap or an inverted bowl and let it rest for a few minutes.

The Hand Cranked Pasta Machine

You can knead, roll and cut this pasta by hand (see previous directions) or you can use one of the many pasta machines that are available.

Pasta machines have two main parts, one that kneads and rolls at the same time, and the other that cuts. Though most machines come with instructions, here are a few guidelines that might prove helpful.

Kneading & Rolling: After the dough has rested, cut it in half and flatten it. Cover the piece of dough you're not using with plastic wrap or a damp towel to keep it moist.

Set the rollers of the pasta machine on their widest setting. Fold the piece of dough you're working with in half and crank it through the rollers.

After it's through, fold it in thirds and crank it though again. Repeat this folding and rolling 8 to 10 times, until the dough feels smooth and silky. If the dough feels sticky, dust it with flour.

Then begin closing the rollers, one setting at a time, feeding the dough through the machine once at each setting until it's as thin as you want it. Don't fold the dough at this stage.

If the dough feels sticky at any time, dust it lightly with flour. (See page 465 for information about thickness or, actually, thinness of specific types of pasta.)

Cutting: After the dough is appropriately thin you can cut it by hand (see pages 466 and 468) or you can use the cutter on the pasta machine. Lasagne, ravioli, cannelloni, manicotti and tortellini are best cut by hand.

- **Linguine, Fettuccine & Tagliatelle:** Pass the sheet of pasta through the cutting teeth set at the indicated setting, or $1/8$ inch for linguine, $1/4$ inch for fettuccine and $1/2$ inch for tagliatelle.

- **Spaghetti:** Stop rolling the pasta sheet two notches from the thinnest setting. Let this sheet of dough dry out a bit and then pass it through the narrow cutting teeth. (Not all pasta machines come with these narrow teeth; you may need to purchase them separately.)

- **Quadrucci (or "Little Squares"):** First cut the pasta into tagliatelle and then, with a knife, cut crosswise into squares.

PLAYING WITH INGREDIENTS

Once you have mastered this basic egg or "yellow" pasta, experiment with some of these others for variations in color, flavor and texture.

As in any recipe, the ratio of flour to liquid is the key to remember. With pasta, the eggs are the "liquid," each measuring about $1/4$ cup. So you'll want to replace them with about $1/4$ cup of liquid. Let the dough tell you whether to add more liquid or flour.

WHOLE WHEAT PASTA

This contains only a modest amount of whole wheat flour. You can certainly use more (or all) as you wish.

1 cup King Arthur Unbleached All-Purpose Flour
$1/3$ to $1/2$ cup King Arthur Stone Ground Whole Wheat Flour
$1/4$ teaspoon salt (optional)
2 large eggs
2 teaspoons olive oil (optional)

TOMATO PASTA

$1 1/3$ to $1 1/2$ cups King Arthur Unbleached All-Purpose Flour
$1/4$ teaspoon salt (optional)
1 large egg
2 rounded tablespoons tomato paste
2 teaspoons olive oil
1 to 2 teaspoons water

SPINACH PASTA

1⅓ to 1½ cups King Arthur Unbleached All-Purpose Flour
¼ teaspoon salt (optional)
1 large egg
2 rounded tablespoons of cooked spinach, drained and minced or
    puréed (or frozen spinach, thawed and minced or puréed)
2 teaspoons olive oil
1 to 2 teaspoons water

BEET PASTA

1⅓ to 1½ cups King Arthur Unbleached All-Purpose Flour
¼ teaspoon salt (optional)
1 large egg
2 rounded tablespoons cooked puréed beets
2 teaspoons olive oil
1 to 2 teaspoons water

PARMESAN PASTA

1⅓ to 1½ cups King Arthur Unbleached
    All-Purpose Flour
¼ teaspoon salt (optional)
½ cup freshly grated Parmesan cheese
2 large eggs
2 teaspoons olive oil (optional)

PESTO PASTA

1⅓ to 1½ cups King Arthur Unbleached
    All-Purpose Flour
¼ teaspoon salt (optional)
1 large egg
1 tablespoon olive oil
2 to 3 tablespoons pesto

Polish Pasta

This intriguing recipe came to us from Mary Metallo, a native of Maine. She says it makes a dough that is exceptionally light and easy to handle and makes wonderful noodles, ravioli or pierogi, a Polish filled pasta like ravioli.

2 cups King Arthur Unbleached All-Purpose Flour
1/4 teaspoon salt (optional)
1/2 cup mashed boiled potato
1 egg
water from boiling the potatoes

Combine the flour, (salt), potato and egg. Add only enough of the potato water to moisten the mixture. Knead, rest and roll out as for Handmade Pasta (page 465).

Stained Glass Pasta

For a lacy or stained glass effect, roll herbs such as whole leaves of Italian (flat) parsley into your pasta. This is so pretty to look at, you might not want to eat it.

If you are rolling by hand, cut your dough in half after it's as thin as you can make it. Moisten one piece lightly.

Sprinkle fresh herbs or lay whole herb leaves in an attractive pattern on this piece of dough and place the other piece on top. Continue rolling until the combined pieces are almost translucent.

If you are using a hand-cranked pasta machine, roll out the dough until it is thoroughly kneaded and you are about to start closing down the rollers. Moisten one of the sheets of dough and sprinkle it with herbs, or carefully place on it whole leaves of Italian parsley.

Carefully cover it with a second sheet of dough. Continue rolling (without folding) until the dough is very thin and you can clearly see the herbs.

• SIMPLE & ELEGANT SAUCES FOR PASTA •

Our Homemde Pasta (by Hand or by Machine) can be served with a traditional marinara sauce or "all decked out" in something fresh and new. In any of the recipes that call for heavy cream, you can substitute evaporated milk which is not authentic but much kinder nutritionally.

CHEF LYNDON VIRKLER'S
PESTOS FOR PASTA

We are fortunate to have the New England Culinary Institute, an internationally acclaimed school for chefs, headquartered right here in Montpelier, Vermont. The Institute provides a rigorous program of hands-on training in real, working food service operations. The students preside over all the food prepared at the Inn at Essex, located a little north and east of Burlington. It is a first-class luxury hotel and the Institute's branch campus.

We initiated our first WinterBake recipe competition with their assistance and expertise, and the award ceremony was held at the Inn in February, 1991. They have fielded and baked off a vast number of entries and have been tremendously supportive in this endeavor. (It has also given us an opportunity to stay at the Inn and sample their fare. Boston and New York...watch out!) Two of their chefs, Lyndon Virkler and Benjamin Cevelo, have graciously shared with us some creative pasta recipes.

Pestos were traditionally made with a mortar and pestle (hence the name) but, unless you're a purist, you'll find that they can also be made successfully in a blender or food processor. The basic recipe will make enough for about 16 servings tossed with your favorite Homemade Pasta. You can cut it in half or make the whole amount and store the pesto you don't use in an airtight container in your refrigerator (a traditional and delicious way to store fresh basil). Try these pestos in a braided bread (page 154).

BASIL PESTO

Traditional pesto is the Italian (or New England) summer distilled to perfection.

4 cups fresh basil, loosely packed
2 cups pignoli (pine nuts) or shelled walnuts
4 to 8 cloves of garlic, peeled and minced
2 teaspoons salt (optional)
3 cups freshly grated Parmesan cheese
2 cups olive oil

Blend the basil, nuts and garlic in your blender or processor. When this mixture is well combined, add the cheese (and salt). With the blender running, gradually pour in the olive oil.

Spinach Pesto

This is a winter substitute for the fresh summer version. Substitute 4 cups of fresh spinach leaves for the basil and add 3 tablespoons dried basil.

Fiddlehead Pesto

This one will store the flavor of that ephemeral green collected in late May from secret, damp places in the woods. Substitute 4 cups cleaned, blanched, drained and rinsed fiddleheads for the basil leaves. Add 3 tablespoons dried basil.

Pistachio Pesto

Substitute 2 cups of pistachios for the pine nuts or walnuts. Process as for basil pesto, but don't process as finely; you want the pistachios to be visible.

Chef Lyndon Virkler's
Sauce with Caramelized Onions & Gorgonzola

Serve with 1 recipe (½ pound) Homemade Linguine *flavored with 1 tablespoon freshly ground rosemary or pasta of your choice.*

2 tablespoons butter
2 medium red onions, sliced (about 1 to 1½ cups)
½ teaspoon fresh thyme
½ teaspoon fresh rosemary
1 tablespoon olive oil
½ teaspoon walnut oil
1 cup white wine
2 cups cream
1¼ cups (about ⅓ pound) Gorgonzola or other blue cheese
¾ cup grated Swiss cheese
1 cup walnuts, toasted

Heat the butter in a sauté pan until it foams. Add the onions and brown lightly. Reduce the heat and continue browning until the natural sugars in the onion are caramelized. Add the herbs and oils. Stir in the wine and reduce until almost dry.

Bring the cream to a simmer with the cheeses and cook until reduced by a quarter. Add the caramelized onions and heat through.

Toss with freshly cooked linguine and garnish with walnuts.

Walnut Ricotta Sauce

This sauce of Chef Lyndon Virkler's is practically a pesto. Serve with 1 recipe (½ pound) Homemade Spinach or Beet Pasta.

2 cups (½ pound) walnuts
½ cup ricotta cheese
⅓ cup pignoli (pine nuts), toasted
¼ to ⅓ cup olive oil
2 tablespoons fresh parsley, minced (or 2 teaspoons dried)
½ clove of garlic, minced
1 tablespoon fresh marjoram, minced (or 1 teaspoon dried)
salt and freshly ground pepper to taste
freshly grated Parmesan cheese (optional)

Combine all the ingredients in a blender or food processor and process until smooth. Toss freshly cooked pasta with this sauce and and serve immediately.

Fresh Summer Sauce

This recipe comes to us from Sylvia Paxton, Frank Sands' sister, who lives with her family in Cincinnati. In addition to being a wife, mother and lawyer (currently on hold), Sylvia is the Activities Director for Evergreen (an assisted living community) and operates her own catering business as well. This is a Paxton favorite both because it's so crisp and salad-like and because it can be put together so quickly.

Serve with 2 recipes (1 pound) Homemade Spaghetti or Fettuccine.

4 cups (about 2 pounds) fresh (or canned) plum tomatoes, skinned
1 cup fresh basil, coarsely chopped (a pair of sharp scissors works well)
3 tablespoons sherry vinegar (or 2 tablespoons white vinegar plus
      1 tablespoon sherry)
1 (1¾-ounce) jar capers, drained and rinsed
salt and pepper
¾ cup olive oil

Coarsely chop the tomatoes and mix in the basil. Let this stand 1 to 2 hours at room temperature or overnight in the refrigerator. Bring back to room temperature before the next step.

Blend in the vinegar and capers and add salt and pepper to taste. Toss the freshly cooked pasta with the olive oil and transfer to a serving platter. Mix in the tomato sauce and let stand 5 minutes before serving.

BARBARA'S
PANNA E POMODORO

This is the first of a several pasta sauce recipes Barbara Lauterbach has graciously given us to share with you. Barbara has a way with quick breads, but with pasta she has Merlin's wand. This recipe is simple and delicious. It is one of Barbara's favorites. A number of her others appear later in these pages.

Serve this with 1 recipe (½ pound) Homemade Fettuccine.

2 tablespoons butter
1⅓ cups heavy cream (or evaporated milk)
salt and freshly ground black pepper, to taste
¼ cup fresh (or canned Italian) tomatoes, skinned and puréed
freshly grated Parmesan cheese

Melt the butter. Add the cream and bring it to a boil. Season to taste with salt and pepper. Gradually stir in the tomato purée.

Combine with freshly cooked pasta and serve with a bowl of freshly grated Parmesan cheese.

SAUCE WITH WINE & SUN-DRIED TOMATOES

Serve with 1 recipe (½ pound) Homemade Fettuccine or pasta of your choice.

1 cup shallots or onions, chopped
1 cup sliced mushrooms (optional)
2 tablespoons butter
2 tablespoons olive oil
½ cup chopped sun-dried tomatoes in olive oil (loosely packed)
½ cup white wine
1½ cups heavy cream (or evaporated milk)
salt and freshly ground black pepper, to taste
freshly grated Parmesan cheese

Sauté the shallots or onions and mushrooms in the butter and oil until they are lightly browned. Add the tomatoes. Blend in the wine and simmer until the liquid is almost gone. Add the cream (or milk) and heat through.

Season to taste with salt and pepper. Toss with freshly cooked pasta and serve with a bowl of Parmesan cheese.

FRESH & SIMPLE TOMATO SAUCE

If you have your own garden with fresh tomatoes and basil, this is the sauce for you. Serve with 2 recipes (1 pound) Homemade Fettuccine or pasta of your choice.

2 cloves of garlic, minced
3 tablespoons olive oil
2 pounds ripe tomatoes, peeled, seeded and chopped (about 4 cups)
3 to 5 leaves of fresh basil, minced (or 1 teaspoon dried)
2 tablespoons fresh parsley, minced (or 2 teaspoons dried)
salt and freshly ground black pepper, to taste
freshly grated Parmesan cheese

Sauté the garlic in the oil until it's just coloring. Add the tomatoes and herbs. Cook over very low heat for about 15 minutes and correct the seasonings. Serve over freshly cooked pasta with a bowl of freshly grated Parmesan cheese.

MARINARA SAUCE

Depending on how much it cooks down, this makes between 1 and 1½ quarts of sauce which will serve 8 to 12 people (3 to 4 recipes Homemade Spagetti or Linguini). It can also be used on or in any of the "construction" pasta recipes in this chapter.

1 to 1½ cups (2 medium or 1 large) onion, chopped
3 or 4 cloves of garlic, minced (more or less depending on taste)
1 green pepper, chopped
¼ cup olive oil
2 tablespoons fresh basil (or 2 teaspoons dried)
⅓ cup fresh parsley (or 1 tablespoon dried)
1 tablespoon fresh oregano (or 1 teaspoon dried)
½ teaspoon fennel seed (optional)
¼ teaspoon freshly ground black pepper
2 teaspoons salt
4 cups (about 2 pounds) fresh plum tomatoes, peeled (or a 32-ounce
    can, undrained)
½ to ¾ cup dry red wine (optional)
6 cups (about 1 pound) sliced mushrooms, sautéed (optional)
1 to 2 pounds cooked, crumbled ground beef and/or sweet or hot
    sausage (optional)

Sauté the onions, garlic and pepper in the oil. Blend in the herbs and salt. Add the tomatoes and bring to a boil. Turn the heat down and simmer for 30 to 45 minutes (depending on how thick you like your sauce), stirring occasionally. Add the mushrooms and meat and heat through. Correct the seasonings.

Fettuccine with Gorgonzola Sauce

Gorgonzola is an Italian blue cheese from the town whose name it bears. Serve with 1 recipe (½ pound) Homemade Fettuccine.

4 ounces Gorgonzola (about 1 cup)
⅓ cup milk
3 tablespoons butter
¼ cup heavy cream
salt, to taste
⅓ cup freshly grated Parmesan cheese
more freshly grated Parmesan cheese (optional)

Put the Gorgonzola, milk and butter in a shallow enameled or other flameproof serving dish that can accommodate all the pasta. Mash the cheese with a wooden spoon and stir to incorporate it into the milk and butter. Cook over low heat for about 1 minute or until the sauce has a dense, creamy consistency.

Stir in the heavy cream, salt to taste and then toss the freshly cooked pasta with the sauce. Blend in the Parmesan cheese. Serve immediately with more freshly grated Parmesan cheese.

Pasta with Smothered Onions

Serve with 1 recipe (½ pound) fresh Homemade Pasta of your choice.

1½ tablespoons lard
5 tablespoons olive oil (or 6 tablespoons olive oil and no lard)
6 cups (about 1½ pounds) thinly sliced onions
salt and freshly ground black pepper, to taste
½ cup dry white wine
2 tablespoons fresh parsley, chopped
freshly grated Parmesan cheese

Put the lard, olive oil and onions in a large sauté pan. Cover and cook over very low heat for at least 45 minutes. Uncover the pan, raise the heat to medium high and cook until the onion turns a deep, dark gold.

Since onions are quite sweet, add a liberal amount of salt and pepper to season. Add the wine, raise the heat to high and stir until the wine has almost evaporated. Quickly stir in the parsley and remove from the heat.

Toss the pasta with the sauce for about 30 seconds and serve accompanied by a bowl of freshly grated Parmesan cheese.

Mortadella & Mushroom Sauce

Mortadella is the original bologna from Bologna. It is sometimes seasoned with pistachio nuts and/or whole peppercorns.

Serve with 1 recipe (½ pound) fresh Homemade Fettuccine.

6 tablespoons butter
5 cups (about ¾ pound) mushrooms, sliced
2 tablespoons shallots or onions, chopped
1½ cups (6 ounces) mortadella, chopped (about 4 thick slices)
1 cup heavy cream
½ cup freshly grated Parmesan cheese
salt and freshly ground black pepper, to taste
freshly grated Parmesan cheese

Melt the butter in a skillet and sauté the shallots and mushrooms until they begin to release their juices. Add the mortadella and cook for a minute, mixing well. Add the cream and cheese and cook down slightly.

Season to taste, pour over freshly cooked pasta and serve with freshly grated Parmesan cheese.

Catherine Sands'
Sauce with Garlic & Cherry Peppers

Cathy and her husband, Bob (Frank's brother), live in Bethesda, Maryland, with their two children. She has graciously agreed to share this recipe, which she serves with 1 recipe (½ pound) fresh Homemade Fettuccine.

4 cloves of garlic, minced
½ cup olive oil
4 marinated hot cherry peppers, chopped
4 sprigs parsley
freshly grated Parmesan cheese

Sauté the garlic in the olive oil. When the garlic is beginning to color, throw on a little water to stop the sautéeing process. Add the cherry peppers and heat through.

Toss with the pasta and serve garnished with freshly grated Parmesan cheese and a sprig of parsley.

Chef Lyndon Virkler's
Smoked Salmon, Green Peppercorn & Mushroom Sauce

Serve with 1 recipe (½ pound) fresh Homemade Fettucini flavored with 1½ tablespoons of fresh, minced dill weed (or 1½ teaspoons dried).

2 teaspoons butter
3 cups (½ pound) mushrooms, sliced
¾ cup scallions, sliced (or onions, chopped)
2 tablespoons white wine
¼ pound smoked salmon cut in ¼-inch strips
½ cup cream
¼ teaspoon green peppercorns
freshly ground pepper
chopped chives or scallion greens (for garnish)

Heat the butter in a medium-sized skillet until it foams. Add the scallions and mushrooms and sauté. Stir in the wine and cook until almost dry. Add the smoked salmon and cream and simmer until reduced by half. Sprinkle in the peppercorns.

Serve immediately, tossed with freshly cooked fettuccine. Garnish with freshly ground pepper and chopped chives or scallion greens.

Paxton House
"Zesta Spagetta"

This is a favorite Paxton main course pasta. It's very quick and easy and the ingredients are ones you are apt to have on hand. The flavor of the anchovies is not overwhelming but gives the sauce some zip.

Serve with 1 recipe (½ pound) Homemade Spaghetti or Fettuccine.

2 tablespoons butter
7 ounces white tuna, in oil (or water, drained, plus 3 tablespoons olive
        oil) or ½ pound fresh grilled tuna
generous amount of freshly ground black pepper
1 (2-ounce) can anchovies, drained and minced
3 tablespoons capers
½ cup cream, evaporated milk or white wine (optional)

Melt the butter in a saucepan. Stir in the tuna (and oil) and break it into small pieces. Add the pepper, anchovies and capers (and liquid, if you use it) and heat through. Toss the pasta and sauce together and serve immediately.

GRILLED TUNA SAUCE

This is a delightful way to use leftover freshly grilled tuna (which can be caught without trapping dolphins). Serve with 1 recipe (½ pound) fresh Homemade Fettuccine.

    2 tablespoons butter
    ½ cup olive oil
    1 cup tuna, shredded
    ¼ cup fresh parsley, chopped
    ¼ cup chicken stock (homemade if available)

Heat the butter and olive oil in a saucepan. Add the tuna and parsley and simmer until they are fairly well combined into a sauce. Thin as desired with stock and serve over freshly cooked pasta.

QUICK REFRIGERATOR SAUTÉE

This is a recipe that uses up leftovers and gets something elegant on the table "p.d.q." If you don't have any of the suggested ingredients, make something up. This is just a template of suggestions so you can throw something together that looks earnest. Serve with 1 recipe (½ pound) fresh Fettuccine.

    2 to 4 tablespoons butter
    2 to 4 tablespoons olive oil
    3 cups (½ pound) mushrooms, cleaned and sliced thin (optional)
    1½ to 2 cups leftover anything in the refrigerator or something new and
            fresh (ham, chicken, shrimp, scallops, etc.)
    2 to 3 cloves of garlic, minced
    ½ to 1 cup chopped onion
    ½ to 1 cup chopped green or red pepper (sweet or hot)
    ¼ cup minced sun-dried tomatoes, artichoke hearts, etc.
    ¼ cup wine (white, Marsala, sherry, etc.), chicken stock or bouillon
    1½ cups cream (or evaporated milk)
    ½ cup freshly grated Parmesan (or other cheese)
    freshly grated Parmesan cheese for the table

Sauté the mushrooms until they are almost dry. Remove to a serving platter. Do the same with any meat or fish that isn't already cooked. Sauté the garlic, onions and peppers. When they begin to color, add the tomatoes or other vegetables. Remove these to the platter. Add the wine to the pan and cook down until it's almost gone. Add the cream or evaporated milk and heat through.

Return everthing to the skillet and heat through. Blend in the cheese, toss with freshly cooked fettuccine. Put it all on the platter and serve pronto.

PETE'S PASTA PUTTANESCA

This recipe comes to us from our old friend, Peter Rizzo, whose fledgling advertising agency, Rizzo, Simons, Cohn, Inc. took on Sands, Taylor & Wood Co. in the early 1980's. Pete, Tom Simons and Rick Cohn are a talented trio whose success has swept them swiftly into new arenas. Pete, when he isn't running his agency (or marathons), loves to cook, as this recipe attests.

Serve with 1 recipe (¹/₂ pound) fresh Homemade Linguine accompanied by a green salad and a hearty red wine.

1 small onion, diced (about ¹/₃ cup)
1 cup sun-dried tomatoes (cut in strips)
1 to 2 vinegar cherry peppers, sliced, or ¹/₂ teaspoon (or more) red
         pepper (optional)
8 black olives, sliced
¹/₄ cup mushrooms, sliced (domestic or rehydrated porcini)
1 clove of garlic
4 tablespoons olive oil
2 tablespoons tomato paste
2 or 3 anchovies, mashed (optional)
1 tablespoon capers
2 tablespoons fresh basil (or 2 teaspoons dried)
freshly grated Parmesan cheese
fresh minced parsley, for garnish

Cut up all the sliceable vegetables ahead of time. Mince the clove of garlic and sauté it and the red pepper in the olive oil over medium heat. Add the onion, tomatoes, cherry pepper, tomato paste and anchovies and stir periodically until hot. Add the capers, olives and fresh basil and mix all together. Turn the heat down to a simmer, add the mushrooms and cook for 2 to 3 minutes.

Top the pasta with a generous portion of sautéed Puttanesca vegetables. Serve with freshly grated cheese and minced parsley to sprinkle on top.

SAUCE WITH CHICKEN & MARSALA

This recipe is one stage of an evolutionary process, which just shows you how ephemeral recipes can be. The original was Mary Ann Esposito's Veal Marsala. Frank Sands has become a master at making this delicious dish, substituting chicken breasts, pounded thin. One evening there was some left over (which doesn't happen very often) so Brinna turned it into the above sauce, which was equally delicious. It's so good, you may want to make it for a first-time-around main dish. Enjoy it in this phase and then see where you can go with it from here. Serve with 1 recipe (¹/₂ pound) Homemade Fettuccine.

2 boneless breasts of chicken (pounded thin), cut into bite-sized pieces
King Arthur Unbleached All-Purpose Flour (seasoned with salt and pepper,
       for dredging)
4 tablespoons butter
1 cup dry Marsala wine
juice of 1 lemon
salt and freshly ground black pepper, to taste
freshly grated Parmesan cheese

Dredge the chicken in the seasoned flour, shaking off the excess, and let it rest while you heat the butter in a skillet. Sauté the chicken pieces in the butter for 2 or 3 minutes (until they're a bit browned and crispy). Remove them to your serving platter (not to be served yet, just to be out of the way).

Pour the Marsala and lemon juice into the pan and try to incorporate all the drippings and bits into the liquid. Correct the seasoning if it needs it. Return the chicken to the Marsala/lemon mixture and heat through.

Toss the freshly cooked fettuccine with the sauce and serve with plenty of freshly grated Parmesan cheese.

White Clam Sauce

Serve with 1 recipe (½ pound) Homemade Pasta of your choice.

2 dozen clams, steamed
¼ cup olive oil
3 large cloves of garlic, whole
white wine (if needed, or to taste)
a pinch of dried hot pepper flakes (optional)
2 tablespoons fresh parsley, chopped
freshly ground black pepper

Drain the clams and reserve the broth. Remove the clams from their shells and chop. Put the juice through a fine strainer lined with cheesecloth to remove any sand.

Heat the oil in a skillet. Add the garlic cloves and sauté until lightly browned. Remove the garlic and discard.

Add the strained clam broth (plus a little white wine if you need more liquid), the hot pepper flakes and parsley. Bring to a boil and reduce slightly. Add the clams and cook for 2 minutes. Season with pepper.

Serve over freshly cooked pasta.

• PASTA "STRUCTURES" •

In this section we are dealing with fairly simple "structures." All the fillings and sauces can be mixed and matched according to your whims and needs. (You can even try some of the sauces in the preceding section.)

Ravioli and tortellini are a little trickier to make than other structural pasta and take more time. You'll find a few suggestions for filling them on page 469 and directions for shaping them starting on page 468. They can be served with any of the sauces in either section (or for a cultural transgression, a few sprinkles of tamari or soy sauce).

MACARONI & CHEESE

A predecessor of this familiar dish, known as "macrows," was actually eaten in Britain in the late fourteenth century. It wasn't until the nineteenth century that "macaroni" captured the hearts of the English and "Macaroni Cheese" (as they call it) became a familiar dish on the Victorian table.

Although this is traditionally served with macaroni, that particular shape is beyond the technology of the home pasta maker so we've substituted our cheerful little bows which will do almost as well.

1 recipe (½ pound) fresh Homemade Bows, cooked
3 tablespoons butter
3 tablespoons King Arthur Unbleached All-Purpose Flour
1½ cups cold milk
1½ cups sharp Cheddar or other cheese (more or less to taste)
salt and pepper, to taste
1 to 1½ cups diced ham (optional)
1 to 1½ cups cooked, diced cauliflower, etc. (optional)
½ cup fresh bread crumbs, sautéed until brown and crisp

Preheat your oven to 350°F.

Melt the butter in a large saucepan. Stir in the flour and cook briefly over low heat. Slowly stir in the milk and cook until thick, stirring constantly. (At this point, you have a simple Béchamel, or white, sauce which can be flavored differently to use in other recipes.)

Blend in and melt the cheese. Add salt and pepper to taste.

Place the cooked bows in a buttered casserole. (Stir in the ham and/or vegetables.) Pour on the sauce and gently blend. Sprinkle with bread crumbs. Bake for 15 to 20 minutes or until hot and bubbly.

Melody Suchmann's
Vegetable Lasagne

This is one of those combinations that stops you short after the first bite because it's so completely delicious. Melody Suchmann makes this at home but she also makes it for Peaberry's Café on Thayer Street in Providence where she is Head Cook. She has graciously agreed to share it with us and so we, in turn, pass it on to you.

This will make enough for 4 to 5 generous servings and can be served hot from the oven, or, as they do at Peaberry's, easily reheated in generous individual portions.

The Noodles

> 1 recipe (½ pound) Homemade Pasta, whatever variation you choose, cut into lasagna noodles, uncooked

While the pasta dough and, later, the cut noodles rest, you can make the sauce and prepare the vegetables.

The Sauce

> ½ cup (1 stick) butter, unsalted
> 2 to 3 large cloves of garlic, minced (optional)
> 2 cups heavy cream (or evaporated milk)
> 8 ounces (1 cup) cream cheese, softened
> 1 tablespoon Dijon mustard
> ¼ teaspoon white pepper (if you have it) or black (if you don't)
> ½ cup freshly grated Parmesan cheese

Melt the butter in a saucepan. Add the garlic and sauté until it's just beginning to brown. Slowly add the cream stirring constantly. Blend in the cream cheese. Add the mustard and pepper and keep on the burner until the mixture is completely heated. Remove it from the burner and stir in the Parmesan cheese.

The Vegetables

> 1 cup chopped broccoli
> 1 cup grated carrots
> 2 or 3 tablespoons olive oil
> 1 small zucchini, sliced thinly lengthwise
> 1 small yellow squash, sliced thinly lengthwise

Blanch the broccoli in boiling water just until it turns a bright green. Sauté the carrots in olive oil until tender but crisp. Don't cook the squash.

The Rest

> ½ cup ricotta (or cottage) cheese
> ⅔ cup grated mozzarella
> ¼ cup bread crumbs

Assembling the Lasagne: Preheat your oven to 350°F.

Brush the bottom of a small roasting pan liberally with olive oil. Place a layer of lasagne noodles on the bottom of the pan. Arrange the broccoli over them. Sprinkle or distribute as evenly as possible about 3 tablespoons each of the ricotta and mozzarella. Drizzle about a cup of sauce over this.

Place a second layer of noodles over the sauce. Sprinkle the grated carrot over these and repeat the same layers as you did with the broccoli. Put down a third layer of noodles and repeat with the squash. Put a fourth layer of noodles on top, sprinkle with mozzarella and dust with bread crumbs.

Bake for 25 to 30 minutes or until slightly browned on top.

CHEF BENJAMIN CEVELO'S GRILLED VEGETABLE LASAGNE

This is a large recipe and will feed 10 to 15 people.

The Noodles & The Sauce

> 3 recipes (1½ pounds) Homemade Pasta (whatever variation you
>   choose), cut into lasagna noodles, uncooked
> 1 recipe (4 cups) Marinara Sauce (page 479)

Make the lasagne noodles first so you can make the sauce and prepare the vegetables while the dough and, later, the noodles rest.

The Vegetables for Grilling

> 1 medium eggplant
> 2 zucchini
> 2 yellow squash
> olive oil
> 2 (or more) cloves of garlic, chopped
> salt and pepper, to taste

Slice the eggplant, zucchini and yellow squash lengthwise, approximately ¼ inch thick. Brush with olive oil, chopped garlic and salt and pepper. Grill until tender.

The Rest

> 1 large onion, finely chopped (³/₄ to 1 cup)
> 2 cups mushrooms, sliced
> 2 pounds fresh spinach (about 4 cups cooked)
> 2 cups ricotta cheese
> 5 eggs (omit for a heart healthy version)
> 2¹/₃ cups freshly grated Parmesan cheese
> 1 pound (4 cups) grated mozzarella

Sauté the onions, mushrooms and spinach together. Mix the ricotta, eggs and Parmesan together, add the onion mixture and season with salt and pepper.

Assembling the Lasagne: Preheat your oven to 350°F. Brush the bottom of a large roasting pan (12 x 17 inches) liberally with olive oil.

Place a layer of lasagne noodles on the bottom of the pan. Layer the vegetables using one kind per layer and topping each with a thin layer of the cheese mix.

Begin each layer with another layer of lasagne noodles.

Top with the sauce and more Parmesan cheese. Bake for 45 to 50 minutes.

Ellen Smith's Lasagne

This recipe was devised by the Sands' daughter, Ellen, who traditionally finds untraditional ways of doing things. She makes it with dried uncooked lasagne noodles which cook in the oven along with the rest of the ingredients.

Although this recipe requires some thinking ahead, it relies for inspiration on what you might find in your refrigerator or on your pantry shelves. This is a large recipe and can be made in two small baking pans so, with one effort, you have two meals.

The Noodles & The Sauce

> 1 recipe (¹/₂ pound) Homemade Pasta cut into lasagna noodles,
>   uncooked or dried
> 1 recipe Marinara Sauce (page 479), without meat

Make the pasta ahead of time so you can prepare the sauce and/or filling while the dough and, later, the cut noodles rest.

The Filling

> 4 cups (1 quart) cottage cheese
> 1 or 2 eggs
> 1 tablespoon fresh basil, minced (or 1 teaspoon dried)
> 1 tablespoon fresh oregano, minced (or 1 teaspoon dried)
> 1/3 cup chopped chives or 3/4 cup chopped onion

Blend this mixture together in a large mixing bowl. Add anything else that appeals to you.

The Rest

> 2 to 3 cups thinly sliced green and/or red, sweet and/or hot peppers, broccoli, spinach, mushrooms, sun-dried tomatoes, etc.
> 1 to 1 1/2 cups grated mozzarella, Swiss, Parmesan or other cheese

Assembling the Lasagne: Preheat your oven to 350°F.

Lightly oil the bottom and sides of your pan. Spread on a thin layer of marinara sauce. Lay down the first layer of noodles and a layer of vegetables. Put half the cottage cheese mixture on top. Sprinkle this with about one-third of the cheese.

Put another thin layer of marinara sauce down. Lay down another layer of noodles and veggies. Spread the remainder of the cottage cheese mixture on top. Put a second third of grated cheese over this. Add another thin layer of sauce and a final one of lasagne noodles. Spread the remainder of the marinara sauce over these and sprinkle the remainder of the cheese over this.

Bake for 45 to 50 minutes.

BRINNA'S LASAGNE

This recipe has been in Brinna's file for more years than she cares to account for. It's one that probably made the rounds of young mothers twenty-five or so years ago. It can be varied as you wish to accommodate whatever dietary demands (in thinking of children) you're faced with. This will feed 8 to 10 large people, and probably more small ones, so could be made in two batches for two occasions. (Lasagne freezes nicely.)

The Noodles & The Sauce

> 1 recipe (1/2 pound) fresh Homemade Pasta, whatever flavor is in vogue at your house, cut into lasagne noodles, either uncooked or dried
> 1/2 recipe Marinara Sauce (2 to 3 cups), page 479

Make the pasta ahead of time so you can prepare the filling and sauce while the dough and then, later, the cut noodles rest.

The Filling

      1 to 2 green (and/or red) peppers, chopped
      1 large onion, chopped ($^3/_4$ to 1 cup)
      $^1/_2$ cup (1 stick) butter, melted
      1 cup sour cream
      1 cup (8 ounces) ricotta or cottage cheese
      8 ounces softened cream cheese
      1 cup grated mozzarella (and/or Parmesan)

Sauté the peppers and onion in 2 tablespoons of butter until they're just beginning to brown. Blend the sour cream and cheeses together until smooth. Stir in the sautéed vegetables.

The Rest

      1 or 2 cups other vegetables: broccoli, spinach, asparagus, your choice
         (optional, but chopped, sautéed and/or blanched if they need it)
      $^1/_2$ cup grated mozzarella or Parmesan cheese

Assembling the Lasagne: Preheat your oven to 350°F.

Brush the bottom of a 10 x 14-inch roasting pan with olive oil. Place a layer of lasagne noodles on the bottom of the pan.

Place one-third of the optional vegetables over these. Distribute a layer of filling (about 1$^1/_2$ cups) over all as evenly as you can.

Lay down a second layer of lasagne noodles. Repeat with the vegetables and filling. Make one more layer and add a layer of noodles. Drizzle the balance of the melted butter over the noodles.

Pour the marinara sauce over everything. Sprinkle with the $^1/_2$ cup grated mozzarella or Parmesan cheese.

Bake for 45 to 50 minutes.

Stuffed Cannelloni or Manicotti

This stuffed pasta is larger than tortellini and ravioli and a little easier to fill as the pasta squares are cooked ahead of time and then rolled around the filling. One recipe of our Homemade Pasta dough, rolled out until it's about 20 inches on a side, will make 16 cannelloni or manicotti, enough to fill a 10 x 14-inch baking pan.

The Pasta & The Sauce

> 1 recipe (½ pound) Homemade Pasta, in whatever flavor you choose, cut into 5-inch squares, cooked and drained
> 1 recipe Marinara Sauce (page 479) with or without hamburger and/or sausage

Make the pasta up ahead of time so you can prepare the sauce and filling while it rests, cooks, etc.

The Filling & The Rest

> 1 to 2 cups cooked, chopped broccoli, spinach, asparagus, Swiss chard, etc. (optional)
> 1 recipe Ellen Smith's Filling (page 490) or 1 recipe Brinna's Filling (page 491)
> freshly grated Parmesan cheese for the top

Blend the vegetables into the filling and set aside.

Assembling the Cannelloni or Manicotti: Preheat your oven to 350°F.

Brush your baking pan with a little olive oil. Spread a layer of sauce on the bottom of the pan.

> • **Rolling Cannelloni:** Place 2 or 3 tablespoons of filling along the center of each pasta square, roll it up from one side to the other and place it, seam down on the sauce in the pan.

> • **Rolling Manicotti:** Place 2 or 3 tablespoons of filling in the center and begin rolling the square up diagonally (starting with a corner). Tuck the side corners in as you go to contain the filling. Place seam down on the sauce in the pan.

Finishing & Baking: If you have filling left over (which you probably will), mix it with the remainder of the sauce and spread it over the top of the pasta. Shake on some Parmesan cheese and bake for 45 to 50 miniutes.

MARY ANN ESPOSITO'S
ROTOLO DI PASTA

Mary Ann and her husband Guy, have become our good friends through our mutual interest in public television. She prepared and served this pasta roll for us one evening amongst a medley of other Italian delicacies. This was the course that everyone agreed was unsurpassed. Mary Ann has graciously shared her recipe with us so we can pass it on to you. Of all our pasta recipes, this is the most intriguing to make.

It is best to prepare this filled pasta ahead of time as it needs to be cooked and cooled before the final step. After it has cooled, it is sliced, "sauced" and baked, which takes only 20 to 25 minutes. It will serve 6 to 8 people as a first course, or 10 to 12 as an appetizer. (You can also bake half and freeze the other half unbaked (but sliced) to cook and serve at a later time.)

The Pasta

> 1 1/2 recipes Homemade Pasta

Follow the Pasta Primer directions to make the dough. While it rests, prepare the filling.

The Filling

> 1 medium sweet red onion, thinly sliced
> 1/4 cup olive oil
> 1/4 pound prosciutto, cut in small pieces
> 3 tablespoons pignoli (pine nuts), toasted
> 2 1/2 cups cooked fresh spinach, well drained (about 20 ounces fresh)
> 1 cup ricotta cheese
> 2/3 cups freshly grated Parmesan cheese
> 1 egg, beaten
> salt and freshly ground black pepper, to taste
> 1 teaspoon freshly grated nutmeg

In a large skillet cook the onion in the olive oil until limp. Add the prosciutto and pignoli and cook down until most of the liquid is gone. Add the spinach and cook until heated through, about 1 minute. Remove from the heat and let cool. Blend in the cheeses, egg, salt, pepper and nutmeg. Correct the seasoning if necessary.

Filling the Pasta: Roll out the pasta on a floured surface until it's a large circle, about 24 inches in diameter. The dough will be very thin. Spread the filling over the dough leaving about an inch around the outside edge. Roll the dough up like a jelly roll. Pinch to seal so the filling won't come out while it cooks.

Rolling It Up: Thoroughly rinse and ring out a clean kitchen towel (not the terry cloth kind) to make sure there is no soap residue in it. Place the pasta on the clean, damp towel and roll the towel around it. Tie the ends with string to seal the pasta inside. You can also tie string loosely (to allow the pasta to expand) around the middle, which will help keep the towel together.

Simmering: Let the pasta rest while you bring a large pot of water to the boil. Place the towel-encased pasta in the water. When it returns to a boil, turn the heat down a bit but make sure the water is still moving, and let the pasta cook for about 20 minutes with the cover on but slightly ajar.

After the cooking period, remove the pasta roll from the water and let it cool completely before removing the towel.

Cremazola Sauce

> 2 cups heavy cream
> ½ pound (about 2 cups) Gorgonzola (or other blue cheese)

> *For tentative blue cheese lovers, combine 2 cups heavy cream, ¼ pound Gorgonzola and ¼ pound cream cheese.*

Simmer either combination, stirring until the cheese melts.

Preparing & Baking the Rotolo: Preheat your oven to 350°F.

After the pasta roll is cool, unwrap the towel and cut the roll into 1-inch slices. Place the pieces on their sides in a large buttered baking dish. Cover with some of the sauce and bake for 20 to 25 minutes or until it is heated through.

Serve as soon as they are out of the oven and pass the remainder of the sauce at the table. (For dessert, serve Mary Ann's Puréed Peach & Lemon Curd Tart, found on page 431.)

If you froze your Rotolo, you can bake the slices right out of the freezer, but lower the temperature 25°F, and bake 15 to 20 minutes longer.

WHOLE WHEAT
IX

WHOLE WHEAT
ANYTHING & EVERYTHING!

• If baking with King Arthur Stone Ground Whole Wheat Flour is new for you, try the recipes in this section by beginning with a ratio of 1 cup of Whole Wheat to 3 cups of King Arthur Unbleached All-Purpose Flour. Gradually increase the amount of Whole Wheat Flour as you and your family's taste buds become accustomed to the denser texture and nutty flavor.

• Although Whole Wheat Flour does not compact as much as All-Purpose Flour, it is still important to measure it the same way. See the top of our bag of King Arthur Unbleached All-Purpose Flour or page 597 for directions. Because things made with Whole Wheat Flour tend to be heavier, it's important to incorporate as much air as possible right from the beginning.

• A "sponge" in yeast baking is a dough that contains about half the total flour called for in a recipe. It is therefore much like a batter. Breads baked with Whole Wheat Flour will rise higher and not be as dense if the flour is allowed to sit in a sponge for several hours. This softens the bran particles in the flour and helps prevent them from shredding the elastic gluten strands in the dough which contain the carbon dioxide bubbles created by the yeast. Preserving these bubbles produces a lighter texture and a higher loaf.

• Whole Wheat Flour can be used wherever All-Purpose Flour is called for! Whenever you see this symbol, 🌾 ,in the other sections of our cookbook, it means you can substitute any amount of King Arthur Stone Ground Whole Wheat Flour for an equal amount of King Arthur Unbleached All-Purpose Flour. Conversely, you can substitute any amount of King Arthur Unbleached All-Purpose Flour for King Arthur Stone Ground Whole Wheat Flour in any recipe in this section.

• King Arthur Stone Ground Whole Wheat Flour contains the vitamin-and oil-rich germ of the whole wheat berry. Because of the oil it is more sensitive to storage conditions than our Unbleached All-Purpose Flour. If you use your flour fairly quickly, store it where you keep your King Arthur Unbleached All-Purpose Flour, somewhere cool and dry. If you use it more slowly, store it in an airtight container in your freezer. Make sure you bring it to room temperature (try warming it in the oven on a cookie sheet) before you bake with it. Flour at freezing temperatures will discourage even the most vigorous yeast or baking powder.

• King Arthur has introduced a new whole wheat flour. It is nutritionally the same as our classic stone-ground whole wheat flour, but there is a difference in flavor. The original is milled from hard red winter wheat. The new flour is milled from hard white winter wheat. The red pigment in red wheat, which is most obvious in the bran layer, or outer covering of the wheat berry, contains a compound called phenolic acid that is related to tannins, and that has a slightly bitter, astringent taste. White whole wheat is missing this compound, which means it has a sweeter, more pleasing flavor. For those of you who are somewhat hesitant about whole wheat flour, look for one milled from hard white wheat.

WHOLE WHEAT
ANYTHING & EVERYTHING!
IX

It has taken most of the twentieth century for whole wheat flour (flour ground from the whole of the wheat berry) to take its rightful place in the scheme of things. For centuries it was assumed that because white flour was so difficult to produce, it was better. Fortunately our understanding of nutrition has begun to change that perception and has created an appreciation for both. As whole wheat flour becomes a greater part of our diet, our taste and demand for it grows every year.

We tend to think of whole wheat flour in terms of bread. It is true that breads made with stone ground whole wheat flour are robust, hearty, and especially nutritious. Whole wheat bread makes wonderful sandwiches and is a great accompaniment to meats, cheeses or hot, steaming soups. But King Arthur Stone Ground Whole Wheat Flour creates equally exciting flavors and textures in cookies, cakes, pastry, pancakes and pasta, and is included in many recipes in other chapters of this cookbook.

We haven't tried to cover all possibilities here but rather have given you some examples in each baking category just to show you how easy Whole Wheat Flour is to use and how easily you can substitute it in the other sections of our *200th Anniversary Cookbook*. If you've never baked with whole wheat flour before, try starting with a ratio of three parts of King Arthur Unbleached All-Purpose Flour to one of our Stone Ground Whole Wheat and let the flavor and texture grow on you.

• WHOLE WHEAT FOR BREAKFAST •

There's no better way to start your day than with a pancake or muffin made with fiber- and carbohydrate-rich whole wheat flour.

HEARTY WHOLE WHEAT PANCAKES

You can make these pancakes lighter by separating the egg and beating the yolk into the liquid ingredients. Then beat the egg white full of tiny air bubbles (until it peaks) and fold it into the batter just before the pancakes go on the griddle. If you use the vegetable oil option, you won't lose much flavor, but you will eliminate most of the cholesterol.

This recipe makes about two dozen medium-sized pancakes and can easily be doubled for a hungry group.

1 1/2 cups King Arthur Stone Ground Whole Wheat Flour
2 teaspoons baking powder
1/2 teaspoon salt
2 tablespoons sugar
1 egg
1 1/2 cups milk
2 tablespoons (1/4 stick) butter or margarine, melted (or vegetable oil)

Mix the flour, baking powder, salt and sugar together in a bowl.

Separate the egg and set the white aside in a small bowl. Measure the milk in a two-cup "liquid" measure, drop in the egg yolk (and the vegetable oil if you are using it) and beat these together right in the measuring cup.

A "liquid" measure is ordinarily made of glass and has a lip extending above the measuring line (see Appendix). A two-cup liquid measure can accomodate the beaters of most manual or electric mixers and thus can serve as a measure and a small mixing bowl at the same time.

Add the liquid to the dry ingredients, taking about 20 seconds to blend the two. Fold in the melted butter.

Beat the egg white until it is stiff. Gently fold it into the batter.

If you have a non-stick or a well-seasoned griddle you may need to grease it for the first batch but not again. Cook your pancakes on a hot griddle, turning once to brown both sides.

Hearty Whole Wheat Waffles

Increase the amount of butter (or vegetable oil) in your batter to 4 or 6 table-spoons ($\frac{1}{2}$ to $\frac{3}{4}$ stick). This batter will produce waffles that are wonderfully crisp as well as more cooperative about coming out of the iron.

Hearty Buttermilk Pancakes or Waffles

You just can't beat the flavor of buttermilk. Substitute buttermilk for the milk, cut the baking powder to 1 teaspoon and add $\frac{3}{4}$ teaspoon of baking soda to the dry ingredients. To make Whole Wheat Buttermilk Waffle batter, increase the butter (or vegetable oil) to 4 or 6 tablespoons ($\frac{1}{2}$ to $\frac{3}{4}$ stick).

Basic Whole Wheat Muffins

Whole wheat muffins for breakfast, with cream cheese or butter and fruit, are another great way to start your day, but save some for later. Savory soups at lunch or supper are lifted from the simple to the sublime when accompanied by a whole wheat muffin with a slice of cheese on the side. You can read more about muffins in Chapter III. This recipe will make about a dozen.

2 cups King Arthur Stone Ground Whole Wheat Flour
1 tablespoon baking powder
$\frac{1}{2}$ to 1 teaspoon salt
2 eggs
1 cup milk
$\frac{1}{2}$ cup brown sugar
4 tablespoons ($\frac{1}{2}$ stick) butter, melted, or vegetable oil (optional)

Preheat your oven to 400°F.

Combine the flour, baking powder and salt in a mixing bowl.

In a separate bowl, beat the eggs. Add the milk, brown sugar and, if you wish, the butter or oil and beat thoroughly. (If you leave out the butter or oil, your muffins will have fewer calories; they will taste great when they're fresh, but they will not keep or reheat as well.)

Pour the liquid ingredients into the dry and blend with a spoon or wire whisk for 20 seconds and no more.

Fill the cups of a greased muffin tin two-thirds full. Bake for 20 to 25 minutes or until the top surface of the muffins springs back when you press them with your fingertips.

Orange Whole Wheat Muffins

In variations such as this, which contain ingredients that would mask the flavor of the butter, you can use vegetable oil or shortening instead.

Substitute orange juice for the milk, honey for the brown sugar and add 2 tablespoons of grated orange rind.

Whole Wheat Refrigerator Bran Muffins

If you don't want to take the time to make these up in the morning, mix up the batter before you go to bed, cover it tightly and tuck it in the refrigerator. In the morning, preheat your oven and then bake only as many as you want. This recipe makes 8 to 12 muffins and you can double or triple it. Keep it in the refrigerator, tightly covered (for up to two weeks) and bake only enough each morning so they'll always be hot and fresh.

Each muffin contains about 5 grams of dietary fiber, a good start on the 20 or 30 you ought to consume every day. They're also a good source of protein and carbohydrates all wrapped up in a 165-calorie package and good enough to eat plain.

1 cup King Arthur Stone Ground Whole Wheat Flour
1 cup wheat bran
1 teaspoon baking soda
1/2 teaspoon salt
1/2 cup raisins, currants or chopped dried prunes, apricots,
    dates, etc. (optional)
1 cup buttermilk
1 large egg
2 tablespoons vegetable oil
1/4 cup molasses (for a traditional taste) or brown sugar (for a
    lighter flavor)

Preheat your oven to 450°F.

Mix the dry ingredients together in a mixing bowl. Blend in the fruit if you want to include it.

In a smaller bowl, beat together the rest of the ingredients. Blend the liquid ingredients into the dry, taking about 20 seconds.

Fill your greased muffin cups about two-thirds full and bake for about 20 minutes (just long enough for you to jump in and out of the shower).

Quick Molasses Buttermilk Bread

Quick bread batter is like muffin batter but it's baked in a loaf pan. (Most quick breads can be baked as muffins and vice versa.) This is an incredibly easy whole wheat loaf sweetened with molasses and flavored with the moist, but non-fat, tang of buttermilk. You'll find a yeast-raised cousin on page 134.

If you have no buttermilk, you can substitute yogurt, or sweet milk soured with 1½ tablespoons lemon juice or vinegar. Let it stand for 5 minutes or so to clabber.

3 cups King Arthur Stone Ground Whole Wheat Flour
½ cup sugar
1½ teaspoons salt
1 teaspoon baking soda
2 teaspoons baking powder
1½ cups buttermilk
½ cup dark molasses

Preheat your oven to 325°F.

In a mixing bowl, blend the dry ingredients together. Combine the buttermilk and molasses. Pour the liquid ingredients into the dry ingredients and blend for only 20 seconds. Pour this batter into a well-greased, 9 x 5-inch loaf pan.

Bake for about 60 minutes or until you can press the top surface with your fingertips and have it spring back.

Whole Wheat Cornmeal Molasses Banana Bread

Here is another molasses buttermilk bread with some added banana and raisin "decorations." Like the above bread, this one contains no fat.

2 cups King Arthur Stone Ground Whole Wheat Flour
1 cup cornmeal
1 tablespoon baking powder
1 teaspoon baking soda
1 teaspoon salt
¾ cup raisins
1 cup mashed ripe bananas (2 or 3 medium sized)
½ cup molasses
¼ cup honey
1 cup buttermilk

Preheat your oven to 350°F.

Combine the flour, cornmeal, baking powder, soda and salt. Mix in the raisins.

In a separate bowl, mash the bananas and stir in the molasses, honey and buttlermilk. Add this mixture to the dry ingredients and stir only enough to blend.

Pour into two 4½ x 8½-inch, lightly greased loaf pans and bake for 40 to 50 minutes.

WHOLE WHEAT BANANA BREAD

This recipe was sent with a "love letter" to King Arthur Flour by Gail LaMagna from New York. She writes: "I love your King Arthur Stone Ground Whole Wheat Flour. I made delicious banana bread with it the other day and my whole family loved it (and they didn't know they were eating whole wheat flour!). P.S. I'm enclosing my recipe for you to share with others." And so we are.

½ cup (1 stick) butter
1 cup sugar
2 eggs
1 cup mashed ripe bananas (2 or 3 bananas)
1 teaspoon vanilla
2 cups King Arthur Stone Ground Whole Wheat Flour
1 teaspoon baking soda
½ teaspoon salt
½ cup chopped walnuts (optional)

Preheat your oven to 350°F.

Cream the butter and sugar. Add and beat together the eggs, bananas and vanilla.

In another bowl, mix together the flour, baking soda and salt. Blend the liquid ingredients into the dry ingredients. At this point, add the ½ cup of chopped walnuts if you wish.

Pour this mixture into a greased, 9 x 5-inch loaf pan and bake for about 60 minutes.

For information about baking and storing quick bread loaves, turn to page 88.

• WHOLE WHEAT FOR DINNER •

Our first recipe is a meal in itself. The rest are hearty accompaniments.

"WHOLE MEAL" PANCAKES

So much of the year we're moving in "fast forward"; we fly in and out of the house and grab whatever is on hand to eat, of whatever dietary value. There just doesn't seem to be time to think about whether our meals are balanced or not.

Here's one solution, a recipe that is incredibly accommodating timewise, offers incredible variation potential and contains an incredible whole meal in one package. The name, "Whole Meal" Pancakes, is a bit of a play on words since they're not only designed to contain a whole meal, but you can make them completely with King Arthur Stone Ground Whole Wheat Flour.

To get them ready for an evening "on-the-run" meal, make up the batter in the morning before you go to work, class, or wherever your day demands. During this long wait, the batter ferments ever so slightly, not enough to taste but enough to tenderize the protein, which makes the pancakes tender as well.

> 2 cups King Arthur Stone Ground Whole Wheat Flour
> 1 teaspoon of salt
> 1 to 2 tablespoons sugar, brown sugar, honey (or whatever)
> 1½ cups milk (or a 12-ounce can evaporated milk)
> 3 eggs (separated if you have a few extra minutes)

Because whole wheat flour used alone tends to be heavier than all-purpose, these pancakes are greatly improved if you separate the eggs. By beating the egg whites until they form stiff peaks and then folding them into your batter just before you cook them, your batter will be much fluffier, full of millions of tiny air bubbles. As you cook your pancakes, these bubbles will blow up like tiny balloons and make them much lighter.

In a glass or ceramic mixing bowl, mix together the dry ingredients. If you've opted to separate the eggs, beat just the yolks into the milk. Cover the whites and put them in the refrigerator.

Pour the liquid ingredients into the dry and beat everything together furiously until it's frothy and light. Cover your batter, refrigerate it and let it rest until you get back to it later on.

When you're ready to cook, take the batter and egg whites (if you separated them) out of the refrigerator. Go back and search for leftovers and/or fresh vegetables. Dice whatever you find until you have at least 3 cups' worth.

Some suggestions are:

- onion, green peppers, carrots, celery, zucchini, apples
- cooked fish, chicken, turkey, beef or pork
- even tofu

After you've diced your fillings, the egg whites should have warmed some. (The closer to room temperature they are, the more cooperative they are about having air incorporated into them.) Once they are beaten into stiff glossy peaks, use your beater (without cleaning it) to beat the batter again until you can see big air bubbles in it. Gently fold in your diced meal, then fold in the egg whites.

Heat your griddle or frying pan. When a few drops of water "dance" on it, grease it lightly and pour on some of your batter. An ice cream scoop makes getting batter from bowl to griddle very easy. Cook 2 or 3 pancakes until the bottoms are nicely browned.

Turn the pancakes over and brown the other side. Keep them warm in the oven until you've finished cooking the rest of the batter and you can collect most of the people who might like to share them with you.

Even though these pancakes contain a "whole meal," something from every food group as we were told when we were young, you can dress them up a bit by serving them with a green salad and some cheese. To make them something even a child won't resist, sprinkle a bit of soy sauce or tamari on top.

With luck you'll have some pancakes left over. Divide them up into meal-sized portions, put them in the refrigerator and the next morning when people bolt in looking for something for breakfast or to take for lunch, your whole meal pancakes will be waiting. They're wonderful cold.

"WHOLE MEAL" VARIATIONS

LIGHTER "WHOLE MEAL" PANCAKES

If you want a lighter version, substitute 1 or more cups of King Arthur Unbleached All-Purpose Flour for an equal amount of the whole wheat.

QUICKER "WHOLE MEAL" PANCAKES

If you forgot to mix up your batter in the morning, you can make pancakes that are almost as light by adding a tablespoon of baking powder to your dry ingredients when you mix them up for a spur of the moment meal.

"WHOLE MEAL" FRITTERS

For a special treat, take either variety of batter and cook your vegetables, fish or meat in deep fat. (For cooking directions and other fritters, see page 41.)

FISH & CHIP BATTER

To make a batter for the fish part of "fish and chips," substitute beer for the milk when you mix up your batter in the morning. At suppertime, blend in the beaten egg whites to make the batter light. Dip pieces of fish in it and fry them in deep fat (page 41). Add some homemade fried potatoes, sprinkle on a liberal amount of malt vinegar, and serve your meal folded in a piece of newspaper, British fashion.

WHOLE WHEAT POPOVERS

Although whole wheat popovers may sound like a contradiction, beating the batter well and giving it a resting period are the magic steps that make these as light as whole wheat popovers can be. They won't be quite the ethereal balloons that popovers made wholly with unbleached all-purpose flour are, but you'll end up with a dozen nutty-flavored treats to accompany a hearty soup or stew. (For variations, see page 44.)

With this recipe we're making an exception to our "nothing but whole wheat flour" rule for this chapter. There are a few things (not many) in which 100% whole wheat flour just won't quite "rise" to the occasion.

½ cup King Arthur Stone Ground Whole Wheat Flour
½ cup King Arthur Unbleached All-Purpose Flour
½ teaspoon salt
1 cup milk
2 eggs
2 teaspoons melted butter

Place the flour and salt in a mixing bowl. Add the milk, eggs and melted butter. Beat for 2 or 3 minutes until the batter is light and smooth and you begin to see big bubbles in it.

If you have time, let the batter stand at room temperature for an hour or longer. This develops better flavor and mellows the flour a bit, which helps increase the volume of the popovers.

Fifteen minutes before you want to bake your popovers, preheat your oven to 400°F. Just before you bake the batter, beat it once more.

Fill hot, greased muffin or popover pans half full. Bake for 35 to 40 minutes.

Easy No-Knead Whole Wheat Bread

This batter bread is sweetened with iron-rich molasses, contains all the bran and germ of the whole wheat berry and contains no fat at all. It is so moist and rich it's hard to believe it is so good for you and so easy to make as well. If both yeast and whole wheat are new to you, this recipe is a great place to begin. (For more information about batter breads and other recipes, see page 132.)

2 cups warm water
¼ cup dark, unsulphured molasses
1 tablespoon or packet active dry yeast
¼ cup non-fat dry milk (optional)
4 cups King Arthur Stone Ground Whole Wheat Flour
2 teaspoons salt

Mixing & Rising: Pour the water into a mixing bowl. Add and dissolve the molasses and then the yeast. Let this brew sit for a few minutes until you see foamy signs of life. This is called "proofing" the yeast. Add the dry milk.

When everything is dissolved in the liquid, stir in the flour and salt. Beat this mixture vigorously for a couple of minutes and then pour it into two well-greased, 4½ x 8½-inch bread pans.

Let this dough rise for 45 minutes to an hour.

Baking: Put the dough in a cold oven, turn the heat to 400°F and bake for 15 minutes. Then turn the oven down to 350°F and bake for a further 20 to 25 minutes until the bread is brown and crusty.

100% Whole Wheat Bread

This recipe will make two robust and hearty loaves. To make them as light as possible, make a sponge first and allow it to work for a couple of hours.

As we have mentioned, when you combine the proteins in a grain with those in a dairy product you create a protein which is as complete and good for you as that in any meat or fish but with vegetable fiber replacing the fat. If you make this bread with milk, you'll definitely have something worth more than the sum of its parts.

2 cups warm water or skim milk (see page 126)
¼ cup sugar, molasses or honey
1 tablespoon or packet active dry yeast
5½ to 6½ cups King Arthur Stone Ground Whole Wheat Flour
2 tablespoons butter or vegetable oil
1 tablespoon salt

Activating the Yeast: Pour the liquid in the mixing bowl. Add and dissolve the sweetener and the yeast. Let this sit for several minutes to allow the yeast to grow and expand.

Making the Sponge: When you see lots of activity, stir in 3 cups of the flour and the butter or oil. Allow this sponge to work for a couple of hours or longer. It will help soften the bran of the whole wheat which will give the bread a lighter texture as well as more flavor.

Making the Dough: Add the salt and gradually add the balance of the flour, stirring until the dough pulls cleanly away from the sides of the bowl.

Kneading & Rising: Place the dough on a floured board and knead for 3 to 4 minutes. Give it a rest while you clean out and grease your bowl.

Knead for a further 3 or 4 minutes and put the dough into the greased bowl, turning it so the top of the dough is also greased, which will allow it to expand.

Cover it with a damp towel or plastic wrap and let rise in a warm place for 1 1/2 hours, or until you can poke your finger in it without it springing back at you.

(For a finer grained bread, punch the dough down and let it rise in the bowl a second time.)

Shaping & Rising: Divide the dough in half, shape into two loaves and place in greased bread pans. Let rise for about an hour in a warm place.

Baking: About 15 minutes before you want to bake your bread, preheat your oven to 350°F.

Bake the loaves for 35 to 40 minutes, or until done. Remove them from the pans to cool.

An alternative baking method is to let your bread rise for 1/2 to 3/4 hour and then place it in a cold oven. Turn the temperature to 400°F for 15 minutes and then down to 350°F for a further 20 to 25 minutes. (Refer to the information about baking yeasted breads on page 122.)

Whole Wheat Cinnamon Raisin Bread

For a delicious variation, incorporate 3 tablespoons of cinnamon and 1 cup of raisins into the sponge.

Laura Jemison's
Herb & Onion Bread

Back when Davy, the Sands' youngest son, was eleven years old, he was so smitten with this bread that he (who never used to write anything down) did, in fact, ask their old friend if he could make a copy of her recipe. With that unsolicited recommendation we share it with you.

2 cups warm water
1/4 cup sugar
1 tablespoon or packet active dry yeast
1/2 cup non-fat dry milk (optional)
4 tablespoons (1/2 stick) butter or vegetable oil
1 tablespoon salt
1 medium onion, minced
1 teaspoon dried dill weed
2 teaspoons crushed dried rosemary
1 cup medium rye flour or pumpernickel
4 1/2 to 5 1/2 cups King Arthur Stone Ground Whole Wheat Flour

Mixing: Pour the water into a large mixing bowl. Add and dissolve the sugar and yeast. Let this work for 5 minutes or so until the yeast is frothing and bubbling. Add the dry milk, and butter or vegetable oil.

Mix the salt, onion and herbs into the rye flour and blend them into the yeast mixture. Stir in the whole wheat flour until the dough is stiff enough to knead.

Kneading & Rising: Turn the dough out onto a floured surface and knead for 3 or 4 minutes. Give it a rest while you clean out and grease your bowl.

When you return to the dough it will be relaxed and cooperative. Knead another 3 or 4 minutes until it feels springy. Because this dough has rye flour in it, it will tend to be a bit sticky. That's the nature of rye flour so don't continue to add flour to eliminate the stickiness or you'll wind up with a dough that's too stiff.

Put the dough into your greased bowl, turning it so the top of the dough has a thin film of oil on it also. This helps keep it from drying out while it rises. Cover it with a damp towel or plastic wrap, put it somewhere cozy, and let it rise until you can poke your finger in it without the dough springing back at you.

Shaping & Rising: Knock it down and either let it rise again in the bowl (this creates a finer grain) or divide it in half, shape it into two loaves, and put them in two greased, 4 1/2 x 8 1/2-inch bread pans. (You can actually use any size bread pan you want. The resulting bread will either be "tall and thin," or "short and fat.")

Let the bread rise, covered, until it is almost doubled, 45 minutes to an hour.

Baking: About 15 minutes before you want to bake your bread, preheat your oven to 350°F.

Bake the bread for 40 to 45 minutes. If you like moist chewy bread, take it out sooner. If you like a crisp crust, give it a few extra minutes.

As with any bread, this is wonderful hot from the oven, but it will be easier to cut if you give it a chance to cool.

Stone Ground Whole Wheat Rolls

Rolls made completely with King Arthur Stone Ground Whole Wheat Flour will definitely be more hearty and robust in flavor and texture than rolls made with unbleached all-purpose flour. They are a great accompaniment to any meal.

To have fresh rolls at dinner time, you can make up a sponge in the morning before you're off on your day's travails. Let the sponge "travail" all day on its own, which will both mellow the flour and develop the flavor. (If you want rolls in the morning for breakfast, make the sponge the evening before.)

1 1/2 cups warm water
1/4 to 1/2 cup white or brown sugar
1 tablespoon or packet active dry yeast
2 eggs
4 tablespoons (1/2 stick) butter, at room temperature, or vegetable oil
5 1/2 to 6 1/2 cups King Arthur Stone Ground Whole Wheat Flour
1 tablespoon salt

Mixing: Pour the water into a mixing bowl. Add and thoroughly dissolve the sugar and then add the yeast. When the yeast is dissolved and bubbly, beat in the eggs. Blend in the butter or vegetable oil. Stir in 3 cups of flour. If you have time, let this sponge work for at least 2 hours or all day.

When you return to your sponge (about an hour and a half before you want to serve your rolls), stir in the salt and the remaining flour until you have a soft but kneadable dough.

Kneading & Resting: Turn it out onto a floured surface and, with well-floured hands, knead it for 3 or 4 minutes. Give the dough a rest while you scrape out and grease your bowl. Knead a further 3 or 4 minutes until it's as bouncy and smooth as a dough made with whole wheat flour can be.

Place it in the greased bowl turning the dough over so its top, or exposed surface, is greased. Cover it with a damp towel or plastic wrap, put it somewhere cozy and let it rest for half an hour.

Shaping & Resting: You'll find directions for shaping several varieties of rolls starting on page 159. After shaping, put the rolls in a muffin tin or on a greased baking sheet, cover them and let them rest and rise for ½ to 1 hour.

Baking: About 15 minutes before you want to bake the rolls, preheat your oven to 400°F. Bake them for about 20 minutes and serve them piping hot.

WHOLE WHEAT CRACKERS

There isn't anything more appropriate for a cracker than hearty whole wheat flour. In fact, King Arthur Stone Ground Whole Wheat Flour is an important ingredient in many of the cracker recipes found in Chapter VI.

These are made very quickly. Depending on the size of the circles or squares you cut, this recipes makes between 2 and 3 dozen crackers.

1 cup King Arthur Stone Ground Whole Wheat Flour
¼ teaspoon baking soda
½ teaspoon salt
3 tablespoons butter or shortening
½ cup buttermilk
coarse salt, herbal salt substitute or sesame seeds for cracker tops

First: Preheat your oven to 425°F.

Mixing: Combine the flour, baking soda and salt. With a pastry blender, two knives or your fingertips, rub in the butter or shortening until it looks like bread crumbs. Add the milk and blend quickly with a fork.

Place the dough on a floured board and knead it about 10 times until it comes together and forms a ball. Cover the dough with a damp towel and let it rest for 5 or 10 minutes.

Shaping: With a well-floured rolling pin, on a well-floured surface, roll the dough out to ⅛ inch, "paper thin." Cut into shapes with a cookie cutter or, to save rolling out the leftover dough, into squares. (If you use a spatula or bowl scraper for this task, dip it in flour before you cut with it.)

Baking: With a spatula, gently slide the crackers onto a lightly greased baking sheet. Let them rest another 5 minutes and then sprinkle them with coarse salt, an herbal salt substitute or sesame seeds.

Prick well with a fork and bake for about 6 minutes, flip them over and bake another few minutes until they are golden. Make sure you keep an eye on them. They're so thin they can go from gold to scorched very quickly.

• WHOLE WHEAT FOR DESSERT •

Cakes and cookies made with whole wheat flour can almost be called "healthy food." Healthy or not, desserts made with whole wheat flour are delicious.

GOLDEN ANGEL FOOD CAKE

Although you might think an Angel Food Cake in the Whole Wheat Chapter is unlikely, this particular one, though dense with earthy overtones, is heavenly. Making this cake is a great way to use the twelve egg yolks left over from our Traditional Angel Food Cake, which you'll find on page 267.

Egg yolks are the part of the egg that contains the most calories and cholesterol. If you have a concern about cholesterol, stick with our cholesterol-free variety. But remember, the much-maligned egg yolk's calories are not empty; with them you get some protein and lots of vitamin A and iron. And because this cake is made with whole wheat, it contains extra fiber you won't find in our traditional variety.

> 12 egg yolks
> ³⁄₄ cup boiling water
> 1 tablespoon orange or lemon rind (fresh is best)
> 1¹⁄₄ cups sugar
> 1³⁄₄ cups King Arthur Stone Ground Whole Wheat Flour
> 2 teaspoons baking powder
> ³⁄₄ teaspoon salt

First, preheat your oven to 325°F.

Beat the egg yolks until they are thick and lemon colored. Slowly add the boiling water and keep beating for another few minutes. With a wire whisk, fold in the orange or lemon rind and the sugar, beating all the time.

In a separate bowl, blend the flour, baking powder and salt. Slowly add them to the egg yolk mixture the way you did the sugar.

Grease only the very bottom of a tube pan (not the sides) or cut out a piece of waxed paper to fit the bottom. Pour the cake batter in and bake for 45 minutes or until the top springs back when you press on it with your fingertips. Cool this upside down on the tube pan feet or over a bottle for about 1¹⁄₂ hours.

This cake is moist, robust and full of flavor as is, but to dress it up for company, you might serve it with the Lemon or Orange Sauce which you'll find on page 322. Or you might consider the Dark Semi-Sweet Chocolate Sauce flavored with a bit of orange liqueur (page 321).

Whole Wheat Applesauce Cake

Here's an exceptional flavor combination. This cake is so moist, it keeps especially well and even improves after a day as the flavors mellow and blend. Vegetable shortening is a good choice here since the flavor of butter would be masked by the spices. Because there's so much air incorporated into shortening to begin with, it creates a cake with a light and airy texture.

1 cup brown sugar
1/2 cup vegetable shortening
2 eggs
1 teaspoon baking soda
1/2 teaspoon salt
2 teaspoon baking powder
1 teaspoon cinnamon
1/2 teaspoon cloves
1 3/4 cups King Arthur Stone Ground Whole Wheat Flour
1 cup unsweetened applesauce
1/2 cup raisins
1/2 cup chopped walnuts

Preheat your oven to 350°F.

In a large bowl, cream the sugar and shortening. Add the eggs and beat well. In a separate bowl, combine the dry ingredients.

Add the dry ingredients alternately with the applesauce to the creamed mixture. Fold in the raisins and chopped nuts. As with other cakes, stir until mixed, but don't overdo it. Pour the batter into a greased, 5 x 9-inch loaf pan and bake for about an hour.

Rhubarb Crumble

Whole wheat flour, with its nutty flavor and hearty texture, is a natural for fruit crumbles and crisps.

Filling

2 eggs
1 1/2 to 2 cups sugar
1/4 cup King Arthur Stone Ground Whole Wheat Flour
1 tablespoon butter (or margarine)
1 teaspoon grated orange rind
1 teaspoon orange juice
4 cups rhubarb, cut into 1/2-inch pieces

First: Preheat your oven to 350°F.

Making the Filling: Beat the eggs slightly and add the sugar and flour. Melt the butter and stir in the orange rind and juice. Add this to the egg mixture. Stir in the rhubarb and place this filling in a greased, 9-inch square cake pan.

Topping

> ½ cup (1 stick) butter
> 2 cups King Arthur Stone Ground Whole Wheat Flour
> ¼ cup brown sugar
> ½ teaspoon salt

Making the Topping: Cut the butter into the flour using a pastry cutter, two knives or your fingertips. Add the brown sugar and salt, mixing until the topping looks like bread crumbs.

Assembling the Crumble: Sprinkle the topping on the fruit filling. Bake for 35 to 45 minutes.

This is good hot from the oven with whipped cream, ice cream or all on its own. Although this recipe is for rhubarb, you can make many variations of this crumble by adjusting the sugar for the sweetness of the fruits in season.

ROSEMARY (OR THYME) SNAPS

This recipe was graciously shared with us by Happy Griffiths, a member of the New England Unit of the Herb Society of America and the Herbalist at Lower Shaker Village in Enfield, New Hampshire. We included it as a Gingersnap variation in our Cookie chapter, but print the whole recipe here with whole wheat flour, which seems quite appropriate for the earthy herb. It will make between 5 and 6 dozen cookies.

> ¾ cup (1½ sticks) butter
> 1 cup sugar
> 1 egg
> 4 tablespoons molasses
> 2 teaspoons dried, crumbled rosemary (or thyme)
> 2 cups King Arthur Stone Ground Whole Wheat Flour
> 1 teaspoon baking soda
> 1 teaspoon salt
> ¼ teaspoon ground cloves
> ½ teaspoon ginger

Preheat your oven to 350°F.

Cream the butter and add the sugar beating until light. Add the egg, then the molasses, and continue beating until the mixture is fluffy. In a separate bowl, combine the dry ingredients. Add and blend in the butter mixture.

Drop by the spoonful on a lightly greased baking sheet, leaving a couple of inches between them as they spread a lot. (A non-stick pan or parchment paper is helpful with these cookies.)

Bake for 10 to 12 minutes.

WHOLE WHEAT OATMEAL MOLASSES COOKIES

These wholesome, earthy whole wheat cookies were developed by someone who radiates the same characteristics. Joyce DiBona is as at home in the kitchen making cookies as she is being President of our exceptional advertising agency, DiBona, Bornstein & Random. In both places she's a winner. In the spring of 1989, Joyce was inducted into the New England Advertising Hall of Fame, only the second woman in its history to have received this honor. If you think that counts for something, just wait until you taste these cookies. Her recipe makes about 4 dozen.

$\frac{1}{2}$ cup (1 stick) butter or margarine
1 cup brown sugar
2 eggs
$\frac{1}{2}$ cup dark, unsulphured molasses
2 cups King Arthur Stone Ground Whole Wheat Flour
1 teaspoon baking soda
1 teaspoon salt
1 teaspoon cinnamon
2 cups oatmeal
$\frac{1}{2}$ to 1 cup chopped nuts (optional)
$\frac{1}{2}$ to 1 cup raisins (optional)

Preheat your oven to 400°F.

Cream the butter and sugar together. Beat in the eggs one at a time and then add the molasses.

In a separate bowl, combine the flour, baking soda, salt and cinnamon. Add the dry ingredients to the creamed mixture and mix well. Stir in the oats, nuts and raisins.

Drop by the spoonful onto a greased baking sheet and bake for 8 to 10 minutes.

Oatmeal Raisin Chocolate Chip Crispies

Whole wheat flour contains the germ of the wheat which is full of minerals and vitamins. It also contains wheat bran, or the seed coat, a source of insoluble fiber. This is as important to good nutrition as the soluble fiber you find in oat bran. In these cookies you'll have the benefits of both.

    1 cup (2 sticks) butter or margarine
    3/4 cup brown sugar
    3/4 cup granulated sugar
    1 teaspoon vanilla
    2 eggs
    2 cups King Arthur Stone Ground Whole Wheat Flour
    2 cups oats, regular or quick
    1 teaspoon salt
    1 teaspoon baking powder
    1/2 teaspoon baking soda
    1/4 cup milk
    1 cup chopped nuts
    1 cup raisins
    1 cup chocolate chips

Any one or all of the last three ingredients can be left out; or try something totally different like chopped almonds, apricots, a cup of sunflower seeds, or even butterscotch or peanut butter chips.

Preheat oven to 350°F.

Cream the butter (or a margarine which doesn't contain any cholesterol) and the sugars together well. Beat in the vanilla and eggs until light.

Mix the flour, oats, salt, baking powder and soda together. Mix in the chopped nuts, raisins and chocolate chips.

Add about 1 cup of the dry ingredients to the butter mixture. Blend in the milk and then the rest of the dry ingredients.

Drop the batter from a tablespoon or teaspoon (depending on whether you want 3 dozen large or 5 dozen small cookies) onto a lightly greased cookie sheet and bake from 10 to 14 minutes.

CHEWY WHOLE WHEAT BROWNIES

This brownie recipe is the same version of Brinna's grandmother's brownies that is included in the chapter on Cookies & Bars. We repeat ourselves because it is such a versatile brownie and absolutely delicious made with whole wheat flour. This recipe can be doubled or tripled.

Remember to try adding a cup of raisins, chopped apricots or other dried fruit, chocolate, butterscotch or peanut butter chips (or a combination), coconut, chopped nuts, sunflower seeds or whatever adds a taste and texture that pleases you.

4 ounces (squares) unsweetened chocolate
$\frac{1}{2}$ cup (1 stick) butter or margarine (or a combination)
2 cups sugar (or brown sugar)
2 to 4 eggs (for chewier brownies, use fewer eggs)
$\frac{1}{2}$ teaspoon salt
2 teaspoons vanilla
1 cup King Arthur Stone Ground Whole Wheat Flour

If you discover that you are out of unsweetened chocolate, you can substitute 3 tablespoons of cocoa and 1 tablespoon of butter (or vegetable shortening) for each ounce of chocolate. For this recipe you would need $\frac{3}{4}$ cup of cocoa and $\frac{1}{4}$ cup ($\frac{1}{2}$ stick) of butter.

Preheat your oven to 350°F.

Melt the chocolate and butter in a large saucepan over very low heat (or use a double boiler to be safe), stirring to blend.

Remove the pan from the heat, add and blend in the sugar and then the rest of the ingredients. Mix this all together with a large spoon and put it into a greased, 9-inch square pan.

Bake for 35 to 45 minutes (longer if you've doubled or tripled the recipe) or until it just begins to pull away from the sides of the pan. Remove the brownies from the oven, let them cool enough so you can cut them in squares and remove them from the pan with a spatula.

WHOLE WHEAT APPLESAUCE BROWNIES

Unlikely though it sounds, the flavors and textures of whole wheat flour, applesauce and chocolate complement each other very nicely. This intriguing recipe comes from Ann Berry, teacher extraordinaire, mother of Emily and Leah, and wife of Scott, Vice President of Sands, Taylor & Wood Co.

Batter

$\frac{1}{2}$ cup (1 stick) butter or margarine
2 ounces (squares) unsweetened chocolate
$\frac{3}{4}$ cup sugar
2 eggs, beaten
$\frac{3}{4}$ cup applesauce
$1\frac{1}{4}$ teaspoons vanilla
1 cup King Arthur Stone Ground Whole Wheat Flour
$\frac{1}{2}$ teaspoon baking powder
$\frac{1}{4}$ teaspoon baking soda
$\frac{1}{4}$ teaspoon salt

Topping

2 tablespoons sugar
$\frac{1}{4}$ cup chopped nuts
$\frac{1}{2}$ cup semi-sweet chocolate pieces

Preheat your oven to 350°F.

Melt the butter and chocolate in a saucepan over low heat. Add the sugar, eggs, applesauce and vanilla and beat well.

Combine the flour, baking powder, soda and salt. Add these dry ingredients to the chocolate mixture and blend only enough to combine them.

Pour the batter into a greased, 8-inch square baking pan.

Mix the three topping ingredients and sprinkle over batter.

Bake for 30 to 35 minutes. Allow these brownies to cool slightly before cutting.

AFS Bars

On a rainy Sunday during foliage season several years ago, the Sands family, including their newly acquired student son from Holland, was involved in something called a "safety break." Armed with coffee, fruit juices and granola bars, they occupied a rest stop on Route 89 in Vermont for three hours. As weary travellers wandered in, they offered their fare in hopes of a donation to their worthy cause, the American Field Service, a foreign student exchange program through which they acquired their Dutch son for a year (or a lifetime). The safety break was a great success, from the other AFS families they met to the unexpected requests for the granola bar recipe.

These bars, which were renamed AFS Bars after this occasion, are an old family favorite, a recipe that has something for everyone, from the sweet tooth to the health food addict. Because of their "hands across the sea" associations, they are a happy finale for this chapter.

> $^1\!/_2$ cup (1 stick) butter (or $^1\!/_4$ cup butter and $^1\!/_4$ cup vegetable oil)
> $1^1\!/_2$ cups brown sugar (more or less, depending on the severity of
>   your sweet tooth)
> 2 eggs
> 2 teaspoons vanilla
> 1 cup King Arthur Stone Ground Whole Wheat Flour
> 1 tablespoon baking powder
> 1 teaspoon salt
> 2 cups granola

Granola is a very loosely defined cereal, but usually a combination of rolled oats or wheat, seeds such as sesame or sunflower, and sometimes wheat germ, coconut and dried fruit. For this occasion, because it was all that was available, they used a mixture of sunflower seeds, sesame seeds and thinly sliced almonds. They also threw in a handful of raisins and dried apple. And finally, to overwhelm the reservations of those who are suspicious of anything that is suggestive of health food, a cupful of chocolate bits did the trick.

Preheat your oven to 350°F.

In a large saucepan, melt the butter or butter/oil mixture. Stir in the sugar, beat in the eggs and add the vanilla.

In a separate mixing bowl, mix together the flour, baking powder, salt and granola. Blend this flour mixture with the sugar/butter mixture.

Spread the batter in a lightly greased, 9 x 9-inch pan and bake for about 30 minutes or until the center is set. Cool and cut into squares. (Dutch ingenuity discovered that a pizza wheel cuts these very effectively.)

SOURDOUGH
X

SOURDOUGH
FOR GRIDDLE & OVEN

• When you use your Sourdough Starter to make any of the wonderful possibilities in this section, replace what you take out of the pot with equal amounts of flour and water. Most of these recipes call for 1 cup of starter, so to replace it you would add 1 cup of King Arthur Unbleached All-Purpose Flour and 1 cup of water to your Sourdough pot, in that order. (Adding liquids to dry ingredients helps prevent lumps.)

• You can certainly substitute an equal amount of King Arthur Stone Ground Whole Wheat Flour for some of the Unbleached All-Purpose Flour in your Sourdough Starter. It will give it a hearty, earthy appearance, like the flavor of the starter itself.

• Whenever you feed your starter, give it at least a day to "work." This time period allows the wild yeast to multiply and get ready for its next task.

• Although some people say no metal should come in contact with Sourdough because of a chemical reaction between it and the acid in the starter, a brief stir with a stainless steel spoon or wire wisk probably won't do any damage. But be sure to store an active culture in a non-metal container, either ceramic or glass.

• Use clean utensils when adding to or mixing up your starter pot to minimize the introduction of unwanted strains of bacteria. In a rare instance, your Sourdough Starter may begin to nurture a bacteria or organism which might not taste great in food. If it develops a peculiar odor rather than the "clean sour aroma" it should have, or a color that doesn't look like flour mixed with water (such as pink, green, etc.), it's probably best to take a deep breath and throw it out. But don't despair. It only happens once in a blue moon, so thoroughly clean out your containers and start another one.

• Baking soda in Sourdough recipes neutralizes the acidity of the starter and, in the process of doing so, releases carbon dioxide bubbles in a relatively quick chemical reaction which can be quite dramatic. By adding the soda last in the order of ingredients, you will ensure that the dough or batter will lose as few of these bubbles as possible. The more bubbles, the lighter the pancake or bread!

• Some Sourdough breads call for active dry yeast in addition to the starter. It works to assist the wild yeast in creating a light texture, while retaining the distinctive flavor of the Sourdough. When you make a recipe that includes active dry yeast, it usually won't take as long to rise or bake as one leavened completely with your Sourdough Starter.

SOURDOUGH
FOR GRIDDLE & OVEN
X

Although we associate sourdough with pioneers trekking west and prospectors heading for Alaska during the gold rush, people have actually been baking with sourdough for over six thousand years. Egyptians began experimenting with it several thousand years before the birth of Christ. The Hebrews leavened breads with it long before their flight from Egypt. No one will ever know just how it was discovered, but it may have happened something like this.

One day long ago, in an ancient Mediterranean village, a baker temporarily abandoned a batter he had made for a traditional, unleavened, flat bread. While he was gone, the batter, instead of drying up and spoiling, began to develop tiny bubbles on its surface. These grew into a foam and the whole batter began to expand as if it contained a mysterious life of its own. In fact it did.

Upon his return, that ancient baker, because he was either lazy or inspired, took that mysteriously bubbling brew and baked it. Much to his amazement, he discovered that the finished bread was very different from the dense, flat bread he had made before. It's texture was lighter and more open; it's flavor was different and exciting; it had "risen."

• A SOURDOUGH PRIMER •

A sourdough starter is a wild yeast living in a batter of flour and water. If you can imagine a world without any packets of active dry yeast available, you can imagine how important your sourdough starter would be to you. Without it, you would be doomed to some pretty awful eating. It is no wonder that sourdough starters were treasured, fought over, and carried to all ends of the earth. To the early prospectors, a starter was such a valued possession (almost more than the gold they were seeking), that they slept with it to keep it from freezing on frigid winter nights. (Ironically, freezing won't kill a sourdough starter, although too much heat will.)

There are sourdoughs that are centuries old which have been zealously fed and cared for by generations. Liza Bernard acquired one from her neighbor which came originally from the sourdough pot of Joe Richards who used it in the gold rush town of Hope, Alaska. The Sands have one that never made it out west but can be traced back at least two-hundred thirty years right here in New England. But there are starters around the Mediterranean today that make our American starters look like newborns.

The area you come from plays a part in determining the personality of a sourdough starter. The particular strain of wild yeast thriving only in the San Francisco area of California can alone produce the unique flavor of San Francisco sourdough breads. Your area may harbor a wild yeast with its own exciting flavor.

Keeping a sourdough starter is somewhat like having a pet because it needs to be fed and cared for. But its requirements are simple and not time consuming. With a minimum of effort, you can keep one in your refrigerator to use whenever the impulse strikes. Unlike more traditional pets, you can put your sourdough starter "on hold" by freezing or drying it. And like that ancient Mediterranean baker, you can capture a wild yeast at any time and create a new starter that will be ready to use in a few days.

Baking with sourdough is a very simple process. All it takes is a little planning and timing. The results are so satisfying, you'll grow to treasure your invisible pet the way our ancestors did.

Getting a Starter

Fermentation: Wild versus Domestic Yeast

Amazingly enough, no one knew until the middle of the nineteenth century that the magical rising action of a sourdough starter is due to a tiny, single-celled fungus called a yeast. As the yeast feeds on the natural sugars in a dough, it multiplies and gives off carbon dioxide just as we do. This process is called fermentation. The elastic wheat gluten in a dough entraps these carbon dioxide bubbles, causing the dough to expand as if it contained a million tiny balloons.

Wild yeasts are rugged individualists that can withstand the most extreme of circumstances. There are many varieties of these tiny plants around us all the time. But because a wild yeast is a free agent, catching one to bake with is a bit haphazard as can be the results of baking with it. There are other ways to acquire one, however, which put the odds for success in your favor.

Active dry yeast, the kind we can buy in packets at our grocer's, is a domesticated descendant of these wild relatives, one that has been grown for flavor, speed of growth and predictability. There are others which have been developed to make yogurt and cheese out of milk as well as beer and wine from the juices of grains and fruit. But domestic yeasts are much more fragile and can't be grown at home without eventually reverting to their original wild state. Both wild and domestic yeasts have their assets and liabilities.

Beg, Borrow or Buy...

The easiest way to acquire a sourdough starter is to find a friend who already has one. Most sourdough devotees are more than willing to share. It's always nice to offer something in exchange, a favorite recipe along with something warm from the oven, but usually your interest and enthusiasm is all it takes. People who love baking with sourdough love to have company.

If you don't know anyone who has some active starter, you can often find small packets of dried sourdough starter in grocery or food specialty stores. When it's dried, it's still living but in a dormant state. Once you get it home, you can have it active and bubbling in no time by following the instructions that come with it. If there are no instructions, you can get the starter going by feeding it, just what you would do for yourself if you hadn't had a meal in a long time.

Activating a Dried Starter

> 2 cups warm water
> 1 tablespoon sugar or honey (optional)
> 2 cups King Arthur Unbleached All-Purpose Flour
> 1 packet (or other) dried sourdough starter

Pour the warm water (a temperature that feels comfortable on your wrist) into a glass or ceramic bowl. Add and dissolve the sugar or honey if you want to use it. This isn't necessary but it gives the yeast an easy "first course." Stir in the flour and the dried starter. Cover the bowl with plastic wrap and place it where you'd place a rising dough, someplace warm and free of drafts. Small telltale bubbles should begin to appear on the surface within a few hours. Once you see them you'll know your starter is alive and well.

Let this newly activated starter continue to grow for a further 24 to 36 hours. The mixture will begin to separate after a day or so. Give it a stir every once in a while to blend it back together and to help distribute the yeast evenly. When the starter has a good clean, sour aroma, pour it into a glass jar with a lid (a large glass, not plastic, peanut butter jar will work well) and put it in the refrigerator.

...Or Start Your Own

If you can't find a source for either active or dried starter, you can easily make your own.

Letting Active Dry Yeast Go "Wild"

The easiest and most successful method of making your own starter is to combine water, flour and a tablespoon (or packet) of active dry "domestic" yeast which is available at any grocery store. By letting this brew sit for several days as you would with a dried sourdough starter, the domestic yeast will go "wild" and develop the familiar tang of its truly wild cousins. You'll probably catch some wild yeast in the process as well.

> 2 cups warm water
> 1 tablespoon of sugar or honey (optional)
> 1 tablespoon or packet active dry yeast
> 2 cups King Arthur Unbleached All-Purpose Flour

Pour the water into a two-quart glass or ceramic jar or bowl, add and dissolve the sugar or honey and the yeast in that order. Stir in the flour gradually. Cover the jar or bowl with a clean dishcloth and place it somewhere warm. By using a dishcloth instead of plastic wrap, you'll allow any wild yeast in the area to infiltrate and begin to work with the domestic yeast which itself is beginning to develop "wild" characteristics and flavors.

The mixture will begin to bubble and brew almost immediately. Let it work anywhere from 2 to 5 days, stirring it about once a day as it will separate. When the bubbling has subsided and a yeasty, sour aroma has developed, stir your starter once more and refrigerate it until you are ready to use it. The starter should have the consistency of pancake batter.

The clear amber liquid that floats to the surface of your sourdough starter contains 12% to 14% alcohol. When yeast is in contact with air, it produces carbon dioxide; when it's not, it produces alcohol. When you blend the alcohol back into the starter, it helps produce the unique flavor you find in good sourdough breads. (The alcohol itself dissipates during the baking process.) For milder flavor, you can pour off some of the alcohol if you wish, although this will thicken the starter, requiring a bit more liquid to return it to its "pancake batter" consistency. (To "sweeten" a starter in another way, see Troubleshooting on page 528.)

The '49ers and "Sourdoughs" of Alaska used this alcohol in other ways as you might have guessed. Because other "spirits" weren't generally available, they happily availed themselves of this source. It has about the same alcohol content as wine, but an unforgettable flavor of its own which is probably better in bread.

Catching a "Wild" Yeast of Your Own

A second way to get a starter going at home is to capture the wild yeast that resides in your own kitchen just as the Mediterranean baker did in our introduction. Capturing wild yeast is fun though a bit unpredictable. The summer and fall are times of the year when there will be more of them around. If you bake with yeast fairly often there may be enough wild yeast in your kitchen to activate a starter. If you can afford the time and the haphazardness of the results, it's worth a try. When you've captured some wild yeast successfully, you'll feel very accomplished. Here's how to set your trap.

2 cups warm water
1 tablespoon sugar or honey (optional)
2 cups King Arthur Unbleached All-Purpose Flour

Mix the water, flour and optional sweetener together thoroughly in a clean, scalded glass or ceramic bowl. The scalding will ensure that you're starting "pure." Cover the bowl with a clean dishcloth. Put it in an area where there's apt to be the highest concentration of airborne yeast as well as the warmth that is needed to begin fermentation.

If the surface begins to look dry after a while, give the mixture a stir. It should begin to "work" in the first day or two if it's going to at all. If it does, your trap has been successful. As you would with a dried starter or active dry yeast, let this mixture continue working for 3 or 4 days giving it a stir every day or so. When it's developed a yeasty, sour aroma, put it in a clean jar with a lid and refrigerate it until you're ready to use it.

If the mixture begins to mold or develop a peculiar color or odor instead of a "clean, sour aroma," give a sigh, throw it out and, if you're patient, start again. Along with the vital yeasts, you may have inadvertently nurtured a strain of bacteria that will not be wonderful in food. This doesn't happen very often though, so don't let the possibility dissuade you from this adventure.

STARTER VARIATIONS

There are a number of variations on the basic flour/liquid/yeast combinations that will produce sourdough starters with different personalities.

• Substitute 1 cup of King Arthur Stone Ground Whole Wheat Flour for 1 cup of the unbleached all-purpose flour.

• Rather than tap water, use water leftover from cooking potatoes. It contains nutrients which any kind of yeast loves. It may make your dough darker in color but, along with making the yeast happy, it creates great flavor in bread.

• Substitute 1 cup of buttermilk for 1 cup of water in your starter mixture.

• Make a Rye Sour using the directions found on page 534.

• Make a sweet Friendship Starter following the directions on page 545.

CARING FOR YOUR STARTER

Storing

• **Refrigerating:** Once your sourdough starter is safely in the refrigerator, it will need a little attention, although once it's cold and relatively dormant, it can survive quite a long time between "feedings." It is certainly not as demanding as children or more traditional pets, but it won't just sit for months on end like a packet of commercially dried yeast either.

• **Freezing:** You may be able to ignore your starter for a month or even much longer, but if you know you're going to be away for a time, you can store it, unlike children or pets, in the freezer. You may want to transfer it to a plastic container first since it will expand as it freezes.

When you are ready to use it again, give it a day to revive, feed it a good meal, give it another day to build up an armada of fresh, new wild siblings and it will be ready to go to work.

• **Drying:** An alternative storage method is to dry your starter by spreading it out on a piece of heavy plastic wrap or waxed paper. Once it's dry, crumble it up and put it in an airtight container. Store it someplace cool or, to be safe, in the freezer.

To reactivate the culture, place the dried starter in a mixture of flour and water as described in the first section. To help the dried chunks dissolve, you can grind them into smaller particles with a hand cranked grinder, a blender or a food processor before you add them to the flour/water mixture.

Feeding

Ordinarily, you feed your starter when you remove some to bake with it. A good rule of thumb is to replenish its food and water at least once every two weeks, preferably because you have used the starter for a wonderful loaf of sourdough bread, a stack of pancakes or maybe the Chocolate Sourdough Cake you'll find on page 543.

While it's been stored in the refrigerator, the alcohol will have separated and come to the surface. With a spoon or wire whisk, blend it back into the starter and then measure out the quantity of starter required by your recipe. Replace the amount taken with equal amounts of flour and water. Since most of our recipes are based on using 1 cup of starter, you would stir in a cup of flour and a cup of water. (This actually makes 1⅓ cups more starter but you can adjust the amount whenever you want.)

Let the replenished starter sit at room temperature for at least 12 hours to give the yeast a chance to multiply and become active before you chill it again.

Troubleshooting

It takes a lot to "do in" a sourdough starter. Even after the grossest of neglect, a little warmth and a good meal should perk it up and get it ready to go. Here are a few tips to help you keep your starter in peak condition.

- **Feeding without Baking:** If you have been busy or away, you can always feed your starter without baking anything. Stir the mixture together, take out and discard 1 cup of starter and replenish as above, stirring in 1 cup water and 1 cup flour. (Or instead of discarding the starter you removed, ask your neighbors if they would be interested in adopting a starter of their very own.) Let the resuscitated mixture sit at room temperature for several hours before you return it to the refrigerator.

- **Treating a Sluggish Starter:** If you live in an area where water is chlorinated, let some sit out overnight to allow the chlorine to dissipate before you feed it to your starter. This will help keep it from interfering with the development of the sourdough microorganisms.

Or, if at any time you feel that your sourdough starter is just not "up to snuff," dissolve a teaspoon of yeast in the cup of water you mix into the starter when you feed it.

- **Sweetening a Starter:** If your starter becomes too sour, take out 1 cup, dispose of the remainder, and add 2 cups each of flour and water to freshen it.

- **Increasing your Starter:** If you want to increase the amount of starter you have, either to give some to a friend or, to get ready for a lot of baking, simply increase the amount you feed it. Whenever you feed your starter, give it at least a day at room temperature to "work." This time period allows the yeast to multiply and get ready for its next task.

- **Resuscitating a Neglected Starter:** If your sourdough starter has sat in the refrigerator months beyond the point of health, give it a fighting chance for survival before you throw it out. A little warmth and a good meal of strong, high-energy carbohydrates may be all it needs to get it off and running again.

The layer of liquid on the surface will probably be very dark, making it look as if the starter must surely have expired. Quell your fear, wrestle the top off the jar and give it a sniff. If it smells the way it should, though exceptionally sour, it may just be sitting there in a dormant state waiting to be fed. The only way to know is to give it a meal.

Blend it back together and pour it into a glass or ceramic bowl. (Take this opportunity to give its jar a good wash.) As the starter will probably be quite thin, mix in 2 cups of flour and 1 cup of water both to nourish and thicken it. Leave the bowl out on your counter where it will be warm and visible.

In a couple of hours you may see some tiny bubbles appearing. If so, cheer it on by keeping it warm and covered overnight. In the morning, celebrate by making Sourdough Pancakes (page 541) which are delicious and quick. Give the remaining starter another feeding, let it sit for another day to ensure its reawakened vigor and then tuck it back in the fridge. Then you can quietly heave a sigh of relief and congratulate yourself on your rescue.

• SOURDOUGH BREADS FOR DINNER •

You will notice that most sourdough bread recipes involve creating a "sponge," or batter, which is allowed to "work" for several hours. This is the same as feeding your starter but the amount you feed it is specific to whatever recipe you're following. During the period the sponge works, the yeast cells are growing and multiplying. By the time you mix in the remainder of your ingredients, you have a formidable army of yeast to leaven the dough.

You may also find that the "feel" of a sourdough dough is different from a traditional yeasted dough. Because the wild yeast in a sourdough starter works more slowly than domestic yeast, the dough tends to feel more relaxed. Don't try to stiffen it up by continuing to add flour. Although the dough will "spread" when it's rising on a baking sheet, it will pick up in the oven and assume a more appropriate shape.

CLASSIC SOURDOUGH BREAD

Leavened only with sourdough starter, this bread has a crackly, chewy crust and a rich, pungent interior. The preparation is divided into several steps, each of which takes only a short time. The time between stages is very flexible in length. Even though creating a loaf of sourdough bread may take longer from start to finish than making bread leavened with commercial yeast, it doesn't take any more of your time. And because this dough has so long to mature the finished loaf has tremendous flavor.

Try using this Classic Sourdough Bread dough to make pretzels, as described in the last chapter, or for a terrific pizza crust.

1 cup Sourdough Starter
1 1/2 cups warm water
5 1/2 to 6 1/2 cups King Arthur Unbleached All-Purpose Flour
1 tablespoon salt
1 tablespoon sugar (optional)
1 teaspoon baking soda
cornmeal to sprinkle on pans
boiling water for oven

Making the Sponge: When you take your starter from the refrigerator it probably will have separated. Blend it thoroughly with a fork or wire whisk. Pour one cup into a glass or pottery mixing bowl. Replenish the starter according to the directions on page 527.

To the starter in the mixing bowl, add the warm water and about 3 cups of flour. Beat vigorously with a spoon or wire whisk.

Cover this sponge with plastic wrap and put it aside to begin to come to life and work. This time period can be very flexible, but allow at least 2 hours and as many as 24. Let it work overnight or all day while you're off at work yourself. The longer it has to work, the more yeast there will be for the second rising period and the more pronounced the sour flavor of the finished bread.

Making the Dough: Blend the salt, sugar and baking soda into 2 cups of flour. Mix this into the expanded and bubbly sponge with a large spoon. When the dough begins to hold together, turn it out onto a floured board and knead it for 3 or 4 minutes. Add flour as needed to make a fairly stiff dough.

Give the dough a rest while you clean out and grease your bowl. Continue kneading for another 3 or 4 minutes. Place the kneaded dough back in the bowl turning it to grease the top. Cover it again to let it expand and rise for anywhere from 2 to 4 hours.

If time necessitates, you can skip the second rising in the bowl and proceed directly to the next step. The second rising takes time but will develop more flavor.

Shaping & Baking: Knock down the dough and shape it into 2 long French-style loaves. Place them on a cornmeal-sprinkled baking sheet and let them rise for another 2 hours or so.

Toward the end of the rising period, place a baking pan on the oven bottom (or on the lowest rack) and preheat your oven to 450°F.

Just before it's time to bake these carefully cultured loaves, slash the tops diagonally with a knife every couple of inches, about ¼ inch deep, and brush with cold water. Pour 2 or 3 cups of water into the pan, put the loaves on the rack above the steaming water and bake them for about 25 minutes.

The crust will be very hard when you remove the bread but in 5 minutes it will be soft and chewy. To make the crust hard and chewy, turn the oven off and leave the bread inside for an additional 5 minutes.

This bread demands to be eaten right out of the oven but it tastes wonderful the next day. Eat it hot with soup or cheese or stew (or toast it for breakfast).

VARIATIONS

• For a darker, shinier crust, brush the tops with a wash of egg white or yolk (or both) mixed with a tablespoon of water before you bake the loaves.

• To make the loaves more festive, mix in 3 or 4 tablespoons of sesame, caraway, dill or poppy seeds when you add the sugar, and then sprinkle some seeds over the egg wash on top.

Sourdough Bread with Yeast

Many recipes for sourdough breads include some active dry yeast to speed up the process, the sourdough starter included mainly for flavor. This version makes a quicker loaf with a slightly different texture and taste.

1 1/2 cups lukewarm water
1 tablespoon sugar
1 tablespoon or packet active dry yeast
1 cup sourdough starter
5 1/2 to 6 1/2 cups King Arthur Unbleached All-Purpose Flour
1 tablespoon salt
1 tablespoon vegetable oil
cornmeal to sprinkle on baking pans

Making the Sponge: In a large mixing bowl, dissolve the sugar and yeast in the warm water. Let this sit for 10 minutes or so until bubbly. Add the starter and stir. Gradually add 3 cups of flour, stirring until well mixed and smooth.

Cover this sponge and set it aside in a warm draft-free place for 4 to 5 hours.

Making the Dough: Stir down the sponge. Stir in 1 cup of flour, the salt and oil. Gradually add flour until the dough no longer sticks to the sides of the bowl.

Turn the dough out onto a lightly floured board and knead for 3 to 4 minutes. Let the dough rest while you clean out and grease your bowl. Continue kneading another 3 or 4 minutes or until the dough becomes smooth and elastic. Add only enough flour to the board to keep the dough from sticking. Place the dough in the greased bowl and let rise until doubled in bulk, 1 to 2 hours.

Shaping & Baking: Knock down the dough and shape it into 2 long French- or Italian-style loaves. Place them on a cornmeal-sprinkled baking sheet and let them rise for another 1 to 1 1/2 hours.

Toward the end of the rising period, place a baking pan on the oven bottom (or on the lowest rack) and preheat your oven to 450°F.

Just before baking, slash the tops diagonally every couple of inches, about 1/4 inch deep and brush with cold water.

Pour 2 or 3 cups of water into the pan, put the loaves on the rack above the steaming water and bake for about 25 minutes.

The crust will be very hard when you remove the bread, but in 5 minutes, it will be soft and chewy. To make the crust hard and chewy, turn the oven off and leave the bread inside for an additional 5 minutes.

Sourdough Pumpernickel Bread

Pumpernickel is to "white" rye flour as whole wheat flour is to white wheat flour. It contains the whole rye berry and is more coarsely ground than the white rye. This recipe can be adjusted to either type of rye flour, or a blend of both. Flours ground from whole rye berries can be found in specialty or health food stores.

1 cup water
1 cup pumpernickel
$\frac{1}{2}$ cup water, lukewarm
$\frac{1}{3}$ cup molasses
2 tablespoons or packets active dry yeast
1 cup Sourdough Starter
4 to 6 cups King Arthur Unbleached All-Purpose Flour
$\frac{1}{4}$ cup vegetable oil
$1\frac{1}{2}$ teaspoons salt
1 tablespoon caraway seeds
2 teaspoons cocoa powder (optional, for a darker color)
cornmeal to sprinkle on baking pans (if making free-form loaves)
egg white or yolk beaten with 1 tablespoon water, for wash (optional)

Making the Sponge: Bring 1 cup of water to a boil in a saucepan. Turn off the heat and stir in the cup of pumpernickel. Let it sit until lukewarm.

Pour the $\frac{1}{2}$ cup of lukewarm water into a large mixing bowl. Add the molasses and yeast, stir and let rest for 10 minutes to dissolve and activate the yeast. Stir in the starter and moistened pumpernickel flour. Add $\frac{1}{2}$ cup of unbleached all-purpose flour, stir, cover and set this sponge in a warm, draft-free place for about 4 hours.

Making & Shaping the Dough: Stir down the sponge. Add the oil, salt, caraway seeds and optional cocoa and stir. Gradually add flour until the dough no longer sticks to the sides of the bowl. Place the dough on a lightly floured surface and knead for 8 to 10 minutes.

Form the dough into 2 large loaves and place them in greased bread pans. If you prefer, you can make free-form loaves and place them on a greased baking sheet that has been sprinkled with cornmeal. Cover and let the dough rise in a warm place until doubled in bulk.

Baking: About 15 minutes before the loaves are ready to be baked, preheat your oven to 375°F. If you are baking the loaves free-form, slash the tops diagonally 2 or 3 times just before they go into the oven.

For a crunchy crust, brush the tops with water. For a shiny crust, brush them with the egg wash. Bake for 35 to 40 minutes.

RUSSIAN RYE BREAD

Dark Russian Rye is a hearty, main-meal kind of bread that should accompany a hearty, main-meal kind of soup and perhaps some chunks of pickled herring. This recipe comes from King Arthur Flour's spokesman Michael Jubinsky's voluminous files of northern European recipes.

To begin, you make another variation of a starter called a Rye Sour. This needs to be done 4 to 5 days ahead of the day you want to bake your bread. It, like our other sourdoughs, takes a little planning but not much more active preparation than regular yeasted bread. It is certainly one of those unique breads that can only be crafted by loving hands at home.

Rye Sour

1 tablespoon or packet active dry yeast
2 cups warm water
3 cups medium rye flour
a thick slice of raw onion

Preparing the Rye Sour: Dissolve the yeast in 1 cup of the water and blend in 1½ cups of the rye flour. Stir in the onion, cover with plastic wrap and set aside at room temperature.

Let the sour rise and fall back. After this point, stir the sour twice a day for three days.

Remove the onion and add the second cup of warm water. Blend in the remaining 1½ cups of rye flour, cover and set aside again. When the sour has risen and fallen once more, it is ready to use. This will take another day or so.

Dough

½ cup warm water (warm to the wrist)
2 tablespoons or packets active dry yeast
1 teaspoon sugar
6½ to 8½ cups King Arthur Unbleached All-Purpose Flour
2 cups boiling water
1 cup pumpernickel (or coarse rye meal)
½ cup shortening or vegetable oil
1 tablespoon salt
½ cup molasses
3 tablespoons instant coffee
1 ounce unsweetened chocolate
3 cups thick Rye Sour
2 cups medium rye flour

Activating the Yeast: In a small bowl combine the ½ cup warm water, yeast, sugar, and ½ cup of the unbleached all-purpose flour. Cover with plastic wrap and a clean towel and set aside for about 15 minutes, until bubbly.

Making the Dough: In a large bowl, combine the boiling water, pumpernickel, shortening, salt, molasses, instant coffee, and chocolate. Mix to blend.

When this mixture has cooled, add the rye sour and the yeast mixture. Add the remaining rye flour and then the unbleached all-purpose flour, one cup at a time, until the dough comes cleanly away from the sides of the bowl.

Kneading & Rising: Turn out onto a lightly floured board and knead, adding only enough flour to prevent sticking, for 4 to 5 minutes.

Give the dough a rest while you clean out and grease your bowl. Continue kneading for another 4 to 5 minutes, adding only enough flour to prevent sticking.

Doughs made with rye flour and/or molasses tend to be sticky. Although the dough should be fairly stiff, don't continue to add flour to try to completely eliminate the stickiness. You can't. It's just the nature of this kind of dough.

Place the dough in your bowl, turning the dough to oil the top surface. Cover with plastic wrap and set in a warm, draft-free place to rise until doubled in bulk.

Shaping & Baking: When it's fully risen, punch the dough down and divide it into quarters.

Shape each quarter into a round loaf and place on a cornmeal-covered baking sheet. You can also use four traditional bread pans which should be greased and sprinkled with cornmeal. Let the dough rise until it's almost doubled in bulk.

About 15 minutes before you want to bake your bread, place a baking pan on the oven bottom (or on the lowest rack) and preheat your oven to 375°F.

Just before the loaves go in, slash them once across the top (with a sharp knife) about ¼ inch deep and brush with cold water.

Pour 2 or 3 cups of water into the pan in the oven to create steam (see page 120) and bake for 35 to 40 minutes. When the loaves are done, cool them on a wire rack.

Onion Caraway Sourdough Bread

This recipe was sent to us by Ceil Downey, of Framingham, Massachusetts. A longtime friend and user of King Arthur Flour, she is married to Edward Downey, a senior Vice President of our New England broker, Morris Alper & Sons. This recipe contains active dry yeast which eliminates the need to develop a sponge. The onion topping adds zest.

4 cups King Arthur Unbleached All-Purpose Flour
3 tablespoons sugar
2½ teaspoons salt
1 tablespoon or packet active dry yeast
1 cup milk
2 tablespoons butter or margarine
1½ cups Sourdough Starter
cornmeal (to sprinkle on baking sheet)
1 egg white, beaten with 1 tablespoon water (for wash)
⅔ cup finely chopped onion
caraway seed to sprinkle on top of loaves

Making the Dough: Combine 1 cup of the flour, the sugar, salt and yeast in a large bowl. Then, combine milk and butter or margarine in a saucepan. Heat over low heat until the liquid is very warm, 120°F to 130°F. (The butter does not need to melt.)

Gradually add the liquids to the dry ingredients, beating well. Blend in the starter and another cup of flour. Beat again. Stir in enough additional flour to make a soft dough.

Kneading & Rising: Turn the dough out onto a lightly floured board and knead until smooth and elastic, about 10 minutes. Then place it in a greased bowl, turning the dough to grease the top. Cover and let it rise in a warm, draft-free place until doubled, 1 to 2 hours.

Shaping & Rising: Punch down the dough, turn it onto a board and divide it in half (or quarters). Cover and let it rest 15 minutes. Shape into 2 long loaves (or 4 small round loaves) and place on baking sheets that have been sprinkled with cornmeal. (For regular shaped loaves, place in 2 greased, 4½ x 8½-inch bread pans.) Cover and let the loaves rise until doubled in bulk, about 1 hour.

Baking: About 15 minutes before you want to bake your bread, preheat your oven to 400°F.

Just before the loaves go in, brush the wash generously over the loaves. Top with chopped onion and sprinkle with caraway seeds.

Bake the loaves for about 25 minutes and then cool them on a wire rack.

SOURDOUGH ANADAMA

A sourdough starter can be used in a wide variety of baked goods as this collection of recipes demonstrates. Recipes written for active dry yeast can be converted to sourdough provided you take into account the slower action of wild yeast and the fact that you are using a leavening that is thick and liquid in place of one that is dry and granular.

Anadama bread leavened with a wild yeast rather than a domestic yeast is a bread with a great combination of flavors. When converting a recipe, you want to keep in mind the amount of flour and liquid in the starter. One cup of flour mixed with one cup of water makes 1⅓ cups of both combined. For ease in translation we'll use 1⅓ cups of starter.

> 1 cup boiling water
> ½ cup cornmeal
> ½ cup non-fat dry milk (optional)
> ½ cup dark molasses
> 1⅓ cups Sourdough Starter
> ¼ cup (½ stick) butter or vegetable oil
> 4½ to 5½ cups King Arthur Unbleached All-Purpose Flour
> 1 tablespoon salt
> 1 teaspoon baking soda

Making the Sponge: Pour the cup of boiling water over the cornmeal in a glass or ceramic mixing bowl. (Remember that the other cup of water is in the starter.) Mix in the molasses, dry milk and butter. Let cool to lukewarm and blend in 2 cups of flour.

To "start" the sponge, blend in the starter. Cover with plastic wrap and let this work for several hours or all day if it suits your schedule. Notice that the salt isn't included yet. Salt discourages wild yeast as well as domestic yeast so we'll add it when we add the remainder of the flour.

Making the Dough: After the sponge has grown, add 2 more cups of flour into which you've blended the salt and baking soda. In addition to the leavening action of the wild yeast, the "sweetness" of the soda will react with the acidity of the sourdough to assist in the final rise and will help the dough take on its final texture and shape. Knead this dough and, if you have time, let it rise once more in the bowl.

Shaping: Proceed as you would for traditional Anadama Bread (page 139), dividing the dough in half, shaping the loaves and letting them rise in the pans. The rising period will be a bit longer than the traditional rising period.

Baking: About 15 minutes before you want to bake your bread, preheat your oven to 350°F. Bake the bread for about 45 minutes (10 minutes more than the usual baking time for Anadama Bread).

• SOURDOUGH AT BREAKFAST •

SOURDOUGH ENGLISH MUFFINS

The best English muffins are made with sourdough and their characteristic "holes" are created by adding baking soda just before they are cooked on a griddle.

1 cup Sourdough Starter
1 1/2 cups milk
5 1/2 to 6 cups King Arthur Unbleached All-Purpose Flour 🌾
1 tablespoon sugar
1 tablespoon salt
1 teaspoon baking soda
cornmeal to sprinkle on baking sheet

Making the Sponge: In a ceramic bowl, mix together the starter, milk and about 3 cups of flour. Cover this with plastic wrap and leave it to work for anywhere from 2 to 24 hours. You might mix this up just before you go to bed so you can have fresh English muffins for breakfast the next morning.

Making the Dough: When the sponge has developed, mix the sugar, salt, baking soda and 2 1/2 cups flour together in a separate bowl. Stir these into the sponge as thoroughly as you can and cover the resulting dough with plastic wrap and let it work for anywhere up to an hour. This allows the gluten in the flour you've just added to absorb some moisture and to relax.

Kneading & Shaping: Flour your kneading board and hands well as this dough will be soft when you turn it out. Knead for only 2 to 3 minutes until the dough is smooth and no longer lumpy. With a floured rolling pin, roll it out, like a pie dough, from the center to the outside, until it is between 1/4 and 1/2 inch thick.

Cut out circles between 3 and 4 inches in diameter (the muffins will shrink in diameter as they cook). A large tuna-sized can with both ends removed works well, or you can even throw tradition to the wind and cut squares.

Place the muffins on a cookie sheet that has been sprinkled with cornmeal and let them rest for at least 15 minutes.

Cooking: Place 4 or 5 circles on a lightly greased skillet on low, low heat with the cornmeal side down first. Cook slowly for 10 minutes, gently flip the muffins over and continue cooking for a further 10 minutes.

Serving: Cool your muffins, split with a fork to make the most of their wonderful open texture, toast and enjoy right away, or store the cooled muffins in a plastic bag to use at your leisure. English muffins also keep well in the freezer.

Sourdough Sticky Buns

It's best to start these the night before you want to serve them. They take some time (not much of yours), but they're worth the wait. This recipe will fill two 8-inch round cake pans or a 9 x 11-inch baking pan.

The Sponge

> 1 cup Sourdough Starter
> ½ cup milk
> 2 tablespoons vegetable oil
> 2 cups King Arthur Unbleached All-Purpose Flour 🌾
> ¼ cup sugar

Making the Sponge: Pour the Sourdough Starter into a mixing bowl. Stir the milk and vegetable oil into the sourdough starter. Blend in the flour and sugar to make a fairly stiff sponge. Cover the bowl and let it work overnight.

The Filling: Before you finish the dough in the morning, prepare the Traditional Filling on page 234 (or one of the variations, page 236).

The Dough

> 1 cup King Arthur Unbleached All-Purpose Flour (½ to blend into the
>   sponge; ½ to sprinkle on the board and the dough)
> 1 teaspoon salt
> 1 teaspoon baking soda

Making the Dough: Blend ½ cup of the flour with the salt and soda and stir into the sponge to make a fairly slack dough. Make sure your kneading surface is well floured before you turn it out. Flour your hands and knead for 2 to 3 minutes, enough to make the dough cohesive. Sprinkle flour on any sticky spots.

Making the Sticky Buns: Grease your pans. Melt ¼ cup of the butter and distribute it evenly into the pans. Sprinkle 2 tablespoons of sugar in each and sprinkle cinnamon over the sugar (or use whatever is appropriate for your filling).

Roll out the dough with a well-floured rolling pin until it's about 12 x 18 inches. (While rolling, sprinkle flour on any sticky spots, under or on top of the dough.) Spread about 4 tablespoons of butter over the surface of the dough. Sprinkle ¼ cup sugar over the butter. (Or finish with your other filling ingredients.)

Starting with the long edge and using a spatula or bowl scraper to help, roll up the dough. Cut the roll into about eighteen ¾- to 1-inch pieces. Place them in the cake or other pans, allowing room for the dough to expand. Cover and let rise for about an hour.

Baking & Serving: Fifteen minutes before you want to bake the buns, preheat your oven to 400°F. Bake for 15 minutes. Turn the heat down to 350°F and continue baking for a further 20 minutes. Remove the buns from the oven.

Place a serving plate over the top of the pan, flip the two over and leave the pan in place until the buns are securely on the plate, topping and all.

Indian Meal Muffins

When you make sourdough quick breads and pancakes, you utilize a different characteristic of your starter than you do when you make regular sourdough bread. Rather than depending on the wild yeast in the starter to do the work, the following muffins (and pancakes) are leavened the way traditional quick breads are, through the reaction of baking soda with the starter, which is acidic. So these muffins are quick to make though "quick" is not a word ordinarily associated with sourdough.

This recipe puts together several ingredients that were readily available back when Sands, Taylor & Wood was a fledgling company on Long Wharf in Boston. Indian meal is an old word for cornmeal. Molasses, honey and maple syrup all were sweeteners to which the early colonists had access. Each of these sweeteners produces a muffin with a different personality. Whichever you choose you'll make about a dozen hearty muffins with an old-fashioned flavor. (These reheat beautifully at 400°F in about 10 minutes.)

3/4 cup King Arthur Unbleached All-Purpose Flour 🌾
3/4 cup cornmeal
3/4 teaspoon salt
1 teaspoon baking soda
1 1/2 teaspoons cinnamon
1 cup Sourdough Starter
1/4 cup milk
1 egg
4 tablespoons (1/2 stick) butter, melted, or vegetable oil
6 tablespoons molasses, honey or maple syrup

Preheat your oven to 500°F.

Combine the dry ingredients in a mixing bowl. In a second bowl, beat together the starter, milk, egg, melted butter and sweetener. Blend the wet ingredients with the dry, taking about 20 seconds.

Fill the cups of a greased muffin tin two-thirds full. Put the tin in the oven, turn the temperature down to 400°F and bake for about 20 minutes.

For Indian Meal Bread, bake this batter in a 10 1/2-inch griddle for 25 minutes. Or, for Indian Meal Pancakes, add 1/2 cup more milk, and cook in a griddle on the stove top.

SOURDOUGH PANCAKES

What do Olney, England, and Liberal, Kansas, have in common? The answer is Shrove Tuesday. And what does Shrove Tuesday have to do with pancakes?

Shrove Tuesday is the day when members of the Christian Church are "shriven," or granted absolution after confession and penance in preparation for Lent and forty days of fasting. It's also the last day that certain traditionally rich foods, such as butter and eggs, can be eaten. So, along with confession and penance, it's also a day of games and feasting.

Shrove Tuesday is also known as "Pancake Tuesday," and here is where Olney, England, comes in. According to local Olney lore, back in 1445 at 11:55 in the morning, an Olney housewife heard the bells of the parish church calling parishioners to the shriving service. She was in the middle of preparing the midday meal and in her haste to get to church, she bolted out the door and ran all the way with a griddle in her hand and a pancake in the griddle. Thus originated the great pancake race which has been held on Shrove Tuesday in Olney, and many other English parishes, on and off ever since.

One year, there were visitors from Liberal, Kansas, in Olney on Pancake Tuesday. They were so inspired by the Olney race that they returned to Kansas and instituted their own. The race is four hundred fifteen yards long, just shy of a quarter of a mile. A participant must run it carrying a griddle complete with pancake, flipping the cake once at the beginning and once at the end.

This pancake recipe probably tastes much like the Olney pancakes which were made long before baking powder appeared on the scene. They are delicious and light, perhaps light enough to get you to your feet to run the four hundred fifteen yards yourself. Whether you run or not, at 5 minutes to noon on Shrove Tuesday, think of the runners from Olney, England, and Liberal, Kansas, celebrating a tradition that is over five hundred years old and then make some pancakes.

This recipe feeds a family of four moderate eaters. If you have adolescents in the house, or are one yourself, double it.

1 cup King Arthur Unbleached All-Purpose Flour
1 cup King Arthur Stone Ground Whole Wheat Flour
2 tablespoons sugar
2 cups buttermilk, slightly warmed
1 cup sourdough starter
2 eggs
$\frac{1}{4}$ cup butter, melted (or vegetable oil)
$\frac{3}{4}$ teaspoon salt
1 teaspoon baking soda

Combine the flours and sugar in a large mixing bowl. Warm the buttermilk and blend it in.

Remove a cup of your sourdough starter, and replenish the pot as explained on page 527. Blend the sourdough starter into the flour/buttermilk mixture.

Let this work for at least 2 hours but it's best and actually easier if you make it up the night before serving and let it work overnight.

Beat the eggs, butter or oil, salt and baking soda together until light. Blend this mixture into the sponge. (Watch the batter begin to bubble and foam.)

Drop by the spoonful, large or small, onto a moderately hot, lightly buttered griddle and cook until large bubbles begin to appear. Flip them over and cook until the other side is browned.

SOURDOUGH WAFFLES

For the lightest, tastiest waffles you'll ever eat, use this same batter and follow the directions for your waffle iron, or turn to page 33.

• SOURDOUGH DESSERTS •

Cakes used to be leavened with yeast. Baking powder did not appear on the scene until the middle of the last century. On the American frontier, baking powder was not practical even when it was available since it had only a limited life, so recipes for all things leavened were adapted to utilize the sturdy pioneer's wild yeast, or sourdough starter.

CHOCOLATE SOURDOUGH CAKE

Here is our sourdough starter at work in a moist, dark chocolate cake. The recipe involves making a sponge so it will take more time from start to finish than the following Carrot Cake.

> 1 cup Sourdough Starter
> 1 cup milk or evaporated milk (for a richer flavor)
> 2 cups King Arthur Unbleached All-Purpose Flour
> 1½ cups sugar
> 1 cup vegetable oil
> 2 teaspoons vanilla
> 1 teaspoon salt
> 1½ teaspoons baking soda
> ¾ cup cocoa
> 2 eggs
> Frosting of your choice (page 317)

Preheat your oven to 350°F.

Combine the starter, milk and flour. Let this sponge work for 2 to 3 hours in a warm place until it's bubbly and it has a pleasing sour-milk aroma.

In a second bowl, cream the sugar, oil, salt, vanilla, baking soda and cocoa. Add the eggs, one at a time, beating well after each addition. You want to incorporate as much air as possible in this process.

Combine the creamed mixture with the sourdough mixture. Do this as gently as possible but make sure it's well blended.

Grease two 9-inch cake pans, divide the cake batter between them and bake for 40 to 45 minutes, or until done. After five minutes, remove the cakes from their pans and cool on a wire rack.

After the layers are thoroughly cooled, you can top them with your choice of frosting. You might also try spreading the bottom layer with a seedless raspberry jam for an old world flavor variation.

SOURDOUGH CARROT CAKE

Claimed by Michael Jubinsky to be "worth its weight in gold!"

1 1/2 cups vegetable oil
2 cups sugar
1 cup Sourdough Starter
3 eggs
1 cup (8 ounces) crushed pineapple
2 cups grated carrots
1/2 cup chopped walnuts
2 teaspoons vanilla
2 1/2 cups King Arthur Unbleached All-Purpose Flour
2 teaspoons cinnamon
1/2 teaspoon salt
1 teaspoon baking soda
1/2 cup shredded coconut
1 recipe Cream Cheese Frosting (page 317, optional)

Preheat your oven to 350°F.

Combine the oil and sugar and add the Sourdough Starter. Mix in the eggs, one at a time, and beat well. Fold in the pineapple, carrots, nuts and vanilla. Combine the dry ingredients, and blend well with the wet mixture. Fold in the coconut.

Bake in a greased, 8 x 12-inch pan for 40 to 45 minutes. Cool on a wire rack before frosting with Cream Cheese Frosting on page 317.

FRIENDSHIP CAKE

The starter for a Friendship Cake is a sweet variation on the sourdough theme. Every now and then it circulates through the baking world much the way a chain letter does, with instructions for feeding, baking, and passing it on, a wonderful way of sharing "the joys of baking."

The Sands' starter came with the traditional directions, which appear on the next page, from Evan Douple, Professor of Radiobiology at the Dartmouth College Medical School, who got his from an associate there. (Marvelous things come out of this lab. The Chocolate Steamed Pudding with its mysterious topping called "Ope," which you'll find in the Quick Bread chapter on page 102, also came from some lab associates there.)

If you don't have a friend with some of this interesting starter, we include instructions for modifying a traditional one to create the Friendship variety. Like other starters, this one develops more flavor and character with age, so it's worth keeping some around.

The instructions for baking a Friendship Cake involve making enough starter every time you use it to have what you need to make the cake and some to give to three friends as well. The cakes that you can bake with it are so good that you may find you want to keep using it after you've given starter to everyone you know. So we've also included instructions for making enough for one cake and only enough extra for your own starter pot. We've also shortened the number of days involved in the whole process.

> *Day 1 - The day you receive the base, pour it into a large glass or pottery bowl, stir thoroughly, cover, and place on counter (or somewhere at room temperature). Do not refrigerate.*
>
> *Days 2,3, and 4 - Stir and return to counter.*
>
> *Day 5 - Add 1 cup each, sugar, King Arthur Unbleached All-Purpose Flour and milk. Stir, cover, and return to counter.*
>
> *Days 6,7,8, and 9 - Stir and return to counter.*
>
> *Day 10 - Add ingredients as in day 5, stir and take 3 cups of the base and give one cup each to three friends with a copy of these directions and a piece of the Friendship Cake you baked with your portion of the starter.*

In creating these alternative instructions, we are bypassing, to a degree, the intent behind the Friendship Cake which is to create a chain of Friendship Cakes, each one related to all the others, which could reach around and contain the world. We at Sands, Taylor & Wood Co., like this philosophy of "world peace through Friendship Cakes" and hope that you will make a commitment to share your starter with everyone you know before you use the abbreviated instructions.

Friendship Starter from Traditional Starter

1 cup traditional Sourdough Starter
1 cup milk
1 cup sugar
1 cup King Arthur Unbleached All-Purpose Flour 🌾

Take a cup of traditional starter and put it in a glass or ceramic bowl. Add the milk, sugar and flour and blend well. Cover with plastic wrap and let it work for at least 24 hours.

To make the Friendship Cake, remove 2 cups of this starter and proceed with the following recipe.

Feed the starter you don't use in the cake with equal parts of milk, sugar and flour, enough just for you. Or, in friendship spirit, make enough to divide and share. Let it sit at room temperature for several hours to grow. After it's bubbly and healthy, store it in your refrigerator the way you store your other sourdough starter. If you give some away, remember to feed your starter so you'll always have the 2 cups you need for the recipe and a cup left over to grow some more.

Friendship Cake

The first time you make a cake with this traditional-turned-friendship starter, it won't be quite as sweet as it will be the second time. You can either add a bit more sugar to the cake batter to compensate or try it as is. Either way, it is an exceptional cake.

$2/3$ cup vegetable oil
1 cup sugar
3 eggs
2 teaspoons vanilla
2 cups Friendship Starter
$1\frac{1}{2}$ to 2 cups King Arthur Unbleached All-Purpose Flour
$1\frac{1}{2}$ teaspoons cinnamon
$1/4$ teaspoon nutmeg
$1\frac{1}{2}$ teaspoons baking soda
2 teaspoons baking powder
$1/2$ teaspoon salt

Preheat your oven to 350°F.

Combine the oil, sugar, eggs and vanilla and beat until light. Add the starter and beat until smooth. Blend the dry ingredients together and fold into the starter mixture. Pour into a greased Bundt pan and bake for 40 to 45 minutes.

VARIATIONS

• Just before baking, fold in up to 2 cups of chopped nuts, diced apple or applesauce, raisins or whatever seems appropriate.

• For a chocolate version, substitute $1/2$ cup cocoa powder for the cinnamon and nutmeg and add any other ingredients at your own discretion. Some possibilities that come to mind are chocolate chips, chopped nuts, minced orange peel and rum or mint extract.

Fun!
for the Young & Young at Heart

• In this section there are clearly some places where our King Arthur Unbleached All-Purpose Flour used all by itself will do the best job. We've indicated where you can successfully substitute some King Arthur Stone Ground Whole Wheat Flour for our Unbleached All-Purpose by the 🪶 symbol in the ingredient list.

• To begin, set up a spot for yourself or your "sculptor" that allows enough room for creating and which won't interfere with other things going on nearby. A large sheet of heavy plastic or an old "wipable" tablecloth is handy either on a tabletop or the floor depending on the age of the creator. They make a good work surface as well as an easily removed container when a project is done.

• The key to fun in this section is experimentation! Look around the house and garage for unusual "tools" to shape and texture your Play Dough, Salt Dough or Bread Sculptures. Instead of a traditional Pretzel, bake a giant one or make a Pretzel chain to hang on a tree. Read our Gingerbread House instructions and then close your eyes and fantisize one of your own. Add your own projects and inspirations for the years to come.

Fun!
FOR THE YOUNG & YOUNG AT HEART
XI

Have you ever tried modeling bread dough like clay to create a bread sculpture, creating a fantastic papier-mâché creature out of flour, water and newspaper, or using gingerbread to build people, a house or a castle? This section goes beyond baking to highlight some of King Arthur Flour's other creative qualities.

If you're in a solitary and creative mood, you can do any of these projects by yourself. You'll find many things here that can be made as gifts to celebrate any holiday or season or just the joy of playing. But this kind of playing is a perfect way to spend time with a child or a friend. And, when you're in the mood, many of these projects will make a great foundation for a party.

Whatever you do and however you do it, we dedicate this chapter to serendipity, smiles and the child in us all.

• PASTES •

Flour and water combined make paste. King Arthur Flour, with its extra amount of gluten, is a natural for paste and all the things you can make with it. Other ingredients can be added to paste to strengthen and preserve it as well as create texture and aroma.

All of these pastes are completely water soluble and can be soaked off anything that has been inappropriately pasted.

Simple Paste

This paste is for the most spontaneous of jobs.

¹/₂ cup King Arthur Unbleached All-Purpose Flour
6 tablespoons water

Add the water to the flour and mix. That's all!

Schoolroom Paste

This paste smells better and lasts longer than the Simple Paste. It also takes longer to prepare and needs to be made ahead of time.

1 cup sugar
1 cup King Arthur Unbleached All-Purpose Flour
1 teaspoon alum (optional, to preserve the paste)
4 cups water
a few drops oil of cloves, peppermint or wintergreen, for a pleasant
        aroma (optional)

Cooking: In a saucepan, mix the sugar, flour and alum and gradually add the water.

Cook the paste over medium heat, stirring until it thickens and clears. Add the fragrant oil and let it cool.

Storing: This paste should be stored in a covered jar. If it gets too thick to spread, thin with hot water, a few drops at a time.

Papier-Mâché Paste

Papier-mâché is a versatile sculpting medium. Puppet heads and hands, a globe, a piñata, animals, even an entire a village can be created with just paper, paste, paint and a bit of imagination.

Have your base ready (see piñata below) before mixing your paste, as it is best used warm.

> 1 cup King Arthur Unbleached All-Purpose Flour
> 1/4 cup sugar
> 4 cups warm water
> 4 cups cold water
> 1/8 teaspoon oil of wintergreen, cloves or peppermint (optional)

Mix the flour and sugar in a sauce pan. Stir in 2 cups of the warm water and blend well.

Add the rest of the water and bring the mixture to a boil, stirring constantly. Cook until thick and clear. Add the oil, if desired.

Piñata made of Papier-Mâché

By sticking a lot of paper together with papier-mâché paste in a very specific sort of way, you can create a piñata, a splendid Mexican invention which is painted, filled with treasures and suspended amidst a group of excited revelers. One by one, each person, blindfolded, has a turn to swing at it with a stick until it bursts open and scatters its wealth. Since there is quite a lot of drying time involved, allow at least three days to make a piñata from start to finish.

First: Decide what you want your piñata to look like.

Building the Frame: One of the easiest forms to build around is a blown-up balloon. You can make simple piñatas in the shape of the balloon itself. Or you can use the balloon to form the base or body of something else, a round balloon for the body of a pig or turkey, a long balloon as a base for a surrealistic snake or dragon. Make sure the balloon is sturdy and close to the shape you want to create.

You can also use cardboard, wire, wood, or anything else that will form an effective frame. Tie a good, sturdy string to the top before you start adding the strips of papier-mâché so you'll be able to hang it.

Applying the Papier-Mâché: Once you have your base, tear up an abundance of paper into 1- or 2-inch strips; newspaper is very good and there's usually a lot of it around but any paper that has an absorbent rather than a slick or shiny surface will do.

It's best to use the papier-mâché paste while it's relatively warm. Run strips of paper through it and wrap them on your base. More layers provide more strength, so keep in mind who it is for. Four or five layers will create a piñata which will offer solid resistance to a well-aimed stick. Cut body appendages out of cardboard and attach them with strips of paste-covered paper.

Drying: When your piñata is fully sculpted and finished, hang it to dry for at least 24 hours.

When it's completely dry, cut out an opening large enough so you can fill it with treats. You can use anything from candies to small toys, but it's best if they are fairly rugged since they'll take quite a drubbing before they are claimed. Replace the opening, paste it shut with more paper strips and allow this to dry.

Painting: Poster paint will decorate it very nicely. For a more professional look, you may want to use acrylics but if you're using them with children, make sure they are non-toxic.

Celebrating: Hang the piñata where people can swing at it without doing damage to anything or anyone nearby and where the contents can scatter and be fairly visible. Find a stick that won't break and gather everyone around, but at a safe distance.

It's important to set some ground rules first. Traditionally before a person is allowed to swing at the piñata, he or she is blindfolded and turned three times in a circle. Then the piñata is given a push so it becomes a moving target. One person is allowed three whacks, including misses, before the next person has a turn. If there are small children involved, you may decide to eliminate the blindfold and only count solid hits.

Once the piñata has scattered its treasure, let everyone jump in and glean for a few minutes but encourage trading and sharing so everyone comes away feeling equally exuberant.

• MODELING DOUGHS •

Homemade modeling doughs are another natural for King Arthur Flour and its extra gluten. We give you two choices, one you can store between uses in the refrigerator and one you can "fire" like pottery clay.

PLAY DOUGH

This play dough is easy to make, easy to store and always fun to use. When your sculptor is through using it, just put it in an airtight container or plastic bag in the refrigerator until those creative impulses strike again.

When you make your own play dough, you know that it is safe if some finds its way into the sculptor's mouth. Although it is usually colored with food coloring you can use vegetable juices if you prefer. This dough contains a lot of salt which will discourage much tasting in any case.

Salt is hygroscopic, which means it attracts and retains water. This, along with the addition of a little vegetable oil, helps keep play dough moist. If, after it's been used several times, your play dough becomes stiff or crumbly, knead in a bit of water. In spite of the salt, some evaporation will occur. If your dough is ever sticky, knead in a bit of flour.

This dough is "cooked" with boiling water but cold water will work (though more slowly) if hot water isn't available. When you want to make a larger amount for several children, or to use as gifts, it's easier to do it in several batches. You can double this recipe, but it's difficult to handle much more than that at one time.

> 2 cups King Arthur Unbleached All-purpose Flour
> 1 cup salt
> 1 tablespoon alum or cream of tartar (optional, but helps preserve the
>   play dough)
> 1 tablespoon vegetable oil
> 2 cups boiling water (or cold if that's all that's available)
> food coloring or vegetable juices (beet, spinach, carrot, etc.)

Mixing the Ingredients: Mix the flour, salt and alum or cream of tartar together. Add the oil, water and coloring if you plan to make just one color.

Knead for 6 to 8 minutes. If you want more colors, divide the dough after kneading for 3 or 4 minutes, add a different color to each piece and finish kneading each separately. (This is a good job for the sculptor.)

Shaping the Play Dough: With play dough you can make animals, people, houses, cars and trucks, ornaments and beads, "cookies and cakes." The possibilities are infinite. What you don't make today, you can always make tomorrow.

Because this dough is water soluble, any tools you use will be easy to clean.

• Just as you use modeling clay, you can make snakes, coils, and balls with this dough.

• You can roll it out into slabs with a rolling pin or pat it flat with your hands so you can use it for building material or for cutting out shapes with cookie cutters or plastic knives.

• Create texture in the dough with the tines of a fork, your fingers or whatever else looks promising.

• Make hair by pressing some dough through a garlic press, worms or rope by using an old-fashioned potato ricer.

• A hand-cranked meat or vegetable grinder that clamps on a table is also fun to sculpt with (maybe more for the doing than the results).

Salt or "Firing" Dough

This dough is much like play dough but, in spite of its name, contains less salt and no oil (it's not as hygroscopic) so it can be "fired" like clay to make "permanent" sculpture. Unlike clay, which needs to be fired in a super-hot kiln, this dough needs only to be baked in your kitchen oven.

3/4 cup boiling water
1/2 cup salt
2 cups King Arthur Unbleached All-Purpose Flour
food coloring (optional)

Making the Dough: Pour the boiling water into a medium-sized mixing bowl. Add and dissolve the salt. If you want the dough to be all one color, add color to the water. Stir to cool a bit and then add the flour all at once. Mix and shape into a ball. Knead for 6 to 8 minutes.

To make dough with more than one color, divide it after kneading for 3 or 4 minutes, add a different color to each piece and finish kneading each piece separately. Remember that you can always paint this dough after it's baked.

Shaping the Dough: While you work with one piece of dough, keep the rest covered with plastic wrap or a damp cloth. For shaping possibilities refer to the recipe for play dough. To join pieces of dough together, use water sparingly. If the dough is too sticky add a little flour. If it becomes crumbly, add water, a few drops at a time.

As with play dough, the possibilities are infinite, so let your imagination go.

- Christmas ornaments and other holiday decorations are often the product of an afternoon experimenting with this dough, although this doesn't need to be your only theme.

- Colorful butterflies or birds can be sculpted for a mobile to hang in a window.

- A fruit fantasia can fill a wicker basket or hang on your kitchen wall.

If you plan to hang your dough creations, before you bake them make a hole in an appropriate place, or shape the dough so that a string can be tied around it (e.g., make the stem of an apple flair at the top). You can even embed a piece of wire into the dough (a bent paper clip will do in a pinch).

Baking the Dough: Preheat your oven to 225°F for at least 15 minutes. Lay the shaped ornaments or sculptures on foil-covered baking sheets and bake for 30 to 90 minutes depending on thickness. Let your creations cool completely before painting.

Alternatively, these pieces will dry without baking over a period of a few days if the weather is dry. Leave them where dry air can circulate around them.

Coloring & Finishing the Dough: You can paint these ornaments or sculptures with acrylics, poster paint or water colors. (If children are making them, poster paints or water colors are safer choices.) Felt tip markers, thick or thin, are good for detailing. After coloring, bake the sculptures once more in a warm oven (150°F to 200°F) for 30 minutes to remove any remaining moisture.

This dough is fairly sturdy when baked and can be handled like ceramic. The main difference is that, because it contains salt, it will absorb moisture over time. In order for it to last indefinitely, it must be thoroughly dried and sealed with 2 or 3 coats of clear acrylic paint or varnish.

An alternative is to display it and then store it in an airtight plastic bag, preferably in your freezer, until you want to display it again.

Sculpting with Bread Dough

Wheat flour, with its abundance of elastic gluten, makes another medium that is wonderful to sculpt with. Many people have discovered this amazing property of bread dough but there are a few who have taken it into the realm of "art."

Jennifer Sawyer, an accomplished bread sculptor as well as a Connecticut cousin of the Sands, has agreed to share her sculpting tricks with us. Whether you're young or old, a new or advanced sculptor, you'll find that this particular pastime is great fun and edible as well.

Almost any bread dough can be sculpted, but a dough that is stiff enough to hold its shape is preferable. Jennifer usually uses her own Anadama Oatmeal Bread dough (page 140), which, as well as tasting good, gives her sculptures a healthy, bronzed appearance.

Use Jennifer's or one of your own choice. If you want to make a sculpture that you can keep rather than eat, use a dough such as our Hearth Bread (page 114), which doesn't contain egg, milk or fat (anything that can spoil).

Follow the directions for mixing and kneading your dough and allow it to rise once. Punch it down, dust your sculpting surface and you're ready to begin.

Tools of the Trade: Only simple tools are needed for shaping the dough. Your hands and fingers are most important, but a sharp knife, clean scissors, a rolling pin and cookie cutters are useful. Look around the kitchen for other "tools" to imprint or texture the dough with.

Manipulating the Dough: Here are a few suggestions although, once you get started, many more will come to mind.

> • To make heads, bodies, lobster claws, etc., shape the dough into tiny round or oval "loaves of bread." Use them as is or flatten and alter their shapes a bit with your hands.

> • Roll the dough thin with a rolling pin and use a knife or cookie cutters to cut shapes.

• Use your hands to roll dough into long snakes which can be used for hair, bristles of a broom, or rope. These "snakes" can also be coiled or woven into a basket or platter. To shape and bake an edible serving dish or basket, use an inverted, greased metal bowl or platter that can go into a hot oven.

• To create thicker dimensions, you can either fold dough that you have rolled out or simply stick more dough on top of a shape you are trying to add body to.

• To create the texture of sheaves of wheat, feathers, leaves, fur or bricks, score the surface of the dough with your knife.

• To detail a beak, lobster claw, etc. clip with scissors.

Decorating & Glazing: You can decorate your creations, before baking them, with nuts and raisins or other dried fruits. (See the following Dough Dolly.)

A glaze made of an egg beaten with a tablespoon of water gives the final sculpture a smooth, rich color, and an elegant, shiny finish. It also creates a sticky surface for adding seeds, raisins, etc., for texture or decoration. You can also add a bit of food coloring to the dough or paint it with Cookie Paint (page 562).

Place the formed sculpture on a greased cookie sheet. Cover it and let it rise for 15 to 20 minutes while you preheat your oven to 400°F. Just before you put the dough into the oven, brush on the glaze. If you want some of the surface to be a darker shade, apply a second coat.

Baking: Bake for ¹/₂ to 1 hour depending on the size of the sculpture. After the first 15 minutes, turn the heat down to 350°F to finish baking. If the top is browning too rapidly, cover it with an aluminum foil tent. After this sculpture has finished baking, it is completely edible and ready to be your centerpiece.

Making your Sculpture Permanent (optional): If, rather than eat it, you wish to preserve your sculpture, bake and brown it as above and then continue baking it in a very slow oven (200°F to 250°F) until the moisture is almost gone. The time needed depends on its size and shape. Most often it will be somewhere between 1 and 1¹/₂ hours. After it's baked, let it cool completely and continue drying for 24 hours.

A dried sculpture should keep almost indefinitely if protected from children, pets and mice. To assure its permanence, after it is thoroughly dried, give it 2 or 3 coats of clear acrylic paint or varnish.

A Dough Dolly

Here are instructions for making a 12-inch dough dolly out of half a Hearth Bread dough recipe (page 114).

After the dough has risen once, cut it in half and then cut one of the halves in thirds. Shape one of the thirds into an elongated roll for the head. Shape a second one into a rough square for the torso which you can manipulate to look like neck, shoulders and waist.

If your dolly is a girl, cut the last third into 3 pieces. With your hands, roll each piece into a "snake" about 12 inches long. Lay these over the top of her head. Braid the lower ends starting about where her ears would be. You can tie them with ribbons made out of dough scraps. If your dolly is a boy, cut the "snakes" into short pieces to make curls.

Cut the other half of the dough into 2 pieces. Make a trapezoid (a triangle with a flat top) out of one of these halves and attach it to the waist with a bit of water to make a skirt. To make a pair of pants, make a vertical incision up from the bottom edge on the long side of the trapezoid.

Cut the remaining half in half. Roll out one of these halves until it is very, very thin. Cut out an apron (boys wear these too) and place it over the skirt or pants and torso. With the scraps, make a tie for the waist and straps for the shoulders. Use the remaining piece of dough to make arms and legs.

Add raisins for eyes, buttons and other trimmings. Glaze and bake your dolly according to the instructions on the previous page.

• HOLIDAY PROJECTS •

Although these particular projects are usually associated with the holidays, there's no reason why you can't have fun with them any time of the year.

PRETZELS

The pretzel has a very old lineage which may explain its association with the holiday season. Its shape has evolved from an ancient calendar sign, a circle with a dot in the center, which represented the winter solstice. Since it isn't possible to bake a shape with a floating central dot, the first pretzels were circles divided into four quadrants whose boundaries anchored the dot. In time, each of the pretzel's quadrants came to represent a season. This shape continued to evolve until it began to look like a child at prayer with his arms crossed over his chest. At this point, they were often made in monastery kitchens and given by monks to children as rewards for "piety" and "good works." Today, the pretzel serves as the baker's sign in Denmark and Norway, an ancient symbol for an ancient craft.

Pretzels now are as common as crackers. They're available crisp and hard from your grocery or, if you're lucky and in the right place, soft and chewy from street vendors. Our recipe is for the soft, chewy kind, a perfect small bread for children to start with. Once they're proficient at rolling out "snakes" with play dough, pretzels will be child's play.

One batch of our Hearth Bread dough will make 16 soft pretzels which can be shaped traditionally or any other way. If there are any left over after they have cooled, they'll look wonderful decorating a tree or greens during the holidays. (Of course, you can use any other bread dough that tempts you.) Pretzels are not only ancient, symbolic decorations, they are great, low-calorie, high-energy snacks as well and good any time of the year.

1 recipe Hearth Bread dough (page 114) made with only 5½ cups of flour
    to make a slack dough
6 cups water
2 tablespoons baking soda
1 egg beaten with 1 teaspoon water (for wash)
kosher or pretzel salt or a salt-free herb mixture

Shaping: After the dough has doubled in bulk one time, knock it down and divide it into 16 pieces. This is easily done by continuing to cut each piece in half until you have 16. Roll each piece into a 20-inch "snake."

You may have to let the dough relax several times before the snakes are as long as you want them.

Once they're long enough, tie them in the familiar pretzel shape. After shaping, cover and let them rest for about 20 minutes.

Preparing the Water: While the pretzels relax, preheat your oven to 450°F and begin to heat the water in a kettle (preferably not aluminum). Add the baking soda. When the 20-minute resting period is up, bring the water to a boil and then turn it down a bit so that the action of the boil doesn't deflate the dough.

Simmering: Using a spatula or slotted spoon, gently put 3 or 4 pretzels in the water making sure they have enough room to expand. Turn up the heat and cook for about a minute. Just as gently, so they do not deflate, remove them from the water and place them on a lightly greased cookie sheet. Repeat until you have a cookie sheet full.

Baking: Just before the pretzels go in the oven, brush them with the egg wash mixture and sprinkle them with salt or an herb blend. A goose feather brush does a great job here since you want to brush the egg mixture on without exerting any pressure.

Bake for 12 to 15 minutes or until they are crusty and brown.

CHRISTBAUMGEBACH
CHRISTMAS TREE BISCUITS

These "durable" cookies from Germany are designed to decorate a wreath or tree. They're a great way to introduce kids to baking and to the idea that making things for the holidays, especially to give away, is an important part of the whole season. Making and painting Christbaumgebach is also a wonderful way to release a lot of holiday creativity and energy.

These are meant primarily to be decorations but they are actually edible and even tasty although you'll need strong teeth or a cup of cocoa or tea to dunk them in. If you want to store them after the holiday season, seal them in an airtight plastic bag and put them somewhere dry and out of the reach of pets, mice or children.

While the children are making shapes, you can put together the cookie paint, which is applied before the cookies go in the oven. This simple recipe produces colors that are beautifully clear and are completely edible. In fact, it is great for decorating cookies that you plan to eat as well as dough sculptures.

Cookie Dough

    4 cups King Arthur Unbleached All-Purpose Flour
    1 teaspoon salt
    1 cup sugar
    4 large eggs

Making & Shaping the Cookie Dough: Blend the dry ingredients and place them in a mound on your kneading surface. Make a well in the center and break the eggs into it. (This is the same technique you use to make pasta.)

With floured hands, slowly pull the flour mixture into the eggs and blend them together. You'll find that you'll need to keep dusting the dough and your hands with flour to keep it from sticking as you work. Once the ingredients are combined, knead the dough thoroughly for 5 or 6 minutes and then cover it with a damp towel to let it relax for about 15 minutes.

Flour your work surface and rolling pin well. Roll out the dough until it's about ⅛ inch thick. This dough can be cut with cookie cutters or free form with a knife, so arm the children and let them go. (If knives are involved, keep a close eye on the operation.) Place the shaped cookies on a lightly greased baking sheet.

Cookie Paint

> 2 egg yolks
> 1 teaspoon water
> various food colorings

Making the Cookie Paint: Beat the egg yolks together with the water. Divide into tiny cups (egg cups or cordial glasses do nicely), and add a couple of drops of food coloring to each.

Painting & Baking: Preheat your oven to 350°F.

Using small paint brushes, you and your helpers can color away. The painting can be as simple or intricate as you desire.

Before you bake them take a nail and poke a depression in the top of the cookies where you'd like to run thread or pieces of yarn to tie them on your tree or wreath.

Bake the cookies for 10 to 12 minutes or until they're just barely coloring. Make sure you get them out of the oven before they begin to brown.

As soon as you can handle them without burning yourself, take the nail and again run it through the depression you made before they went in the oven. String the cookies with strong thread and hang them on your greenery.

GINGERBREAD CONSTRUCTION

Gingerbread people, houses, villages, even castles, seem to be part of our collective image of the holiday season. It's a perfect time of year to spend a day with a child creating a gingerbread cottage and the people who live in it. You might enlist everyone in the family to help build a gingerbread village (or another family to help build an entire medieval town, complete with wall and castle).

It's probably important not to be too ambitious on your first try. And it's a good idea to make your plans and designs ahead of time on paper. (Graph paper is great for this if you have some.) This will assure that you make all the pieces you need. It will help keep the scale more or less consistent and ensure that walls line up and that the roof will be big enough. You can double check to make sure that the people who live in the house can fit in the doors if you think that's important.

Although you can do your best to anticipate problems before they develop, even the most thoughtful of designs may not prevent an occasional architectural disaster. You may need a few unplanned supports and buttresses, so make sure you have a little extra gingerbread "lumber" to cope with such an event. It all adds to the excitement and fun.

Gingerbread Dough

Construction grade gingerbread, with a good "carrying capacity," can be made by doubling the amount of flour used in our American Gingerbread recipe (page 305), repeated here with the adjustments included. You can make several batches up to a week ahead of time and refrigerate or freeze them until construction day.

> ³/₄ cup buttermilk
> 6 tablespoons (³/₄ stick) butter or margarine
> 1 cup brown sugar
> ¹/₂ cup molasses
> 1 egg
> 5 cups King Arthur Unbleached All-Purpose Flour
> 1 teaspoon baking soda
> 1 teaspoon ginger
> 1 teaspoon cinnamon
> ¹/₂ teaspoon salt

First: Preheat your oven to 350°F.

Preparing the Dough: In a large saucepan, heat the butter in the buttermilk until it is just melted and remove from the heat. Add the brown sugar and molasses and beat in the egg. In a separate bowl, blend the dry ingredients. Add these to the wet mixture and blend in quickly with a spoon or wire whisk.

Shaping the Pieces: Here's how to use this versatile dough.

- **Gingerbread People:** Roll the dough out until it's 1/8 inch thick and cut into desired shapes. Lightly grease a baking sheet, place the pieces on it and bake for 10 to 12 minutes.

- **Gingerbread Buildings:** Roll out the dough until it's 1/8 thick. Lay your pattern on top. Using a straight edge and a knife, cut out the pieces you need and some extra "lumber." Place them on a greased baking sheet and bake for 20 to 25 minutes. Remove them from the oven and allow them to cool and stiffen before removing them from the baking sheet.

"Mortar" Frosting

Because the "mortar" goes together quite quickly, make it as you need it. Just make sure you have plenty of eggs and confectioners' sugar on hand.

3 1/2 cups (1 pound) unsifted confectioners' sugar
3 egg whites
1/2 teaspoon cream of tartar
food coloring (optional)
vanilla, lemon, peppermint or other extract (optional)

Mixing the "Mortar" Frosting: Beat the three frosting ingredients together until the mixture is thick. This mortar can be colored and flavored and used as icing both for houses and cookies.

Assembling a House: Mortar the side edges of the front, back and side walls. Hold the pieces together for a few minutes so the mortar can set. Tall straight glasses or cans can be useful for holding the walls in a vertical position. When the walls are fairly firm, mortar the top edges. Attach the roof, one piece at a time. Make sure you mortar the seam at the roof peak. When the roof is firm, attach the chimney if you designed one.

Decorating Houses & People: After the entire house has had a chance to set, use more mortar to attach decorations. Sugar cookies can be shingles; pieces of candy cane can frame doors and windows; gumdrops, chocolate bits, raisins, nuts and seeds can add color and texture. Make a pastry tube (see page 320) to apply the colored mortar in a decorative pattern. Your house and people can be as simple or elaborate as time and energy allow.

• FOR BIRDS & BEASTS •

Here are treats to make for your own creatures, or someone else's.

DOG BISCUITS

This recipe was graciously given to us by Betty Hyde of Bethel, Vermont, who has long taught obedience classes for dogs. She has used it for about twenty years after even more years of looking for just the right one, one that was healthy, natural and, above all, delicious (from a doggie point of view). She says this recipe will make 8 to 10 dozen biscuits and that they (and the dough) freeze beautifully. A box full, all tied up with a bright red ribbon, would make a very special present for an important dog in your life.

1 cup (about ½ pound) beef liver, cooked and minced
2 or 3 cloves of fresh garlic, minced
2½ cups water (if possible, use water you've hard boiled eggs in; it is
     very nutritious)
1 teaspoon honey (or sugar)
1 tablespoon or packet active dry yeast
½ cup warm water (for dissolving yeast)
3½ cups King Arthur Unbleached All-Purpose Flour
2 cups King Arthur Stone Ground Whole Wheat Flour
2 cups cornmeal (whole cornmeal, if possible)
1¾ cups old-fashioned rolled oats
¼ cup wheat germ
1 cup non-fat dry milk
½ cup brewers' yeast (optional, but some feel it helps to control fleas)
4 teaspoons iodized salt
3 eggs, beaten
1 egg beaten with ¼ cup milk (for brushing tops of biscuits)

Making the Dough: Rinse and cut the raw liver into small pieces. Combine with the garlic and water in a saucepan. Bring to a boil, cover the pot, lower the temperature to simmer and cook 15 minutes. Remove from the stove and cool. When cool, grind or purée this mixture (water included) and set aside.

Dissolve the honey and yeast in the warm water and set aside. In a large mixing bowl, blend the flours with the cornmeal, oats, wheat germ, dry milk, brewers' yeast and salt. Add the cooled liver/garlic mixture, the dissolved yeast and the beaten eggs to the dry ingredients. With a large spoon mix this together well.

Kneading & Resting: Turn the mixture out onto a work surface which you've dusted with flour. Knead as you would bread dough for at least 4 to 5 minutes.

Return the dough to the mixing bowl, cover and place somewhere warm (e.g., on top of your stove) to rest for 15 minutes to relax the gluten in the flour. Preheat your oven to 300°F and grease 2 or 3 cookie sheets.

Shaping: Divide the dough into 3 equal parts and leave 2 in the bowl. Roll out the third with a rolling pin until it's between ⅛ and ¼ inch thick. Cut or shape into biscuits, the size depending somewhat on the size of the recipient. Place these fairly close together on a cookie sheet. Repeat with the other 2 balls of dough, filling as many sheets as you need. (You can always chill or freeze whatever dough won't fit in your oven at one time.)

Glazing & Baking: Brush the egg/milk mixture over the tops of the biscuits and bake for 1 hour. Turn the oven off and leave the biscuits in the oven overnight, or for several hours, until they are "dog biscuit" hard.

Pack whatever you need for a week in a cardboard box and store somewhere cool. The rest can be frozen very successfully in airtight plastic bags.

Bird Pudding
For the Birds!

Chickadees, evening grosbeaks and other creatures who live with the cold and snow of winter will greatly appreciate this pudding full of the things that will help them weather any storm. Although your bird visitors may not be able to say thank you, you will enjoy watching them stay strong and healthy through the winter months. It's important to remember that once you start feeding birds, you shouldn't abandon them mid-season. These amounts can be halved or doubled depending on what your clientele is.

> 3 cups suet or other fat
> ¼ cup unsalted peanut butter
> 3 cups bread crumbs (from bread made with good King Arthur Flour)
> 1 cup King Arthur Stone Ground Whole Wheat Flour
> 1 cup sunflower seeds
> 1 cup rolled oats
> 1 cup cornmeal
> ½ cup sugar

Melt the suet or fat in a large saucepan or kettle. Mix in the remaining ingredients. Pour into a bread pan and chill.

To serve, slice off an inch or so and put it in a tray type bird feeder. If you have one attached to your window, this is a perfect place to observe the reactions to your culinary efforts. Or, take a plastic mesh bag that onions come in, place the whole pudding inside, tie it up and hang it in a nearby tree, preferably in the shade and high enough so you don't attract uninvited dining companions.

APPENDICES
& INDEX
XII

APPENDICES & INDEX
INFORMATION & DIRECTIONS

Measuring terminology can be confusing. We use the word "ounces" to describe both a volume measure and a weight measure which are not necessarily the same amount of some ingredients! Be sure you know which is referred to. For instance, one cup of flour, measured according to the directions on page 597, weighs 4 ounces, not the 8 ounces a fluid cup would measure.

a dash = 8 drops
a pinch = $1/8$ teaspoon or less
1 teaspoon = 60 drops = $1/3$ tablespoon
3 teaspoons = 1 tablespoon
2 tablespoons liquid = 1 fluid ounce
4 tablespoons = $1/4$ cup
8 tablespoons = $1/2$ cup
16 tablespoons = 8 fluid ounces = $1/2$ pint = 1 cup
2 cups = 16 fluid ounces = 1 pint = 1 pound (A pint's a pound the world around! — but only in measuring a water-based liquid.)
2 pints = 1 quart
4 quarts, liquid = 1 gallon, liquid
8 quarts = 1 peck (dry measure)

Odd But Occasionally Useful Measurements

$3/8$ cup = $1/4$ cup plus 2 tablespoons
$5/8$ cup = $1/2$ cup plus 2 tablespoons
$7/8$ cup = $3/4$ cup plus 2 tablespoons
$1/3$ cup = $5 1/3$ tablespoons = 16 teaspoons
butter the size of a walnut = 1 ounce (2 tablespoons or $1/4$ stick)
butter the size of an egg = 2 ounces (4 tablespoons or $1/2$ stick)

Metric Measure by Weight:

1 ounce = 28.35 grams (or 30 grams rounded off)   100 grams = 3.5 ounces
16 ounces = 1 pound = 454 grams   200 grams = 7 ounces
2 pounds and 3 ounces = 1 kilogram or "kilo"   400 grams = 14 ounces
14 pounds = 1 stone = 6.36 kilograms   454 grams = 16 ounces

Metric Measure by Fluid Volume:

1 teaspoon = $1/6$ ounce = 5 milliliters
1 tablespoon = $1/2$ ounce = 15 milliliters
8 tablespoons = 4 ounces = $1/2$ cup or 1 "gill"
16 tablespoons = 8 ounces = 1 cup = 236 milliliters = .236 liters
4 cups = 32 ounces = 1 quart = .946 liters
1 milliliter = $1/5$ teaspoon
1 liter = 1.057 quarts
4 liters = 1 gallon plus 1 cup

APPENDICES & INDEX
INFORMATION & DIRECTIONS
XII

A-Z

• THE INTUITIVE BAKER AS INTUITIVE EATER •

In these days of "the diet," it is often difficult keep food in perspective. "Balanced" and "moderate" are not adrenaline-producing concepts. It's much more fun to find a diet that is "the answering one," the one that will change us next week into the slim, healthy selves that exist in our minds.

But like the magic that creates the best breads, the magic that creates a healthy body is quiet and slow. When we decide to use time as our ally, there isn't anything we can't accomplish. As it does in baking, time can transform a small magic into a mighty one worthy of Merlin.

CREATING A HEALTHY DIET

Just as the way to develop an intuitive feeling for baking is to know and understand ingredients and how they relate to each other, so it is with eating. Rather than analyzing each meal on an ongoing basis (as we tend to get in the habit of doing), take a day, or even a week (including weekends) and get an honest sense of your overall eating pattern. Count calories, the ones that come from carbohydrates, the ones that come from protein and the ones that come from fats.

If you know approximately how many calories you need to fire your own engine daily, then you can make subtle shifts in what you eat (based on the information below) if you need to. There won't be anything that you should stop eating (10% of your daily calories can come from saturated fats). You may need only to adjust the amounts of some things in your diet (and increase the number of brisk walks you take a week).

Then forget about analyzing. Once you've plugged some basic information into your head, you'll have the basis for an intuitively healthy diet and then you can relax and enjoy it. It's interesting to analyze the parts of a symphony but not every time you hear one. Just as you want music to transport you, so do you an exquisitely orchestrated meal.

CALORIES

As full-grown adults, we need to consume between 1800 and 4000 calories (see page 585) a day, the lower end of the scale for smaller or less active people, the higher end for large or extremely active people. (There are people who fall off the scale on either end, but the majority of us drop somewhere in this range.)

CARBOHYDRATES, PROTEINS & FATS

These are the large foods that we take into our bodies, the ones we can see. (The small ones that we can't see are the vitamins and minerals.)

Below we've explained the ratio these food categories should generally have to each other in a healthy diet (if we have no specific dietary needs, i.e., we're not pregnant, diabetic, or otherwise under a doctor's care). Along with these solid foods, we should drink several glasses of liquid a day to facilitate the chemical reactions our bodies are designed to create out of this brew we feed it daily.

Carbohydrates

These provide the major fuel (sugar) that we need to keep our bodies running and our brains computing. They come in two basic varieties. We should get about 60% of our calories from the two together.

> **Complex Carbohydrates:** These are actually starches and natural sugars found in grains, vegetables and fruits. When we eat them, our bodies break them down into the simple sugars we need for fuel.

> **Simple Carbohydrates:** These are just what you might think they are, sugars that are already sugar. Our bodies can put these to work much more quickly. Why don't we just eat sugar when we need some energy?

> Simple sugars just don't have much besides calories to recommend them, which you'll see in the Sugar Table on page 589. Don't cut them out of your diet completely though; they come in too many lovely varieties. But they are like those pretty books with blank pages; if they are to have any value we have to add it ourselves.

Along with the starches and natural sugars in complex carbohydrates, we get a tremendous supply of vitamins, minerals and fiber. Without these to keep our body chemistry balanced, no amount of sugar could get us up and moving. The majority of "sugars" we use should come from natural sources (grains, vegetables and fruits) so we get the benefit of their other attributes. For these reasons, about half our calories should come from complex carbohydrates with maybe a tenth from the simple variety.

Fiber: Another important part of our diet, which is also supplied by complex carbohydrates, is fiber. We need about 20 to 35 grams a day, somewhere around an ounce. (If half of the calories you consume are in the form of complex carbohydrates, this will be a cinch.) Fiber comes in two basic kinds.

> • **Soluble Fiber:** We need 7 to 14 grams of this kind a day. You find it in oat and rice bran, carrots, beans, corn, etc. This kind of fiber helps reduce cholesterol by combining with one of its derivatives and taking it out of our bodies.

> • **Insoluble Fiber:** The balance of our fiber intake (14 to 21 grams) should be insoluble. This kind "scours" our systems and keeps them clean and healthy. One of the best sources for this is wheat bran found in whole wheat flour.

Proteins

Proteins are the building blocks of our human bodies so we need a larger ratio of them when we're young and growing, but not as much as once was believed. (See Milk, page 580.) By the time we are adults, our "houses" are already built and we need only enough protein to keep them in repair. This means that only a little over a tenth of our calories needs to come from proteins, or 45 to 65 grams (somewhere around two ounces).

Like carbohydrates, proteins come from two kinds of sources. The first kind consists of foods that contain complete proteins themselves. These are meat, fish, poultry, milk and eggs. But because protein is like a puzzle (it is made up of lots of small parts called amino acids), you can put a complete one together by combining foods that contain different parts of the puzzle.

We can use wheat is an example. Wheat does not contain all of the amino acids needed to make a complete protein. When you combine flour ground from wheat with water to make bread, you'll eat it as a complex carbohydrate. But by using milk as the liquid (or by adding 2 tablespoons of dry milk per cup of flour), you add the missing amino acids which complete the protein and increase the protein value of the bread by almost 50%. The same thing happens when you eat wheat with beans or when you combine corn with beans (succotash).

Each culture has its own protein combination foods. (See page 368 for some more examples.) The advantage of this kind of protein is that, while it is as complete as that in meat, it comes in a lower calorie (but vitamin-rich) container that is full of fiber which isn't present in any meat, milk or egg.

Fats

About 30% of our calories can come from fats but, because fat stores calories so efficiently, they will be disguised in a much smaller package. Fats can store 9 calories per gram versus 4 for both protein and carbohydrates (it takes almost 30 grams to make one ounce). So don't be fooled. But fats are critical to our bodies' good health so it's important to find the right place for them in our diets. (See Fats, page 584.)

VITAMINS & MINERALS

Food is to people as gasoline is to cars. But because we are more complex than cars, the food we eat needs to be complex as well. Along with energy, we need an assortment of vitamins and minerals (in amounts we can't see) to keep the chemistry in our bodies balanced and running smoothly. These are scattered throughout all three food categories so the best bet is to eat a wide assortment from each.

Vitamins, and the chemical environment they perform in (provided by minerals), work together like a symphony orchestra. All of them are necessary. Each one plays its own important part but the relationship they have to each other is equally important. Too little or too much of any one of them throws the body's music out of balance. Below you will find U.S. Recommended Daily Allowances (RDAs) for full-grown men and women, of a number of the vitamins and minerals on which our diet can have an impact.

RDAs are not minimum daily requirements but an average allowance recommended for the population as a whole. Just as the average height of the population may be five-foot-six, you may be shorter or taller and need less or more of the vitamins and minerals listed here. (There are 40 International Units (IU) in 1 microgram, 1000 micrograms in 1 milligram, 1000 milligrams in 1 gram, and 28.35 grams in 1 ounce.)

Vitamins

Fat-Soluble Vitamins: These can only be taken into the body with fats (they are fat soluble) and can be stored for a "rainy day."

> **Vitamin A:** 5000 IU (8000 if you are pregnant or nursing). This vitamin for our eyes comes from dairy products, egg yolks and vegetables that contain beta carotene (dark green and deep orange ones).
>
> **Vitamin D:** 400 IU. This one, for our bones and teeth, comes from milk, egg yolks, butter, and sunshine. (Walks are good for more than exercise.)
>
> **Vitamin E:** 30 IU. This keeps the polyunsaturated fats in our bodies healthy. One of the best sources is the germ of the wheat.
>
> **Vitamin K:** 70 to 140 micrograms. This is for clotting blood and comes from green leafy vegetables and egg yolks. (This is not an RDA but an estimated adequate and safe range.)

Water-Soluble Vitamins: The remaining vitamins are water soluble and cannot be stored away so we need to eat foods that contain them often.

> **The B Vitamins:** The first three are the "enrichment vitamins" in flour. They need to be present in the enzymes in our bodies that unlock the energy in the foods we eat. We need them all, and in balance, since too much or too little of any one of them throws this whole section of our body symphonies out of step. We get enough of these if we eat some of the following every day: whole grains, wheat germ, dark green leafy vegetables, dried beans, eggs, milk, liver and other meats. The major B vitamins and their RDAs are: **thiamin** (B1): 1.5 mg (1.7 if pregnant or nursing), **riboflavin** (B2): 1.7 mg (2.0 if pregnant or nursing), **niacin**: 20 mg, **vitamin B6**: 2 mg (2.5 if pregnant or nursing), **vitamin B12**: 6 mg (8 if pregnant or nursing), **folacin** (folic acid): .4 mg (.8 if pregnant or nursing), **biotin**: .3 mg, **pantothenic acid**: 10 mg.

Vitamin C: 60 milligrams. This is the anti-scurvy vitamin from oranges, cantaloupes, strawberries, peppers, potatoes and the cabbage family.

Minerals

Ninety-six percent of our bodies are made up of oxygen, carbon, hydrogen and nitrogen. (We're pretty elemental and earthy.) The other four percent is made up primarily of the following minerals that complete the chemical climate of our bodies and allow all the parts to play together in harmony. There are several others, known as trace minerals, that are needed in much smaller amounts and are easily obtained through a balanced diet so we don't include them here.

Calcium: 1 gram (1.3 if pregnant or nursing). This is necessary for bones and teeth and comes from milk products, blackstrap molasses, green vegetables, dried beans and canned fish (sardines, mackerel, salmon).

Iodine: 150 mg. This keeps our thyroid glands healthy and is easily obtained from iodized salt as well as seafood.

Iron: 18 mg. This forms blood hemoglobin and comes from liver and red meats, egg yolks, leafy green vegetables, dried fruits, whole grains, blackstrap molasses and the iron griddle in which you cook your pancakes or eggs. If you are pregnant, you need an extra 30 to 60 mg which you should continue taking for 2 or 3 months after the baby is born.

Magnesium: 400 mg (450 mg if pregnant or nursing). This builds bones and releases energy from muscles; it comes from whole grains, leafy green vegetables, milk and nuts.

Phosphorus: 1 gram (1.2 grams for adolescents, 1.3 if pregnant or nursing). This is also necessary for bones and teeth and comes from meat, fish, poultry, eggs, whole grains, legumes and milk products.

Potassium: 1875 to 5625 mg. This is an "electrolyte," a mineral that helps regulate body fluids inside cell walls; it comes from most fruits and vegetables. (This is not an RDA but an estimated adequate and safe range.)

Sodium: 1100 to 3300 mg. This is another "electrolyte" which regulates body fluids outside of cell walls. It also activates enzymes in the saliva to help us digest food; it comes from table salt (sodium chloride) and other foods containing salt. This is one mineral that our diets provide too much of. We should probably aim for the lower end of the range, 1100 mg. (This is not an RDA but an estimated adequate and safe range.)

Zinc: 15 mg. This is an important part of many of the enzymes in our bodies; it comes from whole grains, meat, liver, eggs and milk products.

• THE BUILDING BLOCKS OF BAKING •

Below we have included nutritional information for some of the ingredients we bake with most frequently. After you've become an intuitive baker, use this and the preceeding information to become an intuitive eater as well.

GRAINS

WHEAT

In this country this is the most widely used and versatile of the grains.

Protein: King Arthur Unbleached All-Purpose Flour is a blend ground from the endosperm of two of the highest protein wheats available, hard red winter and hard red spring. It contains no chemicals or additives other than federally mandated "enrichment" which consists of iron (a mineral) and thiamin, niacin and riboflavin (B vitamins). The technical word that is used to describe the protein in King Arthur Flour is "mellow." This means that it absorbs moisture and develops well.

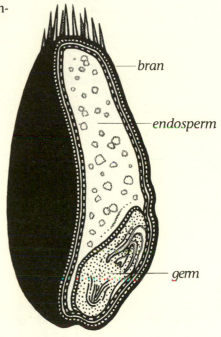

bran

endosperm

germ

King Arthur Stone Ground Whole Wheat Flour is ground only from hard red spring wheat, which means that its protein level is slightly higher than that of our unbleached white. Because it contains the bran (seed coat) and the germ (embryo) of the wheat berry, it contains the nutrients that are found in these as well, making it nutritionally superior, in some ways, to white flour.

But because bran contains significant amounts of fiber, a percentage of the nutrients in whole wheat flour moves so swiftly through our systems (that's the effect of fiber) that we don't have time to take advantage of them. (This is true of all whole grains and other fiber-rich foods.) When we compare the relative values of foods, this is just one more consideration.

The level and characteristics of protein in wheat varies with each season and batch so each time our flours are milled, the blend is carefully balanced so that the protein levels are always the same. After each milling, samples are baked into bread to make sure the protein is as mellow as it should be.

The Bread Table

The following table gives you nutritional values for one-ounce slices of three types of bread, 100% whole wheat, 25% whole wheat mixed with 75% white, and 100% white. You'll see that each has its merits. (The table doesn't take into consideration the effect of fiber on nutrient retention as each person reacts to fiber differently.)

BREAD	100% ww	25% ww	100% white
Calories	70.0	72.0	76.0
Protein (grams)	2.7	2.5	2.4
Carbohydrates (grams)	12.9	13.3	13.9
Fat (grams)	1.2	1.1	1.1
Dietary fiber (grams)	1.5	0.8	0.5
Sodium (milligrams)	181.0	153.0	146.0
% of U.S. Recommended Daily Allowance			
Protein	4.2	4.0	3.7
Vitamin A	tr.	tr.	tr.
Vitamin C	tr.	tr.	tr.
Thiamin	6.7	8.4	8.7
Riboflavin	3.5	5.1	5.3
Niacin	5.4	6.1	6.4
Calcium	2.0	3.2	3.6
Iron	5.5	4.8	4.5
Vitamin B-6	2.5	1.5	0.5
Pantothenic acid	2.3	1.2	1.0
Folacin	4.0	3.3	2.5
Phosphorus	7.4	5.2	3.1
Magnesium	6.5	3.3	1.5
Zinc	3.2	2.0	1.2
Copper	5.0	3.5	2.0

Gluten: The protein in wheat, when it is combined with a liquid, produces a magic substance called "gluten." No other grain produces this in any appreciable amount. Gluten is an elastic substance that creates a network of strands when it is kneaded in a dough. This network traps the bubbles of carbon dioxide created by growing yeast.

The amount of protein in a flour determines the amount of gluten the flour will produce. A "mellow" protein produces a gluten that is both easy to knead and "tolerant." Tolerance is a measure of how much manipulating a dough can withstand before it begins to break down. The tolerance of the gluten in King Arthur Flour is very high, which means that you can let a dough rise several times and still produce an excellent loaf. It's designed to enable you to succeed.

Ash: Each time King Arthur Unbleached All-Purpose Flour is milled, its "ash" content is checked. To do this, a sample is burned to see how much residue, or ash, is left after everything else has been consumed. Because the ash in King Arthur Flour is so low, it is naturally white with golden overtones.

Forms: Wheat can be ground into flour, either the entire grain (whole wheat flour) or just the endosperm (white flour). It can be steamed and rolled into flakes like oatmeal. It can be also steamed and cracked (or steel-cut), again the entire grain (cracked wheat or bulgur), or just the endosperm (cous-cous).

OTHER GRAINS

Although these don't contain appreciable amounts of gluten, you can substitute any of them for some wheat flour in most of the recipes in this book to create different textures and flavors. (See page 131.) Like wheat, all of them do best when stored where it is cool and dry. For long-term storage, they do best frozen in airtight containers.

Amaranth: This is a "recently discovered" grain that was used for centuries in South America by the Aztec Indians. It has a greater quantity of a more complete protein than wheat, but it is not gluten producing. Because of this, it can be mixed with wheat to create a high-protein/low-gluten blend that can be used most successfully in cakes and pastries but, in small amounts, in breads as well.

Barley: This may have been the first grain cultivated around the Mediterranean but it can grow anywhere. Pot or Scotch barley is only partially processed and is therefore more nutritious than pearled barley which has lost all of its bran and most of its germ. In this country, a small amount of flour made from malted barley (see page 11) is added to wheat flour as yeast food. Because it is ground from the whole grain which has first been sprouted, it is particularly nutritious.

Buckwheat: This is not a grain at all but a member of a family that includes rhubarb and sorrel. It originated in Asia and wasn't introduced to Europe until the late Middle Ages. It has a high fat content and needs to be used freshly ground or kept frozen. It makes hearty pancakes and waffles (page 38). When it is prepared like cracked wheat it is known as "kasha" and is common in Eastern Europe.

Corn: This is a New World grain (originally known as Indian meal) widely available as a meal ground from just the endosperm of the corn kernel. Whole grain cornmeal, which contains the germ, is available in some specialty stores and is preferable because of its flavor and greater nutrition.

Nutritionally, yellow and white cornmeal are the same with one exception. The presence of beta carotene in the endosperm of the yellow variety means it contains an additional 629 IU of vitamin A per cup. Blue cornmeal is ground from a dark blue/black dent corn and is the same as white cornmeal nutritionally.

Cornstarch is derived from the endosperm of the corn kernel and it is just what its name implies, starch with none of the protein or fat that is also found in the endosperm (or the nutrients they contain). See page 597 for instructions for using cornstarch to make King Arthur "Cake" Flour.

Cornell Formula: Developed at Cornell University, this blend has the attributes of whole wheat flour, but is designed particularly for people who are sensitive to wheat bran. To make this blend yourself, measure 1 tablespoon of non-fat dry milk, 1 tablespoon soy flour and 1 teaspoon wheat germ into a dry cup measure. Fill the remainder of the cup with King Arthur Unbleached All-Purpose Flour, sprinkled lightly. If you wish, increase the amounts of dry milk, soy flour and wheat germ but do it slowly until you find a blend you like. You can use this mix anywhere you use whole wheat flour.

Millet: This is an ancient grain used widely around the Mediterranean that contains many of the same nutrients as other grains but 16 to 22% protein. It can be substituted for an equal amount of wheat flour either as a whole grain (it is quite small) or ground in a blender.

Oats: A grain of cool, northern climates, oats have traditionally been used as feed for horses but are a good source of nutrition for people as well. Oats contain more protein than wheat (although it is non-gluten producing) and they keep well as they contain a natural anti-oxidant that keeps the oil in the germ from becoming rancid. Although oats are most often rolled, you can buy them steel-cut (like cracked wheat) or you can grind them into a "flour" in a blender.

Rice: Rice is an ancient grain and has meant to the East what wheat has meant to the West. It has long been a symbol of fertility, which is why we traditionally throw it at a bride and groom after their wedding ceremony. Rice can be ground into flour which can be used as a thickening agent like cornstarch or potato flour. It can also be used, like cornstarch, to lower the protein of wheat flour. (See Shortbread, page 343.)

Rye: See page 143.

Soy Flour: A native of China, the soybean is a tremendously rich source of complete protein (about 40%) with almost the same nutritional value as meat, fish or poultry. The flavor of soy flour tends to be strong so substitute only a small amount until you decide whether your family will appreciate it. Flour ground from the whole soybean tastes better than the defatted type.

Triticale: This grain is the result of crossing wheat with rye and its name is a combination of the Latin names for each: "triticum" (wheat) and "secale" (rye). Like amaranth, which is ancient, this new hybrid can grow and survive in poorer soils than most grains so, with amaranth, may help feed the world in the next century. It contains more protein than wheat and its amino acids are in better balance. Because its protein produces less gluten, it can be used very successfully as a cake and pastry flour, and, in combination with wheat, as a bread flour.

Grain Table

one cup	grams	cal-ories	pro-tein (g)	carbo-hydrates (g)	fat (g)	fiber (g)	vit. A (IU)	thia-min (mg)
K. A. Unbl. All-Purp. Flour	115	400	13.0	87.0	2.0	3.0	0	0.80
K. A. Whole Wheat Flour	120	400	16.0	85.2	2.4	11.5	0	0.66
Wheat Germ (toasted)	112	400	36.0	48.0	12.0	13.2	0	1.88
Wheat Bran (raw)	57	120	13.0	36.0	2.6	26.0	n/a	0.42
Amaranth (grain)	195	729	28.2	129.0	12.7	7.4	0	0.16
Barley (pearled)	200	698	16.4	157.6	2.0	1.0	0	0.24
Barley (Scotch)	200	696	19.2	154.4	2.2	1.8	0	0.42
Buckwheat (light)	98	340	6.3	77.9	1.2	0.5	0	0.08
Buckwheat (dark)	98	326	11.5	70.6	2.5	1.6	0	0.57
Cornmeal (whole, yellow)	122	433	11.2	89.9	4.8	2.0	620	0.46
Cornmeal (whole, white)	122	433	11.2	89.9	4.8	2.0	0	0.46
Millet (unground)	200	756	22.0	146.0	8.4	17.0	n/a	0.84
Oatmeal	80	312	11.4	54.6	5.9	n/a	0	0.48
Rice Flour	113	398	7.1	91.0	0.9	n/a	0	0.52
Rye (medium)	111	400	12.2	81.0	2.2	n/a	0	0.33
Rye (whole grain flour)	128	419	20.9	87.2	3.3	3.1	0	0.78
Soy (full fat)	85	360	32.0	27.1	17.3	1.4	102	0.49
Triticale (flour)	130	440	17.1	95.1	2.4	2.0	0	0.49

		ribo-flavin (mg)	nia-cin (mg)	sodi-um (mg)	cal-cium (mg)	potas-sium (mg)	phos-phorus (mg)	iron (mg)
K. A. Unbl. All-Purp. Flour	115	0.34	6.2	2	22	130	112	5.00
K. A. Whole Wheat Flour	120	0.14	5.2	9	49	444	446	4.00
Wheat Germ (toasted)	112	0.92	6.4	4	52	1072	1300	7.20
Wheat Bran (raw)	57	0.20	12.0	0	60	636	920	8.28
Amaranth (grain)	195	0.41	2.5	42	298	714	887	14.81
Barley (pearled)	200	0.10	6.2	6	32	320	378	4.00
Barley (Scotch)	200	0.14	7.4	n/a	68	592	580	5.40
Buckwheat (light)	98	0.04	0.4	n/a	11	314	86	1.00
Buckwheat (dark)	98	0.15	2.8	n/a	32	490	340	2.70
Cornmeal (whole, yellow)	122	0.13	2.4	1	24	346	312	2.90
Cornmeal (whole, white)	122	0.13	2.4	1	24	346	312	2.90
Millet (unground)	200	0.58	9.4	n/a	16	390	568	6.00
Oatmeal	80	0.11	2.6	2	42	282	324	3.60
Rice Flour	113	0.59	2.9	45	13	168	249	3.28
Rye (medium)	111	0.11	1.3	5	22	322	152	2.78
Rye (whole grain flour)	128	0.28	3.5	1	69	1101	686	5.80
Soy (full fat)	85	0.99	3.7	11	175	2138	420	5.42
Triticale (flour)	130	0.17	3.7	3	45	805	417	3.37

DAIRY PRODUCTS

These are a valuable source of protein and fat soluble vitamins, particularly D, the sunshine vitamin.

Milk: When we think of milk, we usually mean cow's milk. But cow's milk is quite different from human milk. If you look at the table on page 583, you'll see that human milk has much less calcium and protein, more unsaturated fat (with over twice the vitamin A) and almost twice the carbohydrates.

Cow's milk is designed to grow a heavy, large-framed, not terribly intelligent (although very endearing) animal. Human milk is designed for growing smaller, lighter bodies. Its extra carbohydrates provide the large amount of energy required for the development and functioning of a much more complex brain.

The way in which human milk differs from cow's milk almost gives us a prescription for our diets as adults. We have learned in the last several years that we need less protein than was originally believed and many more carbohydrates. After anlayzing the milk that was designed to start us on our human lives, those conclusions seem appropriate.

Cow's milk, with modifications, can provide humans with a good source of high-quality nutrients. Whole cow's milk contains about 87% water, 3.5% fat, 3.5% protein, 4.9% lactose (milk sugar) and 0.7% minerals (primarily calcium, phosphorus and potassium). Since more than 30% of the calories in whole cow's milk come from fat, low-fat or skim milk is more appropriate on a day-to-day basis. (To keep cow's milk in perspective, look at the nutritional values for the milk of the Laplander's "cow," the reindeer.)

Butter, cheese and creams (including ice cream) contain many of the same nutrients that milk does, but many more calories from fat, so ought to be eaten only on an occasional basis. (Don't give them up; just keep them in perspective.) For more information on butter and cheese, see Fats on page 584. In eliminating the fat, the fat-soluble vitamins go as well. Because of this, milk is now "fortified" with vitamins A and D, so low-fat skim milks contain as much or more of those vitamins as does whole milk. (Remember that we need some fat to carry these into our system. Otherwise they will pass right though.)

Buttermilk: This low-calorie fluid used to be what was left over after butter was churned. It was primarily the carbohydrate- and calcium-rich whey (with its own protein) and lactose (milk sugar, which is one-seventh as sweet as granulated sugar). Buttermilk is now made much as yogurt is, from a culture introduced into a pasteurized non-fat or low-fat milk. Even when it is completely fat free, it has a rich, creamy quality. You can make it at home the same way you make yogurt (page 582). A half-gallon of buttermilk contains an added ¼ teaspoon of salt.

Cheese: See Fats, page 584.

Cream: This has many of the same nutrients as whole milk but a much higher proportion of fat, making it another of those "every once in a while" luxuries. In the Pasta chapter we suggest substituting evaporated milk for cream to make less traditional but nutritionally superior sauces (with the exception of vitamins A and D, unless the evaporated milk is fortified).

Cream Cheese: This is in the same fat league as butter and cheese. In 2 table-spoons of cream cheese, there are 100 calories, 90% of which come from fat, most of it saturated. It is much lower in protein and calcium than other "cheeses." One 3-ounce package of cream cheese equals 6 tablespoons.

Cottage Cheese: This is made from just the curds (protein) of milk rather than the whey which is where the calcium is. Cottage cheese is not a good choice if you are looking for something to make strong teeth and bones. But since less than 30% of the calories in "light" cottage cheese come from fat, of the cheeses, this is a good choice for frequent consumption.

Clotted Cream: This is unique to the Celtic West Country of England. It is tradi-tionally made from the raw milk of Jersey cows which contains a high percentage of butterfat. The milk, with its thick layer of heavy cream on top, is allowed to "ripen" for about half a day at room temperature. It is then heated very slowly over a very low heat until there is just the suggestion of activity on the surface. Then the cream is scooped from the whey, put in a glass or ceramic container and chilled to be served on fruit, trifle, etc.

Condensed Milk: This is whole milk from which the water has been removed and to which sugar has been added. One can of condensed milk contains the equivalent of about $2\frac{1}{2}$ cups of whole milk plus $\frac{1}{2}$ cup of sugar. It thus has almost three times the fat but three times the protein and vitamin A as well. This method of preserving milk was first devised by Gail Borden in 1856 and was a staple issued to Civil War soldiers.

Eggs: Even though their producers occupy a different part of the barnyard, eggs are often included with dairy foods. In spite of their bad reputation because of cholesterol, they contain a lot of nutrition in a very small, low-calorie package. The protein in egg is complete and can complete the partial protein in grains when they are eaten together.

Eggs are a wonderful food on their own and they also perform great magic in baking. Egg yolks, which contain most of the nutrients (as well as the choles-terol), make baked products richer and more tender. When you mix egg whites into a batter or dough, they create structure as they bake, just as gluten does. When you beat egg whites into stiff glossy peaks, you trap millions of air bubbles inside. Whether those bubbles are at work in a meringue or an angel food cake, they'll expand in the oven to make an airy structure that can't be created any other way.

Egg yolks do have their share of cholesterol (see the Dairy Table). But since the greater culprit in creating cholesterol is saturated fat rather than cholesterol itself, eggs begin to look a little better nutritionally. Out of about 6 grams of fat per egg, more than half of it is unsaturated. When you bake with eggs, you use one or two per cake or 4 to 5 dozen cookies. The amount you will eat in one serving probably isn't much cause for alarm. It certainly doesn't overshadow the nutritional, flavor and textural benefits eggs provide. If you are concerned, in most recipes you can substitute 2 egg whites for 1 whole egg. Be aware that raw eggs may carry salmonella, a bacterium that will raise severe havoc with your digestive system. These bacteria are destroyed by cooking. If you have any questions about your eggs, do not use them for meringue or other uncooked dishes.

Evaporated Milk: As the name implies, a little more than half of the water has been evaporated from either whole or skim milk. The concentrated milk is then canned and can be used as is, or, with water added, as regular milk. It is an acceptable substitute for cream in many soups and sauces.

Sour Cream: This is a high-fat version of buttermilk and yogurt. In baking, it makes particularly rich and tender goods because of its acidity as well as its fat content. It can be made like yogurt using cream that is at least 20% fat with commercial buttermilk as a starter. It many need several more hours to "set."

Sour Milk: This used to be made naturally from raw milk that had not been pasturized to kill naturally occurring bacteria, which allowed it to sour rather than to spoil.

To make sour milk from pasteurized milk, blend 1 tablespoon of vinegar or lemon juice with 1 cup of milk. Let sit for 5 minutes to "clabber."

Sweetened Whipped Cream (Crème Chantilly): This is made from 1 cup of medium or heavy cream, beaten until stiff, to which you add 3 to 4 tablespoons confectioners' sugar and 1 teaspoon of vanilla or other extract.

Yogurt: Like "modern" buttermilk, this is made from a culture that is introduced to pasteurized milk, either whole, low-fat or skim. The bacteria in the culture are similar to the ones in our own digestive systems so yogurt is particularly easy to digest. (Some feel it is helpful for restoring bacteria to our systems after we have been taking antibiotics.)

To make your own fortified yogurt, blend ½ to 1 cup non-fat dry milk into ½ gallon skim or low-fat milk from a previously unopened container (so other bacteria haven't inadvertently been introduced to it). Heat it to lukewarm in an enamel or stainless steel saucepan. Remove 1 cup of milk and blend into it 2 or 3 tablespoons of plain yogurt that contains an active culture. Blend this diluted yogurt mixture into the milk in the saucepan. Cover it and place it somewhere warm (as you would a rising bread dough) for 3 to 5 hours or until it has clabbered or "set." Fresh yogurt is not particularly sour. Like sourdough, the longer it works, the more sour it will become.

Dairy Table

The following table will give you some information about the benefits and nutritional tradeoffs you'll have to make depending on what milk product you choose to use.

one cup	grams	water %	cal-ories	pro-tein (g)	fat (g)	sat. fat (g)	mono-unsat. (g)	poly-unsat. (g)	choles-terol (mg)
Cow's Milk (3.5% fat)	244	87.4	159	8.5	8.0	4.9	2.8	0.2	34
Cow's Milk (2% fat)	244	89.5	121	8.1	4.7	2.9	2.0	0.1	18
Cow's Milk (1% fat)	244	90.0	102	8.2	2.6	1.6	1.8	0.1	10
Cow's Milk (skim)	245	90.5	86	8.4	0.4	0.3	1.1	0.0	4
Condensed Milk	305	27.0	980	24.8	26.5	14.7	8.8	0.8	104
Dry Milk (non-fat, instant)	68	4.0	244	24.3	0.5	tr.	tr.	tr.	tr.
Dry Milk (non-fat, non-instant)	120	3.0	436	43.1	1.0	tr.	tr.	tr.	tr.
Evaporated Milk (whole)	252	74.0	345	17.2	20.0	11.0	6.6	0.6	74
Cream (11.7% fat)	242	79.7	324	7.7	28.3	15.6	9.3	0.8	96
Light Cream (20.6% fat)	240	71.5	506	7.2	49.4	27.2	16.3	1.5	160
Whipping Cream (31.3% fat)	239	62.1	710	6.0	74.0	41.2	24.7	2.2	272
Heavy Cream (37.6% fat)	238	56.6	835	5.2	89.5	49.2	29.5	2.7	336
Whey	246	93.0	64	2.2	0.7	0.1	n/a	n/a	n/a
Human Milk	246	85.2	185	2.4	9.8	4.8	3.2	0.8	32
Goat's Milk	244	87.5	165	8.2	10.0	6.5	2.4	0.5	28
Reindeer Milk	248	64.1	580	26.8	48.6	n/a	n/a	n/a	n/a
Eggs (5 large = 1 cup)	250	73.7	400	30.5	28.0	8.5	12.5	2.0	1370
Egg (1 white)	33	87.6	16	3.4	tr.	tr.	tr.	tr.	0
Egg (1 yolk)	17	51.0	60	2.8	5.6	1.7	2.5	0.4	274

one cup	grams	carbo-hydrate (g)	cal-cium (mg)	phos-phorus (mg)	iron (mg)	potas-sium (mg)	sodi-um (mg)	vita-min A (IU)
Cow's Milk (3.5% fat)	244	11.0	288	227	0.12	351	122	350
Cow's Milk (2% fat)	244	11.7	297	230	0.12	377	122	500
Cow's Milk (1% fat)	244	11.7	300	235	0.12	381	123	500
Cow's Milk (skim)	245	11.9	302	247	0.10	406	126	10
Condensed Milk	305	166.2	802	620	0.30	961	342	1100
Dry Milk (non-fat, instant)	68	35.1	879	683	0.40	1173	358	20
Dry Milk (non-fat, non-instant)	120	62.8	1570	1219	0.70	2094	638	40
Evaporated Milk (whole)	252	25.4	635	515	0.48	764	280	700
Cream (11.7% fat)	242	11.1	260	206	0.10	310	100	1100
Light Cream (20.6% fat)	240	9.8	240	192	0.10	290	96	2000
Whipping Cream (31.3% fat)	239	8.0	180	155	0.10	240	82	3000
Heavy Cream (37.6% fat)	238	7.0	160	140	0.10	212	80	3600
Whey	246	12.5	125	130	0.20	0	0	20
Human Milk	246	22.0	80	32	0.30	128	40	592
Goat's Milk	244	11.0	320	265	0.15	465	100	450
Reindeer Milk	248	10.2	630	491	0.20	394	389	n/a
Eggs (5 large = 1 cup)	250	2.5	135	515	6.00	325	305	1300-2950
Egg (1 white)	33	0.3	3	5	tr.	46	48	0
Egg (1 yolk)	17	0.1	24	98	0.90	19	9	313-580

Note: Buttermilk, sour cream and yogurt will have the same nutritional value as the products they are cultured from. If you add non-fat dry milk solids to a yogurt culture, it will contain those nutrients as well. Buttermilk contains extra sodium (see page 580).

FATS

This country's ongoing love/hate relationship with fat probably gets it more press coverage than any other nutrient. We need fat to carry fat soluble vitamins into our bodies; we need it to store the fuel that we burn (calories). Fat is a much more efficient fuel-storing medium than carbohydrates or protein; one gram will produce nine calories of energy; the other two, only four. In order to be healthy, we need to eat all types of fat.

But since fat makes things taste good, it is sometimes difficult to eat only what we need. If we figure that about 30% of a day's calories can come from fat, that gives us a start on where to stop. (If we're eating as many complex carbohydrates as we should, stopping will be easier.)

NUTRITIONAL VALUE OF SOME FATS

Cholesterol

Cholesterol is an unsaturated solid alcohol that feels and looks like a soft, greasy soap. It is found in the fatty tissues of animals. Our bodies manufacture cholesterol (about 1000 mg a day!) since it is necessary for building the membranes of the cells that our bodies are made of, the membranes that surround our nerves, and for producing the hormones that determine our sex.

But there seems to be a connection between too much cholesterol and heart disease. Excess cholesterol can accumulate in and clog our arteries creating stress on the whole circulatory system. Whether what we eat contributes to the accumulation of cholesterol in our bodies and ultimately, heart disease, is still a bit of a mystery. Some people seem to be able to eat anything they want; others are apparently much more vulnerable.

In general, it seems wise to keep our level of cholesterol below the magic 200 number. This number means 200 milligrams of cholesterol per deciliter of blood. (A milligram is $1/1000$ gram so 200 milligrams equals $1/5$ of a gram, or about $1/150$ of an ounce. A deciliter is $1/10$ liter, or a bit less than 1 cup.)

Types of Fat

We're told we can help achieve this goal through the fats we choose to eat. Fats can be divided into three groups: saturated, monounsaturated and polyunsaturated. Saturated fats apparently help create cholesterol. Monounsaturated fats seem to have no effect on cholesterol levels. Polyunsaturated fats help it pass through the system.

Interestingly enough, eating foods that contain cholesterol does not have as much effect on our own blood cholesterol levels as eating foods high in saturated fats. (But worse than saturated fat, as far as heart disease is concerned, is smoking and not getting out three or four times a week to work up a sweat. It's important to keep all of this in perspective and not to single out any one thing as "the bad guy" or "the answering one.")

Of the 600 "fat" calories we may eat (if our overall calorie goal is 2000), a good balance is 1/3 (or 200 calories) saturated fat, 1/3 monounsaturated fat and 1/3 polyunsaturated fat. This minimizes the negative impact any one type might have and maximizes its positive aspects.

Fat Table

This chart gives you a breakdown of various fats. Vegetable oils and shortenings do not contain any nutrition other than fat. Olive oil contains a small amount of iron. A tablespoon of butter and/or margarine contains about 470 IU of vitamin A, making them the only fats (other than cheese) to contain any significant nutrition other than fuel (calories).

When we speak of food containing a certain number of calories, we really mean its potential to produce a certain amount of energy. One calorie is the unit of energy required to raise the temperature of 1 kilogram of water (1000 grams, or a bit more than a quart) 1 degree centigrade (1.8 degrees Fahrenheit) at 1 atmosphere of pressure (sea level).

fat	% saturated	% mono-unsaturated	% poly-unsaturated
Safflower Oil	9	13	78
Sunflower Oil	11	21	68
Corn Oil	13	25	62
Sesame Oil	14	42	44
Olive Oil	14	77	9
Peanut Oil	18	48	34
Soy Lecithin	15	40	49
Margarine	19	53	28
Shortening (vegetable)	25	68	7
Cottonseed Oil	27	18	55
Lard	41	43	16
Palm Oil	53	38	9
Butter	68	28	4
Coconut Oil	92	6	2

Physical Characteristics of Some Fats

Butter: Butter is only 80% fat with the remainder water and milk solids. It is available either with or without salt (sweet butter). The salted variety will keep longer. The unsalted variety has a delicious and delicate flavor.

Butter/Vegetable Oil Blends: These are a great flavor/nutrition compromise. There are several varieties on the market providing different ratios of saturated and unsaturated fats. Most can be used where butter is called for. Do not use these in puff dough or puff pastry.

Cheese: Cheese is made from the curd (protein) in milk in combination with fat. Hard cheeses (Cheddar, Romano, Parmesan, Swiss, etc.) are very concentrated, containing up to 80% fat, as much or more than well-marbled beef (which is only 50 to 60% fat.) When using them, think of them as you would meat and eat an equivalent amount. Nutritionally, it has the same values as milk with lots of high-quality protein, calcium, and vitamins A and D. Processed cheese is usually lower in fat than "real" cheese but often contains more salt.

Clarified Butter: This is a pure butter that is all fat (butter is only 80% fat). To make it, melt the butter, boil off the water, chill the remainder and remove the non-fat solids which will have settled on the bottom.

Lard: This is an animal fat rendered from pork. It is softer and oilier than other solid fats. Because of its large crystalline structure, it works well in biscuits and pie crusts, but won't create as fine a grain in cakes. As you can see from the Fats Table, lard is not on the bottom of the list nutritionally. If you use butter in baking (and you are not a vegetarian), you can certainly feel comfortable with lard. (It is unsurpassed in a pie crust or for frying doughnuts.)

Margarine: This is a vegetable oil version of butter and, like butter, contains 80% fat and is fortified with vitamin A. The oils have been hydrogenated to make them solid at room temperature. Some of them contain more saturated fat than others, so if that is what you are trying to avoid, check the labels.

Shortening: This term initially included all fats and oils. It refers to the ability of fat to break up and weaken the gluten connections in flour, or to "shorten" them. This makes cakes, cookies and pie crusts tender. Today, this term is generally used for vegetable shortening, a vegetable oil equivalent of lard that also has been hydrogenated to make it solid at room temperature. Vegetable shortening contains no cholesterol and, depending on the oils used, less saturated fat. Check your labels to be sure of what you are getting.

Vegetable shortening is used very much as lard is but is stable at room temperature so will keep almost indefinitely. (For this reason it is the basis for many "mixes.") It can replace butter when the flavor of butter is not important. For an easy way to measure shortening, see page 278.

Vegetable Oils: These are pressed from various seeds and fruits, and most are refined to remove anything that will cause them to spoil. There are also some available which are not refined and need to be refrigerated. Refined oils are 100% fat and so must be reduced by about 20% in recipes where you can substitute them for butter. Because a liquid vegetable oil interacts differently with ingredients than a solid shortening does, it can not always be substituted for one. (Recipes where vegetable oils are not appropriate are noted in the text.)

Using Fats to Prepare your Pans

Butter contains a certain amount of water so when you use it to grease a cake or bread pan, you need to flour the pan afterward to absorb the moisture. Shortening on the other hand, contains no moisture, so flouring isn't necessary. An alternative to vegetable shortening is liquid soy lecithin, which does an equally good job. It, too, doesn't need to be floured and is preferable to the spray variety for environmental reasons. To make a liquid lecithin mixture for greasing pans, blend one part vegetable oil with two parts liquid lecithin. Store this mixture in an airtight container in the refrigerator.

SWEETENERS

All sweeteners contain about the same number of calories per tablespoon (46, compared to 100 to 130 calories per tablespoon of fat). Although there are some minor nutritional variations, it is the different mineral composition of each that makes their flavors and characters distinct. Most of them provide only fuel (calories or potential energy) with very few other nutritional benefits.

But they have their place in baking. Sweeteners, like fats, tenderize a dough. They are also hygroscopic which means they absorb moisture. When you add a sweetener to a dough or batter, the resulting product will stay fresher longer.

Sweeteners also taste good, which is probably the most important reason they are used, and they make baked goods taste good as well. Some add just sweetening; others add their own flavor. Below you'll find some information about each and a table that gives you their nutritional profile.

Brown Sugar: This sugar creates the flavor of butterscotch when mixed with butter. Brown sugar is not partially refined granulated sugar, but granulated sugar with a little molasses mixed back in. You can make your own brown sugar the same way it is made commercially. To make 1 cup, blend 1/4 cup molasses with 1 cup granulated sugar. When measuring brown sugar, pack it tightly in a cup measure rather than loosening it up as you do flour.

Cinnamon Sugar: This is simply granulated sugar to which you add powdered cinnamon in whatever ratio you like. A good place to start is 1 cup granulated sugar and 1 to 2 tablespoons of cinnamon.

Citrus Sugar: This is another flavored granulated sugar. To make it, blend 2 to 3 teaspoons of lemon or orange zest (grated peel) into 1 cup of sugar. Let it sit in an airtight container overnight so the flavor can permeate the sugar. Use it to sprinkle on pancakes, waffles or simple cakes. You can also use it in sticky buns or other "breakfast breads."

Confectioners' Sugar: This is sugar that has been "powdered" so it can be dissolved almost instantly. Like baking powder, it contains some cornstarch to keep it dry and prevent it from lumping. Because of this and because it is not crystalline (it doesn't have edges to create air pockets) it can wreak havoc if you bake with it. Save it for frostings and glazes. A confectioners' sugar substitute can be made by processing granulated sugar in a blender until it's the consistency you want. It won't be quite as fine but will do quite well.

Granulated Sugar: This is the sugar most often called for in baking. Although many people feel that other sugars are superior to it nutritionally, the only one that really is, is blackstrap molasses. So when you want sweetening power that is inexpensive and whose flavor is not intrusive, this is the sugar to use.

Honey: Although this is a "natural" sweetener with an appealing flavor, honey has its liabilities. The type of sugar it is composed of and the way it reacts with the saliva in your mouth makes it somewhat more damaging to tooth enamel than other sugars. Honey is also associated with a form of botulism that has been linked with sudden infant death syndrome, so it is important never to feed it to an infant under one year of age. Some types of honey are inclined to scorch at high temperatures. If you substitute honey for another sweetener and the baking temperature called for is over 400°F, you might lower it 25°F and extend the baking period by 5 or 10 minutes (or you might just go ahead with the temperature called for and check in every once in a while).

Icing Sugar: This is a very fine granulated sugar (not powdered) which the English call castor sugar.

Liquid Sweeteners: If you choose to substitute a liquid sweetener for a dry one, you may want to hold back on the other liquid ingredients. To figure out how much to reduce the liquid ingredients, check the percent of water (H_2O) in the Sugar Table. For example, since molasses is 24% water, you can reduce your liquid by 1/4 cup for each cup of granulated sugar you want to substitute molasses for in the recipe (or extend your baking time a bit). Do not substitute a liquid sweetener entirely for a dry one in a recipe that calls for a large amount.

Maple Syrup: It takes between 35 and 50 gallons of maple sap to produce 1 gallon of maple syrup. The fanciest maple syrup, usually made from the earliest "runs" of sap, has a very delicate flavor that is not strong enough to be tasted in baked goods. It is better used as a syrup on top. Darker grades of syrup, which are less expensive, are much better suited for baking. For a description of how this seasonal sweet is made, see page 86.

Molasses: This is a by-product of the sugar refining process, the residue left after pure sugar is extracted from the juice of sugar cane. With each extraction, the residue is darker and less sweet, but with the original nutrients in the cane (mainly calcium, iron and potassium) left in a concentrated form. The strongest flavored molasses is blackstrap, a great addition to baked goods in small amounts and the only sweetener with significant nutritional value.

Powdered Sugar: This is the same as confectioners' sugar but a term used more often in the west.

Raw Sugar: Real raw sugar is full of impurities, all those things, mostly solid (dirt, mold, insect parts, etc.), that are cleaned out of granulated sugar. Because of this it doesn't pass FDA standards and cannot be imported into this country. A cleaned up variety, called Turbinado sugar, similar to English Demerara sugar, can be sold in this country. This sugar is closer to what many of us may have thought brown sugar was, partially refined white sugar. But it, too, doesn't have any more nutritional benefits than white or brown sugar so is an expensive, although interesting, substitute.

Vanilla Sugar: Like cinnamon and citrus sugars, this is a flavored granulated sugar. To make it, cut up several vanilla beans and place them in several cups of sugar in an airtight container. In about two weeks, you'll have something that will perk up your coffee or tea or can be used in Rebecca Cunningham's Apple Tartlets, which you'll find on page 424. As you use the sugar, replace it with more and an occasional fresh bean.

Sugar Table

In the table below, it may seem as if some sugars are better nutritionally than others because of the nutrient traces they contain. But in order for these traces to be meaningful in our diets, we would have to consume more sugar than we could stomach.

one cup	grams	% H$_2$O	cal-ories	carbo-hydrates (g)	sodi-um (mg)	potas-sium (mg)	cal-cium (mg)	phos-phorus (mg)	iron (mg)
Granulated Sugar	200	0.5	770	199.0	2	6	0	0	0.2
Brown Sugar, packed	220	2.1	821	212.0	66	757	187	42	7.5
Maple Syrup	315	33.0	794	205.0	32	554	328	25	3.8
Corn Syrup, light	336	26.0	960	238.4	480	0	0	0	0.0
Corn Syrup, dark	336	26.0	960	240.0	640	0	0	0	0.0
Honey	339	17.2	1031	279.0	17	173	17	20	1.7
Molasses, light	328	24.0	827	213.2	49	3008	541	148	14.1
Molasses, medium	328	24.0	761	197.0	121	3487	951	226	19.7
Molasses, blackstrap	328	24.0	699	180.4	315	9601	2244	276	52.8
Molasses, Barbados	328	24.0	889	229.6	0	0	804	164	0.0
Confectioners' Sugar	120	0.6	462	119.4	1	4	0	0	0.1

FLAVORINGS

These are some of the flavorings used most frequently in this cookbook; we have not tried to cover all possibilities. Although they are generally added to batters and doughs in small amounts, they have a tremendous impact on the personality and character of finished products.

Chocolate: Both bitter baking chocolate and cocoa come from the cocoa bean. A one-ounce square of unsweetened (bitter) chocolate contains about fifteen grams of fat, over half of which is saturated. One ounce of cocoa powder has only 2 or 3 grams of fat of which a little over half is saturated.

To make a substitute for a one-ounce square of bitter baking chocolate that contains less saturated fat, mix 3 tablespoons of cocoa with 1 tablespoon of low saturated fat vegetable shortening. (For a richer version, use butter.) To make it a semi-sweet ounce, add 3 tablespoons of granulated sugar. For information on chocolate as an acidic ingredient, see page 55.

Extracts: These are the essential oils of fruits, nuts and flowers that are dissolved in alcohol and used to enhance or dominate the flavors of baked goods. (It is also possible to obtain just the concentrated oils by themselves in some specialty shops. You use just the barest amount of these.) Although there are extracts available for brandy, rum and other liquors, the real thing is no more expensive and has better flavor.

To make your own vanilla extract, steep 2 or 3 vanilla beans in vodka (closest to vanilla extract) or brandy (an interesting brandy flavored vanilla) for 2 or 3 weeeks.

Herbs: For our early colonists, these were as important in daily life as the vegetable garden, the dairy and the barnyard. They were used medicinally, in cooking and just for the aromas they lent to houses that could be dank and dark. Today there is renewed interest in them. Anyone can plant an herb garden, and fresh herbs in cooking are much more interesting than dried, as their flavors are more complex and intense. Herbs are used generally in savory foods but you will find some recipes for sweet baked goods that call for them, such as the Rosemary Snaps on page 513. When herbs are dried, use one-third of the amount that you would of fresh.

Marzipan: This is a paste of ground almonds, egg white and sugar, traditionally flavored with rose water (see next page).

To make your own, take 4 cups of blanched, slivered almonds, 1 pound (3½ cups) of confectioners' sugar, 2 large or 3 medium egg whites beaten until soft peaks have formed, 1 teaspoon almond extract and 2 to 3 tablespoons rose water. Grind the almonds in a blender 1 cup at a time until they are very fine. Place in a bowl and mix in the confectioners' sugar. Stir in the egg whites, extract and rose water and knead until the mixture is combined and smooth. Chill until you are ready to use it. (This makes about 2 pounds.)

Rose Water: In medieval England, roses were grown for their scent and flavor. Old-fashioned roses were much smaller than the giants we see today but their aroma and even their cultural importance was much larger. Roses were the national flowers of both England and France. The Tudor Rose was an emblem that symbolized the final uniting of the House of Lancaster (The White Rose) and the House of York (The Red Rose) after the War of the Roses in fifteenth-century England.

Rose petals were traditionally sprinkled on the top of pies. Rose juices and extracts were found in ointments, vinegars and syrups. Rose water (made by steeping the petals in water) is used to flavor cakes and is a traditional flavoring for marzipan (see preceding page). It is available in some grocery stores (in the gourmet food sections), specialty food shops and pharmacies.

Spices: These have more mystery than herbs because of their origins in Asia and the "East Indies" (India). Ginger and pepper are two of the oldest spices to be used in England. Ginger flavored many meat dishes, as well as gingerbread (page 305). It has long been believed that it acts as a tonic to yeast. Saffron is another old English spice (see page 242). For a mixed spice with some sparkle, try a little pepper in combination with cinnamon, ginger, nutmeg, cloves and/or allspice.

Because most spices come from so far away and can't be grown in our own gardens like herbs, they are usually dried. If you can get whole ones, you can grate your own powders in a small coffee grinder or pepper mill to produce flavors that are, like fresh herbs, more complex and intense.

Zest: This is the minced outer rind (the inner white pulpy rind is bitter) of citrus fruits, primarily lemons and oranges, although you can make a colorful lime zest and a pungent grapefruit zest as well. The oils in the rind are especially intense so a teaspoon or two adds a lot of flavor.

• TOOLS, UTENSILS, POTS & PANS •

Traditional & Microwave Ovens: *For information about how to work with a traditional oven, see page 120. A microvave oven is not appropriate for most baked goods. Microwaves don't like things that move (anything that contains yeast or baking powder changes shape significantly when heated); they penetrate only ½ to 1 inch so will cook the inside of a large item only through the energy transferred from that point; they toughen protein which is the opposite of what you want. Microwaving is more useful in preparation for baking: you can thaw frozen ingredients, melt butter or shortening, liquefy crystallized honey, or heat liquids that you want to add to a batter or dough (keep an eye on them). Microwaving baked goods to reheat them is also not recommended since that, too, makes the protein tough.*

Freezers: *There are two basic types of freezer. The older variety maintains a set temperature and builds up frost over a period of time. It needs to be emptied and defrosted every few months, more often during warm weather. The newer variety is the self-defrosting kind which you'll find in most refrigerator/freezer combinations. While this type saves you some labor, it does create more stress on the foodstuffs stored in it. In order to remain frost free, it must warm up, usually every 12 or 24 hours, to the point where any accumulated ice crystals melt and run off the interior surfaces. The food stored in the freezer stays fairly well frozen but there is enough fluctuation in temperature so that it won't keep as long or as well as food in the old fashioned, set temperature variety.*

MEASURING TOOLS

1. Scales: *Although the American system of measuring ingredients is based on volume rather than weight (as the European system is), a scale can be useful when volume measurement isn't appropriate. Weight measurement is more precise than volume measurement (4 ounces of flour may or may not fill a one-cup measure depending on how "wet" or "dry" it is and how it gets into the cup). Ingredient relationships will be much easier to understand when (and if) we switch to weight and metric systems of measurement.*

2. Liquid Measures: *These come in 1-, 2- and 4-cup sizes with a lip above the measuring line to accommodate liquid ingredients without spilling. They are generally made of glass or clear plastic so you can see to measure more accurately. A two-cup measure will accommodate a manual or electric mixer so can function as a small mixing bowl as well.*

3. Dry Measures: *These come in ¼-, ⅓-, ½-, 1-, 2- and 4-cup sizes. Because they are used for measuring dry ingredients (flour, sugar, etc.), there is no lip above the measuring mark. This enables you to scrape off the excess ingredient with a knife at the exact measure.*

4. Measuring Spoons: *These usually come in sets with spoons measuring ¼, ½ and 1 teaspoon, and 1 tablespoon (3 teaspoons). They are used for measuring both liquid (extracts) and dry (salt, sugar, spices, etc.) ingredients.*

UTENSILS

5. Pastry Cutter: *This tool easily cuts butter or shortening into flour for pie crusts, scones, biscuits, etc. It is useful for mashing bananas, hard boiled eggs, etc.*

6. Rolling Pins: *There are several types. The one pictured is traditional for rolling pie crusts. There are also large, heavy, professional-weight pins that can be used for pie crusts as well as large doughs or pastries. Pins for rolling out pasta are solid, narrow and extra long. Give any wooden pins an occasional rubdown with vegetable oil to both preserve the wood and to make them "non-stick." You'll also find rolling pins made of marble (which are nice but not necessary) that can be chilled for rolling out pie doughs or puff pastry.*

7. Shakers: *These are useful for shaking flour (or other dry ingredients like cinnamon sugar) evenly over a surface.*

8. Ceramic Crocks: *These can keep a variety of utensils and tools close at hand. If they have tops, they make attractive cannisters, sourdough crocks, etc.*

9. Spatulas: *These come in many sizes and shapes (as large as 9 x 10 inches), are made of metal or plastic, and are immensely helpful for getting food, hot or cold, from one place to another.*

10. Wooden Spoons: *These come in many sizes and shapes, are strong, non-reactive and friendly.*

11. Danish Dough Whisk: *This heavy duty whisk handles light muffin and cake batters and heavy doughs equally well.*

12. Whisks: *These manual beaters come in many sizes and can mix both liquid and dry ingredients quickly and easily.*

13. Pastry Brushes: *The best are made from natural bristles. Use to grease pans or brush washes or glazes on delicate doughs or pastries without exerting much pressure.*

14. Goose Feather Brush: *This is unbeatable for spreading washes or glazes without exerting any pressure at all.*

15. Thermometers: *These take a lot of guesswork out of baking. They can tell you when water is ready for yeast, a loaf of bread is done, a syrup has reached the "soft ball" stage and what your oven temperature really is.*

16. Cookie & Biscuit Cutters: *Good, sharp cutters in a variety of sizes and shapes makes baking biscuits to bagels, to playing with play dough or construction grade gingerbread, easier and more fun.*

17. King Arthur Bowl Scraper: *This flexible scraper can do everything from cleaning bowls and kneading surfaces (or icy windsheilds!) to cutting scones and Danish Pastry.*

18. Dough Scraper: *This non-flexible, metal version of the bowl scraper is used for many of the same purposes but can be used on hot surfaces as well.*

19. Bread or Loaf Pans: *These come in several standard sizes: large (9 x 5 inches), medium (8½ x 4½ inches), small (7½ x 3 ½ inches) and individual (5½ x 3½ inches). You'll find other sizes on the market designed for specific purposes.*

They can be made of a number of different materials: metal (most common), glass or ceramic. In learning how to work with your oven, one more variable is the material your pans are made of. Dark metal pans create dark, crisp crusts. Shiny metal pans reflect the heat away from the dough or batter inside and will produce light, delicate crusts. Glass pans absorb and hold heat most efficiently so, like dark metal pans, create brown, crisp crusts. (Some people feel you should lower the temperature of your oven 25°F when using glass pans to compensate for their heat-holding ability.) Ceramic pans are attractive (they make great gifts with loaves of bread inside) but may take longer to bake with depending on the thickness of the ceramic and the length of time it takes heat to penetrate them.

20. Muffin Tins: *These come in several, now standard, sizes: 6 or 12 medium-size-cup tins (2¾ inches across the top), 6 large-size-cup tins (4 inches across the top), and 12 or 24 miniature-size-cup tins (2 inches across the top). They are most often made of aluminum or steel (the non-stick variety is very useful) as well as cast iron, which, when well seasoned, makes crisp, moist muffins or popovers.*

21. Old-Fashioned Bread Bucket: *Found in most homes a hundred years ago, this could handle doughs containing 12 to 18 cups of flour. Sands, Taylor & Wood Co. sold them for many years and we intend to make them available again through our new* King Arthur Flour Baker's Catalogue.

22. Pizza Pans: *These come in a variety of sizes ranging from 12 to 18 inches in diameter. They can be flat for traditional pizza or focaccia or rimmed for deep-dish pizza. Like bread pans, pizza pans that make the crispest crusts are made of dark aluminum or steel that absorbs and concentrates heat.*

23. Pizza Peels: *These are large wooden "spatulas" which make getting pizza and other baked goods in and out of the oven easy. They are also great for cutting on and serving pizza.*

24. French Bread Baguette Pans: *These long, thin pans are designed to hold the slack, airy dough that traditional French bread is made from (page 141).*

25. Monkey Bread Pan: *This is a variation of a ring mold but smaller and taller to hold the balls of dough that make Monkey Bread (page 230).*

26. Cast Iron Skillets: *These come in a variety of sizes and shapes and are modern versions of the old fashioned iron "spider." (See page 67.)*

28. Angel Food or Sponge Cake Pans: *These pans, with their central tube, are designed to bake these ethereally light and fragile cakes. The "feet" are used to hold an inverted baked cake off a table or counter surface during its long cooling and "setting" period. These pans can also be used for large coffeecakes.*

29. Solid Bottom Round Cake Pans: *The sizes most frequently used are 8 or 9 inches in diameter but they are available all the way from 4 to 20 inches in diameter with depths of 2 to 3 inches.*

30. Pudding Mold: *This old-fashioned device is used to "bake" a quick bread batter in a simmering water bath. It is not dependent on an oven and can be used anywhere you can boil water. (See page 100.)*

27. Springform Pans: *These come in sizes ranging from 6 to 12 inches in diameter. (Our recipes are written for 9-inch pans. See page 89.) They are cake pans with removable bottoms and sides that latch to keep the bottoms in place. Some have bottom inserts with a tube so can be used for Angel Food or Sponge Cakes. Springform pans can be used for any batter or dough you would bake in a traditional cake pan.*

31. Bundt Pan: *This variation of a tube pan was developed in Germany. It is available in 6-, 9- or 12-cup sizes as well as a miniature, individual size (that comes like a 6-cup muffin tin) holding 1 cup of batter each. They were used to bake pound cake type batters but can be used to bake any type of cake, coffeecake, monkey bread (or can even to chill a molded aspic).*

32. Solid Bottom Square Baking Pans: *Like solid bottom round cake pans, these come usually 8 or 9 inches on a side. They are also used for cakes but more frequently for brownies and other bars. They are available in a wide range of sizes from 6 to 15 inches on a side.*

33. Crumpet Rings: *These metal rings, usually 4 inches in diameter and open on the top and bottom, are used for cooking crumpet batter on a griddle. (See page 168.)*

34. Removable Bottom Tart or Quiche Pans: *These are similar to Removable Bottom Cake Pans (see following). They have scalloped edges so are appropriate for things that should be fluted.*

35. Brioche Mold: *This is a special mold, like the French bread baguette pan, that holds a slack and egg-rich dough that bakes into an elegant breakfast or tea bread. (See page 241.)*

36. Solid Bottom Tart or Quiche Pans: *These are often made of ceramic or pottery and are attractive for serving as well as baking.*

Not Shown

Baking Stone or Tiles: *These can turn your oven into an old-world clay or brick oven to create hearth breads and pizza with crisp, crunchy crusts. (See page 120.)*

Dutch Oven: *See page 113.*

Jelly Roll Pan: *This is traditionally the same as a half-sheet pan (see below).*

Removable Bottom Round Cake Pans: *These pans come in a wide range of sizes from 6 to 14 inches in diameter. Unlike springform pans, their sides are a solid piece but their bottoms can be pushed out to remove whatever is baked inside, cakes, quickbreads, cheese cakes, etc.*

Sandbakkelse Pans: *These are like tiny brioche pans or fluted muffin cups (see page 430).*

Sheet Pans: *These are professional baking sheets and come in half size (12 x 18 inches) or full size (18 x 24 inches).*

Solid Bottom Rectangular Baking Pan: *These come in several traditional sizes: 7¾ x 10 inches, 9 x 13 inches, 10 x 14 inches, 11½ x 15½ inches and 12 x 17 inches.*

"Spider": *See page 67.*

• WHAT ARE KING ARTHUR FLOURS? •

King Arthur Unbleached All-Purpose Flour is a blend of hard red winter and hard red spring wheats. Unlike most all-purpose flours, it does not contain any soft wheat. This means that it has a higher protein content than most all-purpose flours, about 11.7%. When it is kneaded into a dough, it produces more gluten and thus is an excellent flour for yeast-raised products. Because it is unbleached (bleaching sort of chemically cooks and toughens the protein in flour), it will produce tender pie crusts, cakes and cookies as well. It is also excellent for pasta and bread machines.

King Arthur Stone Ground Whole Wheat Flour is milled completely from hard red spring wheat and contains the whole wheat berry, both the fiber-rich bran and the vitamin- and mineral-rich germ. It can be used wherever all-purpose flour is called for: in breads, brownies, cakes, cookies, pastry and pasta. If baking with whole wheat is new to you, try a ratio of 1 cup whole wheat to 3 cups of unbleached white until you become familiar with the nutty taste and wholesome texture.

IMPORTANT MEASURING INFORMATION
(This can mean the difference between a light loaf and a doorstop!)

The Milling Process: The process of milling flour involves grinding and sifting wheat over and over again until the resulting flour has reached a desirable degree of fineness. Before it is finally bagged, flour has been sifted through many layers of silk screening; all flour is therefore "pre-sifted." However, during shipment and storage, flour will settle and become compacted. If you scoop compacted flour directly from your bag or canister, it can weigh anywhere from 4½ to 5½ ounces a cup. Sifted flour weighs 4 ounces a cup. In the past, recipes were written for 4-ounce cups of flour and are still today unless you are otherwise directed. Here is how to accomplish that without sifting.

How To Measure: First, fluff up the flour in your storage container with a large spoon or flour scoop. Sprinkle it gently into a dry cup measure (one that measures exactly a cup at the rim). Scrape the excess off with the back of a knife (or your scoop), without shaking or tapping the cup. A cup measured this way will weigh 4 ounces and will contain lots of air, an important beginning to a light loaf or cake.

One More Measuring Consideration: Flour is like a sponge. In the winter when houses are warm and dry, flour is dry and will be able to absorb more moisture than it can in the summer when it is more humid. This means you will use less flour in the winter than you will in the summer to get the same results. In recipes calling for a flexible amount of flour, always start with the least amount and gradually add more to achieve the consistency you want.

TURNING YOUR KING ARTHUR INTO CAKE, PASTRY, OR SELF-RISING FLOUR

There are times when you may want to temper King Arthur's good gluten (lower the protein), or you may want to adapt a favorite family or friend's recipe written for a lower protein or self-rising flour. Rather than compromising with flours that contain chemicals, here is how you can mix up your own chemical-free King Arthur cake, pastry, and self-rising flours.

King Arthur Cake & Pastry Flour: For each cup of cake flour needed, put 2 tablespoons of cornstarch in your measuring cup. Fill the remainder of the cup with King Arthur Unbleached All-Purpose Flour measured according to the above directions. For pastry flour, use 1½ tablespoons of cornstarch and proceed as you would for cake flour. (Or order our unbleached Round Table Pastry Flour direct from our Baker's Catalogue and use it for both pies and cakes.)

King Arthur Self-Rising Flour: To 9 cups of King Arthur Unbleached Flour, add 1 tablespoon of salt and 5 tablespoons of double-acting baking powder. Blend and store what you don't use in an airtight container. Be sure to stick in a label identifying it. To make just 1 cup of self-rising flour, add 1½ teaspoons baking powder and ¼ to ½ teaspoon salt to 1 cup King Arthur Unbleached All-Purpose Flour.

STORING FLOUR

King Arthur Unbleached All-Purpose Flour will keep for years if stored in a cool, dry place. To discourage any "visitors," stick a couple of bay leaves in the top of the bag.

King Arthur Stone Ground Whole Wheat Flour is more sensitive to storage conditions than our unbleached all-purpose flour because it contains the vitamin-rich oil of the germ. If you use your whole wheat flour fairly quickly, store it in an airtight container in a cool place as you would your unbleached all-purpose flour. If you use it more slowly, store it in an airtight bag in your freezer.

• INDEX •

(References to other parts of the index
appear in parentheses after text page references.)